Broken Memories

Broken Memories

Case Studies in Memory Impairment

Edited by

Ruth Campbell and Martin A. Conway

BLACKWELL

Oxford UK & Cambridge USA

Copyright © Blackwell Publishers Ltd 1995

First published 1995

Blackwell Publishers Ltd
108 Cowley Road
Oxford   OX4 1JF
UK

Blackwell Publishers Inc.
238 Main Street
Cambridge, Massachusetts 02142
USA

British Library Cataloguing in Publication Data

A CIP catalogue record for this book is available from the British Library.

Library of Congress Cataloging-in-Publication Data has been applied for.

ISBN 0–631–18722–7
ISBN 0–631–18723–5 (pbk)

Typeset in 10 on 12pt Ehrhardt
by Graphicraft Typesetters, Hong Kong
Printed in Great Britain by T.J. Press Ltd, Padstow, Cornwall

This book is printed on acid-free paper.

Contents

Figures

Tables

Contributors

A.D. Baddeley, Fulburn Hospital and MRC Applied Psychology Unit, Cambridge, United Kingdom

Christopher Barry, University of Wales College of Cardiff, United Kingdom

Nelson Butters, University of California, San Diego

Ruth Campbell, University of London, United Kingdom

David Caplan, Massachusetts General Hospital, United States of America

Alfonso Caramazza, Dartmouth College, United States of America

Laird S. Cermak, Boston University, United States of America

Martin A. Conway, University of Bristol, United Kingdom

Françoise Coyette, Clinique Universitaire Saint-Luc, Belgium

Gianfranco Dalla Barba, INSERM, Paris, France

Ann D.M. Davies, Wirral District Psychology Service, United Kingdom

Sergio Della Sala, University of Aberdeen, United Kingdom

John Joseph Downes, University of Liverpool, United Kingdom

Elaine Funnell, University of London, United Kingdom

Susan E. Gathercole, University of Bristol, United Kingdom

Elizabeth M. Guinan, Guy's and St Thomas's Hospital, London, United Kingdom

J. Richard Hanley, University of Liverpool, United Kingdom

Argye E. Hillis, Johns Hopkins University, United States of America

John R. Hodges, University of Cambridge, United Kingdom

David Howard, University of London, United Kingdom

Glyn W. Humphreys, University of Birmingham, United Kingdom

Narinder Kapur, Wessex Neurological Centre, United Kingdom

Michael D. Kopelman, Guy's and St Thomas's Hospital, London, United Kingdom

Theodor Landis, University of Zurich, Switzerland

Philip D.R. Lewis, Guy's and St Thomas's Hospital, London, United Kingdom

Federica Lucchelli, Hospital S. Carlo, Milan, Italy
Alessandro Lunghi, Lecco Hospital, Italy
Randi C. Martin, Rice University, United States of America
Andrew R. Mayes, University of Sheffield, United Kingdom
Rosaleen A. McCarthy, University of Cambridge, United Kingdom
Jo V. McHattie, University of Wales College of Cardiff, United Kingdom
A.P. McKay, Fulburn Hospital and MRC Applied Psychology Unit, Cambridge, United Kingdom
P.J. McKenna, Fulburn Hospital and MRC Applied Psychology Unit, Cambridge, United Kingdom
David Moakes, Southampton General Hospital, United Kingdom
Robin G. Morris, Institute of Psychiatry, London, United Kingdom
Nick Morton, Institute of Psychiatry, London, United Kingdom
Margaret G. O'Connor, Boston University, United States of America
Costanzo Papagno, Seregno Hospital, Italy
Alan J. Parkin, University of Sussex, United Kingdom
Hilary Ratner, Wayne State University, United States of America
M. Jane Riddoch, University of Birmingham, United Kingdom
Christina Röhrenbach, University of Zurich, Switzerland
Cristina Romani, Rice University, United States of America
Jennifer Rusted, University of Sussex, United Kingdom
Larry J. Seidman, Boston University, United States of America
Carlo Semenza, Padova University, Italy
Linda Sheppard, University of Sussex, United Kingdom
Hans Spinnler, University of Milan, Italy
Hans G. Stampfer, University of Western Australia
Christine M. Temple, University of Essex, United Kingdom
Giuseppe Vallar, University of Rome, Italy
Martial Van der Linden, University of Liege, Belgium
Mieke Verfaellie, Boston University, United States of America
Gloria S. Waters, McGill University, Canada
Deborah Wearing, University of Cambridge, United Kingdom
Barbara A. Wilson, University of Cambridge, United Kingdom
Dahlia W. Zaidel, University of California, Los Angeles, United States of America

Foreword

In 1989, one of us (Ruth Campbell) thought that it would be a good idea to give undergraduates, particularly those studying psychology, a taste of individual case study as a means of understanding aspects of cognition. From that idea came *Mental Lives* (Blackwell, 1992). That volume ranged far and wide over developmental and acquired disorder to cast light on reading, drawing, speaking, writing and recognizing faces (among other things). In 1991, the other one (Martin Conway) thought that the idea was worth pursuing, with a volume dedicated to memory disturbances. While one or two chapters in *Mental Lives* were concerned with memory malfunction, the wealth of case studies currently being explored was hardly hinted at in the earlier volume. So this book specifically explores case studies in memory malfunction.

Once more, our aim is to use individual case study in neuropsychology to help to understand how memory works in general. We have taken memory in the widest possible sense to comprise the faculty of knowledge of facts, events and language, the processes of recalling and the ways that experience of the past interacts with present behaviour.

Our brief to authors was to present experimental studies of a case (or series of cases) of interesting anomalies of memory, set in the appropriate theoretical context, with the aim of elucidating both what has gone amiss in the patient and what this means for theorizing about memory. That is, this book as a whole is aimed at the advanced undergraduate or the beginning postgraduate in memory research, seeking an understanding, perhaps at second hand, of how neuropsychological research can proceed.

In response to this, the chapters produced are extremely varied, with riches of very different kinds in each one. Some (for instance, Wilson and Wearing's chapter) bring important cases to life by detailing a wide range of spared and impaired abilities, with experimental and theoretical investigations a little more in the background. Others (such as Martin and Romani's chapter) present detailed experimental investigations, with a new theoretical import. These drive home the point that performance on a particular task may be impaired for a variety of reasons and only by uncovering these systematically can we extend our understanding of how memory can serve or fail us.

While these chapters are many and diverse, we are aware that they could constitute a rich meal for the browser, nibbler or beginner. We recommend that, after reading the Introduction, and the Part Introductions which offer short frameworks, you read specific chapters that are close to your own concerns. The authors have produced their chapters to stand alone. Cross-referencing has been kept to a minimum and some repetition of key theoretical issues therefore occurs as one reads sets of chapters. Each chapter contains recommended further reading.

In the Introduction that follows we suggest that the use of the case-study approach to memory should be engaged with some caution. That's not to say it shouldn't be fun, and editing this volume has given us a great deal of pleasure from gaining insight into memory processes and understanding better the mental lives of people with a variety of memory problems. While we are still some way from effective remediation of memory disorder, the first steps must require theoretical insight and practical understanding. Our aim in this volume is to offer something of each.

RUTH CAMPBELL AND MARTIN A. CONWAY

Introduction: Case Studies in the Neuropsychology of Memory

Martin A. Conway, Ruth Campbell and Susan E. Gathercole

Memory seems to be the psychological function most closely linked with one's human uniqueness. Memories shape individual lives to an extent that is hard to imagine for other faculties such as seeing or speaking. Our memories are endogenous, private, internal and controllable by our own minds; they capture events in the world as personal experiences. It is hardly surprising, then, that neurological and psychological perspectives on memory have tended to show that memories depend on a multitude of brain systems, rather than the function of one or two key areas.

In his influential paper 'In search of the engram', Karl Lashley (1950) argued that memory, above all other functions, was mediated by neurological processes occurring in many different areas of the brain. Not only this, but that memory was achieved by the 'mass action' of the brain and highly localized or 'focal' brain damage was unlikely markedly to impair memory performance. By contrast, widespread brain damage should have detrimental, and potentially catastrophic, effects upon memory. Clinical neuropsychologists would have contested this conclusion even then, but the idea had a strong hold on psychological theorizing and research.

Later, Scoville and Milner (1957) reported a landmark study of the patient HM who, following brain surgery for intractable epilepsy, developed a profound and dense amnesia. The focus of HM's epileptic seizures seemed to be deep in the middle parts of the temporal lobes, implicating some close underlying structures, especially the hippocampus. To prevent the epileptic episodes, the hippocampus was lesioned on both left and right, effectively disconnecting it and other medial limbic structures from the temporal lobes that covered it. Following the operation, HM's memory for events prior to his operation was relatively intact. However, he had a dense anterograde amnesia: the ability to encode new information into long-term memory seemed to be completely abolished. But interestingly, other aspects of HM's cognitive abilities were intact; in particular, his short-term memory and general intelligence were unimpaired. This profile of both impaired and spared memory function following highly localized brain damage is important for several reasons. It calls into question Lashley's proposal that memory arises from 'mass action' within the brain. Instead, it suggests that differentiable aspects of human memory are served by distinct brain structures, and in particular that the construction of long-term memories is mediated by temporal lobe activity which, in turn, requires some input from subcortical structures, especially the hippocampus.

While the case of HM, and the implications of his surgery, quite quickly became known to neuroscientists and psychologists, nevertheless its influence on the course of memory theorizing was initially quite small. Yet over the last thirty years, along with very many shifts in the conceptualization of memory as a psychological function, has come an increasing awareness of the importance of case studies in memory dysfunction as a mode of illuminating memory processes and informing the development of theory. As with Scoville and Milner's pioneering study, these shifts have followed important case studies that made theoretical psychological points. For instance, Shallice and Warrington's study of patient KF (Warrington and Shallice, 1969; Shallice and Warrington, 1970) emphasized how, following head injury (in this case, posterior left parietal structures were damaged), short-term memory could be lost, but long-term memory remain unaffected. Since KF nevertheless showed no anterograde amnesia, this meant that theoretical approaches that stressed that short-term memory was required for long-term memory processing were misguided. Similarly, Warrington and Weiskrantz (1968, 1970) showed that under certain conditions amnesic patients were able to learn new material: specifically, when partial information, such as fragments of the original material, were presented, such patients showed essentially normal performance (as long as this was tested not by overt recollection but rather by covert tasks, such as identification or completion of fragmentary parts). This meant, at the very least, that the encoding of new material was not particularly defective in such patients, but the retrieval of it was limited to certain conditions. In both these examples, while clinicians had often been aware of these dissociable abilities and deficits in practice, the link to theorizing in psychology was slow to be made.

In recent years, this knowledge gap has been closing and the development of theories of normal memory has increasingly been informed by neuropsychological findings. This book is a collection of reports by leading researchers, using case studies that should influence understanding of memory function and of the brain mechanisms that support this function. In their presentations the authors have two aims: first, to provide relatively nontechnical accounts of the profiles of memory impairments of their own patient or patients, and second, to identify the key theoretical implications that follow from these profiles. In some chapters, the first aim was paramount, and here the authors have provided more detail on their patients than is usual in journal publications in order to give more of a feel for the actual nature of the impairments. In other chapters, the implications of specific patterns of performance for the development of theories of psychological function are drawn out at some length. The editors have not attempted to force each chapter into a tight presentational format: some of these cases bear heavy theoretical interpretation; others are more useful for their insights into memory disorder at a personal level.

The chapters have generally been grouped into content areas that illustrate broad types of similar memory dysfunction. Not all the reports are restricted to examinations of memory characteristics following verified neurological injury and several case studies are presented which describe memory dysfunctions arising from clinical or psychogenic disorders such as schizophrenia. These are starting to provide illuminating and often unique perspectives on the ways that memory can fail, and of its consequences for the cognitive capabilities of the individual.

Some Memory Distinctions

Memory can refer to many different types of remembering and types of knowledge. Over the past thirty years or so, many different memory distinctions have been explored; some have since been discarded, and some are still retained. It is useful at this point to consider a few of the enduring terms and distinctions concerning memory that psychologists are using today, and that will be encountered in the following chapters. One distinction is that between short-term memory and long-term memory. Short-term memory is used to describe the retention of information over a period up to a few minutes, as in immediate recall tasks. An example of an everyday short-term memory task is listening to a number when you call the directory enquiries service, and attempting to dial it immediately without writing it down (a risky strategy!). This task involves verbal recall of the unfamiliar sequence of digit names. Within short-term memory, different systems seem to operate for retaining verbal and visual information over brief periods of time, and even within visual or verbal short-term memory, subcomponents can be identified. Aspects of such discrete functional impairments are highlighted in several chapters in this volume.

Long-term memory spans a much longer period, from several minutes to several decades. Tasks such as remembering what you had for breakfast, your parent's telephone number, the names of old schoolfriends and the meanings of words all involve long-term memory. There are a number of important distinctions within long-term memory and one central distinction is that between declarative and procedural memory (Cohen and Squire, 1980; Tulving, 1985). Declarative memory refers to information which we can report and reflect upon, such as memory for a specific event, the content of a conversation, or a fact or concept we have acquired. Procedural memory, in contrast, refers to information upon which we cannot reflect or report, such as a skill. For example, a person may have learned to whistle the tune of 'Yesterday', but apart from the actual performance there is very little that this individual could tell us about what sort of knowledge was used to complete the task or, indeed, how they actually whistled.

Within the broad area of declarative knowledge, a further distinction that will be encountered in the following chapters is between semantic and episodic memory (Tulving, 1972, 1985). Semantic memory refers to memory for facts, concepts and meanings; episodic or autobiographical memory refers to memory for events that have been personally experienced (Conway, 1990, 1991). Thus, episodic memories preserve knowledge of details of an experience. Semantic memories, in contrast, do not retain such knowledge. Most people know that the word 'furniture' refers to a category of objects, and when asked 'What's a chair?' can respond by recalling that it is an item of furniture. They do not, however, recall the time when they learned this fact, and would probably find it very difficult to remember the last time they used the word. This contrasts with recall of, for example, memory for a meal in a restaurant two weeks past. This distinction between episodic and semantic memory has proved particularly useful in the study of patients with amnesia. These individuals have very striking impairments of episodic memory, while their semantic memory is more or less intact. Such dissociations can lend experimental validity to the episodic–semantic distinction. In this volume, the contributions by McCarthy and Hodges, Cermak et al., Butters et al., and van der Linde and Coyotte illustrate this.

A further distinction, between implicit and explicit memory, relates to the links between conscious awareness and memory (see Schacter, 1987, for a review). Explicit memory is the intentional and conscious recall of a past event, or of some other item of declarative knowledge. The term implicit memory, in contrast, is used to describe situations when memory influences behaviour without awareness that it is doing so. It was this that Warrington and Weiskrantz (1968, 1970) explored in amnesic patients. In such implicit tasks, subjects may be shown a list of words, and later, in the guise of a filler task, be asked to complete letter fragments of words including those on the original list. So, subjects who saw the word 'assassin' in the original list may be presented with the fragment '–ss–ss––', and asked to provide the missing letters to form a familiar word (Tulving et al., 1982). They are not told to remember the earlier encountered words as a means of doing this, and subjects are typically unaware of any relationship between the original word list and the word fragment list. None the less, subjects who previously saw 'assassin' will be more likely to complete the fragment to produce this word, even though they may be unable to recollect the item in the original list (see Roediger and McDermott, 1993, for a recent review). It now appears, following a large number of independent studies across different domains, that people with even very dense amnesia can be influenced by their prior exposure to the memory list to a similar degree as normal subjects. What is missing is awareness of having learned the task (see Butters et al., this volume).

Amnesia and Other Types of Memory Loss

The term 'amnesia' has seeped into everyday usage in the language, where it often refers to any loss of memory. Psychologists' use of the term is more specific than just 'loss of memory', and amnesia has been considered a clinical syndrome by neurologists for over 100 years. Amnesia can arise for many reasons, including Korsakoff's alcoholic syndrome, viral infections of the brain such as herpes encephalitis, strokes and closed head injury. Despite the variability in physical aetiology, the following features define amnesia as a neuropsychological syndrome (Parkin and Leng, 1993).

- sparing of short-term memory;
- semantic memory, IQ, and other cognitive abilities also intact;
- dense and permanent anterograde amnesia (the patient is strikingly impaired in acquiring new knowledge);
- a degree of retrograde amnesia (the patient has some impairment in recalling events which occurred prior to the onset of the amnesia);

- intact procedural memory, and some preservation of the ability to form new procedural memories.

The first chapter in this book shows just how difficult everyday life becomes for a family with an amnesic in it (Kapur and Moakes). Although important both clinically and theoretically, amnesia is by definition but one type of memory impairment. What such cases (see Part I) highlight, however, is a good deal of individual variability in memory ability even in this apparently functionally homogeneous group.

Outside the realm of diagnosed neuropsychological amnesia, memory problems in a variety of domains are explored in this volume: for instance, knowledge of places (Hanley and Davies) and memory for proper names (Semenza). The possibility that selective, categorical memory loss, for example of animate objects, is also addressed (Barry and McHattie). In these parts, too, are papers addressing a rather different aspect of memory performance: difficulties in recruiting and controlling the required processes to make memory work (for example, Parkin and Stampfer; Riddoch and Humphreys), as well as a number of papers on memory dysfunction in people not generally considered to have neuropsychological problems (Kopelman et al.; McKenna et al.).

Papers on short-term memory have an important place in this volume. This is an area of intensive current research, especially in relation to language function and spatial skills. A number of papers in this section illuminate theoretical developments in a precise fashion (Howard et al.; Morris and Morton, among others). Developmental problems in memory are highlighted in the final section of the book.

Memory and the Brain

Deep in the brain, beneath the cortical hemispheres, lie a set of interconnected structures that form the limbic system. These have long been known to be involved in memory as well as emotion, and motivated or goal-directed behaviour in general. Structures within the limbic system include the hippocampus, amygdala, septum, mamillary bodies, olfactory bulbs, fornix, thalamus and hypothalamus (cf. Kolb and Whishaw, 1990) and these sites are interconnected with one another, and with other subcortical sites. The hippocampus and amygdala, together with the medial temporal lobe, can be considered to form a functional unit: the medial temporal lobe memory system (Squire, 1992). In turn, the medial temporal lobe memory system has connections to structures including the thalamus and mamillary bodies and there is also a pathway from the amygdala to the frontal lobe region.

However, neither the medial temporal lobe memory system nor the limbic system itself seem to be specialized for storage in a manner akin to library or file storage. Rather, these circuits are involved in the initial formation of memories. Memory impairments following brain injury to the hippocampus have been extensively studied ever since HM was subject to bilateral hippocampectomy in 1955. One hypothesis is that this structure is critical in mediating the encoding of events, fact or set of facts (Squire, 1992). It has been suggested that the hippocampus is required to frame events into episodes. One reason this may be necessary is to protect the brain from 'catastrophic interference' which could accrue as old events have to be linked in new associations. Lesions to other structures in the limbic system, including the fornix, mamillary bodies and thalamus, can also give rise to memory impairments, and it is becoming increasingly apparent that limbic system structures form circuits required both for the encoding and subsequent retrieval of declarative knowledge. The frontal lobes, which contain a number of structures that form part of the limbic circuitry, are also involved in memory in a variety of different ways (Shallice, 1988), including some critical executive aspects of performance on memory tasks.

While limbic system memory circuits seem to be needed in the formation of long-term memories, other brain regions are implicated in storage of learned material and in recruitment of recently presented material, as in short-term memory tasks. Some long-term storage might be located in areas adjacent to the medial limbic structures. For instance, some parts of the left temporal lobe are implicated in precise knowledge about things in the world (Funnell, this volume). Yet the localization of deficits such as the 'category specific knowledge losses' (see Barry and McHattie, this volume) has proven quite intractable, with the picture becoming obscured as finer and finer functional distinctions are drawn between patients with similar, but not identical, problems. Similarly, while the functional description of short-term memory loss can be extremely precise, and a number of components within it can be distinguished (see Howard et al.; Martin and Romani, this volume), the precise location of sites specific for different functional components of auditory verbal short-term memory has proven to be quite elusive. One affected region apparently common to patients with different types of verbal short-term memory is the perisylvian area of the left tempero-parietal areas (Vallar and Shallice, 1990). Cerebral imaging techniques are starting to provide reliable indications of the localization of these skills in normal brains (Paulesu et al., 1993).

Some researchers take a more 'broad brush' approach to cortical localization, attempting to tie cortical structures directly with more general distinctions in psychological function: Schacter (1989), for instance, suggests parietal structures are implicated in 'bringing memories to consciousness'. It is also worth noting that, overlaid on general functional specialities, brain lateralization exerts an influence. In general, dissociable effects arise according to whether the injury is to a structure in the left or right cortical hemisphere (Milner, 1982), with left hemisphere specialization for language processing and right hemisphere (generally) for object processing. The exploration of knowledge and memory in people with surgically separated cortical hemispheres (but with intact subcortical structures) can cast a rather different light on this simple dichotomy and show differently conceptualized specializations (Zaidel, this volume). Even from this very brief outline it would seem that activity in many brain regions must be synchronized when memory is used. The limbic system circuits recruit the necessary activity required for laying down long-term memories. Circuits involving sensory processing areas, such as the occipital lobes for vision and the auditory reception areas of the temporal lobe for audition, play a role in the immediate (brief) processing of events. Parietal structures are probably required in holding modality-specific information for short periods of time and in making these available to consciousness. Some temporal areas, especially inferior and some anterior temporal structures, may serve as knowledge-based storage sites. The role of the frontal lobes is crucial, both in determining what is to be stored, and then in moderating executive and attentional aspects of encoding, storing and retrieving memories.

Despite our earlier comments, Lashley's concept of 'mass action' may not be such an inappropriate characterization of how the brain supports memory, after all. Yet the essential difference between the 'mass action' view and current views of the neuropsychology of human memory is that the latter take a modular view of memory. Single cases of localized brain damage can show how memory fractionates, revealing the subcomponents or modules (such as the medial temporal lobe memory system) which support memory encoding and retrieval.

One of the problems posed by a fully modular, componential account of memory processes is that patients with very similar brain damage do not necessarily show the same type of cognitive impairment. More generally, there are a range of problems associated with inferences about the nature of cognition when inferences are based on findings from one individual only.

Case Studies

It is our contention that studying patients with impairments of memory can illuminate the structure and function of normal memory, while understanding the functional basis of an individual's memory problems, revealed through thoughtful psychological testing, also represents an important first step in rehabilitating memory function. It is, however, important to note that it is often more difficult to interpret findings from patients than from normal samples of subjects. There are a number of reasons for this, a few of which are considered here.

If we are to use findings from memory-impaired populations to inform theories of normal memory function, it would be good to know that the memory behaviour we observe in patients corresponds to that of the normal population, but with a straightforward 'hole' indicating the deficient memory process. In particular, it is critically important to the way that patient data can be understood that individuals with memory impairments do not adopt special strategies to overcome their limitations; strategies that are not used in the absence of memory impairment. A number of the chapters in this book, particularly in Part II, in circumstances where individual memory becomes aberrant rather than lost, highlight this issue. This rationale is usually assumed rather than demonstrated by neuropsychologists; indeed, it is quite difficult to imagine how we might go about establishing that the patient's unusual memory characteristics do not reflect a deficient memory component, but instead the use of an unusual strategy to compensate for the individual's primary memory deficits (see Seidenberg, 1988). Some reassurance that disturbed memory behaviour does not reflect compensatory strategy use might be provided by studying groups of patients under a single syndrome label, such as amnesia. The argument here is that if all patients behave in a consistent manner, their memory characteristics are unlikely to reflect idiosyncratic strategies developed on the basis of their neurological injury. However, the group study methodology itself brings with it further interpretational ambiguities. Many cognitive neuropsychologists have rejected this approach, arguing that patients do not have identical neurological impairments and so cannot be grouped together meaningfully in terms of their psychological dysfunctions. Thus according to Caramazza and McCloskey (1988), averaging performance of groups of patients classified as sharing the same psychological deficit can be both meaningless and misleading. They argue instead that the only useful study of brain-damaged patients with cognitive deficits is via the 'single case study' approach, in which the aim is to describe the unique cognitive system of an individual, usually in terms of the intact and impaired components of the normal cognitive system. This approach represents, at present, the dominant methodology within cognitive neuropsychology, except possibly in the study of amnesia, and is strongly represented in this book.

Within the present volume, a number of investigators have made a virtue out of clinical necessity, using the 'natural experiment' of impaired neurological function to explore function in new ways and to sidestep some of the methodological problems outlined above. For instance, Funnell's work on focal semantic dementia has explicitly followed a research programme aimed at elucidating the functional changes occurring in a progressive dementing disorder, with a view to mapping the stages of semantic loss in this particular patient. Studies relating to memory disorganization, such as those reported here by Kopelman et al. and by McKenna et al., offer a unique perspective on memory function. These relate to the coherence of individual mental lives and it is hard to envisage how experiments with normal subjects could cast any sort of light on the necessary cohesive processes which are usually so powerful as to be 'invisible to experiment'.

There are pitfalls associated with the single-case-study approach. It is simply not clear how far the findings with a single brain-damaged individual can generalize to the population at large. If these findings cannot even be generalized to similar patients then the prospect of generalizing to non-brain damaged individuals may be remote. The reliability of the sampling techniques is also an important issue. Even with normal subjects, single assessments may yield atypical memory profiles which may be unreliable on re-testing (Della Sala et al., 1991). It is therefore necessary for psychologists working with single cases to sample behaviour even more extensively than would be required in a comparable experiment on normal subjects. With normal subjects, counter-balancing and randomization techniques are routinely used to eliminate confounding variables such as practice, fatigue and material-specific effects. It is also possible to demonstrate the robustness of a particular finding by replicating the result with a different group of subjects. This opportunity is often not available for further, theory-driven exploration of an individual with a unique neuropsychological profile. Access to patients is limited by geographical boundaries, laboratory loyalties, and the individual's variable health. When access fails for one or more of these reasons, the opportunity to provide the critical test of competing theories can be lost for good. It is much more difficult to extend these usual tests of generality to the study of a single patient, necessitating caution in interpreting unique findings.

Theories of normal memory, and indeed of normal cognition more generally, therefore reflect a relationship with neuropsychological methods and findings which is substantially different from that with experimental data from normal subjects. On the positive side, even an isolated case study can provide direct disconfirmations of theory, as in Shallice and Warrington's demonstration, with case KF, that short-term memory impairment need not preclude the consolidation of long-term memories. Neuropsychological studies often provide experimental manipulations that cannot be mimicked or achieved in the laboratory, and which can be crucial to the development of current memory theory. Where they are particularly useful is in guiding explorations of memory deficits in their own right and providing insights into disorder based on close analysis of functional patterns.

The Kabbalists have a creation myth that is illuminating (Scholem, 1974). God, they say, created a series of great vessels to hold the light and form of creation. But some of these broke, constituting the first great catastrophe. The shards of these broken vessels constitute our everyday experience of the world. We may not hope to put all the pieces together again, but the art of interpreting the world, and of enabling scientific understanding, is essentially one of careful reconstruction. The experiences of the patients described here with broken memories provide us with important evidence about the nature of memory in general; but that evidence should be treated with care.

References

Caramazza, A. and McCloskey, M. (1988) 'The case for single patient studies', *Cognitive Neuropsychology*, **5**: 517–27.

Cohen, N.J. and Squire, L.R. (1980) 'Preserved learning and retention of a pattern-analyzing skill in amnesia: dissociation of knowing how and knowing that', *Science*, **210**: 207–10.

Conway, M.A. (1990) *Autobiographical Memory: An Introduction* (Milton Keynes: Open University Press).

Conway, M.A. (1991) 'In defense of everyday memory', *American Psychologist*, **46**: 19–26.

Della Sala, S., Logie, R.H., Marchetti, C. and Wynn, V. (1991) 'Case Studies in working memory: a case for single cases?', *Cortex*, **27**: 169–91.

Kolb, B. and Whishaw, I.Q. (eds) (1990) *Fundamentals of Human Neuropsychology*, 3rd edn (New York: W.H. Freeman).

Lashley, K. (1950) 'In search of the engram', in *Symposium for the Society of Experimental Biology, no. 4* (Cambridge: Cambridge University Press).

Milner, B. (1982) 'Some cognitive effects of frontal lobe lesions in man', *Philosophical Transactions of the Royal Society of London, B*, **298**: 211–26.

Parkin, A.J. and Leng, N.R.C (1993) *Neuropsychology of the Amnesic Syndrome* (Hove, Sussex: Lawrence Erlbaum Associates).

Paulesu, E., Frith, C.D., Frackowiak, R.S.J. (1993) 'The neural components of the verbal component of working memory', *Nature*, **362**: 342–4.

Roediger, H.L. III and McDermott, K.B. (1993) 'Implicit memory in normal human subjects', in H. Spinnler and F. Boller (eds), *Handbook of Neuropsychology, 8* (Amsterdam: Elsevier).

Schacter, D. (1987) 'Implicit memory: history and current status', *Journal of Experimental Psychology, Learning, Memory and Cognition*, **13**: 501–18.

Schacter, D. (1989) 'On the relation between memory and consciousness: dissociable interactions and conscious experience', in H.L. Roediger III and F.I.M. Craik (eds), *Varieties of Memory and Consciousness: Essays in Honour of Endel Tulving* (Hillsdale, N.J.: Lawrence Erlbaum Associates), pp. 355–391.

Scholem, G. (1974) *Kabbalah* (Jerusalem: Keter), pp. 138–47.

Scoville, W.B. and Milner, B. (1957) 'Loss of recent memory after bilateral hippocampal lesions', *Journal of Neurology, Neurosurgery and Psychiatry*, **20**: 11–12.

Seidenberg, M. (1988) 'Cognitive neuropsychology: the state of the art', *Cognitive Neuropsychology*, **5**: 403–26.

Shallice, T. (1988) *From Neuropsychology to Mental Structure* (Cambridge: Cambridge University Press).

Shallice, T. and Warrington, E.K. (1970) 'Independent functioning of the verbal memory stores: a neuropsychological study', *Quarterly Journal of Experimental Psychology*, **22**: 261–73.

Squire, L.R. (1992) 'Memory and the hippocampus: a synthesis from findings with rats, monkeys, and humans', *Psychological Review*, **99**: 195–231.

Tulving, E. (1972) 'Episodic and semantic memory', in E. Tulving and W. Donaldson (eds), *Organisation of Memory* (New York: Academic Press), pp. 382–404.

Tulving, E. (1985) 'How many memory systems are there?', *American Psychologist*, **40**: 385–98.

Tulving, E., Schacter, D.L. and Stark, H.A. (1982) 'Priming effects in word fragment completion are independent of recognition memory', *Journal of Experimental Psychology: Learning, Memory, and Cognition*, **8**: 336–42.

Vallar, G. and Shallice, T. (eds) (1990) *Neuropsychological Impairments of Short Memory* (Cambridge: Cambridge University Press).

Warrington, E.K. and Shallice, T. (1969) 'The selective impairment of auditory verbal short-term memory', *Brain*, **92**: 885–96.

Warrington, E.K. and Weiskrantz, L. (1968) 'New method of testing long-term retention with special reference to amnesic patients', *Nature*, **217**: 972–4.

Warrington, E.K. and Weiskrantz, L. (1970) 'Amnesia: consolidation or retrieval?', *Nature*, **228**: 628–30.

1   Living with Amnesia

Narinder Kapur and David Moakes

This chapter provides a non-clinical account of the day-to-day effects of amnesia. Part of the account is given by the husband of a young woman, Sheila Moakes, who, following a viral infection of the brain, suffered a dense and intractable anterograde amnesia. The account was provided in response to a questionnaire that attempted to assess the impact of Sheila's amnesia on her everyday behaviour and the extent to which she and her husband came to cope, over a ten-year period, with her memory disability. Although the account clearly shows the devastating effects of amnesia on daily life, it also demonstrates that it is possible to maintain some degree of quality of life even in the face of such a debilitating injury.

Clinical History

Sheila's clinical history is typical of that associated with herpes simplex encephalitis (HSE), and the presence of the herpes simplex virus was confirmed by virological tests at the time of her initial hospital admission (May 1981). Nine years after the onset of her illness, she underwent a number of detailed investigations as part of a study of the long-term sequelae associated with HSE (Kapur et al., 1994). A magnetic resonance brain scan, carried out in July 1990, showed significant residual pathology in the right temporal lobe, affecting medial structures such as the hippocampal formation, and also all three temporal lobe gyri across their anterior–posterior length (superior, middle and inferior gyri). The right insula also showed significant pathology. There was milder damage to the right frontal lobe, with involvement of orbital and medial areas and sparing of dorsolateral areas. On the left side, there was major pathology in left medial temporal lobe structures, but apart from the left temporal pole and left insula, there was sparing of the remaining part of the left temporal lobe. Her left frontal lobe was free of pathology.

On standard memory tests, her overall level of amnesia was severe, and she ranked third in terms of degree of severity within the group of ten HSE patients that have recently been reported (Kapur et al., 1994). Thus, on the Wechsler Memory Scale – Revised she had General and Delayed Memory Quotients of less than 50. On the Warrington Recognition Memory Test her scores were very poor (less than the fifth percentile for both words and faces). General cognitive testing showed a Wechsler Adult Intelligence Scale – Revised (WAIS–R) Verbal IQ of 101, a Performance IQ of 100 and a Full Scale IQ of 101. Her estimated IQ on the basis of the National Adult Reading Test was 113, so it is possible that some of her average or low-average scores, such as Information, Block Design and Object Assembly, do reflect mild intellectual impairments. On a picture-naming task and on the Modified Card Sorting Test she performed normally. On formal tests of retrograde amnesia, there was evidence of some impairment in the identification of famous faces and in knowing whether certain personalities were dead or alive. However, Sheila's main problem was a severe anterograde amnesia.

The Questionnaire Responses

Sheila's husband completed a detailed questionnaire that examined the consequences of her amnesia, both for herself and her family, and in this section we include edited excerpts from David Moakes's transcript. (Full details of the questionnaire are available from the first author.) Note that the questionnaire was completed some ten years after her brain injury and covered the whole of this period.

A brief outline of what Sheila was like before the illness and what she did

Sheila was 32 at the time of her illness. We had been married for ten years. Our only child is Jonathon, who was three years old at the time. Sheila was a qualified primary school teacher, and had specialized in teaching reading to children with learning difficulties. She was a dedicated and able teacher and had always intended to go back to it once family commitments permitted. Sheila was a confident, efficient and well-organized person. Some would say she was the dominant partner. She was creative and artistic, and enjoyed sewing (she made many of her own clothes) and cookery to a very high standard. She loved organizing dinner parties. She was houseproud. She was a confident driver.

Onset and course of the acute illness

The illness started with a common cold following a winter holiday. This developed into a severe headache, dizziness and vomiting, which resulted in her collapsing unconscious after taking a bath. About ten minutes later, she regained consciousness and was confined to bed with suspected influenza. That same night she had a convulsion and was admitted to the local cottage hospital. Over the next few days she deteriorated rapidly and became very confused. Although she continued to recognize people, she did not know where she was or why she was there. On one occasion, she said she was in a library. On another occasion, she thought she was in hospital to have Jonathon. On another occasion, she thought she was in hospital visiting Jonathon, who was ill. She became incontinent. She was taken into St Bartholomew's Hospital and within twenty-four hours she was in intensive care.

On transfer from intensive care to the general ward she was, not surprisingly, very drowsy and able to remember hardly anything. She apparently recognized close members of the family when they visited her, and occasionally recognized photographs of friends and other relatives, but rarely was able to give them a name. She did not recognize photographs of homes, present or past, or of holidays. Famous landmarks or buildings (such as St Paul's Cathedral or Big Ben) were unfamiliar to her. She stayed in this hospital for three weeks and was then transferred back to the local cottage hospital for a further period of approximately three weeks, when she was discharged.

At this time she was still very confused and frightened. She did not know her way around her own home and she would very often forget why she had gone from one room to another by the time she had arrived. Her retention could still only be measured in seconds. Her autobiographical memory was virtually nonexistent, her visual memory even worse. Her frustration often resulted in physical or verbal violence. Conversely, she would have bouts of sheer euphoria, particularly when she recognized someone or when she found she could join in a conversation. She was ultra-sensitive to bright light or to sound.

Day-to-day performance since the illness

It must be remembered that Sheila emerged from hospital as a virtual 'cabbage' and has developed gradually over the period to a position where she can lead an apparently normal and independent life. I shall highlight any points that I feel may be significant during the period of development.

It is worth noting from the start that we do not live near any of our families. All of Sheila's family (parents, brother and family and sister and family) live in the West Midlands, my father lives in Derbyshire and my sister lives in Sussex. At the time of her acute illness, we lived in Hertfordshire. Neither of Sheila's parents enjoys the best of health. When Sheila was in hospital she had the occasional visit from her parents and one visit from her brother. My own sister was the only person I could rely on for support during this period, and she visited the hospital daily. The intention had been that as soon as Sheila was able, she would go to stay with her parents until, it was hoped, she was able to look after herself at home. This lasted precisely two days. Sheila was sufficiently aware to know that she was not in her own home, but could not understand why. It made her extremely distressed and she often resorted to throwing childish tantrums. This, together with the constant repeated questioning, made life very difficult for her parents and they had to ask me to take her home. Since then our relationship with Sheila's family has continued as before, with a weekly phone call and the occasional weekend visit. I have never asked for their help, and perhaps consequently it has rarely been offered. I do not think they have ever really understood the nature or indeed the severity of the illness, and in a way refuse to accept that it has happened.

We had a small circle of close friends on whom we had to rely a great deal in the early days. One couple in particular offered their services as 'Jonathon minder', and this was gratefully accepted. It gave me the freedom to visit Sheila in hospital virtually whenever I wished. Other friends spent time with Sheila at home – but this did not last for very long. Gradually our friends either moved away (or we moved away from them) or have fallen by the wayside. It is virtually impossible now for Sheila to make new friends. We still exchange the occasional weekend visits with two families whom we knew for many years before Sheila's illness, but otherwise Sheila's life is rather isolated outside her immediate family.

She is now totally dependent on me as the bread-winner and decision-maker, both of which used to be shared, with Sheila in the past probably having the upper hand on the latter. She nowadays rarely offers an opinion on anything and never takes the initiative in suggesting that we do something or go somewhere. Conversation is very limited. I rarely talk about Sheila to other people, and often behave as if she does not exist.

What is perhaps of more interest is the relationship, or otherwise, with Jonathon and how this has developed during the period. He has, of course, had to grow up from the age of three without a 'mother', but instead has had a person who is apparently unable to offer the love, guidance or rational discipline that would otherwise have been part of Sheila's personality. Prior to her illness, she spent many hours patiently teaching him to read, and by the age of three Jonathon had a reading age of six – an indication partly of Sheila's knowledge of her subject and partly of Jonathon's intelligence. They enjoyed a loving and relaxed relationship. Suddenly, this was wrenched away from him. There were occasions when I would come home to find both Sheila and Jonathon sitting on the stairs in tears. The reason rarely became apparent. At other times, she would scold him for doing something and minutes later encourage him to do the same thing. Often she would serve him with the same meal day after day – which meant he could have his favourite fish fingers whenever he wanted; a plus point as far as he was concerned. As he has grown up it has become harder for Sheila to apply discipline in a logical and reasoned manner: an easy situation for a youngster to take advantage of, and he has done so on many occasions. Like me, he rarely talks about Sheila either with me or with his friends. Despite all this, however, he is as 'normal' as any teenager can be, and is probably more independent and single-minded than most. How he would have turned out under normal circumstances is anyone's guess.

Sheila has always said that she would like to go back to teaching, but with her disability it is very unlikely that she will ever be able to do so, certainly not as a class teacher. For some years she has assisted one morning a week at the local junior school where she helps one of the teachers with children with reading difficulties. I am told that she does an excellent job and her teaching abilities and instincts are still there. She does, however, need regular supervision as she loses track of what she has done, even over a few minutes. Obviously, any continuity from one week to the next would be impossible if she were left to her own devices.

Sheila is well aware of her disability (but not of the extent), so any wish to learn a new skill is greatly influenced by the knowledge of the difficulties she would be likely to experience. I suspect that the desire to learn is still there, but the motivation is suppressed. In the early days, both the wish and the ability to do daily household chores were nonexistent. Even when given a job to do, she would quickly lose interest. Sheila is now able to run the home without assistance, although this is achieved by following a strict routine (Monday is washday, Tuesday is dusting, and so on). The difference between now and before the illness is that she is content just to do the bare minimum to keep the house clean. In other words, the attention to detail and the pride in the end product has gone.

We were fortunate that we literally lived next door to the local shops, and, armed with a list, Sheila was able to do a limited amount of shopping at an early stage in her recovery. Unfortunately, she would often fail to recognize where she lived, and would wander off into the distance. Any thought of shopping unaccompanied anywhere else was, of course, out of the question. The construction of a shopping list was, and still is, a problem. Just knowing that you are in need of a particular item requires a memory; so does knowing where that particular item is normally kept or where spares are kept. Often we had numerous identical bottles of shampoo in various locations around the house. Sheila is now able to go shopping in the town (a mile away) where she buys most of the groceries and household items unaccompanied. She has never had the need to travel on public transport during the period, but I am sure she would still find it a problem if she did.

As I said earlier, Sheila was a confident driver, and she is equally confident (and competent) now. The decision to allow her to drive again was a difficult one, but she often says that it gave a greater boost to her confidence than anything else during the period of recovery. (This was about seven years ago.) From the point of view of her driving technique, she literally sat in the car and drove as if there had been nothing wrong. The problem, again, was of getting lost, which is still a problem. She does go further afield nowadays, but even so, would rarely dare to venture more than five miles from home. She drives a Mini, which is a car she used to drive before the illness. She would find it difficult to adjust to another type of car.

Sheila still likes to cook, but she is unable (or unwilling?) to attempt anything too ambitious. The emphasis is now more on eating for eating's sake rather than on presentation. She finds cooking something like a Sunday lunch (meat and two veg) very taxing. Preparation normally takes place well in advance, and everything is labelled according to when she needs to start cooking it so that the whole meal is ready at the same time. Her skills with the sewing machine have also gone, and despite many attempts she is still only able to undertake simple jobs. Similarly, her abilities with a sewing needle or knitting needles are now very basic, and the results are invariably untidy.

Sheila spends a lot of time watching television, particularly music, comedy and wild life programmes. She rarely watches films or plays because she cannot follow the story. She no longer reads books. She does, however, spend hours each day reading the newspaper, although she may read the same item a number of times. The newspaper is also used as a reference point to enable her to get a fix on the day and date.

Sheila is generally strong and healthy, and since the illness has only suffered from the occasional cold. In fact, she even went five years without a cold in the period immediately following the illness. She does not indulge in any vigorous sports, but she has attended yoga classes for many years, both before and after; she still gets a great deal of enjoyment out of this.

She is both able and willing to carry on a conversation, but the range of such a conversation is very limited. She is more confident when talking about her pet subjects (such as teaching), when she often becomes overanimated and tries to dominate the conversation. Such things as current affairs are usually avoided. When the conversation is about something outside her sphere of knowledge she quickly loses interest, and if sitting down she will often fall asleep.

There have never been any major problems with the telephone. There was a time when she could not recognize even close relatives' voices, but this is no longer a problem. In fact, she often recognizes people on the 'phone that we have met since the illness.

Sheila has never been unable or unwilling to wash and dress herself. The problem lay in remembering when she last took a bath or when an item of clothing was last washed. She tended to overcompensate for this. She has now developed a system whereby she turns an item of clothing inside out if it has been worn but is not ready for washing.

How the illness has affected me

The question of interaction with our families was covered to some extent in the earlier section; life has effectively gone on as if nothing had happened. I cannot help feeling a certain amount of bitterness towards them for not offering more help, but this was to some extent self-inflicted. We each have our own lives to lead, and when life gets tough we have to sort things out for ourselves.

Most of our friends were those we shared as a couple and tended also to be married couples of our own age group. As explained earlier, these relationships have tended to drift away. My own friends have tended to be work-related and rarely overlap with the home situation. I do have one close friend who constantly keeps my head above water. Had Sheila not recovered to the extent she has, it would have been impossible to continue with my career, or indeed pursue any other form of full-time occupation. (I was, and still am, a qualified actuary.) Not only did Sheila require constant attention, the sheer mental and physical strain of looking after her would have left me with too little time or energy to devote to a professional career. Initially, I always refused to believe that Sheila would remain in such a condition (whether this was just wishful thinking, I shall never know) and I returned to work as soon as I was able. Whether my career path would have taken a different direction had this not happened, I do not know, but it has certainly forced me to reassess my priorities. A job move four years ago took me away from a high-pressure partnership in London to employment in Southampton.

My wish or ability to learn new skills have not been affected. The freedom to do so, however, is greatly curtailed. At first, it was necessary for me to take on board most of the household chores, which I hate at the best of times. Fortunately, the responsibility for these has been handed back, although it is now necessary for me to act much more as a 'quality controller'. I have probably devoted more time to hobbies and pastimes than I used to – in particular, sailing, squash and playing the organ. I probably watch less TV than I used, to which is the result of a conscious effort to make better use of my spare time. My health is generally good, and I probably take better care of myself now than I did before.

Comment

Although this chapter has been included because it provides insights into the everyday experience of amnesia, it nevertheless illustrates important points about amnesia and its effects. For example, although the ability to create new long-term memories appears to have been largely lost, it is clear that some new information can be retained (see chapter by Butters et al.) – Sheila was able to recognize the voices of some new friends and she knew her memory was impaired. Some skills and knowledge acquired prior to the brain damage remained relatively intact, for example, the ability to drive and skills in teaching (see chapter by Wilson and Wearing), whereas others were lost, such as her sewing skills. Also Sheila and her husband developed various memory aids that made possible the execution of many everyday activities; for example, labelling dishes with cooking times, using newspapers to help her know the day and date, and so on (see chapter by Van der Linden et al.). In later chapters we shall see that although memory impairments arising from brain damage nearly always lead to major disability, preservation of some aspects of memory coupled with sparing of other intellectual abilities allow some recovery and rehabilitation of everyday activities.

Reference

Kapur, N., Barker, S., Burrows, E., Ellison, D., Brice, J., Illis, L., Scholey, K., Colbourn, C., Wilson, B. and Loates, M. (1994) 'Herpes simplex encephalitis: long-term MRI and neuropsychological profile', *Journal of Neurology, Neurosurgery and Psychiatry*, **57**: 1334–42.

Part I Stranded in Time
Long-term Memory

Introduction

The four chapters in this part report studies of patients with various types of long-term memory impairments (retrograde amnesia) coupled with moderate to severe anterograde amnesia in the presence of otherwise relatively well-preserved general intelligence. One of the best-known recent cases is that of the celebrated musician Clive Wearing who, as a result of herpes simplex encephalitis, sustained extensive temporal lobe damage encompassing virtually all the left temporal lobe and regions of the right temporal lobe as well damage to areas of the frontal lobes. Wilson and Wearing describe the sequence of neuropsychological testing Clive Wearing has undergone since his injury, and provide a thorough and detailed account of his current abilities. Essentially his illness gave rise to an extremely dense retrograde amnesia covering most of his adult life and much of his childhood. In addition he had a profound anterograde amnesia such that he was wholly unable to encode new information into long-term memory. Although his short-term memory was well preserved he also suffered from impairments of semantic knowledge, that is the meanings of many common words were no longer available to him, and he frequently confabulated definitions and explanations. His musical skills were also diminished as was his general intelligence, both of which had been in the upper range prior to becoming ill. For Clive Wearing, life after his brain injury became literally 'momentary'. A particularly revealing example of this is that when attempting to play the card game patience/solitaire, a brief glance away form the cards would be sufficient for him to forget their layout and become surprised, when glancing back, at their arrangement and nature. Indeed, in an attempt perhaps to manage his memory problems he has kept a diary for a number of years, but the diary entries simply record repetitively that he is awake at the moment an entry is made: this may occur many times in the same day. Interestingly, he is aware, to at least some extent, of his memory problems and, as Wilson and Wearing point out, has tried, unsuccessfully, to understand these. Also, unlike many patients with similar patterns of amnesia, he has strong emotions, often of irritation, anger and anxiety.

In contrast to Clive Wearing is patient PS, a 67-year-old retired garage owner who, following a stroke, sustained damage to the thalamus. This patient has been extensively studied by McCarthy and Hodges, who have established that PS has dense retrograde and anterograde amnesia with an interact short-term memory and reasonably well-preserved general intelligence – a pattern of cognitive impairment not unlike that of Clive Wearing. However, PS's retrograde amnesia, although profound, is not as complete as that suffered by Clive Wearing. In particular PS has comparatively good knowledge of a period from his life when he was on active service in the British Navy during the Second World War – some forty years prior to the onset of his illness. This preservation of a period from PS's autobiography stands in stark contrast to his almost complete amnesia for his family and working life in the period after his naval service up to his illness. Indeed, PS now believes himself still to be on active naval duty and explains his presence at home as 'shore leave'. Many of PS's day-to-day problems, misunderstandings and incomprehension arise from interpreting daily activities in terms of this inappropriate life period. PS also, unlike Clive Wearing and more like other amnesic patients, has virtually no awareness of his memory problems and is emotionally 'flat' and withdrawn.

This characteristic of a lowering of emotional tone and a restriction in the variety of experienced emotions is explored further by O'Connor, Cermak and Seidman. O'Connor et al. describe their patient SS-who, following herpes simplex encephalitis, also suffered damage to the left temporal lobe and regions of the frontal lobes. SS has been studied for many years and has been found to have dense retrograde and anterograde amnesias with preservation of short-term memory and general intelligence. In this chapter O'Connor et al. examine SS's mood state and personality. These are clearly aspects of cognition we would expect to change, given that an individual no longer has access to his memories, can no longer encode new memories, and, of course, that his life has changed so radically as a consequence of his illness. In fact, SS generally showed a positive mood state in his everyday behaviour with little insight into his amnesia. On some of tests of clinical depression administered by O'Connor et al., this was supported and he was not found to be clinically depressed. However, on other tests of personality there were indications of an anxious and depressed individual who perhaps hid his mood state out of a moral sense that such negative emotions should not be inflicted on others. Yet the interpretation of these findings is fraught with problems and it is difficult to associate mood and personality with the brain injury itself rather than the daily consequences of the injury. Nevertheless, changes in emotion and self arising from brain injury must occur and it will be an important task for future research to determine which of these changes relate solely to brain injury, which to life changes, and which arise interactively.

Finally, in this section van der Linden and Croyette report a rehabilitation study of their patient AC – a 33-year old man who for unknown reasons sustained brain damage to regions of the occipital and temporal lobes. AC's amnesia differed from that of the other patients discussed in this section in that although he presented with a profound anterograde amnesia, spared short-term memory, language and IQ, his retrograde amnesia was not as dense as that of the other patients. Thus, although his memory for specific, autobiographical memories was clearly and profoundly impaired, his memory for the personal facts of his life was relatively spared. Despite these differences the important demonstration of van der Linden and Croyette is that evenly densely impaired amnesic patients can learn some new information and eventually resume a role in the community. Following methods developed by Schacter and his colleagues, van der Linden and Croyette were able to train AC to use a word processor and, eventually, a memory book in which he kept track of activities he had already performed. This type of retraining capitalizes upon the now well-established finding that amnesiac patients can often benefit from *implicit* learning. That is to say that although a patient with dense anterograde amnesia will be unable to remember either when they learned some information or what they learned, that information may none the less influence their subsequent behaviour (see the chapter by Butters et al.). So, for example, when shown a list of words which had been seen previously, an amnesic patient, although wholly unaware of the prior viewing of the word list, will nevertheless still respond more quickly to the second presentation, indicating that the word list was originally retained in some form. Capitalizing on this process of preserved implicit learning and limiting it to a narrow domain of knowledge (word processing) van der Linden and Croyette were able to design a rehabilitation programme that effectively retrained AC and allowed him to resume a useful role in society.

Taken together, these four cases of impaired memory following brain injury reveal a great deal about the nature and working of long-term memory and how this relates to personality and mood. They also show that in certain cases there is some possibility of rehabilitation through retraining, although it should be noted that the memory impairments themselves are permanent and, once present, do not change.

2 Prisoner of Consciousness: a State of Just Awakening Following Herpes Simplex Encephalitis

Barbara A. Wilson and Deborah Wearing

1 History and Background

At the time of his illness in 1985 Clive Wearing* was an outstanding musician, producer of early music for the British Broadcasting Corporation's classical music station, chorus master to the London Sinfonietta (working with many of today's great composers), conductor of a large Renaissance ensemble, and one of the world's leading authorities on the sixteenth-century composer Orlandus Lassus. So thorough was his research and so ambitious his performances that historians agreed that his concerts of early music were the next best thing to going back in time. He was one of the first to conduct authentic instruments by candlelight, but did not stop short at the music on the page: he searched for every last detail about the original performance – pronunciation, forces employed, tones of voice of the singers, how the music carried in the room or building and, where possible, what the audience had for dinner. He toiled through archives all over Europe to find contemporary documents and manuscripts to provide him with more clues. When the Victoria and Albert Museum wanted a concert to celebrate their exhibition of the Gonzaga family, Clive went to Mantua and found music written for and even by the Dukes of Gonzaga plus the correct chant and information about local usage. He came back and conducted his reconstruction of vespers in the V&A against pictures of the Ducal palace projected for the audience.

Clive's excitement about the music he spent his life unearthing was so keen that he was never deterred by, for example, not being a linguist: he would successfully translate

* With his wife's permission, we are deviating from the normal practice of using initials to disguise the identity of the patient, as Clive Wearing is well known to many people in the United Kingdom and other parts of the world through (a) his music, (b) two television documentaries made about him, and (c) numerous articles in magazines.

anything – sixteenth-century Neapolitan dialect or mediaeval church Latin as pronounced in Renaissance Bavaria, with the aid of dictionaries, tracts, an intellectual rigour that astounded his peers and a boundless, almost boyish, determination. BBC Radio's Royal Wedding Day celebration for Charles and Diana consisted of Clive's reconstruction of the 1568 wedding of Duke Wilhelm of Bavaria for which, as with most programmes, he had found the music, edited it for performance, translated a contemporary account and written talks to bring the event to life.

Over Christmas 1984 Clive produced the Octave of the Nativity, ten programmes recreating Christmas services in different cities from different times. That series produced the largest amount of fan mail in the history of Radio 3.

For twenty-five years before joining the BBC staff in 1983 Clive was a freelance conductor, musicologist and singer. For all that time he sang daily services at Westminster Cathedral, providing his only regular (and tiny) income which had to support three children from his first marriage as well as sustain him while he pursued his research. So Clive was never without money worries. He was always known as a 'workaholic', working seven days a week until late at night, almost never taking holidays or breaks. An evening spent at home would typically see him doing several things at once – a microfilm reader on his lap, transcribing and editing a newly discovered motet with his right hand, eating a bowl of spaghetti bolognaise with his left hand, chatting to his wife about the spread of influence of the Council of Trent, and following a rugby match on the television in front of him. He did everything thoroughly and fast, and quickly grew impatient with anyone who could not keep up with him. Musicians who arrived late for rehearsal or who were slow to get something right soon experienced his hot temper and loud voice.

With such a punishing and relentless schedule, Clive was frequently in a state of exhaustion and had suffered increasingly from headaches as he pushed himself harder still with the BBC job in addition to his other work. Then in March 1985, just as his career was beginning to blossom, Clive was struck down by herpes simplex encephalitis, which robbed him of virtually all of his episodic memory functioning. In the words of his wife Deborah, speaking on Colin Blakemore's television documentary series *The Mind Machine* (BBC, 1988):

Clive's world now consists of a *moment* with no past to anchor it and no future to look ahead to. It is a blinkered moment. He sees what is right in front of him but as soon as that information hits the brain it fades. Nothing registers. Everything goes in perfectly well . . . he perceives his world as you or I do, but as soon as he's perceived it and looked away it's gone for him. So it's a moment to moment consciousness as it were . . . a time vacuum.

2 Illness and Acute Stage

One Saturday afternoon in March 1985 Deborah returned home from work and began playing her violin. Clive asked her to stop as he had a headache. Over the next few days the headache became more acute and he developed a high fever with vomiting and sensitivity to light. Two general practitioners repeatedly diagnosed influenza. From the Sunday to the Wednesday morning Clive had been unable to sleep because of the headache. Then early on Wednesday morning, when his temperature was 104, he became extremely confused, unable to answer the simplest questions. A general practitioner visiting him then ascribed his confusion to lack of sleep and prescribed sleeping tablets. With these he said Clive would be 'out for eight hours' and encouraged his wife to go and give the lecture she was due to give that afternoon. On her return in the evening Clive was missing. The police began a search. At some point in the afternoon Clive had dressed himself and gone out, hailed a taxi but been unable to recall his home address. The taxi driver had dropped him at a police station where they had traced his home through his Barclaycard in his wallet, and called Deborah to come and collect him.

On his return home he did not recognize the flat. Two GPs visiting at various times that night maintained their diagnosis of influenza with 'meningitis-like' symptoms. On the following day, Thursday, Clive slept and took fluids. His temperature dropped. But early on Friday morning he was confused as to which piece of bathroom furniture was the lavatory. As his wife repeatedly called the doctor he began to grow floppy. The doctor arrived a little before 8.00 a.m. He called the emergency services and left. At 9.00 a.m. on Friday 29 March, the sixth day of the headache, Clive was admitted to hospital. Once there it took eleven hours to diagnose herpes simplex encephalitis. Clive was treated with Acyclovir, an antiviral drug; it probably saved his life, although his brilliant mind remained full of holes. He was given a computerized tomography (CT) scan on that day and the subsequent report indicated areas of low density (that is, malfunctioning), particularly in the left temporal lobe and extending into the inferior and posterior frontal lobe as well as the right temporal lobe.

3   The First Few Months

For the first few days Clive's consciousness fluctuated, and on the Sunday he had a *grand mal* seizure after which he was also treated with phenytoin intravenously. Once past the critical stage he was confused and disorientated, wandering around the hospital and climbing into beds, even those already occupied. He appeared to have very limited comprehension, his speech did not make sense and he repeated meaningless phrases. He could not answer such questions as, 'What is a tree? Do you eat it, dress in it, or pick fruit from it?' Certain words and phrases cropped up unaccountably often: 'chicken' for example was used to mean anything from a tie to a cigarette.

For the first couple of months Clive's mood was principally one of euphoria as he was generally unperturbed by his dense confusion: too confused to be confused.

A speech therapist's report in May 1985 noted 'extreme distractibility'. She also stated that Clive had an impairment in auditory comprehension at complex levels where retention of information is necessary. There was also difficulty in comprehending written material: Clive could read words accurately but could not always define them. He complained that words had changed their meanings. Furthermore, his ability to define single words was affected. When asked to define 'eyelid', for example, he replied, 'I don't know that word, it must be used by a great specialist.'

At about this time Deborah noticed that Clive was articulating and spelling words backwards at a rate faster than people could decipher. For example, he called his wife

'Harobed'. His spelling forwards was phonetic: 'pipal' for people, and 'conchaseness' for consciousness. The backward spelling and talking was accomplished in the spirit of a joke. As for the phonetic spelling, Deborah believes that stemmed from a need to cover up slight spelling difficulties and Clive then exaggerated his confused spelling to joke proportions in order to disguise the extent of his problem.

In these months Clive was not able to retain impressions for more than the briefest moment. The effect was of course that the environment appeared to be in a state of flux. On many occasions he would comment, 'You weren't wearing blue just now. No, no, it was yellow or pink but it certainly wasn't blue.' In response to the constantly new appearance of the room Clive would keep asking, 'How do they do that?' One day he put this phenomenon to the test. He held a chocolate in one hand and repeatedly covered and uncovered it with the other. He could feel that the chocolate never moved, yet each time he uncovered it, it appeared to be a new chocolate, however quickly he looked.

At first in his most highly confused and euphoric state he regarded these astonishing changes with baffled amusement. But as the initial jumble subsided and his sentences began to make more sense a huge despair set in so that, for a couple of months, he was crying every morning even before he had opened his eyes and did not stop crying all day unless he was playing the piano. One day during this period, Clive and Deborah were sitting on a wall waiting for an ambulance to return to hospital and Clive was sobbing tearlessly. Deborah handed him a notebook and pen and asked him to write down why he was crying. (He had by then been crying for a month almost continuously.) Clive wrote: 'I am completely incapable of thinking.'

It was Clive's wish to try to fix his apparently changing environment which first prompted him to begin his compulsive habit of writing. He spent much of his time playing the card game Patience (Solitaire in the USA). Naturally the cards seemed to change each time he glanced away from one. So in a typically thorough exercise to research the reason, Clive picked up a pencil and paper one day and began to draw the arrangement of the cards with symbols, colours and numbers. At the bottom of the page he put a key to the symbols but could not remember the names of all the suits. He called clubs 'clicks' and could not remember spades at all. It was then that he began recording the time, date and the fact of having become conscious that very moment, details which he has repeated in copious diaries through all the years since. He describes some of his impressions in the diaries. For example, of the cards he wrote 'curious looks, take eyes away from cards then return them, cards alter in name and positions'. In the desperate bid of a still intelligent man to make sense of the apparently shifting patterns of cards, he began to look for a code in the way the cards had fallen which would also explain the momentous fact of regaining consciousness just at that very moment. So he translated the numbers on the cards to notes on the stave and looked at the melody they made against which he might write: 'HEAVENLY INSPIRED – cards NOT laid out by me.'

During the early months there were epileptic and Parkinsonian symptoms, ranging from tremor when he attempted to pick something up, to marked jerking, shaking and severe belching episodes. After an acute bout he might vomit and would sleep.

A psychiatric report from July 1985 described an episode of marked shaking and frequently repeated burping sounds. An EEG carried out on Clive indicated that the noises and movements were epileptic in origin. Exacerbated by stress and anxiety, these shakings and burpings have continued to this day. Avi Schmueli (personal communication), then a trainee clinical psychologist working with Clive in 1991, noted that the episodes occurred with a change of activity such as a nurse entering the room or Clive switching tasks.

Semantic memory problems were also described by Deborah in 1985. She reported that Clive could not tell the difference between jam, honey and marmalade. He ate a whole lemon, peel and all, and would eat huge quantities of food if left unsupervised, indicating no feeling of satiety. He could not tell which of the several bottles and one tube in his bathroom was toothpaste, he confused the mantelpiece and the wardrobe, gave Deborah talcum powder when she asked for soap, called a scarf an umbrella, and mistook his wife's sweater for his shirt.

From the very earliest days since his illness, Clive has confabulated. The hospital notes from April 1985 reported that his conversation was marked by confabulation and perseveration. By July that year he had begun his most persistent confabulation about working in whichever building he happened to be in. In the hospital where he spent seven years he believed he had worked there years before when he was a student in Cambridge. He said that he used to organize fellow students to come to the hospital and work in their vacations while staff were on holiday. He usually added that he did this for the whole country for eight, twelve, fifteen, twenty or twenty-five years. This confabulation also occurred when he first saw me (BAW) at another hospital and on the many occasions I saw him thereafter. It occurred, too, when he spent a few weeks at a therapeutic centre early in 1986, and remains the same to this day. His wife believes this fixed confabulation is founded on two real memories: one of spending his actual summer vacations working in a hotel with other Cambridge students, which he did for several years (hotel being semantically linked with 'hospital'); the other being a very remote sense of hospitals being familiar because by then he had been in one for six or seven months, but so remote as to seem twenty or thirty years ago rather than five minutes ago.

Two further developments occurred between June and October 1985. First, Clive tried to find an explanation for the case of his illness. He typically attributed it to whatever story was on the front page of *The Times* that day. On 27 October 1985 he wrote:

a *strange* kind of illness seems to blame for this gap in my life! Was this illness imposed upon me by other people? The only way to find out is to do a detailed examination of all the magazines, newspapers and other published material appearing during the last 6 months. The results of an inquiry will release the causes of my 'now-living' – despite apparently unlikely connection between the subjects.

In late October and early November of that year he blamed, among others, the secrets-for-sex trials at the Old Bailey; King Hussein of Jordan; Sir Geoffrey Howe, the Conservative politician; and Mrs Victoria Gillick, mother of ten and a Roman Catholic with outspoken views on contraception. He seemed to assume that someone wanted to shut him up because he must have uncovered some important international conspiracy. He often ran down the hospital corridors looking for a policeman to tell.

The second development was the beginning of his compulsion to write things down. On 7 July 1985 he wrote: 'awake first time'. This was the first recording of a phrase that has been repeated by Clive many hundreds of times in the intervening years. Figure 2.1

Figure 2.1 Part of a page of Clive's many diaries

shows a single page from one of Clive's diaries. At the time of writing this chapter (October 1993) there are nine such diaries, all containing very similar entries.

4   November 1985–May 1986

Deborah arranged for Clive to be seen by BAW in November 1985, some eight months after the onset of encephalitis. Deborah wanted an assessment of Clive's memory as well as advice on the management of his memory problems. By then he had been assessed by several neuropsychologists, all of whom noted his very dense amnesia. BAW's assessment was possibly more detailed, and since that time she has kept in touch with Clive and Deborah for the past eight years. Because Clive was seen by BAW as an outpatient once a month the initial assessment took seven months to complete.

Clive was not an easy person to test. He frequently became angry, saying he had 'just woken up for the first time'. He said that he had not seen or heard anything until that moment so how could he know the answers to the tester's questions. This theme was repeated every few minutes. The tests he seemed to enjoy most were the performance items from the Wechsler Adult Intelligence Scale (WAIS) (Wechsler, 1955). Some tests were abandoned because of Clive's increasing frustration and annoyance. He became very angry during the administration of the Seashore Test of Musical Abilities (Seashore et al., 1960), saying something to the effect that 'I am a world famous musician, how dare you ask me if I can differentiate between different pitches!' Although Clive was unable to remember much about his early life, he did and does remember he was a musician.

In the report of the May 1986 assessment the following points were noted:

1   Premorbidly, Mr Wearing was probably functioning in the superior range of ability. Evidence for this comes from his scores on the National Adult Reading Test (Nelson, 1982), which gave an estimated IQ of 122 (informal testing before his illness indicated a premorbid IQ that might be as high as 144, together with his reputation as a talented and gifted musician and scholar.
2   His current general intellectual functioning, as assessed by the WAIS, is in the average range (Verbal IQ = 105; Performance IQ = 106), suggesting that some intellectual decline has occurred.
3   He has a very profound amnesia. On the Rivermead Behavioural Memory Test (Wilson et al., 1985) his screening score was 0/12. On the immediate and delayed recall of prose passages from the Wechsler Memory Scale (Wechsler, 1945), Clive scored 1 and 0 respectively, with confabulation noted on immediate recall. On the Rey Osterreith Figure (Osterreith, 1944) his copy was normal but he failed to recall anything after a delay. On the Autobiographical Memory Interview (AMI) (Kopelman et al., 1989) his scores for all time periods were abnormal, this being true for both factual (personal semantic) questions and for autobiographical incidents. He shows a severe retrograde amnesia for virtually the whole of his adult life and for much of his childhood. However, his immediate memory span is normal and he shows implicit learning. (BAW also notes that she has never seen a patient more amnesic than Clive Wearing.)

4   His scores on frontal lobe tests were impaired.
5   He scored in the impaired range on a test of semantic processing (Baddeley et al., 1992).

Semantic memory was not investigated in any detail until 1991–2.

5   Since May 1986

Clive was reassessed in 1989 as part of a long-term follow-up study of memory-impaired people (Wilson, 1991), and given further tests in 1991 and 1992.

In most areas of functioning, Clive's scores were essentially unchanged when reassessed. His immediate memory spans as assessed by recall of digits remained at 6 forward and 4 backward on each of three occasions. He failed to score on the Rivermead Behavioural Memory Test, delayed recall of prose passages and the Rey Figure. He was unable to recall any public events on tests of retrograde amnesia, and claimed he had never heard of John Lennon or John F. Kennedy. His scores on the AMI were still in the impaired range.

Intellectually, there may have been some decline over this period as his Verbal IQ on the revised version of the WAIS (Wechsler, 1981) was estimated to be 92 in 1992. These results can be seen in table 2.1. Even allowing for the fact that the new WAIS typically estimates both Verbal and Performance IQ to be 7 or 8 points less than the original WAIS, Clive's responses were qualitatively poorer on the latter assessment. For example, on the similarities subtest his 1985 response to the question, 'In what way are North and West alike?' was 'Part of the compass'. In 1992 his response was, 'At right angles to each other'. Similarly, when asked 'In what way are air and water alike?', he replied in 1985, 'Both have oxygen', in 1992 he said, 'Naturally part of the climate'.

However, on a test of speed of information processing, Clive scored in the normal range: his simple reaction time on a task whereby he had to press a button as fast as possible whenever a red light appeared compared favourably with control subjects and with subjects having the pure amnesic syndrome (Wilson et al., 1992).

The apparent deterioration noted earlier might be caused by Clive forgetting his world knowledge as the years pass; he is no longer rehearsing information through exposure to conversation, newspapers, television and other media. This suggestion is perhaps supported by the fact his score on the National Adult Reading Test (NART) (Nelson and O'Connell, 1982) has also decreased. The NART is a test that requires subjects to read and pronounce a range of orthographically irregular words ranging from common to rare. A predicted premorbid IQ can be estimated from the number of errors made on the test. In 1985, Clive's estimated IQ was 122, when he made seven errors. In 1992 he made twenty errors, giving him a predicted premorbid IQ of 111. This was a man who completed *The Times* crossword daily prior to his illness, and the hard AZED crossword in the *Sunday Observer*. Both 122 and 111 are certainly underestimates of his premorbid IQ, but the reason for the deterioration could well be because he is slowly forgetting such semantic information.

Table 2.1   CW's age-scaled scores on the WAIS and WAIS-R*

	1985 WAIS results	*1992 WAIS-R results*
Verbal subtests		
Information	11	8
Comprehension	11	8
Arithmetic	13	12
Similarities	9	6
Digit span	10	9
Vocabulary	12	12
Verbal IQ	105	92
Performance subtests		
Digit symbol	8	11
Picture completion	12	10
Block design	14	15
Picture arrangement	11	8
Object assembly	10	12
Performance IQ	106	105
Full-scale IQ	106	97

* Wechsler Adult Intelligence Scale and Wechsler Adult Intelligence Scale – Revised.

Clive's semantic memory was investigated in greater detail in 1991 and 1992. On the Graded Naming Test (GNT) (McKenna and Warrington, 1983) Clive scored only 2 out of a possible 30. Some of his errors were obviously due to word-finding difficulties (for example, 'a swimming tortoise' for 'turtle'); but others suggested object recognition difficulties (for example, 'a worshipping point for certain cultures' when shown a picture of a scarecrow). On a later occasion he was asked to define the words from the GNT. His response to 'scarecrow' was 'a bird that flies and makes funny noises'.

On a semantic memory test developed by John Hodges (Hodges et al., 1992a), Clive showed a discrepancy between living and man-made items, matched for frequency, with his knowledge of man-made items being better than living items. His scores on naming pictures, naming to description, and word-picture matching for both living and non-living items can be seen in table 2.2. His scores are a little worse than those of people with mild to moderate dementia of the Alzheimer type reported by Hodges et al. (1992a).

On verbal fluency, too, Clive showed the living/non-living discrepancy, as can be seen in table 2.3.

Clive had great difficulty with further tests of fluency. For example, when asked for names of famous musicians he produced only four in one minute, namely Mozart, Beethoven, Bach and Haydn. He omitted Lassus, the composer on whom he was considered to be the world expert. He could produce only one famous writer, Dickens, in a one-minute period, and no famous painters or artists.

Table 2.2 CW's scores on naming pictures, naming to description and word–picture matching for living and non-living items

		Living		*Non-living*
1	Naming pictures: total	11/24		20/24
	(a) Land animals	9/12	(a) Household items	9/12
	(b) Water creatures	1/6	(b) Vehicles	5/6
	(c) Birds	1/6	(c) Musical instruments	6/6
2	Naming to description: total	2/12		8/12
	(a) Land animals	1/4	(a) Household items	3/4
	(b) Water creatures	0/4	(b) Vehicles	3/4
	(c) Birds	1/4	(c) Musical instruments	2/4
3	Word–picture matching: total	17/24		24/24
	(a) Domestic animals	6/6	(a) Electrical items	6/6
	(b) Foreign animals	4/6	(b) Household items	6/6
	(c) Water creatures	2/6	(c) Vehicles	6/6
	(d) Birds	5/6	(d) Musical instruments	6/6

Table 2.3 CW's scores on category fluency for living and non-living items (1 minute each category)

Living	*Total correct responses*	*Non-living*	*Total correct responses*
Animals	9	Household items	11
Birds	6	Vehicles	7
Water creatures	3	Musical instruments	12
Dogs	0	Boats	10
Overall total	18		40

No further CT scans were given to Clive but Dr Narinder Kapur from the Wessex Neurological Centre in Southampton arranged for Clive to have an MRI scan in 1991. The report from the consultant neuroradiologist stated:

Extensive structural changes are present in both temporal lobes. The left temporal lobe is most severely affected, virtually its entire substance being abnormal. The temporal horn is widely dilated in its entire length, its tip being circular and the anatomy of the hippocampus having disappeared. On the right side, damage is confined to the medial side of the right temporal lobe, again the temporal horn is widely dilated and almost circular in outline. Each hippocampus . . . returns an abnormal signal indicating diffuse involvement. Both mammillary bodies are visible. Damage to the rest of the brain includes quite marked enlargement of the left lateral ventricle and widening of the third ventricle . . .

6 Musical Abilities

What has happened to Clive's musical abilities over this period of time? To the untrained ear he appeared at first to be as competent as ever when singing, playing or conducting his choir. As Jonathan Miller stated in a television documentary about Clive (Channel 4, *Equinox* series: *Prisoner of Consciousness*, 1986):

As soon as the music started Clive's professional personality was unaccountably restored and a casual observer would hardly suspect that large parts of his memory are virtually non-existent. And yet when the music stops he is left high and dry and he often improvises or confabulates an imaginary past as if to make up for the one he has forgotten.

Deborah has observed that there is little change in Clive's ability to sight read, though there is a significant deterioration in pianistic skills: he is able to obey repeat marks within a short page (and has been able to do that since July 1985); he still knows what a metronome mark signifies; and he can ornament, play from a figured bass, transpose and extemporise. Nevertheless, Deborah feels there has been a change. Clive is less confident when playing, and plays some pieces at a speed beyond his present capacity, although premorbidly he could have played them at that speed with ease. These changes are slight enough not to be noticed by non-musicians when he tackles simple scores.

However, he does now baulk at reading a large score. Before his illness Clive was able to read highly complex scores the size of a kitchen table and written in virtually any notation. He was known at the London Sinfonietta (Europe's leading contemporary music group) for his uncanny ability to read the most complicated modern score with great accuracy. Without the aid of an instrument, he could hear the whole piece at pitch in his head, and was able to conduct even different sections playing at different speeds simultaneously with more accuracy than some composers.

Clive now restricts his playing to straightforward pieces from the sixteenth to twentieth centuries, and does not attempt anything obviously difficult, though he might have done so in the first few years of his illness before he became withdrawn and aware of shortcomings.

Perhaps like his confabulation, he has one fixed passage of improvisation which, at times, he has played incessantly. As it is 'improvised' one cannot remove the score so there is no way to stop him other than by persuading him away from the piano.

Another phenomenon has been his use of the piano in times of great agitation, for example when he came off all tranquilizers after transfer to a special home. He would pound a piece as loudly as he could with fistfuls of wrong notes. This habit eventually subsided.

For many years Clive has experienced auditory hallucinations. He hears what he thinks is a tape of himself playing in the distance. He refers to this in his diaries as a 'master tape' (a term used in broadcasting for the original audiotape which should be protected from casual use and should certainly not leave the studio). If asked to sing what he can hear – a sound only ever heard in the distance – he picks the tune up in the middle and is puzzled that no one else hears it. Half an hour later when asked to sing what he can hear it is usually the same tune but sometimes sung in a different style as if it were replaying in variations.

There is some evidence for assuming Clive's musical memory functions better than memory for other kinds of material: he has hummed something which he had not played for half an hour (although he could have been rehearsing it subvocally in the interim).

Other brain-damaged musicians have been reported. For example, Sloboda (1985) describes a distinguished Russian composer, Shebalin, who suffered a severe stroke that left him dysphasic but did not affect his ability to compose new music. A composition produced three years after the stroke was described by Shostakovitch as 'a brilliant creative work, filled with highest emotions, optimistic and full of life. This symphony, composed during his illness, is a creation of a great master' (Sloboda, 1985, p. 260).

Shebalin went on to suffer a second stroke six years after the first, yet lost none of his ability to compose (Sergent, 1993). Other composers reported by Sergent include Jean Langlair, a French organist and composer (1907–91), the British composer, Benjamin Britten (1913–76), and the American composer George Gershwin (1898–1937). Langlair and Britten both sustained a cerebral vascular accident and Gershwin a glioblastoma. None appeared to show any decline in their musical abilities, although Shebalin and Langlair were rendered severely dysphasic.

In contrast, Ravel (1875–1937) completely lost the ability to compose, although he was able to listen to and appreciate musical pieces. The onset of Ravel's amusia was gradual and it seems likely that he had a relatively focal (presumably left) cerebral degeneration (Henson, 1988). He too was dysphasic. In the words of Brust (1980, p. 387): 'The presence or absence of aphasia, or of left or right hemisphere damage, fails to predict the presence, type and severity of amusia, including musical alexia or agraphia.'

Sergent (1993) considers the anatomical regions involved in sight-reading and keyboard performance. She claims that there are three main areas involved in sight-reading: first, the supramarginal gyrus which is important for mapping auditory and visual representations; second, the posterior part of the superior parietal lobule which is responsible for transforming sensorimotor to visuospatial representations and then transforming these to information relevant for the patterning and positioning of fingers on the keyboard; third the prefrontal cortex, extending from the inferior frontal gyrus to the supplementary area which is concerned with the organization of the sequencing and timing of finger movements necessary for playing the particular score being sight-read.

We can presume that Clive has no deficits in these areas. Most of his damage is in the temporal lobes, with some frontal lobe damage involvement. Both Clive and Ravel share involvement of the left temporal area. It is this, presumably, that gives rise to semantic memory problems. As Hodges et al. (1992b), and Patterson and Hodges (1995) have indicated, semantic memory deficits are invariably associated with left temporal lesions. It is likely therefore that damage to this same area causes Clive's semantic memory deficit.

Unlike Ravel, however, Clive has not lost the ability to sight-read, neither is he dysphasic. Presumably Ravel, with a Wernicke's aphasia, had a disturbance of the posterior and superior region of the left temporal lobe (Sergent, 1993) and we can surmise additional damage to the three areas involved in sight-reading described above. Clive's latest MRI scan, reported above, indicated that virtually the entire substance of the left temporal lobe was affected, but presumably Wernicke's area was spared.

We know that both hemispheres are involved in music. Sloboda (1985) says it is simplistic to think of music being localized in one or other hemisphere. Like memory, music is not one single skill but a number of independent subskills each of which could be anatomically independent. He says that although right hemisphere damage nearly always disrupts musical functioning, left hemisphere damage often disrupts it too.

Peretz (1985) points out that the left hemisphere is more involved with the analysis of musical stimuli whereas the right hemisphere is better equipped for the perception of whole sounds. Furthermore, she says that depending on the type of strategy used by the musician, the right or the left hemisphere could be more efficient. This could explain some of the apparent anomalies between musical abilities and brain damage. To para- phrase Sergent (1993), the only consistency across studies of neuropsychological research on musicians is their inconsistency.

7   How Does Clive Compare with Other Amnesic Subjects?

The most famous amnesic subject is no doubt HM, first reported by Scoville (1954) and Scoville and Milner (1957), and described in numerous papers since then, including Milner et al. (1968) and Cohen (1984). Clive seems to differ from HM in a number of ways. Clive has a longer retrograde amnesia and a more severe loss of autobiographical memory. HM, on the other hand, appeared to be able to remember events until about two years prior to his operation (Milner et al., 1968). There are no reports of HM having semantic memory impairments. Clive is constantly preoccupied with having just woken up. HM described his amnesia as being *like* sleep, stating, 'Every day is alone in itself, whatever joy I've had and whatever sorrow I've had' (Milner et al., 1968, p. 217). Unlike HM, Clive is unaware there have been other days prior to the one in which he finds himself. He only ever has knowledge of being conscious for a couple of minutes.

HM's lesions were restricted to the mesial parts of both temporal lobes. The temporal neocortex was spared but excision of the mesial surface was very radical, extending some '8 centimetres from the tips of the temporal lobes and destroying the anterior two thirds of the hippocampus bilaterally, as well as the uncus and amygdala' (Milner, 1966, p. 112). Clive's lesions were more extensive, with virtually all of the left temporal lobe affected, although only the medial side of the right was involved.

One of the best-known cases of amnesia following thalamic damage is that of NA, a man who suffered a stab wound to the left thalamic region at the age of twenty-two years (Squire and Moore, 1979). Once again, NA's lesion is more restricted and his amnesia less dense than Clive's.

Several patients have been reported following encephalitis, including SS by Cermak and O'Connor (1983); RFR by Warrington and McCarthy (1988); and Boswell by Damasio et al. (1985) and Tranel and Damasio (1993). SS shows a temporal gradient with events from the 1930s being recalled better than those from the 1970s. Clive does not show this temporal gradient. SS also appears to have better recall of personal than of public events whereas Clive is impaired in both domains.

Cermak and O'Connor report how SS retains an ability to entertain his visitors with anecdotes about his childhood and young adult years. Clive does this too after a manner except that, since he does not have a single episodic memory, he does not have any anecdotes as such. However, what remains of his autobiographical memory is markedly richer for his childhood and he regularly chats to nurses about Birmingham, where he grew up. He remembers in general the reasons he did not like Birmingham, what 'A' level certificates he gained, and that he played for the West Midlands junior rugby team. He even remembers the number plates of his father's cars. So he has frequent vague conversations about these things and about music.

His conversation is characterized by its limited range of topics and his repetition, verbatim, of an internal script using the same tone of voice, inflections and facial expressions. His three conversations with his wife are about whether the BBC was satisfied with his work (remarkable since he only worked on their staff for eighteen months before his illness); his anxiety about not having enough money; and his preoccupation with his apparent lack of consciousness up to that minute. With other people he extends topics to Birmingham, music and perhaps other vague subjects.

After the first few years post-insult, when talking to his wife he began to abbreviate his questions; this suggests that, at some level, he is aware he must have asked them before. He only has to mumble 'How long?' and his wife knows he means, 'How long have I been ill?' The telling point is that the abbreviation shows he *knows* that she knows. When asked how long *he* thinks he has been ill, Clive may 'guess' the right number of years as often as not, but continues to ask the question as he does not *know* the answer in any real sense of comprehension, or is unable to retrieve the correct answer.

After eighteen months in his new home, where he has been taken for a daily walk to feed the ducks, he now asks, when prompted to put his coat on, 'Aha, do the ducks want their tea?' He has all but stopped asking how long he has been ill, breaking a seven-year obsessive habit. He is preoccupied instead with car number plates and the origins of words, a frequent subject for confabulation. When he hears the word 'amnesia', for example, he responds, 'Ah yes, that's from the Latin "anti-amnesia" meaning autumn.' Many of Clive's origins and definitions of words are equally unfathomable but he is always consistent with himself. He will make such a pronouncement once and then always give the same verbatim response. As of old, he makes his statements in a voice of authority entirely credible to strangers: some taxi drivers have been absolutely astonished when he has regaled them with a history of some word or the name of their town, while Deborah is hard put to keep from laughing.

For all that he is apparently disorientated in time and space, he did (over seven years) learn to walk from the hospital dining room, up to the next floor and back to his room, although he could only be sure he had arrived when he found his name on the door. The staff assumed he must know his way as he had some implicit knowledge that took him there if he were not distracted. But when his name was removed from the door during decorations he 'went berserk' because suddenly the only clue to assure him he had found his right place was not there. Also, when the clocks have been put back an hour for winter he has been observed to be 'melancholic, out of sorts' for the first few days.

Like many amnesic patients, Clive's conversation is characterized by a jocular vein, peppered with catchphrases, puns and giggling about, for example, car number plates. A catchphrase for several years was 'Merry Xmas, a happy New Year and lang may yer lumb reek' (whatever the season).

Clive differs further from SS in that he has more neuropsychological dysfunction, especially in regard to semantic memory, and he confabulates.

In comparison with RFR (who has also been assessed by one of the authors – BAW), Clive once again has a longer period of RA, semantic memory problems, and is far more agitated and difficult to test. RFR's scores on the Wechsler Memory Scale – Revised are also higher than Clive's. For example, RFR's verbal memory index is 62 and his visual memory index 64 whereas Clive's are below 50 on both measures.

In many ways Clive is more similar to Boswell in that both have widespread temporal lobe damage, extensive retrograde amnesia, and both confabulate. However, Clive's anterograde amnesia appears to be even more extensive than Boswell's (for example, Boswell recalled four items of the Rey Osterreith Figure after a delay). Clive also has a higher IQ than Boswell.

Parkin (1984) argues that Korsakoff patients show a more extensive RA than patients with purely temporal lesions, yet even these patients rarely show as devastating a loss as Clive. He is certainly not like a typical Korsakoff patient in terms of personality. Butters (1979, p. 453), for example, says of the typical Korsakoff patient, 'Regardless of the patient's premorbid personality, he is extremely passive, malleable and emotionally flat in the chronic Korsakoff state.'

According to Parkin (1984), amnesic patients with damage to the diencephalon show a different pattern of deficits than amnesic patients with damage to the temporal lobes. Clive of course has damage to both these systems. The original scan indicated frontal lobe involvement, whereas the report of the MRI scan indicated there was widening of the third ventricle which is part of the diencephalon. So too are the mammillary bodies, although it is not clear from the MRI report whether these were affected. The report simply states that 'both mammillary bodies are visible'.

The most likely explanation for Clive's pattern of deficits is that the severity of his amnesia is caused by the almost complete destruction of the hippocampus; the extensive RA is due to the diencephalic damage; and the semantic memory impairment follows from the more widespread temporal lobe damage.

8   Summary

We report the case of Clive Wearing, a gifted musician and scholar who, at the height of his career, became infected by herpes simplex encephalitis in 1985. His amnesia is extremely severe in comparison with other reported cases, particularly in regard to both his retrograde amnesia, which extends back for virtually the whole of his life, and his episodic memory. As well as his episodic deficits, Clive has marked semantic memory impairments for both visual and verbal material. He believes he has just woken up and this state of awakening has persisted for over eight years. His musical ability appears to be relatively unaffected by his amnesia. We describe the onset of his illness and the nature of his memory dysfunctioning. We consider other musicians who have suffered brain damage, and we compare Clive to some of the well known amnesic patients in the literature.

Further Reading

Baddeley, A.D., Wilson, B.A. and Watts, F.N. (eds) (1995) *Handbook of Memory Disorders* (Chichester: John Wiley, 1995).

References

Baddeley, A.D., Emslie, H. and Nimmo-Smith, I. (1992) *The Speed and Capacity of Language Processing (SCOLP) Test* (Bury St Edmunds, Suffolk: Thames Valley Test Company).

Brust, J.C.M. (1980) 'Music and language: musical alexia and agraphia', *Brain*, 103: 367–92.

Butters, N. (1979). 'Amnesic disorders', in K.M. Heilman and E. Valenstein (eds), *Clinical Neuropsychology* (New York: Oxford University Press).

Cermak, L.S. and O'Connor, V. (1983) 'The anterograde and retrograde retrieval ability of a patient with amnesia due to encephalitis', *Neuropsychologia*, 21: 213–34.

Cohen, N.J. (1984) 'Preserved learning capacity in amnesia: evidence for multiple memory systems', in L.R. Squire and N. Butters (eds), *Neuropsychology of Memory* (New York: Guilford Press), pp. 83–103.

Damasio, A.R., Eslinger, P.J., Damasio, H., van Hoesen, G.W. and Cornell, S. (1985) 'Multimodal amnesic syndrome following bilateral temporal and basal forebrain damage', *Archives of Neurology*, 42: 252–9.

Henson, R.A. (1988) 'Maurice Ravel's illness: a tragedy of lost creativity', *British Medical Journal*, 296: 1585–8.

Hodges, J., Salmon, D.P. and Butters, N. (1992a) 'Semantic memory impairment in Alzheimer's disease: failure of access or degraded knowledge?', *Neuropsychologia*, 30: 301–14.

Hodges, J., Patterson, K., Oxbury, S. and Funnell, E. (1992b) 'Semantic dementia: progressive fluent aphasia with temporal lobe atrophy', *Brain*, 115: 1783–1806.

Kopelman, M., Wilson, B.A. and Baddeley, A.D. (1989) 'The autobiographical memory interview: a new assessment of autobiographical and semantic memory in amnesic patients', *Journal of Clinical and Experimental Neuropsychology*, 11: 724–44.

McKenna, P. and Warrington, E.K. (1983) *The Graded Naming Test* (Windsor: NFER-Nelson).

Milner, B. (1966) 'Amnesia following operation on the temporal lobes', in C.W.M. Whitty and O.L. Zangwill (eds), *Amnesia* (London: Butterworths), pp. 109–33.

Milner, B., Corkin, S. and Teuber, J.L. (1968) 'Further analysis of the hippocampal amnesic syndrome: a 14-year follow-up study of HM', *Neuropsychologia*, 6: 215–34.

Nelson, H. (1982) *The National Adult Reading Test* (Windsor: NFER-Nelson).

Osterreith, P.A. (1944) 'Le test de copie d'une figure complexe', *Archives de psychologie*, 30: 206–56.

Parkin, A.J. (1984) 'Amnesic syndrome: a lesion-specific disorder', *Cortex*, 20: 479–508.

Patterson, K. and Hodges, J. (1995) 'Disorders of semantic memory', in A.D. Baddeley, B.A. Wilson and F.N. Watts (eds), *Handbook of Memory Disorders* (Chichester: John Wiley), pp. 167–86.

Peretz, I. (1985) 'Hemispheric differences for processing musical sounds in normal subjects', *Anneé-psychologique*, 85: 429–40.

Scoville, W.B. (1954) 'The limbic lobe in man', *Journal of Neurosurgery*, 11: 64–6.

Scoville, W.B. and Milner, B. (1957) 'Loss of recent memory after bilateral hippocampal lesions', *Journal of Neurology, Neurosurgery and Psychiatry*, 20: 11–21.

Seashore, C.E., Lewis, D. and Saetveit, D.L. (1960) *Seashore Measures of Musical Talents*, rev. edn (New York: Psychological Corporation).

Sergent, J. (1993) 'Music, the brain and Ravel', *Trends in Neurological Science*, 16: 168–72.

Sloboda, J.A. (1985) *The Musical Mind* (London: Oxford University Press).

Squire, L.R. and Moore, R.Y. (1979) 'Dorsal thalamic lesion in a noted case of human memory dysfunction', *Annals of Neurology*, **6**: 303–6.

Tranel, D. and Damasio, A.R. (1993) 'The covert learning of affective valence does not require structures in hippocampal system or amygdala', *Journal of Cognitive Neuroscience*, **5**: 79–88.

Warrington, E.K. and McCarthy, R.A. (1988) 'The fractionation of retrograde amnesia', *Brain and Cognition*, **7**: 184–200.

Wechsler, D. (1945) 'A standardised memory scale for clinical use', *Journal of Psychology*, **19**: 87–95.

Wechsler, D. (1955) *Wechsler Adult Intelligence Scale* (New York: Psychological Corporation).

Wechsler, D. (1981) *Manual for the Wechsler Adult Intelligence Scale*, rev. edn (New York: Psychological Corporation).

Wilson, B., Cockburn, J. and Baddeley, A.D. (1985) *The Rivermead Behavioural Memory Test Manual* (Flempton, Bury St Edmunds, Suffolk: Thames Valley Test Company).

Wilson, B.A. (1991) 'Long-term prognosis of patients with severe memory disorders', *Neuropsychological Rehabilitation*, **1**: 117–34.

Wilson, B.A., Baddeley, A.D. Shiel, A. and Patton, G. (1992) 'How does post-traumatic amnesia differ from the amnesic syndrome and from chronic memory impairment?' *Neuropsychological Rehabilitation*, **2**: 231–43.

3 Trapped in Time: Profound Autobiographical Memory Loss Following a Thalamic Stroke

Rosaleen A. McCarthy and John R. Hodges

Introduction

Loss of memory for past events – so called retrograde amnesia (RA) – is undoubtedly one of the most devastating consequences of brain injury for patients and their carers. Yet until quite recently it has been studied relatively little. Although clinicians have always been interested in RA and have made various attempts to assess it, precise measurement of the deficit has been problematic. In many situations, we cannot be absolutely sure that a patient actually ever knew about a certain event or person: claims that the information has been forgotten have to be based on normative 'guesstimates' of what people of the same age and educational background *do* know (e.g. Warrington and Sanders, 1970). Moreover, it is impossible to control opportunities for learning in the setting of normal life, and we have no precise way of quantifying the personal salience of events.

It is clearly much simpler to study the acquisition of new material, and perhaps this is why most studies of the amnesic syndrome have focused on patients' disabilities in learning new materials or *anterograde amnesia*.[1] Despite problems in studying RA, a range of experimental techniques has evolved over the past twenty years which do allow us to explore memory for past events in the individual case. Focus on the single case also allows us to compare and contrast different types of memory test and different domains of memory (such as personal autobiographical knowledge and public memory).

One of the major findings in the study of anterograde amnesia has been that, despite showing profound impairment of new learning ability on most standard tests of memory and in everyday life, amnesic patients can, nevertheless, show normal, or near normal, performance on more indirect measures of memory retention such as word completion, priming, perceptual learning and conditioning (e.g. Warrington and Weiskrantz, 1982; Milner, 1967; see e.g. Schacter, 1987; Shimamura, 1989 for reviews). In retrograde amnesia, the evidence for dissociations between different types of memory (or different types of memory test) is far less well established. A major issue has been one of determining whether a retrograde deficit exists in different types of pathology, rather than on the profile of spared and impaired abilities in the individual patient. However, in line with our understanding of the complexities of human memory, the emphasis in studies of retrograde amnesia is beginning to change.

As is so often the case in neuropsychology, the detailed study of individual cases has provided major insights (Marslen-Wilson and Teuber, 1975; Cermak and O'Connor, 1983; Butters and Cermak, 1986; Baddeley and Wilson, 1986; Warrington and McCarthy, 1987; McCarthy and Warrington, 1992). These investigations have demonstrated the type of task used (e.g., recall of a name or choosing the familiar face from a line-up of three faces) affects performance in some cases with retrograde amnesia. There is also growing evidence for material-specificity. That is to say, patients may lose some types of information but retain others. For example, in some cases knowledge of word meaning, facts about other people and personal semantic information appears to be relatively spared, whereas knowledge of events appears to be gravely impaired (e.g. Warrington and McCarthy, 1987). The converse profile has been documented in other patients (e.g. Hodges et al., 1993). There are also pointers to suggest that personal memories may be different from public events (De Renzi et al., 1987).

We have had the opportunity to study a patient who developed a profound amnesia that included a loss of memory for his own life (autobiographical amnesia) and the details of public events. His amnesic syndrome occurred as the result of a small critically placed stroke deep within the brain. This bilateral stroke appears to have interrupted pathways which are essential for both the establishment of new memories and the retrieval of old memories. Although a number of patients with lesions similar to those found in our patient have already been reported (Graff-Radford et al., 1990; Winocur et al., 1984; von Crammon et al., 1985; Stuss et al., 1988; Markowitsch et al., 1993), the overwhelming emphasis in these studies has been on the patient's anterograde amnesia. In the studies that we describe in this chapter, we focus on our patient's memory for events pre-dating his stroke. The pattern of remote memory deficits that we observed has lead us propose some new ideas about the organisation of autobiographical memories and the processes underlying their successful retrieval.

Case Report

PS, a 67-year-old, right-handed garage proprietor was admitted to Addenbrooke's Hospital, Cambridge, on 12 June 1989 in coma. He had retired to bed the night before with his wife as normal, but the following morning was unrousable. There was no evidence of drug overdose. He had been in good general health with no history of prior strokes. Careful questioning of this wife and other family members established that his alcohol consumption was, at most, modest.

Following admission to hospital he remained in coma for less than 24 hours. The diagnosis at this stage was uncertain. When he could be adequately examined, however,

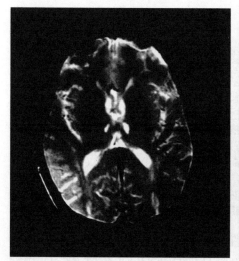 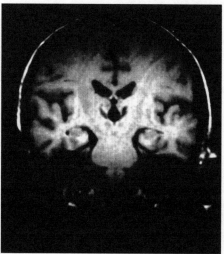

Figure 3.1   MRI scan: horizontal T2 (left) and coronal T1 (right) weighted images at the level of the thalamus showing symmetrical infarction of the dorsomedial nuclei, internal medullary lamina and mammillo-thalamic tract bilaterally

the following physical signs were observed: absent pupillary reflexes, marked bilateral ptosis (eyelid drooping) with an inability to voluntarily open his eyes, and paralysis of vertical eye movements. No other abnormal signs were elicited. Upon recovery of his conscious level, he was noted to be severely confused, disorientated in time and place with marked impairment in new learning capacity. No language or perceptual abnormalities were noted.

Full investigations on admission were normal including a CT brain scan. A subsequent magnetic resonance (MR) scan (which gives much greater anatomical detail than conventional CT scans) obtained in October 1989 documented symmetrical bilateral thalamic infarction in the territory of the paramedian artery (see figure 3.1). The lesions involved the dorsomedial nuclei as well as the internal medullary lamina and the mammillo-thalamic tract bilaterally.

He remained in hospital for a month. When discharged in July 1989 he was fully alert but exhibited features of a profound memory disorder which has persisted ever since. His retention of new information remains negligible and he has a extensive retrograde amnesia encompassing the whole of his adult life. There has also been a marked change in his personality; having been a vigorous and successful garage owner and a keen member of various business clubs, he is now apathetic and lethargic. He is content to sit in the house all day watching the television and shows little interest in the family or his business. He lacks insight into his deficits and denies any cognitive impairment. We assume that these frontal features are due to the fact that the thalamic lesion has interrupted pathways essential for normal frontal lobe function.

Neuropsychological assessment

The results of standard clinical neuropsychological tests showed that he had the features of a relatively selective amnesic syndrome. Thus, the level of measured IQ was commensurate with his estimated premorbid level, as judged by the National Adult Reading Test (Nelson and O'Connell, 1978) and his short-term (immediate) memory for verbal information, as judged by digit span, was normal. In contrast, all tests of longer-term memory demonstrated profound impairment; on the Recognition Memory Test (Warrington, 1984) in which subjects are shown a series of 50 faces (or words), then afterwards are asked to choose from two alternatives which face (or word) they have just seen, his performance was at chance level. Similarly, he showed no retention of verbal material from the story recall subtest of the Wechsler Memory Scale. Although he was able to copy a complex geometric figure very well, his recall of the figure after a delay was minimal.

Tests of language and visuo-spatial function showed no significant impairments. In keeping with the personality and motivational changes described above, he showed a moderate deficit on tests considered dependent upon frontal executive function such as the Wisconsin Card Sorting Test (Nelson, 1976).

Autobiographical memory

Clinically, the most striking feature of PS's autobiographical memory was his persistent belief that he was currently in the Navy on active service, but away from his boat on shore leave. He usually stated that he was called up two years previously at the start of the war. Many core details of his naval career (1941–6) appeared to be related accurately; however, he claimed to have been married with two children before entering the Navy, when in fact his children were all born after he left. There were also some curious inconsistencies in his beliefs. On questioning, he would agree that he was born in 1922 and must, therefore be in his sixties, but nevertheless he persisted in the claim that he was on active Navy service. He would also agree that being on active Navy service when over sixty is highly implausible, but his memory 'illusion' was more compelling for him than was rational thought. Within minutes (if not seconds) of having agreed that he must have made a mistake, he would once again be stating that he was just back on leave from his ship. At home, PS typically behaved as if he were still in the war years; he would look for cigarettes that he had not smoked since 1945, frequently mentioned rationing and restricted travel, and tormented his wife by insisting on a nightly blackout. When asked about places and landmarks around Cambridge, his recollections were reasonably accurate, but appropriate to twenty years or more previously. He did not recall the location of a bridge or a shopping centre built in the 1970s but clearly described the appearance of those places prior to development.

Using semi-structured interviews, we documented a temporally extensive deficit in PS's autobiographical recall. He could relate facts about his early life, such as place and date of birth, schools attended, names of teachers, and his first job. But he was unable to furnish any specific details of major personal events, such as his own wedding (e.g. date, name of church, best man's name). For events after 1945, he was able to recall a few very salient occurrences but virtually no details. Thus, he could often recall that he had three children, but was vague and variable about their place of birth and where he was at that time. He also knew that he owned two garages, and that they were now run by his sons, but further details about the business eluded him.

The finding of profoundly impaired recall of autobiographical events was substantiated using the cued recall technique, sometimes known as the modified Galton–Crovitz test. In this test subjects are administered a list of fifteen high-frequency nouns (e.g. train, house, book, car, etc.) and asked to describe a personally experienced and unique episode relating to each word. Despite extensive encouragement and cueing, PS did not produce a single specific episode. Instead, general facts about his early life and Navy service in the 1930s and 1940s were related, but without any of the richness of detail or self-reference that normally characterizes the recall of personally experienced autobiographical episodes. Each episode was scored for richness and temporal specificity according to previously described guidelines (Sagar et al., 1988; Hodges and Ward, 1989): PS obtained an extremely poor score.

Qualitatively similar responses were obtained using the Autobiographical Memory Interview (Kopelman et al., 1989). In this task, subjects are asked to generate personal semantic or factual information (names of school friends, teachers, occupations, addresses, etc.) as well as episodes from three life periods (early: pre-school and school; mid; first job, marriage, birth of children; late: recent holidays, hospital admissions, etc.). PS was able to produce a normal amount of semantic information from the first life period, was markedly impaired on the second and produced virtually no information from the third. Despite encouragement, he remained unable to produce *any* specific episodic material.

To explore this aspect further, the patient's wife supplied us with photographs of events containing family members and close friends (holidays, weddings, dinners, and so on) from the 1970s and 1980s. The photographs were presented in a random order and the patient was asked about the people and events portrayed in each. PS did not recognize any of the events. He identified only a third of the people and made a number of major errors, misidentifying, for instance, his grandchildren and close long-standing friends. He mistook a fairly recent Masonic dinner for his own wedding.

Finally, again with the help of his wife, we compiled a list of major family events from the past three decades (1960s, 1970s, 1980s) including births, weddings, business deals and holidays. Using these we constructed a cued recall task. For each item (e.g. 'your holiday in Tenerife') we asked first for spontaneous recall using the labels generated by his wife. Then, if PS was unable to produce any details we administered a standard cue (e.g. 'it was when the hotel flooded and there was a power cut'). PS produced virtually no correct details even in the cued recall paradigm and many confabulatory errors. Incidents were typically incorporated into his Navy service schema in that he thought that most of the events had occurred while he was in the Navy on location, often in the Caribbean where he had served in the war.

Comment Tests of autobiographical memory indicate a profound deficit in recalling specific life events whether using a clinical interview format, the Galton–Crovitz word association technique, the Autobiographical Memory Interview, or cueing with family photographs or named family events. PS shows some preservation of semantic information about his early life, but even salient facts about his own life after 1940 are related inconsistently. The persistence of a paramnesic state of delusional proportions in which he believes that he is still on active service in the Navy is the most striking clinical observation. It is against this background that we embarked upon a parallel investigation of his remote memory for public events and famous faces.

Public remote memory

Famous people   Knowledge of famous people was explored using a Famous Faces Test which has been described in detail elsewhere (Hodges and Ward, 1989; Hodges, 1991). The test consists of 72 portrait photographs, twelve per decade, from the 1930s to the 1980s. PS was first asked to name the people in the photographs. If unable to do so, he was asked to identify them by description and encouraged to be as specific as possible (e.g. in response to 'a politician', he was asked 'what party was he in' or 'which position did he hold', etc.). Finally, a forced choice of three names from the same era and category were presented for recognition (e.g. Harold Wilson, James Callaghan, Ted Heath). Thus, three scores were obtained, (a) naming, (b) identification, and (c) forced choice recognition. PS named only 12 of the 72 – which is in the clearly impaired range, being more than two standard deviations below normal – and showed evidence of a modest gradient. However, in the second part of the test he identified 55 of the 60 unnamed faces by their correct superordinate category (i.e. politician, film star, etc.). Of these correct superordinate responses, 41 further included very specific and often uniquely identifying information (e.g. Princess Diana, 'she married Prince Charles'; Ronald Reagan, 'he's the American President who was an ex-film star'; Terry Waite, 'he is the church-going man held in the East'; Benito Mussolini, 'the Italian ex-war leader'). In the third (forced choice recognition) part of the test, he chose the correct name in a striking 53 of 60 (88 per cent) instances. PS's scores for identification and recognition are within the normal range and contrast with his impaired naming.

To ensure that the information PS generated about the people in the Famous Faces Test was not face-specific or even merely deducible from the photographs, we subsequently presented him with the names of the people depicted in the Famous Faces Test and asked him to describe them in as much detail as possible. In all but one instance he gave the correct superordinate category (politician, film star, etc.), and for 83 per cent he generated highly specific or unique information (e.g. John Profumo, 'he was in the government, a Tory, had an affair with some tart'; Michael Heseltine, 'an MP, one of Maggie's crowd'; Franklin Roosevelt, 'Prime Minister of America during the war'; Sean Connery, 'an actor in he-man films, he's Scottish'). In contrast to his ability to access specific information about names he was completely unable to say when each person was famous; he attributed practically all of the names to the 1940s.

To establish whether PS was able to recognize famous faces as famous, we matched each of the 72 photographs from the Famous Faces Test with a photograph of a non-famous person of the same sex and age, and from the same era as the target photograph. These were obtained from a wide range of historical sources. For each pair, PS was asked to choose the famous person. Then the whole set was given again in a different order and

Table 3.1 Comparison of PS's performance on a recency judgement test involving famous personalities (n = 27 triplets in both conditions)

	PS	Controls (n = 8)	
		Range	Mean (SD)
Photographs			
Most recent	25/27	22–27	25 (1.8)
Least recent	24/27	22–27	25 (1.9)
Overall	49/54 (91%)		
Names only			
Most recent	21/27	21–27	23 (1.9)
Least recent	23/27	20–27	23 (1.8)
Overall	44/54 (82%)		

he was asked to select the non-famous person. His accuracy in the two conditions was virtually 100 per cent.

We were interested to see if PS was able to judge the relative recency of famous faces. To examine this, the photographs from the Famous Faces Test were arranged in triplets so that each triplet contained three famous faces of the same category (e.g. US Presidents, Prime Ministers, sportsmen, etc.) and from three consecutive decades. PS was then asked, for all triplets, to judge which of the three was famous most recently. Then, the sequence was repeated and he was asked which was famous longest ago. PS was correct on 90 per cent of the trials. The same experiment was repeated using the names, rather than photographs, of the same individuals. For the names, PS was correct on 82 per cent. This level of performance was well within the normal range for controls given the same test (Table 3.1).

Comment In contrast to his performance on tests of autobiographical memory, PS showed a very striking preservation of his knowledge about famous people from all eras of his life. Although poor at naming famous faces, he can generate specific identifying information in the majority of instances whether tested using faces or names. His ability to distinguish famous faces and names from non famous foils is extremely good. Even more remarkable is his ability to place triplets of faces and names in their correct temporal sequence, although his ability to date individual names is severely impaired.

Famous events The Famous Events Test used has been described in detail elsewhere (Hodges and Ward, 1989; Hodges, 1991). In brief, the test consists of the names of 100 news items; 50 true events from the 1930s to the 1970s (e.g., the Profumo affair, the Watergate scandal, the Mau Mau etc.), and 50 fictitious events made up to sound authentic (e.g., the Goldberg affair, the Jin Jin, the Blackheath murders, etc.). The subject is asked merely to say which of these events are true and then to date these to a single decade. For normal subjects, the recognition part is very easy and scores approach 100 per cent. PS endorsed only 75 per cent of real events, which is clearly very impaired (Hodges and Ward, 1989). In addition, he also endorsed almost a third of the foils, which

Table 3.2 Comparison of PS's performance on the famous personalities and events recency judgement tests

	Famous personalities	*Famous events*
Correct	44	13
Incorrect	10	15
Total	54	28

$\chi^2 = 10.83$ $p = 0.001$

gave him an overall score approaching chance. His dating was correct only for the events from the 1940s and this is artefactual since all events were judged to have occurred either during or shortly after the Second World War II.

To compare identification of famous events with his performance on the Famous Faces Test, we selected 26 photographs of very famous events taken from a popular chronicle of the twentieth century. The events were distributed evenly from the 1930s to the 1980s. PS correctly identified only four events (the Jarrow March, King Edward VIII's abdication speech, the coronation of Queen Elizabeth II, the assassination of John F. Kennedy). In the remainder, he correctly identified the person depicted in six of the eleven photographs showing people. The events he described only in non-specific (generic) terms using visual information present in the photographs. In many cases he spontaneously confabulated. For instance, when shown a picture of the mushroom cloud and the destruction of Hiroshima, he responded that it must have been a bomb, probably dropped on South America or China by the Germans. Cueing appeared not to help, but merely elicited further confabulation. Dating was also severely defective. Only the events from the 1930s and 1940s were correctly dated. However, this again reflects response bias since all events he judged to have occurred just before, during or shortly after the war.

For direct comparison of PS's recency judgement for famous people, we took events from the Famous Events Test and combined them into triplets containing events from three consecutive decades (e.g. the Abdication crisis, the Berlin air-lift, the Mau-Mau; the Great Train robbery, the Watergate scandal, the Falklands war). The same procedure as that described for the Name Recency Test was employed. PS was first asked to judge the most recent from each triplet, then all the triplets were repeated and he was asked to judge the least recent item from each. In contrast to his excellent and normal performance on the face version of this task, his scores on the event-based version were at chance. A comparison of PS's performance on the Famous Name and Famous Events Recency Judgement tests revealed a significantly better performance on the Famous Faces. By contrast, the percentage obtained by controls on the two tests was virtually identical (Table 3.2).

Comment PS's preservation of specific semantic information about famous people appears not to generalise to other domains of public knowledge since his performance on tests of famous event identification (from name and photograph) is extremely poor.

Furthermore, his ability to sequence famous events is significantly worse than his ability to perform comparable judgements about famous people.

Discussion

Cognitive questions

The most striking clinical observation is PS's persistent claim to be home from the Navy on leave from active service during the Second World War. This claim has a delusional intensity and is resistant to contrary evidence and argument. On directed questioning, PS can recall some factual information and can retrieve a few 'favourite tales' and isolated themes; however, this information is fragmentary and is not, or cannot be, spontaneously integrated into a coherent life-story. PS has a marked impairment of personal autobiographical knowledge. He cannot give details about major family occurrences, he has very grave difficulty in recognizing photographs of his family, gets confused in recalling which of his children is married or single, and can neither recall their jobs and careers nor say who is the parent of his grandchildren. Indeed, his wife claims that his memory of virtually all of their married life has been lost as a result of the stroke. PS's knowledge of public events is also gravely impaired and their recall is characterized by confabulation. He is unable to discriminate the names of famous events from fictitious ones, cannot recall information about famous events and cannot order their occurrence in time. By contrast, PS's recall of information about famous people appears to be relatively better preserved. He can detect and recognize people's names, he can provide very detailed definitional accounts of who they are and can say why they are famous. Remarkably, he is even able to place named or photographed individuals in an appropriate date order.

How are we to account for the characteristics of PS's remote memory loss? Both qualitative and quantitative evidence makes it unlikely that he has simply lost information of a particular type (e.g. memory for episodes) or that he is generally unable to monitor his behaviour (e.g. a dysexecutive syndrome). Contemporary cognitive theory may be more enlightening. Many theorists have emphasized that our ongoing memory is mediated via dynamic and active operations involving problem solving, cross-checking, verification and inference (e.g. Norman and Bobrow, 1979; Baddeley, 1990). We can consider PS as having lost the ability to use or control specific aspects of this system in reconstructing his past, and perhaps in processing the present.

According to some theorists, episodic memory retrieval can be thought of as being mediated via a hierarchically organized system. At the highest level of the system are retrieval 'frameworks' (sometimes termed E-Mops or episodic memory organisation packets; Schank, 1982). At the lowest level are event records which may be relatively fragmentary and cognitively unstructured (Morton et al., 1985). The major role of the high-level retrieval frameworks is in providing pointers, and a basic organizational structure, for guiding retrieval and integration of memory evidence in the lower level records. It has further been suggested that memory retrieval frameworks are *themselves* organized in terms of major life events or lifetime periods (Conway, 1992). In essence, by accessing the retrieval framework appropriate to one or other life epoch, a major organizational structure is provided that can guide retrieval and reconstruction of more specific auto-biographical episodes (e.g. Reiser et al., 1986; Conway and Bekerian, 1987).

The qualitative characteristics of PS's disorder are consistent with a major disruption in his ability to use the thematic framework level of the retrieval process. He is unable to use an adequate set of frameworks in order to access his autobiographical memory records. So, rather than being able to look up his memories via a childhood theme, a Navy theme, a young married theme, a successful businessman theme (for example), PS is inappropriately stuck with 'Navy' as his default framework for reconstructing the past – and perhaps for interpreting the present. This is a cognitive disaster from a number of perspectives. First, over the intervening forty years since the Navy theme was appropri-ate, access to the contents of PS's lower-level records is likely to have become noisy or degraded, and subject to considerable retroactive interference. His search, retrieval and reconstructive activities are referred by default to relatively weak information. Secondly, PS is extremely restricted in the range of verification operations that he can carry out on the results of his memory searches and reconstructions. He is operating on false default assumptions and therefore has no firm ground for checking and cross-checking his retrieval. Thirdly, the Navy scheme is inappropriate to, and inconsistent with, his current life. He is like a person operating on expectations appropriate for visiting the dentist when going into a restaurant. The wrong things will seem significant and mem-orable and the right things will seem trivial and irrelevant. We would speculate that the distinction between people and events may arise as a consequence of the differing uniqueness of the cues that are provided by the names of people and events. The name of a person is typically unambiguous with a single referent; the name of an event is often 'borrowed' from the major players (e.g. the Profumo affair) or the location of the happening (e.g. the Watergate scandal). Since people's names are highly specific or unique it is possible that they provide a means of entering the memory system at a level below that of thematic retrieval frameworks.

Neuroanatomical issues

PS demonstrates that an extensive retrograde amnesia can arise from acute injury to a restricted but critical region of the brain. The region damaged in PS is, in fact, very similar to the principal common site of damage in alchoholic Korsakoff's syndrome, a disorder that is well known to be associated with severe anterograde and retrograde amnesia (e.g. Mair et al., 1978; McCarthy and Warrington, 1990). In this context, it is interesting to note that the qualitative features of PS's retrograde amnesia resemble very closely those described by Oliver Sacks (1987) in his patient with Korsakoff's syndrome, Jimmie G ('The Lost Mariner'), who likewise remained fixed in his wartime Naval service days. Interpretation of Korsakoff's amnesia has been far from straightforward because of problems in distinguishing the memory disturbance attributable to the diencephalic lesions *per se* from the multiple complications of chronic alcohol abuse (e.g. Squire, 1986; Butters and Stuss, 1989; Kopelman, 1989). The evidence from PS suggests that the retrograde amnesia observed in Korsakoff's patients may indeed be an integral component of the syndrome, rather than a by-product of drunken haziness or the widespread neurotoxic effects of alcohol.

How could such a small symmetrical lesion cause such a devastating 'loss' of remote memory? *A priori*, there is insufficient neuronal space in this small area for a store of one's adult life memories! Rather, it seems more likely that the lesion has severed a critical link within an integrated system. PS's lesion is located in a region that could produce a disconnection within the cortical-subcortical memory processing system, specifically disrupting the links between the frontal and parieto-temporal regions (Warrington and Weiskrantz, 1982). The neuroanatomical evidence is entirely consistent with the hierarchical memory-system account that we have put forward on the basis of the cognitive and behavioural evidence. The highest levels of memory organization – here termed thematic retrieval frameworks – and the dynamic control of memory search are both thought to rely on procedures supported by the frontal lobes (e.g. Shallice, 1988). Contextually independent (semantic) information and individual memory records may be based on representations supported by temporal and inferior parietal cortical areas (e.g. McCarthy and Warrington, 1990; Weiskrantz, 1990; Hodges et al., 1992). Due to his lesion, the two domains of memory processing are partly segregated in PS; he is unable to bring them into register, and is tragically trapped in time.

We can only speculate as to why PS may have become stuck in the Navy epoch of his life. There seem two distinct explanations for this phenomenon: psychological and neuroanatomical. From the perspective of psychology we may speculate that for PS his call-up and wartime service had a close similarity to his present condition in terms of lack of personal control, disruption and trauma. Alternatively, there is the possibility that there is something neuroanatomically and/or physiologically special about early adult life memories.

Note

1   Although retrograde and anterograde amnesia commonly co-occur, there is considerable debate about their possible dissociation. We shall not be concerned here with such issues since our patient showed both facets of the classical amnesic syndrome (but see Kapur, 1993 for discussion).

References

Albert, M.S., Butters, N. and Levin, J. (1979) 'Temporal gradients in the retrograde amnesia of patients with alcoholic Korsakoff's Disease', *Archives of Neurology*, **36**: 211–16.
Baddeley, A.D. (1990) *Human Memory: Theory and Practice* (Hove and London: Lawrence Erlbaum Associates).
Baddeley, A.D. and Wilson, B. (1986) 'Amnesia, autobiographical memory and confabulation', in *Autobiographical Memory*, ed. D.C. Rubin (Cambridge: Cambridge University Press), pp. 225–52.
Berlyne, N. (1972) 'Confabulation', *British Journal of Psychiatry*, **120**: 31–9.
Brown, N.R., Shevell, S.K. and Rips, L.J. (1986) 'Public memories and their personal context', in *Autobiographical Memory*, ed. D.C. Rubin (Cambridge: Cambridge University Press), pp. 137–58.

Butters, N. (1984) 'Alcoholic Korsakoff's Syndrome: an update', *Seminars in Neurology*, 4: 226–44.

Butters, N. (1985) 'Alcoholic Korsakoff's Syndrome: some unresolved issues concerning aetiology, neuropathology and cognitive deficits', *Journal of Clinical and Experimental Neuropsychology*, 7: 181–210.

Butters, N. and Cermak, L.S. (1986) 'A case study of the forgetting of autobiographical knowledge: implications for the study of retrograde amnesia', in *Autobiographical Memory*, ed. D.C. Rubin (Cambridge: Cambridge University Press), pp. 253–72.

Butters, N. and Stuss, D.T. (1989) 'Diencephalic amnesia', in *Handbook of Neuropsychology*, vol. 3, ed. F. Boller and J. Grafman (Amsterdam: Elsevier Publishers).

Cermak, L.S. and O'Connor, M. (1983) 'The anterograde and retrograde retrieval ability of a patient with amnesia due to encephalitis', *Neuropsychologia*, 21: 213–33.

Conway, M.A. (1992) 'A structural model of autobiographical memory', in *Theoretical Perspectives on Autobiographical Memory*, ed. M.A. Conway, D.C. Rubin, H. Spinler and W. Wagenaar (Amsterdam: Kluwer Academic Publishers).

Conway, M.A. and Bekerian, D.A. (1987) 'Organisation in autobiographical memory', *Memory and Cognition*, 15: 119–32.

Corkin, S. (1984) 'Lasting consequences of bilateral medial lobectomy: clinical course and experimental findings in HM', *Seminars in Neurology*, 4: 249–59.

Damasio, A.R., Graff-Radford, N.R., Eslinger, P.G., Damasio, H. and Kassell, N. (1985) 'Amnesia following basal forebrain lesions', *Archives of Neurology (Chicago)*, 42: 263–71.

Delbecq-Derouesne, J., Beavois, M.F. and Shallice, T. (1990) 'Preserved recall versus impaired recognition: a case study', *Brain*, 113: 1045–74.

Goodglass, H. and Kaplan, K. (1983) *The Assessment of Aphasia and Related Disorders*, 2nd edn (Philadelphia: Lea & Febiger).

Graff-Radford, N.R., Eslinger, P.J., Damasio, A.R. and Yamada, T. (1984) 'Non-hemorrhagic infarction of the thalamus: behavioural, anatomic, and physiological correlates', *Neurology*, 34: 14–23.

Graff-Radford, N.R., Damasio, H., Yamada, T., Eslinger, P.G. and Damasio, A.R. (1985) 'Non-haemorrhagic thalamic infarction', *Brain*, 108: 485–516.

Graff-Radford, N.R., Tranel, D., Van Hoesen, G.W. and Brandt, J.P. (1990) 'Diencephalic amnesia', *Brain*, 113: 1–25.

Hodges, J.R. (1991) *Transient Amnesia: Clinical and Neuropsychological Aspects* (London: W.B. Saunders).

Hodges, J.R. and Ward, C.D. (1989) 'Observations during transient global amnesia. *Brain*, 112: 595–620.

Hodges, J.R., Patterson, K., Oxbury, S., Funnell, E. (1993) 'Semantic Dementia: progressive fluent aphasia with temporal lobe atrophy', *Brain*, 115: 1783–1806.

Kopelman, M.D. (1989) 'Remote and autobiographical memory, temporal context memory and frontal atrophy in Korsakoff and Alzheimer patients', *Neuropsychologia*, 27: 437–60.

Kopelman, M.D., Wilson, B. and Baddeley, A. (1989) 'The Autobiographical Interview: a new assessment of autobiographical and personal semantic memory in amnesic patients', *Journal of Clinical and Experimental Neuropsychology*, 11: 724–44.

Logue, V., Durwood, M., Pratt, R.T.C., Piercy, M. and Nixon, W.L.B. (1968) 'The quality of survival after rupture of an anterior cerebral aneurysm', *British Journal of Psychiatry*, 114: 137–68.

Mair, W.G.P., Warrington, E.K. and Weiskrantz, L. (1978) 'Neuropathological and psychological examination of two patients with Korsakoff's psychosis', *Brain*, 102: 749–83.

Markowitsch, H.J. (1984) 'Can amnesia be caused by damage of a single brain structure?', *Cortex*, 20: 27–45.

Markowitsch, H.J. (1988) 'Diencephalic amnesia: a reorientation towards tracts', *Brain Research Reviews*, **13**: 351–70.

Marslen-Wilson, W.D., Teuber, H.L. (1975) 'Memory for remote events in anterograde amnesia: recognition of public figures from news photographs', *Neuropsychologia*, **13**: 353–64.

McCarthy, R.A. and Warrington, E.K. (1988) 'Evidence for modality specific meaning systems in the brain', *Nature*, **334**: 428–30.

McCarthy, R.A. and Warrington, E.K. (1990) *Cognitive Neuropsychology: A Clinical Introduction* (San Diego, Cal.; Academic Press).

McCarthy, R.A. and Warrington, E.K. (1992) 'Actors but not scripts: the dissociation of people and events in retrograde amnesia', *Neuropsychologia*, **30**: 633–44.

McKenna, P. and Warrington, E.K. (1983) *The Graded Naming Test* (Windsor: Nelson).

Milner, B. Corkin, S. and Teuber, H.L. (1968) 'Further analysis of hippocampal amnesia – 14 year follow-up of HM', *Neuropsychologia*, **6**: 215–34.

Morton, J., Hammersley, R.H. and Bekerian, D.A. (1985) 'Headed records: a model for memory and its failures', *Cognition*, **20**: 1–23.

Nelson, H.E. (1976) 'A modified card sorting task sensitive to frontal lobe defects', *Cortex*, **12**: 313–24.

Nelson, H.E. and O'Connell, A. (1978) 'Dementia: the estimation of premorbid intelligence levels using the new adult reading test', *Cortex*, **14**: 234–44.

Norman, D.A. and Bobrow, D.G. (1979) 'Descriptions and intermediate stages in memory retrieval', *Cognitive Psychology*, **11**: 107–23.

Osterrieth, P. and Rey, A. (1944) 'Le test de copie d'une figure complexe', *Archives de psychologie*, **30**: 205–20.

Reiser, B.J., Black, J.B. and Kalamarides, D. (1986) 'Strategic memory search processes', in *Autobiographical Memory*, ed. D.C.Rubin (Cambridge: Cambridge University Press), pp. 100–21.

Richardson-Klavehn, A. and Bjork, R.A. (1988) 'Measures of memory', *Annual Review of Psychology*, **39**: 475–543.

Sacks, O. (1987) *The Man Who Mistook his Wife for a Hat* (New York: Harper & Row).

Sagar, H.J., Cohen, N.J., Sullivan, E.V., Corkin, S. and Growden, J.H. (1988) 'Remote memory function in Alzheimer's disease and Parkinson's disease', *Brain*, **111**: 185–206.

Schacter, D.L. (1987) 'Implicit memory: history and current status', *Journal of Experimental Psychology, Learning, Memory and Cognition*, **13**: 501–18.

Schank, R.C. (1982) *Dynamic Memory* (Cambridge: Cambridge University Press).

Shallice, T. (1988) *From Neuropsychology to Mental Structure* (Cambridge: Cambridge University Press).

Shallice, T. and Evans, M.E. (1978) 'The involvement of the frontal lobes in cognitive estimation', *Cortex*, **14**: 294–303.

Shimamura, A. (1989) 'Disorder or memory: the cognitive science perspective', in *Handbook of Neuropsychology*, vol. 3, ed. L. Squire and G. Gainotti (Amsterdam: Elsevier), pp. 35–73.

Squire, L.R. (1986) 'Mechanisms of memory', *Science*, **232**: 1612–19.

Stuss, D.T., Gubermann, A., Nelson, R. and Larochelle, S. (1988) 'The neuropsychology of paramedian thalamic infarction', *Brain and Cognition*, **8**: 348–78.

Tulving, E. (1983) *Elements of Episodic Memory* (London: Oxford University Press).

Tulving, E. and Thomson, D.M. (1973) 'Encoding specificity and retrieval processes in episodic memory', *Psychological Review*, **80**: 353–73.

von Cramon, D.Y., Hebel, N. and Schuri, U. (1985) 'A contribution to the anatomical basis of thalamic amnesia', *Brain*, **108**: 993–1008.

Warrington, E.K. (1975) 'The selective impairment of semantic memory', *Quarterly Journal of Experimental Psychology*, **27**: 187–99.

Warrington, E.K. (1984) *Recognition Memory Test* (Windsor: Nelson).

Warrington, E.K. and James, M. (1991) *The Visual Object and Space Perception Battery* (Bury St Edmunds, Suffolk: Thames Valley Test Company).

Warrington, E.K. and McCarthy, R.A. (1987) 'Categories of knowledge: further fractionation and an attempted integration', *Brain*, **110**: 1273–96.

Warrington, E.K. and McCarthy, R.A. (1988) 'The fractionation of retrograde amnesia', *Brain and Cognition*, **7**: 184–200.

Warrington, E.K. and Weiskrantz, L. (1982) 'Amnesia: a disconnection syndrome', *Neuropsychologia*, **20**: 233–49.

Wechsler, D. (1945) *Wechsler Memory Scale (Manual)* (New York: Psychological Corporation).

Weiskrantz, L. (1990) 'Problems of learning and memory – one multiple memory – systems?', *Philosophical Transactions of the Royal Society of London Series B – Biological Sciences*, **329**: 99–108.

Winocur, G., Oxbury, S., Roberts, R., Agnetti, V. and Davis, C.J.F. (1984) 'Amnesia in a patient with bilateral lesions to the thalamus', *Neuropsychologia*, **22**: 123–43.

Zola-Morgan, S., Squire, L.R. and Amaral, D.G. (1986) 'Human amnesia and the medial temporal region: enduring memory impairment following bilateral lesions limited to field CA1 of the hippocampus', *Journal of Neuroscience*, **6**: 2950–67.

4 Social and Emotional Characteristics of a Profoundly Amnesic Postencephalitic Patient

Margaret G. O'Connor, Laird S. Cermak and Larry J. Seidman

The personality characteristics of amnesic patients have rarely been described in research or review articles although it is likely that the neuroanatomical and psychosocial ramifications of amnesia have profound effects on personality and emotional development. Organic amnesia and emotional dysfunction are both associated with damage to the limbic system (MacLean, 1952; LeDoux, 1989). Furthermore, the social consequences of amnesia may contribute to feelings of social isolation and depression. A broader and more interesting question concerns the effects of amnesia on emotional maturation. In the absence of memories for everyday events, it is possible that amnesic patients would be predisposed toward emotional stagnation. By definition, the amnesic patient would be inclined to focus on the immediate present and/or the distant past. This could diminish the range of their emotional experiences and result in blunted affect. Over the long term, one might expect that they would exhibit personality characteristics typically associated with an earlier developmental stage.

In this chapter we shall investigate the emotional profile of patient SS, a 64-year-old former physicist, whom we have followed over the past two decades. Before discussing the results of this personality inquiry we shall summarize cognitive studies and CT scan findings of this interesting patient (Cermak, 1976; Cermak and O'Connor, 1983; Cermak et al., 1988).

Background Information

Prior to the onset of his illness, SS was president of an optical physics firm dedicated to the development of laser technology. He was described as a bright and gregarious man who had a wide range of interests and many friends. SS contracted herpes simplex

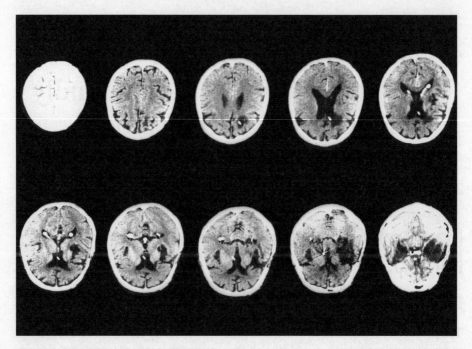

Figure 4.1   CT scan of SS, March 1988

encephalitis in 1971 at age 44. He was comatose for approximately one month, after which he demonstrated a right hemiparesis, aphasia and amnesia. Over time, his motor and speech problems cleared but his severe memory disorder persisted. Today SS continues to demonstrate a severe memory disorder on the Wechsler Memory Scale – Revised (WMS–R), where his General Memory Index is average (GM = 100). In contrast, his Delayed Memory Index is below average (DM < 50). SS's attention, verbal analytic skills, deductive reasoning, mathematical abilities, complex perception and grasp of abstract concepts all remain well above average. His overall IQ of 136 is in the superior range.

SS's memory problem is characterized by dense anterograde and retrograde amnesia. He is virtually unable to recall any new information after a two to three minute time interval has elapsed and his memory for events preceding the onset of his amnesia is severely impaired. Hence, he cannot recall any of the major events in his family life such as his wedding day. Nor can he converse about the past in anything other than vague generalities or repetitive family folklore.

A CT scan from March 1988 (figure 4.1) revealed lesions in anterior and mesial portions of the left temporal lobe including the anterior tip of the superior and middle temporal gyri, amygdala, hippocampus, and a small portion of the anterior parahippocampal gyrus. Lesions were also present in the insular structures, the putamen and the lateral globus pallidus. There is an additional low density area in the left frontal lobe due to a shunt involving white matter deep to the premotor cortex and anterolateral to the left frontal horn. The left frontal lesion also involves orbitofrontal regions with extension into the basal forebrain area. Right hemisphere lesions were noted in the anteriormesial temporal lobe involving the amygdala and hippocampus. Lesions were also present in a small portion of the insular structures and the lateral putamen.

SS has always intrigued us because he was the first non-Korsakoff amnesic followed at the Memory Disorders Research Center. In an initial study we demonstrated that he was more adept at analysing incoming information than other amnesic patients (Cermak, 1976). In fact, his proficiency on tasks of on-line semantic analysis was on par with normal control subjects. Despite this capacity, SS's retention of new material remained abysmal. The constrast between his normal analytic abilities and his amnesia led to the revision of the initial encoding deficits theory. Rather than viewing amnesia as a consequence of an inability to perform semantic analysis of incoming information, we came to realize that memory deficits may be due to an inability to perform the mental operations necessary to integrate semantically analysed information with a pre-existing memory system (Cermak, 1984).

Subsequent analyses contrasted SS's retrograde amnesia with that of other amnesic patients (Cermak and O'Connor, 1983). Like other amnesics (Albert et al., 1979), SS demonstrated impoverished recall of public events preceding the onset of his illness. However, SS's retrieval deficit was inconsistent across test sessions; sometimes he retrieved information that he did not have access to on other occasions. This suggested that SS was impaired not only in the amount of information that he had available to retrieve, but in the retrieval process as well. SS also demonstrated deficits in the recall of personal episodes; his recall of these events was of a generic/semantic nature and did not include episodic detail. This led directly to our formulation of the semantic/episodic dissociation theory of retrograde amnesia (Cermak, 1984).

SS's processing abilities were also investigated with implicit memory paradigms (Cermak et al., 1988). Altogether, five tasks were used: perceptual priming with real words and pseudowords; word-stem completion (with and without contextual cues); word-stem completion following presentation of high- and low-frequency words; biasing of ambiguous homophones; and conceptual priming. Through this investigation we found that SS's implicit memory could be primed whenever previously acquired information (that is, knowledge stored in semantic memory) was used. This pattern was also observed for all amnesics including alcoholic Korsakoff patients. In contrast to other amnesics, however, SS demonstrated intact priming on tasks requiring the formation of new associations. In other words, SS was proficient at pseudoword priming and contextual word-stem completion, tasks failed by the other amnesics. We suspected that SS's intact on-line analytic abilities enhanced implicit memory even though they were insufficient for the support of explicit memory.

It is evident from the above studies that patient SS played a prominent role in the development and refinement of the theories of amnesia emerging from our Center. Our work with this very unusual man enhanced our knowledge of the processing strategies involved in explicit memory as well as those integral to implicit memory.

Emotional Characteristics

Since the onset of his amnesia, SS has lived at home with support from family members. Unable to resume meaningful work, he performs routine household chores under the supervision of his wife. His mood is generally pleasant, and he comes across as an outgoing person able to carry on an intelligent discourse encompassing a variety of topics. A brief encounter with SS might lead one to consider him a well-adjusted individual with no aberrant behaviour or personality patterns. Prolonged contact, however, underscores the density of his amnesia largely because of his tendency to provide the listener with stimulus-bound vignettes of his past life. The contrast between SS's upbeat demeanour and the dire circumstances of his life might lead one to wonder whether SS has a normal capacity for emotional experience. Although he occasionally expresses concern about memory problems, he does so in an unemotional manner, and his mood varies little over time. In fact, his insight regarding his situation seems entirely superficial.

A number of factors could contribute to the static nature of SS's personality. First, we know that limbic lesions have profound effects on emotions (MacLean, 1952; LeDoux, 1989). Damage in this area could interfere with his ability to derive meaning from emotional events and/or diminish his ability to express his feelings. Second, SS's life has been bereft of intellectual and social stimulation for over twenty years, a situation that may precipitate depression or emotional stagnation. Though depression is not apparent on a manifest level, such feelings may exert an indirect influence on behaviour, inhibiting his range of emotions. Finally, the impact of SS's profound amnesia on his emotional life cannot be underestimated. His consistently pleasant but stable mood may reflect his premorbid disposition uncontaminated by persistent thoughts of personal tragedy or memory of daily events. Because SS cannot integrate new experiences into his knowledge of the world, his view of reality might be based on a combination of very remote events and the immediate present.

In sum, SS's blunted affect may be due to neuroanatomical damage, depression or amnesia. Of course, all three factors could be operating at the same time and it is impossible to determine the relative impact of each. Despite this ambiguity, we were interested in obtaining more information about his personality and emotional life utilizing standard clinical personality assessment instruments.

Personality Testing

Three types of personality tests were included in this study. The first type was objective measures of emotional functions and personality. These included the Beck Depression Inventory (Beck et al., 1961), the Hamilton Psychiatric Rating Scale for Depression (Hamilton, 1960), the Minnesota Multiphasic Personality Inventory and the Minnesota Multiphasic Personality – Revised (Butcher et al., 1989). We did not expect SS to demonstrate emotional distress on these objective tests in light of his superficial grasp of his circumstances and his generally pleasant mood. Second, we administered the Rorschach Test (Beck, 1944), a projective technique that examines latent aspects of emotion. We believed that the Rorschach could provide more information regarding SS's emotional life because it did not depend directly on his insight regarding his emotional experiences. Finally, our interest in the effects of chronic amnesia on psychological and emotional maturation led us to choose the Measures of Psychosocial Development (Hawley, 1980) as a longitudinal index of personality development. It was expected that SS would not exhibit a level of psychosocial maturity characteristic of his nonamnesic peers because he had not learned, retained or acted upon any new information since the onset of his disorder.

Testing took place in a quiet room in SS's home. He was friendly and talkative, relating anecdotes about his youth and early adulthood, all of which he had told the examiner (MOC) during numerous previous meetings. SS was co-operative with test procedures and worked diligently at each task with which he was presented. Testing took place over several years. Some tests (that is, the Rorschach and MMPI) were administered as part of a larger group study (O'Connor et al., 1990).

The first set of objective measures of personality and emotions yielded surprising results. Consistent with SS's overt clinical presentation, there was no evidence of depression on the Beck Depression Inventory (BDI = 3) or the Hamilton Psychiatric Rating Scale for Depression (HRSD = 4). This was expected because these tests reflect the conscious awareness of symptoms. The Minnesota Multiphasic Personality Inventory and Minnesota Multiphasic Personality – Revised (MMPI-2) were administered as part of a study investigating test–retest reliability with amnesic patients (O'Connor et al., 1990). SS's performance on both versions of the test was quite consistent and was suggestive of significant emotional distress. Elevations on validity scales suggested psychological defensiveness, a desire to be seen as a virtuous person and adherence to unusually high moral standards. Elevations on clinical scales indicated depression and anxiety. Profile analysis suggested that SS was pessimistic and fearful and that he was preoccupied with personal deficiencies. Diagnostic possibilities included anxiety reaction and depression.

Results from the MMPI/MMPI-2 were inconsistent with SS's manifest behaviour and his performance on the depression inventories. This discrepancy could be attributed to differences inherent in the design of these tests. The BDI and HRSD contain questions that are face-valid indices of depression. SS may have scored low on these tests because he made a conscious effort to deny distress or because he truly lacked insight into his feelings. Such conscious denial or lack of insight would not be as effective in minimizing emotional problems measured by the criterion-validated questions of the MMPI/MMPI-2.

An alternative explanation for the difference between SS's scores on the BDI and HRSD versus the MMPI/MMPI-2 may be that his MMPI/MMPI-2 profiles were distorted by situational factors related to his medical illness. The examination of critical items revealed that SS endorsed questions related to amnesia (for example, 'There is something wrong with my mind', 'I am afraid of losing my mind'). A similar trend was seen in a study of the MMPI/MMPI-2 with amnesic patients where elevations on the depressive and schizophrenic subscales were noted (O'Connor et al., 1990). It may be that amnesics' MMPI/MMPI-2 profiles are biased by neurological concerns, because similar findings were reported in several studies examining the use of the MMPI with other neurologically impaired groups (Gass, 1991).

The Rorschach Test provided further information regarding latent aspects of SS's personality. The test was administered on two occasions separated by a two-week delay interval, allowing an investigation of the issue of test–retest reliability and stability of findings. Scoring was done according to the method of Klopfer et al. (1954). Overall, SS

Table 4.1 Correlations between
Rorschach responses across test
sessions

Animal movement (FM)	0.80
Human movement (M)	0.80
Reaction time (RT)	0.36
Number of responses (R)	0.60
Whole determinants (W)	0.80
Large detail determinants	0.58
Animal content (A)	0.80
Human content (H)	1.00

demonstrated good reality testing. He was able to organize perceptually the ambiguous stimuli in a well-formed and clearly differentiated manner. The total number of responses produced was low for someone of his intellectual capacities. Regarding the issue of test–retest reliability, it was clear that there was a great deal of consistency across test sessions (table 4.1) despite the fact that SS had absolutely no recollection of taking the test before. Content analysis also underscored consistency across test sessions. These data indicate that almost identical Rorschach percepts were generated in the absence of conscious memory for previously generated ones. This probably reflects the stability of his personality organization and/or the contribution of long-term implicit memory.

Qualitative evaluation of SS's Rorschach protocols revealed that there was an obsessional quality to many of his responses, with recurrent emphasis on symmetry. He attempted to account for every aspect of an inkblot according to rules of scientific logic and social conventions. While obsessional tendencies may reflect a lifelong personality pattern, these tendencies may be exaggerated by SS's amnesia. It may be that he is continually bewildered by a world around him which changes in unpredictable ways for unknown reasons. To this extent his emphasis on symmetry and exactness may reflect his attempt to organize and understand his unpredictable environment. Also noteworthy were the relative prominence of themes of deterioration and decay (for example, a torn up leaf, a dead bird, a bisected bleeding heart, and a bat in a state of decay) which may represent SS's damaged sense of self secondary to his brain injury.

Clinical data suggest that some amnesics demonstrate relatively static and immature personality patterns. Curiosity about the long-term impact of amnesia on personality development prompted us to utilize a personality instrument sensitive to emotional maturation. SS was given the Measures of Psychosocial Development (Hawley, 1980), a test based on Eriksonian theory of human development. Erikson's theory proposes that development proceeds in a sequential, hierarchical fashion driven by biological (genetically determined) and social forces. Each stage is characterized by the resolution of specific maturational conflicts. At age 64, SS should be faced with the conflicts of older adulthood. Favourable resolution of this period of older adulthood would be associated with ego integrity as opposed to despair. It was our suspicion that SS would not exhibit personality attributes characteristic of older adulthood but rather that he might demonstrate those of a younger developmental period (that is, middle adulthood or young adulthood).

SS's performance on the MPD was in line with our expectations. His profile revealed a failure to resolve the conflicts of older and middle adulthood. In contrast, he appeared to have resolved conflicts of earlier developmental periods. While SS's difficulties in the areas of generativity and ego integrity could not be attributed solely to his amnesia, it is possible that the absence of recollections for ongoing experiences would contribute to a developmental arrest above and beyond the neuroanatomical and social issues considered above. Future investigations of this issue might include comparisons of amnesic individuals, matched for age, IQ, socioeconomic status and lesion site, but differing in terms of age of onset. Of particular interest would be the evaluation of an elderly patient who became amnesic at a very young age.

Conclusions

Our previous work with patient SS prompted us to explore various aspects of his personality and emotional functioning. In doing so we discovered a dissociation between his manifest behaviour and more latent aspects of his emotional state. SS demonstrates some elements of depression on the MMPI/MMPI-2 and Rorschach tests where pessimism, low self-esteem and a preoccupation with personal deficiencies are apparent. However, SS's clinical presentation is nondepressed and he does not exhibit any tendencies towards apathy or abulia. SS clearly does not meet DSMIII-R criteria for Major Depressive Disorder. In a similar vein, his scores on the Beck Depression Inventory and the Hamilton Psychiatric Rating Scale showed absolutely no indication of an underlying depression.

So is SS depressed or not? In order to make such a determination, we first considered the distinction between experiential and expressive aspects of emotion. It is entirely possible that SS *experiences* depressive feelings, but that he does not access these feelings on a frequent basis due to his amnesia or due to blunted insight. Depression may be operative on some level, but it clearly does not exert a major influence on daily behavior. Certain situations may facilitate SS's access to feelings of dysphoria. The unstructured and ambiguous nature of projective techniques may heighten underlying feelings of confusion and despair. Under these circumstances, SS may express his depression. But in most other situations he seems less inclined to reflect upon the dire circumstances of his life and more inclined to contemplate the immediate present. His cheerful disposition would then be enhanced by his natural (premorbid) tendency to emphasize the positive aspects of daily experiences.

We also explored the idea that amnesia might inhibit the maturation process. The results of our testing with SS confirm the possibility that he may have experienced a developmental arrest, failing to resolve conflicts from an earlier age. It is conceivable that SS's amnesia deprived him of memories that otherwise would serve as catalysts for emotional growth. Alternatively, it may be that SS's neuropathology (that is, limbic lesions) interferes with his emotional development by restricting his ability to derive meaning from emotional stimuli. Finally, one must consider the psychosocial ramifications of chronic memory problems on maturation. Amnesia is inevitably accompanied by major changes in the individual's professional life and social milieu which could contribute to feelings of social isolation and despair. In the light of these three putative mechanisms, it makes sense that SS demonstrates emotion and behaviour characteristic of the developmental stage during which his illness occurred.

Future studies on emotion should investigate whether amnesic patients demonstrate normal psychophysiological reactions to emotionally laden stimuli. This would provide direct information regarding how amnesic patients process emotional experiences in the initial stages. The presence and longevity of emotionally based priming should also be examined in order to determine the impact of affective states on amnesics' behaviour. Finally, a comparison of patients who became amnesic at different ages would provide information relative to the issue of developmental arrest. It would be particularly instructive to compare SS with an age-matched amnesic who was of the same intellectual calibre and social class, but who became amnesic at a much earlier time in life.

The investigation of emotional lives of amnesic patients is an area often overlooked in neuropsychological and cognitive investigations of the amnesic syndrome and our initial foray into this area has been far from conclusive. None the less, we believe that such a study is a worthwhile endeavour because it enriches our understanding of the amnesic syndrome from clinical and research perspectives.

Further Reading

Cermak, L.S. (1976) 'The encoding capacity of a patient with amnesia due to encephalitis', *Neuropsychologia*, **14**: 311–26.

Cermak, L.S. and O'Connor, M. (1983) 'The anterograde and retrograde retrieval ability of a patient with amnesia due to encephalitis', *Neuropsychologia*, **21**: 213–34.

Cermak, L.S., Blackford, S.P., O'Connor, M. and Bleich, R.P. (1988) 'The implicit memory ability of a patient with amnesia due to encephalitis', *Brain and Cognition*, **7**: 145–6.

References

Albert, M.A., Butters, N. and Levin, B. (1979) 'Temporal gradients in the retrograde amnesia of patients with alcoholic Korsakoff's disaease', *Archives of Neurology*, **36**: 211–16.

Beck, A.T., Ward, C.H., Mendelson, M., Mock, J. and Erbaugh, J. (1961) 'An inventory for measuring depression', *Archives of General Psychiatry*, **4**: 53–62.

Beck, S.J. (1944) *Rorschach's Test* (New York: Grune & Stratton).

Butcher, J.N., Dahlstrom, W.G., Graham, J.R., Telelgen, A. and Kaemmer, B. (1989) *Manual for the Restandardized Minnesota Multphasic Personality Inventory: MMPI-2: An Interpretive and Administrative Guide* (Minneapolis: University of Minnesota Press).

Cermak, L.S. (1976) 'The encoding capacity of a patient with amnesia due to encephalitis', *Neuropsychologia*, **14**: 311–26.

Cermak, L.S. (1984) 'The episodic/semantic distinction in amnesia', in L.R. Squire and N. Butters (eds), *The Neuropsychology of Memory* (New York: Guilford Press).

Cermak, L.S. and O'Connor, M. (1983) 'The anterograde and retrograde retrieval ability of a patient with amnesia due to encephalitis', *Neuropsychologia*, **21**: 213–34.

Cermak, L.S., Blackford, S.P., O'Connor, M. and Bleich, R.P. (1988) 'The implicit memory ability of a patient with amnesia due to encephalitis', *Brain and Cognition*, **7**: 145–6.

Gass, C. (1991) 'MMPI-2 interpretation and closed head injury: a correction factor', *Psychological Assessment: A Journal of Consulting and Clinical Psychology*, 3(1): 27–31.

Hamilton, M. (1960) 'A rating scale for depression', *Journal of Neurology, Neurosurgery, and Psychiatry*, 23: 56–62.

Hawley, G. (1980) *Measures of Personality Development* (Odessa, Floa: Psychological Assessment Resources).

Klopfer, B., Ainsworth, M.D., Klopfer, W.G. and Holt, R.R. (1954) *Developments in the Rorschach Technique* (New York: Harcourt, Brace & World).

LeDoux, J.E. (1989) 'Cognitive-emotional interactions in the brain', *Cognitions and Emotions*, 3: 267–89.

MacLean, P.D. (1952) 'Some psychiatric implications of physiological studies of frontotemporal portions of the limbic system', *Electroencephalogram Clinical Neurophysiology*, 4: 407–18.

O'Connor, M.G., Walsh, S., Penk, W. and Bitman, D. (1990) 'MMPI versus MMPI-R: examination of test/retest reliability with amnesic patients', paper presented at American Psychological Association annual meeting.

5 Acquisition of Word-Processing Knowledge in an Amnesic Patient: Implications for Theory and Rehabilitation

Martial Van der Linden and Françoise Coyette

The amnesic syndrome is classically defined by a deficit in the acquisition of new information (anterograde amnesia) accompanied by a deficit in recall and recognition of information acquired before the lesion was sustained (retrograde amnesia). The importance of the deficit may vary from one patient to another but even in the most severe cases intellectual abilities and short-term memory may be preserved.

Considerable evidence has also demonstrated that amnesic patients may show preserved or partially preserved learning abilities in a variety of tasks (Mayes, 1988; Shimamura, 1989; Van der Linden, 1994). First, amnesics can acquire perceptual, motor and even cognitive skills (such as tracking moving objects, reading peculiar scripts or solving puzzles) in a normal or near-normal manner although they may have little or no recollection of the learning episodes (see Soliveri et al., 1992). Second, they also exhibit normal perceptual and conceptual priming (see Shimamura, 1989; Van der Linden, 1992). Priming refers to the facilitatory or biasing effect that exposure to a stimulus has on subsequent processing of the same stimulus. Memory for an item is inferred from changes in the efficiency with which the item is processed when it is repeated or in the efficiency that it is elicited by appropriate cues. On perceptual priming tests, a target item presented at study is cued at test by its fragmented or 'perceptually degraded' form. On conceptual priming tests, the cue at test is conceptually related to the studied stimulus word, in the absence of any perceptual similarity between them. Third, amnesic patients may learn more or less easily new factual and semantic information such as new computer-related vocabulary (Glisky et al., 1986a) or second language vocabulary (Hirst et al., 1988).

Various researchers have interpreted the pattern of preserved and impaired memory functions in amnesia by postulating the existence of several distinct memory systems, some of which are affected by the brain damage while some are not. In this perspective, it is widely agreed that episodic memory is impaired in amnesia and that procedural memory and perceptual representation system (PRS) remain intact (Squire, 1992; Tulving & Schacter, 1990). The episodic memory system enables individuals to remember personally experienced events; episodic information serves as the basis for the conscious recollection of the personal past. The procedural memory system makes possible the acquisition and retention of motor, perceptual and cognitive skills; procedural knowledge is not accessible to conscious recollection and can only be demonstrated indirectly through some form of action. The perceptual representation system represents modality-specific information of a presemantic or perceptual nature; it consists in several subsystems and it has been postulated as the system subserving perceptual priming.

The integrity of semantic memory (a memory system that makes possible the acquisition of factual information) is more controversial: one theory suggests that episodic memory is impaired whereas semantic memory remains at least partially intact (Tulving et al., 1991) while another theory considers that episodic and semantic memory are both impaired in amnesia (Squire, 1992). The first theory predicts that amnesic subjects may show relatively preserved flexible semantic learning. According to the second theory, amnesics are no longer able to learn new semantic information, any more than they are able to acquire new personal episodes. This is the view held by Squire (1992) when he suggests that amnesics show a deficit of declarative memory that includes both facts and events. According to Squire, the acquisition of episodic and semantic information depends on a common memory system that requires the intact functioning of the hippocampus and anatomically related structures. More specifically, the hippocampal system is needed to bind together distributed sites in the neocortex in order to create rapidly new and flexible relationships between a stimulus and its spatio-temporal context (thus representing a new episode) and between a fact and its semantic context (thus representing a new concept). On the other hand, amnesic patients with hippocampal damage could acquire new associations, but only slowly and after many repetitions (that is, by incremental and cumulative change, as in the development of a habit). The knowledge acquired with such a strategy should be relatively inflexible, that is, accessible only when the cues presented at retrieval are the same as those used during the study phase.

In fact, little is known about the extent of semantic learning in amnesics, the kind of semantic information they can learn, the factors that affect such learning and the characteristics of the newly acquired knowledge. Several studies have provided conflicting findings. Thus, Gabrieli et al. (1988, 1983) have shown that the amnesic patient HM and a small group of other amnesic patients could not learn, by means of a rote learning method, the meaning of ten English words which they did not know before.

On the other hand, Glisky et al. (1986a) found that amnesics were able to acquire a substantial amount of computer vocabulary by means of the method of vanishing cues, designed to allow patients to use their preserved priming abilities to respond to fragment cues. A series of definitions was presented to the patient on a computer screen (for example, programs that the computer carries out: SOFTWARE). When a definition appeared, the patient tried to complete the definition with the appropriate word. If he failed, he was prompted with the first letter of the word as a cue. The cue was extended as needed (i.e., S———————, SO——————, SOF—————) until the patient successfully recalled the response. On the next trial, the definition was presented along with a cue that was one letter shorter than the cue required for successful completion on the last trial. Thus, the cue was withdrawn gradually, one letter at a time, until the patient could complete the definition without a cue. The results demonstrated that even severely amnesic patients could learn the vocabulary although they had little conscious recollection of the learning experience.

Consistent learning was also observed with a standard anticipation learning method but the vanishing-cues method yielded higher levels of learning. However, such learning was slow compared to controls. Moreover, it was tightly bound to stimulus context and was not readily accessible to changed cues (even if the vanishing-cues method led to a more flexible knowledge than the anticipation method). On the other hand, Hirst et al. (1988) showed that an amnesic patient (CS) was able to acquire new French vocabulary and her progress was as rapid as that of her husband. Moreover, such new knowledge was sufficiently flexible to permit CS to use newly acquired words in varied tasks not presented during the tutoring. Hirst et al. suggested that the differences between their results and those obtained by Glisky et al. (1986a) could reflect a difference in the relationship between the new information and pre-existing knowledge. In their own study, the amnesic patient already had concepts in French vocabulary which she had learned, and therefore she only had to integrate the new vocabulary into an existing contextual framework. In the Glisky et al. study, the patients probably had no pre-existing concepts for the computer vocabulary terms they learned and therefore, they had to build the concept and to associate the term with the concept. Thus, amnesics could easily learn a new flexible knowledge only when they have relevant pre-existing knowledge.

Tulving et al. (1991) also demonstrated that a severely amnesic patient (KC) was able to learn semantic knowledge. Moreover, they showed that semantic learning occurred independently of perceptual priming. According to Tulving et al., the semantic learning effects observed in KC (and other amnesics) appear to be dependent on two factors: meaningfulness and interference. It seems that amnesic patients are able to learn factual or semantic information if it is meaningful: that is to say, if it concerns a domain they already know or if it is consistent with existing concepts. Furthermore, amnesics seem to show semantic learning when testing procedures are administered that preclude interfering responses. In that perspective, Tulving et al. suggest that the absence of semantic learning effects in the Gabrieli et al. (1983, 1988) studies would reflect a testing procedure engendering many incorrect responses and thus creating interferences in the course of learning.

Finally, recent studies (Van der Linden et al., 1993; Butters et al., 1993; see also Leng et al., 1991) confirmed that amnesic patients may acquire new semantic information and that, when they are submitted to sufficient numbers of learning sessions (Butters et al., 1993) or to active learning in varied contexts (Van der Linden et al., 1993), the transfer of learning to new situations and contexts is possible. These findings seem inconsistent with Squire's (1992) view, according to which flexible factual knowledge cannot easily be acquired by amnesic patients. However, even if amnesic patients seem to be able to learn flexible semantic knowledge, it must be noted that their progress is laborious by comparison to the controls. According to Tulving et al. (1991), there exist several interpretations of the difference between the efficiency of semantic learning in amnesics and controls which are compatible with the view that semantic memory is completely intact in amnesics. Thus, it could be that normal subjects use both episodic and semantic systems to learn new semantic information and/or to retrieve recently learnt semantic knowledge while amnesics can only rely on their semantic system. A possible contribution of the episodic system to new semantic learning could be to help the normal learner (and not the amnesic) to overcome the effect of interference. In that perspective, careful comparisons of semantic learning in normal subjects and amnesics are necessary. Finally, it could also be that the amnesic patients show a deficit of both the episodic and semantic systems but that the semantic memory is less severely impaired than episodic memory.

In addition to these studies of new semantic learning, there are also several reports of robust conceptual priming effects in amnesic subjects (Gardner et al., 1973; Shimamura and Squire, 1984). According to Tulving and Schacter (1990), such effects reflect 'a process of semantic learning: the modification of, or adding of new information to, semantic memory'.

Amnesic patients are not only able to acquire isolated factual or procedural information but also appear to be capable of acquiring considerable amounts of complex knowledge relevant to the running of their everyday life. Complex learning has been defined by Booker and Schacter (1988) as 'learning in relatively rich knowledge domains (e.g., computer programming, text editing, physics/maths problems, chess playing) that require the acquisition of various kinds of information, such as items, concepts, relations, and conditional associations (p. 61)'. For example, Glisky et al. (1986a and b) have shown that amnesics can learn, with more or less difficulty, and practice new computer vocabulary and operating procedures although little conscious recollection of the learning experience occurred. Subsequently, Glisky and Schacter (1987, 1988, 1989) also showed that an amnesic patient was able to acquire complex knowledge and processes required for the execution of a computer data-entry task. Furthermore, successful transfer into an actual work-setting was achieved. More recently, Glisky (1992) extended this earlier work to a larger group of memory-impaired patients and observed that all patients were able to learn both the data-entry procedures and the factual information associated with the task. In addition, patients showed evidence of transfer of factual knowledge to the procedural task, as well as transfer of the data-entry procedures across minor variations in materials. Finally, factual knowledge was acquired by patients at a much slower rate than control subjects whereas procedural learning (measured by the speed of data-entry) progressed at approximately the same rate in amnesics and controls.

It should be noted that procedural learning may not necessarily lead to normal performance in amnesic patients. For example, Wilson et al. (1989) observed that two amnesic patients had extreme difficulty in learning a procedural task which consisted of entering the data and time into an electronic memory aid despite the fact that they showed normal performance in the traditional procedural learning tests. This procedural task involves about six simple steps and was mastered by control subjects within two or three trials. Baddeley (1992) interprets this failure by suggesting that the number of steps to be mastered in this task exceeds the capacity of working memory and, consequently, errors are produced on trial 1 by both the amnesics and the controls. However, due to their defective episodic memory, the amnesic patients (contrary to the controls) fail to recollect their error and recall how it was corrected and cannot thus avoid repeating it. More generally, Baddeley's view predicts that amnesic patients' performance should be weaker than that of the normals in a procedural task when it depends on episodic memory for its acquisition.

However that may be, the demonstration that amnesic patients can acquire complex (factual and procedural) knowledge and can transfer it in the real world has important practical consequences. Indeed, it now seems possible to reduce the negative impact of memory impairment on everyday life by teaching amnesic patients complex knowledge and skills in different domains that might enable them to live more independently (for further discussion, see Schacter and Glisky, 1986). This chapter decribes a re-education study in which we attempted to teach an amnesic patient (AC) the complex knowledge needed to use word-processing software, with the intention to optimize his social or even professional reinsertion.

Case History

AC is a 33-year-old right-handed man who had earned a master's degree in history and was employed as a teacher. He was found comatose in the street in March 1987. No identifiable cause of the accident was found. The coma spanned a three-month period. A first emergency CT showed a left subdural haematoma with extensive left hemispheric swelling. The volume of the haematoma had increased in a second CT performed after clinical worsening. This was surgically drained. A ventriculo-cardiac shunt was installed for hydrocephalus.

A short neuropsychological examination carried out in December 1987 showed severe amnesia and some language problems (word-finding difficulties, semantic paraphasias and slow comprehension). Furthermore, an ophthalmological examination showed normal visual acuity but tubular vision, the visual field being reduced to its central 5°. A control CT showed signs of softening of the left occipital lobe and both internal regions of the right and left occipital lobes. A bilateral, left-predominating dilatation of the brain-ventricule posterior horns was also observed. It was concluded that the transtentorial herniation resulting from the subdural haematoma gave rise to compression of both posterior cerebral arteries. Such compression can explain the infarction of both occipital lobes responsible for the visual complaints and is likely to explain the mesial temporal lesions responsible for the amnesic syndrome.

In December 1988 AC was referred to the Neuropsychological Rehabilitation Unit for evaluation and re-education. A detailed neuropsychological investigation was conducted at this time.

Neuropsychological Examination

General intellectual functioning and frontal lobe tests

The patient was co-operative, alert and attentive. Furthermore, he showed a normal intellectual efficiency. In the Progressive Matrices, he scored 55, which places him at the ceiling of his age group (95th percentile). Some subtests of the Wechsler Adult Intelligence Scale (WAIS) were also administered. He obtained the following scaled scores:

information: 13; digit span: 10; arithmetic: 10; similarities: 10; comprehension: 10; picture completion: 13; block design: 13.

In Nelson's (1976) modified version of the Wisconsin Card Sorting test, AC achieved all six categories, making no perseverative error. In a phonemic fluency test (letters P, F and L), AC scored in the normal range, generating a total of 24 words (controls: 29.3, s.d.: 6.7). Furthermore, the subject's judgement was essentially normal.

Language and instrumental functions

AC had fluent, well-articulated speech with some word-finding difficulty and semantic paraphasias. In an oral-naming test, he made six errors on a forty-five-item set and he also made many pauses. Furthermore, he displayed a normal use of morphological and syntactic structures. His comprehension of complex syntactic-semantic sentences expressing spatial and temporal relations and passive and relative structures was correct. Finally, reading and writing revealed no deficits.

Mental and written calculation were intact and there were no signs of object agnosia and apraxia. In the test battery designed to explore face recognition (Bruyer and Schweich, 1991), the patient performed normally in the different subtests devised to assess perceptual operations, structural encoding, analysis of expressions and extraction of semantic features (apparent gender, age, and so on) from surface facial features.

Finally, in an auditory reaction time task, his results were also normal: he obtained a median reaction time of 204 msec (controls: 256 msec).

Memory assessment

Short-term memory   The short-term memory investigated by the forward digit span test and the Corsi block-tapping procedure (Milner, 1971) was normal: his Corsi block span was 5 and his digit span was 7. Moreover, when the patient was not distracted or interrupted, he could hold a question in mind and keep to an activity.

Long-term memory   In contrast to his well-preserved intellectual and short-term memory abilities, the patient was profoundly amnesic. He was completely unable to maintain durably any record of ongoing events, and he could not recollect a single detailed personal episode of his life or recount current news events. For example, he did not remember the important earth tremor which had occurred a few days previously in Armenia. He could neither recall the name of the newly elected President of the United States (President Bush), but when he was given the first letter of the name he produced the correct response while saying that he was not sure and that he had put his trust in his 'instinct'. Furthermore, he was disorientated in time and space but he knew his date of birth and age and he did not confabulate. If questioned on his memory functioning, he denied any memory symptoms whatsoever. Due to these severe memory disorders, AC was completely dependent on his parents for most everyday activities (for example, they had to accompany him from his home to the rehabilitation unit). Moreover, his life was restricted to a few routine activities whereas before his accident AC was a very active person involved in political and cultural associations.

Table 5.1 Memory test scores for AC (December 1988)

	AC	Normative data
Short-term memory		
Digit span	7	6.9 (0.9)
Spatial span	5	5.7 (0.8)
Long-term memory		
Auditory verbal learning test (15 words, 10 trials)		
mean recall	6.3	12.4 (0.85)
list learning %	3.1	76.2 (13.7)
delayed recall (30-min. delay)	0	15
recognition	6	15
Warrington's forced choice recognition test (faces)	26	<perc.10
Implicit/explicit memory test		
completion (%)	45	48.1 (14.5)
free recall (%)	20	55.2 (20.9)
Rivermead Behavioural Memory Test (screening score)	0	12
Wechsler Memory Scale (MQ)	75	

Formal neuropsychological evaluation confirmed the existence of a marked impairment in a variety of memory tests (see table 5.1). His Memory Quotient on the Wechsler Memory Scale was 75. He was also administered the Rivermead Behavioural Memory Test (Wilson et al., 1985), which is a test of everyday memory problems and comprises twelve subtests. Normal subjects of the same age and education of AC pass all twelve items but AC failed them all.

In a fifteen-word list learning task (Selective Reminding Task, Buschke, 1973), AC recalled an average of 6.3 words per trial (controls: 12.4, s.d. = 0.85) and he failed to recall any word after a thirty-minute delay. In the two-alternative forced-choice faces recognition memory test (Warrington, 1984), he performed at close to chance level, scoring 26/50.

AC was also submitted to a word-completion priming task. The patient was shown lists of ten words and was asked to rate how much he liked each word on a five-point 'like–dislike' scale. Then he was given the completion test, and finally, a free recall test. In the completion task, his result was perfectly normal (AC: 45 per cent; controls: 48.1 per cent, s.d.: 14.5). However, his ability for explicit memory (free recall) was minimal (AC: 20 per cent; control: 55.2, s.d.: 20.9).

As regard retrograde memory, AC was administered the Autobiographical Memory Interview devised by Kopelman et al. (1990). It is a semi-structured interview schedule composed of two parts: the personal semantic memory schedule, which assesses the patient's memory of facts from his past life (such as addresses where he had lived, names of school teachers), and the autobiographical incidents schedule, which assesses the patient's memory of specific events in his past. Each schedule explores memories across

Table 5.2 AC's performance on the personal semantic memory schedule and the autobiographical incidents schedule

	Autobiographical incidents schedule	*Personal semantic schedule*
Childhood	4/9	21/21
Early adult life	2/9	15/17
Recent life	0/9	17/21

three time-spans: childhood, early adult life, and recent events. In the autobiographical incidents schedule, subjects are required to recall three incidents from each time-period. If the subject fails to produce any incident, specific prompts may be proposed. The answers were scored by two examiners in terms of descriptive episodicity, that is, specificity in time and place. Table 5.2 summarizes the patient's performance on both schedules.

On the autobiographical incidents schedule, AC's performance was clearly abnormal: the patient recalled only two specific incidents with no time and place indications and two responses based purely on general knowledge (all these responses concerned the earliest periods). On the personal semantic schedule, AC obtained a normal score for the questions relating to the childhood and young adult periods. As to the recent period, his performance was slightly weaker but remains very good by comparison with the recall of incidents. In conclusion, AC's ability to recollect specific personal episodes was profoundly impaired but his general (semantic) personal knowledge was globally preserved (even for recent information which was acquired after the brain injury). These data confirm the view that part of personal knowledge can be stored in semantic memory (see Van der Linden et al., 1992, for further discussion) and also that amnesic patients can acquire new semantic information.

Other evidence concerning the existence of new semantic learning ability in AC was obtained in a famous faces naming task (Van der Linden et al., 1995). In fact, AC was able to identify several personalities who have become famous since his accident. AC's following commentaries clearly show that he was able to learn names as well as properties of individuals after his accident:

- Bill Clinton [. . .] he is the current President of the United States, he was elected last year and I think he has taken up his post in January . . .
- A Belgian scientist, a Belgian Astronaut, uh Dirk Frimout.
- [Jean-Luc Dehaene's face is presented] This is a Belgian Prime Minister, perhaps the current Prime Minister . . . but what is his name? . . . he is a member of the Flemish Catholic Party . . . his first name is Jean-Luc . . . [. . .] no I can't remember his name.

This ability to learn properties of newly famous people is still more obvious in a task in which AC had to identify personalities from their names. In this task, AC was able to provide precise relevant information for half of the thirty-four names of people who have become famous since 1987 (moreover, AC was particularly interested in politics, and for this category of personalities his performance was not different from that of five control subjects).

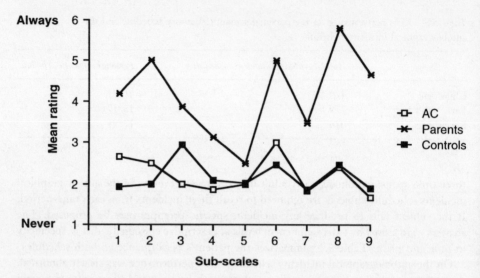

Figure 5.1   Patterns of responses of AC, his parents and control subjects in the memory self-assessment questionnaire

Awareness of disorder (anosognosia)

AC was administered a memory self-assessment questionnaire (QAM: Van der Linden et al., 1989). The QAM consists of forty-seven questions corresponding to various memory failures in everyday life grouped into nine different subscales: (1) conversations: (2) films and books; (3) absent-mindedness; (4) faces and names; (5) skills; (6) general knowledge; (7) places; (8) prospective memory; and (9) personal episodes. The subject rated each failure for frequency of occurrence on a six-point scale (extending from 'never' to 'always'). Each question was scored by giving one point for a 'never' response, two points for a 'very rare' response, and so on, up to six points for an 'always' response. In addition, a mean score by subscale was computed. AC's parents were also asked to rate his difficulties. The patient and parents completed their questionnaires independently in order to give two separate estimates of patient's everyday memory. Finally, AC's performance was compared with the scores obtained by a group of normal adult subjects of the same educational level and age who were asked to rate their memory problems in everyday life. The scores of AC, his parents and the control subjects are shown in figure 5.1. Results indicated that AC substantially underestimated the degree to which he experienced memory difficulty in everyday life: he rated his own difficulties significantly lower than the parents rated his problems, and in addition, his ratings were very similar to those made by normal subjects.

Emotional and motivational functions

AC appeared dull, apathetic and emotionally flat. He was co-operative but relatively passive. Throughout the re-education, we observed no depressive episode or catastrophe reaction. At the very most, he showed brief episodes of irritation when confronted with a difficulty in the manipulation of the computer or word-processing. He never worried explicitly about his future.

Description of the Re-education

Before being admitted to the Neuropsychological Rehabilitation Unit in Brussels, the patient underwent re-education in a hospital close to his home. He was submitted to repetitive memory drills and he was also instructed to use elaborative encoding strategies. However, this programme did not lead to any significant improvement of his memory in daily life. Consequently, we decided to adopt the re-education strategy suggested by Schacter and Glisky (1986); that is, to teach him domain-specific knowledge that should improve his ability to function independently in the real world. The domain of knowledge we selected was word-processing. It seemed to us that the acquisition of this domain of knowledge might give the patient several opportunities of social or even professional reinsertion.

In a preliminary phase, the patient was submitted to a re-education programme designed to improve his visual exploration. More specifically, he was instructed to compensate the reduction of his visual fields by means of voluntary movements of the eyes and head. At the end of this programme, AC was able spontaneously to make compensation movements, but this compensation strategy had not yet become automatic and he still showed some difficulty in dual tasks. Nevertheless, his visual abilities were sufficiently improved to permit the start of the word-processing acquisition programme.

Computer and word-processing knowledge acquisition

The computer and word-processing training was conducted on a Macintosh SE microcomputer. It consisted of three phases: (1) acquisition of keyboard skills; (2) acquisition of general terminology concerning both the computer and the word-processing software; and (3) acquisition of computer and word-processing skills. It should be noted that AC had absolutely no previous knowledge concerning typewriting, computer and word-processing operations. However, his spelling abilities were excellent.

Acquisition of keyboard skills The keyboard training began in January 1989, approximately at the same time as the re-education of the visual functions. In the first phase of the training, the patient was instructed to use a mask system which disclosed only a limited number of keys on the keyboard. At the beginning, the patient was asked to type single words in capital letters without accents, punctuation or correction. Only a limited number of letter keys (as well as the bar space) were accessible and the patient had to type longer and longer words involving the accessible letters. Progressively the number of accessible letters increased but the patient did not have access to the number keys or the punctuation keys. In the second phase (May 1989), the distinction between lower-

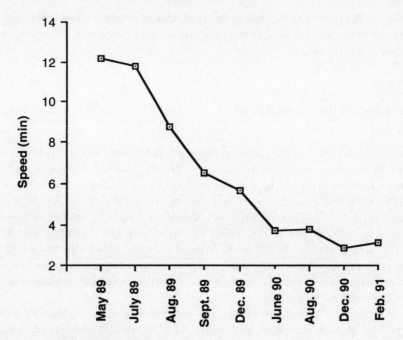

Figure 5.2   Evolution of AC's typing speed

case letters and capital letters, as well as accents, numbers and symbols were progressively introduced. In the last phase, the patient was instructed to type sentences and texts (with punctuation and paragraphs). At this time (July 1989), two coloured cues were placed on the 'delete' and 'capital letters' keys but these cues were progressively removed. At the different phases of the programme, the patient was asked to practice at home (20–30 minutes per day).

Regular controls of typing speed (on a 59-word text) were carried out from May 1989 to February 1991. As figure 5.2 indicates, the patient's progress was constant, and in February 1991 his performance stabilized at the level of 18.8 words per minute, which was a very satisfying level, considering his visual problems.

Vocabulary acquisition phase   This learning phase was conducted at the same time as the first phase. Thirty-four words and definitions were selected as the words to be learned (for example, the word 'cursor' was defined as 'the blinking symbol on the screen that marks typing location'). Three separate lists were constructed: list 1 consisted of ten words related to the different components of the computer (for example, MOUSE): list 2 was composed of eleven words concerning the operation of the computer (such as CLICK) and list 3 consisted of thirteen words describing the specific operations of word-processing (for example, SAVE).

Learning was carried out by means of the vanishing-cues method designed by Glisky et al. (1986a). The procedure and the storage of the data were entirely controlled by the computer. One learning session lasted about an hour and a half and consisted of a pretest, followed by two to seven training trials, and then a post-test. In the pre- and post-tests, the definitions were displayed for twenty seconds and the patient's task was to produce or guess the corresponding labels. If he failed to produce the correct word within ten seconds, he was presented with hyphens indicating the number of letters of the word. If he did not produce the word, he was shown the first letter of the word (C----- for CURSOR). If he still did not complete the word correctly, one letter at a time was added until the patient gave the right answer or until the word had been displayed in its entirety (C-----, CU----, CUR---). The definitions were presented in the same order for all pre- and post-tests.

In trial 1 of the first session, the same procedure was administered but stimulus presentation varied from trial to trial. In all subsequent trials, the definitions were presented along with a letter fragment of the corresponding word which was one letter shorter than the fragment required for successful completion in the previous trial. The correct response given by the subject was confirmed by the presentation of the target word and definition for five seconds. Errors were not displayed on the screen but they were indicated to the patient by means of an auditory signal. Due to AC's visual deficits and his poor knowledge of the keyboard at that moment of the re-education, the therapist read the definitions at the same time as they were displayed on the screen and typed the patient's responses.

For each list, learning was interrupted when it appeared that the patient was not progressing any further. Eight sessions were devoted to the acquisition of list 1; fourteen sessions to list 2; and seventeen sessions to list 3. In fact, AC did not achieve the criterion of one evocation of all words without cue for any of the lists. However, the number of letters needed to complete target words at the end of each session decreased progressively (see figure 5.3 as an illustration concerning list 2). Furthermore, for most words that the patient failed to produce without letter cues, only the first letter was required for a correct response. Thus, at the end of sessions 8, 14 and 17, he correctly produced respectively eight words without cue and two words with one cue letter (out of ten), nine words without cue and two words with a cue letter (out of eleven), and finally, eight words without cue and four words with one cue letter (out of thirteen). Several delayed tests were also administered. As illustrated in figure 5.3, the patient demonstrated substantial and stable retention of vocabulary over periods of up to twenty-four months.

It should be noted that the patient seemed to show flexibility in the use of part of this vocabulary knowledge in everyday life. For example, in 1989, at the end of the year, AC's mother reported that while she was reading an English text concerning computers, she found the word 'MOUSE', and was puzzled (believing that maybe it was an error) and so she asked AC the meaning of this word. The patient was able to give an adequate definition without being able to recollect how and where he had learned this information.

Computer and word-processing skills acquisition In the first step of the programme the patient was taught the basic manipulations of the mouse: displacing or raising the mouse, pointing, clicking, displacing an icon, dragging through the menu and releasing the mouse button. These manipulations were directly related to the newly acquired definitions. For this part of the programme, we used some of the exercices proposed in the 'Welcome' initiation disk designed by Macintosh. Acquisition of the manipulations took three sessions of one and a half hours. At the end of the third session the patient was able to apply the manipulations to unpractised tasks (from written instructions).

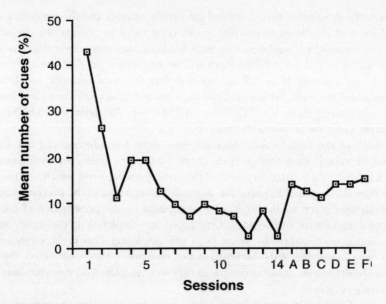

Figure 5.3   Number of letter cues required by AC to complete fragment of list 2 words in presence of their definitions

Note: The final six points depict performance in the delayed tests conducted three weeks (A), seven weeks (B), three months (C), eight months (D), sixteen months (E) and twenty-four months (F) after the termination of session 14.

In the second step, the patient learned to start up and close the computer and a programme (AC again needed three sessions to acquire this knowledge).

Finally, AC was taught to use the word-processor. The word-processing software package used was a popular commercial menu-driven software (Microsoft Word, Version 3.1). In such menu-driven software, a document is created and edited in the document window. The document window consists of a list of seven main menus: titled file, edit, format, font, document, tools, and view. When a main menu is chosen, a list of submenus appears on the screen and the user can choose the appropriate submenu. Editing is accomplished with the help of a mouse. To perform an edit, using the mouse the user first selects the object of text to be edited, then chooses the appropriate menu and clicks on the menu item desired. Some complex editing may involve moving between the menu and the object several times. For some of the editing options, the user may choose to issue a command equivalent instead of using the menu options, but we decided to restrict learning to the menu options. There is no on-line help in this software other than the help which may be given by the menus themselves. Nevertheless, the user is warned, by means of an auditory signal and/or a written comment appearing on the screen, when he makes certain types of errors (for example, quitting without saving the document).

Different general tasks and commonly used editing and formating tasks were taught: saving, printing, inserting, deleting, replacing, moving, centring, changing format and character, and so on. The learning technique consisted in breaking down the process into a hierarchy of tasks and subtasks and cuing the patient through each subtask by giving verbal and physical prompts and even written plans. At the outset the prompts were very numerous, detailing each operation of a subtask (for example, take the mouse, put the pointer on the word 'File' placed above and to the left, click and let your finger, pressing the mouse, explore 'File', and so on). Then the prompts were progressively removed and the patient was only given the headings corresponding to the subtasks (for example, 'explore File'). Finally, the patient was only provided with the general heading corresponding to the task to be realized (for example, 'Save'). A new task was taught when the patient was able to execute the preceding one alone, several times in succession and after a few days' delay. Old tasks were regularly re-presented to the patient. Furthermore, exercises involving several already acquired tasks were administered. When a task or subtask could be realized by means of different procedures, only one was selected.

Teaching AC these computer and word-processing skills was a long and arduous task. It began in May 1989 and was conducted with a frequency of, first, three, and then two sessions per week. AC's performance was very variable from one session to another. Sometimes, he was completely unable to execute a very well-learned operation, but usually he could remember the correct operation after a short delay or after being given general cues. When the patient did not remember a particular manipulation, he was instructed to explore the menu freely and not to search explicitly for the correct solution. Numerous perseverative errors were observed (for example, inserting the disk before starting). His reactions with regard to his errors changed as learning progressed. At the beginning, he was clearly unaware of his errors (he was sure he was right). Then we observed a partial awareness of the inadequacy of his behaviour ('I don't know if I have to insert the disk before starting') that was followed by a diffuse knowledge of the task's difficulty. Finally, he did not remember that the task had been problematical.

In June 1990, the patient could execute (with some hesitation and temporary blockings) the main computer and word-processing tasks and he could work alone in the rehabilitation unit. At this time, we examined if the patient had acquired declarative knowledge concerning the computer and word-processing. If we asked him to describe verbally different computer or word-processing specific operations, we observed that he could give a substantial amount of information. For example, here is an answer which AC gave to one of the questions asked:

Q. If, when revising a text, you notice that you have omitted a letter in a word, like, for example 'GADEN' instead of 'GARDEN', how would you make the correction?

A. I would go with the mouse . . . go the word 'gaden', blacken the whole word; when the word is black, it can be changed easily . . . I must place the arrow between the A and the D . . . I must place the arrow at the missing spot . . . to type the missing R.

The year 1991 was essentially devoted to overlearning; that is, to make the acquisitions more automatic. In April 1992 AC bought a microcomputer and consequently he could work at home. The transfer from the rehabilitation unit to his home took place without any difficulty (except that during the first weeks he did not remember that he had his own computer at home). He also easily moved from Version 3.1 to Version 4 (a slightly different version) of the word-processing program. The only observed problem concerned the creation of tables, a task in which the modifications between the two versions are far more important. A specific short-term programme was devoted to teaching AC this task. In 1993 the main objective of the re-education was to train AC to apply his word-processing knowledge in a real-world work environment. More precisely, he was instructed to perform a secretarial and librarian job in an association devoted to the assistance of brain-damaged patients. This training phase is in progress.

It should be noted that AC's re-education was not restricted to word-processing acquisition alone. Indeed, the patient was also submitted to a re-education programme designed to teach him some specific routes, for example from his home to the re-education unit. Moreover, he was also taught to use a memory book (see p. 71).

Long-term assessment

During 1993 several control tests were administered in order to evaluate long-term retention of AC's knowledge.

In February 1993 we assessed AC's typing speed by asking him to type the same 59-word text as that presented in the control tests after the initial keyboard learning phase. He showed a performance of 25 words per minute; it had been 18.8 in February 91. Furthermore, his performance with a new, unfamiliar text was very similar to that obtained with the familiar text: he typed this text at a speed of 25 words per min. These results showed that AC's typing abilities had continued to improve over the two-year period.

In the same period, we also tested his retention of the thirty-four acquired computer-related words. Moreover, the flexibility of this knowledge was examined by asking the patient to produce the target words in response to transformed versions of the definitions. More precisely, the specific wording of the thirty-four definitions was altered so that the meaning of the original definitions was preserved. For example, the definition 'a little movable box which permits communication with the computer without using the keyboard', a definition corresponding to the word 'MOUSE', was transformed into 'a little instrument sliding on the mat and designed to interact with the computer'. The results showed that the patient needed respectively ten letter cues (out of 245) to produce the correct responses in the May 1989 test, thirteen letter cues in the May 1993 'same definition' test and twenty-one letter cues in the May 1993 'altered definitions' test. Furthermore, in these three tests, he correctly produced respectively twenty-five words without cue and eight words with one cue letter (out of thirty-four), twenty-four words without cue and seven words with a cue letter and twenty words without cue and eight words with one cue letter (see figure 5.4).

Finally, in a definition test, we observed that the patient could give a very detailed definition of most the thirty-four labels. He frequently added information that did not exist in the original definitions which suggests that the word-processing learning programme had considerably enriched his semantic knowledge. As an illustration, he defined the word 'MOUSE' and 'PRINT' as follows:

> MOUSE: A piece of wire with one end attached to the set and the other to a little
> box . . . which transmits via the cable the position of an arrow; the box
> is about 7 cm long and 3–4 cm wide, it has the shape of a small roof with

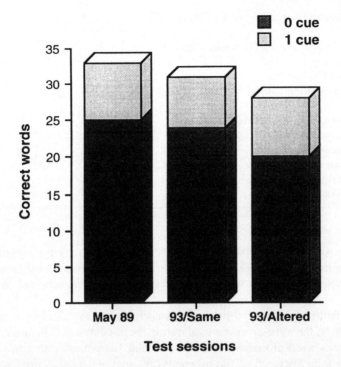

Figure 5.4 Number of words correctly produced in response to the original or altered definitions with one or no cue

a short slope and a long slope; there is a surface which can be pressed [the patient makes the gesture of clicking]; the mouse can blacken a line . . . move the arrow which marks the spot where to type.

PRINT: This is the operation whereby visible text on the screen is transformed to visible text on paper . . . one only needs to switch on the printer . . . the text has already been recorded, I mean the text is kept by the computer; one has to check that the printer is in working condition; something is also displayed on the screen . . . the computer asks how many pages to print, where to start, where to finish, . . . from to . . . , and then you click on OK.

AC was also submitted to a manuscript-editing task which consisted of making fifty-four changes, marked on hard copy, to the computer's version of a document. In order to make these changes, the patient had to use the different editing and formating tasks he had learned during his re-education. The therapist was present during all the sessions and he recorded the events occurring during this control test. The results showed that AC succeeded directly and without hesitation in forty-two changes. The twelve remaining changes were also executed, but the patient either hesitated or adopted an inadequate solution that was rapidly corrected (suggesting an imperfect knowledge of the semantic structure of the system). It should be noted that these types of errors are also frequently

Table 5.3 Memory test scores for AC (January 1993)

Auditory verbal learning test (15 words, 10 trials)

mean recall	5.7
list learning (%)	5.3
delayed recall (30-min. delay)	0

Wechsler Memory Scale – revised indexes

Attention/concentration	106
Verbal memory	<50
Visual memory	64
General memory	<50
Delayed recall	0

observed in normal discretionary users of software, that is to say professionals who do not work in the computer field itself but who have integrated personal computers and personal computer software into their everyday work (Santhanam and Wiedenbeck, 1993).

The flexibility of AC's word-processing knowledge was evaluated by comparing his performance on the word-processor used during the re-education (Microsoft, Version 4) and two other word-processors (MacWrite II and ClarisWorks, an English version) which differ from Microsoft on various points (headings of the menu, presentation of the cursor and the rule, and so on). The differences were slight for MacWrite II and more important for ClarisWorks. AC was asked to start up the program, to type an 81-word text, to change the format, to use the rule, to make paragraphs, to save and to print the text. He was clearly able to execute the task completely on both new word-processors even though he took more time than on the Microsoft word-processor: 20 minutes on Microsoft, 31 minutes on MacWrite and 32 minutes on ClarisWorks.

Finally, a follow-up memory assessment clearly demonstrated that the word-processing training did not lead to a general improvement of AC's memory. Indeed, AC's results in the episodic memory tasks were very similar to those obtained in December 1989 (see table 5.3). In other words, AC's progress was strictly domain-specific and he remained profoundly amnesic. Thus, while he had acquired substantial word-processing and computer knowledge, he was unable to retrieve any specific episodes of his re-education and to locate the specific spatio-temporal context of these episodes. He only possessed some factual knowledge, such as the general location of the Rehabilitation Centre (Cliniques St-Luc), the names of his therapist and of some other people whom he met frequently in the Rehabilitation Centre (the secretary, another amnesic patient). Moreover, he could say that his re-education concerned word-processing acquisition and that he used a Macintosh microcomputer. Finally, when he was questioned about his memory function, he admitted that he had some difficulties in the memory domain and that these difficulties constituted the motive for his re-education but he was completely unable to recall specific episodes of memory dysfunction in everyday life. In other words, as in other domains of autobiographical memory, AC possessed some general factual (semantic) knowledge of his memory function but no episodic knowledge. As a matter of

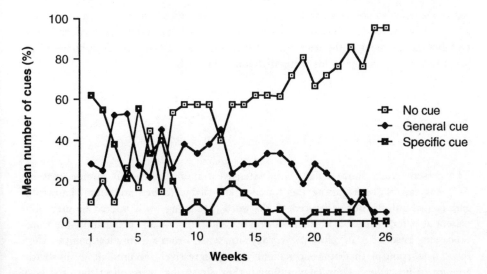

Figure 5.5 Evolution of AC's independence for using the memory book system at home

fact, on the memory self-assessment questionnaire (QAM: Van der Linden et al., 1989), AC's ratings were very similar to those made in December 1988 and he clearly still underestimated his memory problems.

Due to his remaining severe episodic memory deficits, AC was still very dependent on his parents and near relations in everyday life. For example, he was completely unable to carry on his work spontaneously because he did not remember the point he had reached in the preceding work session or even a few minutes previously. In order to increase his autonomy, it was decided to teach AC to use a compensatory memory book consisting of different sections in which he could record and refer to information concerning things to do, names of new people, information concerning transportation, and so on. AC was administered a training programme adapted from Sohlberg and Mateer (1989) which distinguishes three training phases: an acquisition stage, in which the patient has to become familiar with the purpose and use of each different section in the memory book; an application stage, in which the patient has to learn when and where to use the notebook; and finally, an adaptation stage, in which the patient has to demonstrate appropriate notebook use in natural settings. The most important problem was encountered in the second stage of the training because, due to his amnesia, the patient forgot to consult and note information in his book. Consequently, it was decided to associate his parents with a programme designed to teach him to use his book at several key moments in the day. At each key moment, AC's parents were asked to wait for several seconds to see if AC spontaneously used his memory book. If he did not, they were instructed to give AC either general (What do you have to do now?) or specific (Use your memory book) cues. They also had to record the level of cueing necessary for each situation. A similar method was adopted by the therapist at the time of the re-education sessions. Figure 5.5 shows that it took twenty-six weeks of training for AC to achieve the spontaneous use of the system at each key moment at home. A transfer to other nonlearned situations was also observed, and at present AC systematically uses his memory book in all everyday situations. More particularly, the memory book system has enabled him to be more independent in the realization of word-processing tasks, either at home, in the re-education sessions or in his secretarial and library job.

Conclusions

The present study showed that, with extensive training, a severely amnesic patient, AC, was capable of acquiring the complex knowledge (either procedural knowledge and factual information) required to do word-processing on a microcomputer. The patient also demonstrated substantial flexibility and retention and could apply the word-processing knowledge in relevant everyday situations. From a theoretical point of view, these data confirm that amnesic patients can progressively accumulate a substantial amount of procedural knowledge although they are unable to recollect the process of learning. Nevertheless, it should be noted that AC did not learn the word-processing skills in a normal fashion. Indeed, considerable repetition was needed before he mastered the various procedures. On the other hand, AC was able to perform, without error but more slowly, a word-processing task by using word-processing software that differed on several points from that used during the training phase. Finally, these results demonstrated once more that amnesic patients can acquire, although not a normal rate, new flexible factual (semantic) information despite a total lack of episodic memory.

From a re-education point of view, the present study confirms that the approach of Schacter and Glisky (1986) to re-education, which emphasizes the acquisition of domain-specific knowledge, constitutes a promising way to improve the integration of amnesic patients into social and professional life. However, it also suggests that this domain-specific strategy will be efficient only if it is coupled with an attempt to provide the amnesic patient with a compensatory memory system such as a memory book.

Although these results have implications for both theory and re-education, much has yet to be discovered about both the nature of complex learning in amnesia and the factors which might affect speed and transfer of learning. Thus, for example, it remains to investigate the nature and real efficiency of the vanishing-cues procedure which was used in the present study to teach AC the computer and word-processing vocabulary. With regard to the efficiency of this procedure, several studies have provided conflicting findings. Glisky et al. (1986a) have shown that amnesic patients displayed higher levels of learning of computer-related vocabulary with the vanishing-cues method than with a standard anticipation-learning method. Nevertheless, they reported that the patients remained dependent on first-letter cues to produce target words in response to their definition. On the other hand, Leng et al. (1991) also found that a patient who had suffered a severe head injury was able to learn computer-related vocabulary more rapidly with the method of vanishing cues. In addition, this patient did not remain dependent on first-letter cues. Finally, in two recent studies, Parkin and his collegues (Aldrich, submitted; Hunkin and Parkin, submitted; cited in Parkin and Leng, 1993) were unable to show that the vanishing-cues technique was more advantageous than a standard rote-learning procedure. So it could be that only certain amnesic patients may benefit from this technique. In this context, we have recently observed a dissociation between the performance of two amnesic patients in the acquisition of six new concepts by means of the vanishing-cues method (Van der Linden et al., 1993). One patient remained dependent on first-letter cues while the other patient showed rapid progress (although not as rapid as that of the controls) and was able to produce the target words without fragment cues. Both patients were very similar with regards to their educational level, severity of amnesia or existence of frontal signs.

Further studies are necessary in order to identify the relevant factors which may predict the success of the vanishing-cues procedure. More fundamentally, there are theoretical issues that need to be clarified. According to Glisky et al. (1986a), learning by the method of vanishing cues may be mediated by the same system that supports repetition priming, what Tulving and Schacter (1990) have referred to as the perceptual representation system (PRS). On the other hand, the factual acquisitions demonstrated with the vanishing-cues method may also constitute instances of new semantic learning. At the present time, neither hypothesis has been directly tested. In fact, the flexible nature of the knowledge acquired with this method (see Butters et al., 1993) seems inconsistent with characteristics normally attributed to the perceptual representation system (Glisky, 1992). Moreover, both interpretations have to explain the fact that learning with the vanishing-cues method in amnesics is slower than in normal subjects. As amnesic patients show normal repetition priming effects, they should perform normally in the vanishing-cues task. According to Leng et al. (1991), it may be that, in addition to the priming component, there is an explicit memory component in the vanishing-cues task. Tulving et al. (1991) suggest that there exist different interpretations of the difference between the efficiency of semantic learning in amnesics and controls, which are compatible with the view that semantic memory is completely intact in amnesics. Thus, it could be that normal subjects use both episodic and semantic systems to learn new semantic information and/or to retrieve recently learnt semantic knowledge while amnesics can only rely on their semantic system. A possible contribution of the episodic system to new semantic learning could be to help the normal learner (and not the amnesic) to overcome the effect of interference. It should be noted that, in the present study, AC produced many errors in the vocabulary-learning phase and some of these errors were repeated from one session to another. Finally, with regard to flexibility of factual knowledge which can be taught to amnesic patients, the findings of Butters et al. (1993) suggest that generalization of learning may be obtained with overlearning (this could explain the flexibility of knowledge shown by AC in the present study).

Another important theoretical issue raised by the present study (and by the other studies which have examined complex learning in amnesia) concerns the role of episodic memory in the acquisition of procedural knowledge. In this context, Ross (1984) has shown that remindings, the memory retrieval of earlier learning episodes, are an integral part of the skill-learning process in normal subjects and that they have predictable effects on performance. Furthermore, the explicitness of the remindings and the effect of remindings seem to decrease with practice. According to Ross, remindings aid learning because they provide the initial information which permits the subject to apply the actions from the earlier task to the present one by analogy. They are also the source of many of the initial generalizations and they can be used to allow the organization of partially decontextualized information. Viewed from another angle, Baddeley (1992) argues that episodic memory permits the normal subject to recollect an error made in a previous trial, to recall how it was corrected and thus to avoid it. These views can easily explain why amnesic patients whose episodic memory is severely defective do not necessarily show normal skill learning. As a matter of fact, normal skill acquisition should be observed in amnesia only when the task does not depend on episodic memory for its acquisition. However, as suggested by Wilson et al. (1989), the testing of this hypothesis is confronted with the problem of establishing in advance whether the acquisition of a given task will or will not depend on episodic memory. It should be mentioned that the patient AC produced many perseverative errors during the word-processing skill-learning phase, which is consistent with the view that he tended to repeat his earlier attempts, including errors which he failed to recall and correct. At a practical level, this suggests that the technique of errorless learning should optimize learning in amnesic patients (Baddeley, 1992).

Other questions concerning the nature of complex learning in amnesia should be explored; for example, the study of whether mental models develop without explicit remembering, or whether appropriate cues could involuntarily trigger a previously acquired piece of information (see Booker and Schacter, 1988). These studies would provide important information concerning the best way to teach complex knowledge to amnesics and the limit of the acquisitions that they can accumulate. Furthermore, they would also contribute to shedding light on the processes involved in normal complex learning.

Further Reading

Glisky, E.L., Schacter, D.L. and Butters, M.A. (1994) 'Domain-specific learning and remediation of memory disorders', in M.J. Riddoch and G.W. Humphreys (eds), *Cognitive Neuropsychology and Cognitive Rehabilitation* (Hove and London: Lawrence Erlbaum Associates).
Parkin, A.J. and Leng, N.R.C. (1993) *Neuropsychology of the Amnesic Syndrome* (Hove and London: Lawrence Erlbaum Associates).

References

Aldrich, F.K. (submitted) 'Vanishing cues versus serial anticipation learning following head injury: a case study'.
Baddeley, A.D. (1992) 'Implicit memory and errorless learning: a link between cognitive theory and neuropsychological rehabilitation?', in L.R. Squire and N. Butters (eds), *Neuropsychology of Memory* (New York: Guilford).
Booker, J. and Schacter, D.L. (1988) 'Toward a cognitive neuropsychology of complex learning', in J.M. Williams and C.J. Long (eds), *Cognitive Approaches to Neuropsychology* (New York: Plenum).
Bruyer, R. and Schweich, M. (1991) 'A clinical test battery of face processing', *International Journal of Neuroscience*, **6**: 19–30.

Buschke, H. (1973) 'Selective reminding for analysis of memory and learning', *Journal of Verbal Learning and Verbal Behavior*, **12**: 543–50.

Butters, M., Glisky, E. and Schacter, D. (1993) 'Transfer of new learning in memory-impaired patients', *Journal of Clinical and Experimental Neuropsychology*, **15**: 219–30.

Gabrieli, J.D.E., Cohen, N.J. and Corkin, S. (1983) 'Acquisition of semantic and lexical knowledge in amnesia', *Society for Neurosciences Abstracts*, **9**: 28.

Gabrieli, J.D.E., Cohen, N.J. and Corkin, S. (1988) 'The impaired learning of semantic knowledge following bilateral medial temporal-lobe resection', *Brain and Cognition*, **7**: 157–77.

Gardner, H., Boller, F., Moreines, J. and Butters, N. (1973) 'Retrieving information from Korsakoff patients: effects of categorical cues and reference to the task', *Cortex*, **9**: 165–75.

Glisky, E.L. (1992) 'Acquisition and transfer of declarative and procedural knowledge by memory-impaired patients: a computer data-entry task', *Neuropsychologia*, **30**: 899–910.

Glisky, E.L. and Schacter, D.L. (1987) 'Acquisition of domain-specific knowledge in organic amnesia: training for computer-related work', *Neuropsychologia*, **25**(6): 893–906.

Glisky, E.L. and Schacter, D.L. (1988) 'Long-term retention of computer learning by patients with memory disorders', *Neuropsychologia*, **26**(1): 173–8.

Glisky, E.L. and Schacter, D.L. (1989) 'Extending the limits of complex learning in organic amnesia: computer training in a vocational domain', *Neuropsychologia*, **27**: 107–20.

Glisky, E.L. Schacter, D.L. and Tulving, E. (1986a) 'Learning and retention of computer-related vocabulary in memory-impaired patients: method of vanishing cues', *Journal of Clinical and Experimental Neuropsychology*, **8**: 292–312.

Glisky, E.L., Schacter, D.L. and Tulving, E. (1986b) 'Computer learning by memory-impaired patients: acquisition and retention of complex knowledge', *Neuropsychologia*, **24**(3): 313–28.

Hirst, W., Phelps, E.A., Johnson, M.K. and Volpe, B.T. (1988) 'Amnesia and second language learning', *Brain and Cognition*, **8**: 105–16.

Hunkin, N.M. and Parkin, A.J. (submitted) 'A critical evaluation of memory remediation using the "vanishing cues" method'.

Kopelman, M.D., Wilson, B.A. and Baddeley, A.D. (1990) *The Autobiographical Memory Interview* (Bury St Edmunds: Thames Valley Test).

Leng, N.R.C., Copello, A.G. and Sayegh, A. (1991) 'Learning after brain injury by the method of vanishing cues: a case study', *Behavioural Psychotherapy*, **19**: 173–81.

Mayes, A.R. (1988) *Human Organic Memory Disorders* (Cambridge: Cambridge University Press).

Milner, B. (1971) 'Interhemispheric differences in the localization of psychological processes in man', *British Medical Bulletin*, **27**: 272–7.

Nelson, H.E. (1976) 'A modified card sorting task sensitive to frontal lobe defects', *Neuropsychologia*, **12**: 313–24.

Parkin, A.J. and Leng, N.R.C. (1993) *Neuropsychology of the Amnesic Syndrome* (Hove: Lawrence Erlbaum Associates).

Ross, B.H. (1984) 'Remindings and their effects in learning a cognitive skill', *Cognitive Psychology*, **16**: 371–416.

Santhanam, R. and Wiedenbeck, S. (1993) 'Neither novice nor expert: the discretionary user of software', *International Journal of Man-Machine Studies*, **38**: 201–29.

Schacter, D.L. and Glisky, E.L. (1986) 'Memory remediation: restoration, alleviation, and the acquisition of domain-specific knowledge', in B. Uzzell and Y. Gross (eds), *Clinical Neuropsychology of Intervention* (Boston, Mass.: Martinus Nijhoff).

Shimamura, A.P. (1989) 'Disorders of memory: the cognitive science perspective', in F. Boller and J. Grafman (eds), *Handbook of Neuropsychology*, vol. 3 (Amsterdam: Elsevier).

Shimamura, A.P. and Squire, L.R. (1984) 'Paired-associate learning and priming effects in amnesia: a neuropsychological study', *Journal of Experimental Psychology: General*, **113**: 556–70.

Sohlberg, M.M. and Mateer, C.A. (1989) 'Training use of compensatory memory book: a three-stage behavioral approach', *Journal of Clinical and Experimental Neuropsychology*, **11**: 871–91.

Soliveri, P., Brown, R.G., Jahanshahi, M. and Marsden, C.D. (1992) 'Procedural memory and neurological disease', *European Journal of Cognitive Psychology*, **4**: 161–93.

Squire, L.R. (1992) 'Memory and the hippocampus: a synthesis from findings with rats, monkeys, and humans', *Psychological Review*, **99**: 195–231.

Tulving, E. and Schacter, D.L. (1990) 'Priming and human memory systems', *Science*, **247**: 301–6.

Tulving, E. Hayman, C.A.G. and Macdonald, C.A. (1991) 'Long-lasting perceptual priming and semantic learning in amnesia: a case experiment', *Journal of Experimental Psychology: Learning, Memory, and Cognition*, **17**: 595–617.

Van der Linden, M. (1992) 'Effets de priming et apprentissage sémantique chez l'amnésique: données récentes et interprétations théoriques', *Psychologica Belgica*, **32**: 3–50.

Van der Linden, M. (1994) 'Neuropsychologie de la mémoire', in X. Seron and M. Jeannerod (eds), *Traité de neuropsychologie humaine* (Brussels: Mardaga).

Van der Linden, M., Wijns, C., von Frenkel, R., Coyette, F. and Seron, X. (1989) *Un Questionnaire d'auto-évaluation de la mémoire* (Brusell: Editest).

Van der Linden, M., de Partz, M.P., Schils, J.P. and Seron, X. (1992) 'Semantic and autobiographical memory: neuropsychological dissociations?', in M.A. Conway, D. Rubin, H. Spinnler and W. Wagenaar (eds), *Theoretical Perspectives on Autobiographical Memory*. (Dordrecht: Kluwer Academic).

Van der Linden, M., Meulemans, T. and Lorrain, D. (1993) 'Acquisition of new concepts by two amnesic patients', *Cortex*, **29**: 543–8.

Van der Linden, M., Brédart, S. and Depoorter, N. (1995) 'Semantic memory and amnesia: a case study', *Journal of the International Neuropsychological Society*, **1**: 196 (abstract).

Warrington, E.K. (1984) *Recognition Memory Test* (Windsor, Berks.: NFER and Nelson Publishing).

Wilson, B.A., Baddeley, A.D. and Cockburn, J.M. (1989) 'How do old dogs learn new tricks? Teaching a technological skill to brain injured people', *Cortex*, **27**: 115–19.

Wilson, B.A., Cockburn, J.M. and Baddeley, A. (1985) *Rivermead Behavioural Memory Test* (Bury St Edmunds: Thames Valley Test).

Part II   Did It Really Happen?
Confabulations, Misrememberings and Delusions

Introduction

Neurological damage to structures in the temporal lobes can give rise to various types of memory impairment, often featuring dense anterograde with variable degrees of retrograde amnesia (Part I). However, other types of brain damage, to the frontal lobes or more global and widespread injuries, can lead to memory impairments distinguished not so much by amnesia but rather by various forms of misremembering or confabulation. Dalla Barba describes two patients, MB and SD, with widespread brain injuries, resulting from high blood pressure and an open head injury respectively, who both confabulated but in different ways. MB following his illness was found to have preserved general intelligence, linguistic skills, semantic knowledge and good knowledge for public events. He only confabulated episodic memories and even these confabulations were more plausible than fantastic. In contrast, SD's general intelligence was impaired following his injury, as were his semantic knowledge, performance on tests sensitive to frontal lobe injuries and episodic memory. He produced fantastic confabulations that were often semantically anomalous as well as implausible. Downes and Mayes also report three cases of variations in confabulatory responses. Their patient JW, who suffered from Korsakoff syndrome, did not spontaneously confabulate but nevertheless believed himself still to be working, when in fact he was hospitalized, and had no insight into his memory deficits. Patient WF, with damage to the frontal lobes, believed that he was living with his parents and had a perseverative memory for a heated argument he had supposedly had with his father, always on the preceding evening. Lastly, NH following injury to the temporal and occipital lobes had a persistent hallucination which involved him in lengthy conversations with a mysterious figure. However, although NH claimed that these conversations took place when others were present no one had noted NH holding such conversations. Thus, it may be that not only was the figure hallucinated but so were the interactions with it, and NH was unable to distinguish these from actual experiences. In a fascinating paper, Rohrenbach and Landis review the disorder of *reduplicative paramnesia*, a striking symptom of which is a persistent false belief. Often this can take the form of a patient believing himself to be in a hospital other than that in which he actually is a patient. Rohrenbach and Landis provide a first-hand account by a patient who sustained neurological damage to the corpus callosum followed by a reduplicative paramnesia in which he believed himself to be in a hospital in Toulon when in fact he was in a clinic in Zurich.

These types of memory impairment are not exclusively limited to patients with permanent and verified neurological injuries. They can also arise in functional or psychogenic disorders such as schizophrenia and clinical depression. Psychogenic disorders must, of course, also have a neurological basis, and one possibility is that temporary changes in memory performance occurring during psychogenic illnesses may be associated with changes to the normal functioning of structures in the frontal lobes. Thus, Parkin and Stampfer describe a case of a young woman who, during a twelve-week psychotic episode that had many of the symptoms of schizophrenia, suffered marked intellectual decline and impairment of memory including a retrograde amnesia for the events of her life. Parkin and Stampfer argue that these impairments may reflect the breakdown of central control processes, that is, the central executive of working memory, that have long been thought to be mediated by regions of the frontal lobes. This temporary *dysexecutive syndrome* appeared to be a prominent feature of the psychosis they describe. Kopelman, Guinan and Lewis, in a thorough review of the neurological literature on schizophrenia, point out that schizophrenics are known to show changes to areas in both the temporal and frontal lobes and to suffer from some degree of retrograde and anterograde amnesia as well showing signs of a dysexecutive syndrome. They provide a detailed account of a patient who, among other things, believed she shared her thoughts with another individual. However, this patient, although obviously schizophrenic, showed no pattern of impairment on a full range of neuropsychological tests, demonstrating that the false beliefs of schizophrenics are not always associated with more general signs of neurological changes. Finally, McKay, McKenna and Baddeley describe a series of case studies of schizophrenic patients, including a fascinating transcript of an extended interview with one particular individual. These authors show that highly deluded individuals may perform well on some neurological tests, particularly tests of short-term memory, but show impairments on tests of long-term memory and on some frontal lobe tests. It seems clear from this group of papers that knowledge and theory originating from neuropsychological studies can be profitably extended to patients with psychogenic illnesses and in the process extend our understanding of cognitive impairment in these illnesses.

6 Keeping Out the Past: a Study of Temporary Memory Loss

Alan J. Parkin and Hans G. Stampfer

The study of disordered memory has been primarily confined to people who have suffered irreversible deficits following some form of brain injury or disease. However, a much larger number of individuals suffer temporary memory impairment which is presumed to be 'psychogenic' or 'functional' in origin, and is invariably associated with wider psychiatric disturbance. This group has been relatively neglected in formal neuropsychological studies, although there is a considerable clinical literature on individual cases and a large body of 'psychodynamic' theory about the nature of such impairment and the mechanisms that might be involved (Kopelman, 1987; Parkin, 1987; Schacter and Kihlstrom, 1991).

There is a close association between memory impairment and psychiatric illness. In day-to-day practice, complaints of 'poor memory' often emerge spontaneously or in response to specific inquiry (for example, in different forms of anxiety and depression). Intermittently, 'amnesia' is the presenting complaint (for example, dissociative reaction, fugue state and multiple personality).

After orientation in time, place and person, the testing of memory is probably the most common 'bedside' cognitive assessment undertaken by any duly qualified clinician. In the main, the primary concern is to distinguish 'organic' from 'functional' impairment. 'Organic' means that the memory impairment is due to some 'physical' fault caused by fixed or reversible damage to brain regions directly involved in mediating memory – and the most immediately important reason for distinguishing 'organic' from 'functional' memory impairment is to diagnose reversible or treatable brain damage, caused, for example, by vitamin deficiency or hypothyroidism.

The term 'functional' could simply be taken to mean the converse of 'organic'; namely, that the memory impairment is not due to some 'physical' brain damage. However, more complex issues are involved and this is also true of the seemingly straightforward concept of 'organic' impairment. For example, there may be 'functional' impairment of memory which is a secondary manifestation of 'organic' damage to parts of the brain not directly involved in mediating memory. The primary problem is physical or structural brain damage, but this has led secondarily to functional system impairment in nondamaged parts. Similar difficulties are involved in the concept of 'functional'. The primary implication of 'functional' is that the impairment is not due to physical damage. This usually implies (although not necessarily) that the impairment is reversible. However, the nature of 'functional' impairment may depend on when one looks and what coexisting factors are relevant at the time. More specifically, if it is recognized that long-term motor immobility (including voluntary and enforced 'functional' immobility) can lead to physical disuse atrophy and irreversible fibrosis, is this also possible in the realms of emotional and higher intellectual functioning? We think not, but we don't know.

In this chapter we describe a case of presumed functional memory impairment associated with an atypical psychotic disorder characterized by prominent 'negative' symptoms that are usually associated with schizophrenia (Andreasen, 1982). The impairment was presumed to be 'functional' in origin, in that thorough clinical assessment with appropriate laboratory investigations failed to demonstrate any organic cause. The patient's illness and memory impairment improved and there was evidence of premorbid personality vulnerabilities linked to an emotionally traumatic upbringing and adult life. Serial neuropsychological testing was undertaken on our patient Elizabeth during her three-month admission, and we believe that the presented findings show the potential benefits of incorporating experimental neuropsychological test data in psychiatric research and day-to-day clinical practice.

Elizabeth

Elizabeth was born in Western Australia. Her birth was unproblematic and she achieved developmental milestones normally. Although of good intelligence, she left school at fifteen and obtained a trade qualification. Her home life was dramatic. Her parents separated when she was three due to problems with her mother's alcoholism and her father's persistent gambling. Her mother remarried, but this was to another alcoholic. At eighteen she had her first serious relationship. It was a traumatic time which culminated in her being badly stabbed. In her early twenties she married an alcoholic. A child was born but she had a rare congenital illness. Although given only three days to live, the child lived for 2.5 years during which time Elizabeth had to resuscitate her a number of times. Finally, she left her husband to live with another man and they now have a daughter.

Elizabeth was referred by a psychiatrist as someone who 'couldn't move . . . couldn't cope'. She gave a history of 2–3 months of increasing disorganization, anxiety and depressed mood. She felt her problems began after seeing a hypnotherapist in order to give up smoking. Since then she had never really come out of being hypnotized. Initially she had experienced racing thoughts and had felt more alive, but very soon she became unable to complete daily tasks, had difficulty thinking and making decisions, began to feel frightened to leave the house, and was losing track of time. She would wander around the house not really knowing what she was doing, and had been found on numerous occasions by her partner lying in the foetal position. On one occasion follow-ing hypnosis, she reported seeing black smoke coming out of the 'pores of her body' and had been told that depression was black and would come out of her. On admission the diagnoses considered were a dissociative state, an organic brain syndrome, or a delayed grief reaction. Over the next four weeks she reported feeling progressively worse, with feelings of hopelessness. She wanted to be in a long-stay mental hospital and began requesting electroconvulsive therapy. Four weeks after admission, while on weekend leave, she attempted suicide, slashing at her arm with glass and also being found with a blow-dryer and a bucket of water. She said she wanted to commit suicide because she did not think she would get better. Little improvement was noted over the next five weeks. Again on weekend leave, she attempted suicide and continued being preoccupied with suicidal ideation. Ten weeks after admission she began to feel subjectively better. This improvement coincided with her return from three weeks' holiday with her partner. Earlier in the admission her relationship had been strained. A steady progress ensued. There was no more suicidal ideation and she was noted to be caring well for herself, her daughter and partner while on leave. She was discharged twelve weeks after admission and remains well.

Neuropsychological Investigations

One feature of Elizabeth's case was particularly fascinating. She claimed to have great difficulty remembering the past. On one occasion she remarked that everything in her life had been fine until her present illness developed – a somewhat odd statement, given the range of negative life events she had been through. She also remarked that even people well known to her seemed odd: she knew who they were, but they somehow did not seem familiar. This feeling of alienation caused her particular problems with her family.

We decided to examine her impairments more closely, but all we had available were the tools of the neuropsychologist. None the less these provided some useful insights into her difficulties and, possibly, some pointers towards the organic basis of her psycho-genic disturbance.

A Neuropsychological Examination

Elizabeth's estimated premorbid IQ (Nelson, 1982) was 106, but on the Weschler Adult Intelligence Scale (Wechsler, 1981) she had an IQ of only 78. Impaired performance was widespread, with performance normal on only two tests. On the Weschler Memory Scale (WMS: Wechsler, 1945) she also showed some impairment – particularly on those subtests most sensitive to amnesia: logical memory, paired associate learning and visual reproduction – where she scored 9, 13.5 and 6 (corresponding control scores are 12, 16 and 15). She was given the Rey Figure (Rey, 1964) to copy (see figure 6.1). Copying was accurate but her execution was bizarre in that she failed to take account of the overall

Copy

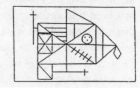

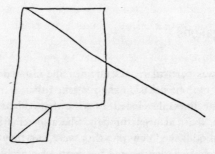

Recall

Figure 6.1   Elizabeth's copying and recall of the Rey Figure (*see inset*)
Note: All figures are tracings of original. Top figure shows the order with which she copied different
elements of the figure. Solid lines indicate early stages of copying, dashes the middle stage, and dotted lines
the final stage. Note that her copy does not utilize the overall structure of the figure. The lower figure
shows her recall of the figure after ten minutes

organization of the picture. Furthermore she could remember very little about it after
five minutes. Figure 6.2 shows Elizabeth's attempt to draw a bicycle: while not all the
bicycles drawn by controls might be considered roadworthy, Elizabeth's problem with
this task is self-evident.

Elizabeth's unusual copying of the Rey Figure is considered indicative of frontal lobe
function (Ogden et al., 1990) and her difficulties with the draw-a-bicycle test also merit
a similar interpretation. Other testing confirmed this. Her word fluency, the number
of words she could generate beginning with a given letter, was substantially impaired
(a total of 23 words compared with a control average of 44) and she had very marked
problems with the Wisconsin Card Sorting Task in that she was unable to understand
what was required.

Other tasks emphasized her substantial memory deficit. The Brown-Peterson task

Figure 6.2 Left: Two of Elizabeth's attempts to draw a bicycle; *right*: a representative sample of how other women of her age perform the same task

involves the presentation of target stimuli followed by a distracter interval, then instructions to recall the target. Figure 6.3 shows Elizabeth's immense difficulty with this task. She was also markedly impaired on the immediate free recall of simple twelve-word lists, scoring 4, 2, and 0, and performance did not improve much when the words in the list were drawn from obvious categories. She was also given a number of tests of recognition memory and here a different picture emerged. On the Warrington Test (Warrington, 1987) she scored 82 per cent correct on the words and 84 per cent correct on the faces version of the test. On a 36-item test of yes–no recognition (Gardiner, 1988) she scored 56 per cent correct with two false alarms (control range 52–92 per cent), and on an additional 30-item yes–no test of recognition designed by John Dunn and Kim Kirsner (personal communication) she scored 77 per cent correct. Overall, therefore, her recognition performance was quite good especially when one considers how poor her recall performance was.

As we noted earlier, Elizabeth complained of being unable to remember her past, and we investigated this formally using the autobiographical cueing technique devised by Robinson (1976). Elizabeth was given a number of cue words and asked to recall a specific incident in her life in response to each one. This revealed some access to her turbulent past – the cue 'break' brought recollection of an incident in which she broke a pizza over her husband's head. However, the number of memories produced, 58 per cent, was well below the control rate of 96 per cent. There was also evidence of repressed memory. Just two days earlier Elizabeth had slashed her wrists but, in response to the cue word 'cut', she related an incident about cutting her thumb when she was eight.

Elizabeth's remote memory was also evaluated using the Famous Personalities Test devised by John Dunn at the University of Western Australia. In the first phase Elizabeth had to identify which of a group of four names was that of a famous person. Next she had to explain why that person was famous. Figure 6.4 shows that Elizabeth was as good as the controls (mainly library staff of her age) at identification (note that this was not because the test was easy – some of the names were relatively unfamiliar, for

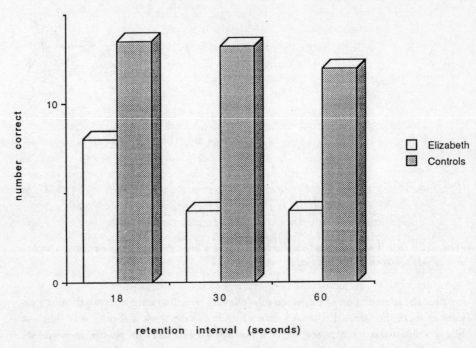

Figure 6.3   Elizabeth's performance on the Brown–Peterson test compared with controls

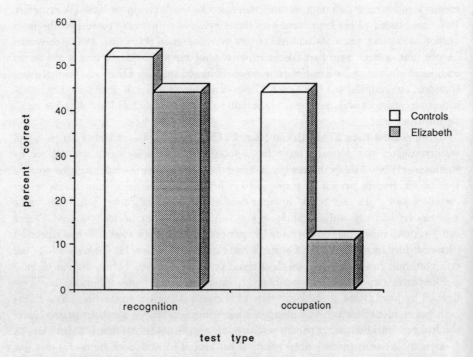

Figure 6.4   Elizabeth's performance on the famous personalities test

example, Sally Ride, Sidney Nolan, Amelia Earhart. However, she was much poorer at retrieving the occupations of correctly identified people.

The WMS revealed that Elizabeth had a marked problem with learning unrelated pairs of words. We explored the possibility that this deficit might be overcome by teaching her to use images as links between the words. Instructions to use imagery greatly improved her ability to learn the word pairs and, more remarkably, she was able to retain them for twenty-four hours. However, it was disappointing that on a subsequent test using a similar task she failed to use the imagery strategy spontaneously.

A final test procedure was temporal discrimination (Squire et al., 1981). Elizabeth was shown two lists of sentences separated by a two-minute interval. She was then given a recognition test and, if she identified a sentence, she was asked to say whether it came in the first or second list. Her recognition performance was quite good, but her temporal discrimination was at chance levels. Interestingly, it did not improve when the lists were distinguishable in some obvious way, for example, when all the first list sentences contained an arabic number, and all the second list contained numbers in spelt out form.

As noted earlier, Elizabeth's symptoms lasted only twelve weeks. As her negative symptoms lifted it was notable that her frontal signs also reduced markedly, thus suggesting a direct link between frontal pathology and her impairment.

Discussion

Following a traumatic life history Elizabeth underwent a psychotic episode which had, as its major outcome, a temporary period of negative symptoms. Prominent among these symptoms was a pronounced impairment of memory. In attempting to explain what has happened we can approach the problem at two levels. First, we can ask what kind of mechanism was responsible? and, second, we can try to explain why the mechanism was called into action.

A proposed mechanism for Elizabeth's memory deficit

It is instructive to begin with a summary of Elizabeth's memory impairment. The principal features were:

1 a decline in intellectual function;
2 a gross impairment of memory when measured by various forms of recall. However, recognition memory appeared reasonably intact;
3 an impairment in temporal discrimination;
4 evidence of disturbed frontal lobe dysfunction.

The general pattern of impairment shown by Elizabeth is not unique and has been described in a number of patients who have suffered focal lesions of frontal lobes and associated structures (Petrides, 1989). Deficits in temporal discrimination in the presence of relatively normal recognition are, for example, a typical finding in frontal patients (ibid.). The pattern of memory impairment associated with frontal damage has been termed the 'dysexecutive syndrome' (Baddeley and Wilson, 1988). As the name suggests, this disorder is thought to affect higher-level functions in memory rather than more basic functions such as consolidation.

In a recent study Parkin et al. (1994) have described a man known as CB, who developed memory difficulties following rupture and repair of the anterior communicating artery (ACoA). Almost invariably, this kind of event leads to frontal lobe damage (see Parkin and Leng, 1993) and this was clearly evident in CB. He had markedly reduced word fluency and showed disorganized copying of the Rey Figure that was similar to that of Elizabeth. His memory abilities were widely investigated, but for our present purpose it is important to note that, like Elizabeth, he experienced peculiar difficulty on tests of recall relative to recognition (for a further similar case, see the case of Hanley et al., 1994).

That recall should be particularly affected by damage to the frontal lobes is explained by proposing that recalling information, particularly in the absence of external cues, presents a considerable problem-solving task in that hypotheses concerning the nature of target information must be constructed. In contrast, recognition presents far less of a problem because the basis of the information to be evaluated is actually presented and does not need to be retrieved. This account of memory has been particularly developed by Shallice (1988), who has argued that executive processes in memory involve a *description* phase in which a hypothesis is formed about the nature of stored information, and a subsequent *matching* and *verification* stage in which retrieved information is evaluated.

Within this account deficits can arise either because the description phase fails to produced candidate information or because the matching and verification stages fail to confirm the identity of generated target information. This arrangement can produce two fundamental patterns of breakdown, and both have been observed. A failure in the description phase would be expected to produce poor recall but not necessarily poor recognition – the argument being that recall cannot be effective without the ability to generate candidate descriptions of to-be-remembered information. Recognition testing, however, may provide sufficient conditions for an item to be matched and verified without any additional derivation of a description.

A failure in the matching and verification phase predicts a different form of deficit, one in which descriptions are made available but are not adequately evaluated. This pattern of performance was observed in the study of a post ACoA patient, RW (Delbecq-Derousne et al., 1990), in which it was shown that the patient had normal levels of recall but only at the expense of recalling large numbers of incorrect items. This suggested an impaired ability to evaluate the memory-based qualities of retrieved information and this was confirmed by the patient's surprisingly poor performance on the Warrington Recognition Test.

Other aspects of Elizabeth's impairment are also consistent with a frontally based dysexecutive deficit. Elizabeth performed exceptionally badly on the Brown-Peterson test and there is now good evidence that this test loads on frontal function. Stuss et al. (1982) found that patients who had undergone frontal leucotomy performed very badly on the Brown-Peterson task even though they performed similarly to controls on other measures of memory. More recently, Parkin et al. (1993) described poor performance on this task in a young woman exhibiting marked frontal problems following recovery from

Wernicke's Encephalopathy. Finally, converging evidence for a frontal locus to impaired Brown-Peterson performance comes from a study of age differences, in which the poorer performance of older adults was predicted by impairments exhibited on test of frontal function (Parkin and Walter, 1991).

The manner in which her paired associate learning improved with instructions to use imagery suggests strongly that she did not have a fundamental memory deficit; rather, an inability to execute an optimal encoding strategy. This finding is again mirrored in the frontal lobe literature. Parkin et al. (1988) described similar findings in their ACoA patient JB (see also Parkin et al., 1993). Also, the fact that Elizabeth could not improve her temporal discrimination when an obvious cue distinguished the two lists also points towards an executive deficit.

Elizabeth's memory impairments thus resemble those encountered in frontal patients; but how strongly can we argue that she has disrupted frontal lobe function? First, we can point to her bad performance on figure copying, fluency and Wisconsin Card Sorting measures as evidence for frontal disturbance. However, doubts have often been expressed about the localizing value of these tests (for example, Bigler, 1988) and, on their own, they are perhaps an insufficient basis for asserting the neuroanatomical locus of Elizabeth's problems.

A stronger case for a frontal basis to Elizabeth's memory loss comes from the observation that Elizabeth's psychiatric presentation can be characterized as that of *negative symptoms* (Andreasen, 1982). These symptoms are generally associated with, but not exclusive to, the aftermath of schizophrenia. They include blunting of affect, apathy, disorganization, impaired memory and bradykinesia. These symptoms were all shown in Elizabeth, and thus any information available concerning the neural basis of negative symptoms might be germane to a greater understanding of Elizabeth's difficulties.

A pattern of 'hypofrontality' is now well established in schizophrenia (see, for example, Buchsbaum et al., 1992) and there are a number of indications that a direct consequence of this may be the appearance of negative symptoms. Neurophysiological studies (Besson et al., 1987; Volkow et al., 1987) have indicated that hypofrontality and negative symptoms are correlated, and Merriam et al. (1990) reported a significant relationship between neurological 'soft' signs of frontal dysfunction and negative symptoms. Liddle (1987; Liddle and Barnes, 1990) has also linked negative symptoms and frontal dysfunction but argues for two subsets of negative symptoms each relating to a different aspect of frontal function. More recently, Wolkin et al. (1992) have confirmed that the pattern of hypofrontality associated with negative symptoms is not an artefact of medication, and Andreasen et al. (1992) have shown that hypofrontality in schizophrenics correlates with both the extent of negative symptoms and the Tower of London Test – a newly developed test of frontal dysfunction.

What initiated memory loss?

We have suggested that the memory loss shown by Elizabeth bears considerable resemblance to that encountered in frontal lobe dysfunction. The next and perhaps more difficult question is to explain why this loss of memory occurred.

The first possibility is that Elizabeth's memory loss is due to the depression that accompanied her negative symptoms. This would seem very unlikely. It is well recognized that the memory impairment in severe depression resembles that of dementia, and the impairment is anything but protective. In particular, the person reveals a memory impairment that makes day-to-day life more difficult while long-term memory is left relatively intact. As a result the depressed person characteristically focuses on past events that confirm their negative perceptions of themselves and the world (Eyesnck and Mogg, 1991). In contrast, Elizabeth's deficit appeared to achieve the opposite in that it served to insulate her from her disturbing past.

It is reasonable to suppose that our intellectual functions may not only help us to understand the 'world out there'; they may also protect our 'world within' when the world out there proves too much for us to bear. Everyone knows we 'rationalize' at times to give ourselves an excuse and we often advise those in great distress after some emotionally traumatic event to 'forget all about it', 'put it out of your mind'. It is the possible purpose underlying functional memory impairment that makes all comparisons with machine impairment or breakdown inappropriate. A car does not develop a functional timing problem to protect the engine from overheating, but a person evidently can develop amnesia for some emotionally overbearing event. Normal memory is a 'functional' brain attribute, and there is a lot of clinical observation to suggest that protective forgetting is part of normal memory functioning (Parkin, 1987).

Stampfer (1990) has specifically considered the protective role that might be played by the memory loss associated with negative symptoms. He notes the marked similarity between the nature of negative symptoms and the pattern of impairment seen in patients with post-traumatic stress disorder (PTSD). Both disorders have memory loss as a prominent symptom, and Stampfer argues that for the PTSD patient the memory loss serves to keep the distressing predisposing event out of mind. Memory loss arising within the context of negative symptoms is addressed from the standpoint that negative symptoms follow an acute psychotic episode. Here Stampfer argues that the protective mechanism prevents the patient from recalling the disturbing hallucinations and thought disturbance of the acute phase.

Elizabeth's personal history created an ideal background within which protective forgetting could arise. Her life featured a number of extremely negative life events culminating in a psychotic episode characterized by disturbing hallucinations. It is not difficult to envisage how her subsequent negative symptoms, especially loss of memory, could have imparted a degree of functional value to her.

Elizabeth's experience is not unusual in that there are many instances of patients showing dissociative memory disturbances following disturbing life events. Most notable are the cicumscribed amnesias surrounding combat and crime – many of which are now likely to come into the category of PTSD. In addition, one can include the more pervasive disruptions of memory underlying fugue, multiple personality and the kind of mechanisms responsible for disruptive memories of incest or similar traumatic experiences which return many years after the event.

The mechanism observed here can be given a number of names with 'motivated forgetting' or 'repression' the most obvious. By combining observations of these phenomena with neuropsychological analysis we have shown how an explication of these somewhat vague psychodynamic terms might be incorporated into the framework provided by the newly emerging cognitive neuropsychology.

Further Reading

Carpenter, W.T., Buchanan, R.W. and Kirkpatrick, B. (1991) 'The concept of negative symptoms in schizophrenia', in J.F. Greden and R. Tandon (eds), *Negative Schizophrenic Symptoms: Pathophysiology and Clinical Implications* (Washington, D.C.: American Psychiatric Press).
Parkin, A.J. (1993) *Memory: Phenomena, Experiment, and Theory* (Oxford: Blackwell Publishers), chs 4 and 16.

References

Andreasen, N.C. (1982) 'Negative symptoms in schizophrenia: definition and reliability', *Archives of General Psychiatry*, **43**: 136–4.
Andreasen, N.C., Reziak, K. and Alliger, R. (1992) 'Hypofrontality in neuroleptic-naive patients and in patients with chronic schizophrenia. Assessment with Xenon 133 single-photon emission computerised tomography and the Tower of London Test', *Archives of General Psychiatry*, **49**: 943–58.
Baddeley, A.D. and Wilson, B. (1988) 'Frontal amnesia and the dysexecutive syndrome', *Brain and Cognition*, **7**: 212–30.
Besson, J.A.O., Corrigan, F.M., Cherryman, G.R. et al. (1987) 'Nuclear magnetic brain imaging in chronic schizophrenia', *British Journal of Psychiatry*, **150**: 161–3.
Bigler, E.D. (1988) 'Frontal lobe damage and neuropsychological assessment', *Archives of Clinical Neuropsychology*, **3**: 279–97.
Buchsbaum, M.S., Haier, R.J. and Potkin, S.G. (1992) 'Frontostriatal disorder of cerebral metabolism in never-medicated schizophrenics', *Archives of General Psychiatry*, **49**: 935–42.
Delbecq-Derouesne, J., Beauvois, M.F. and Shallice, T. (1990) 'Preserved recall versus impaired recognition', *Brain*, **113**: 1045–74.
Eysenck, M. and Mogg, K. (1991) 'Mood disorders and memory', in J. Weinman and J. Hunter (eds), *Memory: Neurochemical and Abnormal Perspectives* (London: Harwood).
Gardiner, J.M. (1988) 'Functional aspects of recognition experience', *Memory and Cognition*, **16**: 309–13.
Hanley, J.R., Davies, A.D.M., Downes, J. Mayer, A.R. (1994) 'Impaired recall of verbal material following an anterior communicating artery aneurysm', *Cognitive Neuropsychology*, **11**: 543–78.
Kopelman, M. (1987) 'Amnesia: organic and psychogenic', *British Journal of Psychiatry*, **150**: 428–42.
Liddle, P.F. (1987) 'Schizophrenic syndromes, cognitive performance and neurological dysfunction', *Psychological Medicine*, **17**: 49–57.
Liddle, P.F. and Barnes, T.R.E. (1990) 'Syndromes of chronic schizophrenia', *British Journal of Psychiatry*, **157**: 558–61.
Merriam, A.E., Kay, S.R., Opler, L.A., Kushner, S.F. and van Praag, H.M. (1990) 'Neurological signs and the positive–negative dimension in schizophrenia', *Biological Psychiatry*, **28**: 181–92.
Nelson, H.E. (1982) *The National Adult Reading Test Manual* (Windsor, Berks.: NFER and Nelson).
Ogden, J.A., Growdon, J.H. and Corkin, S. (1990) 'Deficits on visuospatial tests involving forward planning in high-functioning Parkinsonians', *Neuropsychiatry, Neuropsychology and Behavioural Neurology*, **3**: 125–9.
Parkin, A.J. (1987) *Memory and Amnesia: An Introduction* (Oxford: Basil Blackwell).
Parkin, A.J., Leng, N.R.C., Stanhope, M. and Smith, A.P. (1988) 'Memory impairment following ruptured aneurysm of the anterior communicating artery', *Brain and Cognition*, **7**: 321–43.

Parkin, A.J. and Walter, B.M. (1991) 'Short-term, memory, ageing, and frontal lobe dysfunction', *Psychobiology*, **19**: 175–9.

Parkin, A.J., Dunn, J.C., Lee, C.W., O'Hara, P.F. and Nussbaum, L. (1993) 'Neuropsychological sequelae of Wernicke's Encephalopathy in a 20-year-old woman', *Brain and Cognition*, **21**: 1–19.

Parkin, A.J. and Leng, N.R.C. (1993) *Neuropsychology of the Amnesic Syndrome* (Hove, Sussex: Lawrence Erlbaum Associates).

Parkin, A.J., Pitchford, J. and Bindschaedler, C. (1994) 'Further characterisation of the executive memory impairment following frontal lobe lesions', *Brain and Cognition*, **26**: 23–42.

Petrides, M. (1989) 'Frontal lobes and memory', in F. Boller and J. Grafman (eds), *Handbook of Neuropsychology* (Amsterdam: Elsevier), vol. 3, pp. 75–90.

Rey, A. (1964) *L'Examen clinique en psychologie* (Paris: Presses Universitaires de France).

Robinson, J.A. (1976) 'Sampling autobiographical memory', *Cognitive Psychology*, **8**: 578–95.

Schacter, D.L. and Kihlstrom, J.F. (1991) 'Functional amnesia', in F. Boller and J. Grafman (eds), *Handbook of Neuropsychology* (Amsterdam: Elsevier).

Shallice, T. (1988) *From Neuropsychology to Mental Structure* (Cambridge: Cambridge University Press).

Squire, L.R., Nadel, L. and Slater, P.C. (1981) 'Anterograde amnesia and memory for temporal order', *Neuropsychologia*, **19**: 141–5.

Stampfer, H.G. (1990) ' "Negative symptoms": a cumulative trauma stress disorder?', *Australian and New Zealand Journal of Psychiatry*, **24**: 516–28.

Stuss, D.T., Kaplan, E.F., Benson, D.F. et al. (1982) 'Evidence for involvement of orbito-frontal cortex in memory functions: an interference effect', *Journal of Comparative and Physiological Psychology*, **96**: 913–25.

Volkow, N.D., Wolf, A.P., Van Gelder, P. et al. (1987) 'Phenomenological correlates of metabolic activity in 18 patients with chronic schizophrenia', *American Journal of Psychiatry*, **144**: 151–8.

Warrington, E.K. (1987) *Recognition Memory Test* (London: NFER and Nelson).

Wechsler, D. (1945) 'A standardized scale for clinical use', *Journal of Psychology*, **14**: 87–95.

Wechsler, D. (1981) *Wechsler Adult Intelligence Scale – Revised Manual* (New York: Psychological Corporation).

Wolkin, A., Sanfilipo, M., Wolf, A.P. et al. (1992) 'Negative symptoms and hypofrontality in schizophrenia', *Archives of General Psychiatry*, **49**: 959–65.

7 Dreamjourneys: Living in Woven Realities, the Syndrome of Reduplicative Paramnesia

Christina Röhrenbach and Theodor Landis

In our daily life lapses of identification occur that can be quite disturbing. For example, we meet someone and we know that we have met this person before but we can't recall when or where we met. By recollecting probable situations, perhaps then suddenly we have that lightning 'Aha', a flash of knowledge in which we are able to place the person and identify them. Another example is the confusion that is created when somebody reminds us of someone else or even looks very similar and we ask ourselves: Is it that person or not? We have to take a second look to make sure that it is not the person we expected. Such situations can be quite embarrassing, but if we can't find the solution by searching for memory-traces, we might ask that person, assuming we are not too shy.

What is going on, when such mismatches persist for a longer time, when there is a certainty about our identification of a person or a place that cannot be shared with others? In this case a private reality becomes dominant and some aspects of the outer world (places or persons) are interpreted or identified differently from others. If such mismatches occur just for a while or for special things, then the person switches between 'two realities', a subjective, private one and a more or less common-sense generally experienced reality. What is reality then? It is a construction made out of a variety of information we get through our senses. It is one possible solution to bring sense to the manifold information, and we can share that interpretation or construction with others who are in the same 'state of consciousness'. We report a disturbance, or rather we let a patient himself report what happened, when that sort of 'common-sense reality' coexists with another private one.

In neurological terminology such a disturbance is called reduplicative paramnesia. To our knowledge there only exists one other self report of a reduplicative paramnestic episode (Levin, 1968), even though there has been quite a renaissance of interest in such disturbances in the last twenty years.

The patient we shall talk about, and who wrote his impressions down, is a librarian by profession and at the time was 50 years old. He himself entitled that report 'dreamjourneys'.

During his vacation on the Canary Islands he suffered a sudden massive headache and neck stiffness and he was confabulating. Some days later he became more and more drowsy and was transferred to our clinic in Switzerland. On admission he was somnolent, disorientated in time and space and did not recognize close friends. He was largely mute and the few words he uttered were slurred, but he could follow simple commands adequately. Computed tomography revealed a subarachnoidal haemorrhage involving the anterior corpus callosum and an infarction in the territory of the left anterior cerebral artery.

Within ten days his initial mutism cleared. On mental status examination his speech was nonfluent with problems in initiating speech and occasional phonemic errors, but repetition was relatively preserved. He was slow, had difficulties carrying out planned motor acts and showed intermanual conflicts (diagonistic apraxia). Only mild difficulties in learning and recalling verbal as well as figural information could be discerned. After the second week in hospital he appeared to be orientated in time and space, but still gave strange responses when asked where he was. Let us now turn to his own report which he wrote down three months later:

Dreamjourneys: a self report of a reduplicative paramnesic episode
I am quite astonished. What's going on? It seems that I am lying in a hospital. I know on my right side next to me is S [his girlfriend] and that calms me down. Everything seems slightly foggy – even sounds are muffled.

Before I had dreamt, I was driving along a road in a car. We are driving uphill, curve by curve. Obviously it is Algeria: the bare mountains, some single bushes and trees. Up on the mountainside is a huge, stretched building just like a sanatorium. It is a hospital and I am a patient there.

Later on we are in France. We drive along a road towards Switzerland. We are in the old center of Toulon and are driving towards the harbour. On this descending road we find a typical 'Bistro' – doors made of glass with brass handles. I open the door and walk to the bar. There is coffee and the usual croissants. I eat and drink a little. Suddenly I am in bed, the waitresses are nurses. They are very busy and laugh a lot. Two young nurses tell me that their hobby is measuring blood pressure. I stretch my arm and say: 'here please'. The nurses keep asking if I know where I am. Of course I know where I am – it is Toulon and I try to explain this to them. They are just laughing, shake their heads and say: 'No you are in a large Swiss city.' They look at me expecting an answer, thus I guess 'Geneva?' No – 'Zürich?' Yes. I am supposed to be at the University Hospital in Zürich. But I know very well that I am in Toulon. But since they are very kind and friendly, I do them the favour and kindly repeat after them the line 'University Hospital Zürich'. By doing so I find out that I please them all, and since they are very nice, I can do them this little favour. All that counts is that I know where I am. But after a while their insisting that I am in a clinic in Zürich makes me insecure. Maybe then I am in a branch of this Hospital in Toulon. Yes that is the the solution – in order to get the same standard of care, that they can work more efficiently with the same machines, etc. . . . I am really relieved to have found the solution.

The Syndrome of Reduplicative Paramnesia

What do we know about reduplicative phenomena? Reading this report we might ask: What is going wrong? Why can't he 'correctly' identify a place? Can't he distinguish between dream and reality? Is it a problem of memory, of perception or of something else that misleads his feeling of familiarity? Later we shall try to find some answers, but first we give a short historical overview and a description of what is known about this disturbance.

To our knowledge, the first reports about such phenomena stem from Bonnet (1788) and Kahlbaum (1866). Years later the neuropsychiatrist Arnold Pick (1903) described in detail a patient who suffered from progressive paralysis: 'The patient in question asserted that there were two clinics exactly alike in which he had been, two professors of the same name were at the head of these clinics.' Pick understood his clinical observation as a syndrome, characterized by subjective certainty that a physical location or a familiar person has been duplicated; he thought it to be a specific disturbance in memory (delusion of memory) and coined the term reduplicative paramnesia. In the same year he reported a second case, a patient with dementia (probably of the Alzheimer type), who showed the same phenomenon and duplicated the hospital, including doctors and patients. Subsequently other reports of reduplicative paramnesia occurring after brain damage appeared in the literature. In most cases the hospital where a patient was treated was duplicated and relocated to another site, significant to him in his earlier life. Patients often believed that there were two almost identical hospitals coexisting at the same time in different places (Head, 1926; Patterson and Zangwill, 1944; Weinstein et al., 1952).

A variety of reduplication phenomena have been described, such as the Capgras syndrome, a reduplication of persons (Capgras and Reboul-Lachaux, 1923); a reduplication of the self (Westphal, 1927); of body parts, of time, events or objects (for review, see Christodoulou, 1986a; Cutting, 1991; Joseph, 1986; Signer, 1992; Weinstein, 1974). Although in several cases the duplication of places and persons co-occurred, reduplicative paramnesia was believed to be a neurological disease, while the Capgras syndrome was attributed to functional psychosis, that is, a psychiatric disease. Even Pick's case showed a reduplication of places and persons, and Capgras's patient had the impression that duplicates (imposters) of several family members and of herself existed. Recent reviews of psychiatric case reports show that in about a third of the patients who were diagnosed as psychotic (paranoid schizophrenic, schizoaffective or affective) neuroradiological or neuropsychological evidence of a brain disease was found (Christodoulou, 1977, 1978; Förstl et al., 1991; Joseph, 1985, 1986; Joseph et al., 1990; Malloy et al., 1992; Merrin and Silberfarb, 1976; Morrison and Tarter, 1984; Signer, 1992). Moreover it has been recently suggested that both reduplicative paramnesia and Capgras syndrome reflect the same underlying disturbance due to brain dysfunction (Alexander et al., 1979). Meanwhile, a variety of neurological etiologies causing reduplicative paramnesias were reported: post-traumatic encephalopathy, subarachnoidal hemorrhage, cerebro-vascular infarction, haematoma, tumour, and degenerative, toxic and infectious diseases (for review, see Cummings, 1985; Signer, 1992). In most cases frontal and/or right hemispheric pathology was revealed and attempts were made to explain putative neuropsychological and neuroanatomical factors causing that disturbance.

Broken Memory or Something Else?

Is a disturbance of memory, of perception or of something else, the cause of these phenomena? Pick (1903) himself believed it to be a delusion of memory, that 'a continous series of events in the patient's remembrance fall into manifold occurrences; the isolated events, though remain pretty clearly in his memory are impressed on him as repetitions thereof'. He observed that after a temporary interruption in the course of events (induced by a short sleep) the patient was unaware of the continuity of events during that interruption and believed that the events were duplicated. Sleeping and dreaming may give rise to a disruption of the continuity of mental events. But it may also give rise to changed 'states of awareness' in which dream and everyday reality are not distinguished. Like our patient, Levin (1968) also reported a series of vivid dreams which he had and which he termed 'occupational delirium'; these dreams centred around talks and appointments into which hospital events were mingled.

Pick suggested also a disordered sense of familiarity and a 'mental disturbance' that prevents the proper integration of a vague sense of familiarity into a certain identification. Others also discussed a disturbed sense of familiarity (Christodoulou, 1986b; Feinberg and Shapiro, 1989) that prevents the patient from recognizing and identifying environmental stimuli. Either in the sense of a selective persisting *jamais-vu*, when environmental stimuli that should evoke a strong sense of personal familiarity appear physically similar but unfamiliar, or resembling a *déjà-vu*, so that an unfamiliar (never before experienced) environment appears in pathologically familiar form. A right hemispheric disturbance, particularly one of the right temporal lobe, is supposed to be the reason for this impaired sense of familiarity.

Others explain reduplicative phenomena as a primary memory disorder (Ewert et al., 1985; Kapur et al., 1988; Staton et al., 1982). If new information can be registered but not integrated with past (premorbid) memories, reduplications are likely to occur. Recent and past memories are stored separately and a disconnection of recent memory stores from past (premorbid) memory stores, anatomically caused by a disruption of occipito-hippocampal association connections, is the suggested essential impairment (Staton et al., 1982).

For the Capgras syndrome, the special case of reduplication of persons, a primary disturbance of facial processing was brought into the discussion, either in the sense of a subclinical prosopagnosia (Bidault et al., 1986; Hayman and Abrams, 1977), where matching or recognizing unfamiliar faces is impaired, or as a 'mirror image' of the disturbances underlying prosopagnosia (Anderson, 1988; Bouckoms et al., 1986; Ellis and Young, 1990; Lewis, 1987; Weston and Whitlock, 1971). The latter explanation supposes a disconnection between the percept of a face and its evocation of effective memories. Anatomically two routes of facial recognition are proposed, a 'ventral route' that runs from visual cortex to temporal lobes and is responsible for overt or conscious face recognition, and a 'dorsal route', from visual cortex to the limbic system, which provides the affective information of the face. Prosopagnosic patients can't recognize overt or consciously familiar faces, due to damage to the 'ventral route' but some of them can grasp the emotional significance of a previously known face and show covert recognition (that is, recognition at an unconscious level), because their 'dorsal route' is intact. On the other hand, patients with Capgras syndrome show intact conscious face recognition. When looking at a person they receive an image that stimulates all appropriate semantic information about that person but they have no access to information about the affective tone. This conflict of cognitive recognition and affective nonrecognition may lead to a rationalization strategy in which the perceived person is deemed to be an imposter or a double (Ellis and Young, 1990).

Discussion and Conclusion

If we presume a memory disturbance is the main cause, the observation that reduplicative phenomena occur at a time when memory functions are improving or nearly normalized would need further explanation. Furthermore there is still no answer to the question why just particular persons or places are duplicated. If memory were in general impaired more information would be erroneously reported, as is the case in severe amnesic patients with confabulatory behaviour. Perhaps then reduplicative paramnesia signals the recovery process of a disturbed memory; that is, the process of acquiring new bits of information and gaining access to previously stored information and tying these together. But then why do not all patients with improvement of severely disturbed memory functions show such phenomena? There must be an additional factor.

Moreover the suggestion of a primary disturbance of facial perception explains only one aspect of the syndrome and ignores that duplication of places can coexist with that of persons. Also the fact that patients with prosopagnosia normally do not experience reduplicative phenomena suggests that a failure in facial perception cannot be a sufficient explanation.

Reviewing the well-documented neurological and neuropsychological case reports, most patients have lesions in the right hemisphere and in the frontal lobes (Alexander et al., 1979; Benson et al., 1976; Bouckoms et al., 1986; Burns, 1985; Ewert et al., 1985; Filley and Jarvis, 1987; Hakim et al., 1988; Lewis, 1987; Patterson and Mack, 1985; Ruff and Volpe, 1981; Staton et al., 1982; Vighetto et al., 1980). Apart from our patient, only a few patients showed lesions limited to the frontal region (Durani et al., 1991; Head, 1926).

In the past several years a growing body of evidence supports the hypothesis that a frontal dysfunction superimposed on a right hemispheric dysfunction may be necessary to cause such misidentification phenomena (Alexander et al., 1979; Benson et al., 1976). Visual-perceptual disturbances, resulting from dysfunctions of the right hemisphere, may lead to insecure information about places, faces and spatial relations.

An additional frontal dysfunction causes an inability to solve a problem in a situation of conflicting information and thus leads to premature inference. Once created, these inferences remain stable even when confronted with logical arguments, due to an inability to switch sets.

This is reminiscent of 'hyperlogic' behaviour observed in patients with right-frontal lesions. Hyperlogic argumentations are also known from split-brain patients and are interpreted to be an attempt of the isolated left hemisphere to explain phenomena not directly accessible to the verbal system.

In fact, no patients with purely left hemispheric lesions are reported experiencing reduplicative paramnesia. Since it is often the right hemisphere which is structurally or functionally lesioned, it may well be that the rational attempt to explain the experience of reduplicative paramnesia is a compensatory strategy of the intact or isolated verbal system of the left hemisphere.

Our patient, however, showed neither functional nor structural (CT) signs of right posterior hemispheric damage, but a bifrontal pathology and symptoms reflecting an information transfer deficit between the two hemispheres (anterior split brain). The crucial point in our patient, as compared to those with right hemispheric damage, may be that in addition to bifrontal pathology there was evidence for a structural and functional anterior split-brain situation, in which information of the right hemisphere may not have reached the left hemispheric frontal lobe.

We suppose that a frontal disturbance causes inability to deal with conflicting information, as we explained above; and that during the process of memory recovery integrative and evaluative processes are necessary to tie in new information about places and persons with already stored information. An additional partial isolation (split brain) of the verbal left-hemispheric system from information of the right hemisphere might explain why wrong memory matches occur and why bizarre but rationalized verbal explications are given.

We still need to explain why in most cases the hospital or significant persons such as family members, doctors and other care-givers are duplicated. Our patient lived on the Canary Islands and thought that the Zürich hospital was a branch located in Toulon, a town which is about halfway between Zürich and his home on the islands. Other patients translocated the hospital to their home towns. As Benson and co-workers (1976) pointed out, three facts are important for an individual gaining stepwise orientation in hospital: little experience of being a patient in hospital; confusing circumstances surrounding hospital admission after a brain lesion; and integration of many pieces of information and prior hospital experiences.

As we can imagine, in such a situation there must be a search for explanation and familiarity and a desire to know where you are and who are the important persons around you. If information cannot be integrated in an interpretation of parts of the outer world and if the motivation to disprove once-drawn inferences is limited, the transformation of the first impression of a new location or person into a familiar one seems most convincing.

Reduplications are temporary phenomena, suggesting a plasticity of some functional deficits. Five years after the accident our patient still had impaired frontal functions while the other deficits normalized.

Referring to our observation and to several cases reported in the literature, reduplicative paramnesia is functionally best explained as an attempt to rationalize unfamiliar information by duplicating it with personally relevant information in a situation where affective and temporal-spatial contexts are lacking or insecure and where an additional monitoring deficit prevents inferences, once drawn, to be changed. Anatomically the right hemispheric lesion (or in our case a damage of the callosal connection between left and right hemisphere) may be responsible for the problem with affective and temporal-spatial contexts, while the monitoring deficit is attributable to frontal lobe damage.

That the duplication occurs with personally relevant information is probably due to the fact that personally relevant information is the best consolidated and thus is easily accessed and provides comfort. With improved orientation and control the sense of reality is regained and replaces the provisional construction of a dual reality.

Acknowledgements

We thank Marianne Regard, Ruth Campbell and Michael Röhrenbach for their critical reading, helpful comments and editorial work. This work was supported by the Swiss National Science foundation Grant 32–31 257.91.

References

Alexander, M.P., Stuss, D.T. and Benson, D.F. (1979) 'Capgras syndrome: a reduplicative phenomenon', *Neurology*, **29**: 334–9.

Anderson, D.N. (1988) 'The delusion of inanimate doubles: understanding the Capgras phenomenon', *British Journal of Psychiatry*, **153**: 694–9.

Benson, D.F., Gardner, H. and Meadows, J.C. (1976) 'Reduplicative paramnesia', *Neurology*, **26**: 141–51.

Bidault, E., Luauté, J.P. and Tzavaras, A. (1986) 'Prosopagnosia and the delusional misidentification syndromes', *Bibliotheca Psychiatrica*, **164**: 80–91.

Bonnet, C. (1788) *Krankheit der Einbildungskraft. Gnothi Seauton*, vol. VI (Berlin: Mylius).

Bouckoms, A., Martuza, R. and Henderson, M. (1986) 'Single case study: Capgras syndrome with subarachnoid hemorrhage', *Journal of Nervous and Mental Disease*, **174**: 484–8.

Burns, A. (1985) 'The oldest patient with Capgras syndrome', *British Journal of Psychiatry*, **147**: 719–20.

Capgras, J. and Reboul-Lachaux, J. (1923) 'L'illusion des "sosies" dans un délir systématisé chronique', *Société Clinique de Médécine mentale*, **2**: 6–16.

Christodoulou, G.N. (1977) 'The syndrome of Capgras', *British Journal of Psychiatry*, **130**: 556–64.

Christodoulou, G.N. (1978) 'Syndrome of subjective doubles', *American Journal of Psychiatry*, **135**: 249–52.

Christodoulou, G.N. (1986a) 'The origin of the concept of "doubles" ', *Bibliotheca Psychiatrica*, **164**: 1–8.

Christodoulou, G.N. (1986b) 'Role of depersonalization–derealization phenomena in delusional misidentification syndromes', *Bibliotheca Psychiatrica*, **164**: 99–104.

Cummings, J.L. (1985) 'Organic delusions: phenomenology, anatomical correlations, and review', *British Journal of Psychiatry*, **146**: 184–97.

Cutting, J. (1991) 'Delusional misidentification and the role of the right hemisphere in appreciation of identity', *British Journal of Psychiatry*, **159**: 70–5.

Durani, S.K., Ford, R. and Sajjad, S.H.A. (1991) 'Capgras syndrome associated with frontal lobe tumour', *Irish Journal of Psychological Medicine*, **8**: 135–6.

Ellis, H.D. and Young, A.W. (1990) 'Accounting for delusional misidentifications', *British Journal of Psychiatry*, **157**: 239–48.

Ewert, P.J., Hart, T., Kalisky, Z. and Hayden, E. (1985) 'Reduplicative paramnesia: neuropsychological and anatomical correlates', *Journal of Clinical and Experimental Neuropsychology*, **7**: 647.

Feinberg, T.E. and Shapiro, R.M. (1989) 'Misidentification-reduplication and the right hemisphere', *Neuropsychiatry, Neuropsychology, and Behavioral Neurology*, **2**: 39–48.

Filley, C.M. and Jarvis, P.E. (1987) 'Delayed reduplicative paramnesia', *Neurology*, **37**: 701–3.

Förstl, H., Almeida, O.P., Owen, A.M., Burns, A. and Howard, R. (1991) 'Psychiatric, neurological and medical aspects of misidentification syndromes: a review of 260 cases', *Psychological Medicine*, **21**: 905–10.

Hakim, H., Verma, N.P. and Greiffenstein, M.F. (1988) 'Pathogenesis of reduplicative paramnesia', *Journal of Neurology, Neurosurgery and Psychiatry*, **51**: 839–41.

Hayman, M.A. and Abrams, R. (1977) 'Capgras' syndrome and cerebral dysfunction', *British Journal of Psychiatry*, **130**: 68–71.

Head, H. (1926) *Aphasia and Kindred Disorders of Speech* (Cambridge: Cambridge University Press).

Joseph, A.B. (1985) 'Capgras syndrome', *British Journal of Psychiatry*, **148**: 749–50.

Joseph, A.B. (1986) 'Focal central nervous system abnormalities in patients with misidentification syndromes', *Bibliotheca Psychiatrica*, **164**: 68–79.

Joseph, A.B., O'Leary, D.H. and Wheeler, H.G. (1990) 'Bilateral atrophy of the frontal and temporal lobes in schizophrenic patients with Capgras syndrome: a case-control study using computed tomography', *Journal of Clinical Psychiatry*, **51**: 322–5.

Kahlbaum (1866) 'Die Sinnestäuschungen', *Allgemeine Zeitschrift für Psychiatrie*, **23**: 50–86.

Kapur, N., Turner, A. and King, C. (1988) 'Reduplicative paramnesia: possible anatomical and neuropsychological mechanisms', *Journal of Neurology, Neurosurgery and Psychiatry*, **51**: 579–81.

Levin, M. (1968) 'Delirium: an experience and some reflections', *American Journal of Psychiatry*, **124**: 1120–3.

Lewis, S.W. (1987) 'Brain imaging in a case of Capgras' syndrome', *British Journal of Psychiatry*, **150**: 117–21.

Malloy, P., Cimino, C. and Westlake, R. (1992) 'Differential diagnosis of primary and secondary Capgras delusions', *Neuropsychiatry, Neuropsychology, and Behavioral Neurology*, **5**: 83–96.

Merrin, E.L. and Silberfarb, P.M. (1976) 'The Capgras phenomenon', *Archives of General Psychiatry*, **33**: 965–8.

Morrison, R.L. and Tarter, R.E. (1984) 'Neuropsychological findings relating to Capgras syndrome', *Biological Psychiatry*, **19**: 1119–28.

Patterson, A. and Zangwill, O.L. (1944) 'Recovery of spatial orientation in the post-traumatic confusional state', *Brain*, **67**: 54–68.

Patterson, M.B. and Mack, J.L. (1985) 'Neuropsychological analysis of a case of reduplicative paramnesia', *Journal of Clinical and Experimental Neuropsychology*, **7**: 111–21.

Pick, A. (1903) 'Clinical studies: III. On reduplicative paramnesia', *Brain*, **26**: 260–7.

Ruff, R.L. and Volpe, B.T. (1981) 'Environmental reduplication associated with right frontal and parietal lobe injury', *Journal of Neurology, Neurosurgery and Psychiatry*, **44**: 382–6.

Signer, S.F. (1992) 'Capgras syndrome and delusions of reduplication in neurologic disorders', *Neuropsychiatry, Neuropsychology, and Behavioral Neurology*, **5**: 138–42.

Staton, R.D., Brumback, R.A. and Wilson, H. (1982) 'Reduplicative paramnesia: a disconnection syndrome of memory', *Cortex*, **18**: 23–6.

Vighetto, A., Aimard, G., Confavreux, C. and Devic, M. (1980) 'Une observation anatomoclinique de fabulation (ou délire) topographique', *Cortex*, **16**: 501–7.

Weinstein, E.A. (1974) 'Patterns of reduplication in organic brain disease, in P.J. Vinken and G.W. Bruyn (eds), *Handbook of Clinical Neurology* (Amsterdam: North-Holland), vol. 3, pp. 251–7.

Weinstein, E.A. Kahn, R.L. and Sugarman, L.A. (1952) 'Phenomenon of reduplication', *Archives of Neurology and Psychiatry*, **67**: 808–14.

Weston, M.J. and Whitlock, F.A. (1971) 'The Capgras syndrome following head injury', *British Journal of Psychiatry*, **119**: 25–31.

Westphal, K. (1927) 'Über reduplizierende Paramnesie (Pick) und verwandte Symptome bei progressiver Paralyse', *Zeitschrift für Neurologie und Psychiatrie*, **110**: 585–607.

8 Consciousness and Confabulation: Remembering 'Another' Past

Gianfranco Dalla Barba

Confabulation is a symptom, frequently observed in amnesic patients unaware of their memory deficit, which consists of both actions and verbal statements that are unintentionally incongruous with the subject's personal history and present situation (Dalla Barba, 1993). Although it represents a cardinal symptom of the Korsakoff's syndrome, confabulation can be observed in several clinical conditions involving memory impairments (for example, herpes encephalitis, craniocerebral trauma, frontal lobe damage, dementia) and occasionally in normal subjects.

The content of confabulation can vary considerably, ranging from subtle alteration of events and information to really implausible and bizarre reports of episodes and to marked distortion of semantic information. Consequently some authors (for example, Berlyne, 1972; Bonhoeffer, 1904; Kopelman, 1987; Talland, 1965) have suggested that confabulation is not a unitary phenomenon, but that at least two different types of confabulation must be considered: one consisting of minor distortion of true autobiographical events or their misplacement in time and space, the second consisting of the spontaneous production of more fantastic and implausible reports.

In this chapter I shall describe two patients, MB and SD[1] who showed an amnesic-confabulatory syndrome. Both patients were densely amnesic for past and on-going personal events. SD, however, in addition to episodic memory deficit also showed impairments in semantic processing. Thus although both patients confabulated in recalling personal events, only SD confabulated when providing semantic information. Finally, SD's confabulation was on some occasions highly implausible, whereas this was never the case for MB. The theoretical implications of these different confabulatory behaviours will be discussed in the light of current theories of knowing and remembering.

Table 8.1   Scores on the Wechsler Adult Intelligence Scale (WAIS)

	MB	SD
Verbal IQ	105	78
Performance IQ	92	70
Information	11	8
Comprehension	9	4
Arithmetic	9	5
Digit span	5	4
Vocabulary	14	7
Digit symbol	1	2
Picture completion	6	9
Block design	1	4
Picture arrangement	3	2
Object assembly	4	6

Case Histories

Case 1

MB is a 75-year old, right-handed man with a high-school education. Now retired, he used to work as trading director of an airway company. He is married and has two children. He never suffered from neuropsychiatric diseases. In late 1989 he reported a femur fracture and was treated in an orthopaedic hospital for surgical osteosynthesis of the fracture. He was then admitted to the Hôpital Broca for re-education of gait. At admission his general health conditions were good and he showed no neurological problems. However, the clinical staff noted that MB had some, not further specified, memory problems in his everyday life at the hospital. For this reason, he was referred to our Unit for neuropsychological evaluation. He underwent a brain CT-scan, that found a marked ventricular enlargement with multiple small vascular lesions of the region surrounding the third ventricle. This radiographic picture was compatible with a diagnosis of Binswanger's encephalopathy, a condition known to be associated with high blood pressure.

MB was seen on various occasions and his collaboration during the testing sessions was always good. Neuropsychological examination showed that MB had normal intelligence (see table 8.1 for the Wechsler Adult Intelligence Scale (WAIS) scores) and a good performance on bedside tests of oral expression, understanding of oral language, reading, writing, spatial attention, praxis and calculation. Similarly, his level of performance in tasks involving various kinds of semantic knowledge was completely normal. On a group of tests thought to be sensitive to frontal lobe lesion his performance was defective only in category naming (see table 8.2). On the contrary, on a variety of clinical tests of memory his performance was markedly defective. He achieved a Memory Quotient of 87 (see table 8.3), which is not a dramatically poor score, but he scored 0 on the delayed recall of the Logical Memory subtest, given ten minutes later.

Table 8.2 Scores on the subtests of the Wechsler Memory Scale

	MB	Mean for his age (sd)	sd	Mean for his age (sd)
Personal information	5	5.4 (0.8)	2	5.9 (0.3)
Orientation	2	4.4 (0.4)	2	4.9 (0.2)
Mental control	4	4.4 (2.1)	3	6.7 (2.2)
Logical memory	6	6.4 (3.5)	6	9.64 (4.2)
Digits	6	8.2 (2.5)	6	10.3 (1.9)
Visual reproduction	2	4.8 (2.6)	6	11.4 (2.9)
PA learning	9.5	11 (5.4)	5.5	15.4 (4.4)
MQ	87		64	
Delayed logical memory	0		0	

Table 8.3 Performance on 'frontal lobe' tasks

	MB	SD	Comments
Modified Wisconsin[a] (categories achieved)	4	1	Controls mean = 5, SD 1.6
Verbal fluency			
3 categories, each 60 s. (total retrieved)	22	20	Controls mean = 38.2
FPL,[b] each 60 s. (total retrieved)	NT[e]	10	Mean of right posteriors = 18.9
Cognitive estimates[c] (percentage of extreme responses)	NT	53	Mean of left frontals = 36.2
Sequencing tests[d]			
figures	Good	Imposs.	
gestures	Good	Imposs.	

Notes:
[a] Nelson (1976)
[b] Ramier and Hécaen (1970)
[c] Shallice and Evans (1978)
[d] Luria (1966)
[e] NT = Not tested

In summary, MB's performance on language, frontal, semantic knowledge and general intelligence tests was satisfactory. By contrast, his performance on memory tests was impaired, although not uniformly. Clinically the impairment took the form of a disturbance of remembering, mainly characterized by confabulation, of which he seemed to be unaware.

He was disorientated for time and place and his disorientation often took the form of overt confabulation; for example, when asked, he claimed that his hospital room (where the testing session took place) was an Italian doctor's office in Bologna, and that after the testing session he would spend some time arranging his library, and then he would go out with some friends for a drink. MB also tended to confabulate spontaneously, and the characteristic feature of his confabulation was that it always concerned personal events and was always plausible, in the sense that it described events that could in fact have happened, so that a hypothetical observer who did not know MB's personal history and current situation would find it hard to tell whether his reports were confabulations or not. Take, for example, the following reports. At the time MB was admitted to the Hôpital Broca, his wife died. At times MB proved to be perfectly aware of this tragic event. However, at other times he claimed that he had seen his wife the day before, when he had visited her with his mother who had actually died a long time before. On another occasion, he claimed that his mother had died the Wednesday before, and that he had arrived at her bed ten minutes too late because her house was at the far end of Paris and he had been caught in traffic. Another time, he said that he was looking forward to the end of the testing session because he had to go to the general store to buy some new clothes, since he hadn't been able to do so the day before, because he had lost his way in the centre of Paris, were he had fortunately met a nurse who had kindly brought him back to the hospital. On this occasion, the patient actually attempted to leave his hospital room, claiming that there was a taxi waiting for him downstairs.

Interestingly enough, and in sharp contrast with his personal episodic memory that was affected by confabulation, his memory for nonpersonal public events was perfectly normal. He actually followed the news daily and he was very concerned about the central European political changes (this was in autumn 1989): having been deported during the Second World War, he now claimed that he failed to understand how European countries could underestimate the risk of permitting German reunification.

Case 2

SD is a 37-year old bank clerk with eight years of education. During a mountain hike he fell about 200 metres and reported an open head injury involving a fracture of the skull and multiple brain contusions. He remained in coma for forty days; when he came out of it, he was transferred to a rehabilitation department where he remained for approximately three months. Ten months later he was admitted to the department of neurology of the University of Padua for neuropsychological examination and rehabilitation. A CT brain scan performed on that occasion showed a generalized cortical atrophy and a left temporal degenerative area. During the testing sessions, SD's collaboration was generally good in spite of his emotional incontinence and a marked tendency to inappropriate laughing. His orientation for time and place fluctuated but was never perfect. However, on some occasions, he was severely disorientated for time and place and this disorientation took the form of overt confabulatory behaviour. SD's intelligence tests results are given in table 8.1. On the WAIS he had quite poor scores both on the verbal (verbal Intelligence Quotient (IQ) = 78) as well as at the performance scales (performance IQ = 70) and a full scale score of 74. His spontaneous speech was fluent, although contaminated by confabulation and mild word-finding difficulties. His phrase length, syntax and articulation appeared to be entirely normal. He had no major problems in oral comprehension (Token Test = 29/36) and his performance on bedside tests of perception, language, spatial attention, praxis and calculation was judged to be normal. By contrast, SD was severely amnesic for both personal and public, past and on-going events. He had a poor score (64) at the Wechsler Memory Scale (see table 8.2), and at delayed recall of two short stories he was unable to recall a single element of the story and produced a completely confabulatory tale. He could neither learn a supraspan spatial sequence, having a length corresponding to his spatial span plus two (De Renzi et al., 1977a), nor learn a ten-word list after twenty presentations (De Renzi et al., 1977b). SD showed problems also in semantic memory tasks. He clearly had problems in the definition of words as well as in detecting semantically anomalous sentences (Baddeley, 1982). He also had difficulties in associating line-drawings of common objects with their characteristic colour, and his performance was poor on the WAIS Information subtest (see table 8.1) and on the Wechsler Memory Scale Personal and Current Information subtest (see table 8.2). In addition, SD's performance was markedly impaired on tests considered sensitive to frontal lesion (see table 8.3).

In summary, SD's performance on memory tests was markedly impaired. In addition he had problems in tests of intellectual efficiency, semantic knowledge and frontal functions. In some tests his performance was characterized by gross confabulatory errors.

Running races were one of the favourite themes of SD's confabulation, a probable reason being that running was his hobby and he spent most of his leisure time running. Another recurrent confabulatory theme was physiotherapy, which had been part of his everyday life for several months. Yet, in contrast to MB, the subject around which SD constructed his confabulation was often inserted in an inappropriate semantic context. So, for example, he would claim that the day before he had won a running race and that he had been awarded a piece of meat which was put on his right knee. When asked to define the word 'synagogue' he replied that it was something that has to do with physiotherapy. He defined the word 'sentence' as 'a high mountain field'. When asked were he was and what kind of place the testing room was, he replied he was in Milan, in a church probably dedicated to St Anthony. Asked about the last time he went to the cinema, he reported that it was one and a half years earlier when he went with his wife to see a film presented by Mike Buongiorno (a well-known Italian TV quiz host). As is evident from these examples, SD's confabulation describes events that not only he is unlikely to have experienced at that particular time but that it is unlikely that anybody has or will ever experience. Furthermore, when semantics is specifically involved, as in word-definition tasks, the discrepancy between the expected and the given answer is even more striking. That is to say, SD's confabulations are on some occasions semantically anomalous, in the sense that their semantic structure is profoundly disrupted. On the contrary, MB's confabulations, as can be seen from the examples reported above, are always appropriate as far as their semantic structure is concerned. Indeed, his confabulations describe events that could in fact have happened, but are incongruous with his personal history and present situation.

In Search of Confabulation

From a clinical point of view it was evident that, although both patients were affected by an amnesic-confabulatory syndrome, they differed from each other in a number of ways. In fact, not only the etiology of their illness was different but the type of memory impairment and the way in which confabulations were expressed were also different. For this reason, it seemed interesting to focus in more detail on the different specificity of the two patients' confabulatory behaviour. One way of doing this was to give the patients a task involving the retrieval of various kinds of information to see whether a difference in the patients' confabulatory behaviour would consistently emerge according to the different type of information retrieved. We constructed a test consisting of ninety-five questions involving the retrieval of different kinds of information. The questions were divided as follows:

1   twenty questions probing personal semantic memory (age, date of birth, current address, number of children, and so on);
2   fifteen questions probing episodic memory (remembering specific personal events);
3   ten questions probing orientation in time and place;
4   fifteen questions probing general semantic memory (knowledge of famous facts and famous people, past and present);
5   fifteen questions probing linguistic semantic memory; items 16–30 of the WAIS vocabulary subtest were selected for a word definition task;
6   ten 'I don't know (semantic)' questions, that is, questions so constructed that the appropriate answer by normal subjects is 'I don't know' (for example, 'What did Marilyn Monroe's father do?');
7   ten 'I don't know (episodic)' questions, for example, 'Do you remember what you did on 13 March, 1985?'.

Questions were randomized and given to the patients and to twelve normal controls. Responses were tape-recorded and subsequently scored as 'correct', 'wrong', 'I don't know' and 'confabulation'. For episodic memory, responses were scored 'correct' when they matched information obtained from patients' relatives. Correct responses were self-evident for the other kinds of questions. In order to distinguish between a wrong response and a confabulation, an arbitrary decision necessarily had to be made. In general, minor errors were scored as 'wrong', whereas more important discrepancies from the attended response were considered as confabulation. However, it must be emphasized that the decision as to whether an answer was wrong or confabulatory was never puzzling, although it may have been made on an arbitrary or subjective basis.

The patients' and controls' percentages of correct and confabulatory responses are given in figures 8.1 and 8.2 respectively. As clearly emerges from figure 8.1, the proportion of correct responses by MB and normal controls on linguistic, general and personal semantic memory was widely comparable, whereas SD's performance was severely impaired both in general and linguistic semantic memory. Episodic memory was severely affected in both patients, but more markedly in SD, who was able to provide the correct response to only one out of fifteen questions.

As far as confabulations were concerned (see figure 8.2), while in MB they were restricted to questions probing episodic memory (47 per cent), orientation for time and place (53 per cent) and, to a lesser degree, personal semantic memory (20 per cent), in SD confabulatory answers were elicited, though at different levels, by every type of question. Confabulation was impressive when SD was required to remember personal episodes (69 per cent), but was also present when he was required to retrieve general or

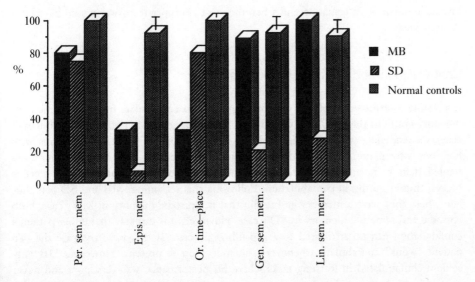

Figure 8.1 Percentage of correct responses

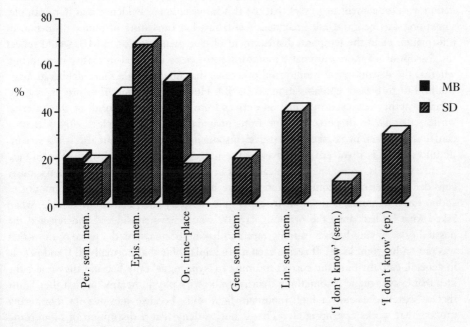

Figure 8.2 Percentage of confabulatory responses
Note: Normal controls are not reported in this figure because they did not produce any confabulation.

linguistic semantic information and when the most appropriate answer would have been 'I don't know'.

Confabulation and Memory Impairment

A possible interpretation of our patients' tendency to confabulate in different memory domains would fit the *gap-filling* hypothesis. According to this hypothesis, confabulation reflects a tendency, which is present also in normal subjects, to fill memory gaps with fictitious information. Since in amnesic subjects the memory gaps are much more extended than in normal subjects, the amount of fictitious information they report is bigger, thus resulting in confabulation. Following this reasoning, MB and SD confabulate where they have a memory gap to fill; that is, episodic memory in MB's case, both episodic and semantic memory in SD's case. However, it is unlikely that either patient's confabulation can be attributed to a gap-filling process. If this were the case the two patients would confabulate whenever a memory gap is present. However, MB only seldom confabulated in learning tasks where his performance was very poor and never confabulated on general semantic memory tasks where his performance was not at ceiling. Similarly, although SD confabulated in general and linguistic semantic memory questions, the most frequent reply he gave to these questions was 'I don't know'.

It has been suggested (Johnson, 1991) that confabulation results from the disruption of processes normally involved in 'reality monitoring' (Johnson, 1988; Johnson and Raye, 1981). Reality monitoring operates on the basis of qualitative characteristic of information (for example, amount of perceptual details, supporting memories) in combination with judgement processes that use this information as evidence that, for example, something was real and not imagined. Confabulation consisting in minor distortion of information or in the temporal displacement of true memories, as in MB, would reflect the disruption of more automatic monitoring processes involved in reality monitoring, whereas the disruption of monitoring processes that operate on a more deliberate basis would lead to bizarre confabulation, as in SD. However, if monitoring processes must decide whether retrieved information derives from the 'external world' or the 'internal world' (that is, from perception or from imagination) it is not clear why MB only confabulates when he is asked to retrieve episodic information but not also when semantic information is involved. Moreover, if the judgement processes disrupted in SD are voluntary (that is, conscious) this means that in normal conditions he would consciously consider and reject his confabulations on the basis of their plausibility, the amount of supporting memories, and so on. It seems quite unlikely that, before the disease, when asked what he had done the previous day SD would have considered and rejected the possibility of having 'won a running race and having been awarded a piece of meat that was put on his right knee'. It seems even more implausible that normally SD, and people in general, can attribute the correct meaning to 'synagogue' only because they reject the idea that 'a synagogue is something that has to do with physiotherapy' or that they know that a 'sentence' is not 'a high mountain field' only because they have a monitoring process that works appropriately. This is not to deny that a disruption of monitoring processes is responsible for confabulation, but to say that it should not be considered *sufficient* to account for the quality of the confabulation's content.

Since confabulation is constructed on the basis of information still available after the onset of memory impairment, the quality of such information necessarily determines the confabulation's content. When the semantic system is preserved, confabulation is semantically appropriate, while it becomes semantically anomalous (or bizarre) when memory impairment also affects the semantic system. Our patients' different confabulatory content can actually be interpreted as reflecting their different memory deficit. This is to say that while an impairment of monitoring processes determines the appearance of confabulation, the type of content of confabulation is determined by the presence or absence of a semantic deficit.

Confabulation and Recollective Experience

The phenomenal experience that accompanies the retrieval of an episode seems to take at least two distinct forms: retrieval can involve the conscious recollection of the episode, or, alternatively, may give rise only to a 'feeling of knowing' of that episode, without any recollective experience. The distinction between these two quite different types of conscious experience has been formalized in psychological terms by Tulving (1985). In distinguishing between episodic and semantic memory, Tulving argues that each of the two systems is characterized by a different kind of consciousness. Semantic memory is characterized by *noetic* (knowing) consciousness. Noetic consciousness refers to the subjective experience of knowing something. Knowledge, including the knowledge of one's own past, is characteristically accompanied by the subjective conscious experience of knowing; that is, in Tulving's terminology, noetic consciousness. *Autonoetic* (self-knowing) consciousness is correlated with episodic memory: 'It is necessary for the remembering of personally experienced events. When a person remembers such an event, he is aware of the event as a veridical part of his own past existence. It is autonoetic consciousness that confers the special phenomenal flavour that distinguishes remembering from other kinds of awareness, such as those characterising perceiving, thinking, imagining or dreaming' (Tulving, 1985, p. 3). So autonoetic consciousness is a necessary component of remembering events and is thus a defining property of episodic memory. Moreover, since the phenomenal experience that accompanies information recovery may differ according to the memory system (semantic versus episodic) from which the information is retrieved, it is assumed that consciousness is measurable: 'one way of measuring autonoetic consciousness could take the form of asking people when they recall or recognize a previously encountered item, whether they *remember* the event or whether they *know* in some other way that it occurred' (ibid., p. 6).

Since confabulation has something to do with memory, being actually a particular type of memory impairment, it seemed interesting to determine the relation between confabulation and autonoetic and noetic consciousness. In other words, do patients have any recollective experience when they confabulate or do they just retrieve confabulated episodes in the knowing mode of consciousness, without any recollective experience? We tried to answer this question by asking MB to report the subjective experience associated with his performance on a subset of questions of the ninety-five item test described above. Questions probing episodic memory, personal semantic memory and general

Table 8.4   MB's 'remember' and 'know' judgements for correct and confabulatory responses

	'Remember'	'Know'
Episodic memory (15)		
correct responses (5)	5	0
confabulation (8)	8	0
Personal semantic memory (20)		
correct responses (16)	1	16 (1)[a]
confabulation (4)	4	2 (2)[a]
General semantic memory (15)		
correct responses (13)	1	13 (1)[a]

Note:
[a]   Figures refer to the number of times in which MB provided a double judgement, claiming that he could either remember the specific fact or know it in some other way.

semantic memory were given again in a randomized form to MB. In addition, he was asked to provide a 'remember' judgement if his response was accompanied by the subjective experience of remembering a personally experienced past event, and a 'know' judgement if it was not accompanied by the conscious recollection of a particular personal event but was known on some other basis. To illustrate the task further and to make sure that he understood it correctly, some example were provided. For example, it was pointed out that if asked one's own address one would provide a 'know' judgement, in the sense that one is not becoming consciously aware of any particular episode of one's life; by contrast, if asked to tell how the previous day was spent, one would typically provide a 'remember' judgement, in the sense of becoming consciously aware of a particular episode (or episodes) of one's own past.

As can be seen from table 8.4, MB's response, both correct and confabulatory, were accompanied by the subjective experience of remembering, whereas responses to semantic memory questions were almost always accompanied by the subjective experience of knowing. The few confabulations observed in personal semantic memory were also accompanied by a 'remember' judgement or, on two occasions, by a double judgement. On these occasions MB said that he knew the fact, but he could also remember the circumstances in which that fact was known. The interesting point, however, is that when MB confabulates he has the same subjective phenomenal experience as when he remembers episodes he has really experienced. In this sense when he confabulates he is remembering 'another' past; that is, he shows a pathological conscious awareness of a past he has never experienced.

Memory, Consciousness and Past

The evidence provided by the study of patient MB shows that confabulation is not just a disturbance of memory but also, if not exclusively, a disturbance of consciousness. But what do we mean when we say that MB has a pathological consciousness of a past that he has never experienced? To answer this question we need a psychological theory of remembering that includes a coherent notion of consciousness and of its relation to the past. This means that we need a theory which is able to explain how we become conscious of our past and, ultimately, a sufficiently acceptable theory of the past itself. The problem with contemporary theories of remembering is that they are based on the assumption that memories are possible because the past is preserved in some form in the organism doing the remembering. According to this view if I remember having dinner with friends last Saturday, it is because this episode has been stored somewhere in my brain in the form of a 'memory trace' or, to use a smarter term, an 'engram'. In other words, the episode 'having dinner with friends last Saturday' has determined a modification in my brain – or, if you prefer, in my cognitive system – that I shall call the memory trace or engram in which the episode is stored. The activation of the information stored in the engram, as in *copy* theories of remembering (for example, Anderson and Bower, 1972; Kintsch, 1970; Ratcliff, 1978), or the interaction between the stored information and a present cue, as in reconstructive models of memory (e.g.: Tulving, 1983) would give rise to the phenomenal experience of remembering, that is to the conscious awareness of an episode of one's own past. The problem with these theories is that they *create* the past arbitrarily with elements borrowed from the present. In fact, it is sufficiently evident that if an event produces a modification in a system, be it physical (the nervous system) or abstract (the computational level), it will always be a modification that acts in the present. When the event is recalled, it happens in the present and, again, as a consequence of a present process, it is as a result of the reactivation of the modification that the event is determined at whatever level it may be considered, be it biochemical, neuroanatomical, neurophysiological or computational. So it is far from being clear how it can be possible for the past to born from elements that are present. In fact, the consequence of the activation of an engram should, in this case, give rise to a new perception of the event stored in the engram, and not to the remembering of that event. The 'warmth and intimacy' of memories, as in James (1890), their 'pastness', as in Bergson (1896), or their 'me-ness', as in Claparède (1911), appropriately describe some characteristics of remembering but do not tell us anything about its nature. In fact, they either describe just a present feature of remembering, and by so doing they remain in the present; or, if they are already connected to the past, they presuppose what they want to explain.

So if consciousness of the past cannot derive from information stored in the engram, since by definition they are present, it must derive from how consciousness itself looks at that information. This implies that we must consider consciousness as a distinct dimension. However, to consider consciousness a distinct dimension does not imply that it is a generic and unitary one, nor that it passively receives and becomes aware of information that gains access to it, as is depicted in some neuropsychological models (Moscovitch, 1989; Schacter, 1989). Consciousness cannot be considered in itself because it must always be consciousness *of* something. To exist, consciousness must be consciousness of an object (be it a concrete or an abstract one), and an object, to exist, must be addressed by consciousness in some particular way. In other words, consciousness has different 'modes' to address an object (such as remembering, knowing, perceiving, imagining), and the past, or the subjective experience of pastness of an object, is the result of that particular 'mode' of consciousness that we call remembering. How this can happen and what the neurological correlates of consciousness are is far from clear. Yet this is not a good reason to attribute the past to objects as in those theories that rely on activation of engrams to explain remembering.

What is the relevance of discussing consciousness in MB's case? If we accept the idea that the breakdown of some kind of monitoring process is responsible for confabulation, it could be argued that a different monitoring process is inherent in each mode of consciousness. For example, when consciousness is in the mode of perceiving an object, some monitoring process specific to that mode of consciousness would allow perception only in the presence of a real object. The result of the breakdown of this process would be a perception without object, that is an hallucination. Similarly, when consciousness is in the remembering mode, some other monitoring process would prevent the mistaking of information pertaining to general knowledge for an actual personal past event. Confabulation in episodic memory would result from the impairment of this monitoring process. Therefore, it is possible that when MB confabulates, his subjective experience of remembering a really-experienced event is the consequence of the disruption of the monitoring process inherent in the remembering mode of consciousness. By contrast, he never confabulates in semantic memory tasks because the monitoring process inherent in the knowing mode of consciousness is preserved. In SD's case, monitoring processes are impaired in the remembering as well as in the knowing modes of consciousness, resulting in confabulation both in episodic and in semantic memory.

The study of consciousness and its relation to memory is becoming a central topic in contemporary research. However, despite this concern with the nature of consciousness in memory, there are still few attempts to directly measure conscious experience in relation to memory performance. This situation may partly reflect the more or less implicit conviction that consciousness is rather a matter of metaphysics or rational speculation than of scientific investigation. I hope that the study of our patients confabulatory behaviour, in particular MB's case, will convince you not only that consciousness has something to do with memory, but also that it is measurable, and therefore it can be and must be the object of scientific investigation. Because – as pointed out by Marcel (1988) – not only 'consciousness in psychological science is demanded, legitimate, and necessary' but 'psychology without consciousness, without phenomenal experience or the personal level, may be biology or cybernetics, but is not psychology'.

Note

1   These patients have been described in more detail elsewhere (Dalla Barba, 1993a; Dalla Barba, 1993b).

Further Reading

Dalla Barba, G., Cipolotti, L. and Denes, G. (1990) 'Autobiographical memory loss and confabulation in Korsakoff's syndrome: a case report', *Cortex*, **26**: 525–34.

Roediger, H.L. III and Craik, F.I. (eds) (1989) *Varieties of Memory and Consciousness* (Hillsdale, N.J.: Lawrence Erlbaum Associates).
Searle, J.R. (1990) 'Consciousness, explanatory inversion, and cognitive science', *Behavioral and Brain Sciences*, 13: 585–642.
Sherry, D.F. and Schacter, D.L. (1987) 'The evolution of multiple memory systems', *Psychological Review*, 94: 439–54.

References

Anderson, J.R. and Bower, J.H. (1972) 'Recognition and retrieval processes in free recall' *Psychological Review*, 79: 97–123.
Baddeley, A. (1982) *Your Memory: A User's Guide* (London: Multimedia Publications).
Bergson, H. (1896) *Matière et mémoire* (Paris: Alcan).
Berlyne, N. (1972) 'Confabulation', *British Journal of Psychiatry*, 120: 31–9.
Bonhoeffer, K. (1904) 'Der Korsakowsche Symptomenkoplex in seinen Beziehungen zu den verschiedenen Krankheitsformen', *Allgemeine Zeitung Psychiatrie*, 61: 744–52.
Claparède, E. (1911) 'Recognition et moïté', *Archives de psychologie*, 11: 79–90.
Dalla Barba, G. (1993a) 'Confabulation: knowledge and recollective experience', *Cognitive Neuropsychology*, 10(1): 1–20.
Dalla Barba, G. (1993b) 'Different patterns of confabulation', *Cortex*, 29: 567–81.
De Renzi, E., Faglioni, P. and Previdi, P. (1977a) 'Spatial memory and hemispheric locus of lesion', *Cortex*, 13(4): 424–33.
De Renzi, E., Faglioni, P. and Ruggerini, C. (1977b) 'Prove di memoria verbale di impiego clinico per la diagnosi clinica di amnesia', *Archivio di Psicologia, Neurologia e Psichiatria*, 38: 303–18.
James, W. (1890) *Principles of Psychology* (New York: Holt).
Johnson, M. (1988) 'Discriminating the origin of information', in F. Oltmanns and B. Mahers (eds), *Delusional Beliefs* (New York: John Wiley), pp. 34–65.
Johnson, M.K. (1991) 'Reality monitoring: evidence from confabulation in organic brain disease patients', in G.P. Prigatano and D.L. Schacter (eds), *Awareness of Deficit After Brain Injury* (New York and London: Oxford University Press).
Johnson, M.K. and Raye, C.L. (1981) 'Reality monitoring', *Psychological Review*, 88: 67–85.
Kintsch, W. (1970) *Learning, Memory and Conceptual Processes* (New York and Chichester: John Wiley).
Kopelman, M.D. (1987) 'Two types of confabulation', *Journal of Neurology, Neurosurgery and Psychiatry*, 50: 482–7.
Luria, A.R. (1966) *Higher Cortical Functions in Man* (London: Tavistock Publications).
Marcel, A.J. (1988) 'Phenomenal experience and functionalism', in A.J. Marcel and E. Bisiach (eds), *Consciousness in Contemporary Science* (London: Oxford University Press).
Moscovitch, M. (1989) 'Confabulation and the frontal system: strategic versus associative retrieval in neuropsychological theories of memory', in H.L. Roedinger and F.I. Craik (eds), *Varieties of Memory and Consciousness: Essays in Honor of Endel Tulving* (Hillsdale, N.J.: Lawrence Erlbaum Associates).
Nelson, H.E. (1976) 'A modified card sorting test sensitive to frontal defects', *Cortex*, 12: 313–24.
Ramier, A.-M., and Hécaen, H. (1970) 'Rôle respectif des atteintes frontales et de la latéralisation lésionnelle dans les déficits de la "fluence verbale" ', *Revue neurologique*, 123(1): 17–22.
Ratcliff, R. (1978) 'A theory of memory retrieval', *Psychological Review*, 85: 59–108.
Schacter, D.L. (1989) 'On the relation between memory and consciousness: dissociable interactions and conscious experience', in H.L. Roedinger and F.I.M. Craik (eds), *Varieties of Memory and Consciousness: Essays in Honor of Endel Tulving* (Hillsdale, N.J.: Lawrence Erlbaum Associates).

Shallice, T. and Evans, M. (1978) 'The involvement of the frontal lobe in cognitive estimation', *Cortex*, **14**: 294–303.

Talland, G.A. (1965) *Deranged Memory* (New York: Academic Press).

Tulving, E. (1983) *Elements of Episodic Memory* (London: Oxford University Press).

Tulving, E. (1985) 'Memory and consciousness', *Canadian Psychology*, **26**: 1–12.

9 How Bad Memories Can Sometimes Lead to Fantastic Beliefs and Strange Visions

John Joseph Downes and Andrew R. Mayes

In this chapter we describe three amnesics, who differ in their aetiologies and, therefore, probably have damage to somewhat different brain structures. They also differ in the way that their memory disorders interact with other aspects of cognitive performance to produce different varieties of phenomenological experience. Amnesic patients will sometimes quite readily 'recall' information from memory, but on closer examination these memory retrievals can be shown to be false, a behaviour described as confabulation. They can be false either in terms of when events are believed to have occurred or, less commonly, the actual details described by the patient may not correspond to anything that has actually happened. The first two patients described below both show evidence of confabulatory behaviour, one with only a very mild form and the other with confabulations of delusional intensity. The third patient initially presented with what would appear to be hallucinatory phenomena but which, on analysis, are probably more like confabulations, but visual in form.

There are four main criteria that are standardly used to characterize the amnesic syndrome. First, they are very poor at remembering verbal and nonverbal material which occurred subsequent to the illness or trauma (anterograde amnesia). Second, they are very poor at remembering all types of material which predates the illness or trauma, which may include details about famous people and events of previous decades, as well as details about their own personal history (retrograde amnesia). Third, they show relative preservation of intelligence; and, fourth, they show preservation of short-term memory as assessed by performance on such tests as the digit span (which involves repeating short sequences of numbers). The first two patients satisfy all four criteria, but the third patient shows evidence of a material-specific memory disorder in that he is amnesic for verbal but not for visual material. Although there is a broad symptomatology common to all three patients, the details of their memory deficits are not identical. This could either indicate that amnesia is a heterogeneous disorder comprising several underlying functional deficits, or it could indicate that although amnesia is a functionally unitary deficit, it is often associated with separate kinds of memory disorders. The first patient we shall discuss is the most classically amnesic.

JW: a Korsakoff Amnesic

JW was born in June 1922 and died in 1984. His life was a sad one. He was brought up in a Dr Barnardo's home as an orphan and was a merchant sailor for a few years after leaving school. In the early 1950s he became a maintenance fitter in the Manchester area. He was laid off from this job in 1975 because of an increasingly severe drinking problem. As far as we could ascertain, his wife had died several years before this time, and her death had probably acted as a trigger for his heavy drinking. During this period he seems not to have eaten properly so his drinking was probably accompanied by undernutrition and an associated thiamin deficiency. His health deteriorated until his general practitioner referred him to a local mental hospital in February 1975, where he remained in long-term care until his death from bronchopneumonia associated with a carcinoma of the upper respiratory tract. This history is fairly representative for Korsakoff's syndrome because the disorder means that the patient cannot support an independent existence, with most family ties being destroyed because of the patient's heavy drinking.

Korsakoff's syndrome is most commonly associated with chronic alcoholism, as in JW's case, but the predominant view is that the proximate cause is thiamin deficiency related to the alcoholism (see Mayes, 1988). This view is supported by cases in which amnesia develops as a result of nonalcoholic factors, such as hyperemesis gravidarum, anorexia nervosa and renal insufficiency, in which the proximal cause is also likely to be thiamin deficiency (see Parkin and Leng, 1993, for a discussion). It remains a moot point to what extent, if any, alcohol toxicity contributes to the genesis of the syndrome.

Although some Korsakoff amnesics show partial or even apparently complete recovery of memory over a period that may range from months to several years, JW remained profoundly amnesic until his death. He was disorientated for time and place and, in our conversations with him, it was clear that he believed himself still to be living at home and working as a fitter, despite having been in hospital for several years. Like many Korsakoff patients, he showed little insight into his condition and often said that he must have a good memory because this was necessary for his job. He did not, however, display the apathy that has been reported to be a common characteristic of patients with this aetiology, and had a somewhat dour and negative demeanour. Despite his lack of insight into his memory disorder, and his belief that he still lived at home and worked as a fitter, he did not confabulate freely when his memory was more formally tested. Typically, he said that he was unable to recall something when asked so that he had to be encouraged to guess in these situations. Confabulation has been defined by Moscovitch (1989) as 'honest lying' in which the patient produces information that is obviously false and sometimes inconsistent. There is, however, no intention to lie and the patient may be unaware of the falsity, and may even defend what has been produced as correct when challenged by an examiner. This 'honest lying' may either be spontaneous or may be elicited by appropriate questioning. It used to be believed that confabulation was a specific feature of Korsakoff amnesia so that its presence was necessary for diagnosis. As Victor et al. (1989) have indicated, however, confabulation is only rarely present in the chronic stage of the illness, and we did not see JW when he was admitted, at which stage confabulation seems to be more common. JW did not confabulate spontaneously or even when encouraged to do so.

JW was given the Wechsler Adult Intelligence Scale (WAIS) test at the end of 1976 and showed a Full Scale IQ of 97. His verbal IQ was somewhat superior to his perform-ance IQ, which we have found to be common in Korsakoff patients. It remains unclear whether this difference is found because the performance tests are timed whereas most of the verbal ones are not. Nevertheless, JW's score on the National Adult Reading Test (NART: a measure of premorbid intelligence) gave an estimated Full Scale IQ of 105, so there is no clear evidence that his intelligence had declined from its previous levels. Similarly, his scaled score on the digit span subtest of the WAIS was slightly above average so his verbal short-term memory was preserved.

When given the Wechsler Memory Scale (WMS) in June 1976, JW achieved a Memory Quotient of 62 despite scoring within the normal range on the mental control and digit span subtests which are not sensitive to amnesia. The WMS primarily taps free recall of verbal or easily verbalizable materials, but in other experiments we found (see Mayes et al., 1988) that JW scored at least two standard deviations below normal subjects on tests of verbal recognition. JW showed impaired recognition for both verbal and nonverbal material, although his nonverbal recognition may have been less severely impaired. For example, he scored at chance on the Warrington word recognition test, but appreciably above chance on her face recognition test. Like other Korsakoff patients, JW showed abnormally fast forgetting between 0 and 30 seconds on the Brown-Peterson task. Unlike control subjects, JW tended to make commission rather than omission errors on this task (Meudell et al., 1978). This was the nearest he came to confabulating, which might be regarded as a kind of commission error. Finally, we found that JW showed a more severe deficit in his temporal order memory than in his recognition memory. Two lists of words were shown that were temporally separated by a short interval, and JW's recognition for the words was equated to that of his controls by giving him longer exposures to the words. Even though his ability to recognize the words was successfully matched to that of this controls, he still had an impaired ability to discriminate from which of the two lists the words were drawn. This deficit is typically found in Korsakoff patients although it remains controversial to what extent it characterizes other kinds of amnesia (see Mayes, 1988; and Parkin and Leng, 1993, for different accounts). It has also been argued that the disproportionate deficit in temporal order memory is not a feature of amnesia, but a result of Korsakoff patients having an additional disruption of frontal association cortex (see Mayes, 1988). In this respect, it is interesting to note that JW scored within normal limits on the Wisconsin Card Sorting Test, a classic test of frontal lobe functioning.

JW had a clinically evident retrograde amnesia that affected memories formed well before the 1970s. On a test of memory for the voices of people who had been famous over the previous forty years, JW was impaired in his ability to recall the names of the owners of the voices and at picking the names from among three alternatives. His recall perform-ance was close to floor level for the 1960s, but his recognition was somewhat better. It fell within two standard deviations of his controls for the 1940s, but was over two standard deviations below control performance levels for the 1950s, 1960s and 1970s (Meudell et al., 1980). He therefore showed the long temporal gradient for his retrograde amnesia that has been reported in some amnesics, and particularly Korsakoff patients. In a test of recall and recognition of public events, JW showed comparable performance with a more striking temporal gradient in which his recall of events from the 1950s or earlier fell at the lower end of the normal range whereas his recall of events from the 1960s and 1970s fell more than two standard deviations below that of his controls (see Snowden, 1983).

WF: a Confabulating Amnesic

In June 1991, at the age of 42, WF suffered a subarachnoid haemorrhage caused by a ruptured aneurysm (a weakness in the wall of a blood vessel) in the anterior communicating artery which supplies the frontal regions of the brain. He underwent surgery two days later to repair the aneurysm, but suffered another haemorrhage some weeks later and received further surgery. Although his physical condition slowly improved, he was left with a marked memory impairment. In the following months, he showed poor memory, confabulation, was disorientated and displayed some obsessional traits. In April 1992 he married his long-standing girlfriend, but he was unable to recall any details of his wedding when asked in November of that year, even when prompted with a video of the event. At that time, he believed he was living with his parents who, in fact, had died four years previously, which is the first evidence of confabulatory behaviour. His language abilities were unaffected by the haemorrhages and intellectually he performed in the normal range with little evidence from his score on the NART that his intelligence had declined appreciably. His anterograde amnesia affected recognition as well as recall of both verbal and nonverbal materials. He may perhaps have had a slightly more severe amnesia for verbal than for nonverbal materials because he scored worse on the Warrington word recognition test than the face recognition test, and his verbal memory quotient on the WMS-Revised was worse than his visual memory quotient. This impairment meant that he was unable to maintain his previous occupation as a British Telecommunications engineer. He also showed clinical signs of a severe retrograde amnesia. Although WF's brain damage caused no emotional or behavioural problems, he has limited insight into his condition, he cannot lead an independent life and remains totally dependent on his wife.

Rupture and repair of anterior communicating artery aneurysms has frequently been reported to lead to memory deficits although the characteristics of these deficits vary somewhat from case to case. This is not surprising because there is now good evidence that this aetiology is associated with highly variable damage to the basal forebrain, basal ganglia and frontal association cortex regions of the brain. We have, however, encountered several patients who have shown a fairly standard amnesia with relatively preserved intelligence and short-term memory abilities in the face of recognition and recall impairments for both the pre- and postmorbid periods. One characteristic feature of the syndrome is confabulation, which some researchers have related to the frontal lobe damage that is often found after anterior communicating artery aneurysms. WF showed some indications of impairment on tests sensitive to frontal lobe lesions. Thus, he showed reduced verbal fluency with many rule breaks and perseverative errors, and performed poorly on the Trail Making Test with signs of poor planning. A necessary condition of confabulation is the tendency to make commission errors in tests of free recall. WF made such errors when given the logical memory subtest from the WMS. On this test subjects are read short stories of about sixty or seventy words which they have to remember and immediately repeat back to the examiner. For example, in one story he incorrectly recalled that the police had gone round to the house of a victim of mugging and asked her some questions, when in fact the victim is described as reporting the crime at the police station, where the officers took up a collection for her.

The above example may seem a trivial retrieval error, or a reasonable attempt to fill in forgotten details, to which we should not attach any clinical significance. But there were much more convincing examples of confabulation which arose in the course of conversations about WF's everyday life. At home, he tends to sit watching television or follows his wife around more or less anywhere she goes. But when first seen, he falsely claimed to spend his time playing golf, gardening and going for walks. These were activities in which he engaged before the rupture and repair of his aneurysm. His wife and he made frequent trips by bus to Liverpool town centre, but when they were ready to go home WF would ask his wife where the car was parked and would even sometimes insist on spending hours searching the city centre car parks. Previously, WF and his wife always travelled to the town centre by car which suggests that he was falsely recalling these events, yet he showed considerable reluctance to admit he was wrong when challenged. As Moscovitch (1989) has pointed out, it is particularly common for confabulation to be associated with temporal confusion, so it is possible that what WF was doing on these occasions was correctly recalling things that he had done in the past but in a different temporal context.

Unlike many patients, however, WF's confabulation seemed to focus around three false beliefs, which dominated his thinking upon leaving hospital. First, he believed that he had fallen out with the two children of his first marriage; second, he believed that he was going on, or had just been on, a British Telecommunications course; and third, when he woke up in the morning he frequently reported that he had had an argument with his father the previous night. Initially, he claimed that his current medical problem was 'pins and needles' although he was aware that he had had two operations. Also, for a long time after returning home, he would introduce his wife as his sister. As time has passed, the first of his dominant beliefs has ceased to be a problem, the second is mentioned less, but the third has grown into something fantastic and delusional. The important point about this belief is that his father is in fact dead.

When we first saw WF, he said that he was living with his parents but did not get on too well with his father. He did not mention his wife. He also described an awful row with his father that had taken place the night before, the result of which was that he was having to leave his parents' house and find somewhere else to live later in the week. This has been a persistently held belief and, on every subsequent meeting, WF describes the same awful row as having just occurred and with the same consequences. What has changed over time is the emotional intensity the story arouses in him when he relates it. Whereas initially he described the events in a very matter-of-fact fashion, he now shakes with anger and is reduced to tears as the story unfolds.

It has been hard to identify the exact content of the argument apart from the fact that his father is derogatory towards him, saying things like 'I wish I could have my real son back'. According to his wife, this may be a reference to a younger brother, who died in childhood. He describes his parents as looking very old and wrinkled and has said that the row takes place in the front room of the house in which there are chairs laid out in a row as in a classroom, with men sitting on them. Although the row takes place in front of them, none of the men participate. When asked why they are there, he answers that his wife's son by her previous marriage left the door open. His relations with this son are poor and he is often included in the delusional system. The delusion is having a major impact on the life of his family. WF is unwilling to believe that his beliefs are false, even though when pressed he is able to recall in fairly vivid detail his father's funeral. Even in the face of his father's death certificate, WF finds his memories of the row so compelling that he concludes that his father must have come back to life.

WF is able to produce further 'memories' with great ease to support his beliefs. For example, in one session, when evidence was advanced to show that his memories must be false, he insisted that he must be right because he had introduced his father to the therapist. He even described the precise context in which the alleged introduction took place. For WF his delusional belief may confer some minor advantages because he thinks that the house in which he lives is his father's and that therefore everything that goes wrong in it is his father's responsibility. If a job needs doing, WF's typical response is 'Let the old bugger do it'. On one occasion, when his wife asked him in a shop to pay the deposit on some cane chairs she wanted to buy for their conservatory, he created a terrible scene saying that he was not going to buy any furniture for 'the old bastard'. His wife left the shop to avoid further embarrassment.

According to Talland (1965), confabulation involves making recall commission errors that constitute a more or less coherent narrative in which the contents are often drawn from the patient's true recollections, but included in the wrong context. The elements are recombined with each other and with the wrong context without the patient being aware of the inaccuracy of the memories. The beliefs are often very resistant to contrary evidence. Nevertheless, it is typically claimed that the false recalls serve no purpose other than producing factual information, although Moscovitch (1989) has suggested that the readiness to confabulate may depend on the patient's personality and way of coping with his self-image. In WF's case, it seems likely that personality factors may help explain the dominance of his favourite confabulation. His case also suggests the possibility that psychotic delusions may share some common underlying disorder(s) with confabulation. Both may involve a frontal lobe dysfunction although this requires further support before it is confidently assumed. Frontal lobe dysfunction has been linked to disturbances of the ability to plan thinking operations, which would particularly affect strategic retrieval. This would be associated not only with the use of inadequate retrieval cues to automatically access the correct memory details, but would also prevent appropriate checks being performed either to settle on the best of several options or eliminate an inappropriate option (see also Moscovitch, 1989; and Johnson, 1991). It is likely that WF has frontal lobe damage, and he does show some degree of dysexecutiveness that would probably lead to the above failures of strategic retrieval. But he also may have particular emotional fixations and personality traits that have the power to turn some of his confabulations into beliefs of delusional intensity. A similar combination of disturbances may underlie schizophrenic delusions.

NH: a Case of Visual Confabulation

In July 1992 NH developed nausea, headaches and abdominal pain followed by slurred speech, progressive disorientation and confusion that lasted for several days. As he slowly recovered, it became apparent that he had an amnesia. There was no confirmation that he had had a herpes simplex encephalitis although this remains a possibility.

Neuropsychological testing indicated that his full-scale IQ had dropped by around a standard deviation from its premorbid level with most, if not all, of this decline being associated with a decrease in verbal abilities. Although he was severely impaired on both the face and word Warrington recognition tests, his performance on the WMS-Revised suggested that his verbal recall was much more severely impaired than his nonverbal recall. In fact, he scored below the first percentile on the verbal memory quotient but above average on the visual memory quotient. He also showed some signs of frontal lobe dysfunction, with reduced verbal fluency associated with many rule breaks and perseverative errors and very poor performance on the trail-making test. Herpes simplex encephalitis often causes verbal deficits with memory impairments that are related to medial temporal lobe damage. Orbitofrontal damage is often also found and this may explain NF's poor fluency and other 'frontal' signs.

Apart from his marked material-specific memory disorder, the most striking feature that NH initially presented with was an apparent hallucinatory phenomenon. He described an encounter with a man in a long overcoat, which he would open to expose a hand-gun in some sort of holster. The man would urge NH, by his actions rather than by words, to take the gun, and it usually took considerable self-restraint for NH to resist. According to NH the reason the man wanted him to take the gun was to kill someone, although he had no idea why. It did make him feel guilty because 'its not my way of keeping people alive – shooting them' (*sic*). These 'visitations' began, according to NH (and corroborated by his wife), after he was admitted to hospital, and were very frequent to begin with – several times a day, gradually reducing to two or three times a week. Currently, they seem to have stopped altogether.

When asked, he was able to describe the man in some detail: approximate height, colour of clothing, and so on. He also says that people probably wondered what was going on because he would be talking to the man several times a day, although the man would never talk back to him; NH would just tell him to go away. He claims that he never told his wife about the visitation when it was happening most frequently, but from our conversations with her it is apparent that she had been aware of the problem from the start. Perhaps tellingly, he has also told us that he thinks he may have had a dream just like his visitation and he has repeatedly said things like: 'well, it still happens but it is just like a dream'; 'I don't think its real, just an odd experience I have to put up with.' Despite NH's claims that he would be talking to the man several times a day, urging him to go away, and that the visitations often occurred while others were present, no one has ever witnessed NH talking in this way, not even his wife who is with him twenty-four hours a day. It seems most likely, therefore, that NH's visitations originate from some internal visual event, probably a dream or fantasy state.

Discussion

The unusual problems experienced by NH could be directly related to brain structures damaged as a result of his encephalitis but, as noted above, there appear to be too many inconsistencies to classify them as primary visual phenomena like hallucinations. Alternatively, their appearance may be linked more directly with his memory disorder, being closely related to the pattern of preserved visual memory and markedly impaired verbal memory.

His visual memory, as measured by the Wechsler Memory Scale, is at a level commensurate with his premorbid IQ. We presumably remember the contents of dreams and fantasies in the same way as we remember other visual material, and so NH is unimpaired in this respect. Visual events of such emotional potency are also quite readily remembered, and people rarely experience significant problems in identifying their source, that is, whether they emanated from within, in the form of imaginal ruminations, fantasies, or dreams, or extrapersonally, in the outside world (but see Johnson et al., 1984). Because memories of these different types of visual event probably overlap in terms of the neuronal activity which mediates their conscious experience, there must be some cognitive mechanism which allows them to become associated with information about the original source of the event. Perhaps in NH it is this mechanism which is dysfunctional. His memories of the original visual event (and the memories of those memories) could be impoverished in the sense that there is no source information associated with them, and NH falsely infers that the man with the gun existed on the outside.

This seems more likely as an explanation for NH's problem if we assume further that source information is stored in some propositional or verbal format as opposed to visually. Thus, his verbal memory impairment increases the likelihood that the source information associated with visual events will be rapidly forgotten. Source, in this case, is interpreted in its most general sense to mean, on the one hand, a set of unspecified cognitive operations which allow the subject to identify unambiguously an event as having occurred either within or outside themselves, and, secondly, information about the spatio-temporal settings of events. Several authors have noted that confabulatory behaviour in amnesics results from the emergence of 'real' memories which have become dislocated from a temporal dimension (for example, Talland, 1965). Some of patient WF's confabulations, described above, fit this hypothesis well, but for the first patient described, JW, we know from the experimental procedures that were run with him that his memory for spatio-temporal contextual details was poor, yet there was very little evidence of the marked confabulatory behaviour that characterised the other two patients. Of course, it is well known that not all amnesic patients exhibit confabulatory behaviour. Thus, although we can go some way to specifying the types of cognitive operation, the impairment of which leads to confabulations, there remains other psychological variables which mediate the behaviour. Moscovitch (1989) (following Talland,

1965) has suggested that the appearance of confabulations may be linked to certain personality variables, including a predisposition for denial, which may also emerge as a lack of concern about, or even unawareness of (anosognosia), the extent and severity of the primary memory disorder.

It is paradoxical that the problems experienced by WF and NH, and other confabulating patients, revolve around events that they can 'remember' as opposed to things that they forget. Rehabilitation of the memory-impaired patient, therefore, may sometimes consist of techniques designed to help patients to 'un-remember' some of those things which they cannot forget, in addition to the more conventional techniques which help the patient remember those things they reliably forget.

Further Reading

Stuss, D.T., Alexander, M.P., Lieberman, A. and Levine, H. (1978) 'An extraordinary form of confabulation', *Neurology*, **28**: 1166–72.
Talland, G.A. (1965) *Deranged Memory* (New York: Academic Press).

References

Johnson, M.K. (1991) 'Reality monitoring: evidence from confabulation organic brain disease patients', in G.P. Prigatano and D.L. Schacter (eds), *Awareness of Deficit after Brain Injury: Clinical and Theoretical Issues* (New York: Oxford University Press).
Johnson, M.K., Kahan, T.L. and Raye, C.L. (1984) 'Dreams and reality monitoring', *Journal of Experimental Psychology: General*, **113**: 329–44.
Mayes, A.R. (1988) *Human Organic Memory Disorders* (Cambridge: Cambridge University Press).
Mayes, A.R., Meudell, P.R., Mann, D. and Pickering, A.D. (1988) 'Locations of lesions in Korsakoff's syndrome: neuropsychological and neuropathological data on two patients', *Cortex*, **24**: 1–22.
Meudell, P.R., Butters, N. and Montgomery, K. (1978) 'Role of rehearsal in the short-term memory performance of patients with Korsakoff's and Huntington's disease', *Neuropsychologia*, **16**: 507–11.
Meudell, P.R., Northen, B., Snowden, J. and Neary, D. (1980) 'Long-term memory for famous voices in amnesic and normal subjects', *Neuropsychologia*, **18**: 133–9.
Moscovitch, M. (1989) 'Confabulation and the frontal systems: strategic versus associative retrieval in neuropsychological theories of memory', in H.L. Roediger and F.I.M. Craik (eds), *Varieties of Memory and Consciousness* (Hillsdale, N.J.: Lawrence Erlbaum Associates).
Parkin, A.J. and Leng, N.R.C. (1993) *Neuropsychology of the Amnesic Syndrome* (Hove, Sussex: Lawrence Erlbaum Associates).
Snowden, J.S. (1983) *Cognitive Disorders in Alcoholic Amnesics*, PhD thesis, University of Manchester.
Talland, G.A. (1965) *Deranged Memory* (New York: Academic Press).
Victor, M., Adams, R.D. and Collins, G.H. (1989) *The Wernicke–Korsakoff Syndrome and Related Neurological Disorders Due to Alcoholism and Malnutrition* (Philadelphia: Davis Company).

10 Memory Pathology in Schizophrenia

A.P. McKay, P.J. McKenna and A.D. Baddeley

Schizophrenia is a fascinating and ill-understood condition, characterized by a wide range of symptoms, some of which are exceedingly strange. There has been much speculation about the cause or causes of the disorder, but little is known with certainty. Currently it is widely believed that the disease reflects some kind of biological disturbance of brain function. Direct evidence for structural or functional brain abnormality, however, has been difficult to come by, and where there have been positive findings, as is invariably the case in schizophrenia research, these are disputed. One of the most interesting developments in recent years has been the demonstration that many patients with schizophrenia show evidence of neuropsychological deficits; among these, memory impairment is being increasingly accorded a central role.

Typically in early adult life, patients with schizophrenia develop florid or 'positive' symptoms. These include delusions, abnormal beliefs which are at least inherently unlikely (for example, that the CIA is monitoring the patient from a red car parked opposite), and which are sometimes ridiculous or fantastic in nature; despite their absurdity these beliefs are usually held with complete conviction. Patients with schizophrenia may also experience hallucinations. These are most commonly auditory – the quintessential schizophrenic symptom of hearing voices – but hallucinations may occur in any sensory modality: visual, tactile, of smell or of taste. In some patients, in addition, the logical coherent structure of thinking breaks down, so that speech becomes difficult to follow or even completely incomprehensible. There are many other positive symptoms of schizophrenia, ranging from the experience of alterations in the 'ownership' of one's own thoughts and actions, to a variety of peculiar changes in motor behaviour and overall activity level, known as catatonic symptoms.

Sooner or later, in the vast majority of patients with schizophrenia a degree of overall deterioration in function becomes apparent. The 'negative' symptoms which make up this state vary, but there is almost always some loss of emotional responsiveness, which may manifest itself in coldness, indifference or enstrangement from friends and relatives. In addition, an important symptom is lack of volition – schizophrenic patients become unable to motivate themselves to work and to carry out basic activities like washing, dressing and changing clothes. The stereotype of the chronic schizophrenic patient is a withdrawn and obviously odd individual who may or may not have enduring florid symptoms, but who gets up late, goes to bed early and does little that is productive in between.

Although serious, generally incurable and associated with a decline in function in many areas of life, schizophrenia was historically considered not to compromise intellectual function – a 'functional' psychosis, as opposed to 'organic' disorders such as delirium and dementia. In the original descriptions by Kraepelin (1913) and Bleuler (1911), however, it was observed that patients with the most severe and chronic forms of schizophrenia sometimes showed suggestions of cognitive impairment. For decades, this aspect of schizophrenia was studiously ignored by both psychiatry and psychology. Over recent years it has, however, been established beyond any reasonable doubt that schizophrenia is frequently complicated by the development of general intellectual decline. This may range from nil, through impairment which is not obvious but which can be revealed as a decline in IQ (for example, Payne, 1973; Nelson et al., 1990) or poor performance on neuropsychological test batteries (for example, Kolb and Whishaw, 1983), to, in a small minority of patients, severe and widespread deficits. For example, Crow and co-workers (Liddle and Crow, 1984) have demonstrated that up to a quarter of chronically hospitalized patients underestimate their own age by five years or more, a phenomenon that is typically seen in the setting of multiple neuropsychological deficits.

Superimposed on this tendency to general intellectual decline are a sprinkling of specific neuropsychological deficits. One such deficit, which has been the subject of considerable investigation, is in executive or 'frontal lobe' function (recent studies of this have been provided by Goldberg et al., 1987, and Shallice et al., 1991). Another, it has recently become clear, is memory impairment (early studies showing this have been reviewed by Cutting, 1985, and substantial deficits in chronic patients have subsequently been documented by Calev et al., 1987). In some cases poor memory in schizophrenia seems merely to be part of a pattern of general intellectual deterioration. In other cases, however, memory impairment stands out against a background of only minor deficits in other areas. Finally, the thinking disorder of schizophrenia sometimes seems to be capable of affecting memory in a more immediate way, as in the phenomenon of delusional memories. The following three case histories illustrate each of these aspects of the memory pathology of schizophrenia in turn.

TC: Overall Intellectual Impairment in Schizophrenia

TC is a 34-year-old, chronically hospitalized patient. He had been a normal cheerful boy who enjoyed school, played the guitar and had many friends. He passed four 'O' levels, but then unexpectedly failed 'A' levels. Shortly afterwards, his parents noticed a change in him: he became withdrawn, isolated himself and seemed depressed. He lost a job as a general handyman and another as a driver because he seemed unable to concentrate even on simple tasks.

He first saw a psychiatrist at the age of nineteen and embarked on a series of lengthy hospital admissions in his early twenties. There was never any doubt that he was suffering from schizophrenia: he was preoccupied with the belief that his life was parallelling that of John Lennon, that he actually was John Lennon, and also that he would be reincarnated as John Lennon's son. He believed himself to be persecuted and endangered by his parents and fellow hospital patients, on a few occasions behaving aggressively in response to these delusions. He experienced auditory hallucinations in the form of voices in the second and third person commenting on his actions. He also described other classical schizophrenic symptoms, for instance feeling that the television was physically controlling his actions. As his illness went on, he became increasingly disorganized in his speech.

Despite drug treatment and intensive attempts at rehabilitation, over the years obvious schizophrenic deterioration set in. For several years TC lived in a hostel and attended hospital as a day patient; at this stage he drove a car and his Volkswagen Beetle was a familiar sight around the hospital grounds. Ultimately, for a variety of reasons, he became unable to manage outside hospital and for the last seven years he has been resident on a long-stay ward. He wanders around the hospital and its immediate environs. Otherwise he is often to be found sitting in the ward reading a book upside down, holding yesterday's newspaper, or watching TV without taking it in. He cannot reliably manage even small sums of money and requires prompting and help to maintain self-care. He talks incoherently, rambling from one topic to another, and often alluding to delusions. He shows a bland, cheerful manner and, unlike many institutionalized schizophrenic patients, he is not withdrawn or inaccessible. He is extremely co-operative with cognitive testing and regularly visits the office of one of the authors to ask if there are any tests he can do.

TC knows his own age and whereabouts, the names of staff and so on. However, he thinks he has only been in hospital for two years. His IQ has recently been measured at 68, a huge fall from his estimated pre-illness level of 113 (made using the National Adult Reading Test, a test of ability to pronounce words which is resistant to intellectual decline). His performance on a range of neuropsychological tests is shown in table 10.1. On a clinically-orientated battery of memory tests, the Rivermead Behavioural Memory Test, he has on different occasions achieved screening scores of 0 or 1 out of 12 – in the severely impaired range. His recall of a passage of prose is virtually nil. Similarly on a test of recognition memory he is impaired on words and very impaired on faces. However, his short-term memory, as assessed by digit span, is well within the normal range at 6. This preservation of short-term memory, despite what may sometimes be marked impairments in long-term memory, has emerged as being a typical pattern in schizophrenia.

TC also performs poorly on tests of executive function – disastrously so on some of them. One of the most widely used tests is the Wisconsin Card Sorting Test in which subjects have to sort cards with designs on them according to a changing set of rules, such as colour, shape or number of designs. On a simplified form of this test he selected an initial rule without difficulty, but was then completely unable to shift to another when asked to do so. On the Cognitive Estimates Test, where subjects have to make guesses in response to questions they are unlikely to know the precise answer to, he was well outside the normal range: he thought the age of the oldest person alive in Britain was 150 and estimated the length of an average man's spine as six feet. Performance on linguistic

Table 10.1   Performance of TC on various neuropsychological tests

	TC	*Normal score range*
Long-term memory		
Rivermead Behavioural Memory Test		
screening score	0/1	7–12
prose recall	0/1	6 or greater
Recognition Memory Test		
word recognition	37	40–50 (chance level 25)
face recognition	32	38–50
Short-term memory		
Digit span	6	5 or greater
Corsi blocks	3	1–2 less than digit span
Executive function		
Wisconsin Card Sorting Test (categories achieved)	1	5–6
Cognitive Estimates Test	15	less than 13 (error score)
Category fluency (animals/1 minute)	12	14 or more
Language		
Graded Naming Test	13	14–30
Modified Token Test	32	28–36
Visuospatial function		
Visual Object and Space Perception Battery		
incomplete letters	19	17–20
dot counting	9	8–10
position discrimination	17	18–20
silhouettes	13	16–30
object decision	14	15–20
Rey Figure copying	25.5	27–36

tests was patchy: on the Graded Naming Test, a measure of the semantic aspects of language, he scored 13 out of 30, naming a tassel as a sweeping brush, a boar as a rhinoceros, a turtle as a porpoise or a tortoise, and an anteater as a suburb. However, his ability to understand the rules of grammar, assessed using the Token Test, was normal. When administered a battery of tests of visual and visuo-spatial function, he passed some and failed others. Thus he was able to identify 19 out of 20 letters from fragmentary outlines; he could count dots accurately; and he made only three mistakes out of twenty on a test that involved deciding whether or not a dot was centred in a square. On the other hand, his copying of the complex Rey–Osterreith figure was impaired, although not grossly so.

TC thus shows in very marked form the two specific neuropsychological deficits currently believed to characterize schizophrenia: memory impairment and impairment of executive function. These are conspicuous, but a the same time they are clearly part of a wider pattern of impairment. This itself is not uniform and there appears to be a relative preservation of some aspects of linguistic and visuospatial function.

DS: Relatively Isolated Memory Impairment in Schizophrenia

DS, a 30-year-old chronic schizophrenic man, was an only child born late and with birth complications. He was something of a loner as a child and had various solitary interests (in fact he showed the typical features of so-called schizoid personality). He was also highly intelligent, passing 10 'O' levels and 3 'A' levels. He went on to obtain a university degree in physics.

At the age of 25, whilst doing postgraduate research work, he began rather abruptly to experience distracting mental symptoms – hearing voices, seeing visions, feeling that he was being followed and spied on – and started behaving oddly, for example wandering the streets in the middle of the night. Then he started expressing the idea that he had grown an extra arm and a tail (which he claimed he could see and moved out of people's way to avoid it being stepped on). These beliefs faded over several months but were replaced by other, equally florid symptoms. Several hospital admissions followed and a diagnosis of schizophrenia was quickly made. No evidence of underlying neurological disease was ever found, despite extensive investigations, including neurological consultations and two CT scans.

As with many patients with schizophrenia, treatment with antipsychotic medication had only a modest effect. DS has continued to show many florid, positive schizophrenic symptoms, including delusions that he can predict events and that he has caused riots in Australia. He continually hears voices making flattering or derogatory remarks. He also has the experience of thought broadcasting, feeling that the whole world is aware of his thoughts. He describes these experiences lucidly, even graphically, and shows no trace of incoherence of thought. However, he shows emotional indifference to his symptoms and even laughs at times when discussing them. A mild degree of lack of volition and some fall-off in self-care has also become evident. Like the vast majority of individuals who suffer from schizophrenia, he has not worked since the onset of his illness. Between admissions to hospital he lives with his parents.

DS occasionally mixes up days and dates, and has been known to get the year wrong. His parents have observed that even when he is relatively well he fails to 'take things in', gets mixed up on simple errands and forgets the names and addresses of close relatives. He might forget what had been said in a conversation only minutes earlier. Sometimes, he has seemed perplexed by simple things – once he asked: 'What's a bath?' Nevertheless, he can find his way around his home village and a nearby town without any difficulty and continues to understand the European languages he learned at school.

Like TC, DS is well motivated and has co-operated with extended neuropsychological testing. When first administered the Rivermead Behavioural Memory Test (during an admission) he achieved a screening score of 2 out of 12 – in the severely impaired range. Subsequently, he showed somewhat better, but still impaired, performance, scoring 4. Both his recall and recognition memory were abnormal: immediate recall of a passage of prose was $3^1/_2$ out of a possible maximum of 23; normal subjects usually score a minimum of 6. His recognition of words was 32 out of 50 – very impaired – but that for faces was 39, just within the normal range for his age group. Performance was poor on a test of remote memory involving identification of famous names. Autobiographical memory was tested by asking DS to recollect incidents from various points in his life. Many of his responses were vague and impoverished: asked to recall an incident at a funeral that he attended in his twenties, he recalled 'It was uncle G—'s. We went to the chapel, then Pontefract Crematorium, then back to the house'; he could not recall when the funeral was or whose house they returned to. Other responses on this test were contaminated by delusional memories. For example, recalling an incident at university he stated, 'I remember making silly predictions, predicting things to friends. We were drinking a pint, Nigel, Robert and Miles were there. I just said "they're going to invent an L515 motorbike". They thought I was joking.' As it predated his illness by several years, it seems highly unlikely that such an event really took place.

DS also showed a strikingly unusual pattern of performance on a test of semantic memory: memory for general knowledge. For example, on the Semantic Processing Test, which assesses the speed of access to semantic information by asking the subject to state whether 50 simple sentences are true or false, his average verification time was 4.14 seconds per sentence, rather slower than that of 3.50 seconds per sentence for normal individuals (these times refer to an orally administered version of this test). More significantly, he also made seven errors, responding 'true' to the propositions 'architects can be bought in shops' and 'beefsteaks are officers', and 'false' to 'grapes come from plants' and 'beefsteaks can be bought in shops'. Normal subjects typically make no more than one or two errors on this task.

On the other hand, several aspects of DS's memory performance appeared to be intact. Short-term memory testing revealed a forward digit span of 6. On a nonverbal version of this test, the Corsi blocks, where the subject has to touch a series of blocks on a board in the same sequence as the tester, he scored 4 – at the expected level of one or two less than digit span. His span for letters and words was also preserved, and he showed the usual deleterious effects of word length and phonologically similar letters on short-term memory performance. Similarly, procedural memory – memory for motor, perceptual and intellectual skills – was normal: DS showed progressive improvement on the Pursuit Rotor, a task involving fine motor co-ordination; and also on repeatedly assembling a child's jigsaw puzzle and reading words in mirror image. His pattern of performance on this last test is shown in figure 10.1, where it is compared to pooled data from eight normal subjects. It is apparent that, although initially slower, DS improved at at least the same rate as the controls on this task, and that the gains he made carried over to testing a week later.

Unlike TC, DS does not show any great evidence of executive impairment. He performed normally on the Wisconsin Card Sorting Test, making all the required shifts in sorting rule with only two errors. Another well-known executive test requires subjects to name items in a particular category. Given categories such as 'words beginning with the letter S', and 'vehicles or means of transport', he was able to name 20 and 15 examples in a minute respectively, perhaps less than expected for someone of his educational level, but by no means poor. When screened for impairment in other domains of neuropsychological function using a battery of brief tests developed to pick up clinically significant deficits in elderly patients, he performed perfectly on tests of language comprehension and naming, fragmented letter completion, unusual views and drawing. Nevertheless,

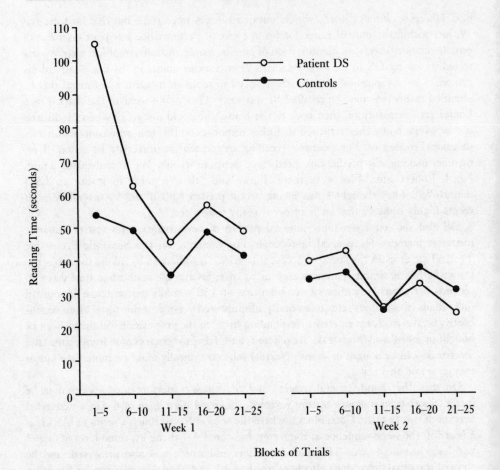

Figure 10.1 DS's performance of a task involving reading 25 triplets of words written in mirror image

DS does show some suggestion of overall intellectual decline: his estimated pre-illness IQ was 115, whereas his current IQ has been measured as 101.

Clearly, DS's main area of abnormal neuropsychological function is memory. His case also brings into sharp focus a pattern of impairment and preservation of function which was only hinted at in TC. In particular, DS shows intact short-term memory coupled with a deficit in long-term memory. Within long-term memory the impairment appears not to be uniform and spares procedural memory.

EN: Delusional Memories

EN is a 34-year-old woman who had an uneventful childhood in East Anglia, the second child of farming parents. She left school at 16, with an Art 'O' level and 5 CSEs. She held a number of different jobs over the next few years: as a dental assistant, a shop assistant, and working in an electrical factory. During this period she also married and divorced, had a miscarriage and lived with a man who abused drugs.

EN was first admitted to psychiatric hospital at the age of 22. Over a few days she had started to seem rather remote and preoccupied. Then she became behaviourally disturbed, running away from her house and later falling into a trance-like state. This hospital admission was the first of ten, the last of which lasted four years. Indefinite institutionalization seemed the inevitable outcome until treatment with a new drug, clozapine, brought her symptoms and behavioural disturbance under control and allowed her to leave hospital and move into a hostel. Currently, she appears superficially well and has managed to find part-time work. However, many of her symptoms continue to be present under the surface. For instance, during a recent conversation with one of the authors she had difficulty finding a word and apologized for this, explaining that English was her second language!

EN's illness has always been dominated by delusions. Early on, she expressed a variety of bizarre beliefs: that her mother was a witch and was sucking fluid from her brain; that her brother was inside her head; that she had been taken over by a poltergeist; and that she had become pregnant by her brother-in-law. Violent acts in response to these beliefs had led to her spending several months in a secure psychiatric unit. Approximately five years ago EN began to talk of having a (nonexistent) identical twin sister, who had the same Christian name as her. During a tape-recorded interview with one of the authors, she gave the following account of this belief:

ADB: Can you tell me what your name is, please?

EN: I was christened Lady Dorothy Lake, but my step-parents call me E—, the same as my sister.

ADB: Were you just given that name or were you actually a titled person?

EN: Yes I am, yes, yes, the Queen Mother's got my birth certificate.

ADB: Why the Queen Mother?

EN: I don't know, because my dad's name was Sir Grace Darling (the name of a Victorian heroine), and when I was a little girl I saw Douglas Bader walk up the street with my dad, the pilot with no legs. And I can remember that when I was a little girl – this is true, I can remember – I went to Buckingham Palace and the Queen took me to the toilet, when I was a little girl.

ADB: Can you tell me a bit about your sister?

EN: Yes, she was born in Ipswich Hospital in Suffolk. E— was thirteen years old when they moved up to B—. My dad filled me in on the thing which was going on, because I came home, you see. I had a terrible accident when I was a little girl.

ADB: What was that?

EN: Someone hit me on the back of the head with a brick. So I had to go away and the Queen Mother arranged for me to go away to a special hospital to see if I could have anything done. Because I've got a big hole in the back of my skull.

This led into a description of a complex system of delusions concerning EN having spent time in Russia following a head injury as a child (she has never in fact had a serious head injury).

ADB: You mentioned that you hurt your head – can you tell me a bit more about that?

EN: I was in the changing room in a little primary school, B— Primary School for the well-to-do little kiddies, and I went to the toilet outside – 'cause we had flush toilets – I went outside to the toilet and came back, through the changing room to the classroom. Somebody hit me on the head with a brick, and I fainted. That's the last thing I heard about.

ADB: Did you ever find out who it was?

EN: I was in a coma. I knew I was put on a stretcher and carried away.

ADB: Right, and where did you wake up, can you remember?

EN: No, I can't remember, it's such a long time.

ADB: And is that linked to your being in Russia, do you think?

EN: Yes, 'cause they couldn't treat me, the surgeons couldn't do the operation. I've got a hole in the back of my head where I've got no bone.

ADB: Right, and were they good at doing that in Russia?

EN: How should I know? I was only a little kiddie.

ADB: No, I just wondered why . . .

EN: I don't know. The surgeons were better in Russia than they were here.

In another interview the patient lapsed into the rare schizophrenic symptom of *delusional confabulation*, where new delusions, often fantastic delusions and delusional memories, appear to be made up on the spot.

PJM: [asking about EN's imagined twin sister] And where is she now?

EN: I haven't got a clue, I don't know. She's done a baby murder, she killed a baby and then she disappeared and blamed it on me and mum. Me and mum were put in prison and in this psychiatric home – 28 years, we've been here.

PJM: Have you?

EN: She did the murder, she murdered a little girl – called Emma Richards – and she blamed it on me and mum. She cut her throat to cover up her own evidence. She is bad. She is two and a half years old in her mind, and when she saw *The Merchant of Venice* it turned her mind. The police are after her, she is named as a murderess. She uses a plastic mac and she's got long red hair – hennaed hair. I'm telling the truth, I don't see why I should lie.

PJM: Let's move off this topic, because it's obviously upsetting.

EN: It's not upsetting. It's just that me and mum were going on holiday to Felixstowe. The police came and took mum away in a Black Maria [police van]. They came for me and took me to F— hospital later on that night. My sister has gone somewhere she can hide, someone is hiding her.

EN shows little in the way of general intellectual impairment. Her current IQ is 90, not greatly different from her estimated pre-illness IQ of 102, and in keeping with her educational achievement. She also passed the Wisconsin Card Sorting Test and a selection of other executive tests with ease. Testing on the brief battery used with DS revealed no suggestions of impairment in short-term memory, language and visuospatial function.

She obtained a screening score of 8/12 on the Rivermead Behavioural Memory Test, in the poor-memory range, but still within normal limits. Recall and recognition for verbal and nonverbal material were tested using a newly devised test, the Doors and People test, in which subjects have to memorize and then recall the names of four people and four abstract designs. The recognition component involves presenting the subject with a series of pictures of doors, after which each item is presented together with three distractors. The same procedure is carried out for people's names. On this test EN showed somewhat poor recognition for both the doors (14/24) and the names (17/24), coupled with poor, though not severely impaired, visual and verbal learning and recall.

An area of more markedly abnormal memory performance was in recollection of autobiographical incidents. Here EN's responses, like those of DS, were overall somewhat vague. However, some of her recollections were richer, and these were distinctly odd in content. Thus, she recalled that at secondary school a friend had cut her throat in the bath (or that this friend had found her mother in the bath with her throat cut, it was not clear which), and had to go away. When asked to describe an incident at a wedding in her twenties, she gave a detailed account of her imaginary twin sister's wedding, complete with a description of the wedding dress, and ending on the touching note of her sister putting flowers on their grandmother's grave. These events, of course, did not take place (although it is possible that EN might have been incorporating material from her own wedding when she was a teenager).

These responses of EN's differ from the usual pattern of confabulation in that they occur in the absence of any evidence of executive impairment (Baddeley and Wilson, 1986). Furthermore, there is a suggestion that something rather similar can also be seen in the domain of semantic memory. EN's performance on the Semantic Processing Test was normal: her average verification time was 1.56 seconds per sentence (on the written version of the test) and she made only one error. She also performed normally on a battery of tests designed to probe different aspects of semantic memory, developed by Hodges et al. (1992), with the exception of one subtest. When asked to give definitions of various items used in the battery, on the whole she provided a normal quantity of information. Much of this was accurate, but on several items she also included idiosyncratic or erroneous details. She stated that an alligator was an 'arthrodidic' reptile; that the closest ancestor of the rhinoceros was the 'pinodaurus' dinosaur; that penguins were related to the duck-billed platypus; and that the helicopter was invented by studying the hummingbird.

Discussion

In the past it was tacitly assumed that when patients with schizophrenia showed poor performance on neuropsychological tests, they did so because of unco-operativeness, lack of volition, the effects of institutionalization, and so on. The cases described here argue against this kind of explanation – both TC and DS were highly co-operative, and DS was not chronically hospitalized – yet both showed substantial deficits. In addition, DS showed poor performance on some tasks but was intact on others (including some like mirror reading which are quite arduous), a pattern which is difficult to reconcile with a general motivational impairment. It has also been proposed that the antipsychotic medication taken by schizophrenic patients, often in large doses, accounts for their cognitive impairment. In fact, there has never been much evidence to support such a view. A large number of studies (recently reviewed by King, 1990) have made it clear that not only do such drugs fail to affect most aspects of cognitive function when given to normal individuals, but if anything they improve test performance in schizophrenic patients. The possibility that cumulative exposure to antischizophrenic drugs over many years might cause intellectual impairment is equally difficult to sustain. In a classic study, Owens and Johnstone (1980) painstakingly reconstructed the treatment histories of 510 chronically hospitalized schizophrenic patients. No relationship between lifetime drug treatment and intellectual impairment was found.

For these reasons, it is now accepted that intellectual impairment is an integral part of the disease process of schizophrenia. Fortunately, it is not seen in every patient and in many cases it is mild, being detectable only as a decline in IQ. Nevertheless, the deterioration can become damagingly great, and patients like TC provide a unique insight into its character. In many ways his pattern of performance resembles that of patients with diffuse brain damage, for example following severe closed head injury. Other cases like TC have been documented and have been found to show a roughly similar picture. Shallice and colleagues (1991) recently carried out a detailed neuropsychological examination of five chronically hospitalized schizophrenic patients. One showed widespread deficits; two showed lesser degrees of overall intellectual impairment plus disproportionately marked executive (and memory) deficits; the remaining two showed more or less isolated poor executive performance. In all their cases, the accent was on executive impairment, whereas in TC poor memory performance was also at least as conspicuous.

Some degree of memory impairment has been found to be prevalent in schizophrenia (for recent studies, see McKenna et al., 1990, and Saykin et al., 1991). For this reason it is not uncommon to encounter patients who, presumably as a chance occurrence, show a moderately severe degree of amnesia in relative isolation. DS is one such patient, and exploration of his performance reveals a pattern of dissociations. In particular, he shows sparing of both short-term memory and procedural memory. The same preservation of short-term memory performance was found in four more memory-impaired schizophrenic patients investigated by the authors (see Tamlyn et al., 1992), and the finding of intact or relatively intact procedural memory has also been duplicated in other studies (Goldberg et al., 1990; Clare et al., 1993). This pattern is of considerable theoretical interest because it resembles that of the classical amnesic syndrome, seen in patients with Korsakoff's syndrome and also in the famous patient HM who underwent bilateral removal of medial temporal lobe structures. However, there is an intriguing difference from the classical amnesic syndrome, in that memory-impaired patients with schizophrenia show strong suggestions of having an additional deficit in semantic memory. This seems to go far beyond the relatively inconspicuous deficits affecting recently acquired semantic information seen in neurological forms of amnesia (see Squire, 1987). This finding may have theoretical implications as well: a recent proposal by Frith (1992) to explain the symptoms of schizophrenia in cognitive neuropsychological terms invokes a disorder of second-order representations of knowledge – knowledge which is independent of personal experience. It is just this kind of knowledge which is stored in semantic memory.

The emerging picture of both general intellectual impairment and specific neuropsychological deficits in schizophrenia is that, while they are to some extent a function of severe, chronic illness, they are not closely linked to the positive and negative symptoms of the disorder (an absence of correlations has now been found in a number of studies, discussed by Mortimer et al., 1990, and Tamlyn et al., 1992). EN illustrates this point: she has experienced very florid psychotic symptoms despite exhibiting no very great neuropsychological deficits. At the same time, her case points to the possibility that there may be more subtle linkages and interactions between certain symptoms and certain types of neuropsychological impairment. In particular, it is striking that the symptom of delusional memory in her case crops up in association with what appears to be a rather circumscribed and unusual abnormality in autobiographical memory (and perhaps also in semantic memory).

Above all, memory impairment in schizophrenia seems to be lawful; that is, the appearance and progression of deficits follows sensible rules and their pattern mirrors that seen in neurological disorders. At the same time, it is clear the malfunction of memory in schizophrenia goes considerably beyond what can be construed as impairment. Perhaps memory in schizophrenia should be thought of as deranged, disorganized or corrupted rather than merely defective. Perhaps subtle alterations in certain aspects of memory such as semantic memory will be found to be responsible for the formation of certain symptoms of such delusions. But wherever the trail uncovered by the findings described here ultimately leads, it is hoped that the reader will be persuaded that schizophrenia forms an interesting addition to the range of clinical memory disorders.

Further Reading

Cutting, J. (1985) *The Psychology of Schizophrenia* (Edinburgh: Churchill Livingstone).
Frith, C.D. (1992) *The Cognitive Neuropsychology of Schizophrenia* (Hove, Sussex: Lawrence Erlbaum Associates).
McKenna, P.J. (1994) *Schizophrenia and Related Syndromes* (London: Oxford University Press).

References

Baddeley, A.D. and Wilson, B.A. (1986) 'Amnesia, autobiographical memory and confabulation', in D. Rubin (ed.), *Autobiographical Memory* (Cambridge: Cambridge University Press), pp. 225–52.
Bleuler, E. (1911) *Dementia Praecox, or the Group of Schizophrenias*, trans. J. Zinkin (New York: International Universities Press, 1950).
Calev, A., Berlin, H. and Lerer, B. (1987) 'Remote and recent memory in long-hospitalised chronic schizophrenics', *Biological Psychiatry*, 22: 79–85.

Clare, L., McKenna, P.J., Mortimer, A.M. and Baddeley, A.D. (1993) 'Memory in schizophrenia: what is impaired and what is preserved?', *Neuropsychologia*, **31**: 1225–41.

Cutting, J. (1985) *The Psychology of Schizophrenia* (Edinburgh: Churchill Livingstone).

Frith, C.D. (1992) *The Cognitive Neuropsychology of Schizophrenia* (Hove, Sussex: Lawrence Earlbaum Associates).

Goldberg, T.E., Weinberger, D.R., Berman, K.F., Pliskin, N.H. and Podd, M.H. (1987) 'Further evidence of dementia of prefrontal type in schizophrenia?', *Archives of General Psychiatry*, **44**: 1008–14.

Goldberg, T.E., Ragland, J.D., Torrey, E.F., Gold, J.M., Bigelow, L.B. and Weinberger, D.F. (1990) 'Neuropsychological assessment of monozygotic twins discordant for schizophrenia', *Archives of General Psychiatry*, **47**: 1066–72.

Hodges, J.R., Salmon, D.P. and Butters, N. (1992) 'Semantic memory impairment in Alzheimer's disease: failure of access or degraded knowledge?', *Neuropsychologia*, **30**: 301–14.

King, D.J. (1990) 'The effect of neuroleptics on cognitive and psychomotor function', *British Journal of Psychiatry*, **157**: 799–811.

Kolb, B. and Whishaw, I.Q. (1983) 'Performance of schizophrenic patients on tests sensitive to right or left frontal, temporal or parietal function in neurological patients', *Journal of Nervous and Mental Disease*, **171**: 435–43.

Kraepelin, E. (1913) *Dementia Praecox and Paraphrenia*, trans. R.M. Barclay (Edinburgh: Livingstone, 1919).

Liddle, P.F. and Crow, T.J. (1984) 'Age disorientation in chronic schizophrenia is associated with global intellectual impairment', *British Journal of Psychiatry*, **144**: 193–9.

McKenna, P.J., Tamlyn, D., Lund, C.E., Mortimer, A.M., Hammond, S. and Baddeley, A.D. (1990) 'Amnesic syndrome in schizophrenia', *Psychological Medicine*, **20**: 967–72.

Mortimer, A.M., Lund, C.E. and McKenna, P.J. (1990) 'The positive:negative dichotomy in schizophrenia', *British Journal of Psychiatry*, **156**, 41–9.

Nelson, H.E., Pantelis, C., Carruthers, K., Speller, J., Baxendale, S. and Barnes, T.R.E. (1990) 'Cognitive functioning and symptomatology in chronic schizophrenia', *Psychological Medicine*, **20**: 357–65.

Owens, D.G.C. and Johnstone, E.C. (1980) 'The disabilities of chronic schizophrenia: their nature and the factors contributing to their development', *British Journal of Psychiatry*, **136**: 384–93.

Payne, R.W. (1973) 'Cognitive abnormalities', in H.J. Eysenck (ed.), *Handbook of Abnormal Psychology* (London: Pitman).

Saykin, A.J., Gur, R.E., Mozley, P.D., Mozley, L.H., Resnick, S.M., Kester, B. and Stafiniak, P. (1991) 'Neuropsychological function in schizophrenia', *Archives of General Psychiatry*, **48**: 618–24.

Shallice, T., Burgess, P.W. and Firth, C.D. (1991) 'Can the neuropsychological case-study approach be applied to schizophrenia?', *Psychological Medicine*, **21**: 661–73.

Squire, L.R. (1987) *Memory and Brain* (London: Oxford University Press).

Tamlyn, D., McKenna, P.J., Mortimer, A.M., Lund, C.E., Hammond, S. and Baddeley, A.D. (1992) 'Memory impairment in schizophrenia: its extent, affiliations and neuropsychological character', *Psychological Medicine*, **22**: 101–15.

11   Delusional Memory, Confabulation and Frontal Lobe Dysfunction

Michael D. Kopelman, Elizabeth M. Guinan
and Philip D.R. Lewis

Introduction

That schizophrenia has devastating consequences has long been known; but that it also
'breaks' memories is a more recent observation. Kraepelin (1910) put forward the notion
of 'dementia praecox' as a progressive and debilitating disorder; and, more recently,
Johnstone et al. (1976) revived the notion of a 'dementia of dementia praecox'. Since that
time, a number of studies have examined the effects of schizophrenia upon aspects of
cognitive function, especially frontal lobe and memory function. Moreover, various
authors, notably Baddeley and Wilson (1986), have described the characteristic features
of confabulation in patients with organic amnesia; and it is notable that these features
closely resemble the defining characteristics of 'delusions' in psychiatric disorder (for
example, Clare, 1976; Mullen, 1979). Consequently, Kopelman (1987a) argued that
spontaneous confabulations can be indistinguishable from 'delusional memories', except
for the context in which they arise.

  The present chapter reviews these issues in turn, before describing a patient with a
prominent delusional memory and considering her neuropsychological test performance.

Schizophrenia and Memory

There is good *a priori* reason to suspect memory impairment in schizophrenic patients.
In a computerised tomography (CT) brain scan study, Johnstone et al. (1976) found
significantly enlarged ventricular–brain ratios in seventeen schizophrenic patients; and
the ventricular enlargement showed a high correlation ($r = -0.70$) with scores on a

clinical, cognitive scale (larger ventricles being correlated with a greater degree of cognitive impairment). The finding of enlarged ventricles, and also sulcal widening, has been replicated by Weinberger et al. (1979a, b), Andreasen et al. (1982), Owens et al. (1985) and others.

More specifically, various autopsy studies have found evidence either of temporal lobe atrophy or of enlargement of the temporal horns of the lateral ventricles (implying temporal lobe atrophy). Bogerts et al. (1985) found a decreased volume of the limbic temporal lobe, by 31 per cent in the hippocampus, by 44 per cent in the parahippocampal gyrus, and by 22 per cent in the amygdala. On the other hand, the basal ganglia were largely unaffected. Brown et al. (1986) compared forty-one schizophrenic patients with twenty-nine patients who had had affective disorder, finding a significant reduction in total brain weight, a significant increase in lateral ventricular size, particularly involving the temporal horns, and a significant reduction in parahippocampal cortical thickness, especially in the left hemisphere. There also appeared to be a bilateral reduction in parahippocampal thickness compared with a small ($n = 5$) healthy control group. Similarly, Crow et al. (1989) found an increase in the size of the left ventricular temporal horn by 82 per cent in a group of twenty-two schizophrenic patients, relative to controls, a finding replicated by Bruton et al. (1990). Particularly pertinent may be findings of cellular disarray (Kovelman and Scheibel, 1984; Arnold et al. 1991) and/or cellular reduction (Jeste and Lohr, 1989) in schizophrenic patients in critical brain regions (namely, the CA1/CA4 regions of the hippocampus, and in the entorhinal cortex) all of which have been implicated in memory processing (Zola-Morgan et al., 1986; Shepherd, 1988; Lynch and Baudry, 1988).

A different finding, also pertinent to memory functioning, was made by Stevens (1982) who found patchy fibrillary gliosis in para-ventricular and peri-acqueductal grey matter (commonly affected in the Wernicke–Korsakoff syndrome), including the thalamus, hypothalamus, and the septal nucleus and nucleus basalis of the basal forebrain.

In the light of this evidence of bitemporal lobe atrophy, and of possible diencephalic and/or basal forebrain involvement, it is unsurprising that various studies have found evidence of anterograde memory impairment in schizophrenic patients. One of the earliest and most careful of these studies was by Cutting (1979). He examined groups of healthy subjects, depressed patients, Korsakoff patients, patients with 'presenile dementia', and acute and chronic schizophrenic patients on tests of verbal paired-associate learning and pattern recognition. Table 11.1 shows that Cutting (1979) found significant impairment in all the clinical groups across both tests, the Korsakoff patients and the dementing patients performing worst. However, quite striking is the fact that both the acute and the chronic schizophrenics performed poorly on the verbal paired-associate learning, and the chronic schizophrenics also performed very poorly on the pattern recognition task. Somewhat similarly, Calev et al. (1991) used a matching procedure to examine the relative severity of verbal and visuo-spatial memory in schizophrenic patients on a story recall task and recall of a complex (Rey–Osterreith) figure, finding that chronic schizophrenics showed approximately equal impairments in verbal and non-verbal memory. Earlier, Calev (1984) had shown that schizophrenics are impaired at both recall and recognition tasks, but particularly the former.

McKenna et al. (1990) examined sixty schizophrenic patients, including both acutely and chronically disturbed patients on the Rivermead Behavioural Memory Test (RBMT)

Table 11.1   Memory tests in schizophrenia

	Verbal paired-associate learning (%)	*Pattern recognition (%)*
Controls	78.1	62.2
Depressives	48.5	49.2
Acute schizophrenics	33.0	58.8
Chronic schizophrenics	32.0	34.0
Korsakoffs	21.5	22.4
Presenile dementia	33.0	17.2

Source: Cutting (1979).

(Wilson et al., 1985). Using this assessment procedure, these authors found that ten patients fell within the range of severe impairment on this test (RBMT score <3), forty were moderately impaired (RBMT score <10), and ten were intact. These same authors (Tamlyn et al., 1992) also administered the Mini Mental State Examination (MMSE) (Folstein et al., 1975) as a screening assessment for more global cognitive impairment. Tamlyn et al. (1992) obtained five patients with moderately severe memory impairment and 'normal' scores on the MMSE, implying a relatively specific memory disorder; and the degree of memory impairment correlated significantly with the duration and severity of schizophrenic symptoms as determined by a global assessment scale (Endicott et al., 1976).

In addition, Tamlyn et al. (1992) characterized the anterograde memory deficit in schizophrenia in further detail, finding preserved digit, letter and Corsi block span, and an unimpaired recency effect on the serial position curve for free recall of words. By contrast, the earlier portion of the serial position curve showed significant impairment; prose recall, word and face recognition were all impaired; and there were increased errors and response times on a measure of semantic memory. Many of these findings have been replicated by Duffy and O'Carroll (1994).

Somewhat similarly, Goldberg and colleagues (1993) have examined learning and memory in monozygotic twins discordant for schizophrenia, finding that affected twins scored significantly lower than their unaffected co-twins on story recall, paired-associate learning and visual recall of designs. On the other hand, performance on two measures of procedural memory did not differ significantly between the two groups. Comparison of the unaffected co-twins with a healthy control group showed very mild deficits in some, but not all, aspects of episodic memory.

Finally, Crow and various colleagues (Crow and Mitchell, 1975; Crow and Stevens, 1978; Liddle and Crow, 1984) have consistently found impaired orientation for age, the current year, and the duration of time since admission in groups of schizophrenic patients. Usually, these patients underestimate time, and there is often a consistent pattern in their errors. Crow and his colleagues suggested that this disorder results from a learning impairment; and, consistent with that view, the phenomena of impaired orientation for age, year and duration since admission have also been reported by other authors in groups of Korsakoff and Alzheimer patients (Zangwill, 1953; Kopelman, 1989).

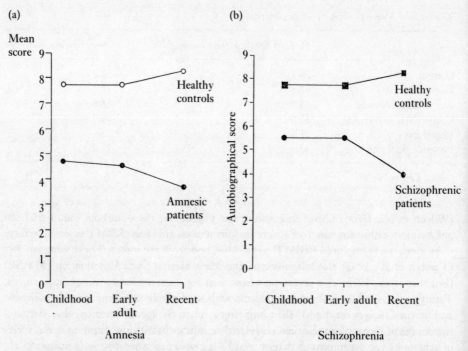

Figure 11.1 Results of the Autobiographical Incidents Schedule administered to schizophrenic and amnesic patients
Sources: Amnesia data: Kopelman et al., 1989; schizophrenia data: Tamlyn et al., 1992

With respect to retrograde memory, there have been fewer studies. However, Liddle (1987) found that impairment in the recognition of famous names on Stevens's (1979) Famous Personalities test correlated with features of Liddle's Psychomotor Poverty Syndrome ($r = -0.51$, p <0.001). The features of this syndrome are somewhat akin to 'frontal lobe dysfunction', consisting of poverty in the quantity of speech, decreased spontaneous movement, and blunted emotion and affective gestures. Moreover, this syndrome was associated with a reduction in left medial prefrontal activity on a resting O^{15} positron-emission tomography (PET) scan (Liddle et al., 1992). Such observations are consistent with the findings in organic amnesia and dementia that frontal lobe dysfunction can produce a temporally extensive retrograde memory loss (Kopelman, 1992; 1993; Della Sala et al., 1993).

Somewhat similarly, Tamlyn et al. (1992) also found impairment on Stevens's (1979) Famous Personalities test. These authors also administered the Autobiographical Incidents Schedule from the Autobiographical Memory Interview (AMI) (Kopelman et al., 1989, 1990). As shown in figure 11.la and b, their sample of schizophrenic patients showed severe impairment on this test (Tamlyn et al., 1992), comparable with patients who have an organic amnesia.

In summary, there is now substantial evidence of anterograde memory impairment in schizophrenic patients, consistent with neuro-imaging and autopsy evidence of bitemporal lobe atrophy and of disruption or reduction in CA1/CA4 and entorhinal neurons. In addition, there is some evidence of retrograde memory impairment, although this has been less thoroughly examined.

Schizophrenia and Frontal Lobe Function

There is evidence of impaired verbal fluency in schizophrenic patients (Kolb and Whishaw, 1983; Shoqeirat and Mayes, 1988), reduced design fluency (Kolb and Whishaw, 1983), reduced categories obtained on card-sorting tasks (Kolb and Whishaw, 1983; Shoqeirat and Mayes, 1988) and increased perseverative errors on card-sorting tasks (Weinberger et al., 1986; Andreasen et al., 1986). However, Shoqeirat and Mayes (1988) failed to find any evidence of specific impairments in memory for temporal or spatial context, as they had predicted on the basis of frontal lobe dysfunction.

Particular interest in the role of frontal lobe dysfunction in schizophrenia was stimulated by a study of Weinberger et al. (1986), using Xenon 133 computerized tomography scanning in a card-sorting activation task. Prefrontal cerebral blood flow (rCBF) was reduced at rest in twenty schizophrenic patients, compared with twenty-five age-matched controls. This difference was accentuated by the card-sorting task, but not by a number-matching task. Moreover, the percentage change score (reflecting the difference in rCBF between card-sorting and rest) correlated negatively with the percentage of perseverative errors on the card-sorting test (that is, the greater the percentage of perseverative errors, the less rCBF was increased by the card-sorting task). These authors postulated a degeneration in limbic–frontal connections. This study was partially replicated in a single photon emission computed tomography (SPECT) study by Lewis et al. (1992) in which uptake of a radioactive ligand was used to measure regional cerebral brain flow during a verbal fluency task. Schizophrenic patients showed decreased rCBF in the left frontal region (and increased left posterior cortical rCBF) relative to healthy controls.

In a further study, Goldberg et al. (1987) attempted to teach schizophrenic patients the skills required to perform the Wisconsin Card Sorting test with card-by-card instructions and feedback. Training failed to produce any benefit, compared with nontrained schizophrenics. However, these patients were able to learn a word list, using a 'selective reminding' procedure, suggesting that the failure to learn the card-sorting task was not simply a result of the schizophrenics' explicit memory impairment.

Finally, Liddle and Morris (1991) have attempted to relate subgroups of schizophrenic symptoms to frontal lobe test performance. They examined forty-three schizophrenic patients who were classified as having either a 'psychomotor poverty' syndrome or a 'disorganization' syndrome on the basis of their pattern of symptoms. In general, the patients showed significant impairments on verbal fluency, card-sorting, and Trail-Making B tests; and Liddle and Morris (1991) also claimed to be able to differentiate the two psychiatric syndromes on the basis of these and a further test (the Stroop).

In summary, there is evidence of frontal lobe dysfunction in schizophrenic patients as determined across a number of standard 'frontal lobe tests'. This impairment is associated with a reduction in regional cerebral blood flow through the frontal lobes as determined by radio-labelling in neuro-imaging studies; and there is some evidence that the degree of the abnormality in regional cerebral perfusion is correlated with the severity of cognitive impairment on frontal lobe tasks. It has also been demonstrated that schizo-phrenic patients have particular difficulty in learning to perform frontal lobe tasks, even when trained, and that this difficulty is not purely the result of their anterograde memory impairment. It is highly plausible that some of the symptoms of schizophrenia – those known as either 'negative symptoms' (Crow, 1980) or the 'psychomotor poverty syn-drome' (Liddle and Morris, 1991) – are related to frontal dysfunction. It is also highly plausible that the frontal lobe dysfunction may be pertinent to some aspects of the memory impairment found in these patients, as discussed below.

Spontaneous Confabulation and Frontal Lobe Dysfunction

Confabulations can be defined as erroneous memories, either false in themselves or resulting from 'true' memories misplaced in context and inappropriately retrieved or interpreted. The pertinence of 'true' memories, displaced in temporal context and inap-propriately recalled, was emphasized by Korsakoff (1889) himself.

Berlyne (1972) distinguished between what he called 'fantastic' confabulation and 'momentary' confabulation, which were differentiated by a number of different factors. Kopelman (1987b) agreed that at least two types of phenomena tend to be identified as 'confabulation', but argued that Berlyne had confounded a number of different factors. Kopelman distinguished between so-called 'spontaneous confabulation', which can be defined as a persistent, unprovoked outpouring of erroneous memories, and 'provoked' or 'momentary' confabulation, which refers to fleeting intrusions or distortions produced in response to a challenge to memory, such as a memory test. In other words, the presence or absence of a provoking stimulus was proposed as the distinguishing feature of the two types of confabulation. The importance of this distinction was that, whilst there is evidence (reviewed below) indicating that spontaneous confabulation often results from frontal lobe dysfunction, momentary confabulation may be a 'normal' response to a failing or 'weak' memory, as evidenced by the fact that healthy subjects produce similar intrusion errors and distortions when asked to recall information at lengthy delays (Kopelman, 1987b).

A number of authors have identified the putative role of frontal lobe dysfunction in spontaneous confabulation. In particular, Luria (1976) argued from clinical studies that lesions involving the orbital-medial regions of the frontal lobes often produce florid confabulation, for example in cases of subarachnoid haemorrhage from anterior commu-nicating artery aneurysms. Subsequently, Stuss et al. (1978) described five patients with CT scan evidence of frontal pathology, of whom four also had EEG evidence of frontal dysfunction. All these patients were severely impaired at the Wisconsin Card Sorting task, and they continued to show florid or spontaneous confabulation, even after their memory test performance had improved. Similarly, Kapur and Coughlan (1980) re-ported a single case-study, involving a patient who had suffered a subarachnoid haem-orrhage from an anterior communicating artery aneurysm. This patient had a well-defined region of hypodensity on his CT scan in the left frontal region. He showed impaired performance on the shortened card-sorting task (Nelson, 1976) as well as abnormal performance on the cognitive estimates task (Shallice and Evans, 1978). However, unlike the Stuss et al. (1978) patients, whose confabulation *persisted* despite improved *memory* task performance, the Kapur and Coughlan (1980) patient's confabulation *resolved* as his *frontal* lobe test performance improved.

Baddeley and Wilson (1986) provided a detailed account of autobiographical memory impairments in four patients with focal frontal lobe lesions. Two of their patients showed impoverished or nonfluent retrieval of autobiographical memories, whereas another two patients showed spontaneous and florid confabulation, one patient denying to his wife that he was married – even after being shown photographs of their wedding. Baddeley and Wilson (1986) described the characteristic features of confabulation in these two patients. First, the confabulation was 'spontaneous' in the sense that it was not limited to test situations. Second, they noted the strong degree of conviction by these patients in their beliefs, and their willingness to act upon them. Third, they noted that the patients were extremely resistant to persuasion that their confabulated beliefs might be inaccurate. Fourth, the authors emphasized that the confabulations were very preoccupying; and, finally, they noted that their content was often bizarre. Such features resemble the defining properties of a 'delusion' in psychiatric disorders (for example, Fish, 1967; Clare, 1976; Mullen, 1979). A delusion is commonly defined as an absolute conviction which is not amenable to argument, not explicable in cultural terms, and is often bizarre and usually preoccupying. Such features led Kopelman (1987a) to argue that there need be no qualitative difference between 'spontaneous confabulation' and a 'delusional memory' except the context (organic amnesia, psychiatric disorder) in which they arise.

In summary, there appears to be plenty of evidence that the presence of the spontaneous type of confabulation is often related to frontal lobe dysfunction, even though a recent case study indicates that this may not be true of all amnesic patients who confabulate (Dalla Barba, 1993).

Delusional Memory

Like many psychiatric phenomena, the notion of 'delusional memory' tends to be defined variously by differing authors (for example, Schneider, 1959; Jaspers, 1913; Fish, 1967; Wing et al., 1974; Mullen, 1979; Gelder et al., 1989). In essence, its definitions amount to *either* a true memory which stimulates a deluded interpretation *or* a false memory arising in the context of psychosis. It is in the latter sense that 'delusional memory' most obviously resembles 'spontaneous confabulation', in that the latter could be summarized as false memories arising in the context of organic amnesia; however, as noted above, confabulation can also involve 'true' memories inappropriately recalled and interpreted.

Recently, Buchanan (1991) summarized the psychiatric literature on delusional memories, arguing that they can arise either *de novo* – 'out of the blue' or they can be stimulated by a 'real' memory, as discussed above, in which case they are analogous to so-called 'delusional perceptions' (shorthand for delusional interpretations of 'real' perceptions), which constitute a 'first-rank' symptom of schizophrenia (Schneider, 1959).

Patient LD was first seen by MDK in 1981, when LD was aged 33. He displayed various first-rank symptoms of schizophrenia, including the beliefs that his thoughts, actions and emotions were controlled by outside forces. This patient gave a detailed account of how he believed he had been hired by Lord Lucan to kill Lady Lucan in a well-publicized murder, some eight years earlier. He explained how he had been re-cruited in a London nightclub and how he had, indeed, assaulted Lady Lucan, and then proceeded to kill Lord Lucan (who, in fact, has not been traced since the night of Lady Lucan's assault); and he also described how he had killed Lady Lucan's nanny (who was in fact murdered on the night in question). The patient described these events in graphic detail and with absolute conviction, although incidental details (angels appearing on the bonnet of his car) failed to be quite so persuasive. As far as could be told, these 'memories' had arisen 'out of the blue'. There was no evidence of any underlying organic pathology in this patient. After several weeks of treatment with thioridazine, the various memories became much less preoccupying and LD was much more uncertain about them, although they had not completely disappeared.

The putative relationship between frontal lobe dysfunction and confabulation may have a parallel in evidence that frontal lobe damage can contribute to the presence of delusions in patients with organic psychiatric syndromes. Benson and Stuss (1990) reported five patients who had confabulations and/or delusions in the presence of frontal lobe damage. Three of these patients had organic amnesic or dementing disorders; but the most interesting two cases had delusions of misidentification (the Capgras syndrome; reduplicative paramnesia) following head injuries which had caused frontal haematomas and contusion.

In summary, there are no unequivocal or defining features which distinguish delusional confabulation from spontaneous confabulation other than the context in which each arises. There is also evidence that frontal lobe damage may contribute to delusions in organic psychiatric syndromes, just as frontal lobe dysfunction seems to be the basis of spontaneous confabulation in many patients with organic amnesia.

Hypothesis

Summarizing the above, various pieces of evidence suggest that frontal lobe dysfunction may contribute to delusional memories in schizophrenic patients:

1   schizophrenic patients show anterograde and retrograde memory impairments;
2   schizophrenic patients show frontal lobe dysfunction;
3   frontal lobe dysfunction appears to be the basis of 'spontaneous confabulation' in many patients;
4   spontaneous confabulations can show many of the defining features of psychiatric delusions, and cannot be unequivocally distinguished from 'delusional memories' except in terms of the context in which they arise;
5   there is some evidence that frontal lobe damage can also contribute to the presence of delusions in patients with organic psychiatric syndromes.

To the authors' knowledge, there have not previously been any detailed neuropsy-chological studies of patients with delusional memories arising in the context of schizo-phrenia or other psychiatric syndromes. It follows from the above that such a study would be valuable in determining whether the presence of either frontal lobe dysfunction of anterograde/retrograde memory impairment contribute to the presence of delusional memories in schizophrenic patients. A single-case study of such a patient was carried out to examine this.

Case History

Patient WM was first seen by MDK in 1991, when she was aged 47. Her father was a retired vicar, who had had electroconvulsive therapy for depression in the distant past, but her mother and her 43-year-old younger sister had no psychiatric history. WM obtained 'O' and 'A' levels at school and, after working for a short while for the BBC, she took an English degree at one of the Colleges of London University, before commencing PhD research work on Middle English. She never completed her research because of her psychiatric condition but, when first seen, she had recently resumed research on a part-time basis at her original College on a different topic. In the meantime, she had been working for a church organization, which she continues to do for her living. She had never been married nor had any long-term relationships. Indeed, she had had only one brief sexual involvement which, she claims, followed a psychiatrist's encouragement, and in which she subsequently regretted her compliance.

WM claimed that in the summer of 1970 she had been picking fruit on a fruit farm in Suffolk, when she encountered an internationally famous conductor, who also happened to be fruit-picking there. No words were exchanged between them, but she claims that subsequently he traced her and followed her to London, and that her friends challenged him about this. She believes that he was in love with her, and she says that she was prepared 'to meet him half way'. She also claims that his parents had died around that time, that he had recently been divorced, and that he himself was psychologically unsettled at the time they met. She says that she retreated to an Essex town, where her parents were then living, but that the conductor followed her there. Subsequently, he has stopped following her, and they have only ever exchanged a few words when she has waited for him outside stage doors. However, she has continued to write to him, including sending him a card two years ago to celebrate twenty-one years since they first met. Perhaps not surprisingly, she has not received any reply. WM has also described how she believes that she hears the conductor's thoughts in her brain, although these thoughts are not experienced as auditory hallucinations (she cannot identify a voice as such), and that the conductor also knows her thoughts as if by telepathy. Some difficulty arises because they 'share a brain', making it particularly difficult for one or other of them to concentrate when the other is reading. Moreover, she claims that the conductor finds that it interferes, making him irritable, if she listens to his concerts either in the concert hall or on the radio; and, consequently, she avoids doing so nowadays. To direct questioning, WM has also claimed that the conductor may have interfered with her sexually, although she is not certain of that; but she has always been absolutely confident that he will marry her eventually, 'although he keeps putting this off'.

It has to be emphasized that WM is a very sober, apparently sensible lady, tidily dressed, somewhat anxious-looking and obviously intelligent. In discussing her PhD studies with her, for example, one does not get any sense that she carries around with her these unusual beliefs, and WM's personality and everyday functioning are otherwise entirely normal. When describing her beliefs to us, WM does sometimes become marginally euphoric, and her unusual beliefs are certainly held as unswerving convictions – she does not think that she is in any sense 'ill'. In this connection, she had been seen by two other psychiatrists during the 1970s and 1980s, and she had been tried on various different antipsychotic medications, either by mouth or by injection. She does not believe that medication has had any effect upon her. At times she has stopped taking medication, mainly because of unpleasant side-effects; but at other times she has asked to resume it, although she is very vague in those instances about how it is helping her. Her mental state has changed very little in the last few years.

WM's symptoms would appear to be an instance of De Clérambault's syndrome (also known as 'erotomania'), in which a patient, usually a woman, believes that someone famous, accomplished or in authority is in love with her, but this is an entirely delusional belief (Enoch and Trethowan, 1979). The syndrome can arise in the context of schizophrenia, an affective psychosis or as an isolated phenomenon ('primary erotomania'). In WM's case, it would appear to have arisen in the context of schizophrenia, as she has frequently described 'thought insertion' and 'thought diffusion' (or 'broadcasting'), which are so-called first-rank symptoms of schizophrenia (Schneider, 1959). There is no evidence whatsoever that the lady is conducting a relationship with the musician and, in similar instances, other patients have harassed their victim, who have confirmed the absence of any past or present relationship with the patient. In extreme circumstances such cases can result in suicide or even homicide. Unlike patient LD, WM does not appear to have shown any response to medication.

Finally, it should be emphasized that all WM's abnormal beliefs appear to derive from her 'memories' of the initial meeting with the conductor in 1970; and, whilst her memory is not 'broken' or damaged in the sense that an amnesic patient's memory is 'broken', the disruptive effect of these 'memories' upon her subsequent life cannot be overemphasized.

Neuropsychological Examination

WM was administered the National Adult Reading Test (Nelson, 1982) with revised scoring criteria to predict premorbid Wechsler Adult Intelligence Scale – Revised (WAIS–R) IQ. She was given the WAIS-R (Wechsler, 1981) as a measure of current intelligence, and the Wechsler Memory Scale – Revised (WMS–R) (Butters et al., 1988) and the Recognition Memory Test (RMT) (Warrington, 1984) as measures of current anterograde memory. As a measure of retrograde memory, WM was administered an updated version of Kopelman's (1989) News Events test, which asks recall and recognition questions about pictures of news events from the 1940s to the 1980s, inclusive. In addition, WM was administered the Autobiographical Memory Interview (AMI), which asks about facts (or 'personal semantic' memory) and events (or incidents) that have arisen in a subject's life during three broad time-periods – childhood, young adult life, and 're-cently' (Kopelman et al., 1989, 1990; Kopelman, 1994). As measures of frontal lobe function, WM was administered FAS verbal fluency (Benton, 1968; Newcombe, 1969),

Table 11.2 MW'S Cognitive test scores

A: *General cognitive ability*
  1 NART predicted IQ: 127
  2 WAIS-R F-S IQ: 124 (verbal 131; performance 109)

B: *Anterograde memory*
  1 WMS-R   general 99 (verbal 94; visual 114)
           delayed 120
  2 RMT   words 49/50; 92 percentile
           faces 41/50; 23 percentile

C: *Retrograde memory tests*

1 News events	1940s	1950s	1960s	1970s	1980s
recall (%)	70	75	90	55	70
recognition (%)	90	80	90	90	90

2 AMI	Child	Young adult	Recent
facts (max. 21)	21	19.5	19.5
incidents (max. 9)	8	6	7.5

D: *Frontal lobe function*
  1 FAS 54
  2 Cognitive estimates 4
  3 Card-sorting
     categories 6/6
     perseverations 6/9

the Cognitive Estimates test (Shallice and Evans, 1978), and Nelson's version of the card-sorting test (Nelson, 1976).

Table 11.2 shows that WM had a predicted premorbid full-scale IQ of 127. Compared with this, her current WAIS-R full-scale IQ was normal at 124. There was, however, a verbal performance discrepancy of 22 points (Verbal IQ 131; Performance IQ 109). However, this is consistent with general evidence of WM's abilities, in which she reports that she has always been superior at language-based subjects; and she read English at undergraduate and postgraduate levels.

WM is fully orientated in time and place, and on the WMS-R scale she had an Attention/Concentration quotient of 107, a little below what would be expected on the basis of her IQ. Also on the WMS-R, WM's Verbal Memory quotient was surprisingly low at 94, but her Visual Memory quotient was 114, giving a General Memory quotient of 99. However, her Delayed Recall quotient was approximately equivalent to her IQ at 120. On the Recognition Memory Test, the pattern was more as would be expected on the basis of WM's Verbal Performance IQ discrepancy: she scored 49 out of 50 for words (and was at the 92nd percentile for her age), but only 41 out of 50 for faces (23rd percentile for her age).

On the News Events test (Kopelman, 1989), healthy subjects score approximately 50–60 per cent correct on the recall version, and approximately 70–80 per cent correct on the recognition version of this task. Amnesic and dementing patients perform considerably worse than this (Kopelman, 1989). Consequently, WM's scores on both components of this task are entirely normal (table 11.2), although there does appear to be a 'dip' in her performance for the recall of news events from the 1970s. Similarly, on the AMI, WM's scores for 'facts' from her past personal life were entirely normal (table 11.2), according to the criteria published by Kopelman et al. (1990). Likewise, WM's AMI scores for autobiographical incidents from the 'childhood' and 'recent' periods were entirely normal, although her score for the 'young adult' period fell within the 'borderline' range according to the published criteria (ibid.).

On frontal lobe tasks, WM generally performed well. She scored 54 on FAS verbal fluency, which is well above the mean level of performance for healthy controls in most studies (for example, Newcombe, 1969; Miller, 1984; Kopelman, 1991). Similarly, she scored only 4 on the Cognitive Estimates test, which is also well within the normal range in most studies (Leng and Parkin, 1988; Kopelman, 1989, 1991; Shoqeirat et al., 1990). Likewise, WM obtained 6 out of 6 categories correctly on Nelson's (1976) version of the card-sorting test. There were only 9 errors, of which 6 were perseverative, but the proportion of perseverative errors cannot be regarded as abnormal in view of the low total error score.

In summary, WM's general cognitive ability appears to be intact on a comparison of her predicted premorbid and current IQ, although there is a Verbal Performance discrepancy which probably reflects WM's underlying abilities. There was evidence of a mild-to-moderate degree of anterograde memory impairment, relative to her IQ (general memory quotient 99; Face Recognition, 23rd percentile); but WM's performance at retrograde memory tests was virtually intact. The 'dip' in her recall of news events during the 1970s, and in her recollection of incidents from her own life during the 'young adult' period on the AMI, may well have reflected problems arising from the onset of her psychotic disorder at that time. Finally, and most particularly, WM's performance at frontal lobe tasks was entirely intact.

Conclusion

We have argued that delusional memories arising in schizophrenia might be a consequence of the clearly documented frontal lobe dysfunction in that disorder. If this were the case, it would be further evidence that delusional memories resemble spontaneous confabulation, which various authors have shown is commonly the result of frontal lobe dysfunction in organic amnesic patients.

However, our case study of WM has failed to support this hypothesis. WM has a prominent delusional memory of meeting a world-famous conductor on a fruit-picking farm in East Anglia, around which her subsequent delusions revolve. She does indeed show a moderate degree of anterograde memory impairment, consistent with findings in other studies (for example, Cutting, 1979; Calev et al., 1991; McKenna et al., 1990). However, her performance was virtually normal on tests of retrograde memory, aside from a subtle impairment in recalling incidents and news events from the period around the onset of her psychotic disorder; and her scores were entirely normal on tests of frontal lobe function.

The logic in suggesting that frontal lobe dysfunction might underlie both spontaneous confabulation (in organic amnesic patients) and delusional memories (in schizophrenic patients) was simple and appealing. However, the present case history reminds us that phenomena can resemble one another for differing reasons. Whilst spontaneous confabulation may reflect a continuing process of disorganized, incoherent and context-free retrieval of past memories and associations (Kopelman, 1987b), delusional memories may result from an isolated shift or 'slippage' (Reed, 1972) in the relationship between memory 'schemata', producing a specific response-set, a predisposition to interpret the external world in particular ways, related to underlying affective or cognitive factors (Reed, 1972). In short, whilst spontaneous confabulation may reflect persistently disorganized retrieval processes, delusional memory may make manifest an isolated 'slippage' of cognitive 'schemata' and highly organized, overly rigid predispositions.

Acknowledgements

We are grateful to Miss Claire Hook for patiently typing the manuscript. MDK is supported by the West Lambeth Community Care Trust, EMG by the Special Trustees of St Thomas's Hospital, and PDRL by the South East Thames Regional Research Fund (LORS).

Further Reading

Enoch, M.D. and Trethowan, W.H. (1979) *Uncommon Psychiatric Syndromes*, 2nd edn (Bristol: John Wright).
Johnson, Marcia (1988) 'Discriminating the origin of information', in T.F. Oltmann and B.A. Maher (eds), *Delusional Beliefs* (New York: John Wiley).
Johnson, Marcia (1991) 'Reality monitoring: evidence from confabulation in organic brain disease patients' in G.P Prigatano and D.L. Schacter (eds), *Awareness of Deficits in Brain Injury* (New York: Oxford University Press).

References

Andreasen, N.C., Olsen, S.A., Dennert, J.W. and Smith, M.R. (1982) 'Ventricular enlargement in schizophrenia: relationship to positive and negative symptoms', *American Journal of Psychiatry*, 139: 297–302.
Andreasen, N., Nasrallah, H.A., Dunn, V., Olson, S.C., Grove, W.M., Ehrhardt, J.C., Coffman, J.A. and Crossett, J.H.W. (1986) 'Structural abnormalities in the frontal system in schizophrenia: a magnetic resonance imaging study', *Archives of General Psychiatry*, 43: 136–44.
Arnold, S.E., Hyman, B., Hoessen, G. and Damasio, A. (1991) 'Some cytoarchitectural abnormalities of the entorhinal cortex in schizophrenia', *Archives of General Psychiatry*, 48: 625–32.
Baddeley, A.D. and Wilson, B. (1986) 'Amnesia, autobiographical memory, and confabulation', in D.C. Rubin (ed.), *Autobiographical Memory* (Cambridge: Cambridge University Press).
Benson, D.F. and Stuss, D.T. (1990) 'Frontal lobe influences on delusions: a clinical perspective', *Schizophrenia Bulletin*, 16: 403–11.

Benton, A.L. (1968) 'Differential behavioral effects of frontal lobe disease', *Neuropsychologia*, **6**: 53–60.

Berlyne, N. (1972) 'Confabulation', *British Journal of Psychiatry*, **120**: 31–9.

Bogerts, S.B., Meertz, E. and Schonfeldt-Bausch, R. (1985) 'Basal ganglia and limbic system pathology in schizophrenics: a morphometric study of brain volume and shrinkage', *Archives of General Psychiatry*, **42**: 784–91.

Brown, R., Colter, N., Corsellis, J., Crow, T.J., Frith, C., Jagoe, R., Johnstone, E. and Marsh, L. (1986) 'Postmortem evidence of structural brain changes in schizophrenia', *Archives of General Psychiatry*, **43**: 36–42.

Bruton, C.J., Crow, T.J., Frith, C.D., Johnstone, E.C., Owens, D.G.C. and Roberts, G.W. (1990) 'Schizophrenia and the brain: a prospective clinico-neuropathological study', *Psychological Medicine*, **20**: 285–99.

Buchanan, A. (1991) 'Delusional memories: first-rank symptoms?', *British Journal of Psychiatry*, **159**: 472–4.

Butters, N., Salmon, D.P., Munro Cullum, C., Cairns, P., Tröster, A.I. and Jacobs, D. (1988) 'Differentiation of amnesic and demented patients with the Wechsler Memory Scale – Revised', *Clinical Neurologist*, **2**: 133–48.

Calev, A. (1984) 'Recall and recognition in chronic non-demented schizophrenics: use of matched tasks', *Journal of Abnormal Psychology*, **93**: 172–7.

Calev, A., Edelist, S., Kugelmass, S. and Lerer, B. (1991) 'Performance of long-stay schizophrenics on matched verbal and visuo-spatial recall tasks', *Psychological Medicine*, **21**: 655–60.

Clare, A. (1976) *Psychiatry in Dissent: Controversial Issues in Thought and Practice* (London: Tavistock Publications).

Crow, T.J. (1980) 'Molecular pathology of schizophrenia: more than one disease process?', *British Medical Journal*, **280**: 1–9.

Crow, T. and Mitchell, S. (1975) 'Subjective age in chronic schizophrenia: evidence for a subgroup of patients with a defective learning capacity?', *British Journal of Psychiatry*, **126**: 360–3.

Crow, T. and Stevens, M. (1978) 'Age disorientation in chronic schizophrenia: the nature of the cognitive deficit', *British Journal of Psychiatry*, **133**: 137–42.

Crow, T.J., Ball, J., Bloom, S., Brown, R., Bruton, C., Colter, N., Frith, C., Johnstone, E., Owens, D. and Roberts, G. (1989) 'Schizophrenia as an anomaly of development of cerebral asymmetry', *Archives of General Psychiatry*, **42**: 1031–7.

Cutting, J. (1979) 'Memory in functional psychosis', *Journal of Neurology, Neurosurgery, and Psychiatry*, **42**: 1031–7.

Dalla Barba, G. (1993) 'Confabulation: knowledge and recollective experience', *Cognitive Neuropsychology*, **10**: 1–20.

Della Sala, S., Laiacona, M., Spinnler, H. and Trivelli, C. (1993) 'Impaired autobiographical recollection in some frontal patients', *Neuropsychologia*, **31**: 823–40.

Duffy, L. and O'Carroll, R. (1994) 'Memory impairment in schizophrenia – a comparison with that observed in the alcoholic Korsakoff syndrome', *Psychological Medicine*, **24**: 155–65.

Endicott, J., Spitzer, R.C., Fliess, J.L. and Cohen, J. (1976) 'The global assessment scale', *Archives of General Psychiatry*, **33**: 766–71.

Enoch, M.D. and Trethowan, W.H. (1979) *Uncommon Psychiatric Syndromes*, 2nd edn (Bristol: John Wright).

Fish, F. (1967) *Clinical Psychopathology: Signs and Symptoms in Psychiatry* (Bristol: John Wright).

Folstein, M.F., Folstein, S.E. and McHugh, P.R. (1975) 'Mini-mental state: a practical method for grading the cognitive state of patients for the clinician', *Journal of Psychiatric Research*, **12**: 189–98.

Gelder, M., Gath, D. and Mayou, R. (1989) *Oxford Textbook of Psychiatry* (London: Oxford University Press).

Goldberg, T.E., Weinberger, D.R., Berman, K.F., Pliskin, N.H. and Podd, M.H. (1987) 'Further evidence for dementia of the prefrontal type in schizophrenia? A controlled study of teaching the Wisconsin Card Sorting test', *Archives of General Psychiatry*, **44**: 1008–14.

Goldberg, T.E., Torrey, E.F., Gold, J.M., Ragland, J.D., Bigeow, L.B. and Weinberger, D.R. (1993) 'Learning and memory in monozygotic twins discordant for schizophrenia', *Psychological Medicine*, **23**: 71–85.

Jaspers, K. (1913) *General Press, Psychopathology*, trans. J. Hoenig and M.W. Hamilton (Manchester: Manchester University Press, 1963).

Jeste, D. and Lohr, J. (1989) 'Hippocampal pathologic findings in schizophrenia', *Archives of General Psychiatry*, **46**: 1019–24.

Johnstone, E.C., Crow, T.J., Frith, C.D., Husband, J. and Krell, J.L. (1976) 'Cerebral ventricular size and cognitive impairment in chronic schizophrenia', *Lancet*, **2**: 924–6.

Kapur, N. and Coughlan, A.K. (1980) 'Confabulation and frontal lobe dysfunction', *Journal of Neurology, Neurosurgery and Psychiatry*, **43**: 461–3.

Kolb, B. and Whishaw, I.Q. (1983) 'Performance of schizophrenic patients on tests sensitive to left or right frontal, temporal, or parietal function in neurological patients', *Journal of Nervous and Mental Disease*, **171**: 435–43.

Kopelman, M.D. (1987a) 'Amnesia: organic and psychogenic', *British Journal of Psychiatry*, **150**: 428–42.

Kopelman, M.D. (1987b) 'Two types of confabulation', *Journal of Neurology, Neurosurgery and Psychiatry*, **50**: 1482–7.

Kopelman, M.D. (1989) 'Remote and autobiographical memory, temporal context memory, and frontal atrophy in Korsakoff and Alzheimer patients', *Neuropsychologia*, **27**: 437–60.

Kopelman, M.D. (1991) 'Frontal dysfunction and memory deficits in the alcoholic Korsakoff syndrome and Alzheimer-type dementia', *Brain*, **114**: 117–37.

Kopelman, M.D. (1992) 'The "new" and the "old": components of the anterograde and retrograde memory loss in Korsakoff and Alzheimer patients', in L.R. Squire and N. Butters (eds), *The Neuropsychology of Memory* 2nd edn (New York: Guilford).

Kopelman, M.D. (1993) 'The neuropsychology of remote memory', in F. Boller and H. Spinnler (eds), *Handbook of Neuropsychology*, vol. 8 (Amsterdam, Elsevier), pp. 213–36.

Kopelman, M.D. (1994) 'The Autobiographical Memory Interview (AMI) in organic and psychogenic amnesia', *Memory*, **2**: 211–35.

Kopelman, M.D., Wilson, B.A. and Baddeley, A.D (1989) 'The Autobiographical Memory Interview: a new assessment of autobiographical and personal semantic memory in amnesic patients', *Journal of Clinical and Experimental Neuropsychology*, **11**: 724–44.

Kopelman, M.D., Wilson, B.A. and Baddeley, A.D. (1990) *The Autobiographical Memory Interview (Manual)*, (Bury St Edmunds, Suffolk: Thames Valley Test Company).

Korsakoff, S.S. (1889) 'Psychic disorder in conjunction with peripheral neuritis; translated and republished by M. Victor and P.I. Yakovlev (1955) *Neurology*, **5**: 394–406.

Kovelman, J.A. and Schiebel, A.G. (1984) 'A neurohistological correlate of schizophrenia', *Biological Psychiatry*, **19**: 1601–21.

Kraepelin, E. (1910) *Psychiatrie*, 8th edn (Leipzig: Barth).

Leng, N.R.C. and Parkin, A.J. (1988) 'Double dissociation of frontal dysfunction in organic amnesia', *British Journal of Clinical Psychology*, **27**: 359–62.

Lewis, S.W., Ford, R.A., Syed, G.M., Develey, A.M. and Toone, B.K. (1992) 'A controlled study of ^{99m}TcHMPAO single-photon emission imaging in chronic schizophrenia', *Psychological Medicine*, **22**: 27–35.

Liddle, P.F. (1987) 'Schizophrenic syndromes, cognitive performance and neurological dysfunction', *Psychological Medicine*, **17**: 49–57.

Liddle, P.F. and Crow, T.J. (1984) 'Age disorientation in chronic schizophrenia is associated with global intellectual impairments', *British Journal of Psychiatry*, **144**: 193–9.

Liddle, P.F. and Morris, D.L. (1991) 'Schizophrenic syndromes and frontal lobe performance', *British Journal of Psychiatry*, **158**: 340–5.

Liddle, P.F., Friston, K.J., Frith, C.D., Hirsch, S.R., Jones, T. and Frackowiak, R.S.J. (1992) 'Patterns of cerebral blood flow in schizophrenia', *British Journal of Psychiatry*, **160**: 179–86.

Luria, A.R. (1976) *The Neuropsychology of Memory* (New York: John Wiley).

Lynch, G. and Baudry, M. (1988) 'Structure–function relationships in the organization of memory', in M.S. Gazzaniga (ed.), *Perspectives in Memory Research* (Cambridge, Mass.: MIT Press).

McKenna, P., Tamlyn, D., Lund, C., Mortimer, A., Hammond, S. and Baddeley, A.D. (1990) 'Amnesic syndrome in schizophrenia', *Psychological Medicine*, **20**: 967–72.

Miller, E. (1984) 'Verbal fluency as a function of a measure of verbal intelligence and in relation to different types of cerebral pathology', *British Journal of Clinical Psychology*, **23**: 53–7.

Mullen, P.E. (1979) 'The mental state and states of mind', in P. Hill, R. Murray and A. Thorley (eds), *Essentials of Postgraduate Psychiatry* (London: Grune & Stratton).

Nelson, H.E. (1976) 'A modified card-sorting test sensitive to frontal lobe deficit', *Cortex*, **12**: 313–24.

Nelson, H.E. (1982) *The National Adult Reading Test* (Windsor, Berks.: NFER and Nelson).

Newcombe, F. (1969) *Missile Wounds of the Brain* (London: Oxford University Press).

Owens, D.G.C., Johnstone, E.C., Crow, T.J., Frith, C.D., Jagoe, J.R. and Kreel, L. (1985) 'Lateral ventricular size in schizophrenia: relationship to the disease process and its clinical manifestations', *Psychological Medicine*, **15**: 27–41.

Reed, G. (1972) *The Psychology of Anomalous Experience: A Cognitive Approach* (London: Hutchison University Library).

Schneider, K. (1959) *Clinical Psychopathology*, 5th edn, trans. M.W. Hamilton (New York and London: Grune & Stratton).

Shallice, T. and Evans, M.E. (1978) 'The involvement of the frontal lobes in cognitive estimates', *Cortex*, **14**: 294–303.

Shepherd, G.M. (1988) 'A basic circuit of cortical organization', in M.S. Gazzaniga (ed.), *Perspectives in Memory Research* (Cambridge, Mass.: MIT Press).

Shoqeirat, M. and Mayes, A. (1988) 'Spatiotemporal memory and rate of forgetting in acute schizophrenics', *Psychological Medicine*, **18**: 843–53.

Shoqeirat, M.A., Mayes, A., MacDonald, C., Meudell, P. and Pickering, A. (1990) 'Performance on tests sensitive to frontal lobe lesions by patients with organic amnesia: Leng and Parkin revisited', *British Journal of Clinical Psychology*, **29**: 401–8.

Stevens, M. (1979) 'Famous personality test: a test for measuring remote memory', *Bulletin of the British Psychological Society*, **32**: 211.

Stevens, J.R. (1982) 'Neuropathology of schizophrenia', *Archives of General Psychiatry*, **39**: 1131–9.

Stuss, D.T., Alexander, M.P., Liberman, A. and Levine, H. (1978) 'An extraordinary form of confabulation', *Neurology*, **28**: 1166–72.

Tamlyn, D., McKenna, P.J., Mortimer, A.M., Lund, C.E., Hammond, S. and Baddeley, A.D. (1992) 'Memory impairment in schizophrenia: its extent, affiliations and neuropsychological character', *Psychological Medicine*, **22**: 101–15.

Warrington, E.K. (1984) *The Recognition Memory Test* (Windsor, Berks.: NFER and Nelson).

Wechsler, D. (1981) *Wechsler Adult Intelligence Scale – Revised* (London and New York: Psychological Corporation).

Weinberger, D.R., Torrey, E.F., Neophytides, A.N. and Wyatt, R.J. (1979a) 'Structural abnormalities in the cerebral cortex of chronic schizophrenic patients', *Archives of General Psychiatry*, **36**: 935–9.

Weinberger, D.R., Torrey, E.F., Neophytides, A.N. and Wyatt, F.J. (1979b) 'Lateral cerebral ventricular enlargement in chronic schizophrenia', *Archives of General Psychiatry*, **36**: 735–9.

Weinberger, D.R., Berman, K.F. and Zee, R.F. (1986) 'Physiologic dysfunction of dorsolateral prefrontal cortex in schizophrenia. I: Regional cerebral blood flow evidence', *Archives of General Psychiatry*, **43**: 114–24.

Wilson, B., Cockburn, J. and Baddeley (1985) *Rivermead Behavioural Memory Test* (Fareham, Hants.: Thames Valley Test Co.).

Wing, J.K., Cooper, J.E. and Sartorius, N. (1974) *The Measurement and Classification of Psychiatric Symptoms* (London: Cambridge University Press).

Zangwill, O.L. (1953) 'Disorientation for age', *Journal of Mental Science*, **99**: 698–701.

Zola-Morgan, S., Squire, L.R. and Amaral, D.G. (1986) 'Human amnesia and the medial temporal region: enduring memory impairment following a bilateral lesion limited to field CA1 of the hippocampus', *Journal of Neuroscience*, **6**: 2950–67.

Part III Where Was I?
Imagination and Spatial Processing

Introduction

When you remember a specific event (say a birthday party, holiday or school exam), an image comes readily to mind. Usually it is quite specific, although attempts to interrogate it closely might not always work (what colour was the birthday cake; how many pieces could it be cut into without crumbling?). Visual–imagistic processes are closely associated with a host of memory skills, including knowing one's way around a particular venue or recognizing people, things and places appropriately. But exactly how are visual and spatial processing of the environment, visuo–spatial manipulations 'in the head', and memories of visual events or objects related? Here evidence from specific neuropsychological case studies has been useful. The three studies presented reflect some ongoing aspects of the debate concerning this relationship. They do not encompass the field, which is large, and growing. Related questions arise in considering patients labelled *agnosic*, where problems in identifying visually presented material offer intriguing glimpses of how knowledge of aspects of objects in the world is organized in intact brains, and how this relates to the specifically visual aspects of their analysis (see Barry and McHattie, this volume).

A distinction to bear in mind when reading these chapters is that vision can deliver two sorts of information: location ('where' it happened) and identity ('what' occurred). Neuroanatomical research suggests that two distinct cortical pathways subserve these functions from initial registration of visual inputs in the occipital regions. The dorsal pathway (implicating parietal structures) is the 'where' path, while the ventral pathway (involving temporal structures) are more closely implicated in 'what' decisions (Mishkin et al., 1983).

The three patients described here have very different patterns of brain damage and impairment. The first, LD, is a very well-documented case of postencephalitic amnesia, similar in aetiology to Clive Wearing (Wilson and Wearing, this volume). LD's amnesia is less severe than Clive's, but she has some residual, hard-to-overcome visual identification problems. Butters et al. claim that LD's difficulties suggest that autobiographical memories (specific memories of birthday parties, for instance) are linked to effective visual memories quite directly. This is a claim from *association* of deficits: LD's autobiographical memory had been devastated, and she also had difficulties in manipulating visual stimuli. This suggests that her access to knowledge of what things look like was poor – whether this was from the external stimulus or from the demands of the explicit memory task. Thus they argue that memory for past episodes can be related to the ability to identify visually presented material: in the authors' paraphrase of another case (Ogden, 1993) 'the depletion of visual memories' occurs in such cases.

This interpretation should be taken with caution. Visual object recognition disorders (visual agnosias) do not lead to autobiographical memory problems directly. Butters et al.

emphasize that the recollection of episodes may be multiply determined. In LD, as well as damage to the inferior temporal and subcortical sites relevant directly to her amnesia, she had more extensive damage to the right temporal lobe, which might account for the particularities of her visual impairments.

In LD there was evidence for normal priming (implicit memory) for objects, including famous faces, which was absent in her explicit memory for such material. This is now a well-established finding in a variety of patients whose loss of face recognition ability has an 'amnesic' tinge (for example, De Haan et al., 1987). Butters et al. consider this achievement distinct from LD's other interesting spared ability; to perform some 'direct' memory tasks with visual material. This included completing a first-name cue to a famous face with the correct last name. But it is also possible that the implicit, priming tasks and the cue-completion type of task utilize similar spared processes. Such spared processes must be those resistant to damage by such extensive lesions: these could be distinct memory stores as suggested by Butters et al. However, from a different perspective, implicit tasks make use of better-maintained associations (they are weighted more strongly) in a distributed model of memory (Farah, 1994).

Morris and Morton's case MG had some IQ-performance task problems following a *left*-hemisphere stroke. This lesion side had been implicated by previous neuropsychological studies as important for mental transformations (Farah, 1988), despite the common assumption that only right-hemisphere functions are important for visuo-spatial processing.

MG's pattern of spared and impaired abilities could therefore be used to examine different theories concerning the relationship between such visuo-spatial transformation processes (such as generating and rotating visual images on command) and working and list memory for visual and visuo-spatial material. How intimately are these processes connected? Earlier case studies suggested that, while patients could be found with distinct impairments in visuo-spatial working memory and in imagery tasks, one particular task – that of mental rotation or transformation of objects – seemed to link the two. This task needed resources from both, since patients with a mental-rotation deficit had *either* a visuo-spatial working memory problem *or* an imagery generation problem. The detailed investigation of MG suggests that this need not be so. MG could not do mental rotation tasks but seemed relatively unimpaired both on tasks of visuo-spatial working memory and on other tasks of visual imagery. This might mean that correlations between mental transformation difficulty and other tasks in patients might have reflected anatomical rather than functional associations. We could also take this view of MG's other difficulty, that of simply memorizing (rather than manipulating) complex visual material (visual long term memory). The storage difficulty might not be functionally related to MG's spatial manipulation problems but rather to some subcortical damage; MRI scans indicated some damage to the posterior hippocampus on the left side which could be related to this problem, specifically.

With Mr Smith, who had some apparent narrowing of the right carotid artery, which could affect both parietal and temporal areas on that side, Hanley and Davies introduce the topic of topographic amnesia: loss of knowledge of places. Once more, the interesting question for psychologists is: how are difficulties in finding one's way around related to other difficulties, for instance, in recognizing places or in knowledge of maps? Once more, single case studies have been reported that show that topographic memory is not unitary, but comprises separately damageable components. The authors show how Mr

Smith's problems are not to do with recognizing places or objects, but with managing the spatial components of finding his way around. In this study, too, we can see one nice effect of such detailed study. Once the problem was delineated in this way, Hanley and Davies were more confident in their suggestions to Mr Smith on managing his difficulties by introducing useful 'landmarks', like a gate to the stairs.

Overall, these different explorations of visuo-spatial disorder show how quite distinct components of impairment can be drawn out: visuo-spatial processes ramify deeply into memory skills (their visual origin is not lost) but in highly specific ways.

References

De Haan, E.H.F., Young, A.W. and Newcombe, F. (1987) 'Face recognition without awareness', *Cognitive Neuropsychology*, 4: 385–415.

Farah, M. (1988) 'Is visual imagery really visual? Overlooked evidence from neuropsychology', *Psychological Review*, 95: 307–17.

Farah, M. (1994) 'Neuropsychological inference with an interactive brain: a critique of the "locality" assumption', *Brain and Behavioral Science*, 17: 43–104.

Mishkin, M., Ungerleider, L.G., and Macko, K.A. (1983) 'Object vision and spatial vision: two cortical pathways', *Trends in Neurosciences*, 6: 414–17.

Ogden, J.A. (1993) 'Visual object agnosia, prosopagnosia, achromatopsia, loss of visual imagery, and autobiographical amnesia following recovery from cortical blindness: Case MH', *Neuropsychologia*, 31: 571–89.

12 My Own Remembered Past: Insights into the Structure and Processes of Retrograde Amnesia from a Patient with Visual Access Problems Subsequent to Encephalitis

Nelson Butters, Margaret G. O'Connor and Mieke Verfaellie

Single case studies enhance our understanding of amnesia by allowing detailed investigations of the relationship between specific cognitive processes. Furthermore, they provide a forum for the description of patients with unique neuropsychological profiles. Several recent articles described one such patient, a young woman (LD) who demonstrated an unusual dissociation between anterograde and retrograde memory (O'Connor et al., 1992) and who also showed disproportionate impairment on tasks of nonverbal learning (Eslinger et al., 1993). These investigations underscored the neuroanatomic substrates of retrograde and nonverbal/anterograde memory. In this chapter these studies will be reviewed and further investigations of LD's amnesia will be presented using tasks of perceptual priming.

Case Description

At age 17 LD suffered an episode of encephalitis that began with 'flu-like symptoms accompanied by headaches, photophobia and fever. Initial clinical presentation was also noteworthy for aphasia, memory deficits and confusion. Over the course of several weeks, LD became increasingly alert but there was residual evidence of amnesia and visual perceptual problems. Following extensive rehabilitation she was discharged home, at which time she continued to demonstrate memory deficits with disproportionate difficulties in the retrieval of autobiographical events predating the onset of her illness. She was unable to recognize close friends, family members, her house and many of her belongings.

During the following year LD received cognitive remediation at home and as an outpatient at a local rehabilitation facility. Her programme consisted of speech therapy, occupational therapy and vocational training. She received intensive instruction for work as a cafeteria aide. She learned slowly, but with much repetition, eventually performed well in this position. LD's supportive family and her personal resilience facilitated her transition to an adaptive work and social life. However, to this day neuropsychological deficits restrict her range of activities. Facial recognition problems affect old and new relationships and nonverbal learning deficits limit travel in unfamiliar places. LD has adjusted to the consequences of her profound retrograde amnesia, but at times this too is the source of considerable distress and anxiety.

LD's neuropsychological profile has been described in previous publications (O'Connor et al., 1992; Eslinger et al., 1993) and will be reviewed in abbreviated form here (see table 12.1). Performance on tests of general intelligence was in the low average range (FSIQ = 82), somewhat reduced relative to estimated premorbid abilities. Basic attention, reasoning, judgement, language and motor functions were intact. Verbal learning was mildly to moderately impaired, while memory for nonverbal material was severely impaired. LD demonstrated variable perceptual abilities. On most tests of perception, she performed normally; on some (such as facial discrimination) there was evidence of mild impairment. There was evidence of a moderate-level visual object agnosia affecting performance on visual confrontation naming tasks, especially when the stimuli consisted of historic monuments, birds and insects. LD also reported impaired imaging abilities; she could not generate a visual image of any object or person. She could not draw an elephant, a house, a flower or a 3D box from memory even though copying skills were intact (figures 12.1 and 12.2); nor could she recognize the outline of the United States.

Further evaluation of LD's visual object agnosia and her perceptual abilities was conducted with tests from the Visual Object and Space Perception Battery (Warrington and James, 1991). LD performed normally on a variety of tests of spatial perception (for example, single point localization and position discrimination). Performance was also normal on a task requiring perceptual identification of visually degraded letters. Further proficiency was noted on a task requiring LD to select silhouettes of real objects from an array that included nonsense objects as distractor stimuli. In contrast, LD failed two subtests requiring verbal identification of common objects that were partially rotated and presented from unusual views (silhouettes and progressive silhouettes). LD's ability to recognize objects on the object-decision subtest in contrast with her failure to verbally identify objects on the silhouettes subtests suggested that she might have an impairment in the access or activation of visual representations although underlying object representations were preserved.

MRI studies, as reviewed in previous publications (O'Connor et al., 1992; Eslinger et al., 1993), revealed a large lesion in the right hemisphere affecting the entire right temporal lobe with the exception of posterior regions of the superior temporal gyrus. The right hemisphere lesion also included the posterior ventromedial frontal lobe, part of the inferior parietal lobule and lateral occipital areas. The left hemisphere lesion was limited to the insula, parahippocampal gyrus and posterior ventromedial frontal lobe.

Table 12.1 Patient LD's neuropsychological profile

General intelligence

Verbal IQ	88
Performance IQ	79
Full Scale IQ	82
National Adult Reading Test	99

Attention

Digits forward	7–8
Digits backward	4
Word list generation (F,A,S)	90th percentile
Trail-making test (Part B)	65 seconds
Wisconsin card-sorting test	5 sorts, 64 cards

Memory

Wechsler Memory Scale – Revised

Attention index	97
Memory index	84
Verbal memory index	91
Visual memory index	72
Delayed memory index	67
Logical memory I	41st percentile
Logical memory II	31st percentile
Visual reproduction I	19th percentile
Visual reproduction II	7th percentile

Recognition Memory Test

Verbal recognition	43/50 (low average)
Facial recognition	29/50 (below average)

Language

Spontaneous speech	WNL
Boston naming test	35/60 (below average)

Categorical Naming Test

Buildings	1/10
Utensils/tools	10/10
Birds/insects	1/10
Animals	6/10
Vegetables	8/10
Actions	8/10
Clothing	9/10
Body parts	10/10
Colour naming	10/10
Repetition (BDAE)	WNL
Comprehension (BDAE)	WNL
Reading (WRAT)	42nd percentile
Spelling (WRAT)	32nd percentile

Visuo-spatial skills

Letter cancellation	WNL
Benton line-orientation test	20/30 (low average)
Hooper visual organization	23/30 (WNL)
Benton facial recognition	39/54 (borderline impairment)

The Visual Object and Space Perception Battery

Object perception

Screening test	WNL
Incomplete letters	WNL
Silhouettes	Impaired
Object decision	WNL
Progressive silhouettes	Impaired

Space perception

Dot counting	WNL
Position discrimination	WNL
Number location	WNL
Cube analysis	WNL

Figure 12.1   Patient LD's drawing of a house; *left*: to copy; *right*: from memory

Explicit Memory Studies

LD's unusual pattern of mnemonic deficits has been documented in several single-case studies. Eslinger and colleagues provided a detailed analysis of LD's nonverbal amnesia (Eslinger et al., 1993) as well as a description of the MRI findings showing disproportionate lesion in the right hemisphere. There was evidence of a material-specific pattern of memory loss characterized by greater impairment on tasks of nonverbal memory. This was seen as similar, but more severe, than patients who undergo right temporal lobe surgery for treatment of intractible epilepsy (Kimura, 1963; Smith and Milner, 1981). Of additional importance, this investigation underscored the fact that herpes simplex encephalitis is often associated with asymmetric lesions that have differential effects on cognition, a fact often overlooked in group studies of patients with encephalitis (but see Wilson and Weaving, this volume).

O'Connor and associates examined the dissociation between new learning (that is, anterograde memory) and memory for events predating the onset of amnesia (retrograde memory) with patient LD (O'Connor et al., 1992). Over the past decade a consensus has emerged that anterograde and retrograde memory abilities are functionally independent (Butters et al., 1984; Squire et al., 1989), but this has been documented in relatively few

Figure 12.2   Patient LD's drawing of an elephant; *left*: to copy; *right*: from memory

clinical reports (see Kapur, 1993). The contrast between preservation of new verbal learning and remote memory impairment in patient LD was seen as further proof of a dissociation between anterograde and retrograde memory.

LD's remote memory was evaluated with various tests of autobiographical memory and public events. Her recollection of personal experiences from childhood years was devastated: she was unable to produce *any* memory for personal events in response to verbal cues or upon directed questioning. Interestingly, LD demonstrated better recall of factually based information (for example, the name of her first-grade teacher; the fact that she owned a poodle). However, she was unable to elaborate upon these facts with experiential information. LD's nonverbal memory and visual imaging problems were examined in relation to her pronounced episodic memory impairment. It was hypothesized that her significant imaging deficit augmented an impairment in episodic memory because visual images provide an organizational framework for retrieval of episodic/ experiential information. More recently, Ogden (Ogden, 1993) described a patient (MH) with diminished recall of autobiographical events in conjunction with impoverished visual imaging abilities. Ogden theorized that MH's autobiographical impairment was based on the depletion of visual memories. While these patients (MH and LD) demonstrate different patterns of neural damage and some differences on neuropsychological examination (MH demonstrated more severe agnosia and evidence of achromatopsia), they both showed deficits implicating a significant relationship between visual imagery and episodic memory.

LD's selective amnesia for episodically-based experiences indicates that retrograde memory is not a unitary process but that it is composed of functionally independent subprocesses. Other studies have reported a dissociation between remote memory processes. Stuss and Guzman (1988) described a patient with preferential recall of historical events relative to autobiographical information. Tulving and his colleagues reported a dissociation between personal and nonpersonal memories in a patient who suffered a closed head injury (Tulving et al., 1988). Warrington and McCarthy (1988) referred to the 'fractionation' of factually based versus cognitively mediated aspects of retrograde memory. Their patient (RFR) performed well on tasks measuring cued recall of famous names, discrimination of famous from nonfamous photographs, and identification of famous photographs with first-name cues. These data suggested preservation of factual elements of remote memory. In contrast, RFR was unable to recall, recognize or temporally order photographs of famous individuals, indicating deficits in cognitively mediated aspects of remote memory.

A similar set of tasks was administered to LD with comparable results: she was proficient on a fame judgement task (19/24 correct) and on tasks requiring identification of photographs with first name cues (9/12). In stark contrast, she performed abysmally on tasks of facial recognition (2/12) and temporal ordering of famous photographs (chance performance). These data were consistent with Warrington and McCarthy's proposal that remote memory could indeed be 'fractionated' according to factually based versus cognitively mediated subsystems.

Investigations of patient LD also provided information relevant to the neural underpinnings of amnesia. LD's preserved verbal learning was attributed to sparing of the left hippocampus. Damage to the right hippocampus was thought to be responsible for her inability to acquire new nonverbal information. Her retrograde amnesia was viewed as secondary to damage to brain areas beyond the hippocampus, namely neocortical areas in the right temporal lobe (Eslinger et al., 1993). Damage to this area might interfere with access to visual representations, thereby compromising LD's ability to imagine visual information as well as to retrieve it from memory. Given the significance of visual information in the retrieval of multimodal memories, this could account for the severity of her retrograde amnesia.

Studies of Implicit Memory

More recent work focused on the relationship between LD's neuropsychological deficits and her performance on tasks of implicit memory. Memory theorists such as Roediger and Blaxton (Blaxton, 1989; Roediger and Blaxton, 1987) and Keane and Gabrieli (Keane et al., 1991) propose that some aspects of implicit memory are perceptually mediated while others are conceptually based. Perceptual priming tasks, such as perceptual identification and word-stem completion rely on the reinstatement of the perceptual features of a stimulus at time of testing. In contrast, conceptual priming tasks, such as category exemplar production, are mediated by semantic aspects of a stimulus.

A number of studies suggest a dissociation between perceptual and conceptually based priming. There is evidence that patients with Alzheimer's disease demonstrate normal perceptual priming and impaired conceptual priming (Gabrieli et al., 1993; Keane et al., 1991). Furthermore, two separate case study reports of patients with focal posterior lesions demonstrate the reverse pattern: impaired perceptual priming and intact conceptual priming (Keane et al., 1993; Grosse et al., 1992). One of these patients (Keane et al., 1992) had bilateral lesions, whereas in the other (Grosse et al., 1992), the lesion was restricted to the right hemisphere. These findings are consistent with results of recent PET studies (Squire et al., 1992) which also point to the role of the right medial extrastriate cortex in the mediation of perceptual priming.

Given LD's visual agnosia and impaired imaging abilities, as well as the location of her lesion, we were particularly interested in her performance on perceptual priming tasks. In a first study, we examined perceptually based priming in LD using a perceptual-identification task and a stem–completion task, similar to those used in the previously mentioned case reports. Poor performance on tasks of perceptual priming would be expected if LD, like the patients described previously, had degraded visual representations of stored material. However, based on LD's performance on a variety of visual perceptual tests, we favoured the hypothesis that LD's visual perceptual and imagery problems were due not to a disruption in visual representations *per se*, but rather, that they reflected deficient access and manipulation of visual representations. Consequently, we predicted that LD might demonstrate intact perceptual priming.

In the *perceptual-identification task*, LD studied a list of words presented on a computer screen. Subsequently, a subgroup of these words, together with words not previously presented, were flashed on the computer screen very briefly and LD was asked to identify them. Priming was indicated by the enhanced identification of previously presented (studied) words relative to new (nonstudied) words. LD's baseline performance, as reflected in her ability to identify nonstudied words, was equivalent to that of control subjects. More importantly, her identification of previously presented words was also at a level commensurate with normal control subjects, indicating normal perceptual priming.

In the *word-stem completion task*, LD was again asked to study a list of visually presented words. Subsequently, she was asked to complete word stems (that is, the initial three letters of a word) with the first word that came to mind. Some of these stems corresponded to words that had earlier been studied, whereas other stems corresponded to novel, not previously studied words. This latter condition provided a baseline measure of stem completion. Priming was then measured as the difference in the number of target words generated in the primed compared to the baseline condition. Again, LD demonstrated normal priming in this task.

LD's normal performance on these tasks indicates preservation of processes that support perceptual priming in the verbal domain and suggests that she has intact visual representations of words. However, since her impaired perceptual and imaging abilities affect primarily nonverbal stimuli, a question remained regarding her ability to prime for nonverbal materials. One finding which speaks to this issue concerns LD's performance on a facial learning task (Tranel and Damasio, 1985). In this task LD demonstrated covert recognition of faces as indicated by higher galvanic skin responses to familiar than to unknown faces. This finding supports the idea that the representation of nonverbal/

visual information is preserved for LD and suggests that she may demonstrate normal priming of nonverbal stimuli as well.

To examine LD's perceptual priming for nonverbal stimuli in the context of a traditional behavioural paradigm, we administered a picture-clarification task previously used to study amnesic patients (Cermak et al., 1993). In this task, subjects are presented with degraded pictures which can be clarified by pressing a key on the computer which gradually eliminates visual noise. The subjects continue to press the key until the picture becomes sufficiently clear to allow identification. Later, during a test phase, subjects again clarify degraded pictures until they can identify them. Some pictures are identical to those previously presented, some share the same name but are not identical to previously presented pictures, and some are new. In normal subjects, performance on this task is mediated by memory for the perceptual characteristics of the pictures, as evidenced by the fact that identical pictures are identified faster than same-name pictures, which in turn are identified faster than new pictures (Jacoby et al., 1984). LD demonstrated an identical pattern of performance, suggesting that her priming for nonverbal materials was also intact.

The current data are reminiscent of a study by Schacter and colleagues (Schacter et al., 1993) who described a patient (JP) with word-meaning deafness who was capable of auditory priming. The fact that JP showed intact auditory priming despite impaired comprehension of word meaning suggests that auditory priming depends on the presemantic representation of words. LD's performance in the visual domain represents a pattern of performance identical to that of JP in the auditory domain. In this context, LD's proficiency on perceptual priming paradigms in the face of her visual agnosia provides further support for the notion that perceptual priming may proceed independently of processes that provide semantic (meaning-based) information to perceptual systems.

Finally, LD's implicit memory performance also has important implications for our understanding of the neuroanatomical underpinnings of perceptually based priming. First, her performance reinforces a point made clear by numerous studies of amnesic patients, that implicit memory is not dependent on the same neuroanatomical systems that support explicit memory. Like amnesic patients, LD showed significant compromise of the limbic system, yet her implicit memory performance was intact. More importantly, in comparison to patients with impaired perceptual priming (Grosse et al., 1992; Keane et al., 1992) her lesion was more anterior in the right hemisphere. Her performance, therefore, reinforces the view that intact perceptual priming may critically depend on preservation of occipital areas in the right hemisphere.

Summary

Ongoing investigations of LD's explicit and implicit memory enhance our understanding of the psychological parameters and neural underpinnings of mnemonic processes. Her performance on tasks of explicit memory revealed a profound loss of memory for information predating the onset of her encephalitis. The discrepancy between her severe retrograde amnesia and her mild to moderate anterograde amnesia was seen as evidence that these processes were psychologically and neuroanatomically separate. Closer scrutiny of her retrograde memory revealed further dissociations. LD could recall factually based information from the past but she could not provide any experiential information related to these facts. This disparity was also apparent in the replication of a study by Warrington and McCarthy (1988) investigating cognitive/mediational versus factually based features of remote memory. In other investigations the relationship between LD's visual agnosia, visual imaging deficits and her RA was examined. The proposal was advanced that her RA was exacerbated by her inability to generate visual images as cues for the retrieval of remote events.

A review of LD's performance on tasks of implicit memory documented a consistent pattern of intact priming in both verbal and nonverbal domains. This finding is consistent with the notion that LD has intact representations of visual information and that her inability to recognize visual objects and to generate visual images are secondary to a deficit in access to these representations. Furthermore, it provides support for Schacter's argument that perceptually based priming operates at a presemantic level (Schacter et al., 1993). Finally, LD's proficiency on tasks of perceptual priming is supportive of other studies suggesting that perceptual priming is reliant on brain regions within the occipital lobe (Grosse et al., 1992; Keane et al., 1992; Squire et al., 1992).

Acknowledgements

This report is funded in part by NINCDS program project grant NS 26985, funds from the Department of Veterans Affairs Medical Research Service, and by NIAAA grant AA-00187. The authors express their appreciation to Dr Margaret Keane for editorial comments.

Further Reading

Farah, M. (1990) *Visual Agnosia: Disorders of Recognition and What They Tell Us About Normal Vision* (Cambridge, Mass.: MIT Press).

Kopelman, M. (1993) 'Neuropsychology of remote memory', in F. Boller and J. Grafman (eds), *Handbook of Neuropsychology* (Amsterdam: Elsevier).

Schacter, D.L., Chiu, P.C. and Oschner, K.N. (1993) 'Implicit memory: a selective review', *Annual Review of Neuroscience*, **16**: 159–82.

References

Blaxton, T. (1989) 'Investigating dissociations among memory measures: support for a transfer-appropriate processing framework', *Journal of Experimental Psychology: Learning, Memory, and Cognition*, **15**(4): 657–68.

Butters, N., Miliotis, P., Albert, M. and Sax, D. (1984) 'Memory assessment: evidence of the heterogeneity of amnesic symptoms', *Advances in Clinical Neuropsychology*, **1**: 127–59.

Cermak, L.S., Verfaellie, M., Letourneau, L. and Jacoby, L.L. (1993) 'Episodic effects on picture identification for alcoholic Korsakoff patients', *Brain and Cognition*, **22**: 85–97.

Eslinger, P.J., Damasio, H., Damasio, A.R. and Butters, N. (1993) 'Nonverbal amnesia and asymmetric cerebral lesions following encephalitis', *Brain and Cognition*, **21**: 140–52.

Gabrieli, J.D.E., Keane, M.M., Stranger, B.Z., Kjelgaard, M.M., Corkin, S. and Growdon, J.H. (1993) 'Dissociations among structural-perceptual, lexical-semantic, and event-fact memory systems in amnesic, Alzheimer's , and normal-control subjects', *Cortex*, forthcoming.

Grosse, D.A., Gabrieli, J.D.E. and Reminger, S.L. (1992) 'Case-study evidence for a critical and specific right occipital lobe contribution to perceptual identification repetition-priming', *Society for Neuroscience Abstracts*, 18: 1213.

Jacoby, L.L., Baker, J.G. and Brooks, L.R. (1984) 'Episodic effects on picture identification: implications for theories of concept learning and theories of memory', *Journal of Experimental Psychology: Learning, Memory and Cognition*, 15: 275–81.

Kapur, N. (1993) 'Focal retrograde amnesia in neurological disease: a critical review', *Cortex*, 29: 217–34.

Keane, M.M., Clark, H. and Corkin, S. (1992) 'Impaired perceptual priming and intact conceptual priming in a patient with bilateral posterior cerebral lesions', *Society for Neuroscience Abstracts*, 18: 386.

Keane, M.M., Gabrieli, J.D.E., Fennema, A.C., Growdon, J.H. and Corkin, S. (1991) 'Evidence for a dissociation between perceptual and conceptual priming in Alzheimer's disease', *Behavioral Neuroscience*, 105(2): 326–42.

Kimura, D. (1963) 'Right temporal lobe damage', *Archives of Neurology*, 8: 264–71.

O'Connor, M.G., Butters, N., Miliotis, P., Eslinger, P.J. and Cermak, L. (1992) 'The dissociation of anterograde and retrograde amnesia in a patient with herpes encephalitis', *Journal of Clinical and Experimental Neuropsychology*, 14(2): 159–78.

Ogden, J.A. (1993) 'Visual object agnosia, prosopagnosia, achromatopsia, loss of visual imagery, and autobiographical amnesia following recovery from cortical blindness: case MH, *Neuropsychologia*, 31(6): 571–89.

Roediger, H.L. and Blaxton, T.A. (1987) 'Retrieval modes produce dissociations in memory for surface information', in D.S. Gorfein and R.R. Hoffman (eds), *Memory and Learning: The Ebbinghaus Centennial Conference* (Hillsdale, N.J.: Lawrence Erlbaum Associates).

Schacter, D.L., McGlynn, S.M., Milberg, W.P. and Church, B.A. (1993) 'Spared priming despite impaired comprehension: implicit memory in a case of word-meaning deafness', *Neuropsychology*, 7(2): 107–18.

Smith, M.L. and Milner, B. (1981) 'The role of the right hippocampus in the recall of spatial location', *Neuropsychologia*, 19: 781–93.

Squire, L.R., Haist, F. and Shimamura, A.P. (1989) 'The neurology of memory: quantitative assessment of retrograde amnesia in two groups of amnesic patients', *Journal of Neurosciences*, 9(3): 828–39.

Squire, L.R., Ojemann, J.G., Miezin, F.M., Petersen, S.E., Videen, T.O. and Raichle, M.E. (1992) 'Activation of the hippocampus in normal humans: a functional anatomical study of memory', *Proceedings of the National Academy of Science*, 89: 1837–41.

Stuss, D.T. and Guzman, D.A. (1988) 'Severe remote memory loss with minimal anterograde amnesia: a clinical note', *Brain and Cognition*, 8: 21–30.

Tranel, D. and Damasio, A.R. (1985) 'Knowledge without awareness: an autonomic index of facial recognition by prosopagnosics', *Science*, 228: 1453–4.

Tulving, E., Schacter, D., McLachlan, D. and Moscovitch, M. (1988) 'Priming of semantic autobiographical knowledge: a case study of retrograde amnesia', *Brain and Cognition*, 8: 3–20.

Warrington, E.K. and James, M. (1991) *The Visual Object and Space Perception Battery* (Bury St Edmunds: Thames Valley Test Company).

Warrington, E.K. and McCarthy, R.A. (1988) 'The fractionation of retrograde amnesia', *Brain and Cognition*, 7: 184–200.

13 Not Knowing Which Way to Turn: a Specific Image Transformation Impairment Dissociated from Working Memory Functioning

Robin G. Morris and Nick Morton

Introduction

A key feature of human activity is ability to hold and manipulate information whilst performing a task. This ability underpins a number of mental activities, ranging from keeping track of a conversation between several people, remembering a telephone number and navigating through a novel environment with the aid of a map. The term 'working memory' has been given to the cognitive systems that are responsible for these activities. This must function rather like the scratchpad of a data analysis programme, keeping information actively in mind whilst it is processed, perhaps to be discarded or stored in long-term memory for later use. In humans, the working memory system may be seen as a set of interlocking subsystems each specializing in a particular form of activity or storage (Barnard, 1985; Moscovitch, 1992).

One of the more influential models of working memory has been developed by Baddeley and colleagues (1986; 1992). They postulate a system that co-ordinates mental activity, termed the Central Executive System (CES), supported by a number of slave storage systems. The two principal memory subsystems are the Articulatory Loop System (ALS) and the Visuo-spatial Scratchpad (VSSP). The ALS stores verbal material in a temporary fashion and, in turn, divides into two functional parts, a passive phonological store and a rehearsal mechanism, the articulatory loop which recycles verbal material, thus helping to retain it in memory (see Introduction of Ch. 2 in this volume). The VSSP retains visuo-spatial material in working memory (Phillips, 1983; Logie, 1989; see also Chapter 14).

Although incorporated into the Working Memory Model (Baddeley, 1992), the VSSP can be considered part of a wider system responsible for processing higher level vision (Kosslyn et al., 1990; Kosslyn, 1991; Morris and Morton, in press). The case MG,

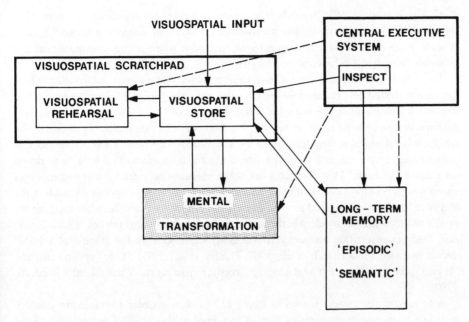

Figure 13.1 The model of high visual processing used in the current study
Note: The shaded region represents the cognitive process found to be impaired in MG.

presented below, whose VSSP was studied extensively, illustrates this added level of complexity. As we shall show, MG has a specific deficit in the transformation of mental imagery. To study her deficit in more detail a componential analysis was used that divided perceptual processes into certain key components, as outlined by Farah (1984) and Kosslyn (1991; Kosslyn et al., 1990). These are incorporated into the summary model shown in figure 13.1, which emphasizes the central role that the CES has in co-ordinating the activity of the different components of the system. Briefly, the input to high-level visual processing is via a visual buffer, the product of low-level vision, functionally equivalent to the VSSP. There is substantial evidence that the VSSP comprises separate visual and spatial components, as indicated by the finding that specifically visual tasks interfere with the temporary storage of visual information whilst spatial tasks interfere with storage of spatial information (Baddeley and Lieberman, 1980; Logie, 1986; Logie and Marchetti, 1991). Maintenance of material may further involve a combination of passive storage and active rehearsal of information (Logie and Marchetti, 1991). Stored material can then be transformed, as when a person rotates a 'mental image' to decide whether it matches the shape or form of another (Shepard and Metzler, 1971). Image transformation is thought to be supported by a number of subcomponents whose principal task is to maintain the integrity of the image whilst transforming it into a different shape (Kosslyn, 1991).

A feature of the computational model of high-level vision proposed by Kosslyn (1991; Kosslyn et al., 1990) is that the mechanism responsible for storing material is separate from those that process it. This contrasts with a more parsimonious approach in which the two types of operation are integrated utilizing the same cognitive modules (Baddeley,

1992; Craik et al., 1990). Separable processes, however, are indicated in figure 13.1, supported by earlier formulations by Kosslyn (1980), who suggests a specific 'rotate' module to execute mental transformations, and also more recent computational approaches (Kosslyn, 1991; Kosslyn et al., 1990).

The VSSP also interacts with a long-term memory system, with information which can be transferred between the two systems. For example, consider a person who is asked to combine the image of two triangles to form the Star of David and report the outcome, perhaps noticing the hexagon in the middle. According to the model, the image of the triangles is taken from long-term memory and brought into the VSSP. The image is manipulated, inspected, and the result stored in long-term memory, able to be retrieved on a future occasion. This illustrates two other phenomena: retrieval and inspection of visual imagery. Inspection can involve a series of different mental operations, such as the ability to 'zoom in' on isolated parts of an imaged pattern; for example, when imaging the profile of an animal to decide whether it has a long or short tail (Holyoak, 1977). Single case studies suggest that imagery retrieval deficits can occur in the absense of a VSSP deficit and vice versa (Farah et al., 1988; Hanley et al., 1991). This suggests that the 'inspect' process can access visual imagery directly, bypassing the VSSP (see also Riddoch, 1990).

A feature of the system shown in figure 13.1 is that in order to transform imagery retrieved from long-term memory it must by stored in the VSSP. Currently, this is an area that has not been investigated fully, but it leads to the prediction that tasks which interfere selectively with the functioning of the VSSP will also prevent the subsequent transformation of retrieved imagery. Indeed, Logie (1986) found that a pegword mnemonic task, which involves retrieving and combining mental images, and thus mental transformation, tends to be interfered with more substantially by specifically visual tasks. Likewise, in the spatial domain, Baddeley and Lieberman (1980) found that use of the method of loci in recall, which would also require mental transformation, was severely disrupted by the subject being asked to concurrently track a moving target.

At each level in the system there appears to be separable visual and spatial components. The functional neuroanatomy of higher-level vision supports this distinction, with well-documented evidence of two visuo-perceptual pathways. The first is a ventral or occipito-temporal pathway that specializes in object perception; the second is a dorsal or occipito-parietal pathway concerned with spatial perception, including encoding the spatial relations between parts of objects (Mishkin et al., 1983; Ungerlieder and Mishkin, 1983) (see figure 13.2). In non-human primates, lesions of the ventral system produce a severe impairment in discriminating between forms, patterns and objects (Gross, 1973; Pohl, 1973). Dorsal lesions within the posterior parietal regions produce an impairment in the ability to determine the spatial relations between objects, and neurones within this pathway are sensitive to the motion and position of a stimulus (Desimone et al., 1984; Mountcastle et al., 1981).

These neurological distinctions are supported by the cognitive functioning of humans with discrete neurological lesions. Patients with visual agnosia have difficulty identifying objects, such as familiar faces, but have no difficulty reaching for them or approaching them (Farah, 1988). In LH, studied by Farah et al. (1988) the deficit extends to the retrieval of visual imagery; he was unable to identify the colour of objects, to compare the size of similar sized objects or to judge the size of animal parts. Conversely, there are

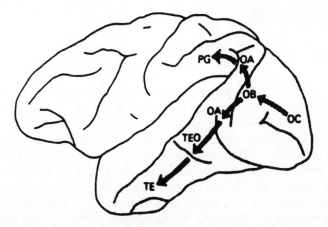

Figure 13.2   Ventral and dorsal systems in the primate brain
Note: Arrows illustrate two cortical visual pathways, each beginning in primary visual cortex (area OC), diverging within prestriate cortex (areas OB and OA), and then passing either ventrally into the inferior temporal cortex (areas TEO and TE) or dorsally into the inferior parietal cortex (area PG). The ventral pathway is responsible for object vision and the dorsal pathway for spatial vision.
Source: Mishkin et al. (1983)

patients with spatial deficits, for example those who have difficulty in locating objects in space (De Renzi, 1982; Levine, 1982, and Hanley and Davies, ch. 14 in this volume). Levine et al. (1985) report a patient who had difficulties recognizing objects and a severe impairment in generating visual imagery, such as imaging faces or animals. In contrast, he had no difficulty reaching for objects and his retrieval of spatial information was excellent, with detailed and accurate descriptions of routes round his city. Another patient could identify common objects with ease and describe the appearance of animals, but could not reach accurately for objects, even those he had identified, orientate himself around his own house or describe familar routes from memory.

MG's lesion was in the left occipito-parietal region implicating the dorsal route, thus likely to affect primarily *spatial* processing of information. In humans, is has been widely accepted that the right hemisphere plays a leading role in spatial processing (De Renzi, 1982; Ratcliff, 1982; 1987). Despite this, there is considerable evidence for visuo-spatial deficits associated with left hemisphere lesions, including impairments in navigating mazes, block span tests, line orientation and mental rotation (see Mehta and Newcombe, 1991). Thus the dorsal route is essentially bilateral, although some differentiation of left and right hemisphere spatial processing has been proposed by Kosslyn (1991), as indicated below.

MG was assessed using a series of tasks that address each of the key components of the model presented in figure 13.1. The main focus was to establish (a) whether she showed specifically spatial deficits, given the nature of her brain damage; (b) whether the maintenance of visuo-spatial information could be differentiated from mental transformation, as suggested by Kosslyn's et al.'s (1990) recent componential analysis of high-level vision; and (c) whether the deficit was dissociated from the retrieval and manipulation of visual imagery.

Single Case Study: MG

Background

MG was born in 1970. She sustained a cerebrovascular accident (CVA) in 1986 whilst on holiday in Austria. The morning after a large birthday party she experienced sudden nausea followed by vomiting. According to a relative, she was dysphasic. This accords with her own account; she also recollects that she had difficulty seeing in her right visual field, later diagnosed as a right lower quadrantianopia (impaired vision within her right lower visual field). Her condition was diagnosed initially by a doctor as due to alcoholic poisoning, but when it became apparent that she had muscle weakness on her right side she was transferred rapidly to a hospital by helicopter. A CT scan was carried out the following day and showed a large intracerebral haematoma (blood clot) in the left parietal region with resulting marked displacement of midline structures. A craniotomy was performed and the haematoma found at a depth of approximately 2 mm in the left occipito-parietal region. An incision of 1 cm was made in the cortex, a brain retractor inserted, and the haematoma removed. She made a good recovery and within ten days was able to walk around the ward. Within twenty days she was allowed home. The cause of the CVA is unknown, but is likely to be due to an arteriovenous malformation (AVM).

Initially MG had a mild right-sided weakness of body muscles, a lower right quadrantianopia, and a mild dysphasia, including difficulties with verbal comprehension, reduced verbal fluency, and impaired reading and writing abilities. Although her recovery was good, it disrupted the remainder of her education and, when seen for the current investigation, she was in an employment training scheme. In 1990, at the age of twenty, she underwent a full neurological examination and neuropsychological assessment at the Neurosurgical Unit, Maudsley Hospital, under the care of Mr C. Polkey, Consultant Neurosurgeon. The reason for referral was that she had developed a form of temporal lobe epilepsy which may have been amenable to neurosurgical treatment, although this was decided against because her epilepsy was found to be managed more successfully by changes in her medication.

On examination, the hemiparesis had resolved and she showed no language impairment, but she still had the lower right quadrantianopia. She was fluent in conversation with good language comprehension and verbal expression. However, she did have some mild word-finding difficulties, which she described as words being 'on the tip of the tongue'. This mild word-retrieval deficit is likely to represent the residual result of her dysphasia, but was not readily apparent on interview or formal testing. She complained of having difficulties in visualizing material and processing or manipulating visual imagery. Nevertheless, she was able to describe the front of her house accurately, the scene from a familiar landmark and the route from her house to the supermarket.

Neuroimaging

She underwent magnetic resonance imaging (MRI) using the 1.5 tesla Phillips Unit at Guy's Hospital, London. A series of sequences were taken in the sagittal plane using 5.0

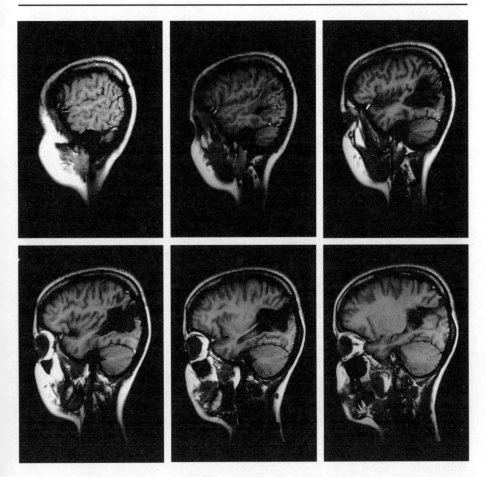

Figure 13.3   Sagittal plane 1.5 tesla MRI images showing the brain damage sustained by MG

mm slices (see figure 13.3). These show clearly the extent of the lesion within the parietal and occipital lobes. At the posterior end the lesion extends laterally into the occipital gyrus and covers the superior region of the optic radiation, effectively lesioning the upper geniculocalcarine tract unilaterally. The lesion extends anteriorly and ventrally into the temporal lobe with damage to the posterior left hippocampus. However, the parahippocampal, the inferotemporal, middle and superior temporal gyri are largely intact.

Neuropsychological Investigation

A series of investigations were conducted, some of which required the development of novel tests for which there were no normative data. These tests were administered to a

Table 13.1   Summary of preliminary neuropsychological assessment for patient MG

Handedness
Laterality coefficient: 100% right (Edinburgh Scale)

Intelligence
National Adult Reading Test Predicted IQ; 103

Verbal subtest aged scaled scores		Performance subtest aged scaled scores	
Vocabulary	11	Block design	10
Comprehension	11	Object assembly	6
Similarities	9		
Verbal IQ	100	Performance IQ	84

Perception
Judgement of line orientation score: 25
Ishihara test for colour blindness: 32/32

Visual Object and Space Perception tests (VOSP)
Visual

Screening	20/20 pass
Incomplete letters	20/20 pass
Silhouettes	23/30 pass
Object decision	16/20 pass
Progressive silhouettes	11/20 fail

Spatial

Dot counting	10/10 pass
Position discrimination	20/20 pass
Number location	10/10 pass
Cube analysis	10/10 pass

Attention
Star cancellation test: 55/56

Left–right orientation
Benton Left–Right Orientation test (form A)
   Total score = 18/20
   Personal orientation = 12/12
   Examiner's (reversed) orientation = 6/8

---

control group of four female subjects of approximately the same age (mean = 20.5 years; range = 20–21 years), socio-economic background and estimated verbal intelligence (National Adult Reading Test mean score = 105; range 100–111).

Preliminary Investigation

The results of the preliminary investigation of MG are summarized in table 13.1.

Dominance

One of the first goals was to establish her language dominance, since this would substantially effect the interpretation of the neuropsychological profile. She was assessed using the Edinburgh Handedness Questionnaire (Oldfield, 1971). She was 100 per cent right-handed; thus she is very likely to be left hemisphere dominant for language. This is further supported by the dysphasia that was reported following the CVA and her report of a residual word-finding deficit, often the last sign of dysphasia during recovery.

Intelligence

An estimate of her premorbid intellectual functioning was obtained using the National Adult Reading Test – Revised (NART–R) (Nelson and Willison, 1991). This estimates her full-scale IQ as 103. A short form of the Wechsler Adult Intelligence Scale – Revised (WAIS–R) (Canavan et al., 1986) shows that the estimated IQ matches her level of verbal intelligence (verbal IQ = 100), but that her nonverbal intelligence is significantly lower (performance IQ = 84). Thus her nonverbal abilities appeared to be worse, despite the fact that the damage was in the left hemisphere. This deficit is accounted for by a low score on the Block Design subtest, measuring visuo-spatial constructional abilities (Lezak, 1983).

Perception

On presentation, MG did not appear to have any gross visual perceptual deficit, including difficulties recognizing objects. To rule out a perceptual deficit the Visual Object and Space Perception Battery (VOSP) was administered to her (Warrington and James, 1991). For all the tests, MG was either in the average or above the average range, with the exception of the Object Decision task, in which she was at the 11th percentile but still above the cut-off criterion for impairment. She was also assessed on the Judgement of Line orientation test (Benton et al., 1983), a test of spatial perception which requires the subject to handle extraneous and/or distracting visual information (Mehta and Newcombe, 1991). Her score of 25 indicated no impairment. Colour perception was also assessed, using the Ishihara (1951) test for colour blindness. Her score was 100 per cent correct.

Attention

Despite having a lower right quadrantianopia, MG appeared to have no difficulty scanning across the visual field. Visual scanning was tested using the Star Cancellation test from the Behavioural Inattention Test (Wilson et al., 1987), yielding a score of 55/60. This result, combined with the normal Line Orientation performance suggests no impairment in visual scanning or attentional abilities.

Table 13.2   Visual short-term memory for faces

	MG	Controls 1	2	3	4	Mean	SD
Total correct	52/64	58	44	40	46	47	7.7
Sequence correct	10/16	14	10	9	11	11	2.2

Right–left orientation

Right–left disorientation is known to be associated with left parietal dysfunction. Since some of the tests used to test mental transformation required right–left judgements, it was crucial to test this function. On the Benton Right–Left Orientation scale (Benton et al., 1983), MG made two errors. This is below the mean score for her sex and age (mean = 19.3; SD = 2.3), but above the cut-off level for a significant deficit. Of note, the errors were made when responding to instructions concerning the examiner's body, requiring some degree of mental rotation or reorientation ('put your right hand on my left ear; put your left hand on my right shoulder').

Experimental Investigation

The preliminary investigation established that she was of average intelligence and had no significant perceptual or attention deficits. Two deficits stood out: first, the difficulty on Block Design, a test of visuo-spatial constructional abilities; and secondly, the difficulties in right–left orientation, but only when in relation to the examiner's body, thus requiring mental transformation. The subsequent experimental investigation focused on the different components of the model of higher-level vision as indicated in figure 13.1, investigating these in turn, starting with the visual and spatial components of the VSSP.

The Visuo-spatial Scratchpad (VSSP)

MG's visual short-term memory was studied by measuring her short-term memory for faces (table 13.2) using a task devised by Hanley et al. (1991) to measure face recognition memory. MG was within range of age-matched controls when memory span was measured with this material.

Spatial memory

Spatial memory was investigated using a version of the Corsi Block Span test (Canavan et al., 1986) and the Brooks matrix task (Brooks, 1967) which has been used extensively

Table 13.3 Performance of MG and four control subjects on the Brooks Matrix task

Sequence length	MG	Controls 1	2	3	4	Mean	SD
(a) Number of errors at each level							
3	0	0	0	0	0	0.00	0.00
4	2	0	0	1	0	0.25	0.50
5	3	0	0	3	2	1.25	1.50
6	2	1	0	1	1	0.75	0.50
7	1	2	0	2	3	1.75	1.25
8	3	3	0	8	7	4.50	3.70
Total errors	11	6	0	15	13	8.50	6.86
(b) Number of sequences correct at each level							
3	3/3	3	3	3	3	3.00	0.00
4	3/3	3	3	3	3	3.00	0.00
5	2/3	3	3	2	2	2.50	0.58
6	2/3	1	3	2	2	2.00	0.82
7	2/3	1	3	2	1	1.75	0.96
8	2/3	2	3	1	1	1.75	0.96
Total correct	14/18	13	18	15	12	14.5	2.65

Spatial material

In the starting square put a 1
In the next square right put a 2
In the next square up put a 3
In the next square right put a 4
In the next square down put a 5
In the next square down put a 6
In the next square left put 7
In the next square down put an 8

Nonsense material

In the starting square put a 1
In the next square good put a 2
In the next square quick put a 3
In the next square bad put a 4
In the next square good put a 5
In the next square slow put a 6
In the next square quick put 7
In the next square bad put an 8

Figure 13.4 The version of the Brooks Matrix text used in the experiment
Note: Examples of the sequences of sentences given for level 5 are given for spatial memory and nonsense control conditions of the task. The matrix illustrates the position of the numbers relating to the 'spatial' sentences but when the task is administered only a blank matrix is shown.

to investigate the function of the VSSP (Baddeley et al., 1975; Baddeley and Liberman, 1980).

In the Corsi task, the experimenter taps a particular sequence in an array of blocks. The subject, who faces the experimenter, watches and then repeats the sequence. MG was unimpaired on this task.

In the Brooks task the subject has to construct a mental image of a matrix from a set of spoken directions and is then required to 'read off' the imaged matrix. A series of sentences are given, as shown in figure 13.4, and have to be recalled in order, the matrix facilitating recall for the sentences shown on the left.

The results are summarized in table 13.2 indicating the number of errors made on each trial and the number of correct sequences at each level. It can be seen that MG performed well on this task, relative to the controls. Despite making slightly more errors, she had the same number of correct sequences as the control group. MG showed no significant impairment on tests of visual or spatial working memory, indicating that the VSSP was functioning normally.

Mental transformation

The next stage of the investigation was to assess the ability of MG to transform mental images. One of the most extensively researched aspects of mental transformation is the ability to rotate mental images, thus this aspect was examined in detail in MG. There is substantial evidence that the mental computations involved in mental rotation are analogous to those in the real world. Thus, when subjects are required to match two images in different planes, the latency for matching lengthens as the angle of rotation increases (Shepard, 1978; Shepard & Metzler, 1971).

Three tests of mental rotation were selected, varying in level of difficulty. The first was the Flags test (Thurstone and Jeffrey, 1956) in which the subject is shown a drawing of a black and white flag and has to judge which out of six flags positioned to the right of it is a rotation of the sample flag; 126 problems are given and the subject has five minutes to complete as many as possible. The second was a version of the Manikin test (Ratcliffe, 1979). The subject is shown a sequence of 'little men' figures in each of four positions, either upright or upside-down, and either facing towards the viewer or facing away; the task is to decide which hand (left or right) is holding a ball with a vertical stripe on it. The third task was a version of Shepard and Metzler's (1971) test of three-dimensional form rotation (Shepherd and Cooper, 1982). A 'sample' shape is presented on the left-hand page and four 'test' stimuli presented to the right, two of which are the different and two the rotated form of the shape. The shapes are rotated at different angles within three-dimensional space; a total of 20 trials were used with no time limit to perform the task.

Results   MG's performance was compared with the four age-matched control subjects (see table 13.4). On the Flags test her performance was very slow and she was able to attempt only 35 items, out of which 32 were correct. She was very poor on this task, with less than half the mean number completed correctly compared with the control subjects. It was suspected that MG was using a non-rotational strategy to perform this task, accounting for the substantial increase in latency. On the Little Man task she was

Table 13.4   Performance of MG and four control subjects on three tests of mental rotation

| | | Controls | | | | | |
	MG	1	2	3	4	Mean	SD
Flags test							
Total correct	32/126	80	60	73	74	71.2	8.4
Number attempted	35/126	81	69	78	76	76.0	5.1
Little Man test							
Number correct							
Upright							
Frontal	8/9	9	9	9	9	9.0	0.0
Back	4/5	5	5	5	5	5.0	0.0
Inverted							
Frontal	2/8	8	8	7	8	7.8	0.5
Back	4/8	8	6	7	6	6.8	1.0
Total	18/30	30	28	28	28	28.5	1.0
Shepard Rotation task							
Total correct	2/20	20	16	17	18	17.75	1.7

substantially impaired, with the majority of her errors on inverted 'men'. The relatively unimpaired performance in the upright facing figures indicates that this cannot be attributed to right–left disorientation. On the more demanding three-dimensional Shepard and Metzler (1971) task she was again substantially impaired, with only 2 trials correct out of 20.

In summary, MG was clearly impaired on all three tasks, particularly when the object had to be inverted or rotated in three-dimensional space.

A further aspect of mental transformation is the ability to rotate the person's frame of reference, in an imaginary sense, rather than the object. For example, in map reading a person can determine which direction to turn by rotating their own frame of reference, rather than the map. The Money's Standardised Road-Map test of direction sense (Butters et al., 1972) was used to test this ability. The map is shown in figure 13.5. The person has to describe the right or left turns which would be needed to follow the route. The various turns can be categorized according to their starting direction in relation to the subject prior to the turn. For example, the first turn in the test route in figure 13.5 is a 90° turn and the second is 0°. In the ninth turn the starting direction is towards the subject and classified as a 180° turn (oblique directions are classified as either going away from (0°) or towards (180°) the subject, depending on the predominant direction).

MG took 216 seconds to complete this task with 11 incorrect responses out of 32 decisions. As indicated above, the errors were broken down into the starting direction in relation to the subject prior to the turn. There were 1/9 errors (11%) for the 0° turn, 3/13 (23%) errors for 90° and 6/10 (60%) for 180°. Thus MG had substantial difficulty judging the direction of a turn in which she had to rotate her frame of reference. Overall, she was impaired relative to the performance of control subjects tested by Butters et al. (1972).

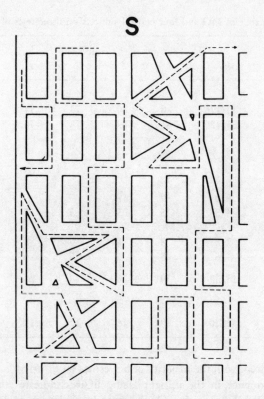

Figure 13.5   The Money's Standardized Road-Map test of direction sense
Note: The shorter route is used for practice; the longer one was used to test the subject.
Source: Butters et al. (1972)

Scanning visual imagery

The ability to scan a mental image is a function of the 'inspect' process (Farah, 1984; Kosslyn, 1980; 1991) (see figure 13.1). For example, when we imagine the Star of David by mentally combining two triangles, the inspect process allows us to find the hexagon embedded in the centre. The next stage of the investigation was to determine whether this 'inspect' process was intact.

The island task   The ability to scan visual imagery was tested using a modified version of the Kosslyn et al. (1978) map task. A fictitious map (see figure 13.6) is presented to the subject who is required to copy it until it has been drawn accurately. The subject then pictures the map mentally and is instructed to focus on a particular location. A second location is given and the subject has to shift focus to it. Kosslyn et al. (1978) found that the time taken to move to the next location was proportional to the distance on the map, supporting the contention that scanning visual imagery involves a similar cognitive process to visually scanning the environment.

A clinical version of the test was developed for MG. The map was memorized by viewing it four times whilst the landmarks (treasure, reed bed, well, straw hut, tree and

Figure 13.6 The Island test, showing the various landmarks
Source: Kosslyn et al. (1978)

mountain) were pointed out. The subject then traced round the island's outline, naming the landmarks and drawing pictures of them. An empty outline of the island was shown and the subject had to fill in the landmarks with their names. This step was repeated several times if there were significant errors (more than 0.5 cm deviation of each landmark), until the locations had been learned. The subject then had to produce a mental image of the island and transfer attention from a set of starting points to various destinations (for example, from the treasure to the reed bed). The intention was to measure the latency required to do this transformation.

MG was able to learn the map, requiring four repetitions of tracing the destinations, naming and drawing the landmarks. When asked to image the island, however, she indicated that she was only able to image destinations individually and was not able to transfer her attention across the map to a new destination. Several attempts at prompting her to do the task produced the same response.

Modified Brooks letter tasks Her performance on the Island task suggests strongly an impairment in scanning mental images. Nevertheless, it is possible that she had difficulties in following the instructions for this task, or that an impairment in some other mental operation was contributing to the deficit. It was therefore decided to employ an alternative image scanning task based on the Brooks (1968) letter task.

The subject has to scan round imagined block letters, such as the letter 'F'. They start from a prescribed starting point and more in a clockwise direction, categorizing each corner as a point at the extreme top (assigned a 'yes' response) or a point in between (assigned a 'no' response). In Brooks's original experiment, subjects took much longer when responding by tapping with the left or right hand than by speaking. In addition, Baddeley and Lieberman (1980) reported that with verbal responses the task is interfered

Figure 13.7   The block letters for the two versions of the Brooks Letter test
Note: T and L were used for training and practice; the remaining letters were used for the test. Arrows
indicate specified starting positions.
Source: Brooks (1967)

with significantly by a pendulum tracking task, but not by brightness judgement. This
suggests that the task requires primarily spatial, rather than visual, processing.

In the current version, the subject was first trained using the image of the letter
presented on a card and then required to 'image' the letter. Thus the image of the letter
is stored temporarily in the VSSP. The nature of the task was explained in relation to the
letter T, followed by three training trials administered using the letter L with three
different starting positions. This was followed by nine test trials, three with F, E and H
(see figure 13.7). MG performed perfectly on all nine test trials. Her 'inspect' system is
sufficiently intact to handle this particular task.

A further modification of the task combines scanning and mental rotation. Here the
subject had to scan round the imagined black letters but this time indicate whether a
corner turned to the left or right. She, not only had to scan the letter, but also change
her 'vantage' point in making the decision. This is akin to the Road Map test of
directional sense (Butters et al., 1972), a crucial difference being that the letters have to
be imaged by the subjects, whilst in the Road Map test it is kept in front of the person.

Exactly the same sequence of trials, letters and starting points was used. MG was

Table 13.5 Performance of MG and four control subjects on a modified version of the Brooks Letter task[a]

Task type	Rotation (in degrees)[b]	Total turns for three trials	Number of errors				
					Controls		
			MG	1	2	3	4
Letter F	0	2	0	0	0	0	0
	90	14	4	0	0	1	3
	180	11	9	1	1	2	2
Letter E	0	2	0	0	1	0	0
	90	17	7	1	0	0	2
	180	14	12	2	1	1	3
Letter H	0	10	0	0	0	0	1
	90	17	1	0	0	2	0
	180	18	7	2	0	0	1
Total	0	14	0	0	1	0	1
	90	48	12	1	0	3	5
	180	43	28	4	2	3	6

Notes:
[a] For each letter type there were three trials.
[b] Starting direction in relation to subject.

unimpaired on the training letter L, demonstrating her understanding of the task. She was substantially impaired on the remaining letters. A breakdown of the type of errors is given in table 13.5, comparing her performance to the control subjects. The data were split according to whether the starting direction for the turn was 0°, 90°, 180° or degrees in relation to the subject's body. Thus for 0°, the subjects did not have to 'mentally rotate' themselves to imagine the turn. For a 90° direction, they had to rotate 90°; and for the 180° turn, rotate 180° (a similar scoring system to that used with the Money's Road Map task).

MG was substantially impaired compared with the control subjects. The number of errors for the three directions were respectively 0%, 25% and 85%. This suggests that MG had difficulty in 'mentally rotating' round the figure, such that she was unable to do the task when the turns were coming from the opposite direction from her. It is notable that with the 180° direction the percentage of errors was significantly below chance levels (50%) of responding. This indicates that she reverted back to judging the turns in relation to the direction of her own body (that is, egocentrically).

The pattern of errors suggests her difficulties do not lie in 'moving round the figure', but in making decision about the direction of the turn. Indeed, the result mirror those found with the Money Road Map task, but with the simpler images stored in the VSSP. Overall, however, it suggests that the basic ability to scan visual images is intact, but that when MG has to transform her own frame of reference to conduct the task, she is impaired. What then, accounts for her difficulty on the Island task? It may lie in the retrieval of visual imagery, particularly for more complex or novel information. Thus, for the Island test she had to learn the locations of the feature and retrieve these to perform the task. In the Block Letter task the outlines of the letters were familiar and may have been easier to retrieve. To explore this issue in more detail, the remaining experiments test her ability to retrieve both novel and familiar visual information.

Storing and retrieving visual images

The VSSP is a temporary store of visuo-spatial information. There are likely to be two routes through which material can enter the store: either through the senses or through memory. The latter includes calling to mind memories pertaining to specific experiences, referred to as retrieval from long-term memory. This contrasts with generating visual images, which relate to more generalized images, for example calling to mind the appearance of an elephant. Whilst long-term memory taps stores of personally experienced events or information, imagery generation is thought to tap the store of visual knowledge about the appearance of objects (Humphreys and Bruce, 1989). This distinction is akin to the 'episodic/semantic' memory distinction made by Tulving (1983; Schacter and Tulving, 1992) that differentiates more generally remembering personally experienced events from the store of semantic knowledge, including rules, concepts and facts.

In relation to visual information, the distinction is seen clearly in patients with brain damage. Patients with right mesiotemporal lobe damage may have a selective impairment in visuo-spatial long-term memory, for example, face recognition memory (Morris et al., 1994a, 1994b; Smith, 1989). In contrast, difficulties in retrieving mental imagery have been associated with left posterior parieto-occipital lesions (Farah, 1984). The distinction tends to become less clear when considering visual imagery that has been acquired recently. Indeed, ELD, studied by Hanley et al. (1991) shows no difficulties in retrieving imagery for material she was exposed to prior to her illness, but a marked difficulty for more recent material. Specifically, she was able to 'image' the faces of celebrities famous before 1985, the start of her illness, but not more recent faces. Similarly MG may have difficulty retrieving newly learned visual images, but not those learned before her neurological impairment (an anterograde deficit, but not a retrograde one).

Long-term visuo-spatial memory   This was assessed using three standardized tests. First was the Benton Visual Retention test, form A, administration C (Benton, 1974), which requires the patient do draw simple abstract line drawings from memory following a ten-second exposure. Ten line drawings are presented invidually for recall. MG could draw six out of the ten items correctly, with six classifiable errors in the four incorrect items. The number of correct items were two lower than expected for a person of average intelligence in her age group, raising the question of a visuo-spatial memory deficit.

A more complex task, the Rey Osterreith Complex Figure (Osterreith, 1944) was also used. This is a single complex drawing which, in the version used with MG, has to be copied and then drawn from memory after a 40-minute delay. Her copy score was 44/ 47 and her recall score was 8.5 (19% recall). This is well below the 5th percentile for a sample of normal subjects (Maudsley Unpublished Normative Data). Finally, she was assessed using the Face Recognition Memory test (Warrington, 1984). Her score of 36/ 50 places her below the 5th percentile for her age and represents a mild to moderate impairment.

Table 13.6 Performance of MG and four control subjects on imagery retrieval tasks

Task type	MG	Controls				Mean	SD
		1	*2*	*3*	*4*		
Colours of objects and animals	23/25	22	24	23	24	23.25	1.0
Animals' tail lengths	17/20	17	15	17	16	16.25	1.0
Size comparison	14/15	15	15	15	14	14.75	0.5
City location	13/15	12	9	10	14	11.25	2.2
Celebrities	12/15	11	13	12	12	12.00	0.8

Imagery generation   A range of different tasks was employed based on those described by Farah et al. (1988) and Hanley et al. (1991). The subject had to answer questions requiring her to 'inspect' the images of objects, rather than recalling information that was necessarily verbally encoded in long-term memory. It has been claimed that when subjects classify the shapes of objects or relative size of similar-sized objects they frequently use visual imagery (Holyoak, 1977; Kerr, 1973). For example, when asked to rate whether an animal has a long or short tail the subject is likely to 'picture' the animal in their minds eye and then 'inspect' the tail. This assumption is made in the following tests of imagery generation. MG was assessed on a range of imagery generation tests, based on Hanley et al. (1991), including those relating to the colour of objects, the length of animals' tails, the relative sizes of common objects, distances between cities, and similarity between celebrities' faces. Compared with controls, MG showed no deficits on these tests (see table 13.6).

Imagery mnemonics   As a further test of visual imagery retrieval, the efficacy of using mnemonics to improve long-term memory was explored. The use of visual imagery as a strategy for remembering material is well established. There is evidence that this strategy also utilizes visuo-spatial working memory since simultaneous tracking can specifically impair the use of visual imagery in paired-associated learning tasks (Baddeley and Lieberman, 1980). A paired-associate task was employed to see whether MG could make use of visual imagery to improve performance.

In this task the subject was presented with four lists of ten pairs of words, each pair being presented for six seconds. The words were concrete nouns matched for frequency. After each list presentation the first word from each pair was presented and the subject was asked to produce the second word. For the first and third lists the subject was instructed just to repeat the items 'over and over again' and not to use visual imagery to aid performance. For the second and fourth list she was instructed to form an image linking the two words together (an example was given prior to the second list of linking the words 'monkey' and 'cigar' by imagining a monkey smoking a cigar).

MG's performance is shown in table 13.7, compared to the control subjects. MG initially performed poorly on this task, not benefiting from the imagery instructions in list 2. However, her performance on the second 'imagery' list improved dramatically and she was able to remember 9 out of 10 of the associations. One possibility is that she misunderstood the instructions on list 2, but when these were repeated for list 4, she was

Table 13.7 Performance on the verbal paired associate learning task with rote learning (lists 1 and 3) and imagery instructions (2 and 4)

| List | MG | Controls | | | | Mean | SD |
		1	2	3	4		
Rote learning							
List 1	2/10	4	2	4	2	3.0	1.2
List 2	1/10	4	4	3	1	3.0	1.4
Total	3/20	8	6	7	3	6.0	2.2
Imagery instructions							
List 1	2/10	10	10	7	8	8.8	1.5
List 2	9/10	10	10	10	10	10.0	0.0
Total	11/20	20	20	17	18	18.8	1.5

able to follow them successfully. Overall, the results indicate that MG was able to use imagery instructions, despite the poor performance on the first trial.

General Discussion

In summary, MG shows no impairment of the VSSP with normal visual and spatial short-term memories. In contrast, she shows significant impairment in mental rotation, detected using a variety of tasks, including the Flags test, the Manikin test, the Shepard and Metzler task, the Money's Road Map task, and our own version of the Brooks Letter task. She also had difficulties in performing the Island scanning task. Despite this, she showed no impairment in retrieving and inspecting visual imagery, although she did have an impairment in longer-term visuo-spatial memory.

This pattern points towards a selective deficit in mental transformation with an accompanying visual long-term memory deficit. Because of the robust nature of the mental transformation deficit, it is difficult to explain it away in terms of task complexity or difficulties in understanding the instructions. Indeed, the deficit seems to occur whenever mental transformation is required, even on relatively simple tasks. For example, in the test of left–right orientation, MG only made errors when required to respond in relation to the examiner's body (for example, Put your right hand on my left ear'). Of note, MG was impaired either when having to rotate the mental image (as in the Shepard and Metzler task) or rotate her own frame of reference (as in the Brooks Letter and Money Road Map tasks). In other words, the deficit spans situations in which the subject has to retain viewpoint independence to 'see' the image from a different angle (allocentric processing), and when the material remains static but the frame of reference is rotated in the subject's mind (egocentric).

The finding supports the dissociation of the VSSP from the processes responsible for mental transformation, as indicated in the introduction (see figure 13.1) and argues against the position taken by Baddeley (1992) and Craik et al.'s (1990) Levels of Process-ing framework. Converging evidence might come from a patient with the opposite pattern of performance; one with a VSSP deficit in the absence of difficulties with mental transformation. However, according to the model in figure 13.1, this may not be possible. The VSSP is needed to store the image that is being transformed and so a VSSP impairment would *always* produce an impairment in mental transformation. This may have happened to ELD, studied by Hanley et al. (1991), who was impaired on both the Brooks Matrix task and on tests of mental rotation. Indeed, the model predicts specific-ally that a deficit in VSSP cannot occur independently of a mental transformation deficit.

MG also had difficulties in the Kosslyn Island task (Kosslyn et al., 1978). She was apparently able to learn the location of the different landmarks but could not switch her attention from location to location when 'imaging' the island. At first sight this would appear to be a deficit in mental scanning. However, she was able to scan the imagery processed in the imagery retrieval tasks. For example, she could make judgements about the relative sizes of animals' tails, which requires a shift of attention around the image of the animal. In addition, she could retrieve the block letters of the Brooks Letter task and showed normal performance on the version requiring 'up' and 'down' judgements. An alternative explanation is that MG had difficulty retaining a stable image of the island because of a failure to lay down new visual memories accurately in the long-term store. As indicated above, there may be a distinction between remembering new images and retrieving images that have been established in memory before brain damage (Hanley et al., 1991). The animal tails and Brooks Letter task used familiar material, while the Island was newly learned.

These findings illustrate the dynamic nature of short-term and long-term memory. Information is activated from long-term memory, temporarily stored and processed. It can then be stored again in long-term memory whilst alternative processing takes place. This complex 'shuffling' between the VSSP and long-term memory must be carefully co-ordinated, presumably calling on a Central Executive System (CES; see, for example, Baddely, 1992). Thus in figure 13.1 the CES is shown as co-ordinating the different cognitive processes associated with higher-level vision. MG may have an intact VSSP, but cannot store visuo-spatial information for longer periods. Her combination of im-pairments would create specific difficulties in using the system as a whole. For example, in navigating in unfamiliar surroundings she would have difficulty both in determining from a map what direction to go and in remembering landmarks along the route, some-thing she did, in fact, report.

The essentially spatial nature of MG's processing deficit is consistent with a lesion in the occipito-parietal pathway, thought to be responsible for processing the spatial rela-tions between parts of objects (Mishkin et al., 1983; Ungerlieder and Mishkin, 1983). Of note, the damage is in the left hemisphere, again highlighting the contribution of this part of the brain to a wide range of visuo-spatial tasks (Mehta and Newcombe, 1991). Indeed, Kosslyn (1991; Kosslyn et al., 1989) distinguishes between the contribution of the left and right hemisphere to mental transformation. His model of higher vision accounts for the fact that when an image is rotated the topographic relations between parts must remain constant under the various transformations that take place. To capture these topographical relations there must be some form of *categorical* representation that maintains the general properties of the spatial structure. Nevertheless, as the image rotates, the distance between regions of an object changes. *Coordinate* representations are used to specify the relations between locations of objects or parts in term of metric units. Kossyln et al.'s (1990) view is that the left dorsal route contains the mechanisms responsible for categorical relations coding, whilst the right dorsal route processes co-ordinate representations. His model is supported by finding that in normal subjects there is a left hemisphere advantage in the speed of processing categorical relations (Kosslyn et al., 1989).

According to this model, a deficit in categorical relations encoding could cause the mental rotation deficit observed in MG. Indeed, Kosslyn et al. (1985) report two patients with left hemisphere lesions who have a deficit in mental rotation. In both patients, the rate of rotation was almost ten times slower than that of a group of normal subjects. Categorical representations are characterized by Kosslyn (1991) as the direction between objects or parts such as 'near to, 'above', 'left' or 'below'.

Nevertheless, the performance of MG creates serious problems for this characterization because of her unimpaired performance on the Brooks Matrix task. To perform this task, which requires remembering directions between cells within the 4×4 matrix (above/below; to the right/left of), the subject would need to encode categorical relations. Yet the mechanism for doing so should be impaired. Thus, MG's impairment in mental transformation may not be fully explained by a deficit in categorical encoding.

In conclusion, previous neuropsychological studies have tended to dissociate the VSSP from the retrieval of visual imagery. For example, the patient LH, investigated by Farah et al. (1988) is unimpaired on tests of VSSP functioning (specifically the Brooks Matrix task) and mental rotation, but is impaired in imagery generation. Conversely, ELD, studied by Hanley et al. (1991) was unimpaired in her imagery generation abilities, but showed a markedly impaired VSSP and mental transformation ability. However, the specific deficit in mental transformation shown by MG helps us to fractionate further the cognitive systems involved in the retention and manipulation of visuo-spatial information. To our knowledge, she is the first patient with a reported impairment in mental transformation in the absence of a VSSP deficit. Careful investigation of other patients with mental transformation deficits may help to determine the extent to which the storage and manipulation of visual material rely on separable subsystems within working memory.

Acknowledgements

The authors are grateful to Mr C. Polkey, Consultant Neurosurgeon at the Maudsley Hospital, for providing access to MG, under his care at the time of the investigation. We thank Dr Edward De Haan and Professor Alan D. Baddeley for making tests available to us, and for advice from Dr Richard Hanley.

Further Reading

Baddeley, A.D. (1992) 'Working memory', *Science*, **255**: 556–9.
Farah, M.J. and Hammond, K.M. (1988) 'Mental rotation and orientation-invariant object recognition: Dissociable processes', *Cognition*, **29**: 29–46.

Kosslyn, S.M. (1991) 'A cognitive neuroscience of visual cognition: Further developments', in *Mental Images in Human Cognition*, ed. R. Logie and M. Denis (Amsterdam: Elsevier).

Kosslyn, S.M., Flynn, R.A., Amsterdam, J.B. and Wang, G. (1990) 'Components of high-level vision: a cognitive neuroscience analysis and accounts of neurological syndromes', *Cognition*, **34**: 203–77.

Mehta, Z. and Newcombe, F. (1991) 'A role for the left hemisphere in spatial processing', *Cortex*, **27**: 153–67.

Ratcliff, G. (1987) 'Spatial cognition in man: the evidence from cerebral lesions', in Ellen and C. Tinus-Blanc (eds), *Cognitive Processes and Spatial Orientation in Animal and Man*, vol. 2: *Neurophysiology and Developmental Aspects* (NATO ASI Series Dordrecht: Martinus Nijhoff), pp. 78–90.

References

Baddeley, A.D. (1986) *Working Memory* (Oxford: Clarendon Press).

Baddeley, A.D. (1992) 'Working memory', *Science*, **255**: 556–9.

Baddeley, A.D. and Lieberman, K. (1980) 'Spatial working memory', in *Attention and Performance*, (vol. 8) (New York: Academic Press).

Baddeley, A.D., Grant, S., Wright, E. and Thomson, E. (1975) 'Imagery and visual working memory', in *Attention and Performance*, vol. 5 (London: Academic Press).

Barnard, P. (1985) 'Interactive cognitive subsystems: a psycholinguistic approach to short-term memory', in A. Ellis (ed.), *Progress in the Psychology of Language*, vol. 2 (Hillsdale, N.J.: Lawrence Erlbaum).

Benton, A.L. (1974) *The Revised Visual Retention Test* (New York: The Psychological Corporation).

Benton, A.L., Hamsher, K., Varney, N.R. and Spreen, O. (1983) *Contributions to Neuropsychological Assessment: A Clinical Manual* (New York: Oxford University Press).

Brooks, L.R. (1967) 'The suppression of visualization by reading', *Quarterly Journal of Experimental Psychology*, **19**: 289–99.

Brooks, L.R. (1968) 'Spatial and verbal components of the act of recall', *Canadian Journal of Psychology*, **22**(5): 349–68.

Butters, N., Soeldner, C. and Fedio, P. (1972) 'Comparison of parietal and frontal lobe spatial deficits in man: extra-personal vs personal (egocentric) space', *Perceptual and Motor Skills*, **34**: 27–34.

Canavan, A.G.M., Dunn, G. and McMillan, T.M. (1986) 'The principal components of the WAIS-R', *British Journal of Clinical Psychology*, **25**: 81–5.

Canavan, A.G.M., Passingham, R.E., Marsden, C.D., Quinn, N., Wyke, M. and Polkey, C.E. (1989) 'Sequencing ability in Parkinsonian patients with frontal lobe lesions and patients who have undergone unilateral temporal lobectomies', *Neuropsychologia*, **27**(6): 787–98.

Craik, F.I.M., Morris, R.G. and Gick, M.L. (1990) 'Adult age differences in working memory', in G. Vallar and T. Shallice (eds), *Neuropsychological Impairments of Short-term Memory* (Cambridge: Cambridge University Press), pp. 247–67.

De Renzi, E. (1982) *Disorder of Space Exploration and Cognition* (New York: John Wiley).

Desimone, R., Albright, T., Gross, C.G. and Bruce, C. (1984) 'Stimulus selective properties of inferior temporal neurones in the macaque', *Journal of Neuroscience*, **4**: 2051–62.

Farah, M.J. (1984) 'The neurological basis of mental imagery: a componential analysis', *Cognition*, **18**: 245–72.

Farah, M.J. (1988) 'Is visual imagery really visual? Overlooked evidence from neuropsychology', *Psychological Review*, **95**(3): 307–17.

Farah, M.J. and Hammond, K.M. (1988) 'Mental rotation and orientation-invariant object recognition: dissociable processes', *Cognition*, **29**: 29–46.

Farah, M.J., Hammond, K.M., Levine, D.N. and Calvanio, R. (1988) 'Visual and spatial mental imagery: dissociable systems of representation', *Cognitive Psychology*, **20**: 439–92.

Gross, C.G. (1973) 'Visual functions of inferotemporal cortex', in R. Jung (ed.), *Handbook of Sensory Physiology*, vol. 7 (Berlin: Springer-Verlag), pp. 451–82.

Hanley, J.R., Young, A.W. and Pearson, N.A. (1991) 'Impairment of the visuo-spatial sketch pad', *Quarterly Journal of Experimental Psychology*, **43A**(1); 101–25.

Holyoak, K.J. (1977) 'The forms of analog size information in memory', *Cognitive Psychology*, **9**: 31–51.

Humphreys, G.W. and Bruce, V. (1989) *Visual Cognition: Computational, Experimental and Neuropsychological Perspectives* (Hove, Sussex: Lawrence Erlbaum Associates).

Ishihara, S. (1951) *Tests for Colour Blindness*. 10th rev. edn (London: H.K. Lewis).

Kerr, N.H. (1983) 'The role of vision in visual imagery experiments: evidence from the congenitally blind', *Journal of Experimental Psychology: General*, **112**: 265–77.

Kosslyn, S.M. (1987) 'Seeing and imagining in the cerebral hemispheres: a computational approach', *Psychological Review*, **94**(2): 148–75.

Kosslyn, S.M. (1980) *Image and the Mind* (Cambridge, Mass.: Harvard University Press).

Kosslyn, S.M. (1991) 'A cognitive neuroscience of visual cognition: further developments', in R. Logie and M. Denis (eds), *Mental Images in Human Cognition* (Amsterdam: Elsevier).

Kosslyn, S.M., Ball, T.M. and Reiser, B.J. (1978) 'Visual images preserve metric spatial information: evidence from studies of image scanning', *Journal of Experimental Psychology: Human Perception and Performance*, **4**: 47–60.

Kosslyn, S.M., Berndt, R.S. and Doyle, T.J. (1985) 'Imagery and language: a preliminary neuropsychological investigation', in M.S. Posner and O.S. Marin (eds), *Attention and Performance*, vol. 11 (Hillsdale, N.J.: Lawrence Erlbaum).

Kosslyn, S.M., Cave, C.B., Provost, D.A. and von Gierke, S.M. (1986) 'Sequential processes in imagery generation', *Cognitive Psychology*, **20**: 319–43.

Kosslyn, S.M., Flynn, R.A., Amsterdam, J.B. and Wang, G. (1990) 'Components of high-level vision: a cognitive neuroscience analysis and accounts of neurological syndromes', *Cognition*, **34**: 203–77.

Kosslyn, S.M., Koenig, O., Barrett, A. and Backer Cave, C. (1989) 'Evidence for two types of spatial representations: hemispheric specialization for categorical and coordinate relations', *Journal of Experimental Psychology: Human Perception and Performance*, **15**(4): 723–35.

Levine, D.N. (1982) 'Visual agnosia in monkey and man', in D.J. Ingle, M.A. Goodale and R.J.W. Mansfield (eds), *Analysis of Visual Behavior* (Cambridge, Mass.: MIT Press).

Levine, D.N., Warach, J. and Farah, M.J. (1985) 'Two visual systems in mental imagery: dissociation of 'what' and 'where' in imagery disorders due to bilateral posterior cerebral lesions', *Neurology*, **35**: 1010–18.

Lezak, M.D. (1983) *Neuropsychological Assessment*, 2nd edn (New York: Oxford University Press).

Logie, R.H. (1986) 'Visuo-spatial processing in working memory', *Quarterly Journal of Experimental Psychology*, **38A**: 229–47.

Logie, R.H. (1989) 'Characteristics of visual short-term memory', *European Journal of Cognitive Psychology*, **1**: 275–84.

Logie, R.H. and Marchetti, C. (1991) 'Visuo-spatial working memory: visual, spatial or central executive?', in R.H. Logie and M. Deni (eds), *Mental Images in Human Cognition* (Amsterdam: Elsevier), pp. 105–15.

Mehta, Z. and Newcombe, F. (1991) 'A role for the left hemisphere in spatial processing', *Cortex*, **27**: 153–67.

Mishkin, M.M., Ungerleider, L.G. and Macko, K.A. (1983) 'Object vision and spatial vision: two cortical pathways', *Trends in Neurosciences*, **6**: 414–17.

Morris, R.G. and Morton, N. 'Visuo-spatial working memory dissociated from image transformation: a single case study', *Cognitive Neuropsychology* (in press).

Moscovitch, M. (1992) 'Memory and working with memory: a component process model based on modules and central systems', *Journal of Cognitive Science*, **4**: 257–67.

Mountcastle, V.B., Andersen, R.A. and Motter, B.C. (1981) 'The influence of attentive fixation upon the excitability of the light-sensitive neurons of the posterior parietal cortex', *Journal of Neuroscience*, **1**: 1218–35.

Nelson, H.E. and Willison, J.R. (1991) *National Adult Reading Test (NART): Test Manual*, 2nd edn (Windsor, Berks.: NFER–Nelson).

Oldfield, R.C. (1971) 'The assessment and analysis of handedness: the Edinburgh Inventory', *Neuropsychologia*, **9**: 97–113.

Osterreith, P.A. (1944) 'Le test de copie d'une figure complexe', *Archives de psychologie*, **30**: 191–8.

Phillips, W.A. (1983) 'Short-term visual memory', *Philosophical Transactions of the Royal Society*, **B302**: 295–309.

Pohl, W. (1973) 'Dissociation of spatial discrimination deficits following frontal and parietal lesions in monkeys', *Journal of Comparative and Physiological Psychology*, **82**: 227–39.

Ratcliff, G. (1979) 'Spatial thought, mental rotation and the right cerebral hemisphere', *Neuropsychologia*, **17**: 49–54.

Ratcliff, G. (1982) 'Disturbances of spatial orientation associated with cerebral lesions', in M. Potegal (ed.), *Spatial Abilities: Developmental and Physiological Foundations* (New York: Academic Press), pp. 301–31.

Ratcliff, G. (1987) 'Spatial cognition in man: the evidence from cerebral lesions', in Ellen and C. Tinus-Blanc (eds), *Cognitive Processes and Spatial Orientation in Animal and Man*, vol. 2: *Neurophysiology and Developmental Aspects*, NATO ASI Series (Dordrecht: Martinus Nijhoff), pp. 78–90.

Riddoch, M.J. (1990) 'Loss of visual imagery: a generation deficit', *Cognitive Neuropsychology*, **7**: 249–73.

Schacter, D.L. and Tulving, E. (1992) Special issue on memory systems, *Journal of Cognitive Neuroscience*, **4**(3).

Shepard, R.N. (1978) 'The mental image', *American Psychologist*, February: 125–37.

Shepard, R.N. and Cooper, L.A. (1982) *Mental Images and their Transformations* (Cambridge, Mass.: MIT Press).

Shepard, R.N. and Metzler, J. (1971) 'Mental rotation of three-dimensional objects', *Science*, **171**: 701–3.

Smith, M.L. (1989) 'Memory disorders associated with temporal-lobe lesions', in F. Boller and J. Grafman (eds), *Handbook of Neuropsychology*, vol. 3 (Amsterdam: Elsevier), pp. 91–105.

Thurstone, L.L. and Jeffrey, T.E. (1956) *Flags: A Test of Spatial Thinking* (Illinois: Industrial Relations Center).

Tulving, E. (1983) *Elements of Episodic Memory* (New York: Oxford University Press).

Ungerleider, L.G. and Mishkin, M. (1982) 'Two cortical visual systems', in D.J. Ingle, M.A. Goodale and R.J.W. Mansfield (eds), *Analysis of Visual Behavior* (Cambridge Mass.: MIT Press).

Vallar, G. and Shallice, T. (eds) (1989) *Neuropsychological Impairments of Short-term Memory* (Cambridge: Cambridge University Press).

Warrington, E.K. (1984) *The Recognition Memory Test* (Windsor, Berks.: NFER–Nelson).

Warrington, E.K. and James, M. (1991) *The Visual Object and Space Perception Battery* (Bury St Edmunds: Thames Valley Test Company).

Wilson, B.A., Cockburn, J. and Halligan, P.W. (1987) *Behaviour Inattention Battery* (Titchfield, Fareham, Hants.: Thames Valley Test Company).

Wilson, J.T.L. Wiedman, K.D., Hadley, D.M. and Brooks, D.N. (1989) 'The relationship between visual memory function and lesions detected by magnetic resonance imaging after closed head injury', *Neuropsychology*, 3: 255–65.

Wechsler, D. (1945) *The Wechsler Memory Scale – Revised* (New York: Psychological Corporation).

14   Lost in Your Own House

J. Richard Hanley and Ann D.M. Davies

Introduction

Our ability to find our way around the environment in which we live is something that appears to be so effortless and natural that we take it for granted. Nevertheless, this is an ability that patients sometimes lose when they suffer memory loss following brain injury. The technical term for such a condition is topographical amnesia, and individuals are forced to adopt some fairly unusual compensatory strategies if they wish to maintain their independence. A patient that one of us has studied in the past (Hanley et al., 1989) frequently relies on his dog to help him find his way home when he goes out for a walk. Another attempts to locate a prominent landmark in her environment; she has learnt a set of verbal instructions that will enable her to find her way home from it (Hanley et al., 1990). The verbal instructions that she uses (for example, turn left at the traffic lights and take the second road on the right) are reminiscent of the directions that, say, a friend might give us when we visit them for the first time after they have moved to an unfamiliar area.

Neurologists and psychologists who have studied patients of this kind have made some important discoveries. One of these is that some patients may be unable to learn new environments, yet be able to find their way around their old haunts. Ross (1980) described a case who was unable to learn the layout of the neurology wing of the hospital in which he stayed for a month, yet his sister reported that he had no apparent problems orientating himself when he went to stay with his parents in the house in which he grew up. Similarly, the lady that we described in the previous paragraph has severe difficulties in learning the layout of her new flat and in finding her way back to it after a day out shopping, but she also says that she is well orientated in her parents' house, which she has known for many years.

Another important finding is that topographical amnesia does not always co–occur with other types of visual memory problems. For example, patient LH (Farah et al., 1988; Levine et al., 1985) is unable to recognize faces following a car accident, failing to identify even his wife unless she wears something distinctive such as a ribbon in her hair. He is also unable to remember the colour, shape and relative sizes of familiar objects. Despite the severity of these visual memory problems, LH can describe familiar routes in his native city of Boston without apparent difficulty, can travel around the city by himself without getting lost, and has good knowledge of the relative location of the individual states of the USA. By contrast, another subject (patient 2) reported by Levine et al. (1985) was not impaired at recognizing faces, and had intact visual knowledge of objects and colours. His topographical memory, however, was severely impaired.

One of the most controversial issues is whether or not patients with topographical problems suffer from essentially the same underlying functional impairment, or whether they fall into distinguishable subgroups. Patients undoubtedly exist who get lost even though their basic *spatial knowledge* of their environment is unimpaired. Landis et al. (1986), for instance, describe a number of patients who could draw accurate maps of areas in which they get lost. One individual described his predicament thus: 'I can draw you a plan of the roads from Cardiff to the Rhondda Valley. It's when I'm out that the trouble starts. My reason tells me I must be in a certain place and yet I don't recognize it. It all has to be worked out each time' (Pallis, 1955). Such difficulties seem to be caused by an inability to recognize well-known environments and landmarks as being familiar. These individuals seem to lose their way because of a visual recognition impairment that prevents them from integrating what they are looking at with their apparently intact spatial knowledge.

On the other hand, the topographical impairment experienced by one of Levine et al.'s (1985) subjects (patient 2) appears to be very different from this. This patient's ability to describe routes from his house to the shops was extremely poor, as was his knowledge of the location of cities in the USA. When he was sitting in a room in the hospital that he had inhabited for two months, he could not point to the location of his bed, the door or the window if he was blindfolded. In contrast to the individuals described by Landis et al. (1986) and Pallis (1955), topographical impairment of this kind may well be the direct result of a loss of spatial knowledge. In the following pages, we describe in detail the difficulties experienced by a new patient, whom we shall call Mr Smith, whose topographical problems also seem to be associated with a spatial rather than a visual recognition impairment.

Case Details

Mr Smith is a 65-year-old man who has retired following many years of employment, first as a merchant seaman, and subsequently with his wife as publican. Following complaints of persistent headaches, he was diagnosed as suffering from right internal carotid artery stenosis (narrowing of the valve orifice) and atheroma (fatty degeneration of the arterial coats). Subsequently, he was referred to one of us (ADMD) because he told his general practitioner that his headaches were getting him down, and his wife thought he needed some counselling as a consequence.

During the first session with him, however, it became clear that he was also suffering from some rather unusual cognitive problems. He told us that there were two situations in which he had particular difficulties. The first of these was when he was trying to get dressed. Sweaters, he said, caused him problems; if he succeeded in getting his head through the appropriate opening (which was not always the case), he frequently found it difficult to work out which sleeve his left arm should go through and which sleeve his right arm should go through. As often as not, he would find that the label ended up under his chin rather than at the back of his neck. Frequently, he would have to call his wife to help him – a situation which made him frustrated and embarrassed, and which could sometimes lead to friction between the two of them. The severity of this problem became apparent to us when we asked him to remove his pullover and attempt to put it back on again. After a couple of minutes of witnessing his agonized struggle, we intervened and showed him where to insert his arms.

His other main problem occurred when he was trying to find his way around. When out walking by himself or with his Alsatian dog, even in an area that he had known for very many years, he would sometimes forget where he was. Often, when he asked people for directions, they would rapidly distance themselves from him without offering assistance, apparently mistaking for intoxication the agitation that he was showing as a result of his predicament. He also told us that he was 'terrible with maps'. Most dramatically, perhaps, he would sometimes get lost in his own house despite having lived there for many years. For example, he might wander around the house for several minutes, ending up in different bedrooms instead of the bathroom (located on the upper floor) for which he was searching. Mr Smith's problems were confirmed to us when we took him to the other end of the hospital building in which we were located, and found that he was quite unable to show us the way back to the room that we had just left.

Although his topographical problems were clearly very severe, it was not the case that Mr Smith got lost every time that he went out by himself. In fact, he would sometimes walk home from the hospital alone without encountering any problems. His ability to do this was confirmed when one of us walked home with him after an assessment session. When we asked him about his strategies, it was clear that Mr Smith was using landmarks. These included a church, the Department of Social Security building, traffic lights, a zebra crossing, a library and a graveyard. It was also apparent that he had learnt a set of instructions (for example, cross over the road at the traffic lights, turn right past the graveyard) that would enable him to get from one landmark to another until he reached home. It seemed that he had chosen one particular route from several alternatives because of the existence of these distinctive landmarks. At one point, when one of us was walking home with him, he pointed to a street and said, 'I could go down that street, but I'd get lost. All the houses look the same.' He also said that he found crossing the road hazardous because he found it difficult to assess the speed at which oncoming cars were travelling.

Investigation

Mr Smith's description of his route-finding abilities suggested a spatial rather than a visual impairment, and we were interested to discover whether a formal assessment of his cognitive abilities would support this interpretation. First of all, we shall describe some of the tasks on which Mr Smith performed reasonably well. He scored within the normal range on the Warrington (1984) Recognition Memory Test for both words (44/50) and faces (40/50). On this test, the subject looks at 50 familiar words and 50 unfamiliar male faces. They are then shown a target item together with a distractor item that has not been presented to them. Their task is to indicate which of the two items was shown to them earlier. The level of performance achieved by Mr Smith suggested that he was not suffering from a general amnesia. His language comprehension was also good, as measured by his near-faultless display when asked to follow a series of spoken instructions on the Token test (De Renzi and Vignolo, 1962). His scores of 15/30 on McKenna and Warrington's (1983) Graded Naming test (a test of picture naming) and 18/30 on the National Adult Reading Test (Nelson, 1982) represent the average level of performance for the population as a whole. He also showed no signs of visual neglect on either a cancellation or a reading task. He was, however, disorientated with respect to time as well as place. Although his score on the 'Mini Mental State Examination' (a quick screening test often used to diagnose dementia) was not low enough to indicate that he was demented, it was notable that he was able to recall neither the day, the date, the month nor the year in which the testing was taking place. Nor was he able to recall the name of the hospital that he was visiting.

On subsequent testing sessions, we investigated Mr Smith's spatial knowledge and visual processing abilities in more detail. His knowledge of the visual characteristics of objects was relatively well preserved. Thus, he was able to provide the colour associated with familiar objects (for example, in response to the words 'motorway sign', he was able to respond 'blue'), decide which was the larger out of two objects when shown two words (such as toothbrush versus banana), and indicate without undue difficulty whether animals have short or long tails from hearing their name (goat = short tail; wolf = long tail). His ability to match photographs of unfamiliar faces, as measured by a score of 39 on the Benton Facial Recognition test, was below average but not severely impaired.

So far, then, Mr Smith's visual processing and visual memory skills seem to be relatively well preserved. Consistent with this, his ability to recognize the shapes of countries was also reasonably accurate – as one would expect in an ex-merchant seaman. In order to test this, we cut out 12 country/continent shapes, and read out the names of these countries/continents to him (Africa, Australia, Britain, Ireland, Italy, Japan, New Zealand, North America, Saudi Arabia, Scandinavia, South America, Spain). He was able to point to the correct country in response to 11/12 names.

Next, however, we selected seven of the shapes and asked him to place them on a sheet of paper in the relative positions that one would find them on a map of the world. Here, his performance was astonishingly bad. Figure 14.1 shows the almost random way in which he arranged the countries. We should point out that we attempted to orientate him by giving him the sheet of paper with North America and Britain already in their correct positions (there was room available to the right of Britain in which he could have placed countries if he had so wished). His remark as he was doing the task was that he was 'just dead on this'.

This pattern of performance, then, did indeed suggest that Mr Smith's problems in finding his way around were caused by a loss of knowledge of spatial layouts. This hypothesis was strengthened when we asked him to draw a map of the layout of the ground floor of his house. His drawing can be seen in figure 14.2. He is correct in placing

Figure 14.1 The world according to Mr Smith

the stairs to the right, the pantry at the back, and the lounge and dining room to the left. The three rooms on the left are drawn in the wrong order, however. The lounge should be at the top, the dining room in the middle, and the kitchen at the bottom; the hatch should be between the kitchen and the dining room rather than between the kitchen and the lounge. Finally, the kitchen is located at the end of the hall, not off to one side as it appears in Mr Smith's drawing. Figure 14.2(b) was drawn by Mr Smith's wife, and shows the correct layout of the ground floor of the house. Note, when comparing the two maps, that Mr Smith has drawn the layout with front door at the top, whereas Mrs Smith has drawn the layout with the front door at the bottom.

(a)

(b)

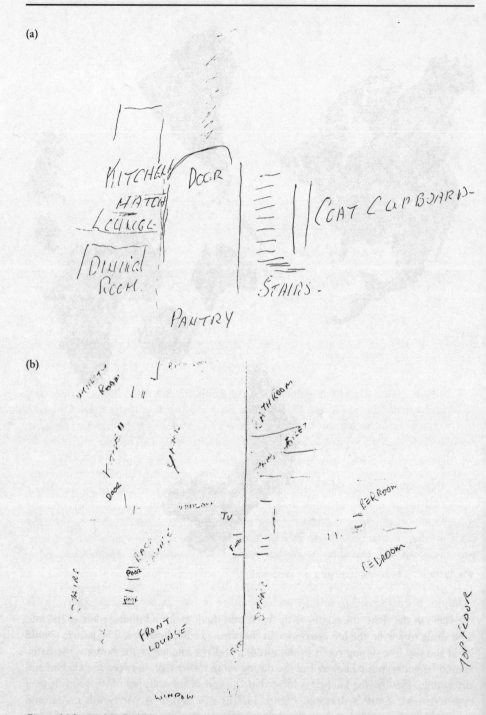

Figure 14.2   (a) Mr Smith's attempt to represent the layout of the ground floor of his house;
(b) Mrs Smith's representation of the layout of their house.

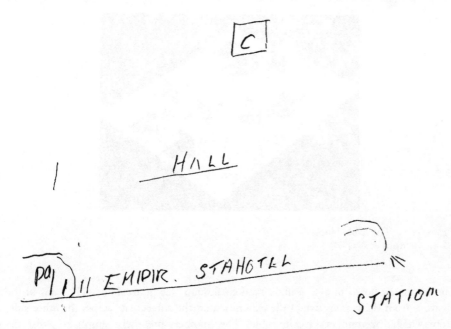

Figure 14.3 Mr Smith's attempt to represent the layout of Lime Street, Liverpool, as it would appear from the St George's Hall

Finally, we asked Mr Smith to draw a map of Lime Street in Liverpool as if one were looking at it from the St George's Hall. Lime Street is, perhaps, the best-known street in Liverpool. His drawing can be seen in figure 14.3. Aside from the fact that this is a very impoverished drawing of an area that Mr Smith has known all his life, he has drawn the station and the Empire (a well-known theatre) at the wrong ends of the street.

It is clear from these three tests that Mr Smith has a severe spatial problem. Information about the relative locations of rooms in his house, buildings in familiar locations and the countries of the world is no longer available to him. The inaccessibility of such information is likely to be the major reason why Mr Smith gets lost so easily. Knowledge such as this is assumed by psychologists to be represented in a person's *long-term* memory store, and this information has either been lost from Mr Smith's long-term store, or else it is still there but he can no longer gain access to it.

In addition to long-term memory storage, Alan Baddeley and his associates (for example, Baddeley, 1986) have identified another important component of the spatial information processing system. This is visuo-spatial *working* memory, and it is frequently referred to as the 'visuo-spatial sketch pad'. Many reports of patients with topographical problems do not provide any information about their visuo-spatial working memory ability, so we thought that it would be interesting to observe Mr Smith's performance on some of the tasks that have previously been used to investigate this system.

One such test which has recently been extensively used by Smyth and her colleagues (for example, Smyth and Pelkey, 1992) is known as the Corsi Blocks. In front of the subject is placed a wooden board on top of which are fixed nine wooden blocks, spread

Figure 14.4   The Corsi blocks
Source: De Renzi et al. (1977)

out across the board in a seemingly random fashion (see figure 14.4). The view in the figure is from the perspective of the experimenter; the subject sits across the other side, from which the numbers are invisible. The numbers are there simply to assist the experimenter in the administration and scoring of the test. In the basic task the experimenter taps a series of blocks in a predetermined order which the subject must then repeat by tapping the same blocks in the same order. The sequences start short but gradually become longer, continuing until performance eventually breaks down. This task therefore taps temporary or short-term retention of visuo-spatial information. Normal subjects can generally manage to remember sequences of at least four or five items correctly. One of us has previously reported a patient who was unable to repeat sequences of more than three items reliably (Hanley et al., 1991). De Renzi et al. (1977) described a similar level of performance in a group of patients who had suffered right hemisphere damage.

When Mr Smith was asked to do this task, however, his performance was extraordinarily poor. He scored 9/10 when the sequence consisted of one item, 9/10 when the sequence consisted of two items, and 3/10 when the sequence consisted of three items. When the sequence contained four or five items, he got no sequences correct whatsoever. Mr Smith was therefore not perfect even when the sequence consisted of only a single item! This level of performance is lower than any that we are aware of in the literature. We also tried to teach him a sequence of six blocks by showing him the correct sequence twice, and correcting him every time he made an error. The sequence was 6–2–5–3–7–8, and we gave up after 15 trials; on his fifteenth and final recall attempt, Mr Smith tapped out the sequence 2–7–8–5–6.

Another task that has been used to investigate visuo-spatial processing is known as mental rotation. Normal subjects find it relatively easy to decide whether or not two shapes are rotated versions of the same or different objects. We used two well-known tests with Mr Smith on which normal subjects make virtually no errors. The first is known as the Ratcliff Mannikin test, and examples of the test materials can be seen in figure 14.5. There was a total of 32 trials, in which the mannikin might be either

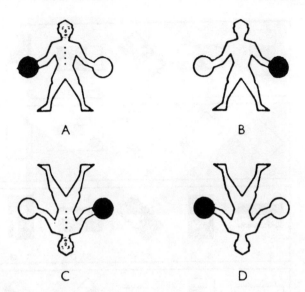

A   B

C   D

Figure 14.5   Stimuli from Ratcliff's Mannikin text
Source: Ratcliff (1979)

normally orientated, upside down, and facing either to the front or to the back. The task is to decide in which hand the mannikin is holding the black ball. Since the answer is always either 'left' or 'right', guessing would achieve a score of 16/32. Mr Smith's score was 18/32, which is not significantly better than chance. His comments as he was doing the test were that he 'couldn't make it go round' and that he was guessing most of the time. We ensured that Mr Smith knew his left from his right, and that he was aware of whether he was looking at the front or at the back of the mannikin.

On the Flags test (Thurstone and Jeffrey, 1956), the task is to look at a picture of a standard flag, and decide whether each of a series of flags presented to its right are rotated versions of the same side of the flag or of the opposite side of the flag. Figure 14.6 gives an example of some of the materials that comprise this test. Unfortunately, Mr Smith's spatial skills were so poor that we were unable even to explain to him what he should be doing. The problem was that when we showed Mr Smith the figures to the right, he was unable to remember which was the flag on the left that he was supposed to be using as a standard. In other words, his spatial short-term memory was so poor that as soon as his eyes fixated on the figures to the right of the page, he was unable to remember the location of the item on the left at which he had just been looking.

A final test, known as the Geneva Lines, further confirmed Mr Smith's problems with spatial processing. The task was to follow a straight line across a page over a number of competing lines, using a crayon. Figure 14.7 illustrates how poorly Mr Smith fared. For the top line (which was to be drawn from left to right), we have inserted the circles to indicate the points at which Mr Smith left the correct route, and started following a different line. X marks a point where he realized that he had made an error and went back. Note also that at the end he breaks the rules completely.

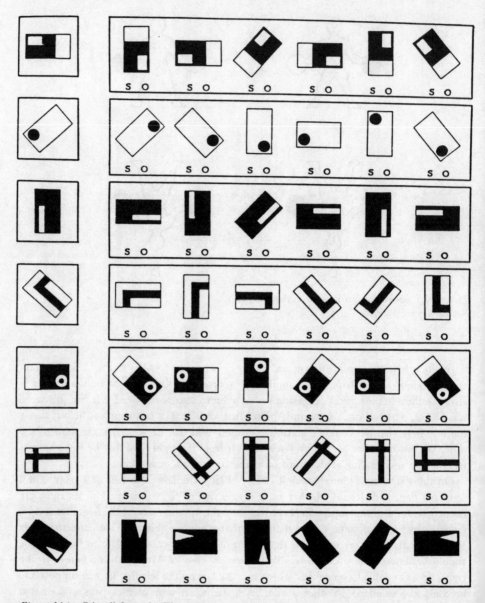

Figure 14.6   Stimuli from the Flags test
Source: Thurstone and Jeffrey (1956)

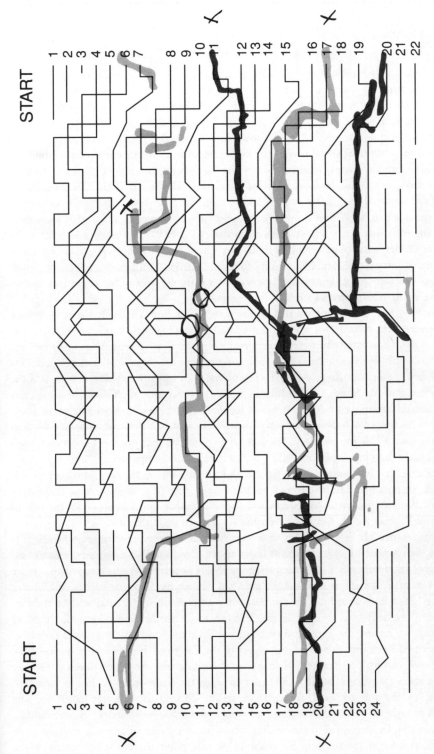

Figure 14.7 Mr Smith's performance on the Geneva Lines test

Conclusions

In summary, Mr Smith presents a very vivid example of someone whose topographical problems appear to reflect a severe spatial impairment. Mr Smith is therefore very different from the patients studied by Pallis (1955) and by Landis et al. (1986), whose difficulties seemed to reflect a problem in identifying once-familiar buildings and other landmarks despite preserved spatial knowledge. Unlike Mr Smith, such patients often suffer from additional visual processing problems such as prosopagnosia (an inability to recognize familiar faces), whereas Mr Smith performed competently on the tests of visual recognition and memory that we gave him. Mr Smith is therefore similar to patient 2 reported by Levine et al. (1985) whom we described earlier. The pattern of performance that Mr Smith shows is consistent with Levine et al.'s view that there exist neurologically distinct 'what' and 'where' memory systems. In other words, because he can remember what objects look like but not where they are located (cf. his ability to identify country shapes and his inability to recall their location), cases such as Mr Smith suggest that our spatial knowledge is stored in a different area of the brain from information about what objects look like.

What we have also demonstrated in the case of Mr Smith is evidence of very poor performance on immediate tests of visuo-spatial processing such as mental rotation, and on tests of visuo-spatial short-term memory such as the Corsi Blocks. It is clear from this that Mr Smith is suffering from a severe impairment of the visuo-spatial sketch pad. One possibility is that because this spatial working memory impairment is so severe, it is the major cause of Mr Smith's difficulties in finding his way around. That is, it is conceivable that Mr Smith's knowledge of spatial locations is still present in long-term memory, but that his spatial short-term memory impairment makes it no longer possible for him to make use of this information. Alternatively, it may be that the short-term and long-term spatial memory problems reflect separate functional impairments, and it is just a coincidence that Mr Smith suffers from both of them. This is the kind of issue that it is virtually impossible to resolve from studying a single case. We therefore hope that future studies of patients such as Mr Smith will provide further information about the role of the visuo-spatial sketch pad in topographical memory impairments.

Finally, since Mr Smith and his wife often become extremely distressed when he gets lost in their house, we visited them at home to see if we could offer any advice as to how to reduce the frequency with which these incidents occurred. We discovered that there were two main situations in which he gets lost. As we have already mentioned, one of these is when he is searching for the toilet or bathroom during the day and he ends up in one of the bedrooms (or vice versa). The other is when he is searching for the toilet or bathroom during the night and ends up wandering around on the ground floor.

It seemed to us that there was one aspect of the design of the house that was contributing to Mr Smith's difficulties: there is a small landing area about two-thirds of the way up the stairs (see figure 14.2(b)). In order to reach the bedrooms, one has to turn 180° on the landing and go up about ten more stairs. To visit the toilet or bathroom, one carries straight on across the landing and climbs about five more stairs. In other words, a person who has ascended to the landing has to make a choice of carrying straight on or making two right turns. It is his inability at this point to remember which is the appropriate decision that seems to be the major cause of Mr Smith getting lost in his own house. He is, of course, faced with a similar dilemma when descending the stairs from one of the bedrooms. If he wishes to visit the toilet, he must remember to turn left then right on the landing; if he is going to the ground floor he must remember to turn left twice. The problems that he experiences at this point would explain why he wanders round the ground floor of the house when searching for the toilet during the night, and why he ends up in a bedroom when he wants to find the bathroom (or vice versa) during the day.

When he first described his problems to us, we found it difficult to explain why Mr Smith gets lost in his own house even though he can find his way home from the hospital; but in fact, negotiating one's way around a house may be particularly difficult for a patient such as Mr Smith who relies on a landmark strategy. The key point is that a house contains many 'routes' which cross over each other. The direction to turn when encountering a landmark in a house will vary according to the purpose of the journey that a person is making. It seems possible, therefore, that a landmark strategy will prove problematic whenever it is necessary to learn a number of different routes across the same terrain.

Our suggestion to the Smiths was that they should consider installing a gate at the top of the flight of stairs that comes up from the ground floor. The gate should be able to swing through 90° so that it would provide a barrier at the top of this flight of stairs and a barrier between the landing and the flight of stairs that leads to the bedrooms. Effectively, this means that at night the stairway down to the ground floor could be temporarily closed off, thus preventing Mr Smith descending to the ground floor. During the day, the route up to the bedrooms would be temporarily closed by moving the gate through 90°. In both cases, Mr Smith would have a direct route to the toilet or bathroom during the day or night. Although this solution would not solve Mr Smith's problem if he wanted to visit a bedroom during the day, it might still alleviate his problems to some extent.

Nevertheless, Mrs Smith did not greet our suggestion with any enthusiasm. She was concerned that a gate on the stairs might be the cause of accidents. We accepted that there was a danger that someone with Mr Smith's problems, in particular, might overbalance at a gate and fall down the stairs. We therefore suggested that a door rather than a gate might be the solution, but Mrs Smith was worried that the cost of a new door would prove prohibitive. As far as we know, Mr and Mrs Smith have not made any changes of the kind we suggested, and Mr Smith continues to get lost in his own house several times every week.

Further Reading

Hanley, J.R. and Young, A.W. (1994) 'The cognitive neuropsychology of memory', in P. Morris and M. Gruneberg (eds), *Aspects of Memory*, vol. 2: *Theoretical Aspects* (London: Routledge).

References

Baddeley, A.D. (1986) *Working Memory* (Oxford: Oxford University Press).

De Renzi, E. and Vignolo, L.A. (1962) 'The token test: a sensitive test to detect receptive disturbances in aphasia', *Brain*, 85: 665–78.

De Renzi, E., Faglioni, P. and Previdi, P. (1977) 'Spatial memory and hemispheric locus of lesion', *Cortex*, 13: 424–33.

Farah, M.J., Levine, D.N. and Calvanio, R. (1988) 'A case study of mental imagery deficit', *Brain and Cognition*, 8: 147–64.

Hanley, J.R., Young, A.W. and Pearson, N. (1989) 'Defective recognition of familiar people', *Cognitive Neuropsychology*, 6: 179–210.

Hanley, J.R., Pearson, N. and Young, A.W. (1990) 'Impaired memory for new visual forms', *Brain*, 113: 1131–48.

Hanley, J.R., Young, A.W. and Pearson, N. (1991) 'Impairment of the visuo-spatial sketch pad', *Quarterly Journal of Experimental Psychology*, 43A: 101–25.

Landis, T., Cummings, J.L., Benson, D.F. and Palmer, E.P. (1986) 'Loss of topographic familiarity: an environmental agnosia', *Archives of Neurology*, 43: 132–6.

Levine, D.N., Warach, J. and Farah, M. (1985) 'Two visual systems in mental imagery: dissociation of "what" and "where" in imagery disorders due to bilateral posterior cerebral lesions', *Neurology*, 35: 1010–18.

McKenna, P. and Warrington, E.K. (1983) *The Graded Naming Test* (Windsor, Berks.: Nelson–NFER).

Nelson, H. (1982) *The New Adult Reading Test* (Windsor, Berks.: Nelson–NFER).

Pallis, C.A. (1955) 'Impaired identification of faces and places with agnosia for colours', *Journal of Neurology, Neurosurgery and Psychiatry*, 18: 218–24.

Ratcliff, G. (1982) 'Spatial thought, mental rotation, and the right cerebral hemisphere', *Neuropsychologia*, 17: 49–54.

Ross, E.D. (1980) 'Sensory-specific and fractional disorders of recent memory in man. I. Isolated loss of visual recent memory', *Archives of Neurology*, 37: 193–200.

Smyth, M.M. and Pelkey, P.L. (1992) 'Short-term retention of spatial information', *British Journal of Psychology*, 83: 359–74.

Thurstone, L.L. and Jeffrey, T.E. (1956) *Flags: A Test of Spatial Thinking* (Chicago: Industrial Relations Center).

Warrington, E.K. (1984) *Recognition Memory Test* (Windsor, Berks.: Nelson–NFER).

Part IV Failures of Facts
Semantic Organization and Breakdown

Introduction

Shown a leek, none of us are likely to respond: 'What is this?', like Mrs P in Elaine Funnell's account. We know, immediately and irrevocably, a number of things about the object. We know what it is used for and how to use it, where it comes from and so forth. Given the word 'leek' we could also provide a description for the word and perform the operation the other way around, too: we could name a leek to description. How is this knowledge organized?

Many researchers in brain and mind have felt sufficiently daunted to leave semantic processing as a 'great unknown' to be skirted, but hardly explored in detail. For example, Fodor (1983) considered that such knowledge-based operations would be intractable if one attempted to determine their componential, modular structure. However, some neurological forays into this uncharted territory have been made, returning successfully with important discoveries. Developments in cognitive science, neuropsychology and linguistics suggest that explorers may now be better equipped to travel further into this difficult area. The three papers in this section represent a selection of some current investigations into the structure of knowledge in brains and in people.

Zaidel offers a particular high-level aerial photograph of the terrain, captured through a specific lens. This view derives from the classic split-brain studies conducted by the Caltech team, of which she was a member. She claims that the differences in processing style and potential between the left and right cerebral hemispheres form two distinct knowledge/memory systems: the left-brain system which is less rigid and more componential in its constituent architecture, and the right-brain system which is more rigid, but also more linked to emotional (affective) aspects of knowledge. The other important point made by Zaidel is that, following the section of the cortical commissures, new memories may be hard to lay down. The role of the fornix (which may be damaged during commisurotomy) in these anterograde difficulties is currently unclear.

Funnell, by contrast, has been exploring the microstructure of knowledge in a patient with quite localized damage to left-temporal regions. In semantic dementia, recently recognized as distinct clinical syndrome (Snowden et al., 1989), specific component knowledge of concepts becomes degraded and eventually lost. Funnell shows how this general picture can be explored in systematic detail and how the strength of specific attributes (based on their frequency and ubiquity) may determine the gradient of knowledge loss. One paradox of Funnell's account, that these patients seem to have a good general idea of the concept under interrogation despite their loss of componential concept knowledge, might be resolved by stepping back to the perspective offered by Zaidel. Could a right-hemisphere 'meaning system' support the *unaffected* conceptual knowledge demonstrated by these patients?

Bert, investigated by Barry and MacHattie, has no trouble telling you what a leek is.

However, if asked to name a squirrel he has difficulties, suggesting specific loss of knowledge about animals. Can knowledge be lost category-wise? This has been an issue of intense speculation since Warrington and Shallice (1984) first suggested that double dissociations could be observed between different patients: some retained knowledge of living things but knowledge of nonliving things was lost; others (more commonly) showed a distinction in the other direction. Since then, there has been controversy concerning the extent to which further levels of fractionation (abstract/concrete, animals/vegetables) can be observed in patients, and, more importantly, precisely what these may signify in terms of the instantiation of knowledge structures in the brain. (The aetiology of the problem was not particularly informative; while some of these category-specific impairments have followed herpes encephalitic infection, others have followed stroke.)

In Bert, following detailed investigation, the problem was highly specific; knowledge of physical attributes of animals was poor in contrast to other attributes both of animals and other objects. Barry and MacHattie reasonably suggest that Bert's naming difficulties and knowledge impairment confined to animal properties are causally linked. Once more, the pattern of brain damage following Bert's small stroke gives a clue to the possible functional impairment; the damage was on the left side and included posterior (occipito-parietal) regions to account for his visual field defect. There is 'something visual' about his knowledge loss; but in contrast to the cases described in section 4, this is not particularly spatial knowledge, but more specifically object-related. The *ventral* ('what?') system (Mishkin et al., 1984) may be damaged here; but in a very circumscribed way. But why animals, and animals alone, should be affected this way is still mysterious.

One of the most promising areas for deepening our understanding of brain function is in such microcognitive explorations of semantic dissolution in patients. Over the next ten years, the investigations of patients like Bert and Mrs P will give important clues concerning how semantic knowledge is acquired, registered and accessed. But neuro-psychological investigations will only form part of this enterprise: studies with normal subjects, including experimental and neuro-imaging studies, will start to draft a new map of this dark continent.

References

Fodor, J. (1983) *The Modularity of Mind* (Cambridge, Mass.: MIT Press).

Mishkin, M., Malamut, B. and Bachevalier, J. (1984) 'Memories and habits: two neural systems', in G. Lynch, J.L. McGaugh and N.M. Weinberger (eds), *Neurobiology of Learning and Memory* (New York: Guilford Press).

Snowden, J.S., Goulding, P.J. and Neary, D. (1989) 'Semantic dementia: a form of circumscribed cerebral atrophy', *Behavioural Neurology*, **2**: 167–82.

Warrington, E.K. and Shallice, T. (1984) 'Category-specific semantic impairments', *Brain*, **107**: 829–54.

15 Separated Hemispheres, Separated Memories: Lessons on Long-term Memory from Split-brain Patients

Dahlia W. Zaidel

1 The Clinical Picture

The traditional neuropsychological approach to the anatomy of human memory focuses on the effects on memory of unilateral or bilateral brain damage, which often includes the hippocampal formation. The role of interhemispheric communication in traditional studies of memory has been largely neglected. Animal models of memory similarly neglect to investigate the role of interhemispheric communication. In part, this may be attributed to a rarity of human cases with surgical hemispheric disconnection. However, severing the anatomical connections between the hemispheres leads to specific memory impairments even while the hemispheres are relatively intact and there is little (known) hippocampal damage (D.W. Zaidel, 1990b).

There is ample evidence that the two halves of the human brain are specialized for different yet complementary functions (see, for example, Corballis, 1991), including different storage/retrieval processes in long-term semantic memory (D.W. Zaidel, 1987, 1990a). The left hemisphere, in right-handers and in the majority of left-handers, is specialized for the main language skills, and the right hemisphere is specialized for visuo-spatial skills such as topographical orientation or facial processing. This can be observed not only following unilateral brain damage but also in the split-brain patients described here. The functional status of the hemispheres of split-brain patients is inferred positively through direct testing rather than through inference from negative findings as is the case in patients with hemispheric damage. Consequently, split-brain patients represent excellent means with which to determine both the role of interhemispheric communication in memory processes and left and right specialization for long-term memory. In this chapter I describe the general memory status in split-brain cases and focus on long-term memory in the disconnected hemispheres.

2   The Anatomy of Split-brain Surgery

The first major study of the effects of split-brain surgery on memory was undertaken by D. Zaidel and Sperry (1974) and it revealed that normal interhemispheric communication is crucial for new memory skills. Ten patients were studied and the results showed impairments in recent memory consistent with informal observations by family members that everyday memory had suffered. The importance of extent of commissural disconnection for memory was highlighted in that study as well. There are different types of split-brain surgery and they have different consequences for memory, ranging from mild to moderate impairment. Some surgeries consist of only partial commissural disconnection and those may include section of the corpus callosum (callosotomy) only, leaving intact the other forebrain commissures, while other types consist of section of the anterior two-thirds of the corpus callosum, or only of the central portion of the callosum (the trunk) (Bogen, 1992). In addition to surgical disruption of callosal fibers, callosal disruptions may be caused by invasive tumours. Even in such cases memory impairments have been reported. In general, the least amount of hemispheric disconnection is associated with the least amount of memory impairment (see D.W. Zaidel, 1990b, for a review of such studies).

A recent confirmation of the conclusions first advanced by D. Zaidel and Sperry (1974), that there is an important role for callosal fibers in memory, has been provided by Rudge and Warrington (1991) who found severe memory impairment in nine cases suffering from tumours in the splenium (posterior section of the corpus callosum).

The focus in this chapter is on complete commissurotomy patients, cases in the Bogen–Vogel series in California (also known as the Caltech series) (Bogen and Vogel, 1962). They are the first group of surgical split-brain patients in the world who were studied systematically in order to determine the functional significance of the interhemispheric commissures and of the hemispheres. The surgery was performed in a single stage and consisted of sectioning the three forebrain commissures: corpus callosum, anterior commissure and the hippocampal commissure. With the improvement in anti-epileptic drugs, surgeons are now inclined to section as few commissural fibres as possible in their attempt to control the epilepsy, and complete commissurotomies are now rarely performed. Thus, the patients described here are rare. They provide a unique opportunity to determine the nature of memory processes in each of the two cerebral hemispheres of the brain.

3   The Anatomic Basis for Specialized Hemispheric Memory

The hippocampus is considered a critical structure in human memory ever since bilateral hippocampal removal in the now-famous case, HM, resulted in profound anterograde amnesia (Scolville and Milner, 1957). Recently it has become clear that there is an evolutionary trend for anatomical and physiological coupling between neocortex and hippocampus on the same side. Wilson and associates (Wilson et al., 1987, 1990) have provided physiological evidence for reduced functional commissural connections via the hippocampal commissure in humans. In the monkey amygdala (Pandya and Rosene, 1985) and in the hippocampus (Amaral et al., 1984) there is a reduction in anatomical interhemispheric commissural connections. This has been confirmed for humans (see Gloor et al., 1993). Rosene and Van Hoesen (1987) report comparative anatomy studies that show progressive phylogenetic reduction in hippocampal commissural connections between the two hippocampi as the move is made from rats and cats to monkeys and humans. This suggests an increase in ipsilateral functional linkage between the hippocampal formation and neocortex as hemispheric specialization evolved. Indeed, recent findings on the human hippocampus have revealed for the first time left–right assymetries in neuronal density and neuronal connectivity (D.W. Zaidel et al., 1993, 1994, 1995). Thus, from anatomical and physiological evidence alone it is reasonable to assume separate, specialized hemispheric long-term memory stores.

4   The General Picture on Memory after Section of the Forebrain Commissures

In patients who undergo complete surgical separation of the left and right hemispheres (complete commissurotomy) there appears to be a clear distinction between memory for events occuring before and after surgery. Family members support this observation. The patients do not suffer from retrograde amnesia; however, there is impairment for events occuring after surgery and they range from subtle to dramatic, depending on individual differences including intelligence level. Memory for motor skills learned prior to surgery, such as swimming, bike riding, typing shoelaces, buttoning a shirt or playing the piano, all appear relatively normal after surgery. Similarly, cooking skills and recipes known prior to surgery are remembered afterwards. In contrast, after surgery, memory for current events, appointments, placement of common articles, parked car location, new motor skills, all appear to be worse than prior to surgery, and very little or no improvement is observed with time. The same applies to learning new motor skills (D. Zaidel and Sperry, 1977). The fact that there is a difference between pre- and post-operative memory suggests that the forebrain commissures play a crucial rule in the initial stages of the memory process, a time when information is sorted out for storage and subsequent retrieval.

Some details on memory assessment in split-brain patients

In the D. Zaidel and Sperry (1974) study, there were eight patients with complete section of the forebrain commissures and two with a partial section. The partial commissurotomy patients had the anterior two-thirds of the corpus callosum sectioned as well as complete section of the hippocampal and anterior commissures. In complete commissurotomy, the corpus callosum, hippocampal and anterior commissures were all sectioned. It is assumed that during surgery some fornix fibres have been partially interrupted on one side in a few cases. Examination of magnetic resonance imaging (MRI shows that it is unlikely that any bilateral fornix damage had occurred. Minimal extra-callosal cortical damage due to the surgery or to the epilepsy is assumed present in all cases.

Unfortunately, no pre-operative scores on standardized memory tests are available. The postoperative standardized tests were the Wechsler Memory Scale (WMS) (Wechsler, 1945), Benton's Revised Visual Retention test (Benton, 1963), Memory for Objects (Wells and Ruesch, 1945), Visual Sequential Memory, a subtest of the Illinois Test of Psycholinguistic Abilities (Kirk et al., 1968), Knox Cubes test (Arthur, 1947) and Memory for Designs (Graham and Kendall, 1960). The results of all of these tests may be summarized as follows: (a) the Wechsler Memory Quotients (MQ) of all patients were substantially below their IQs (WAIS Intelligence Quotient), as judged by the IQ–MQ (Memory Quotient) difference; (b) complete commissurotomy patients were particularly poor in remembering the nonverbal visual task of the WMS; (c) both partial and complete commissurotomy patients obtained lower scores on the 'hard' as compared with 'easy' word associations subtest of the WMS; (d) partial commissurotomy patients obtained low scores on short-story passages of the WMS.

Later, a study by Huppert (1981) on three of the same complete commissurotomy patients confirmed the presence of memory deficit by showing that two of them required eight times the exposure duration of pictorial stimuli than was required by normal subjects in order subsequently to remember them at the same level. One patient with complete commissurotomy, LB, did require normal acquisition exposure durations. Huppert's findings are consistent with LB's normal scores on four of the tests administered by D. Zaidel and Sperry (1974). Her study suggests that retention of pictorial information one week after initial training is within the normal range in all three patients. But the same patient, LB, is severely impaired in remembering everyday events as well having a much lower MQ than IQ.

The general conclusion concerning the status of memory as judged by performance in laboratory tests is that the presence of the interhemispheric commissures is crucial in the initial learning and sorting of perceived information. This may be particularly critical when the level of unilateral hemispheric capacity for learning is not high. When it is, as may be the case in LB, memory skills may be supported by only one hemisphere and the detrimental effects of commissural disconnection on memory are not pronounced. Once learning is accomplished, disconnection effects do not appear to be critical.

5   Interhemispheric Communication in Memory

Generally it is assumed that the verbal output of split-brain patients reflects left hemisphere dominance, and whatever is missing in the output is inferred to be a right hemisphere component or the result of normal interaction between left and right hemispheres. As mentioned, what appears to have suffered dramatically after surgery is recent memory. Indeed, the type of nonverbal memory usually associated with right hemisphere specialization, topographical memory, is particularly poor in daily life. Thus, these patients have exceptional difficulties in topographical memory (for example, relocating a parked car or locating items around the house). Some verbal memory, especially of newly learned material, is also not up to the level preceding surgery, as determined by family members. This is confirmed in laboratory tests as well. Because memory is poor they have no interest in reading novels or newspapers. Similarly, following TV or films poses problems that are probably due to poor memory. The patients have difficulty in following plot lines or recalling narrative structures.

6 The Role of the Forebrain Commissures in Memory

The performance of split-brain patients suggests that the forebrain commissures play an important role in the acquisition stage of memory. A number of important considerations may interact with the level of memory seen following surgery, and some of those are: the age at symptom onset; age at time of surgery; presence versus absence of the disconnection syndrome; extent of commissural section; single versus two-stage surgery; individual variability in innate memory ability, and so on. Three considerations warrant specific mention: (a) there is some decrement, varying from mild to substantial, following section of the corpus callosum alone, or with only one small lesioned region; (b) single, as opposed to serial, callosal surgical section does not appear to result in memory impairment; (c) more than any other standardized memory tasks, the word association and story passage subtests of the WMS appear to be sensitive to partial or complete forebrain commissurotomy. Memory for story passages is seriously impaired even in patient with partial commissural section. Such verbal tests may be particularly dependent on hemispheric integration.

The fornix

As mentioned earlier, during split-brain surgery, there is some unilateral interruption of columnar fibres in the fornix in only some of the patients. Damage to the fornix, a neural tract that connects the hippocampal system to other limbic structures, has been implicated in memory deficits in laboratory animals (Bachvalier et al., 1985). In humans not under-going commissurotomy the picture is not so clear, either clinically or theoretically (Squire, 1987). However, in none of the split-brain patients was the fornix sectioned bilaterally. A detailed review of the status of the fornix in these patients has already been published (Zaidel, 1990b). The conclusion put forth in that publication is that the fornix plays little or no role in the memory impairments of split-brain patients.

7 Long-term Memory (LTM)

The mind in the brain creates order from experience with the aid of organized knowledge systems stored in LTM. Forms of knowledge organization include serial organization, such as the alphabet, calendar, categorial organization (such as taxonomy), and schema organization such as parts that together form a theme or a concept (for example, title of a story, a face) consisting of some of our knowledge about objects, events, scenes, stories or motor programmes. These memory stores guide the pick up of information and control different processing strategies of the same complex stimuli. Cognitive psychologists refer to LTM as the last component in a multiple-stage system made up of several structural components all involved in the internal coding of experience (Klatzky,

1975; Crowder, 1976). A critical feature of this model is that during every stage contact is made with LTM in order to analyse the input. Meaning is attained when contact is made with previous knowledge that is already stored. With regard to the hemispheres, the assumption is that the same external experiences are available to both hemispheres but that each uses its own specialized knowledge organization and its own strategies to process these experiences. This chapter advances the thesis that the presence of specialized hemispheric knowledge stores underlies human visual cognition.

Traditional views of the hemispheric long-term knowledge systems

Visual agnosia is loss of the ability to recognize the meaning of visually perceived objects. Traditional concepts of visual agnosia distinguish between perceptual and semantic components (apperceptive vs. association agnosia) and attribute specialization for processing the semantic component to the left hemisphere, and for processing the perceptual component to the right hemisphere (Newcombe et al., 1975; Warrington, 1975). Thus, considering the right hemisphere as having a long-term memory store whence meaning can be obtained, is not a universally accepted view in neuropsychology. One tradition suggests that meaning is obtained primarily in the left, language, hemisphere. Investigations of split-brain patients are not consistent with such a view. They have shown that external experiences are processed asymmetrically and sorted for storage in ways characteristic of underlying differences in hemispheric long-term semantic memory.

History: initial evidence for long-term memory in the disconnected right hemisphere

Language and long-term knowledge system   Contralateral sensory anatomical projections from the left hand reach the right hemisphere, where there is no speech specialization. Consequently, the disconnected right hemisphere of a split-brain patient has no way to show knowledge about left-hand sensations through speaking or writing. The main control for the right hand is in the left hemisphere, where language is specialized, so patients can verbalize right-hand sensations. A similar situation exists for the primary visual system: sensory information in the left visual half-field projects via the lateral geniculate body of the thalamus to the right hemisphere. On the other hand, an object palpated blindly with the left hand of a normal right-hander can be named easily. In this case the corpus callosum is intact and allows transfer from the area of sensory representation of the left hand in the right hemisphere to the speech centre in the left hemisphere. The same distinction applies to information perceived in the left visual half-field of a normal person and a split-brain patient, respectively.

However, the inability to name objects in the left hand or in the left visual half-field is not by itself an indication that there is no semantic or knowledge system in the right hemisphere. Language is but one way to demonstrate knowledge. Similarly, absence of language should not be interpreted to reflect lack of awareness (D.W. Zaidel, 1990a).

Nonverbal long-term knowledge in the right hemisphere   The existence of long-term knowledge in the right hemisphere was reported early (see, for example, Sperry, 1974):

1 With the left hand (right hemisphere) a split-brain patient can show through blind touch of an array of objects which objects belong in the same category by sorting them into piles, without being informed what those categories are. This demonstrates knowledge of concepts.
2 With the left hand, a particular object can be matched blindly with a related object even when the two are shaped differently. This again demonstrates knowledge of concepts.
3 Knowledge about objects is demonstrated in correct manual handling by the left hand (blindly). For example, although a pen is not named correctly it is grasped in a writing posture, between the forefinger and the thumb; a cup is held by its handle even while the wrong verbal label is provided.
4 Under special viewing conditions, which restrict the visual information to only one hemisphere at a time, episodic memory can be demonstrated in the right hemisphere when patients recognize which cup of several shown is their very own. (Other examples are described below.)

Throughout these tests patients are unable to name the blindly palpated objects correctly. This is usually considered to be evidence that the left hemisphere is not involved in the performance. The information did not become available to the left hemisphere through subcortical pathways.

Long-term memory for historical events in the right hemisphere (Sperry et al., 1979) Various pictures of historical figures (such as Churchill, Kennedy, Roosevelt, Hitler, Stalin), of cultural symbols (for example, swastika, Star of David, cross, American flag), of family members or of the patient him/herself were viewed by each disconnected hemisphere; the task was to show preference. 'Thumbs up' indicated positive preference while 'thumbs down' indicated negative preference. Positive reactions were given to pictures of family members and highly valued individuals or cultural symbols. Negative responses were given to Hitler, Stalin, the swastika and similarly negative cultural images, such as costume of the Ku Klax Clan. When the same visual information was presented to the left hemisphere, responses were nearly identical to those provided for the right hemisphere. This demonstrates the presence of long-term knowledge on a personal as well as on a historical level in the left and right hemispheres.

Recent findings on hemispheric longer-term memory

The category knowledge system: exemplars of natural categories The study of the category knowledge system examines the relationships among single concepts by determining 'mental distances' among members of a category as well as members of different categories. Reaction time (RT) paradigms are used to determine these mental proximities et al. (Rosch, 1975). Verification latencies in natural category membership tasks are considered, according to one view (Rosch, 1975; Rosch and Mervis, 1975), to reflect the degree of similarity between items and the prototype invoked by the category concept. This is because prototypical concepts have more attributes in common with other members of the category than the members have with each other. Although prototypicality as the main organizing principle in LTM has been questioned (see, for example, Gleitman et al., 1983), for natural concepts there is ample evidence that it exists and I have used the method of category membership decisions to study the nature of typicality in the LTM in each hemisphere (D.W. Zaidel, 1987).

Split-brain patients and normal subjects were asked to decide quickly whether or not pictures of single objects were members of superordinate natural categories such as weapon, furniture, vegetable, fruit and vehicle. Some of the exemplars were typical and some were atypical members of the categories (as determined earlier by Rosch, 1975). The pictures were shown in quick flashes in the left or right visual half-fields (D.W. Zaidel, 1987). The task was to press a button as rapidly as possible to indicate whether the seen object (say, a chair) was a member of a specific category (say, furniture). The results showed that in the left visual half-field (right hemisphere), responses were much faster for typical members than for atypical members, while there was no difference between typical and atypical exemplars in the right visual half-field (left-hemisphere). Decisions for typical exemplars were faster in the left visual half-field than in the right visual half-field, whereas decisions for atypical exemplars were made faster in the right visual half-field (D.W. Zaidel, 1987). Importantly, the split-brain patients showed patterns of performance nearly identical to the normal subjects. The similarity between performance of disconnected hemispheres and normal hemispheres suggests that in the normal brain, when the commissures are intact, there is functional separation between the conceptual hemispheric stores.

The schema knowledge system   Schemas constitute organized packets of concepts. A schema is an abstract organizational principle for information stored in LTM. Psychologists and computer scientists discuss them in terms of a collection of parts which together form a theme that guides perception, helps memory or controls action (see, for example, Bartlett, 1932; Norman & Bobrow, 1976, or Mandler, 1984). They may constitute parts of a face, figures in a scene, members of a category, facts in a story, and so on. Cognitive psychologists have further demonstrated that schemas affect accuracy, speed and amount of material remembered. The theoretical notion of a schema rests on the assumption that reality is actively constructed to fit prior knowledge so that new information is meaningful, schema-consistent or schema-relevant. What is perceived, remembered or inferred, then, reflects the nature of prior knowledge.

The face is a unique visual object (different from the objects studied in the previous experiment) and the hemispheric processing of its visual parameters is a useful tool to determine the conceptual organization in each hemisphere. It is a well-rehearsed visual pattern and is extremely important early in infancy, in human social behaviour, and, like language, it appears to be modular (both functionally and structurally). The neuropsychological literature points to both (a) right-hemisphere superiority in face processing (reviewed in Bruce, 1989), and (b) evidence that the left hemisphere also plays some role in face processing. Indeed, work on commissurotomy patients (Levy et al., 1972) clearly showed that both hemispheres play a role in face processing and that the relative contribution of each can be manipulated with task demands.

In the adult right hemisphere there is greater specialization for facial recognition than in the left hemisphere. What does this specialization tell us about the conceptual system of the right hemisphere? And what makes a face a face in the right hemisphere? This is discussed below.

For the study reviewed here, two types of pictures were created. One was of a normal face and the other was a face-like picture in which the contour frame of a face was drawn but with systematically rearranged features inside the frame. For example, a nose was positioned were lips normally occur, an eye was positioned where the nose normally occurs, and so on. These were presented for extended viewing to the left and right hemispheres of two complete commissurotomy patients at Caltech, Pasadena (D.W. Zaidel, 1984, 1990a). Each picture was presented to one hemisphere at a time and the patient pointed to features named by the examiner (for example, eye, nose, mouth). All facial features were correctly recognized in either hemisphere when the normal face was shown. But when the face-like picture with rearranged features was shown, recognition of features was accurate only in the left hemisphere. Systematic errors were made when the task was performed by the right hemisphere. Instead of pointing to the lips or the nose, say, patients pointed to the features which occupied positions normally occupied by the lips and the nose. The errors revealed a bias derived from what appeared to be a rigid face concept, namely of a straight-on view of a normal face with all features correctly juxtaposed. This bias appears to have interfered with seeing/processing the actual features named by the examiner. (Recent work on normal subjects has confirmed this bias even in the intact brain; D.W. Zaidel, 1991). By contrast, with the left hemisphere controlling the manual responses, the actual facial features were recognized. Thus, conceptual systems of the left and right hemispheres seem to have differences with regards to a specific common schema. Left hemisphere strategies may be labelled 'flexible' and the right 'rigid'. In this viewpoint, the flexible strategies reflect easy cross-over among conceptual and perceptual boundaries while the rigid strategies reflect boundary-bound information processing.

8 Theoretical and Clinical Implications of Split-brain Memory Research

My data suggest that cases of visual agnosia due, for instance, to unilateral (or bilateral) lesions underestimate the contribution of each intact hemisphere to perception and memory of pictures, and that the observed deficits in such cases may be the result of pathological inhibition of healthy tissue by diseased tissue (D.W. Zaidel, 1986).

The results described here make a strong case for the presence of two separate LTMs which probably underly hemispheric specialization in information processing at all levels, from perception to recognition (D.W. Zaidel, 1988; D.W. Zaidel and Kasher, 1989). The hemispheric functional 'division of labour' in terms of language versus nonlanguage reflects but one dimension of hemispheric differences. Specialization of language in the left hemisphere and of spatial orientation or *Gestalt* thinking in the right represent only specific aspects of the general underlying hemispheric meaning systems (see D.W. Zaidel, 1994c). Moreover, the recent findings on patients who have undergone anterior temporal lobe resections suggest that left–right differences in neuronal connectivity in the human hippocampi may be the structural underpinning of hemispheric specialization in memory processes (D.W. Zaidel et al., 1993, 1994). The lessons learned from studying split-brain patients with complete cerebral commissurotomy is that there can be two meaning systems to support memory functions, one in the left and one in the right, which may operate separately and simultaneously in the normal brain.

References

Amaral, D.G., Insausti, R. and Cowan, W.M. (1984) 'The commissural connections of the monkey hippocampal formation', *Journal of Comparative Neurology*, **224**: 307–36.

Arthur, G. (1947) *A Point Scale of Performance Tests, Revised Form II* (New York: Psychological Corporation).

Bachvalier, J., Saunders, R. and Mishkin, M. (1985) 'Visual recognition in monkeys: effects of transection of fornix', *Experimental Brain Research*, **57**: 547–53.

Bartlett, F.C. (1932) *Remembering: A Study in Experimental and Social Psychology* (Cambridge: Cambridge University Press).

Benton, A.L. (1963) *The Revised Visual Retention Test* (New York: Psychological Corporation).

Bogen, J.E. (1992) 'The callosal syndromes', in K.M. Heilman and E. Valenstein (eds), *Clinical Neuropsychology* (New York: Oxford University Press).

Bogen, J.E. and Vogel, P.J. (1962) 'Cerebral commissurotomy in man: preliminary case report', *Bulletin of the Los Angeles Neurological Society*, **27**: 169–72.

Bruce V. (1989) *Recognizing Faces* (London: Lawrence Erlbaum Associates).

Corballis, M.C. (1991) *The Lopsided Ape* (London: Oxford University Press).

Crowder, R.G. (1976) *Principles of Learning and Memory* (New York: John Wiley).

Gleitman, L.R., Armstrong, S.L. and Gleitman, H. (1983) 'The concept "concept"', in E.K. Scholnik (ed.), *Trends in Conceptual Representation: Challenges to Piaget's Theory?* (Hillsdale, N.J.: Lawrence Erlbaum).

Gloor, P., Salanova, V., Olivier, A. and Quesney, L.F. (1993) 'The human dorsal hippocampal commissure: an anatomically identifiable and functional pathway', *Brain*, **116**: 1249–73.

Graham, F.K. and Kendall, B.S. (1960) 'Memory-for-designs-test: revised general manual', *Perception and Motor Skills*, **11**: 147–88.

Heilman, J.M. and Sypert, G.W. (1977) 'Korsakoff's syndrome resulting from bilateral fornix lesions', *Neurology*, **27**: 480–93.

Huppert, F.A. (1981) 'Memory in split-brain patients: a comparison with organic amnesic syndromes', *Cortex*, **17**: 303–11.

Kirk, S.A., McCarthy, J.J. and Kirk, W.D. (1968) *Illinois Test of Psycholinguistic Abilities: Examiner's Manual* (Urbana, Ill.: University of Illinois Press).

Klatsky, R.L. (1975) *Human Memory: Structures and Processes* (San Francisco: W.H. Freeman).

Mandler, J.M. (1984) *Stories, Scripts and Scenes: Aspects of Schema Theory* (Hillsdale, N.J.: Lawrence Erlbaum).

McCarthy, R.A. and Warrington, E.K. (1990) *Cognitive Neuropsychology* (London: Academic Press).

Newcombe, F. and Ratcliffe, G. (1975) 'Agnosia: a disorder of object recognition', in F. Michel and B. Schott (eds), *Les Syndromes de disconnexion calleuse chez l'homme* (Lyon: Hôpital neurologique de Lyon).

Norman, D.A. and Bobrow, D.G. (1976) 'On the role of active memory processes in perception and cognition', in C.N. Cofer (ed.), *The Structure of Human Memory* (San Francisco: W.H. Freeman).

Pandya, D.N. and Rosene, D.L. (1985) 'Some observations on trajectories and topography of commissural fibers', in A.G. Reeves (ed.), *Epilepsy and the Corpus Callosum* (New York: Plenum Press).

Parkin, A. (1987) *Memory and Amnesia: An Introduction* (Oxford: Basil Blackwell).

Rosch, E. (1975) 'Cognitive representation of semantic categories', *Journal of Experimental Psychology: General*, 104: 192–233.

Rosch, E. and Mervis, C.B. (1975) 'Family resemblense: studies in the internal structure of categories', *Cognitive Psychology*, 7: 573–605.

Rosene, D.L. and Van Hoesen, G.W. (1987) 'The hippocampal formation of the primate brain', in E.G. Jones and A. Peters (eds), *Cerebral Cortex* (New York: Plenum Press).

Rudge, P. and Warrington, E.K. (1991) 'Selective impairment of memory and visual perception in splenial tumours', *Brain*, 114: 349–60.

Scolville, W.B. and Milner, B. (1957) 'Loss of recent memory after bilateral hippocampal lesions', *Journal of Neurology, Neurosurgery and Psychiatry*, 20: 11–21.

Sperry, R.W. (1974) 'Lateral specialization in the surgically separated hemispheres', in F.O. Schmitt and F.G. Worden (eds), *Neuroscience Third Study Program* (Boston, Mass.: MIT Press).

Sperry, R.W., Zaidel, E. and Zaidel, D. (1979) 'Self-recognition and social awareness in the deconnected minor hemisphere', *Neuropsychologia*, 17: 153–66.

Squire, L.R. (1987) *Memory and Brain* (London: Oxford University Press).

Warrington, E.K. (1975) 'The selective impairment of semantic memory', *Quarterly Journal of Experimental Psychology*, 27: 635–57.

Wechsler, D. (1945) 'A standardized memory scale for clinical use'. *Journal of Psychology*, 19: 87–95.

Wells, F.L. and Ruesch, J. (1945) *Mental Examiner's Handbook* (New York: Psychological Corporation).

Wilson, C.L., Isokawa-Akesson, M., Babb, T.L., Engle, J.J., Cahan, L.D. and Crandall, P.H. (1987) 'A comparative view of local and interhemispheric limbic pathways in humans: an evoked potential analysis', in J. Engle Jr (ed.), *Fundamental Mechanisms of Human Brain Function* (New York: Raven Press), pp. 27–38.

Wilson, C.L., Isokawa-Akesson, M., Babb, T.L. and Crandall, P.H. (1990) Functional connections in the human temporal lobe. I. Analysis of limbic system pathways using neuronal activity evoked by electrical stimulation', *Experimental Brain Research*, 82: 279–92.

Zaidel, D. and Sperry, R.W. (1974) 'Memory impairment after commissurotomy in man', *Brain*, 97: 263–72.

Zaidel, D. and Sperry, R.W. (1977): 'Some long-term motor effects of cerebral commissurotomy in man', *Neuropsychologia*, 15: 193–204.

Zaidel, D.W. (1984) 'Cognitive functions in the right hemisphere', *La Recherche*, 15: 332–40.

Zaidel, D.W. (1986) 'Memory for scenes in stroke patients: hemispheric processing of semantic organization in pictures', *Brain*, 109: 547–60.

Zaidel, D.W. (1987) 'Hemispheric asymmetry in long-term semantic relationships', *Cognitive Neuropsychology*, 4: 321–32.

Zaidel, D.W. (1988) 'Hemi-field asymmetries in memory for incongruous scenes', *Cortex*, 24: 231–44.

Zaidel, D.W. (1990a) 'Long-term semantic memory in the two cerebral hemispheres', in C. Trevarthen (ed.), *Brain Circuits and Functions of the Mind* (New York: Cambridge University Press).

Zaidel, D.W. (1990b) 'Memory and spatial cognition following commissurotomy', in F. Boller and J. Grafman (eds), *Handbook of Neuropsychology* (Amsterdam: Elsevier).

Zaidel, D.W. (1991) 'Effects of violations of a face schema in the left and right hemispheres of split-brain patients and normal subjects', *Society for Neuroscience Abstracts*, 17: 867.

Zaidel, D.W. (1994c) 'Worlds apart: pictorial semantics in the left and right cerebral hemispheres', *Current Directions in Psychological Science*, **3**: 5–8.

Zaidel, D.W. and Kasher, A. (1989) 'Hemispheric memory for surrealistic versus realistic paintings', *Cortex*, **25**: 617–41.

Zaidel, D.W., Esiri, M.M. and Oxbury, J.M. (1993) 'Regional differentiation of cell densities in the left and right hippocampi of epileptic patients', *Journal of Neurology*, **240**: 322–5, 1993.

Zaidel, D.W., Esiri, M.M. and Oxbury, J.M. (1994) 'Sex-related asymmetries in the morphology of the left and right hippocampi? A follow-up study on epileptic patients', *Journal of Neurology*, **241**: 620–3.

Zaidel, D.W., Esiri, M.M., Eastwood, S.L. and Harrison, P.J. (1995) 'Asymmetrical hippocampal circuitry and schizophrenia', *Lancet*, **345**: 656–7.

16   A Case of Forgotten Knowledge

Elaine Funnell

Introduction

If you were to meet Mrs P, she would tell you that she has a memory problem and that it is getting worse. This however, would be only partly true: Mrs P has a memory problem, but only for a particular sort of knowledge.

What Mrs P has forgotten are the concepts underlying word meanings. For example, when she was asked: 'Who wrote Hamlet?', she replied: 'Who's Hamlet?'; when she was asked: 'Is a kitten young?', she replied: 'What on earth is a kitten?'; and to the question: 'Does a mouse have a beak?', she answered: 'If I knew what a beak was I could tell you.' But, in spite of this very marked memory problem for concepts, she has not forgotten her life history; what she has been doing recently; or what she has planned to do tomorrow.

So, while Mrs P seems to have lost knowledge about concepts, she has not forgotten the episodes or events of her life. Tulving (1972) first made the distinction between memory for knowledge about words, word meanings and the relationships between words, which he called *semantic memory*, and memory for personal events or episodes, which he called *episodic memory*. Mrs P's memory problem seems to affect semantic memory only, and gives some support to Tulving's suggestion that there may be distinct types of memory representations.

I first met Mrs P in January 1990. She was then 62 years old, and had retired two years previously from a teaching job where she had been head of department for maths in a middle school (teaching children aged from 8 to 12 years). Her husband had noticed that, twelve months previously, she had begun to have difficulty in finding unusual words and the names of people. She was referred to the Radcliffe Infirmary in Oxford for neurological investigation; a CT scan of her brain carried out there in November 1989 showed focal atrophy of the left temporal lobe. Hodges et al. (1992) have since diagnosed Mrs P's condition as a case of semantic dementia, a condition first identified by Snowden et al. (1989).

When I assessed Mrs P's disorder, there was no doubt that her comprehension was very poor, for she scored at the level of a child of five and a half years on the British Picture Vocabulary Test designed by Dunn et al. (1982). She could point to the correct picture for some words, for example 'teacher', 'disagreement', 'wrist', 'surprise', but made mistakes on words such as 'link', 'tusk', 'snarling', 'locket', 'bloom' and 'weasel'. There can be no doubt that, as a school teacher, she would have understood these words in the past. In spite of these difficulties, Mrs P did very well indeed on other cognitive tests. She could repeat lists of seven numbers and understand complex grammatical constructions such as 'The pencil is on the book that is yellow' and semantically revers-ible sentences such as 'The elephant is pushed by the boy', taken from the Test for the Reception of Grammar, compiled by Bishop (1982). She was also excellent at the non-verbal Colour Matrices Test (Raven, 1965) on which she scored in the top band for her age.

In her daily life, Mrs P's semantic memory problem has fairly limited effect. She drives, and can map-read her way to new places. She is a keen country-dancer and takes her turn at calling the dances. She is a skilled dress-maker and can alter clothes and make up complicated patterns, and she continues to cook and manage the house. However, reading and spelling cause problems, particularly when the words have an irregular spelling-to-sound correspondence. For example, she reads the words 'yacht' and 'pint' as if they rhymed with 'hatched' and 'mint' respectively, and spells these words as 'yot' and 'pynt'. Her mistakes, which are typical of cases of surface dyslexia and dysgraphia, suggest that she reads and spells many of these words on the basis of phonic rules. The only other characteristics which set her apart from others are a rather childlike exaggera-tion of emphasis and intonation in speech, and a somewhat concrete approach to thinking and planning.

What Sort of Knowledge is Forgotten?

I decided to investigate Mrs P's lost knowledge. In particular, I wanted to know whether there was any pattern to the loss of knowledge, or whether the concepts that caused problems were a random sample of the full set. I also wanted to know whether particular concepts always caused problems, or whether knowledge came and went across different occasions. I set about this task, using a number of different sorts of tests, including object naming, defining object names and matching spoken words to pictures.

The first test investigated the effect of differences in word frequency and familiarity upon her ability to define words. Word frequency counts, such as those produced by Kucera and Francis (1967), measure the incidence of words in the language, in this case in the written language. Common words, such as 'man', obviously occur very much more frequently than uncommon words such as 'goose'. Oldfield and Wingfield (1965) found that common names were produced faster by normal subjects in picture naming tasks, and Newcombe et al. (1965) showed that aphasic patients were better at naming pictures with common names than uncommon names. However, it is perhaps worth noting that

Table 16.1 Proportion of spoken nouns and adjectives correctly defined by Mrs P

	N	1990	1992
High frequency/High familiarity	(24)	1.00	0.83
Low frequency/Low familiarity	(24)	0.38	0.04

Morrison et al. (1991) have suggested recently that word frequency measures reflect the age at which words are acquired – more common words being learned earlier – rather than the frequency with which a word is used.

Concepts, also, may be more or less familiar. Snodgrass and Vanderwart (1980) asked subjects to rate 260 line drawings according to how often they came into contact or thought about the concept illustrated in the drawing. They found only modest correlations between the familiarity of the concept and the frequency of the picture names in the language, and argued that familiarity and name frequency are independent attributes. Differences in familiarity can also affect object naming and defining. Funnell and Sheridan (1992) found that a young woman who had suffered brain damage as a result of a road traffic accident had forgotten many concepts and, perhaps not surprisingly, the ones she had forgotten were the least familiar. Mrs P's husband had also observed that the names she was forgetting seemed to be the less-common, less-familiar words.

I selected 24 nouns and adjectives which were highly familiar and frequent, words such as 'table', 'book', 'people', 'good', 'short', 'hot', and 24 less-familiar nouns and adjectives that occur less frequently in the language, words such as 'feather', 'axe', 'peg', 'tame', 'nasty', 'stale'. The names were spoken to her and she was asked to give the meaning of each word. The test was presented to Mrs P in 1990 and 1992, and as table 16.1 shows, she was able to give significantly more meanings of common familiar words than of less-common, less-familiar words. These differences were significantly above chance: 1990, $z = 4.31$, $p < 0.001$; 1992, $z = 5.18$, $p < 0.001$.

When Mrs P knew the meaning of a word, her definitions were clear and fairly precise, but when she failed, she usually said she didn't know, or that she had forgotten. For example, she defined 'station' as 'A place where trains go from here to London'; 'fat' as 'What a person may look like: bigger and heavier than usual', and 'narrow' as 'Not very wide'. In contrast she answered 'Don't know' or 'Forgotten' to the words 'peg', 'tulip', 'cart' and 'stale'.

Mrs P had the same difficulty when she was given pictures to name. She was asked to name 24 pictures and a define the 24 names of the pictured objects, all of which had low-frequency names occurring fewer than ten times in every million spoken words. Half were more familiar items, for example 'apple' and 'thumb', with a mean rating for familiarity of 4.32 (range 3.98–4.72), and half were less-familiar items, such as 'goat' and 'cigar', with a mean rating for familiarity of 2.50 (range 1.92–2.95). The pictures and names were split into half and presented in an ABBA design. As table 16.2 shows, Mrs P was better at naming and defining the more familiar items. The difference is significant: $z = 3.15$, $p < 0.001$. Dr Kathi Hirsh has carried out some regression analyses on Mrs P's naming data and has shown that the important factor is how familiar the

Table 16.2 Proportion of pictures correctly named and picture names correctly defined by Mrs P, according to the familiarity of the object

	N	Named	Defined
Familiar concepts	(12)	0.67	0.75
Less familiar concepts	(12)	0.08	0.25

concept is, not how common is the name, nor indeed how early in life the name is learned (Hirsh and Funnell, 1994).

What Is Lost When Knowledge Breaks Down?

Warrington (1975 has suggested that when knowledge of a concept breaks down, information about the defining properties or features of the concept are lost before knowledge of the category to which the item belongs. When Warrington asked patients questions about properties of the lost concepts, she found that the patients were generally poor at deciding whether items were bigger or smaller than a cat, were foreign or English, were black or white. However, they could generally decide whether the item was an animal or an object. Studies by other research groups, for example, Chertkow et al. (1989), have also reported that patients appear to know more about the general category to which an item belongs than anything about the properties of the items.

Warrington argued that object concepts (such as 'dog') are collections of properties, arranged in a hierarchy in which the most general property ('animal') is placed at the highest level, and the most specific, defining properties ('*barks*') are placed at the lowest level, much like the model of semantic memory suggested by Collins and Quillian (1969). However, Warrington's view differed from Collins and Quillian's view in one important respect: in Warrington's theory, the hierarchy can only be entered from the highest level, at which the most general properties are stored.

While Warrington's idea would fit with the fact that patients often appear to know about the general category to which an item belongs, and little else, it would not fit with other evidence. Collins and Quillian found that normal subjects are faster to answer basic-level questions about typical members of a category, such as 'Is a canary a bird?' than category questions such as 'Is a canary an animal?', and Rosch et al. (1976) showed that subjects use basic-level names rather than category names to name pictures. Rosch et al. also found that young children sort objects into basic level-categories (for example, cats versus dogs) before they learn to sort into categories (for example, cats and dogs versus types of cars). These findings suggest that, if semantic memory is indeed organized as a hierarchy, the information stored in it must be accessible from other levels besides the superordinate category level, as Collins and Quillian proposed.

Bayles et al. (1990) pointed out that the questions about object properties, for example 'Is it heavier than a telephone directory?', 'Is it used to cut wood or stone?', tend to be

Table 16.3 Numbers of questions correctly answered by Mrs P about category membership and semantic properties

	Questions		
	Category 1990	1991	Property 1990
High familiar	20/20 Is a rose a flower?	17/20	41/48 Does a salmon have eyes?
Low familiar	12/20 Is a dahlia a flower?	10/20	33/48 Does a salmon have fins?

Note: In the category questions, the items vary in familiarity and in the property questions the properties vary in familiarity.

more complex than questions about category membership: 'Is it an animal?', and this difference may be the reason why patients do better with category questions. It is also likely that the vocabulary that is used in category questions – 'Is it an animal/building/ clothing' – is generally more familiar than the vocabulary used in questions about properties, for example 'Is it made of metal?' Is it foreign?'. If patients are less likely to understand the words in questions about properties, they will be less likely to answer property questions correctly. They will also be less likely to produce such words when defining object names.

With these points in mind, I composed two sets of questions, one about the category membership of items and one about the properties of items. The same category question was posed for items which varied in familiarity and word frequency. For example, Mrs P was asked: 'Is an apple a fruit?', and later: 'Is a guava a fruit?', or 'Is a buzzard a bird?'; and later again, 'Is a sparrow a bird?'. 'Apple' and 'sparrow' are higher in familiarity, than 'guava' and buzzard', but the hierarchical model would not predict any difference in performance for these two sets of items, for if knowledge about category membership (such as fruit) can be accessed for the familiar items (such as apple), it should also be accessible for the low-familiarity items (such as guava).

However, Mrs P's performance was strongly affected by the familiarity of the item. The test was presented twice, once in March 1990 and again in January 1991. As table 16.3 shows, she answered the category questions about more-familiar items significantly more successfully than the same category questions asked about less-familiar items: 1990: $\chi^2 = 7.66$, $p < 0.01$; 1991: $\chi^2 = 4.10$, $p < 0.05$.

Questions were asked about properties too. These questions varied the familiarity (F) of the property, while keeping the item unchanged; for example, 'Does a chicken have legs (high F property) and 'Does a chicken have a beak?' (low F property); or 'Does a rabbit have a nose?' (high F property) and 'Does a rabbit have paws?' (low F property). Sixty-two questions were about correct pairings (for example, 'Does a bicycle have wheels?') and 34 were about incorrect pairings (for example, 'Does a bicycle have an engine?'). Twenty four additional negative questions to six further items drawn from the same categories were included to balance yes and no questions more evenly.

The test was presented in October 1990. As table 16.3 shows, Mrs P's ability to answer the property questions was *not* significantly affected by the familiarity of the property name ($\chi^2 = 2.89$; $p > 0.05$), suggesting that the familiarity of the object name is the important factor. Overall, there is no evidence that Mrs P knows more about the category membership of items and less about their properties. When the scores for 1990 were summed, Mrs P was found to have answered 32/40 (80 per cent) questions about category membership and 74/96 (77 per cent) about properties. The results do not support the theory that when semantic knowledge breaks down, knowledge about properties is lost before knowledge of the category. Nor do the results fit with the idea that knowledge about category membership is accessed before knowledge of features.

What is more, it soon became clear that even when Mrs P clearly understood a concept, she was nevertheless often unable to point to the critical defining features given in a typical coloured picture of the item. For example, she defined fish in the following way: 'Something that lives in the water, that you can eat when you cook it. Its supposed to be good for your memory too. They breathe in the water, I suppose they get some air from somewhere.' She pointed correctly to the highly familiar properties 'head', 'eye' and 'tail' when these were named, but she failed to point correctly to any less-familiar properties: for 'scales' she pointed to fins, for 'gills' she pointed to the fin nearest to the gills; and for 'fins' she pointed to the gills. Similarly, she correctly defined 'bird' as 'Something which flies, outside, which has babies fairly early in the year. Some come from foreign places to this country', and pointed correctly to the head and the tail, but to the word 'feathers' she pointed to the wings; to the word 'wings' she pointed to the fluffy breast feathers, and to the word 'beak' she made no response, saying only 'What on earth is a beak?'. These less familiar features – fins, gills, scales, feathers, beak, wings – which Mrs P cannot identify, happen to be the so-called defining features of the concepts 'fish' and 'bird' which Mrs P can accurately define. It is clear that knowing or not knowing the defining features of a concept indicates nothing about a person's knowledge of the concept itself. I have suggested elsewhere that, as comprehension worsens, semantic features are not lost but, instead, concepts become increasingly difficult to separate from associated concepts within the same semantic field (Funnell, 1992).

Do the Same Concepts Always Cause Problems?

I was also interested to discover whether Mrs P's problems with particular concepts occurred every time a concept was tested, or whether she could retrieve the answer correctly on some occasions but not on others.

I gave Mrs P three tasks, which were repeated at regular intervals. One task was the word-to-picture matching task taken from the Psycholinguistic Battery (PALPA) developed by Kay et al. (1992). This test asks the patient to match a spoken or written name to one of five pictures: the picture named by the word; two semantically related pictures (one close, one more distant); a visually similar picture; and an unrelated picture.

The second test used the target pictures from the PALPA test and Mrs P was asked to name them. In the third test, she was asked to define the spoken names of these target pictures. The matching tests were interleaved between tests of naming and defining. Each type of test was presented in a different testing session and tests were spaced no less

Table 16.4 Numbers of items that produce consistent and inconsistent answers from Mrs P across repeated tests of word–picture matching, naming and defining

	Matching *1990/1992*	*Naming* *1991/1992*	*Defining* *1991/1992*
Both correct	24	6	10
Both incorrect	7	26	21
Correct → incorrect	8	8	8
Incorrect → correct	1	0	1
Consistency (*c*)	0.41	0.46	0.45
Probability (*p*)	< 0.01	< 0.01	< 0.01

than two weeks apart and, more usually, two to three months apart. Table 16.4 shows that Mrs P gave the same responses to the same items across testing occasions, and that her performance declined across all three tasks. In each case, eight items she had formerly answered correctly were answered incorrectly the second time tested, but only very rarely were items answered incorrectly the first time and correctly the second time. For example, when I compared her performance on word–picture matching tests, spaced two years apart (February 1990 and February 1992), I found that 31/40 items in the set had produced either two correct answers or two incorrect answers; eight items had been correctly identified on the first test, but not on the second (reflecting a decline in overall performance over two years) and only one item was wrong the first time and correct on the second. It is clear that Mrs P either knows an item or does not and that, apart from some worsening in overall performance over time, this pattern is stable across tests.

It is also obvious that there are many items that Mrs P can match between word and picture that she can neither name nor define. Why is this? My first thought was that matching is an easier task; a match between a word and its referent picture has only to be recognized, whereas a name or definition has to be recalled. So if Mrs P knows the item, this may show up in a recognition task and not in a recall task. However, further investigation suggested that word–picture matching may be a less stringent test of picture and name comprehension than either naming or defining, and some correct responses may occur because alternative items in the set are not close enough in meaning.

Matching tests are made more or less easy, by the nature of the semantic relationship between the distractor pictures and the target picture. In the PALPA word–picture matching test, some semantic distractors are close semantic co-ordinates of the target; for example, 'lobster and crab'; 'cat and dog'; 'fence and wall'; while others are associative and thus more distant in meaning: for example, 'pram and baby'; 'cobweb and spider'; 'stamp and envelope'. I divided the stimuli into those with a semantic co-ordinator distractor and those with an associative distractor. I then looked to see how many times Mrs P matched the items correctly *after she had failed to both name and define them*. I found that she matched only 56/84 (40 per cent) of the targets paired with a close semantic co-ordinate, but 27/39 (69 per cent) of the targets paired with a semantic associative item. This difference was highly significant: $\chi^2 = 9.34$ $p < 0.01$. So at least part of the reason why she was more successful at matching than naming or defining was

Table 16.5   Number of mistakes made by Mrs P in recognizing pictures of real and nonsense objects

	1990	1991	1992
Real objects (*N* = 62)	11	12	10
Nonsense objects (*N* = 55)	2	4	5

that the semantic distinction between the target and distractors was not always difficult enough to test subtle difficulties in comprehension.

However, if Mrs P could name the picture, she could reliably match the word to the picture on the following matching test. Over five repeats of the naming test, she named a total of 38 pictures, and matched 37/38 (97 per cent) of these correctly on the matching test which followed the naming test (by an interval of at least one month). These results indicate that, of the three tests used here, picture naming is the most sensitive test of the ability to comprehend an object. I looked in vain for evidence that Mrs P could name the picture but not match it. Such evidence would have supported the idea, first put forward by Ratcliff and Newcombe (1982), that pictures can be named without knowledge of their meaning: a theory which has received preliminary confirmatory evidence in a study reported by Kremin (1988). Although this idea seems plausible, especially for items that are very distinctive in structure (such as scissors), Mrs P's performance provided no support for this theory.

Recognizing without Identifying?

Although Mrs P was forgetting the meaning of words and failing to identify objects, she did not lose her sense of familiarity with the surface forms of objects and words. For example, she could distinguish 23/24 of the spoken words of low familiarity that she defined very poorly (see table 16.1) from 24/24 nonsense words of similar structure. Similarly, she failed to identify real objects, but could distinguish pictures of real objects and nonsense objects pretty well (in a test developed by Riddoch and Humphreys in 1987). Table 16.5 shows her scores on this test over three years. She made most mistakes with real objects, but there were less than 20 per cent of such errors, and most of these seemed to be connected to the quality of the picture. For example, she would comment that the picture 'looked wrong', saying of the picture of the accordion: 'You play it, but it looks wrong'; and of the motor bike: 'It doesn't look right where you have to put your hands'. In most cases, there was something odd about the drawing, for example the lines did not quite meet up, or the proportions were distorted.

The only nonsense pictures that caused her problems were those where parts from semantically related objects were subtly combined. For example she decided that a pig with a rabbit's head, a cow with a camel's head, and a duck with a dog's head were real animals, but she made no mistakes with more obviously bizarre combinations, such as a kangaroo with a human foot inplace of its tail. Warrington was the first person to observe that a patient with a disorder of comprehension was able to recognize an object as familiar without being able to identify it. She suggested that there was a perceptual process for recognizing objects that was separate from semantic knowledge about the identity of the object (Warrington, 1975). While Mrs P's semantic knowledge is shrinking, her knowledge of the visual forms and spoken names of these objects remains almost unchanged, lending support to Warrington's theory that perceptual and semantic records are distinct.

Can Concepts and Names be Relearned?

Mrs P's husband tells of one autumn day when he dug the first leeks of the season and took them into the kitchen to be cooked for lunch. Apparently Mrs P took one look and said: 'What are they? And what do I do with them?' If you asked Mrs P now what a leek is, she would tell you, in a rather stereotyped manner (as if these are lines that she has learned by rote) that they are long things that you have to cut down from the top, wash carefully, and then slice. She has learned to recognize and name leeks again.

Although Mrs P was losing her knowledge of concepts, and this was a continuing process, she nevertheless appeared to learn new words. New words, seemingly connected to new events, would suddenly appear in her vocabulary. For example, she told me the name of the village in Italy where she had recently stayed for a few days on holiday; she learned my name – and how to spell it – and she referred to 'Himalayan balsam', an unusual wild flower that she and her husband had found on a recent walk. Paradoxically, even while she was forgetting information, she was learning new facts, and these examples of what seemed to be new learning of concepts and names suggested that she might be able to relearn concepts and names that she had forgotten.

I decided to try to reteach her some names and concepts. But choosing the concepts to reteach was not an easy matter. It was important to choose a related set of concepts to show that she could learn not only the 'sort of thing' but also that she could learn to distinguish one specific thing from other, similar, things. Thus it seemed important to select similar items belonging to one particular semantic category. If she could identify particular members of the category, it would show that she had relearned specific concepts and names. Vegetables are quite an important part of Mrs P's life: her husband has a flourishing vegetable garden and she herself cooks vegetables every day for lunch. For this reasons, when I searched for a category of items to reteach to Mrs P, I chose vegetables.

In January 1991, I took to Mrs P's house 22 fresh vegetables, which varied from very common items such as potato, cabbage and onion, to unusual items such as aubergine, courgette and fennel. I asked her to name each vegetable in turn, and then, when this test was completed, I spoke each vegetable name to her and asked her to describe it from memory. It became clear very quickly that she did not recognize many vegetables or their names, and that this was particularly true for the less-familiar items. She could neither name nor define 'asparagus', 'courgette', 'chicory', 'broccoli', 'aubergine', 'pepper', 'chili'

Table 16.6   Number of vegetables named correctly by Mrs P over repeated tests

	Pretest			Retests		
		Jan.	Feb.	Mar.	Apr.	Sept.
7 common untreated veg	7	7	6	7	7	2
6 fairly common treated veg	0	6	6	5	5	3
6 unusual untreated veg	0	0	0	0	NT	NT

Notes:
NT = Not tested
Vegetables were either named correctly on the pretest; not named and then retaught; or not named and not retaught.

and 'fennel', saying 'I don't know' in every case. Some of these vegetables may never have been familiar to her, although the cookery books in her kitchen are modern and would certainly include recipes for these vegetables.

She could name and define the most common vegetables, 'potato', 'onion', 'carrot', 'lettuce', 'sprouts', 'cabbage' and 'leek', correctly, but there was a further set of fairly common vegetables which she either failed to name and define or for which she showed only partial knowledge. She failed to name and define 'turnip' and 'cauliflower' but could define (but not name) 'parsnip', 'celery' and 'cucumber', and could give the initial letter only of 'mushroom'. It was this set of six vegetables (turnip, cauliflower, parsnip, celery, cucumber and mushroom), for which she had some remaining knowledge or which should have been known well in the past, that I decided to reteach.

Mrs P was taught to name the vegetables by showing her each object and telling her the name. The vegetables were then shown again, one at a time, for her to name. She was corrected or reminded if she failed. The testing was repeated ten times, with the vegetables being presented in different sequences. She had to be reminded of the name of the cucumber in the first test, but after that she needed no reminding or correcting in any test. She learned quickly and in total got 9/10 of these naming tests correct.

At the end of this session, I left the six 'treated' vegetables with Mrs P together with a set of written names and descriptions, and suggested that she practised testing herself on naming and describing the vegetables. When I returned a week later, she could name and describe all six vegetables correctly, but failed to name or describe any of the six unusual vegetables in the control set. Tests a week later showed that the relearning had been completely retained.

After that, I retested her on an irregular basis so that she would not expect a test each time I visited her. Table 16.6 shows that she continued to name the vegetables through March and April, with only the occasional mistake. The winter vegetables then disappeared from the shops, and the next test was delayed until the following September. By then, she had forgotten the names of 3/6 vegetables she had relearned, but she had also forgotten the names of 5/7 vegetables she had previously known well. Time and a period during which many of the vegetables were not available seem to have weakened her memory for winter vegetables in general; not just those that she had relearned. It is of interest that since this study was carried out, Swales and Johnson (1992) have reported similar relearning of forgotten concepts in a patient whose semantic loss followed herpes encephalitis.

Postscript

Although Mrs P can learn new names and concepts and relearn old information, her semantic memory has worsened gradually over the three years that I have been working with her. As her memory has declined, her vocabulary has become increasingly restricted to her own activities and interests, and seems to reflect how recently she has thought about or named a concept. Topical words may appear for a time and then disappear. Schwartz et al. (1979) have described a patient who, as her condition worsened, spent increasing amounts of time walking to the local shopping centre and back. At the same time, her vocabulary diminished to just one specific naming word – 'shopping centre' – which she used as both a noun and a verb. It is to be hoped that this will not happen to Mrs P.

Further Reading

Funnell, E. (1992) 'Progressive loss of semantic memory in a case of Alzheimer's disease', *Proceedings of the Royal Society of London*, **B.249**: 287–91.

Funnell, E. (1995) 'Objects and properties: a study of the breakdown of semantic memory', *Memory: Special Issue on Semantic Memory* (in press, Spring 1995).

Hodges, J.R., Patterson, K., Tyler, L.K. (1994) 'Loss of semantic memory: implications for the modularity of mind', *Cognitive Neuropsychology*, **11**: 505–42.

Patterson, K.E. and Hodges, J.R. (1994) 'Disorders of semantic memory', in A. Baddeley, B.A. Wilson and F. Watts (eds), *Handbook of Memory Disorders* (Chichester, W. Sussex: John Wiley).

References

Bayles, K.A., Tomeoeda, C.K. and Trosset, M.W. (1990) 'Naming and categorical knowledge in Alzheimer's disease: the process of semantic memory deterioration', *Brain and Language*, **39**: 498–510.

Bishop, D. (1982) *TROG Test for the Reception of Grammar* (London: Medical Research Council).

Chertkow, H., Bub, D. and Seidenberg, M. (1989) 'Priming and semantic memory in Alzheimer's disease', *Brain and Language*, **36**: 420–46.

Collins, A.M. and Quillian, M.R. (1969) 'The comparison of word meanings', *Journal of Experimental Psychology*, **86**: 343–6.

Dunn, M.D., Dunn, L.M., Whetton, C. and Pintile, D. (1982) *British Picture Vocabulary Scale* (Windsor, Berks.: NFER–Nelson).

Funnell, E. (1992) 'Progressive loss of semantic memory in a case of Alzheimer's disease', *Proceedings of the Royal Society of London*, **B.249**: 287–91.

Funnell, E. and Sheridan, J. (1992) 'Categories of knowledge? Unfamiliar aspects of living and non-living things', *Cognitive Neuropsychology*, **9**: 135–54.

Hirsh, K. and Funnell, E. (1994) 'Age of acquisition of names and concept familiarity: evidence for differing locus of effects in progressive aphasia', paper presented to the Experimental Psychology Society, University College London.

Hodges, J.R., Patterson, K., Oxbury, S. and Funnell, E. (1992) 'Semantic dementia', *Brain*, **115**: 1783–1806.

Kay, J., Lesser, R. and Coltheart, M. (1992) *PALPA* (London and Hove: Lawrence Erlbaum Associates).

Kremin, H. (1988) 'Independence of access to meaning and phonology: arguments for direct non-semantic pathways for the naming written words and pictures', in G. Denes, C. Semenza and P. Bisiacchi (eds), *Perspectives on Cognitive Neuropsychology* (Hove: Lawrence Erlbaum).

Kucera, H. and Francis, W.N. (1967) *Computational Analysis of Present-day American English* (Providence, R.I.: Brown University Press).

Morrison, C.M., Ellis, A.W. and Quinlan, P.T. (1991) 'Age of acquisition, not word frequency, affects object naming, not object recognition', *Memory and Cognition*, **20**: 705–14.

Newcombe, F., Oldfield, R.C. and Wingfield, A. (1965) 'Object naming by dysphasic patients', *Nature (London)*, **207**: 1217–18.

Oldfield, R.C. and Wingfield, A. (1965) 'Response latencies in naming objects', *Quarterly Journal of Experimental Psychology*, **17**: 273–81.

Ratcliff, G. and Newcombe, F. (1982) 'Object recognition: some deductions from the clinical evidence', in A.W. Ellis (ed.), *Normality and Pathology and Cognitive Functions* (London: Academic Press).

Raven, J.C. (1965) *Guide to Using the Coloured Progressive Matrices* (London: H.K. Lewis).

Riddoch, M.J. and Humphreys, G.W. (1987) 'Visual object processing in optic aphasia: a case of semantic access agnosia', *Cognitive Neuropsychology*, **4**: 131–86.

Rosch, E., Mervis, C.B., Gray, W., Johnson, D. and Boyes-Braem, P. (1976) 'Basic objects in natural categories', *Cognitive Psychology*, **7**: 573–605.

Schwartz, M., Marin, O.S.M. and Saffran, E.M. (1979) 'Dissociations of language function in dementia: a case study', *Brain and Language*, **7**: 277–306.

Snodgrass, J.G. and Vanderwart, M. (1980) 'A standardized set of 260 pictures: norms for name agreement, image agreement, familiarity, and visual complexity', *Journal of Experimental Psychology: Human Memory and Learning*, **6**: 174–215.

Snowden, J.S., Goulding, P.J. and Neary, D. (1989) 'Semantic dementia: a form of circumscribed cerebral atrophy', *Behavioural Neurology*, **2**: 167–182.

Swales, M. and Johnson, R. (1992) 'Patients with semantic memory loss: can they relearn lost concepts?', *Neuropsychological Rehabilitation*, **2**: 295–306.

Tulving, E. (1972) 'Episodic and semantic memory', in E. Tulving and W. Donaldson (eds), *Organisation of Memory* (London: Academic Press).

Warrington, E.K. (1975) 'The selective impairment of semantic memory', *Quarterly Journal of Experimental Psychology*, **27**: 635–7.

17 Problems Naming Animals: A Category-specific Anomia or a Misnomer?

Christopher Barry and Jo V. McHattie

Introduction

When we consider the knowledge we possess (and can access fairly readily) about objects and living things in the world, we readily see that have a lot. We know many different animals, birds, fish, reptiles and all manner of creepy crawlies, along with what we can do with them and what they might do to us; we also know about plants and bits of them (such as fruits and vegetables) and what we can use them for; we know things about natural objects in the world (such as clouds, mountains and even the stars); we know many hundreds of artefacts and we use numerous tools and implements in our everyday lives; and we also know about our own (and bits of other people's) bodies.

With a little more reflection, we may be able to appreciate the potential advantages of mentally representing this vast array of knowledge in as organized a way as possible but also to realize the difficulties involved in how such a wide body of information should be structured. For example, should we organize by 'semantic' or some more experiential category (such as fruits and vegetables or things I like to eat) and what size should any categories be (for example, edible things or tropical fruit)? There is also the difficulty of justifying and maintaining any such categorization imposed (is a strawberry really a fruit?). It is, however, tantalizing to suppose that not all our knowledge is stored as an amorphous, haphazardly assembled collection but might be structured in some fashion. The basic question addressed in this chapter is whether our knowledge is organized by category; that is, whether different semantic categories of things are differentiated in our permanent memory stores, and, in particular, whether it is the case that brain damage can selectively impair a person's ability to deal with items from some categories while leaving others relatively intact.

Whether we organize things by category or not, an additional question to ask is: how do we organize all the sorts of knowledge we have about particular things (if we do so at all)? When we consider the knowledge we have about dogs, for example, it is possible to organize the kinds of things we know about them systematically. Some knowledge might concern the visual and other sensory attributes of dogs: what they look like, what they smell like, how they feel to the touch and what noises they produce. We might also know – or at least think we know – something about how they behave and why. We will certainly have much knowledge that might be called 'encyclopaedic', such as the set of facts that a dog is a domesticated four-legged carnivorous mammal which can occur in many different breeds and is commonly kept as a pet. (Note that some of these 'facts' are more like generalities than necessary or defining features that apply to all dogs; and we may know some dogs who are fed on vegetarian diet and, although this doesn't necessarily follow, have fewer than four legs.) This sort of knowledge might also be embellished with an array of additional pieces of information, such as that dogs are related to wolves and hyenas, that they can be trained to hunt foxed and to escort blind people, and that they were sent on early rocket flights into space.

Only a cursory reflection upon this set of information about dogs suggests that it is difficult to separate and neatly subcategorize it all, but it is nevertheless tempting to think that our knowledge about this class of things is stored in a structured fashion. What are the possible set of principles which might be used to structure the knowledge we have of items within categories? One way in which we might organize our knowledge of concepts concerns the *type* or qualitative kind of knowledge we have. One possible distinction is between what might be sensory properties compared with functional and associative information. We might separate the knowledge of what dogs look like, smell like, feel like and even taste like from what are their 'functions', that is, what they do for us and how we use them (to assist hunting, to act as companions, and so on). Another possible way to organize our knowledge would be for it to reflect the way it has been *acquired*. It might be the case that most of our knowledge of the sensory properties of dogs comes from our interaction with the beasts. This knowledge might be differentiated from what we learn via our cultural experiences (in schools, through reading and watching television). It is of course possible to acquire a considerable degree of sensory-based knowledge indirectly: reading a suitable book would inform us that dogs bark, for example. Blind people can tell us information about the colour of objects, which they store as verbally acquired facts.

There has been considerable (and lively) interest in cognitive neuropsychological studies of patients who, following some brain damage, appear to display selective impairments of different types of knowledge. The relationship between the single case studies of patients with acquired disorders of cognitive functions and theories of normal functioning, which characterizes cognitive neuropsychology, has two purposes. One is to use detailed processing models of normal functioning to offer interpretations for the impairments shown by particular patients. The other is to take dissociations shown by patients as the stimulus to derive new hypotheses concerning the organization of the subcomponents of *normal* functioning. This second approach is more radical theoretically, because it represents the inductive use of an observed dissociation in a single patient to motivate a theoretical generality. For example, if a patient is found who cannot name or understand living things but can deal with inanimate objects – and if this cannot be attributed to any differential overall difficulty of the two sets of items, or to any unusual premorbid individual idiosyncrasy of the patient's knowledge, or to any selective or strategic relearning of skills, or to anything else the busy critic will wish to be satisfied upon – then this would be used to motivate the claim that the semantics for living and inanimate items are stored separately in the patient and so, by induction, may also be stored separately in all people. In this chapter we shall present a report of our testing of a man, whom we shall call by the pseudonym Bert, who may speak to such possibilities.

One way to discover patients who may have selective impairments of categories of items (such as living things) or appear to have impairments of aspects of knowledge of items (such as knowing what something can do but not knowing what it looks like) – or even those who may have impairments of aspects of knowledge of particular categories (such as only being impaired at what living things look like) – is to ask them to name pictures of the items. It is generally accepted that the task of naming a picture (for example, of a 'sheep' or a 'table') necessarily requires the activation of semantic information about the object; although how much (or what type) of knowledge is required to support naming is not clear. In fact, the normal sequence of major processing stages might be represented as: (a) an object (or a picture of the object) is *recognized* as being a familiar thing; (b) semantic knowledge corresponding to this thing is activated; and (c) the semantic information is used to find the name in a speech production system (by the process we also use in spontaneous speech). There are also earlier perceptual analysis processes prior to object recognition and other processes responsible for the control of articulation of selected names.

Disturbances of picture naming following brain damage in adulthood may arise from functional impairments to any of these processing components. There may be impairments of visual analysis (in patients with apperceptive agnosia), impairments of object recognition (in patients with associative agnosia) and impairments of the relatively peripheral mechanisms responsible for spoken word production (for example, in patients who have a general problem in controlling the muscles responsible for speech). In aphasic patients, naming (and word-finding) difficulties – which we shall refer to as 'anomia – may result from an impairment at the semantic level, or from some disturbance in how semantic representations access entries in the speech production system, or from an impairment at the level of the phonological representations of words.

In studies of patients with naming difficulty, impairments which are apparently category-specific have aroused considerable interest. Warrington and Shallice (1984) reported the case of a young man, JBR, with encephalitis following herpes simplex, who manifested category-specific comprehension problems: he was better at identifying and comprehending inanimate objects than living things and foods, both for the visual presentation of objects and the auditory presentation of their spoken names. This indicated that he had a central semantic disorder and suggested that the semantic representations of living things and artefacts are *separable*, in that neurological damage can selectively affect one set while leaving the other set relatively unimpaired. Hart et al. (1985) reported the case of a stroke patient MD, who showed a category-specific problem which was specific to naming. MD had selective difficulties in naming fruits and vegetables: he was able to name only 63 per cent of these items correctly, compared to 97 per cent of 269 items from a wide range of other categories. (MD was able to name objects with low-frequency names, such as an abacus, but was unable to name an orange.) Hart et al. argue that MD had no comprehension problems for the spoken names of fruits and vegetables, in that he was able to point to a named picture from two semantically related objects.

Several patients have now been reported as showing impairments apparently specific to living things; Sheridan and Humphreys (1993) provide a helpful summary of eleven cases. We shall not be able to review these cases in any detail here, but there are two points to be borne in mind. First, the status of the claimed dissociation in some patients has been hotly debated; see for example Parkin and Stewart's (1993) far from placid critique of Sartori et al. (1993). In addition to the difference in category, living things differ from nonliving things in other important respects. Living things tend to be structurally more similar to each other than items from many categories of man-made objects (consider, for example, fruits, vs. pieces of furniture). Many living things (such as most animals) may be less frequently encountered than nonliving things. Finally, pictures of living things may be (or even may necessary be required to be) more complex than pictures of artefacts. If such variables such as item familiarity (and/or name frequency), degree of shared common features, visual complexity, and others yet to be discovered, can be shown or be suspected to have an independent effect upon naming or comprehension performance, then it is clearly important to control for them in studies of putative category specific impairments. Living things need to be matched to equivalent items from other categories to avoid the possibility of methodological artefact. However, as we shall see, this may be very difficult to achieve. Secondly, there have been only few reports of patients who show the *opposite* dissociation of superior performance on living things than on artefacts. Such patients are certainly theoretically important, and there exist at least three impressive and convincing studies (Warrington and McCarthy, 1987; Hillis and Caramazza, 1991; Sacchett and Humphreys, 1992). However, the asymmetry in frequency of these patients has probably contributed to a degree of suspicion of some of the patients claimed to have category-specific impairments for living things. We shall now present our attempt to provide further evidence which tends to show the selective impairment of some types of living things, namely animals.

Case History

The present study reports our testing of Bert who, when aged 74, had a relatively small stroke. Bert had led a full and varied life. After a great time in the army (where he worked as a blacksmith), he had many interesting jobs, including running a number of small businesses of his own and working in many others, including a successful time as a bookmaker. His stroke left him with a right visual field defect, which caused him some concern, although at the time of testing he said that it was either getting better or he was simply getting used to it. At the time we tested him, some two years after his stroke, he showed no hemiplegia (although he reported having a slight weakness of the right side of his face). He is certainly intellectually intact and his language is very fluent and both phonologically and syntactically well-formed. His comprehension appeared to be well preserved: he is capable of following (and indeed dominating) complex conversations and could obey (when willing) detailed instructions. His reading appeared to be intact and his repetition was good. In conversation, Bert's difficulties are often masked by his fluent and lively speech. However, he had some word-finding difficulty and some naming problems, which appeared to be most pronounced for the category of animals and which justified an attempt to explore a possible category-specific anomia for animals.

Some Background Testing

We administered to Bert a series of tests of our own construction designed to assess his recognition and general comprehension of things. In one test, he was shown a series of three different pictures of which two showed things of the same name but different physical appearances (for example, two keys and one lock) and was asked to point to the two with the same name. He performed flawlessly. This indicates that he has intact object recognition, which is also clear from his appropriate use of things in his house.

In our verification test, we presented 60 pictures and for each one asked Bert: 'Is this a _____?' For 30 trials, the correct response was 'yes' (for example, a picture of a rabbit accompanied by the question: 'Is this a rabbit?'). For the other 30 trials, the correct response was 'no': there were ten trials where the name was semantically related to the picture (such as, 'Is this a match?' for the picture of a candle); there were ten trials where the name was phonologically related to the picture (for example, 'Is this a bee?' for the picture of a tree); and there were ten trials where the name was unrelated to the picture (for example, 'Is this a duck?' for the picture of a flute). Bert made only two errors in this task, although both were for animals in the semantically related condition: he falsely accepted 'owl' as being the name for a picture of an eagle and 'fly' for a picture of an ant.

We assessed his auditory comprehension of concrete and abstract words using a synonym matching task. Two spoken words were presented to Bert who was asked to indicate whether they mean the same thing (for example, error–mistake) or not. He was 95 per cent correct for both concrete and abstract words on this task.

It would seem that Bert has satisfactory general comprehension but that he may have some difficulty with animals. He is aware of this difficulty and was willing for us to explore it further.

Picture naming

In our first test of Bert's ability to name pictures, we presented him with 100 line drawings (most of which were taken from those provided by Snodgrass and Vanderwart, 1980). Each picture was presented and Bert was asked to name it. He was given no time limit and no cues if unable to produce the name. His naming responses were quite easy to classify: he either produced the correct name or he said that he couldn't say it, which might then be embellished with a circumlocutory (or descriptive) response, although this seldom involved producing the correct name. For such responses, he often said that he 'knew' the thing. He frequently used the name of the item, or his 'can't say' response, as the stimulus for an involved reminiscence which sometimes tended towards the prolix. His naming success for animals was only 12 per cent (5/41), which was worse than for fruits and vegetables (47 per cent, 7/15), musical instruments (50 per cent, 3/6), tools

(60 per cent, 3/5), vehicles (67 per cent, 4/6), articles of clothing (71 per cent, 5/7) and body-parts (100 per cent, 6/6).

It was clear that Bert experienced considerable difficulty naming animals (including birds, fish, reptiles and insects). His responses to animals often expressed frustration and he frequently asserted that 'he knew it'. He was aware of the special difficulty he had with animals and was particularly embarrassed by it when reading books to his grand-children (who, it would seem, mischievously asked him to name pictures of animals).

Inspection of the pictures in Snodgrass and Vanderwart (1980) reveals that animals tend to have lower familiarity ratings than items from other categories. For example, the mean familiarity rating of 'sheep' was only 1.85 (on a five-point scale), compared with ratings of 4.56 for 'shirt' and 4.78 for 'pen' (whose names have approximately the same frequency). Analyses of the items Bert could and could not name revealed substantial differences between them in their familiarity ratings. The animals he could name were those with the highest familiarity ratings of the animals (such as 'dog', 'cat' and 'horse') and he was poor at naming objects from other categories with low familiarity ratings (such as 'harp'). It was therefore possible that Bert's apparent category-specific anomia might be reducible to a more general effect of familiarity operating upon his naming. A test of such a possibility was applied by Funnell and Sheridan (1992) to one patient who showed initial (albeit slim) evidence of a category-specific impairment of living things. Funnell and Sheridan were able to show that there was no effect of semantic category when familiarity and frequency were controlled.

In order to test the possibility that Bert's problems with naming animals might simply reflect a more general problem naming items of low familiarity, we selected 30 animals from Snodgrass and Vanderwart which could be matched to 30 other objects (including some fruits and vegetables) on familiarity ratings and as closely as possible on the word-frequency of the item's name. (The mean familiarity ratings and frequencies were 2.70 and 16.5 for the animals and 2.72 and 17.7 for the 'others'.) For example, 'horse' was matched to 'carrot', 'pig' was matched to 'bell', and 'eagle' was matched to 'mushroom'. Bert was asked to name these 60 pictures (which were intermixed at presentation) twice, on separate days. On the first occasion he named 6 animals and 14 others (Fischer's exact probability $= 0.027$) and on the second occasion he named 8 animals and 15 others ($p = 0.055$). These results indicate that – all other things being equal – he had greater difficulty naming animals than other items matched for familiarity. But all other things were not equal. There were significant differences between the two sets of items on other dimensions and in particular on the visual complexity of the pictures. This variable was provided by Snodgrass and Vanderwart and concerns ratings of 'the amount of detail or intricacy of line in the picture'; but recently it has been brought to prominence by Stewart et al. (1992) who reported a patient, HO, whose apparent category-specific naming deficit for animals was eliminated when pictures of animals were matched to others for familiarity, name frequency and visual complexity. The 30 animals we used had significantly higher ratings of visual complexity than the control items (3.90 vs. 3.07). If it is harder to name more-complex than visually simple pictures, then the fact that the pictures of animals are more complex represents a serious methodological confound.

Another difference between the animals and the familiarity-matched controls we used concerned the age of acquisition of their names, only this time there is an advantage for animals. The age at which a word is learned has been found to affect picture-naming latencies in normal subjects (see, for example, Morrison et al., 1992) and picture-naming accuracy in an aphasic patient (Hirsh and Ellis, 1994). The animals had significantly earlier mean age-of-acquisition ratings than the controls (2.40 vs. 3.09) and so, if this variable had an independent effect on Bert's naming accuracy, animals should have been easier rather than harder.

In order to explore in some systematic fashion which variables have reliable effects on Bert's naming accuracy, the whole set of Snodgrass and Vanderwart pictures were presented to him for naming on two separate occasions. The pictures were presented in randomized blocks of 65, with one block per weekly testing session, and an interval of two months between the first and second presentations. Table 17.1 shows Bert's naming success for various categories of items from the Snodgrass and Vanderwart pictures. It can be seen that his naming of animals is considerably worse than for all other categories.

On the first presentation of the 260 pictures, Bert was able to name 16.7 per cent of the animals and 60.7 per cent of the others. The figures for the second presentation were 14.8 per cent and 68.0 per cent. Bert's consistency of naming was fairly high: 48.1 per cent of all items were named correctly on both presentations and 48.1 per cent were not named on either presentation; only 13.3 per cent were named correctly on one but not the other presentation.

It would appear that Bert is worse at naming animals than items from any other category, even the notoriously difficult category of musical instruments. It is quite possible that the items in these various categories differ on a variety of variables which may or may not affect naming accuracy. We have already found that when we matched animals to other pictures on their familiarity and frequency of names, we were unable to match for both visual complexity and age of acquisition. Given the considerable diffi-culty of getting dencent-sized samples of items adequately matched simultaneously on a range of variables, a multivariate analysis was undertaken. The dependent variable was Bert's consistency of naming accuracy: a score of 2 was given to items which were named correctly on both presentations, a score of 1 was given to items named correctly once, and a score of 0 was given to items which were not named on either presentation. The independent variables entered into the analysis were: (a) 'category' (that is, animal or not), where the 54 animals (which include birds, reptiles, insects, and so on) were given a value of 1 and all others were given a value of 0; (b) the Snodgrass and Vanderwart mean rating of visual complexity of the picture; (c) the Snodgrass and Vanderwart mean rating of image agreement; (d) a measure of name agreement, which was the percentage of 22 Cardiff undergraduates who, when asked to write down the name of each picture, produced the most common name; (e) the mean rated familiarity of the thing represented by the picture (also obtained from the Cardiff undergraduates); (f) the Kucera and Francis (1967) word frequency of the most commonly produced name by the Cardiff undergraduates; (g) the number of phonemes in the name most commonly produced by the Cardiff undergraduates; and (h) the rated age-of-acquisition of the name most com-monly produced by the Cardiff undergraduates (obtained from a sample of York under-graduate students, see Barry et al., in preparation).

The simple correlations between the dependent variable and each independent variable

Table 17.1   Bert's naming of Snodgrass and Vanderwart (1980) pictures, presented twice

			No. of items Correctly named		Consistency of naming: % items		
Category	Number of items	Mean familiarity	First	Second	Both correct	Once correct	Neither correct
Animals	54	2.25	9	8	13.0	5.5	81.8
Fruit & vegetables	27	3.11	9	10	33.3	3.7	63.0
Foods (bread, cake)	3	4.12	2	3	66.7	33.0	0
Body-parts	13	4.51	13	13	100	0	0
Clothing	19	3.57	13	15	68.4	10.5	21.1
Furniture	14	3.92	10	9	57.1	21.4	21.4
Kitchen items (cup, fork, toaster)	17	4.13	13	12	64.7	17.6	17.6
Tools (chisel, pliers)	12	2.59	5	8	41.7	25.0	33.3
Transport (car, lorry)	11	3.08	8	8	72.7	0	27.3
Household items (candle, book, key)	22	3.57	13	16	54.5	22.7	22.7
Buildings (or part of) (church, window)	7	3.08	5	4	57.1	14.3	28.6
Jewellery (ring, crown)	5	3.04	3	3	60.0	0	20.0
Sewing items (needle, thimble)	6	2.76	2	4	33.3	33.3	33.3
Natural features (cloud, star)	5	3.46	4	5	80.0	20.0	0
Personal things (glasses, toothbrush)	6	3.60	5	6	83.3	16.7	0
Outside things (barrel, flag, swing)	11	2.62	6	6	54.5	0	45.4
Toys & sports items (doll, tennis racket)	12	2.30	5	8	41.7	25.0	33.3
Musical instruments (flute, guitar)	9	3.46	4	5	33.3	22.2	44.4
Miscellaneous (basket, gun)	8	2.49	5	7	62.5	25.0	12.5

were as follows: (a) 'category', 0.43; (b) visual complexity, −0.37; (c) image agreement, 0.03; (d) name agreement, 0.22; (e) familiarity, 0.61; (f) name frequency, 0.21; (g) phonemic length, −0.21; and (h) age-of-acquisition, −0.48. However, there were also reasonably high correlations among some of the independent variables. In particular, an item's familiarity correlated: (a) negatively with visual complexity (−0.49), showing that more-familiar items are represented by less-complex pictures; (b) negatively with age-of-acquisition (−0.56), showing that more-familiar items tend to have names learned earlier in life; and (c) positively with category (0.44), showing that nonanimals tend to be more familiar than animals. Also, there was a negative correlation between visual complexity and category (−0.52), showing that nonanimals tend to have less-complex pictures.

In a multiple regression analysis, three variables emerged as significant predictors of Bert's naming success: category ($t = 4.65$, $p < 0.0001$), rated familiarity ($t = 3.80$, $p < 0.0005$) and the age-of-acquisition of the item's name ($t = 4.36$, $p < 0.0001$). There was no effect at all of visual complexity ($t < 1$). A stepwise multiple regression analysis revealed only the following three independent steps: familiarity ($R = 0.607$), category ($R = 0.633$) and age-of-acquisition ($R = 0.683$).

For Bert, a picture's rated visual complexity had no independent effect on naming accuracy, but there were reliable and independent effects of an item's rated familiarity, its semantic category and the age-of-acquisition of its name. Bert was better at naming familiar than less-familiar things, and things whose names tend to have been acquired earlier in life. However, in addition to the effects of familiarity and age of acquisition − and not reducible to these or other variables − Bert was significantly worse at naming animals than items from other categories.

Comprehension of animals

There are many possible reasons for Bert's selective problem of naming animals. It seems unlikely to be the case that he is unable to recognize animals. This was tested in a task where we presented him with two pictures of animals, selected so as to be as related as possible (for example, sheep–goat, fly–wasp) and asked him to point to a named animal. He was able to perform this task perfectly (24/24 correct), which indicates that he could both recognize animals and their names. It is also unlikely that the phonological forms of the names of animals have been selectively damaged, as he can repeat animals' names and can read aloud animal names. A more likely candidate for his problem lies either in the integrity of the semantic representations for animals or how such representations are used to support naming.

For each of the 30 animals and 30 items matched on familiarity which were presented to Bert for naming, four questions were constructed: one required an affirmative response about the category of the item (for example, 'Is a squirrel an animal?' and 'Is a mushroom an edible fungus?'), one involved false information about an item's category (for example, 'Is a squirrel a form of transport?' and 'Is a mushroom a musical instrument?'), one was a 'correct' question about the physical appearance of an item (for example, 'Has a squirrel got a bushy tail?' and 'Has a mushroom got a stalk?') and one was a 'false' question about an item's physical appearance (for example, 'Has a squirrel got wings?' and 'Has a mushroom got a long tail?'). For the animals, Bert was 93.3 per cent correct for category questions but only 76.7 per cent correct for physical property questions ($\chi^2 = 5.29$, $df = 1$, $p < 0.025$). For the familiarity matched nonanimal items, there was no difference between questions on category and physical properties (96.7 per cent and 93.3 per cent correct, respectively). Bert's only substantive comprehension problem appears to be specific to the knowledge of the physical properties of animals.

Conclusions and Speculations

Bert showed a particular difficulty in naming animals. Although his problems with naming were also affected by the item's familiarity and the age of acquisition of the item's name, the multiple regression analysis revealed that there exists an independent effect of semantic category: even when all other factors are taken into account statistically, Bert was worse at naming animals than other things. His 'dissociation' between animals and other items is certainly not an absolute one: it was not the case that he was 100 per cent correct on matched control items and 0 per cent correct on the animals. Patients who show 'cleaner' (although still not 'perfect') dissociations have been reported by Hart and Gordon (1992) and Sheridan and Humphreys (1993). For example, Hart and Gordon's patient KR could name only 50 per cent of animals compared to 93 per cent of foods and 100 per cent of inanimate objects matched on familiarity, visual complexity and name frequency. The difference between Bert's naming of animals and other items cannot be reduced to concomitant (or confounded) differences between the two categories in their familiarity, name frequency, name age-of-acquisition or visual complexity. It is not a misnomer to say that Bert has a category-specific anomia for animals, even if this may not be the full description of his naming impairments.

Bert also appears to have some difficulty in accessing full knowledge concerning animals; whereas he was good at answering questions about an animal's category, he was less good (but still not very impaired) in answering questions about their physical properties (such as the number of legs they have and what colour they are). Although the relative difficulty levels of the questions we gave him have not been thoroughly evaluated, the fact that his impairment appears to be limited only to his knowledge of the physical properties of animals is at least consistent with the following proposals. The first is that, within the semantic system, knowledge of category membership and physical properties is differentiated. It is not clear to us whether this division could be said to represent the type of knowledge stored or the way it was acquired, or how exactly it relates to the more general 'visual' vs. 'verbal' semantic systems proposed by Warrington and others, but Bert does seem to show a difference. The second claim is that knowledge of physical properties can show category-specificity and that Bert has a selective impairment to this type of knowledge for animals. A similar pattern of performance was reported for Hart and Gordon's KR: she showed a selective deficit when asked questions about the physical attributes of animals (such as their colour, number of legs and size), although she was perfectly able to answer questions about the nonphysical attributes and functional properties of animals (such as whether they are edible or are kept as pets) as well as about the physical attributes of both objects (such as their colour and size and whether they have wheels) and fruits and vegetables (such as their colour and whether they have seeds).

The final proposal we wish to make is that knowledge of physical attributes has a greater role than knowledge of category (and function) in the process of naming; for example, knowing that a picture of a tiger is an animal (or even a large, wild, predatory cat) may help in naming the picture as a tiger *less* than knowing that it has orangish and black stripes. Such a suggestion – which has also been made by Davidoff (1991) – finds some support from patients who show loss of knowledge of physical properties for those categories of items for which they have a naming impairment (see, for example, Hart and Gordon, 1992), but it must await a greater array of convincing confirmation before it can become established 'knowledge'.

Acknowledgements

The research reported here was supported by a grant from the Welsh Scheme for the Development of Health and Social Research. We thank Pat McKenna for discussion and helpful comments on this manuscript.

Further Reading

Hart, J. and Gordon, B. (1992) 'Neural subsystems of object knowledge', *Nature*, **359**: 60–4.

Job, R., Miozzo, M. and Sartori, G. (1993) 'On the existence of category-specific impairments: a reply to Parkin and Stewart', *Quarterly Journal of Experimental Psychology*, **46A**: 511–16.

McCarthy, R.A. and Warrington, E.K. (1990) *Cognitive Neuropsychology: A Clinical Introduction* (London: Academic Press).

Parkin, A.J. and Stewart, F. (1993) 'Category-specific impairments? No. A critique of Sartori et al.', *Quarterly Journal of Experimental Psychology*, **46A**: 505–9.

Powell, J. and Davidoff, J.B. (1992) 'The two-legged apple', in R. Campbell (ed.), *Mental Lives: Case Studies in Cognition* (Oxford: Basil Blackwell).

Sartori, G., Miozzo, M. and Job, R. (1993) 'Category-specific naming impairments? Yes', *Quarterly Journal of Experimental Psychology*, **46A**: 489–504.

References

Barry, C., Morrison, C.M. and Ellis, A.W. (in preparation) 'Naming the Snodgrass and Vanderwart pictures: the effects of name age-of-acquisition, frequency and agreement'.

Davidoff, J.B. (1991) *Cognition through Color* (London: MIT Press).

Funnell, E. and Sheridan, J. (1992) 'Categories of knowledge? Unfamiliar aspects of living and nonliving things', *Cognitive Neuropsychology*, **9**: 135–53.

Hart, J. and Gordon, B. (1992) 'Neural subsystems of object knowledge', *Nature*, **359**: 60–4.

Hart, J., Berndt, R.S. and Caramazza, A. (1985) 'Category-specific naming deficit following cerebral infarction', *Nature*, **316**: 439–40.

Hillis, A.E. and Caramazza, A. (1991) 'Category-specific naming and comprehension impairment: a double dissociation', *Brain*, **114**: 2081–94.

Hirsh, K.W. and Ellis, A.W. (in press) 'Age of acquisition and lexical processing in aphasia: a case study', *Cognitive Neuropsychology*, **11**: 435–58.

Kucera, H. and Francis, W.N. (1967) *Computational Analysis of Present-day American English* (Providence, R.I.: Brown University Press).

Morrison, C.M., Ellis, A.W. and Quinlan, P.T. (1992) 'Age of acquisition, not word frequency, affects object naming, not object recognition', *Memory and Cognition*, **20**: 705–14.

Parkin, A.J. and Stewart, F. (1993) 'Category-specific impairments? No. A critique of Sartori et al.', *Quarterly Journal of Experimental Psychology*, **46A**: 505–9.

Sacchett, C. and Humphreys, G.W. (1992) 'Calling a squirrel a squirrel but a canoe a wigwam:

a category-specific deficit for artefactual objects and body parts', *Cognitive Neuropsychology*, 9: 73–86.

Sartori, G., Miozzo, M. and Job, R. (1993) 'Category-specific naming impairments? Yes', *Quarterly Journal of Experimental Psychology*, **46A**: 489–504.

Sheridan, J. and Humphreys, G.W. (1993) 'A verbal-semantic category-specific recognition impairment', *Cognitive Neuropsychology*, **10**: 143–84.

Snodgrass, J. and Vanderwart, M. (1980) 'A standardised set of 260 pictures: norms for name agreement, familiarity, and visual complexity', *Journal of Experimental Psychology: Human Learning and Memory*, **6**: 174–215.

Stewart, F., Parkin, A.J. and Hunkin, N.M. (1992) 'Naming impairments following recovery from herpes simplex encephalitis: category-specific?', *Quarterly Journal of Experimental Psychology*, **44A**: 261–84.

Warrington, E.K. and McCarthy, R.A. (1987) 'Categories of knowledge: further fractionation and an attempted integration', *Brain*, **110**: 1273–96.

Warrington, E.K. and Shallice, T. (1984) 'Category specific semantic impairments', *Brain*, **107**: 829–54.

Part V   When It Isn't Working

Introduction

If I tell you a new eight-figure number, how well would you repeat it? Immediate repetition span for verbal material (or of spatial locations or actions) is a simple measure of immediate memory capacity in these different domains. But the determinants of span are surprisingly complex, and the 'storage metaphor' for immediate list memory is not helpful. Working memory (Baddeley 1986) is a relatively recent concept. While it includes the older notion of short-term memory, it goes beyond it. Working memory allows long-term knowledge to be integrated with ongoing plans and actions, providing (in various different similes) a blackboard, scratch-pad or work space in the relevant domain, whereby one can respond to a specific task demand (adding up numbers, repeating spoken lists or nonsense words, finding one's way around, copying a picture) by consulting a constructed record (rehearsal, maintenance, 'refreshment') and updating action in relation to it. This requires a number of different operations. One function must be general control and modulation of action (central executive function); another, retrieval from established store; and yet another, the maintenance function. Inspection and manipulation of the internal record can be considered to be another, separable function (see Morris and Morton's chapter).

Riddoch and Humphreys describe three people who have working memory difficulties across different domains. In two of them, the problem probably reflects recent brain damage, but in Helen it seems that she always had difficulties – a developmental working memory disorder. The subcomponent testing approach, whereby each hypothesized component of the memory system has a specific signature task, has proved useful in generating differential diagnoses among the three people, showing that central executive function might be somewhat impaired in Helen and in Nancy, while Mike has difficulties with maintenance functions. What happens when there are problems in working memory? As Riddoch and Humphreys point out, the main difficulties seem to occur in conditions of information overload (Helen and Nancy) and, particularly, in integrating information effectively.

Both HB (Howard) and Alan (Martin and Romani) became aphasic following left cerebrovascular accidents (CVAs). Their aphasia has resolved (but in different ways in each case), leaving a dense problem in repeating isolated word lists; a deficit of verbal short-term memory. Indeed HB's difficulty in repetition is probably one of the most severe on record, with a digit span of 2, and no ability to repeat invented words at all. Testing the organization of his short-term verbal memory showed that speech-based coding did not account for HB's residual items in short-term store: these seemed to be semantically processed and accessed. By contrast, Alan (Martin and Romani), despite a similarly reduced span, repeats nonsense words and real ones at the same level of accuracy. Alan also has difficulties in resolving word meanings both in comprehension and production. This is not because he has lost the meanings, but because he is unable to maintain them in an accessible state for sufficient time to integrate them with the task, whether this is the understanding of a sentence requiring comparisons or the production of a new phrase of several words. Alan appears to have a disorder of speech-based working memory that, to date, comprises a unique case with important implications for the organization of working memory. It suggests an essential function of working memory: explicit integration and control of new associations in speech production and perception.

Waters and Caplan's chapter focuses on a different aspect of auditory-verbal working memory; the precise relationship between the 'inner voice', used in verbal rehearsal, and measurable speech production difficulties in patients with speech output difficulties characterized as dysarthric. Their work affirms that 'outer' speech need not be intact for 'inner speech' to function, although they suggests some limits to this conclusion. They also show *what* is rehearsed in rehearsal; it is above all sensitive to the phonological structure (in particular the number of phonemes to be produced).

The picture drafted by a series of studies of patients with auditory-verbal working memory disorders (Vallar and Shallice, 1990) is becoming progressively more complex. Out of this complexity, however, are emerging some important new discoveries: in particular, as immediate repetition span itself is seen to reflect a number of distinct processes, so the question 'what is memory span for?' starts to become more tractable. It can indicate the extent to which a range of production, perception and retrieval mechanisms may interact, under executive control, to generate workspaces that can be used to plan complex actions, resolve the content of perceptions and allow complex integrative behaviours to be undertaken. Working memories are clearly domain-specific in terms of their input and output processes, but there is still a good deal of research to be completed concerning the limits of domain specificity, particularly in regard to executive function.

References

Baddeley, A.D. (1986) *Working Memory* (Oxford: Clarendon Press).
Vallar, G. and Shallice, T. (1990) *Neuropsychological Impairments of Short-term Memory* (Cambridge: Cambridge University Press).

18 17 + 14 = 41?
Three Cases of Working
Memory Impairment

M. Jane Riddoch and Glyn W. Humphreys

Introduction

Difficulties in remembering are a common problem – we have all probably been in the situation where we encounter somebody whose name we have completely forgotten. Our memory can play tricks on us in other situations too. Suppose somebody asked you for an hour-by-hour account of how you spent your time a week ago last Wednesday – do you find that the day's events roll off your tongue or do you find the exercise rather effortful? We rely on our long-term memory stores in order to perform these sorts of tasks, and our ability to easily retrieve information from such stores is likely to be affected by the amount of material stored. Memory faculties tend to fail to a certain extent as we get older. Memory faculties are also likely to be affected by damage to the brain (particularly when damage involves the diencephalon and/or medial temporal lobes).

However, memory is more than a store of events and impressions from our past; there is another altogether more dynamic component to our memory system known as working or short-term memory. This component of cognitive functioning plays a crucial role in various aspects of our everyday life. Current psychological theory conceives of working memory as being composed of at least three components: these are known as the central executive, the visual buffer and the phonological loop (Baddeley, 1986). Together these components allow us to hold and update information whilst performing various on-going activities. For instance, when we are listening to someone, we are thought to hold segments of their speech in the phonological loop, and this may serve as a back-up if we fail to understand the sentence as we hear it (for 'off-line' as opposed to 'on-line' analysis). If we want to describe how someone might get from A to B, many of us hold a picture of the route (possibly in the visual buffer) which we consult in order to make our directions explicit. The central executive may be considered to be a controlling attentional system which allocates available resources to the other components of working memory. One point of view is that the central executive acts as an attentional resource which can allow us to do several tasks simultaneously (for instance, the chess master's ability to perform several games of chess simultaneously, or lesser mortals ability to hold a conversation while playing a game of tennis).

Damage to long-term memory gives rise to amnesia but what about damage to working memory? If this is the dynamic processor we have described, damage should have a fairly profound effect on the everyday functioning of an individual. In this chapter we discuss three individuals all of whom had particular difficulties in everyday life which can be linked to impairments of working memory.

Three Cases of Working Memory Impairment

Case 1: Mike

Mike, aged 26 years, was referred to us for investigation by a neurologist. Over the previous year, he had become increasingly concerned with his ability to manage simple aspects of his daily life. He worked as an archaeologist and, at the time we saw him, was concerned with excavations of the mass graves for cholera victims in London (the graves dated to Victorian times when cholera outbursts were frequent, due to poor sanitation conditions). As the graves were uncovered, one of Mike's tasks was to draw each skeleton as it was positioned within the coffin. The bodies were also photographed before being removed. Mike had 'started at the bottom' in his chosen career, having left school at the age of 16. At the time we saw him he was working at the level at which graduates typically enter the profession. He enjoyed his work immensely, and continued in a voluntary capacity at weekends when he formed part of team investigating the catacombs in Highgate cemetery.

Mike was concerned with a number of things. He could no longer easily draw the positions of the bones in the coffins, a task that he had found trivially easy previously. He was unable to perform simple calculations. He found it very difficult to remember appointments and meetings. His driving ability appeared to have deteriorated – he felt he was unable to judge the speed and distance of the other vehicles on the road (indeed, he had had a near miss and had given up driving). Travelling around London using the Underground system was also fraught with problems. On a number of occasions, he found himself quite unable to find the way to the surface from the Underground platform below. He experienced difficulties in route-finding in other spheres too. He could not follow a map when attempting to direct his girl-friend as she drove the car. Time estimation was proving difficult. In the past, he had had a temporary job at a fast-food outlet, now he was unable to co-ordinate the timing when cooking breakfast, the eggs being ready far in advance of the bacon and the toast.

Mike's difficulties were having serious consequences for both his work and domestic life. At the office concern was expressed over Mike's frequent memory lapses, and he found he was being asked to do more menial and less responsible tasks. At home, his girl-friend ended their relationship at the instigation of her mother who was convinced that Mike was not 'all right' in the head.

The neurologist performed a great many tests, but was unable to pinpoint any organic cause for his difficulties. An X-ray of the brain revealed that it was rather more shrunken than would be expected of someone of his age, but it was not felt that this alone could account for Mike's difficulties.

Case 2: Nancy

We first met Nancy when she was 67; again, she had been referred to us for assessment by a neurologist. She was a former mathematics teacher who had retired, and who had a history of heart disease. She was unable to walk any distance without becoming extremely breathless. She was admitted for cardiac bypass surgery. The operation was success as far as physical activity was concerned and she was fitter than she had been for many years. However, the operation itself carried a slight risk of a cerebral haemorrhage, and Nancy sadly experienced a small bleed which affected both hemispheres of the brain (in the left hemisphere the lesion was in the region of the posterior parietal lobe with some involvement of the occipital lobe; on the right there was a greater involvement of the occipital lobe and the posterior parietal lobe was also affected).

Nancy's main concern was her inability to perform mathematical operations. She was particularly embarrassed when dealing with people outside her immediate family. For instance, she was unable to work out the correct money in order to pay the milkman; and if she handed him a banknote, she was unable to estimate whether the change she received was correct or not. This failure in an ability in which she previously excelled was a source of great distress.

She also had other problems. On occasion, dressing was difficult (for example, she could not work out how to put on her brassière). In the kitchen she found it difficult to follow recipes in the way she had been accustomed to do prior to her operation.

Case 3: Helen

Helen was aged 17 when we met her first. She was referred by her mother who was concerned about her long history of difficulties in various aspects of everyday life. At the age of eight years she had been assessed by a clinical psychologist because her parents were concerned that she was finding 'number work' difficult at school. At that time, the psychologist noted that there was a discrepancy between her verbal IQ (99) and her performance IQ (78). The psychologist referred Helen to a consultant psychiatrist who felt that there was probably some minimal cerebral dysfunction. Helen's mother reported nothing adverse in Helen's early history apart from a very high temperature when she was two years old. She was further assessed at the age of 15 years, when the difference between her verbal (102) and performance IQ (48) was even more apparent.

Helen did not find her school days easy; while she managed well in some areas (English and languages) she found others more exacting (mathematics, cookery and games). Many children experience difficulties with mathematics, but the same is not usually true of cookery, and Helen was subjected to much ridicule as a result of her failures to time different components of a meal appropriately. She did not enjoy games lessons because it always took her a long time to learn the relevant rules. Even when rules had been learnt, Helen found the dynamic aspects of sport particularly hard saying: 'I cannot see how and where I should be in my mind.' Like Nancy, Helen also found dealing with money problematic: she found it difficult to calculate the correct amount to hand over to shop assistants. However, of all her problems, Helen was particularly concerned with the difficulty she experienced when trying to cross the road. She found she was unable to judge when it was safe, with the result that she had had several near misses and (aged 17) would not attempt it on her own. Her school friends could not understand her apparent timidity and had became increasingly impatient with her as she grew older.

Where to Start?

A commonality about our three cases appears to be the difficulty in holding and temporarily manipulating information rather than there being any impaired visual or verbal recognition or deficit in remembering learnt information (in long-term memory). For instance, Nancy's problem with mathematics was most apparent when she had mentally to hold information before completing the calculation. She could easily perform some calculations (for example, $9 + 7 =$, $18 - 8 =$, or $5 \times 4 =$); but she started to make errors on operations of the form: $16 + 17 =$, $132 - 47 =$, or $13 \times 9 =$. These last three calculations all require two mental steps, involving a 'carry' operation, as opposed to one simple learned function. Thus to subtract 47 from 132 requires first that 7 is taken from 12 and then adding 1 to the 4 before taking it from 13. Usually such procedures can be performed in the head without recourse to pencil and paper; and certainly Nancy would have had no difficulty prior to her operation. Now, even when she used pencil and paper, she was likely to make errors. Helen experienced similar difficulties and told us: 'I can't work out figures in my head. I always have to write them down on a piece of paper.' Different individuals may perform mental arithmetic in different ways; one way may be to picture the different operations in the mind as though one were writing them down. Another way may be to hold the information in a verbal form and to repeat it mentally until the whole operation is complete. In both instances, information is held temporarily in some portion of memory; once the task is complete this information may be discarded. Helen may never have acquired the ability to do this while Nancy appears to have lost it.

Copying tasks may also require the temporary holding of different bits of information for the duration of the task. Thus one aspect of the to-be-copied item must be held in memory until it has been committed to paper. It will then be replaced in memory by another aspect of the target item. Figure 18.1 shows clearly the difficulties Mike experienced in his attempt to copy a cube, while Nancy's copy of a simple line figure is hopelessly awry. Drawing from memory also appeared problematic. Nancy's fox is readily identifiable; when looking at the hind legs however, it is clear that she has become confused as to which line belongs with which. Nancy stated: 'It seems as though my

(a)

(b)

(c)

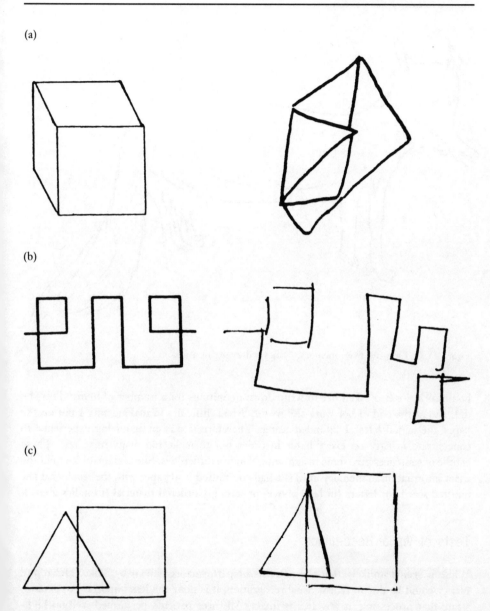

Figure 18.1 Copying: (a) Mike's copy of a cube; (b) Nancy's copy of a simple geometric design; (c) Helen's copy of an overlapping triangle and square
Note: The to-be-copied items are on the left in each example.

mind is a split second ahead and so eye and mind are not completely synchronising. The lines on the paper interfere. I appear to forget the line I was trying to follow and rely on my former image.' Helen's copies are also not true to the original.

In Nancy's case, the problem was not restricted to pictorial material in that she often experienced difficulties when writing. A sample of her writing illustrates this. For

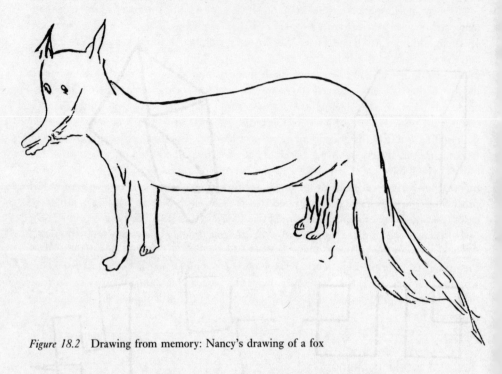

Figure 18.2   Drawing from memory: Nancy's drawing of a fox

homework, we had asked her to write down definitions for a number of items. This she did, and at the end of her work she wrote: 'I had difficulty in making sure I put on the paper the actual letter **I** intended using. Therefore it was an agonizing experience to concentrate *to have* on every letter in order not to make too many mistakes.' These couple of sentences give some insight into Nancy's difficulties. She was unable to hold the exact information in memory until she had committed it to paper with the result that she omitted words or letters (in bold above) or wrongly ordered material (in italics above).

Tests of Visual Recognition

While it seems unlikely that the patterns of performance shown by Mike, Helen and Nancy could be due to faulty visual recognition, it is none the less important to demonstrate that processing in this area is intact. All three patients performed well on high-level tests such as picture naming (here we deliberately selected items that people with visual recognition problems typically find difficult, such as fruit, vegetables, insects, animals and birds). In each case, performance was error-free. Reading of words also presented no difficulty whether the words were regular (those that conform to the normal patterns of spelling-to-sound rules in English, such as 'steamer') or irregular (such as 'yacht', where the word has to recognized as a whole rather than being split into its constituent sound segments). All three patients were also able to match different views of an object correctly. Their good performance on these high-level visual tests suggested that visual recognition was intact.

However, performance was not good on all visual tests. For instance, all three patients made errors when asked to copy simple 2D and 3D drawings (as we have shown in figure 18.1). In addition, Mike and Helen were given a number of low-level perceptual tests, and in both cases performance was not as good as might have been expected from their picture-naming scores. For instance, both made a number of errors when they had to judge whether two lines shared the same orientation or same length, or whether two circles shared the same size. Most current theories of visual recognition hold that the component processes are ordered hierarchically, so that low-level processes concerned with coding line lengths and orientations precede high-level processes concerned with recognizing the objects involved. If this is the case, then deficits at an early level of the hierarchy will have knock-on effects for the later stages of visual processing; an impairment at an early level is likely to result in impairments in the later stages of visual processing. Since we have demonstrated that high-level processing is intact in our three cases (that is, picture naming), we would like to argue that the deficits shown in tests of early visual processing are not due to a visual recognition impairment but rather to a working memory impairment. Poor performance in the copying and matching tests in the presence of normal high-level vision may reflect some deficit in the visual portion of working memory. In particular, when two items have to be compared they need to be held in some form of visual buffer; a deficit in this buffer will render simple matching tests difficult.

Tests of Working Memory

As we have indicated above, there are thought to be three major components of working memory: the phonological loop, the visual buffer and the central executive. We gave our three cases a number of tests which are thought to assess the functioning of the phonological loop and the visual buffer. We did not directly assess the functioning of the central executive.

Assessing the functioning of the phonological loop

The phonological loop is thought to consist of two components: the phonological store and the articulatory loop. The phonological store is thought to be capable of holding a limited amount of phonological information. We may use this store when reading or listening to someone talking to us: phonological information is held in the store until the whole sentence has been read or heard and we can then make sense of it. This is particularly important for complex sentences which may not be understood 'on-line' (for example, 'It is fortunate that most rivers are able to be crossed by bridges that are strong enough for cars').

The articulatory loop allows us to rehearse information. It is thought that when we hear someone speaking the information is automatically encoded in the phonological store, but that when we read something the word must be converted to its phonological form and then conveyed to the phonological store via the articulatory loop.

Before applying tests to assess the functioning of the phonological loop an assessment

Table 18.1   Overall percentage correct of lists of either phonologically similar or dissimilar items

	Phonologically similar (%)	Phonologically dissimilar (%)
Mike	43	68
Helen	64	73
Nancy	33	53

of the subject's digit span should be made. This test gives an indication as to the amount of material that can be held in the verbal portion of working memory. Strings of digits are presented at an even pace (approximately one every three seconds) and the subject's task is to remember the digits in the correct serial order. This test places demands on both the phonological store and the articulatory loop; when digits are presented people tend to rehearse them over and over 'in their minds'. A normal digit span for auditorily presented items is seven plus or minus two (for this reason telephone numbers are chosen to be seven digits long). Nancy had an auditory digit span of five (on the low side of normal); Mike and Helen both had a digit span of four. The reduced digit span in all three instances suggests that the amount of information that can be held temporarily in the verbal component of working memory is limited.

The phonological store   An effect known as the phonological similarity effect is thought to reflect the functioning of the phonological store. If subjects are read strings of phonetically similar letters and are then asked to recall them in the same order, performance is worse than when the letter strings are not phonetically similar (for example, B, G, V, T, P, E as compared with Y, W, H, R, K, M). This effect is thought to reflect the working of the phonological store since, with auditory presentation of the letters, it can be shown even when subjects are required to fill up the articulatory loop by continually repeating a word such as 'the' (this procedure is known as articulatory suppression). We presented our three patients with a number of strings each six letters long, which were either phonologically similar or dissimilar. Each patient was asked to repeat back the letters in the order they were given. These results are given in table 18.1.

All three cases showed clear phonological similarity effects with performance being better for the phonologically dissimilar items, although the magnitude of the effect differed over the individuals. This suggests that the patients were storing information in a phonological store, even though that store might be limited in capacity. Note that in all instances, strings exceeded the digit span of our three subjects in that they were six letters long. Interestingly, Nancy performed most poorly even though she has a slightly higher digit span, suggesting that she was less able than Mike and Helen to cope with a memory load greater than her span. We return later to discuss this.

The articulatory loop   People find that it is more difficult to remember lists of words that are three syllables long than it is to remember an equivalent list of words one syllable long (words such as 'elephant', 'piano', 'butterfly' and so on, as compared with 'doll', 'bath', 'spoon', and so on). This 'word-length effect' is thought to reflect the functioning of the articulatory loop. Long words take more time to articulate than short words, and

Table 18.2 Overall percentage correct with auditorily presented lists of words either one, two or three syllables long

	1 syllable (%)	*2 syllables (%)*	*3 syllables (%)*
Mike	53	33	50
Helen	67	62	52
Nancy	34	30	31

so cannot be as well-rehearsed in the same time span. The word-length effect is also reduced when the articulatory loop is filled by an articulatory suppression task. We assessed the effect of word length on immediate verbal memory by asking the patients to recall lists of auditorily presented words which could be either one, two or three syllables long. In all instances strings were six words long, and so were 'supra-span' for the patients. The task was to remember all the words and then to repeat them back in the right order if possible. The results are presented in table 18.2. Helen showed a clear word-length effect on this task; in contrast, both Mike and Nancy were little affected by syllable number. Again, Nancy performed particularly poorly overall, typically being able to remember the first word but none of the others. None of the patients were able to report the last words in the list any better than the immediately preceding words.

To recap   The fact that Helen showed an effect of word length on her immediate verbal memory suggests that she was attempting to use articulatory rehearsal processes to aid her recall. This result, and the effects of phonological similarity on Helen's performance, are the normal results found. This pattern indicates that the components of working memory (the phonological store and the articulatory loop) are operating, although there seems to be some capacity limitation which underlies her reduced digit span. It could be that either the phonological store or the articulatory loop components have a reduced capacity, or the central executive is limited in allocating resources to the verbal working memory system.

In contrast to Helen, Mike and Nancy seemed to be impaired at using their articulatory loop to support verbal immediate memory, since their performance did not improve when shorter (one-syllable) words were used rather than longer (three-syllable) words. Nancy was somewhat worse than both Helen and Mike at the memory tasks using lists above each patient's digit span. This suggests that she may have problems in addition to those involving immediate verbal memory, perhaps concerned with how she allocates central executive resources when her phonological store is overloaded.

A fuller picture of each patient's performance can be gained by comparing performance with auditory presentation with that of visual presentation. Under visual presentation conditions, we may be more inclined to utilize articulatory coding in order to ensure that visual information is represented in a stable, verbal form. To investigate this, we had the three patients perform the same immediate memory task, using words varying in length, but this time using visual presentations (one word was presented on a card, at the rate of one card every three seconds). The percentage correct report of complete lists for each patient is shown in table 18.3.

Table 18.3 Overall percentage correct with visually presented lists of words either one, two or three syllables long

	1 syllable (%)	2 syllables (%)	3 syllables (%)
Mike	32	33	32
Helen	83	90	60
Nancy	63	69	35

Reading rather than hearing words produced a substantial improvement in both Helen and Nancy's overall level of performance. This is unusual because immediate memory is, if anything, poorer for visual than auditory material. Both Helen and Nancy also showed reliable effects of word length on immediate memory here, indicating that they were using articulatory rehearsal to maintain the words. Helen showed a similar effect with both visual and auditory material. Nancy did not, but it appears that she can use articulatory rehearsal if the conditions encourage that strategy (for example, with visual rather than auditory presentation of words). One reason why Nancy and Helen both improved with visual presentation may be that, with visual presentation, they were not faced with coping with simultaneous demands from auditory input and verbal maintenance rehearsal. Such demands may have disrupted performance with auditory presentation if Helen and Nancy have difficulty allocating resources adequately when different stimuli must be processed simultaneously.

Mike showed worse performance with visual than with auditory presentation, whilst again, there was no effect of word length on his recall. Mike thus provided no evidence of using an articulatory loop, for both visual and auditory modalities. His better performance with auditory presentations is consistent with him using a phonological store with auditory but not with visual presentation.

The results so far have indicated problems with immediate memory for all three patients, though the nature of the problem is slightly different across patients. Mike shows no evidence of using an articulatory loop. Nancy and Helen show evidence of this, but are poor at coping with simultaneous processing demands on verbal memory. However, given the problems that all experienced in drawing and copying tasks, we might also expect difficulties in tasks tapping visual and not just verbal immediate memory. In particular, we may need to consider here a specifically spatial memory system, which may support tasks such as drawing and visual planning, rather than a system involved in remembering visual sequences of events (as might be required to remember a visually presented list of words) (see Hanley and Davies, this volume). The ability to form immediate spatial memories was investigated in a further series of experiments.

Assessing spatial immediate memory

In the above section on visual recognition, we argued that the difficulties experienced by all three patients when copying, and Helen and Mike's errors on various perceptual tests, may reflect an impaired ability to hold information in a visual buffer. There are at least

Table 18.4   Overall percentage correct in the experimental and control conditions of the Tails test

	Experimental condition (%)	*Control condition (%)*
Mike	95	100
Helen	80	100
Nancy	95	100

two ways that the visual buffer may be impaired: first, the information in the buffer may fade abnormally fast so it can no longer support task performance. Secondly, the capacity of the buffer may be reduced. In either case, information may not be available to help integrate parts of a drawing together or to consult as to when parts have been produced. This visual buffer may be used in guiding behaviour on the basis of information in the visual environment (as in a drawing task) or in retrieving information from long-term memory (for example, when recalling what a friend looks like). The ability of the patients to generate information from long-term memory was tested using the 'animal tails' test.

The animal tails test   An ingenious test designed by Martha Farah is based on questions of the nature: 'Is the tail of a goat long or short relative to the length of its body?' This is one experimental condition of Martha Farah's test; in another, a picture of a goat is presented with its tail obscured by a large black box; the same question is now directed to the picture. In order to answer this question, subjects may generate a picture in their 'mind's eye' (the visual buffer) and inspect this image in order to answer the question correctly. In the control condition, the pictured animal is shown with no obscuring black box. This condition tests whether patients understand the concepts being addressed. Our three cases were each given the pictorial experimental condition and the control condition. They all performed the tests reasonably well, suggesting that they had no special difficulty in generating pictorial information from long-term memory into their visual buffer. Their results are given in table 18.4.

The good performance of the patients on this test of 'visual' memory of attributes can be contrasted with their performance when they had to make simple spatial judgements. For instance, Nancy and Helen carried out one test requiring judgements of time. They were visually presented with clock faces in which the top and bottom of the clock were clearly indicated, as were both hands but no numerals were present. Nancy performed this task particularly poorly, scoring 50 per cent, while Helen did a little better, scoring 70 per cent. Neither had any difficulty in telling the time when numerals were present. Nancy scored 100 per cent and Helen scored 95 per cent. The problem with clock faces could be due to poor spatial abilities, or to a more specific impairment in using a spatial immediate memory system (for example, to maintain the position of one hand whilst the position of the other is computed). A more direct test of such a spatial immediate memory is the 'visual span' task.

Visual span   We used a procedure described by Lindsay Wilson et al. (1987) to give a measure of the visual memory span for patterns presented on a computer. In this task,

Table 18.5 Visual spans with a two-second interval between the to-be-remembered grid and the target grid

	Visual span	
Mike	2.7	(range of scores: 2–6)
Helen	5.18	(range of scores: 4–9)
Nancy	3.0	(range of scores: 1–7)

the subject is presented with a matrix of which half the squares are black and the other half white. The location of the different-coloured squares within the matrix is random. The matrix can be presented for a predetermined time (usually two seconds). After an interval, the length of which can varied but which is usually two seconds, the matrix is represented with one of the dark squares missing. The subject is required to point to the place where the block is missing. The initial pattern is very simple, and after each correct response, the pattern is made slightly more complex. Testing continues until the subject fails to remember two patterns in a row. The subjects span score is obtained from the last correct pattern and is given by the number of dark squares in the matrix. For instance, normal adults score around 15, indicating that they are successful in remembering the spatial arrangement of matrices composed of 30 squares. Note that this task specifically requires maintenance of the spatial positions of cells in the matrices.

We assessed visual memory span in all our three cases using the standard procedure which was repeated ten times allowing us to calculate a mean score. The results are given in table 18.5. In all instances the span was very low compared with the span typically obtained by adults (see above). We also show the range of scores obtained and it is clear that, in each case, their best attempt was way below normal.

In the procedure we used above, the gap between the two to-be-remembered displays was two seconds. Normal performance deteriorates if the interval is increased beyond two seconds (scores typically drop from 15 to 11 with an interval of ten seconds) and it improves if the interval is decreased (scores are typically 19 with an interval of one second). We tested the performance of each patient with intervals of ten seconds and one second. Their data are shown in table 18.6 (unfortunately, we were unable to test Nancy at the short interval).

Helen's performance did improve with a shorter interval between the stimuli, but it remained some way below normal. There was little effect of increasing the interval beyond two seconds. Similarly, increasing the interval from two to ten seconds had no detrimental effect on Nancy's performance. However, manipulating the time interval had a drastic effect on Mike's performance. It went from a mean of around 12 (with scores sometimes as high as 25, indicating an immediate memory for matrices composed of 50 squares) with an interval of one second, to a mean of 0.9 with an increased interval of ten seconds. This massive effect of increasing the time interval on Mike's performance suggests that he is only able to store pattern information for a very short time in spatial immediate memory before it is lost. In contrast, Helen and Nancy show similar patterns of performance, with relatively minor effects of the delay interval along with generally

Table 18.6 Visual spans with (a) a ten-second interval, and (b) a one-second interval between the to-be-remembered grid and the target grid

	Visual span (10 sec. gap)	
Mike	0.9	(range of scores: 1–2)
Helen	4.9	(range of scores: 3–8)
Nancy	5.5	(range of scores: 4–6)
	Visual span (1 sec. gap)	
Mike	12.0	(range of scores: 5–25)
Helen	7.7	(range of scores: 3–14)

reduced performance levels. Their problems with immediate visual memory seem to take the form of a reduced capacity in their spatial memory buffer.

Conclusions

We have presented the cases of three people who all experience particular problems in various aspects of their everyday life. In particular, they make errors when asked to copy drawings, errors when asked to perform simple mathematical procedures, errors in time judgement and errors in route-finding. We have suggested that impairments of working memory functioning may underlie their particular difficulties. We have also tried to indicate how more detailed study can reveal different forms of immediate memory impairment. With auditory presentation, Helen and Nancy seem to be particularly impaired at dealing with dual processing demands (from heard speech and from self-articulated rehearsal). This is consistent with their having a reduced capacity in verbal working memory. Nevertheless, the components of the verbal working memory system (the phonological store and the articulatory loop) seem operational, since both patients show 'normal' effects of word length and phonological similarity (at least under appropriate conditions). Mike on the other hand, seems to have an impaired articulatory loop and is insensitive to the effects of word length.

All three patients showed a reduced immediate visual memory, specifically for spatially represented material (though they could apparently form images of single object attributes relatively well). Helen and Nancy were not abnormally affected by the interval over which spatial patterns had to be maintained; Mike, however, was. Again, this points to a difference between Nancy and Helen, on the one hand, and Mike, on the other. Nancy and Helen's difficulties with spatial material can be attributed to a reduced capacity of a spatial working memory system. Mike's can be attributed to abnormally rapid fading of visuo-spatial information.

Can the deficits with visual and verbal material be related? For Helen and Nancy it is possible to link the reduced capacity for both verbal and for visuo-spatial information to a reduced central processing system (the central executive), which may flexibly allocate capacity between the verbal and visuo-spatial 'slave' systems. If this central system is abnormally limited, few extra resources can be given to the visual and verbal memory systems, and this may be most noticeable when the task requires that two separate stimuli are processed simultaneously (for example, with auditory input as well as articulatory rehearsal). On a more speculative note, we may also hypothesize that abnormally rapid fading of both visual and verbal temporary representations may be responsible for Mike's difficulties.

These difficulties in immediate visual and verbal memory probably impinge greatly on everyday life. For instance, even apparently simple tasks such as estimating the time of preparation of different foods for a meal require information about one food to be held temporarily whilst that about another is retrieved and compared. This may largely depend on immediate verbal memory. A task such as crossing the road and judging the speed of traffic may require the maintenance and comparison of spatial information about the relative positions of objects. Either a reduced capacity in the visuo-spatial and verbal components of the working memory system, or abnormal fading within those systems, will render many everyday tasks difficult.

Acknowledgements

This work was supported by the Medical Research Council of Great Britain, and the Human Frontier Science Programme. We are indebted to Mike, Helen and Nancy for giving their time to participate in this research.

Further Reading

Baddeley, A. (1990) *Human Memory: Theory and Practice* (Hove, Sussex: Lawrence Erlbaum Associates).
Baddeley, A.D. (1986) *Working Memory* (London: Oxford University Press).

References

Baddeley, A.D. (1986) *Working Memory* (Oxford: Oxford University Press).
Lindsay Wilson, J.T., Scott, J.H. and Power, K.G. (1987) 'Developmental differences in the span of visual memory for patterns', *British Journal of Developmental Psychology*, 5: 14–20.
Morris, R.G. and Kopelman, M.D. (1986) 'The memory deficits in Alzheimer-type dementia: a review', *Quarterly Journal of Experimental Psychology*, special issue: *Human Memory*, 38A: 575–602.

19 Remembering Stories but Not Words

Randi C. Martin and Cristina Romani

Introduction

People who have had strokes (or other kinds of brain damage) may develop problems in producing and comprehending speech and writing (aphasia). Individuals with aphasia often have reduced memory spans, that is, a reduced ability to recall immediately a sequence of words in the correct order. While normal individuals might easily be able to remember a list of six or seven words, aphasic patients often struggle to remember lists containing two or three words. Some patients can only remember one word. This reduced memory span has been taken as evidence of reduced verbal short-term memory capacity (see Vallar and Shallice, 1990, for an overview). Researchers have investigated whether this reduced short-term memory capacity might be the source of some of the aphasic patients' language production and comprehension difficulties. That is, perhaps aphasics cannot comprehend a phrase in a sentence because they cannot remember enough words at one time. One common view of why we have short-term memory is to hold enough words in mind at once to link them together in comprehension (Martin, 1993). Perhaps aphasic patients cannot do this and so have difficulty comprehending language. In the course of investigating this question in our laboratory, we came across the case of Alan (not his real name). Like many aphasic patients, Alan's memory span was about two or three words; however, details of his performance on memory span tasks revealed a pattern that was unlike that of other patients we had studied. In Alan's case, we believe that his reduced memory span and his difficulties in producing and understanding language derive from the same source: a reduced capacity for the short-term retention of the meanings of individual words (or lexical-semantic representations). It is important to distinguish Alan's deficit from a semantic (or meaning) deficit *per se*. Alan had *not* lost his knowledge of word meanings; however, he did have difficulty keeping the meanings of several words in mind simultaneously. The experiments we carried out were designed to establish this short-term memory deficit and examine its consequences for language comprehension, language production and long-term memory.

Background

Alan is now a 73-year-old man. In 1979 he had an operation to remove a haematoma (a swelling filled with blood) from the frontal lobe of the left hemisphere of the brain. Prior to this time, Alan had worked as a lawyer. After the operation he had severe difficulties in speaking and understanding language. However, in the subsequent three or four months his language abilities recovered substantially. Now, 14 years later, his comprehension seems quite good, at least in informal conversations. However, his speech is halting and lacking in specific content words. For example, when asked to explain the meaning of the proverb 'Don't count your chickens before they're hatched', he said, 'Well, this gets into my long suit. [pause] "Before they're hatched" means don't count on anything until they get it out. [pause] That's not enough.' This difficulty in producing meaningful speech in a normal, rapid fashion is very frustrating to him. In this testing session, he also struggled to provide a definition for the word 'bed', and said, 'I used to be a lawyer, now I can't tell you what a bed is!'

The combination of symptoms that Alan displayed – grammatically correct speech lacking in content information and good comprehension – would seem to place him in the category of 'anomic aphasic' (referring to their difficulty in providing names for objects and concepts). Classical anomic patients are presumed to have preserved knowledge about objects and concepts. Their naming difficulties are often attributed to a difficulty in retrieving the name from a concept, although they can understand the concept. Their good comprehension is attributed to a preserved ability to access concepts when they hear spoken words. Thus, their access deficit is unidirectional; they cannot go from the concept to its name but they can go from the name to the concept, and thereby understand its meaning.

Alan, however, does not show the defining feature of anomia; that is, he does not have difficulty naming objects or pictures presented in isolation. In fact, his naming accuracy is above the average for normal subjects of his age and educational level, even for difficult materials. Furthermore, formal testing revealed that his comprehension is very impaired on certain types of sentences. Alan's comprehension difficulties were not obvious to us when he first became involved in studies in our laboratory. In the earlier studies, we were interested in looking at the comprehension of grammatical information. On sentence comprehension tests using various types of complex grammatical structures, Alan generally performed at a high level. In later studies that are described below, we looked at comprehension of sentences with simple grammatical structures which were loaded with content information (for example, several adjectives modifying the nouns in the sentences), and it was with these materials that Alan's comprehension and repetition broke down. Further details on Alan's comprehension are provided in the section on comprehension.

Table 19.1 Phonological similarity and word-length effects for Alan and control subjects

	Alan		*Control subjects*	
Phonological similarity effect				
	List lengths 2 & 3		List length 5	
	Auditory	Visual	Auditory	Visual
Phonologically dissimilar words	65	40	68	42
Phonologically similar words	30	18	26	18
Difference	35	22	42	24
Auditory word length effect				
	List lengths 2 to 5		List lengths 3 to 6	
One-syllable words	43		59	
Two-syllable words	32		52	
Difference	11		7	

Short-term Memory

Alan's memory span of two to three items was in the range of many aphasic patients that we tested. For many patients with reduced memory span, the source of their reduced capacity is difficulty in retaining phonological information (that is, speech sounds). For Alan, this appeared not to be case (Martin et al., 1994). Table 19.1 shows Alan's performance and that of normal control subjects on span tasks with respect to phonologically related variables. (It should be noted that the controls were tested on longer lists than Alan.) Like normal subjects, Alan was affected by the sound character-istics of the memory span words: he remembered lists with phonologically distinct words better than lists with phonologically similar words (for example, rhyming words) and he remembered lists composed of short words better than lists composed of long words. These effects have been attributed to holding verbal information in a phonological form and using subvocal rehearsal to maintain the lists. Patients with difficulty in retaining phonological information typically do not show these effects.

Other aspects of Alan's short-term memory suggested that he had difficulty retaining semantic information. Normal subjects and patients with difficulty in retaining phono-logical information in short-term memory remember memory span lists composed of words better than lists composed of nonsense words (for example, plim, namber). This is thought to be the case because words can be remembered on the basis of their meanings in addition to their sounds, whereas nonsense words can only be retained on the basis of their sounds (see Howard, this volume). Alan did not show this effect: he recalled lists composed of nonsense words nearly as well as lists composed of real words. On a test in which Alan heard a list of words from different categories (such as 'rose oak dress hurricane') and was asked whether a probe word was in the same category as one of the list words (for example, 'shirt'), Alan was only 80 per cent correct when the list consisted of a single word and was at chance (54 per chance correct) when the list consisted of three words. His poor performance on this task could not be attributed to a lack of understanding of these words or their categories, because he performed perfectly when the list and the probe words were presented visually and stayed in view while he made his decision. The memory load imposed by hearing the words appeared to be the cause of his difficulty. An aphasic patient we tested with a severe difficulty in retaining phonological information performed better than Alan on this same test, scoring 95 per cent correct with a one-word list and 71 per cent correct with a three-word list.

Thus, Alan's short-term memory impairment came from a different source than that observed for many other aphasic patients – he appeared to have primarily a difficulty retaining semantic information rather than phonological information.

Sentence Comprehension

As alluded to earlier, Alan did well on auditory and visual tests of sentence comprehension that tested difficult syntactic structures such as passives (for example, 'The boy was carried by the girl') and embedded relative clauses (such as 'The car that was splashed by the truck was green'). In these tests, Alan would hear a sentence and then have to choose which of two pictures matched the sentence. The nonmatching picture would depict the same objects and actions but would reverse the roles of the participants (for example, show the boy carrying the girl or the car splashing the truck) or would attach the adjective in the relative clause sentences to the wrong noun (for example, show the truck rather than the car as green). In order to perform this test, then, the subject has to be able to decipher the grammatical structure of the sentence in order to determine the proper relationships among the words.

Alan did have difficulty, though, on tests using sentences that were loaded with content information. In one test, Alan heard sentences with either one adjective before each of two nouns (such as 'The blue bird stood by the black shoe') or two adjectives before each of two nouns (for example, 'The fluffy white kitten played with the soft brown yarn'). In this test a picture was presented in which either all the information matched the sentence, or one of the adjectives was incorrectly depicted. Alan had to say whether the picture matched the sentence. On this task, Alan scored only 83 per cent correct for the one-adjective sentences and was at chance for the two adjective sentences (33 per cent correct, where 50 per cent would be chance).

Alan's performance was also very poor on a sentence-comprehension test which did not include pictures. In this test, Alan was asked to answer a question about objects' attributes, such as 'Which is loud, a concert or a library?'. Alan often could not answer the question, and on most trials asked for several repetitions of each sentence. Again, his poor performance on this test could not be attributed to a lack of knowledge of these objects and their attributes. When we changed the questions to ask about a single object and its attribute (for example, 'Is a library loud?'), Alan performed 100 per cent correct. He also performed without error if the original questions were presented visually and left in view until he could make a response. Thus, it appeared that the short-term memory load imposed by auditory presentation of the original question containing two nouns and one attribute exceeded Alan's capacity for retaining semantic information. Alan's very poor performance on this task was not observed for a patient we tested who had a memory span in the range of Alan's, but whose reduced span appeared due to a phonological retention deficit. This patient scored 100 per cent correct on the attribute questions.

Both the short-term memory and sentence comprehension results indicated that Alan had difficulty with the short-term retention of the meanings of more than a few words. These results suggest that the capacity for retaining semantic information plays a role in memory span tasks and in sentence comprehension.

Connection to Production

Earlier, we described Alan's speech as lacking in content information, even though he is very good at naming individual objects. An intriguing question that we are just beginning to address is whether there is a connection between Alan's difficulty in holding several word meanings in short-term memory and his distinctive problems in oral expression. On several tests, we have found that Alan has even greater difficulty producing adjective–noun combinations than he has in understanding them. In describing pictured scenes, Alan uses far fewer adjective–noun phrases than do control subjects. In a test designed to elicit adjective–noun phrases, Alan was presented with two or more pictured objects, and he had to produce a phrase that distinguished one object from the rest. Figure 19.1 shows examples of the pictures used. Alan did well when he had to produce only one word (either a noun or an adjective) to perform the task (for example, producing 'leaf' or 'yellow' or 'curly'). He started to have difficulty if he had to produce an adjective–noun combination (such as 'green leaf', 'curly hair'), producing only three of the ten examples correctly. He often produced the noun and the adjective in separate phrases. For example, when the target was 'short hair', he said, 'Well, that's hair. It's short. That's short . . . I can't get it.' He was totally unable to produce any adjective–adjective–noun phrases correctly (such as 'small green leaf'). For these, not only did he tend to produce the nouns and adjectives in separate phrases, but he sometimes made errors in his word choice. For example, for the target 'small green leaf', he said, 'That's brown. No, br . . . br . . . green. I know it's a leaf. It's a green leaf and it's big.' Thus, even though Alan is able to produce each of the necessary words in isolation, he cannot produce them as a single phrase.

Some theories of speech production assume that individuals must hold the semantic representations for all the content words in a phrase in working memory while retrieving the phonological representations for each word. Thus, Alan's impairment in producing these adjective–noun phrases could occur because he cannot maintain all these semantic representations simultaneously. If this is the cause of his production problems, then it would suggest that the same type of short-term memory is used for holding semantic representations for individual words in comprehension and for holding semantic representations in production.

Short-term and Long-term Memory

Our discussion of Alan's deficits assumes that there is a short-term memory capacity for retaining semantic information that can be selectively affected by brain damage. Traditional

A

B

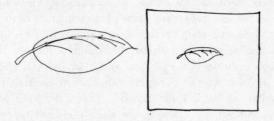

C

Figure 19.1   Examples of materials used in eliciting adjective–noun phrases
Notes
A   The pictures were presented individually and Alan was asked to name each with a single word.
B   The two objects were presented together and Alan was asked to use an adjective–noun phrase that would distinguish the object surrounded with an outline from the other figure (e.g., 'small leaf').
C   The three pictures were presented together and Alan was asked to use an adjective–adjective–noun phrase that would distinguish the object surrounded with an outline from the other two figures (e.g., 'short dark hair').

theories of memory, however, have assumed that the retention of semantic information is a function of long-term memory rather than of short-term memory. According to this view, an influence of meaning on memory span is assumed to arise because there is a long-term memory component to memory span. That is, when a span list is heard, some of the information is stored in long-term memory and some in short-term memory. During recall, performance is enhanced by recalling the information from both short- and long-term memory. According to this line of reasoning, Alan's reduced memory span would result because of a disruption of the long-term memory component. How-ever, Alan does not appear to have any difficulty with long-term retention. That is, he was not at all like an amnesic patient. He remembered us, he found his way to and from the laboratory on his own, and he remembered task instructions from one week to the next. However, we thought it was possible that, as in the case of sentence comprehen-sion, formal testing might reveal some long-term memory impairment that was not evident in casual observation.

We also tested two amnesic patients on some of these tests in order to provide a comparison with Alan. They developed their memory disorder after head injury due to automobile accidents. Dana was 43 at the time of testing and Andrea was 37 (not their real names). Both of these patients have a severely impaired ability to learn new informa-tion. For example, the first author tested each of them for several hours, but neither learned to recognize her. However, their language abilities are quite good: normal in the case of Dana and only mildly impaired in the case of Andrea. Their memory spans are in the normal range, with Dana having a digit span of seven items and Andrea a span of five items. Andrea (but not Dana) was tested on memory span for words versus nonwords and, like normal subjects, showed a large advantage for word lists. Neither of the amnesic patients had any difficulty comprehending or repeating the semantically loaded sentences that had given Alan such difficulty.

Long-term memory: memory for word lists

Many different techniques have been used to study long-term memory. One is a free recall task in which a list of words that exceeds the person's memory span is presented and the person recalls the list in any order. In the free recall test, normal subjects show a serial position effect in which the first few items are recalled well (the primacy effect) as are the last few items (the recency effect), with the middle items recalled the poorest (see figure 19.2). The primacy effect has been attributed to recall from long-term memory whereas the recency effect has been attributed to recall from short-term memory. A second technique is a paired associate test in which word pairs are presented and the person must learn to produce the second word of each pair when the first is given. The pairs may be presented with feedback, that is, with the experimenter providing the correct second word if the person cannot recall it. A third technique is a list-learning task in which a list of words is presented repeatedly, with the person trying to recall the entire list after each presentation. Testing continues until some criterion level of performance is achieved. Studies of patients who are amnesic have shown that they perform poorly on all these tasks. On the free recall tasks, they may show a normal recency effect but reduced recall from the primacy region. Patients with difficulties in retaining phonological

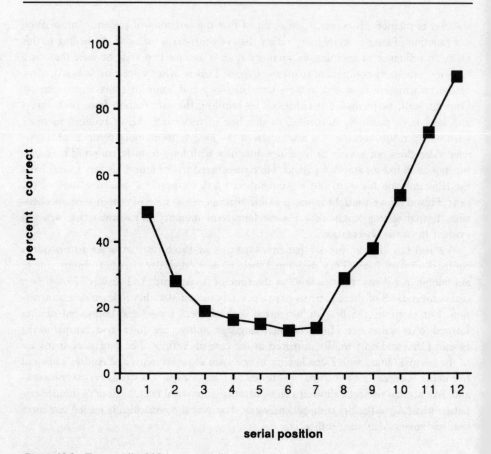

Figure 19.2   Free recall of 12-item word lists: normal control subjects (% correct)

information on short-term memory tests show a contrasting pattern. On free recall tests, the patients show normal performance on the primacy portion but poor performance on the recency portion. On paired associate and list learning paradigms, they perform normally.

Much to our surprise, Alan performed very poorly on all these long-term memory tasks, and thus performed more like an amnesic patient than like previously reported patients with short-term memory deficits. On an oral free recall task, he recalled only the last one or two items, and recalled almost nothing from earlier list positions, including the primacy portion. Figure 19.3 plots his performance and that of the two amnesic patients we tested. As can be seen in the figure, he recalled fewer words than Dana and about as many as Andrea. Alan, like the amnesics, showed no evidence of a primacy effect. On a standardized paired associate task with spoken recall, he performed at the 3rd percentile. On a list-learning task with spoken recall, he recalled only a total of 23 words across five repetitions of a 15 item list (max. score = 75). Normal control subjects recalled on average a total of 53 with a standard deviation of 10.

These results suggested that Alan did have a long-term memory deficit, and a fairly severe one. However, we were concerned that his poor performance on these tasks might

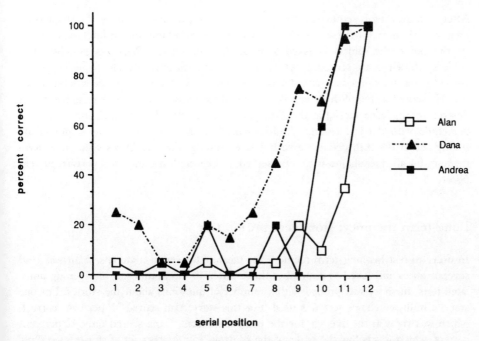

Figure 19.3   Free recall of 12-item word lists: Alan and two amnesic subjects (% correct)

have been caused by his speech production impairment. That is, given his difficulties in producing content information in spontaneous speech, there may have been some difficulty in producing the words in the lists that was not due to a memory problem.[1] In order to test this possibility, we gave Alan a long-term memory test that used a recognition rather than a recall paradigm. In a recognition test, a superspan list is presented and then the memory list items are presented intermixed with distractors, and the person must say whether each word is 'old' or 'new'. On this test Alan scored 71 per cent correct (when averaging correct recognition of old items and correct rejection of new items), and Dana obtained the same score. This was below the range of scores obtained by normal control subjects.

Given Alan's poor long-term memory for words in the absence of other apparent amnesic symptoms, two further aspects of long-term memory were investigated. The first was visual long-term memory. Alan's apparently good long-term memory abilities in everyday life might possibly be due to good memory for visual information rather than verbal information. The second aspect of long-term memory we investigated was memory for stories. If Alan's long-term memory deficit is restricted to the retention of individual words and does not involve other kinds of verbal information, then we would expect his memory for stories to be closer to normal.

Long-term memory: abstract visual shapes

Alan was tested on a section of a standardized test battery, the Wechsler Memory Scale (1981), in which four abstract shapes are presented one at a time for ten seconds each.

After each drawing is removed from sight, the subjects must try to draw the shape from memory. Memory for these shapes is tested again after 30 minutes of intervening tests. At this point, the subject is asked to recall as many of the shapes as possible. The subjects' drawings are scored in terms of how many features of each shape they recall correctly. On the immediate and delayed recall tests, Alan's performance was outstanding. He scored at the 99th percentile at immediate recall and at the 98th percentile at delayed recall. Dana scored at the 27th percentile at immediate testing and at the 3rd percentile with delayed testing. Andrea scored at the 22nd percentile at immediate testing and at the 10th percentile with delayed testing. Clearly, Alan's visual long-term memory for abstract shapes is well preserved; as expected, the amnesics performed very poorly.

Long-term memory: story recognition test

In order to test his long-term memory for meaningful verbal materials, Alan was read several stories and asked to remember them. After 40–45 minutes of intervening unrelated tests, memory was probed with a number of questions about the stories. For one story, a multiple choice test was used. For this story Alan scored 75 per cent correct, which was right at the average for the control subjects. Dana scored only 42 per cent correct, which was below the range of the controls. For another set of stories, 'yes'–'no' questions were asked about the stories. Typically the questions did not repeat information from the story verbatim, but changed the wording or required an inference from the story. For example, a story about two families having a picnic stated that the Brown family arrived at the meeting place before the Green family. The question relating to this asked whether the Greens had to wait for the Browns to arrive. For all these stories, Alan scored either right at the average for the control subjects or slightly above or below this level. Andrea scored at chance on answering these 'yes'–'no' questions. For one of these stories, she claimed that she had no recollection whatsoever of having heard the story.

Alan's performance on these stories was strikingly good. These results indicate that Alan does not have difficulty learning new verbal information, at least when it is presented in the form of a coherent story.

From Words to Sentences to Stories

Several dissociations (that is, impairments on some tasks together with normal ability on others) were noted in Alan's performance on the various verbal tests, some of which may seem quite puzzling. Figure 19.4 presents a summary of our findings. Alan's ability to recall stories was very good, even though this involves both sentence comprehension and long-term memory. This high level of performance contrasts with his very poor performance on short-term and long-term memory tests using unrelated words. The question, then, is how does he retain these stories, when he has difficulty retaining more than a very few words on short-term memory and long-term memory tests? One answer might be that Alan can retain words when they form a meaningful sentence. However,

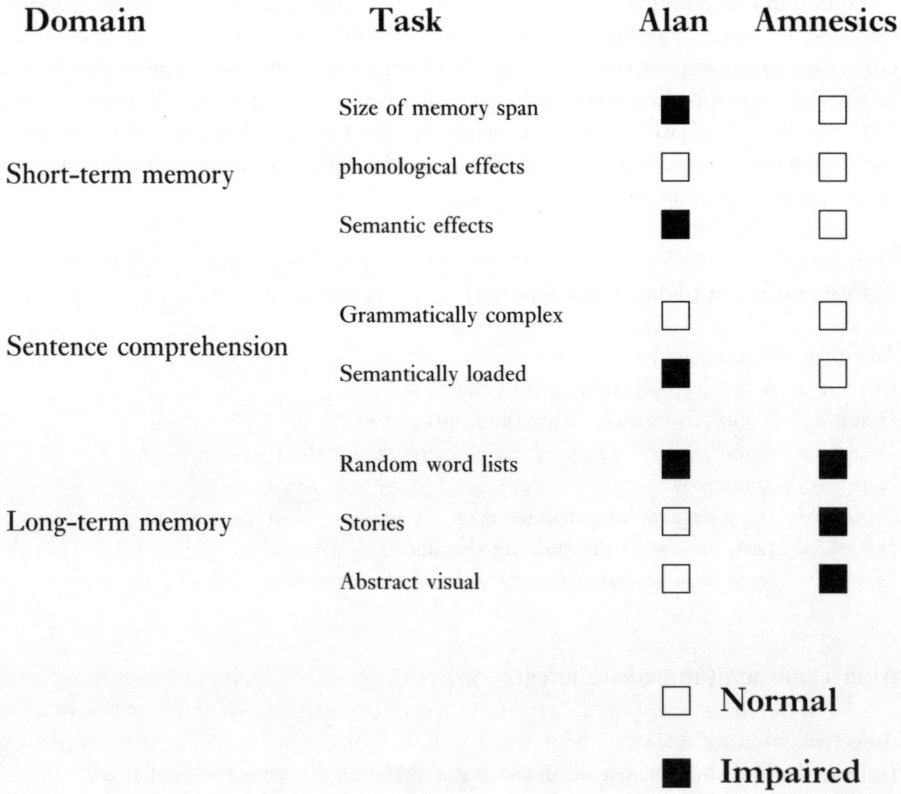

Domain	Task	Alan	Amnesics
Short-term memory	Size of memory span	■	☐
	phonological effects	☐	☐
	Semantic effects	■	☐
Sentence comprehension	Grammatically complex	☐	☐
	Semantically loaded	■	☐
Long-term memory	Random word lists	■	■
	Stories	☐	■
	Abstract visual	☐	■

☐ **Normal**

■ **Impaired**

Figure 19.4 Memory and comprehension tasks: summary of performance of Alan and amnesic subjects

as we discussed in the section on sentence comprehension, Alan did have difficulty comprehending some meaningful sentences when they were loaded with content information. Further investigations suggested to us that what is critical to ensure Alan's comprehension and long-term memory is that he be able to retain the words long enough for them to be integrated into larger units of meaning. A sentence comprehension test that we carried out shed some light on this issue.

We noticed that Alan performed poorly on sentence comprehension when the sentences contained a number of adjectives preceding the corresponding nouns, and the comprehension test assessed memory for these adjectives. We suspected that Alan's particular difficulty with these sentences might arise because the adjectives had to be held as individual word meanings in short-term memory until the noun was heard. Holding these individual word meanings would tax the same short-term memory capacity that was tapped by memory-span tests using random word lists. Alan might show better comprehension for sentences in which each word could be integrated with the meaning of other words as each word was identified. This would only be the case, however, if the capacity used for retaining integrated word meanings was different from that used to hold unintegrated word meanings.

To examine this notion we developed a test in which Alan and the control subjects were asked to judge whether or a sentence was sensible or semantically anomalous. The critical sentences were of two types, one in which a list of adjectives came either before or after the corresponding noun, and a second in which a list of nouns (for example, 'the dog', 'the boy', 'the girl') came either before or after the verb. Examples of the nonsensical sentences of these types are shown below. (An equal number of sensible sentences of the same types were also used).

Before condition (delayed integration)

Adjective–noun anomalies
Distance 1: A *fluffy* shriek came out of the room.
Distance 2: A *fluffy, surprised* shriek came out of the room.
Distance 3: A *fluffy, small, surprised* shriek came out of the room.
Noun–verb anomalies
Distance 1: Jeeps were walking the streets.
Distance 2: Jeeps and men were walking the streets.
Distance 3: Jeeps, men and women were walking the streets.

After condition (immediate integration)

Adjective–noun anomalies
Distance 1: The children played in the water that was *dry* until they got tired.
Distance 2: The children played in the water that was *cold and dry* until they got tired.
Distance 3: The children played in the water that was *blue, cold, and dry* until they got tired.
Noun–verb anomalies
Distance 1: Bill liked to eat *books* at the little shop.
Distance 2: Bill liked to eat *candies and books* at the little shop.
Distance 3: Bill liked to eat *candies, chocolates and books* at the little shop.

Our reasoning for including these sentence types was that in the 'after' condition shown above, the meanings of words could be integrated with each other as each word was heard, whereas in the 'before' condition, integration of meanings would be delayed. Specifically, in the 'before' condition the meanings of the adjectives could not be integrated with the noun until the noun was heard, and the roles of the nouns with respect to the verb could not be determined until the verb was heard. This delay in integration in the 'before' condition would increase as the number of adjectives or nouns increased. If Alan had difficulty in retaining individual word meanings, but not integrated word meanings, then we might expect him to have difficulty in judging as anomalous the sentences in the 'before' condition but not the sentences in the 'after' condition. For example, in the first set of sentences, if Alan had difficulty retaining 'fluffy' while holding on to 'small', and 'surprised' until 'shriek' was heard, then he might have difficulty judging that this sentence did not make sense. On the other hand, for the third set of sentences, he could integrate each adjective with 'water' as it was heard, and thus would not be required to retain a set of individual word meanings. Consequently, he might be able to do much better in judging the 'after' type sentences.

These sentences were presented auditorily one at a time under computer control. Alan and the control subjects were asked to judge whether each sentence was sensible or anomalous. The results in terms of percentage errors averaging across the sensible and anomalous sentences are shown in Figure 19.5(a) for Alan and in figure 19.5(b) for the control subjects. It is evident that overall Alan performed worse than the control subjects (6.5 per cent errors for the control subjects vs. 23 per cent for Alan). There could be a number of reasons for this difference. The sentences were digitized and presented over a computer loudspeaker. Alan has a mild deficit in recognizing spoken words; that might have hindered his performance. Another aphasic patient we tested, who did not have a short-term memory deficit but who had a similar speech perception deficit, performed at about the same overall level as Alan. More important than the overall level of perform-ance is the pattern of results that we obtained for Alan compared with the controls. For the control subjects, errors increased slightly with distance for both the before (delayed integration) and after (immediate integration) conditions.[2] For Alan, there was a very large increase in errors in the 'before' (delayed integration) condition when a comparison is made of distance 1 against distances 2 and 3 (11 per cent vs. 40 per cent and 38 per cent). As 50 per cent correct would be chance when averaging across the sensible and anomalous sentences, Alan's performance was clearly very poor for distances 2 and 3. In contrast, in the 'after' (immediate integration) condition, Alan's performance was much better and about the same for all distances.

Thus, it appears that Alan does have particular difficulty in comprehension when he is forced to retain individual word meanings in short-term memory prior to integration. In trying to relate these findings to Alan's good performance on the stories, we examined the nature of the sentences in the stories. For the most part, the stories did not contain sentences like those in the distance 2 and 3 'before' condition. The story sentences typically had a single adjective preceding a noun or a single subject preceding a verb. Only one story had several conjoined nouns as subjects of sentences and, in this case, the nouns had been mentioned previously in the story before being discussed together. Their previous mention in the story may have made these concepts more memorable when they were encountered together in a sentence. Thus, the stories contained sentences that Alan could understand, and apparently, he was able to link the individual meanings of sen-tences into a coherent interpretation of the stories as a whole.

Implications for the Structure of Memory

In comparing Alan's performance to that of amnesic subjects, a distinct contrast is seen between his pattern and theirs across the short-term memory, long-term memory for words and long-term memory for stories (see figure 19.4.) Their performance is most similar on the long-term memory for words, but we would argue that the similarity in performance is misleading – it derives from different sources. For Alan, the difficulty derives from what we have already described: a specific deficit in the short-term retention

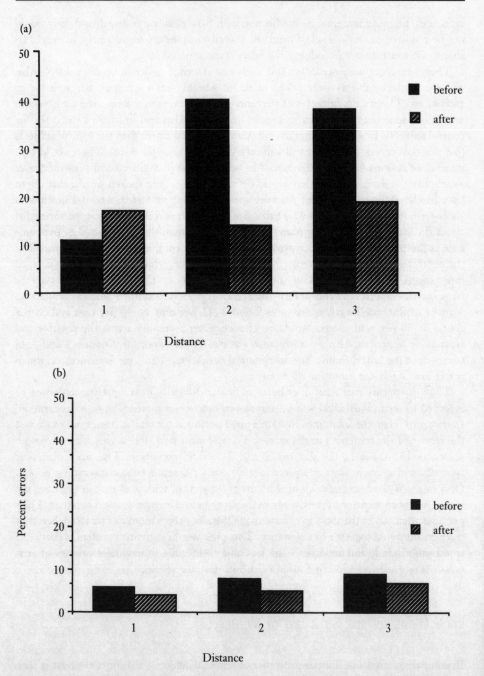

Figure 19.5   Sentence acceptability as a function of distance, averaging across sensible and anomalous sentences: (a) Alan; (b) normal control subjects

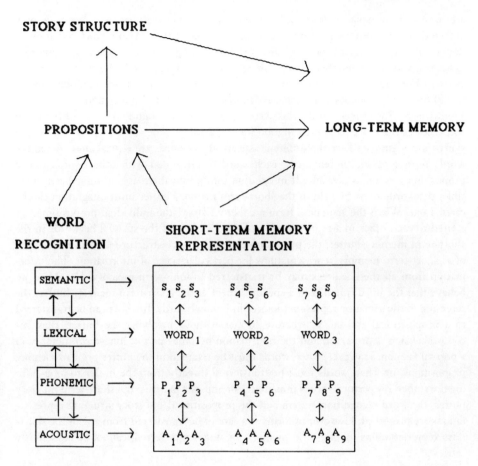

Figure 19.6   Model of the relationship between the word-recognition system, short-term memory and long-term memory

of lexical-semantic information. This deficit prevents the development of a long-term memory representation for items in word lists. For the amnesic patients, the difficulty derives from a more general source: a deficit in retaining, or perhaps a difficulty in consciously accessing, any verbal information (whether integrated or not) over the long term.[3] The amnesic patients can retain semantic and phonological information over the short term. They can understand and repeat back the sentences with many adjectives that gave Alan so much trouble. But for them, this doesn't translate into a long-term memory representation that they can consciously recollect. Thus, we are arguing that there can be two sources of a long-term memory deficit: (a) an inability to retain the appropriate representation over the short term in order to develop the long-term representation; and (b) a more general inability to remember information over the long term despite adequate retention in short-term memory.

In figure 19.6, we have depicted the kind of memory representations that we believe are necessary to explain Alan's and the amnesic subjects' performance. We have only depicted verbal memory here because it seems evident from Alan's good retention of nonverbal visual information over the short and long term that there are different systems involved. (A number of other patients have been reported who show this dissociation.) For the verbal memory system, one component is a word-recognition subsystem. This system consists of a permanent representation of the information that we know about words. For spoken words, this system recognizes the sound structure of the input and accesses the semantic representation for the word. A series of words may be held in short-term memory where the different aspects of the words are represented. When the words form meaningful sentences, each word is integrated with other words into a proposition as soon as possible. If integration into propositions is not immediately possible, the words must be held in the short-term memory buffer until integration can be carried out. When the sentences form a coherent story, the individual propositions are related to each other in a representation of the meaning of the story. The words in the short-term memory buffer, the propositions and the story structure may all be thought of as short-term memory representations for particular types of information. The information from all these sources may be transferred to long-term memory. For Alan, we believe that the impairment is in a specific aspect of the short-term memory buffer, the retention of the semantic representations of individual words. If words can be transferred to a propositional and story structure format without involving the buffer, then his comprehension is preserved and the information becomes part of long-term memory in a normal fashion. However, when words must be retained in the buffer prior to forming propositions, or when words must be transferred directly from the buffer to long-term memory, then his performance is impaired. For amnesic patients, the short-term memory buffer, the word recognition system and the propositional and story structure representations are preserved. However, information cannot be transferred from any of the short-term representations to long-term memory, or if it is transferred, cannot be consciously retrieved.

Summary and Conclusions

We have reported the case of Alan, who has a very specific deficit in short-term memory – a deficit in the short-term retention of semantic representations. This deficit affects only the retention of individual word meanings, and does not hinder his ability to hold more integrated meanings derived from combining the meanings of different words in a sentence. Alan's deficit causes difficulties for the comprehension of certain sentence types, for speech production and for the long-term retention of word lists. A comparison of Alan with amnesic patients indicates that a long-term verbal memory deficit can derive from different sources, with Alan's deficit specific to individual word meanings, and the amnesics' deficit more global in scope. In terms of detrimental effects on Alan's everyday life, it appears that his short-term memory deficit has its greatest impact on language production. For comprehension, as long as Alan is able to integrate word meanings with each other as each word is perceived, his comprehension is quite good, and his long-term memory for integrated meanings is normal. In contrast, his speech production is very impaired whenever he tries to produce more than single-word utterances. Although our conclusions are preliminary at this point, the findings on Alan's difficulties in production suggest that his short-term memory deficit seems to make it very difficult for him to communicate his thoughts with increases in the amount of content information that he wishes convey in a single phrase. Thus, it seems that comprehension can often occur without involving the capacity for retaining several individual word meanings simultaneously. However, in production it may be impossible to avoid a stage at which a set of individual word meanings must be retained while the phonological representations for the words are accessed.

Notes

1 Such a possibility seems unlikely in the case of the paired associate task where Alan only had to produce a single word in response to a cue. As discussed earlier, Alan had no difficulty in producing single words in naming pictures.
2 The normal control subjects did show some evidence of a greater memory load in the 'before' condition than in the 'after' condition as their average times to make the anomaly judgements increased with distance in the 'before' condition and decreased with distance in the 'after' condition.
3 The source of the memory disorder in amnesic patients such as those reported here is a matter of current debate. Some researchers have suggested that a general mechanism which serves to consolidate short-term representations into long-term representations has been disrupted (Squire et al., 1984). Others researchers have suggested that amnesic patients can transfer information to long-term memory but have difficulty with the conscious retrieval of this information (see Mayes, 1988, for discussion). Yet another view is that a specific episodic memory system that retains a record of new experiences has been disrupted (Tulvey et al., 1991).

Acknowledgements

The research reported here was supported by National Institutes of Health grant no. DC 00218 to Randi Martin at Rice University, Houston, Texas. We should like to thank Michael Bartha, Jennifer Shelton, Lisa Sanders and Laura Yaffee for their assistance in carrying out some of the tests reported here.

Further Reading

Baddeley, A.D., Papagno, C. and Vallar, G. (1988) 'When long-term learning depends on short-term storage', *Journal of Memory and Language*, 27: 586–95.
Martin, R.C. and Romani, C. (1994) 'Verbal working memory and sentence comprehension: a multiple components view', *Neuropsychology*, 8: 506–23.

References

Martin, R.C. (1993) 'Short-term memory and sentence processing: evidence from neuropsychology', *Memory and Cognition*, 21: 176–83.

Martin, R.C., Shelton, J. and Yaffee, L. (1994) 'Language processing and working memory: evidence for separate phonological and semantic capacities', *Journal of Memory and Language*, **33**: 83–111.

Mayes, A. (1988) *Human Organic Memory Disorders* (Cambridge: Cambridge University Press).

Squire, L., Cohen, N. and Nadel, L. (1984) 'The medial temporal region and memory consolidation: a new hypothesis', in H. Weingartner and E.S. Parker (eds), *Memory Consolidation* (Hillsdale, N.J.: Lawrence Erlbaum Associates).

Tulving, E., Hayman, C.A.G. and Macdonald, C. (1991) 'Long-lasting perceptual priming and semantic leaving in amnesia: a case experiment', *Journal of Experimental Psychology: Learning, Memory and Cognition*, **17**: 595–617.

Vallar, G. and Shallice, T. (1990) *Neuropsychological Impairments of Short-term Memory* (New York: Cambridge University Press).

Wechsler, D. (1981) *Wechsler Adult Intelligence Scale – Revised* (New York: Psychological Corporation).

20   Short-term Recall without Short-term Memory

David Howard

Introduction

The normal span for repeating back a list of unrelated digits is, in George Miller's famous phrase, seven plus or minus two. Impairments of long-term memory have been known and described since the nineteenth century, but the first case of a patient with a selective impairment in auditory-verbal span, with other language and cognitive functions relatively intact, was reported by Warrington and Shallice as recently as 1969. In a recent review, Shallice and Vallar (1990) argue that patients with short-term memory impairment should show the following four features:

1   a selective deficit in span;
2   a comparable level of performance for all strings of unconnected auditory-verbal items;
3   evidence that the span deficit does not arise from impaired speech production;
4   intact word perception.

The first two criteria demonstrate that the deficit is selective, and not due to a difficulty with some specific category of stimuli. The two final criteria demonstrate that difficulties in word perception and production cannot account for the span impairment.

In their review, Shallice and Vallar argue that 14 patients with acquired lesions have been described who meet their criteria. Almost all these patients had been aphasic, and while most had made quite good recoveries, language abilities were probably impaired in more-or-less subtle ways in all the subjects.

This chapter describes another patient with a highly selective impairment of short-term memory (STM). First, I describe the patient and demonstrate his STM impairment.

Then the chapter investigates the cognitive resources that the patient uses to support recall of lists.

Case Description

HB was born in 1924 in Vienna, one of three children in a middle-class Jewish family. In 1938, when Germany annexed Austria, the British government granted a small number of visas to unaccompanied Jewish children. HB arrived in Britain, speaking no English, with his two younger sisters; none of them ever saw their parents again. After being cared for in a variety of children's homes, HB joined the army and served in the intelligence services in Germany at the end of the war. He was fluent in both English and German and, although he rarely spoke German because he moved entirely in English-speaking circles, he read German. He worked for many years in business before changing career to become a social worker. He was heavily involved in counselling when, in 1984 at the age of 60, he suffered a stroke which affected the temporo-parietal region of the left hemisphere and left him with some aphasic language difficulties. He had excellent speech therapy and made a good recovery. However, he felt that his speech was not good enough to return to social work, which placed heavy demands on accurate, appropriate speech, but he did continue as a lay magistrate, a role which involved understanding court proceedings, but placed little demands on speech production – speaking could be left primarily to the chairman of the bench. He also worked as a volunteer at a disability rights desk in a local hospital, and he attended an aphasic self-help group.

In one-to-one conversation, HB's difficulties were hard to discern. He discussed issues passionately and coherently, although occasional word-finding difficulties would interrupt the expression of his ideas. Like many aphasic people who have made a good recovery, he found group conversation much harder. When intervention in a conversation had to be made quickly and at exactly the right time, he found it hard to hold his own, and adopted a more retiring role than he had previously.

One of his speech therapists noticed that, although HB had made a relatively good recovery from his aphasia, his short-term memory span was severely impaired, and referred him to me.

A selective difficulty in span

One of the first tasks I did with HB was the Wechsler Adult Intelligence Scale (WAIS). This test has the advantage that it probes a variety of different kinds of tasks, which are divided into verbal and nonverbal tests. The score in each subtest can be converted into an age-scaled score, where the mean score for subjects in that age group is 10 with a standard deviation of 3. Conveniently, one of the verbal subtests is a measure of digit span, permitting this to be compared to other cognitive functions. In all the verbal and nonverbal tests HB scores above average for his age group (verbal IQ = 122, performance IQ = 121), with the exception of digit span, where he could only manage three digits forwards and three backwards (scale score of 5 – severely impaired relative to his mean age-scaled score of 15 on the other verbal subtests).

Table 20.1   Immediate serial recall for lists of digits and letters with auditory and visual presentation[a]

| List length | Digits | | Letters | |
	Auditory	Visual	Auditory	Visual
2 items	4/4 (1.0)	—	7/10 (0.85)	—
3 items	8/10 (0.94)	4/4 (1.0)	3/10 (0.60)	4/4 (1.0)
4 items	5/10 (0.75)	4/4 (1.0)	—	7/10 (0.90)
5 items	3/10 (0.76)	9/10 (0.98)	—	0/10 (0.66)
6 items	—	7/10 (0.95)	—	—

Note:
[a]   Number of lists correct; proportion of items correct shown in brackets.

Similar span for all materials

I tested HB's span in immediate serial recall of lists of digits, letter names (such as A, F, Z, Q, which do not sound alike), and words. Both the digits and the letter names were tested with auditory presentation (at one item per second). With visual presentation the digits were presented in a horizontal row on a single sheet, and the letters were presented successively for one second in the centre of a computer screen. Ten lists were presented at each length, except where HB recalled the first four lists at that length correctly. The words which were used were picture names, and recall was tested under two conditions: with verbal recall, HB had to repeat back the lists in order; with pointing, he was presented with a sheet of eight pictures and had to recall them by pointing to the pictures in order. To prevent him simply remembering the location of each picture on the sheet as it was presented, HB was only given the response sheet once all the list had been presented. On each trial the eight pictures were arranged differently on the response sheet. If pointing and spoken recall produce similar levels of performance, this suggests that reduced span is not due to any difficulty in producing a particular kind of response, but rather, a short-term memory impairment.

Normal subjects typically show a small advantage for auditory list presentation as compared to visual presentation, as well as better recall of digits than letter names or words (Brener, 1940). In contrast, STM patients typically show better recall of visually presented lists, but usually show a normal effect of the type of material.

The results in table 20.1 show both the number of lists correct and (in brackets) the proportion of items correctly recalled in the correct position. With digits, HB can reproduce only lists of two items reliably when auditorily presented and his span, measured as the point at which 50 per cent of lists are correctly recalled, is four. Recall of visually presented digits is very much better, and his span is more than six digits. With both modalities of presentation his span for letters is less than for digits; auditory span is 2.5 letters and visual span 4.2 letters. For auditorily presented lists of words, HB's span is independent of the method of recall. Both spoken responses and pointing responses yield a span of 3.3 words.

HB therefore shows a pattern of performance typical of short-term memory patients.

Table 20.2   Nonword repetition: the effects of phoneme length and syllable length (n = 20 in each cell)

| No. of syllables | Nonword length | | | | | |
| No. of phonemes | One syllable | | | | Two syllables | |
	2	3	4	5	5	6
Proportion of nonwords correct	0.80	0.65	0.60	0.50	0.15	0.15
Proportion of phonemes correct	0.95	0.88	0.88	0.81	0.67	0.73

There is a selective impairment of span when other functions probed by the WAIS are entirely normal. Auditory span is impaired for digits, letters and words, while visual span is relatively good and scarcely below normal levels of performance.

In addition to difficulty in repeating lists of unrelated words, patients with impaired short-term memory are invariably impaired in repeating nonsense words (Vallar and Shallice, 1990), although they are typically accurate with nonwords of one syllable (see, for example, Saffran and Martin, 1990) and may even be able to repeat three-syllable nonwords (Baddeley et al., 1988). Nonsense words have, by definition, no lexical or semantic representation, and so these items can only be repeated on the basis of a short-term phonological record; it has been argued that nonword repetition may provide a very pure estimate of the capacity of phonological storage for a patient (Baddeley and Wilson, 1988). HB was given single nonsense words to repeat where the length of the nonwords varied in terms of both number of phonemes and number of syllables.

The results in table 20.2 show that HB is impaired in repeating even single-syllable nonwords. This difficulty cannot be due to a problem in producing nonwords, because he can read them aloud accurately. It cannot be due to a perceptual problem, because he performs satisfactorily in minimal pair judgements on nonwords. His impaired performance is most simply attributed to limited short-term phonological storage.

Testing word recognition

One possible reason for a difficulty in auditory span is an impairment in spoken-word recognition. A variety of tests were used to probe HB's recognition of spoken words. With nonword minimal pairs (for example, 'ba-da'), HB scored 95 per cent with no lip reading, and 96 per cent when lip reading was encouraged. He made no errors in a variety of clinical tests of word comprehension, both with visually and auditorily presented materials. These included word-to-picture matching and synonym judgement. To probe word recognition more closely, HB was given a list of 180 items for lexical decision. Half the items were real words, with equal numbers of one-, two- and three-syllable items. Within each of these sets half the items represented concrete words and half abstract words. The nonwords were generated by changing a single phoneme in a set of real words which were matched in imageability, frequency and length to the real words. HB was asked to decide if each item was a correctly pronounced real word, and if so, to give a definition of it. His performance on this was wholly satisfactory: he was

95 per cent correct in lexical decision with no effects of imageability and length of stimulus – a level of performance consistent with his accuracy in minimal pair judgements. He provided appropriate definitions for 85 of the 86 items he accepted as real words.

HB's performance on these tests, which measure only accuracy, is normal. To be rather more searching, he was tested with a variety of materials where reaction times were measured, and his performance levels compared to undergraduate control subjects. On auditory lexical decision, his performance was within the control range in terms of both accuracy and latency. In semantic classification of visually presented words into 'person' or 'thing', varying word frequency across items, HB's performance was indistinguishable from young controls in terms of both accuracy and latency, and he showed a normal frequency effect. In classifying spoken words into 'name' or 'nonname', HB was within the normal range in terms of accuracy, but his latencies were outside the normal range and about 250 msecs slower than undergraduate controls. It may seem unfair to compare a 64-year-old who has suffered a stroke with undergraduate controls but, given that HB was able to produce latencies comparable to theirs in other tasks, this result suggests that semantic access from auditory stimuli may be slightly slowed, although almost certainly no more so than for other subjects of his age.

Taken together, HB's performance across these quite demanding tasks suggests that he shows good recognition of both spoken and written words.

Testing word production

On the Graded Naming Test, which is a difficult test of picture naming (the first item is a kangaroo and the last a (chemical) retort), HB scored 17/30 with spoken production; this is at the 60th percentile of the normal population; writing the names, he scored 19/30. Reading aloud the exception words of the New Adult Reading Test, he scored 34/50, placing him on the 80th percentile of the normal population. In reading 60 exception words, HB's accuracy was just worse than the worst undergraduate control and his latencies were longer than the slowest control; on average he was 250 msecs slower than the undergraduate controls. His deficit in picture naming was more pronounced: naming 72 pictures of items with varying frequency his error rate (5/72) was outside the normal range. His latencies were much slower than normal subjects, although the word-frequency effect was entirely normal. On average his latencies were 2.2 times that of the younger control population.

Overall, HB's accuracy in reading and naming tasks is normal for his age. He does, however, show slowed responses, particularly in naming, which is in accordance with his mild word-finding difficulties in spontaneous speech.

Summary

HB shows a selective impairment in short-term memory. This is not due to any unusual difficulty in word recognition, and his production is of normal accuracy, although slowed relative to neurologically normal undergraduates. His span is reduced with all kinds of

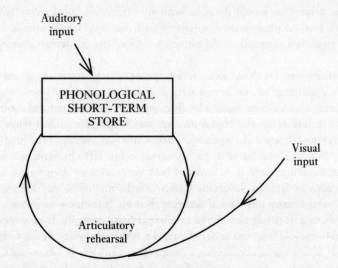

Figure 20.1   Baddeley's articulatory loop model of phonological storage
Source: Baddeley (1986)

materials and, like most short-term memory patients, is much better when material is presented visually. In repeating nonsense words, where only phonological information is available, HB is unreliable even with single-syllable items. In this respect he is more severely impaired than almost any short-term memory patient described in the literature. With words, letters and digits he can repeat considerably more material. He is an unusual patient, because there is strong evidence that word recognition is very close to normal in terms of both accuracy and latency, and word production is normal in accuracy. He should, therefore, be able to use a full range of linguistic resources in list recall. I now turn to investigation of the sources of information which he has available.

The Characteristics of Short-term Memory

Baddeley (1986) has proposed a two-component model of verbal short-term memory. There is a phonological short-term store whose contents are rehearsed using an articulatory loop; without rehearsal the contents of the PSTS decay rapidly. The loop has capacity limited to the amount of material which can be articulated in around 1.5 seconds. Auditorily presented items access the phonological store directly, whereas visually presented material has to be recoded via the articulatory loop.

Baddeley uses this simple model to explain a number of well-known effects on STM span. These include:

1   *The phonological similarity effect.* Recall of lists is worse when the lists consist of phonologically similar items (such as 'cat', 'hat', 'rat', 'mat') than when the items are phonologically distinct ('dog', 'cap', 'elk', 'rug'). This occurs whether items are

presented visually or auditorily (Conrad and Hull, 1964). This is normally taken as evidence that, irrespective of the modality of presentation, items are held in the phonological store. Similar items are more likely to be confused within this store, resulting in poorer recall of such lists;

2   *The word length effect*. Recall of lists of long words (such as 'Warwickshire', 'hippopotamus', 'gladiolus') is worse than recall of lists of short words (such as 'Kent', 'lion', 'rose'). This occurs with both auditory and visual list presentation (Baddeley et al., 1975). The interpretation of this within Baddeley's model is that the contents of STM are maintained by articulatory rehearsal. The number of items that can be rehearsed depends on how long they take to say. The capacity of this 'rehearsal loop' is smaller for long words than for short words;

3   *The effects of articulatory suppression* (also called concurrent articulation). Recall of both visually and auditorily presented lists is worse if subjects have to say something irrelevant (such as 'blah, blah, blah' or 'memory, memory, memory') during presentation and recall. This is because articulatory suppression interferes with the use of rehearsal to maintain the contents of STM.

When the effects of articulatory suppression on the word length effect (WLE) are examined, it is found that suppression eliminates the word-length effect with both auditory and visual list presentation (Baddeley et al., 1984; Besner and Davelaar, 1982). The interpretation is that suppression, by preventing rehearsal, eliminates the word-length effect (which reflects rehearsal).

With the phonological similarity effect (PSE), the results are more complex. With auditory list presentation, performance is worse under suppression, but the advantage for phonologically dissimilar lists remains (Murray, 1968). With visual list presentation, suppression eliminates the phonological similarity effect (Baddeley et al., 1984). The usual interpretation for this pattern is that auditory material can access a phonological short-term store (PSTS) directly, but that visually presented items have to be recoded via the articulatory rehearsal system to gain access to short-term memory. Suppression therefore prevents visually presented items from getting to the phonological store, and they therefore do not show the phonological similarity effect (which reflects use of the phonological store).

From the perspective of this model, the PSE can be taken as a signature of storage of material in the PSTS, and the WLE as a signature of a time-limited rehearsal loop contributing to performance (Vallar and Baddeley, 1984). Are these effects found with HB?

The phonological similarity effect

Normal subjects are better at recalling lists of phonologically distinct items than phonologically confusable items with both visual and auditory list presentation. This is attributed to short-term storage of the list in a phonological form.

Letter recall   Phonologically similar letters were drawn randomly from the set PVBTDCG, and phonologically dissimilar letters from the set JSHYLRZ. Lists were presented at one

Table 20.3   The phonological similarity effect

(a) Phonologically similar and dissimilar letters[a]

	Auditory		Visual	
List length	Similar	Dissimilar	Similar	Dissimilar
2 items	7/10 (0.85)	7/10 (0.85)	—	—
3 items	4/10 (0.67)	3/10 (0.60)	4/4 (1.0)	4/4 (1.0)
4 items	—	—	9/10 (0.98)	7/10 (0.90)
5 items	—	—	2/10 (0.60)	0/10 (0.66)

(b) Phonologically similar and dissimilar words with auditory presentation[a]

List length	Similar	Dissimilar
2 items	9/10 (0.95)	9/10 (0.95)
3 items	1/10 (0.57)	3/10 (0.63)

Note:
[a]   Number of lists correct; proportion of items correct in brackets.

item per second auditorily, and visually at the same rate on a VDU screen. The results (table 20.3) show that there is no effect of phonological similarity on recall of either auditorily or visually presented lists.

Word recall   To examine whether the absence of a PSE was a general property of HB's recall and not confined to letters, HB recalled auditorily presented lists of phonologically similar (rhyming) words drawn from the set sit, wit, knit, quit, fit, pit, lit, kit, bit and phonologically distinct words matched for frequency and length drawn from the set gas, ink, lot, mug, pin, dry, ton, herb, ship. There is again no effect of phonological similarity on list recall (table 20.3).

Nonword probes   Both letters and real words have both semantic and visual representations. HB may be using other nonphonological codes for short-term storage of these lists. He was therefore tested with nonwords, which have no semantic representations, and cannot easily be recoded into visual form (especially because HB is very impaired in writing nonwords to dictation). It was not practicable to test HB's repetition of lists of nonwords because he is unreliable in recall of even the shortest single-syllable nonword. He was therefore tested in a probe task: he was presented with a list of three nonwords followed by a probe nonword, and had to determine whether the probe was present in the list. Half the nonword lists were drawn from a set of rhyming items (ga pa na ta ra sa la va) and half from a set of nonrhyming nonwords with the same initial consonants (gow pu noi tei ree sare luh vai).

  Overall HB was correct on 41/48 of the phonologically similar lists (2/30 misses, 5/18 false positives) and 41/48 dissimilar lists (7/30 misses). Even in this task, which encourages the use of phonological storage, HB shows no effect of phonological similarity.

Table 20.4 The word-length effect[a]

(a) Auditory presentation

List length	One syllable	Three syllables
2 items	8/10 (0.90)	8/10 (0.90)
3 items	15/30 (0.74)	11/30 (0.73)
4 items	0/10 (0.65)	0/10 (0.65)

(b) Auditory presentation of three-item lists and visual presentation of four-item lists

Presentation	One syllable	Three syllables
Auditory	16/40 (0.72)	15/40 (0.68)
Visual	4/40 (0.63)	1/40 (0.50)

Note: Number of lists correct; proportion of items correct in brackets.

Comment Across a variety of experimental materials, HB shows no effect of phonological similarity on list recall. With auditory presentation, his performance is impaired even with the shortest lists. Recall of visually presented lists is substantially better, but also shows no signs of any effects of phonological confusability.

The word length effect

In normal subjects the recall of lists of long words is worse than that of lists of short words with both auditory and visual list presentation. Because this effect of word length is abolished by concurrent articulation, it has been attributed by Baddeley (1986) to an effect of articulatory rehearsal of the contents of a phonological short-term store. The tests above suggest that HB is not using a phonological store in list recall; there should, therefore, be no effect of word length on recall of auditorily or visually presented lists.

Auditorily presented word lists Lists of long and short words were drawn from a pool of 100 one- and three-syllable words, matched item by item for imageability and frequency. HB was presented with lists over two sessions. As word-length effects in recall accuracy are typically observed with lists which are just above span, HB was presented with large numbers of lists of three words. The results in table 20.4 show that there is clearly no effect of syllable length on HB's recall of spoken word lists.

One- and three-syllable words with auditory and visual presentation The preceding results show that there is no suggestion of a word-length effect in recall of auditorily presented lists. The absence of a phonological similarity effect with auditory and visual presentation implies that HB does not use phonological storage. Baddeley's model therefore predicts that HB should show no word–length effect with visually presented lists.

HB was tested with auditory and visual lists in separate sessions three months apart. The lists were matched for imageability and frequency. Auditory lists were of three words, and visual lists of four. Lists were presented visually on a VDU at one word per second. The results in table 20.4 show that with auditory presentation, there is no effect of word syllable length (rank sum test on numbers of items recalled in each trial, $z = 0.74$, ns). With visual presentation, there is, surprisingly, an effect of word length on recall accuracy ($z = 2.58$, $p = 0.005$).

One possible interpretation is that this result reflects articulatory rehearsal of visually presented lists, but not those which were presented auditorily – a pattern of performance which is not easily interpreted by Baddeley's model. A second possibility is that this effect is due to a confounding: the three-syllable items were matched to the one-syllable items in frequency and imageability, but differed in number of letters. The next experiment examines whether the word-length effect in this experiment is due to the number of letters in the word or to the number of syllables in its spoken form, by taking one- and three-syllable words matched for the number of letters.

Visual word length effect controlling for number of letters   The stimuli were drawn from sets of six-letter three-syllable words and six-letter one-syllable words. There were 30 words in each set, matched for imageability and frequency as well as number of letters. Four item lists were presented at the rate of one per second.

The results are straightforward; when visual word letter length is matched, the effect of word syllable length is abolished (one-syllable 1/30 lists, items 0.64; three-syllable 5/30 lists, items 0.67).

Recall of visually presented numbers: the effect of visual length   One possible criticism of the preceding experiment is that, when letter length is matched, one- and three-syllable words differ in articulatory complexity. Thus the one-syllable words always contain at least one consonant cluster (for example, 'shrimp', 'wealth', 'bright'), while the three-syllable words are typically alternating single consonants and vowels (for example, 'family', 'tomato', 'camera'). To meet this possible objection, HB's recall of visually presented lists was examined using numbers presented either as arabic digits or alphabetic number names. The phonological form of the lists in recall (the spoken number names) is therefore identical; the lists differ only in the visual length of the presented stimuli.

Lists of six numbers were presented successively (items presented at the same central location for 0.75 seconds per item). The results were scored as the number of items correct in the correct serial position. Recall is significantly better for digits (3/12 lists, 0.63 items) than for alphabetic numbers (0/12 lists, 0.37 items; $z = 2.44$, $p = 0.007$). This confirms that, when the items have an identical phonological form, there is an effect of visual length on HB's recall accuracy.

Comment   With auditory list presentation HB shows no effect of word length on recall. With visual list presentation there is an effect of word length, but these experiments have established that the effect is due to the visual length of the words, rather than the number of syllables in the word. This finding is consistent with the failure to find a

Table 20.5   Recall of lists of high- and low-imageability words[a]

Presentation	High imageability	Low imageability
Auditory	23/40 (0.80)	8/40 (0.60)
Visual	5/40 (0.62)	0/40 (0.51)

Notes:
[a]   Number of lists correct; proportion of items correct in brackets.
   Auditory presentation was with three-item lists and visual
   presentation with four items.

phonological similarity effect in the previous section. If HB is not storing items in a phonological store, and word-length effects reflect rehearsal of the contents of the phonological store, then he should show no word-length effects.

Thus HB shows no phonological similarity effects or word-length effects in list recall. The implications in terms of Baddeley's model are clear. There is absolutely no evidence that HB uses phonological storage or articulatory rehearsal in STM tasks. While his performance in these tasks is clearly impaired, he manages to recall about three items with auditory presentation and up to six with visual presentation. He is clearly able to use other cognitive resources in the absence of the normal phonological-articulatory short-term memory system. What are they?

I have already demonstrated that with visually presented lists, visual length predicts HB's performance. This suggests that his recall of these lists is supported by a visual short-term memory store.

Semantic effects in recall

Recall of lists of high- and low-imageability words   HB was presented with lists comprising high- and low-imageability words, matched for frequency and length. Lists of length three were presented auditorily and lists of length four were presented visually both at the rate of one item per second.

The results (table 20.5) show that with auditory presentation, there is a strong effect of imageability on the number of items recalled in the correct serial order (rank sum test on number of items correct in each list, $z = 3.38$, $p < 0.001$). With visual presentation, there is a similar effect of imageability on recall ($z = 3.06$, $p = 0.001$).

The effect of imageability on list recall shows that semantic representations are involved. One possibility is that he creates mental images of the word meanings to support recall (cf. Paivio, 1971). A second possibility is that high imageability items have 'richer' semantic representations, which are better able to support recall performance (cf. Plaut and Shallice, 1993; Jones, 1985). Certainly, HB's report was that he did not consciously use mental imagery in the task.

The zero effect   Numbers have a single name with one exception: in British English zero can be called 'zero', 'nought' or 'oh'. These share the same semantics, and the same arabic number form '0'.

This experiment was intended to see whether HB made errors in confusing 'zero', 'nought' and 'oh' in digit list recall. Confusion between these forms will suggest that, instead of using the distinctive phonological form of these words, HB is using either semantic or orthographic forms to aid recall of spoken lists.

HB was presented auditorily with 72 lists of four digits. In 24 lists the number 'zero', 'nought' or 'oh' occurred once in the list. Across lists the three phonological forms of 'zero' were used equally often in each serial position. There were 24 control lists made up only of the numbers 1–9, and 24 filler digit lists.

Errors were classified as a 'digit substitution' where one digit was substituted by another in the range 1–9, as 'zero substitutions' where a digit was substituted by 'zero', 'nought' or 'oh', or as an omission.

There were 8/24 control lists that were completely correct, and 4/24 zero lists; on 6/24 zero lists the only error was a 'zero substitution'. Overall zeros were reproduced much less accurately than other digits (54 per cent of 'zero' items were correct compared to 78 per cent for other digits in the same lists), and 91 per cent of errors on zero items consisted of 'zero substitutions'. On only one occasion was one of the 'zero' forms substituted for other digits.

HB reported that he realized that there were three forms of 'zero' employed. His account was that he was not 'writing the list down' in his head. Clearly, he is relying on some form of coding in which 'zero', 'nought' and 'oh' are confusable. If he had been using an orthographic code, he might have adopted the strategy of assigning different orthographic forms to the three phonological forms. 'Zero substitutions' occur equally often in all parts of the experiment, suggesting that HB did not adopt this strategy during the course of the experiment.

The existence of 'zero' and 'oh' confusions suggests that HB is using either a semantic or orthographic code in this task. His report and his failure to adopt an orthographic code that differentiates between these forms suggest that the code is most likely to be semantic.

Recall of nonwords, pseudohomophones and real words with visual presentation   Besner and Davelaar (1982) demonstrated that for normal subjects recall of lists of pseudohomophones (such as 'bredd', 'fone', 'horce') was better than recall of control nonwords, and this effect remained under concurrent articulation. If concurrent articulation interferes with recoding of visual material into a phonological short-term store, this implies that the advantage for pseudohomophones does not depend on phonological representations in the PSTS. One possibility suggested by Monsell (1987) and Howard and Franklin (1990) is that the effect is due to lexical support of representations in an output phonological buffer.

In normal subjects, recall of real words is better than recall of nonwords; this is attributed to the lexical and semantic representations for real words that support recall.

In this experiment, HB's performance is compared in recall of visually presented lists of concrete nouns (such as 'lake', 'train', 'bruise'), pseudohomophones of concrete nouns (for example, 'wotch', 'kace', 'bote') and control nonwords (such as 'draik', 'prane', 'powce'). The items were matched by list for N-ness (that is, the number of real words that can be made by changing a single letter in the item). There were ten lists of each type of length 3 and of length 4; lists of each type were randomly intermixed, but the lists were blocked by length. HB read each list silently, and then attempted to recall it.

Table 20.6 Recall of visually presented lists of nonwords, pseudohomophones and real words[a]

List length	Nonwords	Pseudohomophones	Real words	Total
3	4/10 (0.70)	6/10 (0.77)	8/10 (0.90)	18/30 (0.79)
4	0/10 (0.45)	1/10 (0.65)	5/10 (0.85)	6/30 (0.65)
Total	4/20 (0.55)	7/20 (0.70)	13/20 (0.87)	24/60 (0.74)

Note:
[a] Number of lists correct; proportion of items correct in brackets.

Table 20.7 Recall of auditorily presented lists of four words[a]

Rate of presentation	Category lists	Mixed lists	Total
Slow	6/20 (0.70)	8/20 (0.74)	14/40 (0.72)
Fast	6/20 (0.66)	1/20 (0.56)	7/40 (0.60)
Total	12/40 (0.68)	9/40 (0.65)	21/80 (0.66)

Note:
[a] Number of lists correct; proportion of items correct in brackets.

Combining across list lengths, there is a significant effect for the hypothesis that recall depends on the list type (Jonckheere trend test, combined S test, $z = 3.72$, $p < 0.001$; see table 20.6). Recall of real word lists is better than recall of lists of pseudohomophones (combined rank sum test, $z = 2.33$, $p < 0.01$). There is a trend for better recall of pseudohomophones than of control nonwords that does not reach significance ($z = 1.33$, $p = 0.09$).

This experiment, therefore, provides strong evidence that the lexical-semantic representations which are available for real words, but not pseudohomophones or nonwords, benefits HB's recall of visually presented lists. It does not, on the other hand, demonstrate whether recall of lists of pseudohomophones is better than recall of control nonwords.

Effects of category and rate of presentation on recall of auditorily-presented lists Use of semantic memory in immediate serial recall tasks is affected by rate of presentation; encoding in semantic memory is easier at slow presentation rates. Semantic organization in lists also makes the items easier to encode.

This experiment compares HB's recall of lists of four items drawn from the same semantic category (category lists, for example, 'lion', 'zebra', 'antelope', 'giraffe'), and lists drawn from different categories (mixed lists, for example, 'hammer', 'rose', 'aeroplane', 'dentist'). Items were presented either at two items per second ('fast') or one item every two seconds ('slow'). All items occurred in the same serial position in both a mixed list and a category list. Lists were presented over two sessions with rate of presentation varied within the sessions in an ABBA design (table 20.7).

Scored by items, there is an overall difference between conditions (Cochran $Q(3) =$

17.75, $p < 0.001$). Pairwise comparisons indicate that recall of mixed lists with fast presentation is significantly worse than all other conditions (McNemar, $p < 0.01$ or better) which do not differ from each other. Significant differences between conditions only occur at positions three and four in the lists.

These results indicate that slow presentation improves recall only with mixed lists, and that categorization only improves recall with fast presentation. The category lists are already semantically organized; slow presentation allows HB to impose semantic order on the mixed lists. As he reported after the experiment: 'To remember the words, I like to make a logic of the list.'

Discussion

Baddeley's (1986) working memory model emphasizes the importance of phonological storage in immediate serial list recall. The evidence presented here shows that there is absolutely no indication that either a phonological store or an articulatory rehearsal loop contribute to HB's list recall. The severe impairment in nonword repetition suggests that his phonological storage is so limited that the main burden of his list recall depends on other cognitive resources.

A number of lines of evidence have established that semantic storage plays a role in list recall. Normal subjects show small advantages in short-term memory for lists of high imageability items relative to low imageability words (Bourassa and Besner, forthcoming); the effect in normal subjects, however, is substantially less than is found with HB. Much of the memory burden in immediate serial recall in normal subjects, however, depends on phonological storage. For HB there is no evidence of a phonological contribution in STM tasks; we would therefore expect to find an exaggerated effect of semantic variables on list recall. While there is some experimental evidence of semantic effects in list recall for other short-term memory subjects, in comparison with HB the effects of list imageability are very small.

Normal subjects also show advantages for semantically categorized lists (animals, countries, and so on) relative to mixed lists (Poirier and Saint-Aubin, forthcoming). This effect remains when subjects perform articulatory suppression (Poirier and Saint-Aubin, forthcoming), suggesting that it is independent of phonological storage. Like normal subjects, HB performed better with categorized lists but in his case the effect was only found with fast list presentation. This suggests that semantic organization benefits recall, supporting a role for semantic storage.

HB's high level of confusions between 'zero', 'nought' and 'oh' in auditory digit recall again supports a role for semantic storage. These items are identical in meaning and differ in phonological form.

Campbell and Butterworth (1985) report on a subject, RE, with a developmental disorder of short-term memory, who, like HB, showed absolutely no evidence of phonological storage in STM tasks. Like HB, RE also confused 'nought', 'zero' and 'oh' in auditory repetition. RE's recall of digit lists was better when she closed her eyes than when she had them open. She reported that this was because she used visual storage in the task. HB, in contrast, was quite clear that he did not use any form of visual representation with auditorily presented lists. With visual presentation, on the other hand, there is strong evidence that he did use a limited-capacity visual store. He showed a word-length effect where long words had more letters than short words; this disappeared when the items were matched for letter length. In addition, he was very much better at recalling arabic digits than alphabetic digit names. If he had been using the same limited-capacity visual store in recall of auditorily presented lists by imaging the written form of the words, he should have shown a length effect with the one- and three-syllable words which differed markedly in word length. That there is no suggestion of such an effect provides experimental support for his claim that he did not use visual representations in recall of auditory lists.

Whether similar effects of visual length can be found in STM tasks with normal subjects is currently unclear. Visual word length effects have typically been investigated using stimuli which differ in both phonological length and in the number of letters. That such effects disappear completely under conditions of concurrent articulation has been taken to indicate that these effects are wholly attributable to articulatory rehearsal. If this interpretation is correct, then HB is using a visual store which plays no significant role in visual STM tasks with word lists in normal subjects, and yet which contributes to a high level of performance in his recall of visual lists. Interestingly, HB's recall of visually presented lists of digits and letters is substantially better than with words. This difference is probably due to the much greater visual length of the words.

In summary, HB shows no evidence that phonological storage contributes to his performance in STM tasks. Although the possible existence of a phonological similarity effect was probed in a number of different ways, the results were consistently negative. Likewise, the phonological length of words did not affect his recall. With auditory presentation of lists, HB seems to have relied primarily on semantic storage. With visual lists, semantic information was supplemented by a limited-capacity visual store.

Compared with other patients with acquired STM impairment, HB performs relatively well in list-recall tasks, without apparently any phonological storage. That his semantic representations were largely unimpaired in a range of tasks may have allowed him to rely on semantic storage to a rather greater extent than many of the other patients who have been reported. The puzzle posed by this analysis of HB's STM is why it should be that list recall can be apparently much more severely impaired in other subjects with STM impairments. Two explanations are possible. It may be that many of these subjects show subtle semantic impairments which, although not obvious on clinical testing, are sufficient to limit the role of semantic information in STM. That almost all these subjects are recovered aphasics makes this at least a plausible account. The second possibility is that other subjects may still have a little useful phonological storage which they attempt to use in STM tasks. Only when the phonological impairment is very severe will these patients opt instead to rely entirely on other sources of information. Paradoxically, under this interpretation HB shows relatively good recall because his phonological short-term store is so profoundly impaired.

Acknowledgements

I am grateful to Claire Gatehouse for referring HB and for her help in some of the testing. This research was supported by the Medical Research Council.

Further Reading

Baddeley, A.D. (1986) *Working Memory* (Oxford: Oxford University Press).
Shallice, T. and Vallar, G. (1990) 'The impairment of auditory-verbal short-term storage', in G. Vallar and T. Shallice (eds), *Neuropsychological Impairments of Short-term Memory* (Cambridge: Cambridge University Press).

References

Baddeley, A.D. (1986) *Working Memory* (Oxford: Oxford University Press).
Baddeley, A.D. and Wilson, B. (1988) 'Comprehension and working memory: a single case neuropsychological study', *Journal of Memory and Language*, **27**: 479–98.
Baddeley, A.D., Lewis, V.J. and Vallar, G. (1984) 'Exploring the articulatory loop', *Quarterly Journal of Experimental Psychology*, **36**: 233–52.
Baddeley, A.D., Papagno, C. and Vallar, G. (1988) 'When long-term learning depends on short-term storage', *Journal of Memory and Language*, **27**: 586–95.
Baddeley, A.D., Thomson, N. and Buchanan, M. (1975) 'Word length and the structure of short-term memory', *Journal of Verbal Learning and Verbal Behaviour*, **14**: 575–89.
Besner, D. and Davelaar, E. (1982) 'Basic processes in reading: two phonological codes', *Canadian Journal of Psychology*, **36**: 701–11.
Bourassa, D. and Besner, D. (forthcoming) 'Beyond the articulatory loop: a semantic contribution to serial order recall of subspan lists', *Psychonomic Bulletin and Review*.
Brener, R. (1940) 'An experimented investigation of memory span', *Journal of Experimental Psychology*, **26**: 467–82.
Campbell, R. and Butterworth, B.L. (1985) 'Phonological dyslexia and dysgraphia in a highly literate subject: a developmental case with associated deficits of of phonemic processing and awareness', *Quarterly Journal of Experimental Psychology*, **37A**: 435–75.
Conrad, R. and Hull, A.J. (1964) 'Information, acoustic confusion and memory span', *British Journal of Psychology*, **53**: 429–32.
Howard, D. and Franklin, S. (1990) 'Memory without rehearsal', in G. Vallar and T. Shallice (eds), *Neuropsychological Impairments of Short-term Memory* (Cambridge: Cambridge University Press).
Jones, G.V. (1985) 'Deep dyslexia, imageability and ease-of-predication', *Brain and Language*, **24**: 1–19.
Monsell, S. (1987) 'On the relation between lexical input and output pathways for speech', in D.A. Allport, D. MacKay, W. Prinz and E. Scheerer (eds), *Language Perception and Production: Common Processes in Listening, Speaking, Reading and Writing* (London: Academic Press).
Murray, D.J. (1968) 'Articulation and acoustic confusability in short-term memory', *Journal of Experimental Psychology*, **78**: 679–84.
Paivio, A. (1971) *Imagery and Verbal Processes* (New York: Holt Rinehart & Winston).
Plaut, D.C. and Shallice, T. (1993) 'Deep dyslexia: a case study of connectionist neuropsychology', *Cognitive Neuropsychology*, **10**: 377–504.
Poirier, M. and Saint-Aubin, J. (forthcoming) 'Memory for related and unrelated words: further evidence concerning the influence of semantic factors on immediate serial recall', *Quarterly Journal of Experimental Psychology*.
Saffran, E.M. and Martin, N. (1990) 'Neuropsychological evidence for lexical involvement in short term memory', in G. Vallar and T. Shallice (eds), *Neuropsychological Impairments of Short-term Memory* (Cambridge: Cambridge University Press).

Shallice, T. and Vallar, G. (1990) 'The impairment of auditory-verbal short-term storage', in G. Vallar and T. Shallice (eds), *Neuropsychological Impairments of Short-term Memory* (Cambridge: Cambridge University Press).

Vallar, G. and Baddeley, A.D. (1984) 'Fractionation of working memory: neuropsychological evidence for a phonological short-term store', *Journal of Verbal Learning and Verbal Behaviour*, **23**: 151–62.

Vallar, G. and Shallice, T. (eds) (1990) *Neuropsychological Impairments of Short-term Memory* (Cambridge: Cambridge University Press).

Warrington, E.K. and Shallice, T. (1969) 'The selective impairment of auditory-verbal short-term memory', *Brain*, **92**: 885–96.

21 What the Study of Patients with Speech Disorders and of Normal Speakers Tells Us about the Nature of Rehearsal

Gloria S. Waters and David Caplan

Rehearsal processes are widely thought to play an important role in the performance of auditory-verbal short-term memory tasks, such as span and delayed recall, and in certain metalinguistic tasks involving single words, such as rhyme judgements. The mechanisms underlying rehearsal have been the subject of a number of recent investigations. In this chapter we summarize the results of three experiments we have carried out with patients with speech output problems (Waters et al., 1992; Caplan and Waters, in press), as well as with normal speakers (Caplan and Waters, 1992), which we think shed new light on the issue of the nature of articulatory rehearsal processes.

Baddeley and his colleagues (Baddeley, 1966; Baddeley et al., 1975) have argued that one mechanism underlying rehearsal involves subvocal articulation. Their argument was based upon several findings.

The first of these findings is the effect of word length on performance in span tasks in normal subjects. Baddeley et al. (1975) reported an advantage for monosyllabic words over five-syllable words on number of lists recalled in span tasks. They repeated these experiments with words of different articulatory durations controlled for syllable number and number of phonemes, and reported that the word-length effect continued to be found for these sets of stimuli in auditory span tasks, and in visual span tasks in which the subjects were instructed 'to remember the lists by repeating the words to themselves' (p. 581). Baddeley and co-workers argued that these effects, as well as the finding that memory span is correlated with articulatory rate, showed that 'short-term memory is a time-based system', in which 'a subject can recall as many words as he can read in 1.6 seconds or can articulate in 1.3 seconds' (ibid.). Rehearsal processes are thought to be responsible (at least in part) for this relationship.

Further support for the role of articulatory-based mechanisms in rehearsal comes from the disappearance of both the visual and auditory word-length effects under conditions of articulatory suppression, provided that articulatory suppression takes place both throughout list presentation and recall (Baddeley et al., 1975, 1984). Since articulatory suppression (whether at input only or at both input and recall) does not eliminate the phonological similarity effect (better performance on nonrhyming than rhyming lists) for auditorily presented lists (Baddeley et al., 1984). Baddeley argued that articulatory suppression interfered with an articulatory-based rehearsal mechanism that is responsible for word length effects in both auditory and visual span (Baddeley et al., 1984; Baddeley, 1986). Similar results to those of Baddeley et al. (1984) were reported by Martin (1987) under conditions in which subjects were instructed to rehearse visually presented words.

Rehearsal is also thought be involved in several tasks involving single word processing. Besner et al. (1981) have demonstrated that visual rhyme judgements (e.g. pair/care) are impaired by concurrent articulation in normal subjects, while visual homophone (for example, pair/pear) judgements are far less impaired. They argue that this pattern indicates that an articulatory-based rehearsal process is involved in visual rhyme but not visual homophone judgements.

One model of short-term memory which accounts for the effects of these phonological and articulatory variables on performance is the working memory model of Baddeley and his colleagues (Baddeley and Hitch, 1974; Baddeley, 1976; Baddeley, 1986; Salame and Baddeley, 1982; Vallar and Baddeley, 1984a, 1984b; Vallar and Cappa, 1987). In this model, working memory is comprised of a limited-capacity, supervisory controlling system, the 'central executive', and a number of slave systems. One of the slave systems, the 'articulatory loop', consisting of an articulatory process and a phonological store, is specialized for processing verbal material. Information is stored in terms of a sound-based code in the phonological store and the articulatory processes preserve the order of information through a rehearsal mechanism. Material in the phonological store can be maintained by the process of articulation, as well as, in turn, being used to feed the process of active rehearsal (Baddeley, 1986).

In this model, the word-length effects reflect the use of articulatory control processes and so are abolished by articulatory suppression. The phonological similarity effects reflect the operation of the phonological store, and so should be less affected by articulatory suppression (Baddeley et al., 1984). Though suppression does not abolish the effect of phonological similarity for auditorily presented material (Murray, 1968), it does abolish the effect of phonological similarity on visual span. This is claimed to occur because, while spoken material has direct access to the phonological store, suppression interferes with visual material *entering* the phonological store. Thus, the differential effects of articulatory suppression on the phonological-similarity and word-length effects result because these effects reflect the operation of different components of the working memory system.

Recently, data from patients with acquired brain lesions have reopened discussion of the nature of the mechanisms underlying rehearsal. Investigations of the memory abilities of patients who have lost the ability to articulate overtly, and/or who have significant motor speech impairments, have been carried out in an attempt to provide evidence for the importance of articulatory rehearsal in short-term memory. The rationale for these studies is that if the effects of articulatory suppression and the correlation between speech rate and memory span are correctly attributed to the role of articulatory-based rehearsal in span, then patients with motor speech disorders might be expected to demonstrate specific short-term memory impairments. Moreover, the performance of these patients should be similar to that of normal subjects tested under conditions of articulatory suppression. They should show reduced memory spans and fail to show an effect of phonological similarity with visually presented material, and of word length when material is presented auditorily and visually. These patients might also show reduced effects of phonological similarity on auditory span, given that in Baddeley's model information in the phonological store is refreshed by the process of articulatory rehearsal.

However, the existing neuropsychological data are not consistent with the data from normal subjects in suggesting a role for articulation in short-term memory. Baddeley and Wilson (1985) tested six patients whose motor speech impairments affected motor control of the vocal tract. This leads to difficulties in actual movement of the articulators but not in planning speech. All these patients had normal memory spans. In addition, they showed the normal effects of phonological similarity and word length on span, suggesting unimpaired articulatory rehearsal abilities. Normal short-term memory spans have also been found in four mute patients (Nebes, 1975; Levine et al., 1982; Vallar and Cappa, 1987). Although two of these patients did not show all the normal effects of phonological similarity and word length on span, their pattern of performance on these tasks was not consistent with an impairment in articulatory rehearsal. One patient showed a pattern which suggested an impairment in the process by which information is entered into the phonological store, and the other showed a pattern which was unexpected in the context of the current working memory model and so was attributed to a 'strategy choice'. On the basis of these results both Baddeley and Wilson (1985) and Vallar and Cappa (1987) concluded that peripheral articulatory activity, as is impaired in dysarthria, does not influence phonological coding and subvocal rehearsal.

Data reported by Bishop and Robson (1989) present a similar pattern. They investigated the memory abilities of cerebral-palsied children who were congenitally dysarthric (unable to perform speech movements normally). They tested these children on a memory-span task and on tasks assessing the effects of phonological similarity and word length on span. They also tested the children's ability to perform rhyme judgements. These children showed normal performance on the span and rhyme judgement tasks and the normal effects of phonological similarity and word length on span.

Baddeley and Wilson (1985) speculated that these negative findings could be reconciled with the data from normal subjects that suggest that there is a role for articulatory rehearsal in short-term memory tasks, if the more central processes controlling articulation, such as the ability to generate motor programmes for speech output, were involved in phonological coding and subvocal rehearsal. According to this hypothesis, patients with disturbances of speech planning might have performances on span tasks that are similar to those found in normals under conditions of articulatory suppression. Thus, the short-term memory abilities of dysarthric and apraxic patients might differ, since these two disorders differ with respect to the level of their speech output impairments. Dysarthria refers to a group of disorders marked by a disturbance of muscular control. It can affect any or all of the basic motor processes of speech, including articulation, respiration, phonation, resonance and prosody (Wertz, 1985). It might consist, for example, of breathy voice, hypernasality, slurred consonants, short phrases and monoloudness. In general, it is not significantly influenced by the type of linguistic material that the speaker produces or by the speech task (naming, repetition, reading) (Darley, 1983). It results from lesions of bulbar motor neurons, the basal ganglia, the cerebellum, deep white-matter tracts or, rarely, small cortical lesions (Darley et al., 1975). Apraxia of speech has been described as a disruption in programming the positioning of speech muscles to produce phonemes (Wertz et al., 1984). Unlike dysarthria 'there is no signifi-cant weakness, slowness, or incoordination of these muscles in reflexive or automatic acts' (Wertz, 1985: 59). Current psycholinguistic approaches would view apraxia as compatible with an impairment in the phonological component of the linguistic gram-mar, where the deficit is one of articulatory implementation and/or phonological plan-ning (Blumstein, 1990). Apraxic patients may show difficulty in initiating speech, poorer articulation with increasing word length, simplification of consonant clusters, phoneme substitutions, and better articulation for automatized speech (for example, counting) than volitional speech (Johns and Darley, 1970; Bowman et al., 1980; Wertz, 1985). Unlike dysarthria, articulatory accuracy varies according to the task (Johns and Darley, 1970). Apraxia of speech is usually associated with anterior cortico-subcortical lesions (Darley et al., 1975).

In the first study we examined the performance of six patients with apraxia of speech on a battery of memory tasks. Since these patients all have high-level speech planning disturbances, examination of their performance on memory-span tasks will provide a test of the hypothesis that the ability to generate motor programmes for speech output plays an important role in the ability to use articulatory rehearsal in short-term memory tasks. If apraxic patients have impairments in articulatory rehearsal they should show reduced or absent effects of word length on both auditory and visual span and of phonological similarity on visual span. They may also show reduced effects of phonological similarity on auditory span, to the extent that their rehearsal impairments interfere with phonologi-cal storage or that they have independent impairments in this aspect of working memory. Individual differences in terms of the severity of the articulatory rehearsal impairments seen in these patients might be expected, however, since severity of apraxia varies between patients.

1 Short-term Memory in Patients with Speech-planning Disorder Apraxia of Speech

Subjects

Three males and three females, ranging in age from 55 to 70 years old, were chosen from a pool of potential patients referred by speech-language pathologists for participation in the study. In order to be included in the study patients were required to have at least a moderate apraxia of speech, not to be primarily dysarthric, to have adequate single word comprehension to perform the experimental tasks, and to have a profile on the Boston Diagnostic Aphasia Examination (BDAE) (Goodglass and Kaplan, 1983) compatible with apraxia of speech. All patients were right-handed and had suffered a left-hemisphere cerebral vascular accident. Ten control subjects (nine female and one male) who ranged in age from 59 to 74 were also tested on the experimental measures. Table 21.1 provides details regarding the apraxic patients' and control subjects' characteristics.

Table 21.1   Subject characteristics

Subject group	Age	Oral Peabody Picture Vocab. Revised[a]	Oral Peabody Picture Vocab.[b]	Print Peabody Picture Vocab. Revised[a]	Print Peabody Picture Vocab.[b]	Time post-stroke	Apraxia severity
Patients (N = 6)							
TR	70	146	137	152	137	3 yrs	Mild/moderate
AK	55	136	79	139	82	6 mo.	Moderate/severe
WK	63	163	140	165	141	1 yr	Mild/moderate
BO	68	167	139	172	125	7 yrs	Moderate/severe
HZ	61	172	140	161	135	5 yrs	Moderate/severe
GB	58	141	112	149	98	6 yrs	Severe/profound
χ	62.5	154.2	124.5	156.3	119.7		
SD	5.7	15.0	24.7	11.9	24.1		
Range	55–70	136–172	79–140	139–172	82–141		
Controls (N = 10)							
χ	64.1	166.9	143.4	170.1	141.8		
SD	4.8	3.8	4.34	4.9	4.3		
Range	59–74	160–173	133–148	162–175	132–147		
		$t = 2.6$	$t = 2.4$	$t = 3.3$	$t = 2.9$		
		$df = 14$	$df = 14$	$df = 14$	$df = 14$		
		$p < 0.05$	$p < 0.05$	$p < 0.01$	$p < 0.01$		

Notes:
[a]   The maximum score on the revised version of the test is 175.
[b]   The maximum score on the unrevised version of the test is 150.

Extensive testing of the patients' speech and language abilities was carried out by a speech–language pathologist and two graduate students in speech–language pathology in order to characterize the nature of any language impairment and to ensure that they were primarily apraxic and not dysarthric. This testing included the Peabody Picture Vocabulary Test (PPVT) (Dunn and Dunn, 1981; Dunn, 1965), the Boston Diagnostic Aphasia Examination (BDAE) (Goodglass and Kaplan, 1983), the Frenchay Dysarthria Assessment test (Enderby, 1983), and the Apraxia Battery for Adults (Dabul, 1979). Though a distinction is drawn between dysarthria and apraxia, the two disorders often co-occur and it was expected that patients might demonstrate some dysarthria. In keeping with the usual diagnoses accompanying apraxia of speech (Wertz et al., 1984), five of these patients (TR, WK, AK, HZ and GB) were classified as Broca's aphasics. One patient's pattern (BO) was not easily classified among the BDAE syndromes. Her major areas of impairment were word-finding and articulatory agility, a pattern that is also compatible with apraxia of speech (Wertz et al., 1984). All patients exhibited some dysarthric symptoms; however, given the overall low level of other dysarthric symptoms exhibited by these patients, their low intelligibility scores were judged to reflect the contribution of mainly apraxic symptoms. On the basis of the Apraxia Battery, one patient (GB) was rated as severe to profound, three patients (HZ, BO, and AK) as moderate to severe, and two patients (TR and WK) as mild to moderate.

The patients' speech was also studied extensively in order to ensure that they demonstrated characteristics of apraxia in their spontaneous speech. All the patients exhibited many apraxic characteristics including some, such as more errors on longer sequences, that are not seen in dysarthria. The patients who were rated as most severe on the apraxia battery did not necessarily demonstrate a larger number of these characteristics, because their limited output resulted in less opportunity for them to occur. In addition, the patients' speech was analysed using two tests typically used to assess articulation disorders in children: the Screening Deep Test of Articulation (McDonald, 1976), and the Assessment of Phonological Processes – Revised (Hodson, 1986). Patients' errors on the Deep Test were consistent with what would be expected in apraxic speech (Wertz, 1985; Johns and Darley, 1970). Four patients (AK, TR, WK, and BO) were rated as having moderate articulatory impairments, and two patients (HZ and GB) were rated as severely impaired on the Assessment of Phonological Processes.

Thus, all the patients in this study were classified as apraxic. However, the data from the speech and language evaluation suggest that they are not homogeneous in terms of severity. GB is the most severely impaired in general. His pattern on the BDAE suggests a more severe Broca's aphasia than does that of the other patients. He received a rating of 'severe' on the apraxia battery, he had extremely limited output, and he received a rating of 'severe' on the Assessment of Phonological Processes. HZ also appears quite impaired, given his limited output, his rating of 'moderate to severe' on the Apraxia Battery, and his rating of 'severe' on the Assessment of Phonological Processes. BO and AK also received a 'moderate to severe' rating on the Apraxia Battery, but they had much less limited output than HZ and GB and they were rated as less severe than these patients on the Assessment of Phonological Processes. The other two patients, TR and WK, are also clearly less affected than HZ and GB.

Assessment of memory span

In order to assess whether patients' memory spans were abnormally reduced as compared to control subjects a digit-span and two word-span tasks (oral and print presentation) were administered. The stimuli for the digit-span task consisted of the digits 1–9, and for the word-span tasks of monosyllabic words. Since verbal output for all subjects was extremely limited, after presentation of the items to be remembered subjects were shown a response sheet which contained the digits from 1 to 9 for the digit-span task, or line drawings of of the items just presented, as well as one additional item, arranged in random order for the word-span tasks. Subjects were required to point to the items in the order in which they had been presented. Digit and word spans were calculated from the largest span size at which subjects were correct on 6/10 trials.

Assessment of articulatory rehearsal and phonological storage

Subjects were tested for the effects of phonological similarity and word length on both auditory and visual span. In order to avoid floor and ceiling effects, subjects were tested for these effects at the span size at which they had correctly reported 60 per cent of the items in the correct serial position in the corresponding mode on the word-span task outlined above. Thus, although subjects were tested at different span sizes, the tasks were presumably at a comparable level of difficulty across subjects. The phonologically similar sequences were chosen from the set *mat, fat, pat, cat, can, pan, man, fan*, and the dissimilar sequences from the set *net, two, egg, fox, pen, bed, hat, jug*. After presentation of the last item in a given trial, subjects were shown one of two sheets, each of which had pictures of the set of eight items in a different random order and they were asked to point to the pictures in the order in which the items had been presented. Subjects were tested in the oral and print conditions in separate sessions. For each subject, the percentage of items which were recalled in the correct serial order was calculated for each list. The procedure for the word-length task was identical to that for the phonological-similarity effect with the exception that the stimuli consisted of short (one-syllable) and long (three-syllable) words. The short words were taken from the set *tray, van, jug, paw, tub, skirt, frog, pig*, and the long words from the set *computer, submarine, magazine, skeleton, musician, potatoes, kangaroo, telescope*.

Rhyme and homophony judgements

Subjects' abilities to perform rhyme and homophony judgements for both auditorily and visually presented word pairs were also investigated. The finding that articulatory suppression interferes with visual rhyme but not homophony judgements has resulted in the hypothesis that articulatory rehearsal processes are involved in the former but not the latter type of judgement (Besner et al., 1981). Thus, it was expected that apraxic patients would have more difficulty with visual rhyme than with homophony judgements. The stimuli for the rhyme-judgement task consisted of four types of word pairs – orthographically similar rhymes (such as best/west), orthographically dissimilar rhymes (such as door/war), orthographically similar nonrhymes (such as farm/warm), and orthographically dissimilar nonrhymes (such as farm/war). On each trial subjects were presented with a pair of words either orally or in print and were required to indicate by pointing to one of two response cards whether the words rhymed. For the homophone judgement task subjects were presented with pairs of words and were required to indicate on each trial whether the two words sounded the same or different. On half of the trials the words were the same and on half they were minimally phonologically different and were nonhomophones.

Articulation rate

We also assessed subjects' articulation rates since, according to Baddeley's model (1976, 1986), this factor should be related to individual differences in the use of articulatory rehearsal in short-term memory tasks. Although previous research has demonstrated a correlation between articulation rate and memory span, there is no data on the correlation between articulation rate and the magnitude of the phonological similarity and word-length effects seen in normals. According to Baddeley's model, the correlation

Table 21.2   Memory span data

Subject group	Auditory digits	Auditory words	Visual words
Patients			
TR	4	3	3
AK	5	3	3
WK	5	4	4
BO	3	3	3
HZ	2	2	2
GB	2	2	2
χ	3.5	2.7	2.8
SD	1.4	0.82	0.75
Range	2–5	2–4	2–4
Controls			
χ	7.1	5.1	4.7
SD	0.99	0.73	0.67
Range	6–9	4–6	4–6

between articulation rate and the magnitude of the auditory phonological similarity effect should be smaller than for the other effects, since in this model it is claimed to be a function of the phonological store. In addition, articulation rate should be related to individual differences in these effects in the patients. Articulation rate was measured for a subset of the short and long words used in the word-length task. Subjects were presented with a pair of items and were instructed to repeat the items continuously as fast as possible, until asked to stop. Time taken for ten repetitions of the pair was recorded.

Results

Memory span   Table 21.2 shows the memory span data for the individual patients and the control group. While there was no overlap between the patients and controls on the digit-span task, on the word-span task one patient (WK) had a span which was comparable to that of the controls. Statistical comparison of the group means for each task showed that the apraxic patients differed from the control subjects on all three span tasks. Thus, as predicted, patients with high-level speech planning impairments have reduced memory spans.

Phonological similarity and word-length effects   The percentage of items reported in the correct serial position was calculated for the two types of stimulus materials for each task, in each of the two modes of presentation. Figure 21.1 shows the data for the four tasks. Statistical analysis of these data showed that both patients and controls showed an auditory phonological-similarity effect, with the effect being larger in the case of the

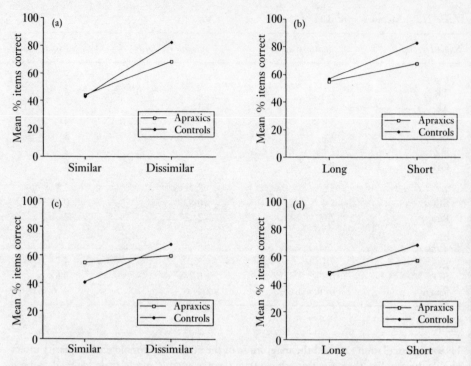

Figure 21.1   Performance of the group of apraxic patients and control subjects on phonological-similarity and word-length tasks: (a) word span: auditory (phonological similarity); (b) word span: auditory (word length); (c) word span: visual (phonological similarity); (d) word span: visual (word length)

controls. However, on each of the other tasks (auditory word length, visual word length, visual phonological-similarity effect) the controls showed a significant effect of type of stimulus material, while the patients did not. Thus, as a group, the patients in this study perform in a similar manner to normal subjects in other studies who have been tested under conditions of articulatory suppression.

The performance of each individual subject on the phonological-similarity and word-length tasks was also analysed in order to determine whether they showed a statistically reliable effect on each of the four tasks. Figure 21.2 shows the data for the individual subjects. The results of the analyses showed that all the control subjects showed statistically reliable effects on all the tasks. However, a variety of patterns across the four tasks were seen for the patients. One patient, TR, showed all of the normal effects. One patient, AK, showed all but the visual word-length effect. One patient, WK, showed the auditory but not the visual effects. Finally, three patients, BO, GB and HZ failed to show any of the normal effects. Thus, although the group data suggest that apraxic patients have articulatory rehearsal impairments, data from the individual patients suggests that not all patients demonstrate such an impairment. We address the question of whether the individual differences seen in the patients is related to the severity of their apraxia and their articulation rates below.

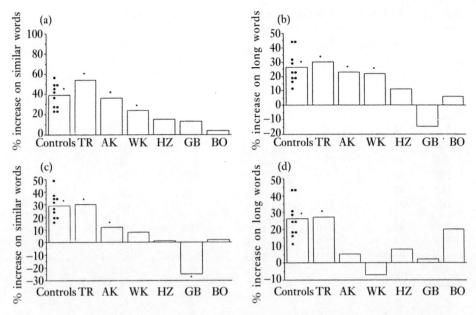

Figure 21.2   Data for individual patients and control subjects on the phonological-similarity and word-length tasks
Notes
• indicates significant effect with χ^2
• data for individual control subjects

Rhyme and homophone judgement tasks   Table 21.3 shows the data for the rhyme and homophone judgement tasks. The patients performed quite well on these tasks when the materials were presented auditorily, showing that they understand the concepts of rhyme and homophony, and can make judgements about them. However, they did differ statistically from the controls even in this modality. For this reason, we used performance in the auditory modality as a baseline against which to look for any decrement in performance in the visual modality in each subject group for each task. Comparison of the group means showed that there was a significant difference between performance in the auditory and visual modalities for the patients on the rhyme judgement task, but that the difference was not significant on the homophone judgement task. Performance of the control subjects did not differ in the two modalities for either task. These data are consistent with the hypothesis that articulatory rehearsal plays a role in visual rhyme but not visual homophony judgements, as suggested by Besner (1987).

Articulation rate   Articulation rates for the patients and controls are shown in table 21.4. The articulation rates seen in the patients are more than twice as slow as those seen in the controls, with the largest discrepancy between patients and controls being on the long words. Correlations between articulation rate and the magnitude of the effects of phonological similarity and word length on span were not calculated for the patients, given that only four subjects could perform the articulation rate task. However, as can be

312   G.S. Waters and D. Caplan

Table 21.3   Performance on the rhyme and homophone judgement tasks

Subject group	Auditory rhyme judgement (%)	Visual rhyme judgement (%)	Difference (%)	Auditory homophone judgement (%)	Visual homophone judgement (%)	Difference (%)
Patients
TR	96	79	17	95	85	10
AK	99	96	3	98	93	5
WK	91	85	6	95	92	3
BO	96	81	15	95	95	0
HZ	90	57	33	78	82	−4
GB	84	52	32	90	67	23
χ	92.7	75.0	17.66	91.8	85.7	6.16
SD	5.4	17.0	12.64	7.2	10.4	9.49
Range	84–99	52–96	3–33	78–98	67–95	−4–23
Controls
χ	96.2	92.2	4	97.9	97.5	0.4
Sd	3.0	7.9		2.6	2.1	
Range	90–100	72–99		92–100	93–100	

Table 21.4   Articulation rate: time for 10 repetitions of short and long word pairs (secs)

Subject	Short words	Long words
Patients
TR	15.6	29.7
AK	20.5	32.7
WK	17.8	41.7
BO	29.4	54.9
HZ	*	*
GB	*	*
χ	20.8	39.8
SD	6.1	11.3
Range	15.6–29.4	29.7–54.9
Controls
χ	6.1	8.58
SD	1.0	1.3
Range	4.9–8.4	7.2–11.6

Note:
*   Unable to perform the task.

seen in table 21.4, the patients who have the fastest articulation rates are those who show the greatest number of significant effects on the tests of phonological similarity and word length. The two patients who were unable to perform the articulation rate task failed to show any significant effects on the tests of phonological similarity and word length.

Pearson Product–Moment correlation coefficients between articulation rate for short and long words and the magnitude of the effects of phonological similarity and word length on span were calculated for the control subjects. The correlations between these effects and articulation rates for long words were larger than those found with short words. As would be expected according to the working memory model, the correlation between the auditory phonological similarity effect and articulation rate was minimal and nonsignificant, while the correlations between articulation rate for longer words and the other effects were much larger and in two of three cases statistically significant.

Discussion

The results of our first study clearly demonstrate that memory span is reduced in patients with apraxia of speech. These data are consistent with the notion that reduced short-term memory capacity is seen in this patient population. These data are in contrast to Baddeley and Wilson's (1985) data with dysarthric subjects, and confirm their hypothesis that rehearsal processes in short-term memory tasks are probably linked to the central programming mechanisms that control articulation, rather than to more peripheral mechanisms that produce speech.

The data indicate that, as a group, patients with apraxia of speech perform differently from controls on tests of the effects of phonological similarity and word length on span. The pattern found for the patient group is the same pattern as is found for normal subjects under conditions of articulatory suppression. This suggests an impairment in articulatory rehearsal processes in this population. The magnitude of the auditory phonological similarity effect seen in patients was also smaller than that seen in controls. However, this effect was present in the patient group, and its reduced magnitude could simply reflect the patients' articulatory rehearsal impairments, given that information in the phonological store is refreshed by the process of articulatory rehearsal.

While the data presented above suggest that, as a group, apraxic patients differ from controls in the functioning of the articulatory rehearsal component of short-term memory, inspection of the data of the individual patients presents a somewhat different picture. None of the individual patients showed the pattern of performance found in the group as a whole. The data from TR and AK show both phonological-similarity and word-length effects in span. Except for the visual word length effect in AK these effects are present in both modalities. These results are consistent with the notion that these two patients do use articulatory rehearsal when performing span tasks (although it is not entirely clear how to account for the lack of a visual word-length effect for AK). In contrast, patients BO, GB, and HZ show none of these effects. The absence of word length and visual phonological similarity effects provides evidence for articulatory rehearsal impairments in these patients. The lack of an auditory phonological similarity effect in these patients could result from an additional impairment in phonological storage, or could simply result from their articulatory rehearsal impairments, as discussed above. The pattern of significant effects in the auditory but not the visual modality, found for patient WK, is the same as that reported by Vallar and Cappa (1987) for a mute patient, and by Rochon et al. (1991) for an apraxic patient. Vallar and Cappa argue that this pattern provides evidence for intact rehearsal but impaired access to this rehearsal process in the visual modality because of an impairment in converting printed words to sound (that is, phonological recoding).

Data concerning the severity of these patients' motor speech disturbances, as well as from the articulation rate and rhyme judgement tasks (see below), support the view that the individual differences seen among the patients reflect the severity of the impairment of rehearsal functions in short-term memory. According to Baddeley's model, patients who show phonological-similarity and word-length effects have minimal impairments in rehearsal functions. These patients show the fastest articulation rates (TR and AK). Patients who do not show auditory phonological-similarity effects may have such severe impairments of rehearsal as to reduce the functioning of the phonological store. On this view, the three patients who show neither phonological-similarity nor word-length effects (BO, HZ, GB) have a more severe disturbance of rehearsal than the other three cases.

As a group, the patients' performance did not differ in the auditory and visual modalities on the homophone task, but did differ across the two modalities on the rhyme task, suggesting that patients with apraxia of speech have an impairment in visual rhyme judgement. This pattern is consistent with the finding that normal subjects show impaired performance on written rhyme but not homophone judgement tasks when tested under conditions of articulatory suppression (Besner et al., 1981). Inspection of the data on the individual patients shows individual variability in the patterns of auditory and written rhyme and homophone judgement. We have argued above that three patients have performances on span tasks that are consistent with a more severe disturbance of rehearsal (BO, HZ, GB). These three patients show a greater difference in performance across the two modalities for the rhyme than for the homophone judgement task. Patients AK and TR, who are claimed to have more intact rehearsal processes, do not show a discrepancy in their performance across the two modalities. Thus, the data from this task are broadly consistent with the data from the phonological-similarity and word-length tasks, in that the three patients whose span performances are consistent with more severe rehearsal impairments show effects in written rhyme and homophone judgements that are also seen in normals under articulatory suppression.

The data from the speech and language evaluations presented in the results section suggested that the six patients in this study were not homogeneous in terms of the severity of their motor speech impairments. On the basis of the speech and language data, it appears that GB and HZ have the most impaired rehearsal functions. It is difficult to rank the other four patients in terms of severity on clinical grounds alone.

Given the relationship between articulation rate and memory span which has been found in normal subjects, as well as the claim that articulation rate is related to the word-length effect, it would be predicted that the patients in this study who are claimed to have more severe rehearsal impairments would also have the slowest articulation rates. Of particular interest is the finding that the rank ordering of the patients in terms of articulation rate corresponds very closely to both their memory spans (lower articulation rates are associated with lower spans) and to the magnitude of the phonological-similarity and word–length effects (lower articulation rates are associated with smaller effects). GB and HZ, both of whom have spans of only two items and who are claimed to have severe rehearsal impairments, could not even perform the articulation rate task. The articulation rate of the other patient, BO, who is claimed to have a severe rehearsal impairment, is the slowest of the four remaining patients. Moreover, of the patients who are claimed to have less-severe rehearsal impairments, there is a direct correspondence between articulation rate and the number of significant effects on the tests of the effects of phonological similarity and word length on span. That is, TR, the patient with the fastest articulation rate, showed all of the normal effects; AK the patient with the next fastest rate showed all but the visual word length effect; and WK showed the effects in the auditory but not visual modalities. This overall relationship of articulatory rate to span and to the word-length and phonological-similarity effects in patients with apraxia of speech is consistent with the claim that these effects partially reflect the operation of high-level speech-planning processes in these tasks.

The data from normal subjects is entirely consistent with these findings in the patients. The correlations between the effects and articulation rates for long words are larger than those found with short words. The correlation between the auditory phonological similarity effect and articulation rate was minimal and nonsignificant, while the correlations between articulation rate and the other effects were much larger and significant. Both these results would be expected according to the working memory model, and both are consistent with the patients' performances.

These results contrast sharply with findings from other studies with dysarthric patients, who, with a few exceptions, have generally shown no disturbances in either span or visual rhyme judgement tasks. Dysarthric and apraxic patients differ with respect to the level of their speech output impairments: dysarthria is a set of disorders affecting motor control of the vocal tract that leads to interference with the movement of the articulators but not with speech planning; apraxia of speech is a set of disorders affecting the planning of speech production. The pattern of results in patients with these two different disorders of speech output suggests that rehearsal processes involve speech planning, not speech production. More specifically, the presence of rehearsal impairments in apraxic patients suggests that rehearsal involves the stage of speech production that plans articulatory gestures associated with the phonemic and syllabic structures of words. A natural next question is: how abstract is the planning process that is involved in rehearsal functions? The second experiment attempted to address this issue.

2 Failure in Verbal Rehearsal: a Case Study

To explore further the question of the speech processes that are involved in rehearsal, we must refer to a model of the stages of the word sound production process. We can then attempt to identify which processes that are specified in this model are involved in rehearsal.

Most models of speech production postulate that the sound of a word is produced in several steps (see Levelt, 1989, ch. 9, for discussion). Though details vary, these models tend to share the assumption that speakers first access a partial phonological representation of a word from a concept, and then perform a number of operations on that representation to render it into a form that is suitable for programming the articulators. We shall briefly review the arguments that support this set of models and that provide data on which to base accounts of what might be represented at the various stages of speech output planning.

First, several everyday observations and considerations suggest that the phonological form of a word that is accessed from semantics does not constitute a complete specification of the articulatory values that are produced when the word is actually uttered. Words can be uttered with various intonation contours, at different loudness levels, in whispered form (that is, without any voicing), and in many other ways that lead to very different articulatory gestures being associated with their constituent sounds. Though we do not know the storage capacity of the human brain, it is unlikely that all these articulatory forms are permanently stored for each word in a speaker's vocabulary. What is much more likely is that a speaker accesses a standard (or 'canonical' or 'citation') form of a word, which is then modified as a function of speech loudness, speed, and so on. Co-articulation phenomena (the effect of phonological context on the articulatory features of a phonemic segment: for example, the rounding of /p/ in *pool* but not in *pit*) also suggest that accessed phonological representations are underspecified for articulatory details.

The above considerations provide intuitive support for a distinction between the phonological representations that are accessed when a word is spoken and the specification of articulatory values associated with those representations. In addition to realizing phonological representations in a variety of articulatory ways, speakers also systematically change phonological features of the sounds of words as a function of their phonological environment when they produce the sounds of words. For instance, in English, all unstressed vowels are reduced to a common short vowel, schwa (/'/). Thus, despite the differences in their orthographic realizations, the vowels in the second syllables of *matador*, and *Canada*, sound almost the same and all are transcribed phonologically as /'/. However, the spelling of these words is actually a guide to true differences among these vowels, which can be seen in several phenomena related to word formation (for example, the second vowel in the word *Canada* is related to the second vowel in the word *Canadian*). Other instances of changes in underlying phonological features include the diphthongization of tense vowels in English (that is, tense vowels are followed by glides: *cry, bay, bow, blue*), and a process known as 'vowel shift' that affects the features [high] and [low] in tense diphthongized vowels (Chomsky and Halle, 1968). Phonologists have argued that these phenomena can be described by postulating lexical phonological segmental representations that are underspecified in certain respects, and whose final phonological values are affected by syllabification, stress assignment and certain morphological processes (for discussion, see Pesetsky, 1979; Mohanan, 1982; Grignon, 1984; and Halle and Mohanan, 1985). Beland et al. (1990) have argued that the phonological representations that are accessed in the mental dictionary for oral production (the so-called 'phonological output lexicon') contain such underspecified phonological information.

The notion that speakers access a phonological representation that is transformed during the process of planning the articulatory gestures associated with a word also receives support from experimental and behavioural observations. The 'tip-of-the-tongue' phenomenon (Brown and McNeill, 1966) and features of malapropisms (Fay and Cutler, 1977) indicate that a word's onset, the number of syllables in the word, which syllable is stressed, and sometimes the final segment of the word, can be accessed separately from other phonological features.

These data encourage us to conceive of lexical phonological activation as consisting of two cognitively separate processes. The first process – which we shall call 'lexical phonological access' – links the semantic and syntactic representation of a word to its underlying phonological representation. Lexical phonological access must make use of an associative mechanism, since word forms are not accessible from word meanings on a content-addressable basis. The second process – which we shall call 'lexical phonological planning' – adds and changes phonological features in this representation. The process of lexical phonological planning can be implemented as a production system.

This division of lexical phonological activation into two stages bears some resemblance to models developed in other branches of cognitive psychology, especially cognitive neuropsychology, that distinguish between a phonological output lexicon and a 'response buffer', whose role is to maintain sequences of phonemes in memory while articulation is being planned (Caramazza et al., 1986). Models that contain the two stages described above do not necessarily specify entities that map in a one-to-one fashion onto the components specified in models containing a phonological output lexicon and a response buffer, however, since the representations and operations specified in different models differ. But in broad terms one can conceive of the lexical phonological access and planning stages in models of the sort we have been discussing as corresponding to the activation of items in the phonological output lexicon and the response buffer in models that specify these two functional components.

One question that can be asked about rehearsal is whether accessing a lexical phonological representation is sufficient for rehearsal to occur, or whether the entire set of processes involved in specifying the phonological content of a word is required for rehearsal to proceed. This question can be rephrased in the terminology used in some neuropsychological models as the question of whether accessing a phonological representation in the phonological output lexicon is sufficient for rehearsal to occur.

The second study investigated the question of what aspects of phonological output processing are needed for rehearsal to proceed by examining the rehearsal abilities of a patient with a speech production impairment called 'conduction aphasia' or, more recently, 'reproduction conduction aphasia' (Shallice and Warrington, 1977). Patients with reproduction conduction aphasia have a disturbance in speech production that affects the production of single spoken words. Their speech is characterized by numerous phonemic paraphasias (omissions, substitutions and misorderings of the phonemes of a word), but they give no signs of misarticulation of either the more peripheral or more central sorts that are associated with dysarthria or apraxia of speech. The functional locus of the speech production deficit in patients with reproduction conduction aphasia is thought to be somewhere between the activation of word forms in a phonological output lexicon and the execution of articulatory gestures. The deficit probably varies from patient to patient, since there are individual differences among patients with respect to the exact frequency of the different types of phonemic errors they make, the relative rate of error production in picture naming, repetition and oral reading tasks, the relative rate of error production for words and nonwords, and the ability of patients to indicate that they are aware of aspects of the phonological forms of words that they cannot produce in picture naming tasks (the presence of the tip-of-the-tongue state). Some of these patients appear to access lexical phonological representations in the phonological output lexicon, while others appear not to do so (see, for discussion, Caplan and Waters, 1992; and Caplan, 1992).

The data presented at the outset of this chapter indicate that rehearsal involves speech planning processes that specify the articulatory gestures associated with phonological segments, but does not require articulatory gestures to take place normally. The study of patients with reproduction conduction aphasia allows us to further characterize the speech-planning processes that are required for rehearsal. One possibility is that the ability to access a phonological representation is sufficient for rehearsal to proceed. If so, those patients with reproduction conduction aphasia who show retained ability to access lexical phonological forms should retain the ability to rehearse. Alternatively, the ability to access a phonological representation may not be sufficient for rehearsal to proceed; successful planning of the phonological form of a word may be needed for rehearsal to proceed. If this is the case, patients with reproduction conduction aphasia who show retained ability to access lexical phonological forms but impaired phonological planning should not rehearse normally.

In this experiment, a patient is presented whose output disturbance appears to affect phonological planning processes that arise after at least many aspects of word form have been activated in the phonological output lexicon. The patient fails to show normal performance on tasks that are thought to require rehearsal. The conclusion that is drawn is that rehearsal requires some aspect of output phonological planning.

Case presentation

RW was a 62-year-old right-handed male who had a small stroke in May 1991. He was admitted to a rehabilitation hospital on 6 June 1991. Magnetic resonance imaging revealed a small left temporo-parietal infarction. RW was a college graduate and had previously worked as an executive for a research corporation.

RW was tested on parts of the Boston Diagnostic Aphasia Examination in June 1991 upon admission to the rehabilitation hospital and again upon discharge in August 1991. His output was described as fluent. He was considered to have mild-to-moderate impairments in auditory comprehension, which improved somewhat over that period of time. Written sentence comprehension was considered to be better than auditory sentence comprehension. Repetition was severely impaired at the word and sentence levels.

RW was tested on the Boston Naming Test (BNT) on several occasions. Responses were tape-recorded and transcribed in the international phonetic alphabet (IPA) by a trained speech-language pathologist. On 24 June 1991 he scored only 22/60; his errors consisted of phonemic errors, false starts and occasional omissions. The BNT was repeated on 25 July 1991 and 8 August 1991; RW scored 47/60 and 46/60 on those two occasions. The types of errors he made were identical to those made when he was tested in June. These errors retain many phonological features of the target. The relationship of these errors to the targets provides evidence that RW accessed a considerable amount of information about the phonological forms of words that he did not produce correctly.

RW was also tested on a psycholinguistically orientated aphasia battery, the Psycholinguistic Assessment of Language: PAL (Caplan and Bub, 1990) in August 1991. The

PAL is designed to assess single word recognition, comprehension, word production from semantics, in the auditory-oral and written modalities, and repetition, oral reading and writing to dictation. RW showed somewhat impaired performance on the test of phoneme discrimination (19/20 correct 'same' and 14/20 correct 'different' judgements). However, his performances on auditory lexical decision (39/40 'yes' and 34/40 'no' responses correct) and auditory word-picture matching (29/32 correct selections) indicated that he none the less recognized and comprehended auditorily presented words well.

RW was perfect at written lexical decision (40/40 items) and written word–picture matching (32/32 items), and answered 44/48 forced-choice questions about written words on the PAL. This indicates that he recognized and comprehended written words well.

RW's output-side processing at the single word level was abnormal. He made many errors on the repetition, oral reading and picture-naming subtests of the PAL. He repeated only 2/20 words and 0/20 nonwords correctly. His errors were all phonological in nature, consisting of omissions, substitutions and rare additions of phonemes and syllables. A few of these errors were phonologically related lexical items; some were quite distantly related to the target (for example, 'friend' → 'spret'). He read 21/32 words and 16/25 nonwords aloud correctly, and there were no effects of frequency, length or imageability and only a mild effect of regularity (13/16 regular words compared with 8/16 irregular words) upon his reading aloud performance. Again, errors were phonological in nature, consisting mainly of substitutions of consonants. There were no regularization or lexicalization errors. RW named 14/32 pictures correctly, with no discrepancy in performance as a function of semantic class, word frequency or length. His errors were exclusively phonological, and consisted of substitutions, omissions and additions of phonemes and, rarely, syllable deletions and additions. There was no evidence of any misarticulation in RW's speech in any of these tasks or in his spontaneous speech.

The final test from the PAL that is relevant to RW's single word processing is the picture homophone matching task. Picture pairs were presented; half were homophones ('bat' (baseball bat)/'bat' (winged mammal)) and half differed by a single distinctive feature ('cat'/'can'). RW was required to indicate whether the names of the pictures were homophones. He performed perfectly and answered immediately. Normal controls (N = 57) performed slightly worse than RW on this task (75 per cent mean correct). This performance indicates that RW retained considerable information about the sounds of words that he could not produce normally, and that he was able to access that information from a semantic representation.

Further investigation of RW's ability to access lexical phonological information from a semantic representation was undertaken by asking him to indicate his awareness of phonological features of words that he could not produce correctly. First, we attempted to establish whether he knew the number of syllables in words that he did not name properly. He was asked to report the number of syllables in each word on the picture naming test of the PAL, administered on 1 July 1991, and he correctly reported the number of syllables in 17/18 items that he had produced erroneously. On the third occasion on which he was given the Boston Naming Test (8 August 1991), RW was consistently able to report correct values of phonological features that he misproduced. These features extend to those not usually available in the tip-of-the-tongue state, such as the nature of phonemes in unstressed second and third syllables of words with three or more syllables. The availability of this information strongly supports the view that RW's disturbance in speech production arises after many aspects of word-form have been accessed.

Overall, RW largely retained his abilities to recognize and comprehend spoken words, and was excellent in recognition and comprehension of written words. He had a major disturbance of single word production. Six features of these data on word production allow us to to characterize the locus of the functional disturbance in RW with reference to the models of speech production described in the introduction to this paper. First, RW made many phonological errors that involve the selection and ordering of the phonemes in the words he produced. This establishes his impairment as one affecting phonological, not semantic, processing. Secondly, he could accomplish picture homophone judgement extremely well; thirdly, his errors in picture naming retained many phonological aspects of the target; fourthly, he could provide information about phonological features of targets that he misproduced; and, fifthly, his errors occurred and had the same quality in all tasks requiring spoken output. These five features indicate that he accessed phonological information that somehow became erroneous during the process of speech sound production. Finally, RW showed no signs of apraxia or dysarthria, for either correct or incorrectly chosen and ordered phonemes. This indicates that his difficulty arises before the articulatory gestures associated with specific segments are planned and executed. We can conclude that RW accessed the forms of words in the phonological output lexicon, and that errors were introduced during the speech-planning process.

Short-term memory assessment

As discussed in the introduction to this paper, rehearsal is thought to be involved in the production of the word-length effects in auditory and visual span tasks, the phonological-similarity effect in visual span, and in written rhyme judgements. RW was tested for these effects using the same materials as were used with the apraxic patients in the first experiment.

Span tasks that present words as stimuli and in which subjects must point to pictures do not necessarily require lexical phonological access – that is, the activation of phonological representations from semantics – as part of the rehearsal process. For both auditorily and visually presented words, the surface forms of phonological representations can be accessed directly from the input without contacting semantic representations. These can be rehearsed and used to access the meaning of the presented words, which can then be matched to the presented pictures (we take up the question of whether this is how this task is performed in our final discussion). Therefore, we also used a purely pictorial version of the span task with patient RW. In this version of the task, subjects were presented with sequences of pictures, the words corresponding to which were either long or short, or phonologically similar or dissimilar. Subjects were given instructions regarding what word was associated with each picture. Subjects were then required to indicate the sequence of pictures that were presented, using a picture-pointing task as in the word-span tasks. Though this task could in principle be accomplished by a purely visual process, Schiano and Watkins (1981) have reported effects of word length and phonological similarity in this task, indicating that subjects activate word forms and use verbal short-term memory in this task. In this task, these word forms must be activated from semantics, thereby affording a subject the opportunity to use an underlying phonological representation as the basis for rehearsal if such a representation is sufficient to allow rehearsal to occur.

RW was tested on all the tasks assessing short-term memory and metalinguistic processing, except picture span, in July 1991.

Results

RW's auditory word span was determined to be 3 and his visual word span to be 2. Results of his performance on the phonological similarity and word length tasks are shown in figure 21.3.

RW's performance on these materials was analysed for each modality in order to determine whether there was a statistically reliable effect on each of the four tasks. The effect of phonological similarity just failed to be significant. The 'reversed' effect of length was significant in both modalities. This invites the speculation that, in the absence of rehearsal, the increased distinctiveness of longer words with respect to the cohort of lexical items of a given length increases their retrievability from verbal short-term memory.

RW was tested on the picture span tasks in September 1992, at a time when he showed residual problems with word production. He had been tested on the PAL in May 1992, and had continued to show deficits in repetition (8/20 words and 0/20 nonwords correctly repeated), though both his picture-naming and oral reading had improved (28/32 and 54/57 correct, respectively). In order to ascertain whether he still showed an impairment of rehearsal in span, he was retested for the effects of word length on span. The results indicate that RW still showed impaired rehearsal in span tasks.

RW obtained a score of 47/80 items correct for pictures with phonologically similar words, 41/80 for pictures with phonologically dissimilar words, 47/80 for pictures with long words, and 45/80 for pictures with short words. The lack of either a word length or phonological similarity effect in this task is consistent with the absence of rehearsal on this task.

He was nearly perfect on homophone judgements (94 per cent oral presentation, 100 per cent print), but very impaired on rhyme judgements in both the auditory and visual modalities (63 per cent and 70 per cent, respectively).

RW's articulatory rate was 23 seconds for ten repetitions of two short words, and 39 seconds for ten repetitions of two long words. This rate is well outside the normal range, and comparable to that of the moderately impaired patients with apraxia of speech in the first experiment. The reason for this slow articulatory rate was that RW had great difficulty in producing the correct forms of the stimuli because of the phonological errors he made.

Discussion

RW's performance sheds light on the mechanism of verbal rehearsal. He showed evidence of being able to activate lexical phonological representations; however, he was

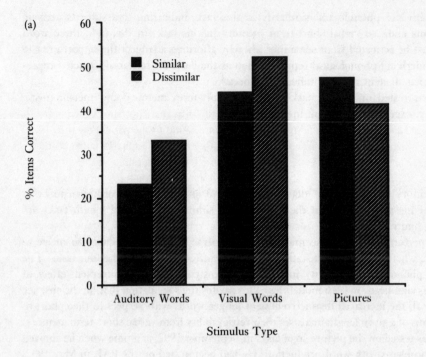

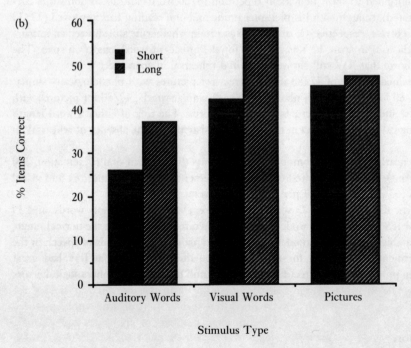

Figure 21.3 Performance of RW on auditory, visual and picture phonological similarity and word–length tasks: (a) Phonological-similarity effect; (b) Word–length effect

unable to produce correct phonological forms of words or nonwords. His disturbed speech production was not dysarthric or apraxic, but consisted of properly articulated, mischosen and misordered phonological segments and mis-structuring of the syllabic forms of words. The locus of his impairment can be identified as a stage of speech output planning that changes and/or adds to the phonological representations that are initially activated from semantics.

RW was unable to use rehearsal processes normally in verbal short-term memory. He had a reduced span, comparable in magnitude to those found in the patients with apraxia of speech described above. He showed no word-length effects in span tasks with auditorily or visually presented words. He showed neither word-length nor phonological-similarity effects in a picture span task. He could make homophone but not rhyme judgements. These performances are strong indications that RW was not using rehearsal mechanisms normally while accomplishing these tasks.

The first implication of these results is that verbal rehearsal involves a stage of speech output processing. RW had no significant impairments of word recognition or comprehension, yet the ability to process words at these levels of function was insufficient to sustain verbal rehearsal. These results thus confirm the wealth of data indicating that verbal rehearsal involves speech output processing.

The data also suggest that the ability to access a lexically listed phonological representation is not adequate to support rehearsal. Just as the fact that RW's intact word recognition and comprehension indicates that the integrity of input-side phonological processing is not sufficient to support rehearsal, the fact that this patient could access many aspects of word form in speech production but could not rehearse indicate that the ability to access lexical phonological representations is not sufficient for rehearsal.

The data indicate that RW's disturbance arises at the planning stage of output phonological processing. Accordingly, the fact that he has a disturbance of verbal rehearsal provides evidence in support of the hypothesis that phonological speech planning is involved in rehearsal. The data suggest that verbal rehearsal requires those abstract mental processes involved in elaborating and otherwise changing phonological representations in the phonological output lexicon into a form needed for programming the articulators.

3 Components of Word Length: Articulatory Complexity and Duration

If the view of rehearsal in span tasks outlined above is correct – namely, that rehearsal does not require articulation itself (whether overt or subvocal) but does make use of specification of articulatory gestures for phonemes – then the findings by Baddeley et al. (1975), that neither the number of syllables nor the number of phonemes in a word predicts the word-length effect in span, become difficult to explain. If rehearsal does not require articulation *per se*, but only requires the specification of articulatory gestures associated with phonemes, words with equivalent numbers of phonemes and syllables might be expected to behave similarly, regardless of the actual time it takes to articulate them.

Given these inconsistencies in the literature, it is important to note that, although numerous studies have documented an effect of word length on memory span in normal subjects, only experiment 4 in the study by Baddeley et al. (1975) compared subjects' performance on words which were matched for number of syllables and phonemes but differed in terms of articulatory duration. Monsell (1987) has raised questions about this experiment on the grounds of the selection of stimuli and the status of the speech-rate measure that was employed. Moreover, Baddeley et al. failed to find an effect of word length on span with visually presented materials except when subjects were explicitly told to rehearse. This either indicates that the visual span task does not require rehearsal (if the word-length effect is a reliable indicator of rehearsal), or that rehearsal can occur without producing a word-length effect.

In the final experiment reported in this chapter we asked the question of whether word-length effects in span are eliminated when words used in span tasks are matched for syllable and phoneme number but differ with respect to the duration and/or complexity of their associated articulatory gestures. Subjects' performance was assessed on two sets of stimulus materials. In one set the items were matched for number of phonemes and syllables, but differed with respect to the time it took to articulate them. The other set of materials examined subjects' performance on items which were matched for number of phonemes and syllables but which differed in terms of articulatory complexity. We predicted that word-length effects would be eliminated with these materials.

Subjects

Fifteen subjects (five male and ten female) who ranged in age from 59 to 74 years (mean = 64 years) participated in the study. All subjects were healthy individuals who were considered to be ageing normally, spoke English as their mother tongue, and had received scores well within the normal range when tested on the Peabody Picture Vocabulary Test – Revised (Dunn and Dunn, 1981) both when the items were presented orally and in print.

Materials and procedure

To test for the effect of articulatory duration in words matched for number of syllables and phonemes, two sets of two-syllable common nouns which differed in terms of vowel duration were constructed. Tense and lax vowels were contrasted in the sets of long and short words, respectively. Since tense vowels have a longer spoken duration than lax vowels in spoken English (Peterson and Lehiste, 1960; Fant, 1973; Jakobson et al., 1976; Fry, 1979), this was chosen as the parameter to manipulate word length. 'Long' words contained two tense vowels, or one tense and one lax vowel, with their associated diphthongs; 'short' words contained two lax vowels. The words were read and recorded by three female speakers and analysed by oscilloscopic display to ensure that they did in fact differ in terms of duration. The mean duration of the short words was 546 msec and of the long words was 720 msec.

To investigate the role of articulatory complexity upon span, two lists of words which differed in the difficulty associated with their articulation, but which were otherwise matched for number of syllables and number of phonemes, were constructed. The contrast between a consonant cluster and a singleton at the beginning of a word has been previously shown to be a measure of 'ease of articulation' in both normal and aphasic subjects (Martin, 1987; Trost and Cantor, 1974). In this experiment, the 'difficult-to-articulate' words consisted of monosyllabic nouns beginning with a consonant cluster and ending with a tense vowel; the 'easy-to-articulate' words consisted of monosyllabic words, matched in frequency, with a CVC structure and a lax vowel. The words were read and recorded by three female speakers and analysed by oscilloscopic display for duration differences. The mean duration of the easy-to-articulate words was 475 msec and of the difficult-to-articulate words was 571 msec.

As in the previous experiments subjects were tested for recall of these lists at the list length at which they had correctly recalled 60 per cent of the items on the auditory and visual word span tasks outlined in the first experiment. Subjects responded using the picture pointing technique employed in that experiment.

Results

The percentage of items recalled in the correct serial position was calculated for each subject for short and long words and easy- and difficult-to-articulate words in each modality. Subjects' performance on the stimulus materials was compared in each modality. The data are presented in figure 21.4. There was a significant effect of word length in both modalities, however, contrary to the prediction of the working memory model, performance on the long words was *better* than on the short words. In addition, as can be seen, there were no significant differences between number of items correctly reported in the lists of easy- and difficult-to-articulate words.

Discussion

These results indicate that, when words are equated for number of phonemes, neither their spoken duration nor the complexity of the articulatory gestures associated with their production affect subjects' performance on span tasks. The results suggest that it is the phonological structure of a word, not features of its actual articulation, that determines the magnitude of the word-length effect in span tasks. This conclusion follows from the fact that the materials used by Baddeley et al. (1975; experiment 3) and the materials in our first experiment which differed in both number of phonemes and spoken word duration, produced a word-length effect, whereas the materials used in our second and third experiments, which differed only in their spoken duration or articulatory complexity and not number of phonemes, did not. It is in keeping with previous reports that word-length effects are maintained in patients with severe articulatory disturbances.

However, there is evidence that word-length effects require some form of phonological output planning and are not entirely due to the activation of a phonological representation of a word in either an input phonological store or in a use-independent mental lexicon. The disappearance of word-length effects under articulatory suppression conditions and

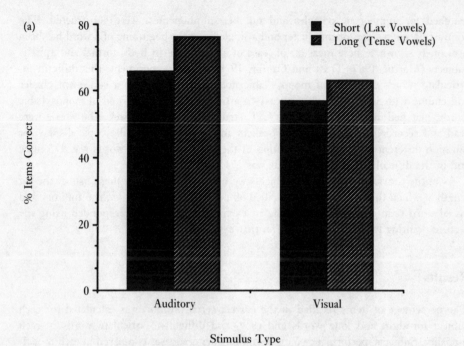

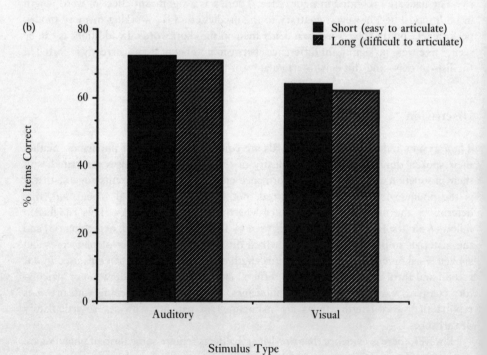

Figure 21.4 Mean percentage of items correctly recalled for words with lax and tense vowels and for easy- and difficult-to-articulate words

in patients with apraxia of speech, coupled with the preservation of the auditory phonological similarity effect in both these groups of subjects, suggests that the word-length effect is dependent upon some aspect of phonological output planning in a fashion that the auditory phonological-similarity effect is not. Our own view is that phonological output processing activates underspecified lexical phonological representations (Beland et al., 1990; Caplan, 1992; Caplan and Waters, 1992), whose sublexical phonological structures (for example, syllables, phonemes, distinctive features) are more fully specified and converted into neural plans for articulatory gestures by subsequent phonological output planning processes. These planning processes feed back to the level of lexical phonological representations (Dell, 1984, 1986, 1988). We tentatively suggest that the word-length effect requires the activation of representations by one or more of these phonological output planning processes. Activation of lexical phonological forms alone does appear to be adequate to allow the word-length effect to occur, and articulation itself does not appear to be necessary for it to occur.

This hypothesis is consistent with other models in the literature. Monsell (1987; see also Howard and Franklin, 1990) distinguishes between an 'inner' and an 'outer' pathway from output to input phonological processing. The inner pathway transmits a 'relatively abstract phonological code', while the outer pathway sends information about articulatory gestures to a 'more peripheral mechanism for . . . perceptual analysis' (p. 301). Our view that the word-length effect requires the activity of phonological output planning processes that operate on accessed lexical phonological forms is an attempt to begin to specify the abstract phonological representations that are involved in the inner output-to-input phonology pathway that Monsell suggests is involved in rehearsal.

This conclusion does not imply that articulation cannot play a role in generating word-length effects. In both Baddeley et al. (1975) experiments and in Martin's (1987) experiments, subjects were explicitly told to rehearse material using an articulatory mechanism. Under these conditions, Martin (1987) found that span was reduced for words that were difficult to articulate compared to words that were easy to articulate. Similarly, Baddeley et al. (1975) reported that there was no word-length effect for the two-syllable stimuli that had produced an auditory word length effect in their experiment 4 when these words were presented visually under conditions in which subjects were not instructed to rehearse items in an articulatory manner. The authors report that 'subjects . . . who did best on the short words reported using a rehearsal strategy, while those who did better on the long words reported using an imagery strategy' (p. 580). Explicit and/or subvocal articulation can be used as a rehearsal mechanism and, when it is used, word-length effects are found. However, this appears to be an optional strategy for subjects.

Conclusions

The data described above, regarding retained rehearsal in patients with dysarthria and impaired rehearsal in patients with apraxia of speech and conduction aphasia, specify what might be thought of as an upper and a lower bound to the speech production processes involved in verbal rehearsal. The presence of rehearsal impairments in apraxic patients suggests that rehearsal involves the stage of speech production that plans articulatory gestures associated with the phonemic and syllabic structures of words. Moreover, the finding of impaired rehearsal in a patient with reproduction conduction aphasia provides evidence supporting the claim that activating lexical phonological representations in the phonological output lexicon – though perhaps necessary – is not sufficient. Data from dysarthric patients suggests that producing articulated utterances is not necessary for verbal rehearsal to take place.

Consistent with this view we have presented data that indicate that the word-length effect in span tasks is not due to the duration or the complexity of the articulation of the items in the lists used in these tasks. None the less it appears that this effect requires output phonological processing. We suggest that the output phonological processing that is involved specifies the full values of sublexical phonological structures that are only partially specified in lexical phonological representations. More work is required to specify the exact phonological values that these processors compute, the nature of these computations, and the role of these computations in the rehearsal process itself.

Further Reading

Caplan, D. and Waters, G.S. (in press) 'On the nature of the phonological planning processes involved in verbal rehearsal: evidence from aphasia', *Brain and Language*.
Caplan, D. and Waters, G.S. (1992) 'Issues arising regarding the nature and consequences of reproduction conduction aphasia', in S.E. Kohn (ed.), *Conduction Aphasia* (Hillsdale, N.J.: Lawrence Erlbaum Associates), pp. 117–49.

References

Baddeley, A.D. (1966) 'Short-term memory for word sequences as a function of acoustic, semantic and formal similarity', *Quarterly Journal of Experimental Psychology*, 18: 362–5.
Baddeley, A.D. (1976) *The Psychology of Memory* (New York: Basic Books), pp. 162–87.
Baddeley, A.D. (1986) *Working Memory* (Oxford: Clarendon Press), pp. 75–108.
Baddeley, A.D. and Hitch, G.J. (1974) 'Working memory', in G. Bower (ed.), *Recent Advances in Learning and Motivation*, vol. VIII (New York: Academic Press).
Baddeley, A.D. and Wilson, B. (1985) 'Phonological coding and short-term memory in patients without speech', *Journal of Memory and Language*, 24: 490–502.
Baddeley, A.D., Thomson, N. and Buchanan, M. (1975) 'Word length and the structure of short-term memory', *Journal of Verbal Learning and Verbal Behavior*, 14: 575–89.
Baddeley, A.D., Lewis, V. and Vallar, G. (1984) 'Exploring the articulatory loop', *Quarterly Journal of Experimental Psychology*, 36: 233–52.
Beland, R., Caplan, D. and Nespoulous, J.-L. (1990) 'The role of abstract phonological representations in word production: evidence from phonemic paraphasias', *Journal of Neurolinguistics*, 5: 125–64.
Besner, D. (1987) 'Phonology, lexical access in reading, and articulatory suppression: a critical review', *Quarterly Journal of Experimental Psychology*, 39A: 467–78.
Besner, D., Davies, J. and Daniels, S. (1981) 'Reading for meaning: the effects of concurrent articulation', *Quarterly Journal of Experimental Psychology*, 33A: 415–37.
Bishop, D. and Robson, J. (1989) 'Unimpaired short-term memory and rhyme judgement in congenitally speechless individuals: implications for the notion of 'articulatory coding', *Quarterly Journal of Experimental Psychology*, 41A: 123–40.

Blumstein, S.E. (1990) 'Phonological deficits in aphasia: theoretical perspectives', in A. Caramazza (ed.), *Cognitive Neuropsychology and Neurolinguistics* (Hillsdale, N.J.: Lawrence Erlbaum).

Bowman, C.A., Hodson, B.W. and Simpson, R.K. (1980) 'Oral apraxia and aphasic misarticulation', in R.H. Brookshire (ed.), *Clinical Aphasiology* (Minneapolis, Minn.: BRK Publishers).

Brown, R. and McNeill, D. (1966) 'The "tip of the tongue" phenomenon', *Journal of Verbal Learning and Verbal Behavior*, **5**: 325–37.

Caplan, D. (1992) *Language: Structure, Processing and Disorders* (Cambridge, Mass.: MIT Press).

Caplan, D. and Bub, D. (1990) 'Psycholinguistic assessment of language', MS.

Caplan, D. and Waters, G. (1992) 'Issues arising regarding the nature and consequences of reproduction conduction aphasia', in S.E. Kohn (ed.), *Conduction Aphasia* (Hillsdale, N.J.: Lawrence Erlbaum), pp. 117–49.

Caplan, D. and Waters, G. (in press) 'On the nature of the phonological planning processes involved in verbal rehearsal: evidence from aphasia', *Brain and Language*.

Caplan, D., Rochon, E. and Waters, G.S. (1992) 'Articulatory and phonological determinants of word length effects in span tasks', *Quarterly Journal of Experimental Psychology*, **45A**: 177–92.

Chomsky, N. and Halle, M. (1968) *The Sound Pattern of English* (New York: Harper & Row).

Dabul, B. (1979) *Apraxia Battery for Adults* (Tigard, Oregon: C.C. Publications).

Darley, F.L. (1983) 'Foreword', in W.R. Berry (ed.), *Clinical Dysarthria* (San Diego, Cal.: College-Hill Press).

Darley, F.L., Aronson, A.E. and Brown, J.R. (1975) *Motor Speech Disorders* (Toronto: W.B. Saunders).

Dell, G.S. (1984) 'Representation of serial order in speech: evidence from the repeated phoneme effect in speech errors', *Journal of Experimental Psychology: Learning, Memory, and Cognition*, **10**: 222–33.

Dell, G.S. (1986) 'A spreading activation theory of retrieval in sentence production', *Psychological Review*, **93**(3): 283–321.

Dell, G.S. (1988) 'The retrieval of phonological forms in production: tests of predictions from a connectionist model', *Journal of Memory and Language*, **27**: 124–42.

Dunn, L.M. (1965) *Peabody Picture Vocabulary Test Manual* (Circle Pines, Minn.: American Guidance Service).

Dunn, L.M. and Dunn, L.M. (1981) *Peabody Picture Vocabulary Test – Revised Manual* (Circle Pines, Minn.: American Guidance Service).

Enderby, P.M. (1983) *Frenchay Dysarthria Assessment* (San Diego, Cal.: College-Hill Press).

Fant, G. (1973) *Speech Sounds and Features* (Cambridge, Mass.: MIT Press).

Fay, D. and Cutler, A. (1977) 'Malapropisms and the structure of the mental lexicon', *Linguistic Inquiry*, **8**: 505–20.

Fry, D.B. (1979) *The Physics of Speech* (Cambridge: Cambridge University Press).

Goodglass, H. and Kaplan, E. (1983) *The Assessment of Aphasia and Related Disorders*, 2nd edn (Philadelphia, Penn.: Lea & Febiger).

Grignon, A.M. (1984) 'Phonologie lexicale tri-dimensionnelle du japonais', unpublished PhD dissertation, Université de Montreal.

Halle, M. and Mohanan, K.P. (1985) 'Segmental phonology in modern English', *Linguistic Inquiry*, **16**: 57–116.

Howard, D. and Franklin, S. (1990) 'Memory without rehearsal', in G. Vallar and T. Shallice (eds), *Neuropsychological Impairments of Short-term Memory* (Cambridge: Cambridge University Press).

Hodson, B.W. (1986) *The Assessment of Phonological Processes – Revised* (Danville, Ill.: Interstate Printers and Publishers).

Howard D. and Franklin, S. (1987) 'Memory without rehearsal', in G. Vallar and T. Shallice (eds), *Neuropsychological Impairments of Short-term Memory* (Cambridge: Cambridge University Press).

Jakobson, R., Fant, G. and Halle, M. (1976) *Preliminaries to Speech Analysis: The Distinctive Features and their Correlates* (Cambridge, Mass.: MIT Press).

Johns, D.F. and Darley, F.L. (1970) 'Phonemic variability in apraxia of speech', *Journal of Speech and Hearing Research*, **13**: 556–83.

Levelt, W.J.M. (1989) *Speaking: From Intention to Articulation* (Cambridge, Mass.: MIT Press).

Levine, D.N., Calvanio, R. and Popovics, A. (1982) 'Language in the absence of inner speech', *Neuropsychologia*, **20**: 391–409.

Martin, R.C. (1987) 'Articulatory and phonological deficits in short-term memory and their relation to syntactic processing', *Brain and Language*, **32**: 159–92.

McDonald, E.T. (1976) *A Screening Deep Test of Articulation* (Pittsburgh, Penn.: Stanwix House).

Mohanan, K.P. (1982) 'Lexical phonology', unpublished PhD dissertation, Massachusetts Institute of Technology.

Monsell, S. (1987) 'On the relation between lexical input and output pathways for speech', in A. Allport, D. MacKay, W. Prinz and E. Sheerer (eds), *Language Perception and Production* (London: Academic Press).

Murray, D.J. (1968) 'Articulation and acoustic confusability in short-term memory', *Journal of Experimental Psychology*, **78**: 679–84.

Nebes, R.D. (1975) 'The nature of internal speech in a patient with aphemia', *Brain and Language*, **2**: 489–97.

Pesetsky, D. (1979) 'Russian morphology and lexical theory', unpublished MS, Department of Linguistics, Massachusetts Institute of Technology.

Peterson, G.E. and Lehiste, I. (1960) 'Duration of syllable nuclei in English', *Journal of the Acoustical Society of America*, **32**: 693–703.

Rochon, E., Caplan, D. and Waters, G.S. (1991) 'Short-term memory processes in patients with apraxia of speech: implications for the nature and structure of the auditory verbal short-term memory system', *Journal of Neurolinguistics*, **5**: 237–64.

Salame, P. and Baddeley, A.D. (1982) 'Disruption of short-term memory by unattended speech: implications for the structure of working memory', *Journal of Verbal Learning and Verbal Behavior*, **21**: 150–64.

Schiano, D.J. and Watkins, M.J. (1981) 'Speech-like coding of pictures in short-term memory', *Memory and Cognition*, **9**: 110–14.

Shallice, T. and Warrington, E.K. (1977) 'Auditory-verbal short-term memory impairment and conduction aphasia', *Brain and Language*, **4**: 479–91.

Trost, J.E. and Cantor, G.J. (1974) 'Apraxia of speech in patient's with Broca's aphasia: a study of phoneme production accuracy and error patterns', *Brain and Language*, **1**: 63–79.

Vallar, G. and Baddeley, A.D. (1984a) 'Fractionation of working memory: neuropsychological evidence for a phonological short-term store', *Cognitive Neuropsychology*, **1**: 121–41.

Vallar, G. and Baddeley, A.D. (1984b) 'Phonological short-term store, phonological processing and sentence comprehension: a neuropsychological case study', *Cognitive Neuropsychology*, **1**(2): 121–41.

Vallar, G. and Cappa, S.F. (1987) 'Articulation and verbal short-term: evidence from anarthria', *Cognitive Neuropsychology*, **4**(1): 55–78.

Waters, G.S., Rochon, E. and Caplan, D. (1992) 'The role of high-level speech planning in rehearsal: evidence from patients with apraxia of speech', *Journal of Memory and Language*, **31**: 54–73.

Wertz, R.T. (1985) 'Neurophathologies of speech and language: an introduction to patient management', in D.R. Johns (ed.), *Clinical Management of Neurogenic Communicative Disorder*, 2nd edn (Boston, Mass: Little Brown).

Wertz, R.T., Lapointe, L.L. and Rosenbek, J.C. (1984) *Apraxia of Speech in Adults: The Disorder and its Management* (New York: Grune & Stratton).

Part VI Lost for Words

Part VI Lost for Words

Introduction

'Laila-tov is "goodnight" in Hebrew.' How do you remember this fact? Are separate systems used for different types of word? Why is foreign language learning easy for some people (and at some ages) and so very difficult for others? What are the principles that determine how words might be 'lost' following stroke or other brain damage?

These questions and others like them motivate the explorations in this part. There is continuity with Part VI, where verbal repetition abilities were shown to be closely linked with verbal comprehension and production, but in this section the focus moves towards the lexicon: the word-form store.

Papagno and Vallar contrast two people with differing abilities in learning new languages: FF, with few intellectual gifts, is a good linguist, while PV – intellectually able, but with a severe short-term verbal memory disorder – cannot learn new phonological forms. This double dissociation reminds us that the 'language module' has its own specifications and can be considered to be relatively independent of general cognitive function. Learning a new language, in particular learning new phonological forms and combinations can show up working memory limitations. Hillis and Caramazza's presentation of Jeanette shows some very specific problems that can persist following a stroke. Jeanette, like PV, has a much-reduced immediate verbal memory span. This has affected her ability to understand some long and difficult spoken sentences, which cannot be parsed 'online'. But she also has difficulties in *writing* some words – especially unfamiliar words and the correct forms of verbs. Other patients (including those like PV and several in Part VI) whose short-term spans are much reduced don't necessarily have as much difficulty as Jeanette in following spoken sentences. So could her problems with outputting verbs and translating spoken to written forms compound her memory deficits?

Semenza outlines another aspect of lexical organization: the distinction between proper names and other noun types. He confirms that proper names can be lost following brain damage, but also that they can, under some conditions, be specifically spared, while common nouns are lost. This double dissociation suggests that proper names and other noun forms might have separable access and representation procedures.

Focusing on lexical distinctions has helped to uncover a number of quite distinct operations and abilities; in this domain, as in others, we are reminded that the specificity of difficulties encountered by patients suggests specific components of word learning that can be independently damaged or spared and used.

22 To Learn or Not to Learn: Vocabulary in Foreign Languages and the Problem with Phonological Memory

Costanza Papagno and Giuseppe Vallar

A basic distinctive feature of the neuropsychological deficits of human patients suffering from focal lesions of the brain is their selectivity. Individual patients may show very specific patterns of impairment, while other, sometimes most, components of the cognitive system are entirely spared. This reflects the highly multicomponential architecture of the brain basis of mental faculties (Vallar, 1994). Specific cerebral circuits may be disrupted by brain disease in very selective fashions, sometimes bringing about extremely 'pure' patterns of cognitive impairment. This state of affairs concerns aphasic deficits, planning disorders (the so-called 'frontal lobe syndrome'), spatial hemineglect, and so on. Memory disorders are no exception to this rule, fractionating into a number of focal patterns of impairment.

The following two case stories of broken and unbroken memories are illustrative examples of the selectivity of memory deficits. They mainly concern a specific memory system: auditory-verbal, or phonological, short-term memory.

The Case of FF: Phonological Short-term Memory Selectively Spared

FF (Vallar and Papagno, 1993) is a 25-year-old Italian woman, affected by Down's syndrome, a genetically-determined disease the main distinctive feature of which is mental retardation. FF also shows some typical features of the disease: slanted eyes, flattened bridge of the nose, convergent strabismus, severe myopia and astigmatism, congenital heart disease, and so on. FF worked in an advertising agency, where she was in charge of the mail and photocopying till last year. Now she has a full-time job in an association which organizes activities for handicapped children, where she is in charge of reception. FF is a pleasant person, able to develop social interactions both at work and with family and friends. FF has a very active life: she likes riding very much and goes swimming one day per week. FF often goes to the cinema with friends and enjoys reading books and magazines.

FF's parents are Italian. Up to the age of six she lived on a NATO military base in Belgium, where she was able to learn French and English in spite of her delayed psychomotor development. She went to school for eight years, supported by a supplementary teacher. She continues to improve her English since the family moved back to Italy, because her sister-in-law is British. FF is now able to hold a conversation with an English speaker, even on the telephone, and to follow an English TV programme or movie. She stopped practising her French and it became poor, but at present FF is trying to improve it by listening to tapes that she buys weekly at the newspaper kiosk.

To give an idea of FF's fluency in English and French, we report from Vallar and Papagno (1993: 469) her oral account of her favourite hobby, riding, and of her studies of French:

I often ride on Saturday. I enjoy it very much, even because horses are my favourite animals. I also buy monthly a magazine about horses and riding, and in my room I have a lot of photographs of horses. To ride is very easy. What I have to do is to sit on the saddle and then I take the reins into the little finger and thumb, and I can go. Ah, of course, my feet! I put my feet into the stirrups. I learnt when I was 15 and since then I always try to find some free hours during the week to do it. Usually, before I ride, I do some exercise, gymnastics. The place where I go is near my house, which is in . . .

J'ai oublié beaucoup de mots en français. Je ne le parle plus comme avant. Mais maintenant le lundi papa m'achète la leçon de français De Agostini. J'écoute la cassette et je lie le livre et puis je fais les devoirs. Je veux apprendre à bien parler pour aller en France. Quand j'étais petite je le parlais mieux.

On the other hand, FF's impairment in other aspects of cognition is apparent in everyday life. For instance, FF never goes out alone, but is always accompanied by a member of the family or some other person: she does not take care of herself, and can be approached by everyone. FF is also unable to drive a car.

One of us (CP) has known FF since she was a baby, being a childhood friend of her sister. CP had been always impressed by her fluency in English, despite her mental retardation. One summer, while spending a holiday in their house in Sardinia, CP noticed that FF, after lunch, used to sit outside translating from English a book explaining how to make paper flowers; she used the dictionary only seldom, even though the text was full of unfamiliar terms.

At that time we were investigating the role of phonological short-term memory in the acquisition of new words (see, for example, Papagno and Vallar, 1992). We thought that FF could provide good evidence that subjects with relatively normal vocabulary should have a preserved function of this system, even in the presence of substantial deficits in other areas of cognition. We therefore asked FF whether she was willing to participate in an experiment which investigated the relative contribution of different factors (general intelligence, verbal long-term and short-term memory) to vocabulary acquisition. FF was keen to perform the experiment and was also eager to do even more than requested.

We investigated FF's mental status in 1990. Her IQ was 71, with a verbal IQ of 80 and a performance IQ of 63. The most impaired tasks were arithmetic among verbal tests; block design and picture arrangement among performance tests. In the vocabulary and span subtests, she was unimpaired. Performance in the Raven Progressive Matrices 47 was grossly defective (6.5 out of 36, cut-off 18) and she failed to understand even the instructions of reasoning tasks, such as three-term problems and syllogisms. Her linguistic skills were within the normal range, in a variety of tasks assessing comprehension of individual words and sentences, vocabulary, speech production and reading. By contrast, her visuo-spatial skills were grossly defective.

Memory was explored in detail. FF's ability to repeat sequences of verbal items was entirely normal: her auditory digit span was 5.75. Her visuo-spatial span (3.75) was in the lower normal range. Auditory-verbal long-term memory, as assessed by short-story recall and free recall of lists of words, was defective. The final words of the lists (recency effect) were however recalled normally, suggesting a preserved function of phonological memory. Learning of a visuo-spatial route was grossly defective.

To summarize, FF's general intelligence, visuo-spatial perception and visuo-spatial memory were severely impaired. However, even though FF was impaired in tasks assessing verbal and visuo-spatial long-term memory, she was not clinically amnesic. FF was able to recall events which occurred in the recent and remote past, meetings she had to attend, movies she had seen, and so on. She was particularly good at remembering people's names, and one of us (CP) has often seen her parents asking her about names they had failed to remember.

From this account, it is clear that FF's cognitive pattern differs in important respects from that observed in group studies of subjects suffering from Down's syndrome. These subjects typically have a more widespread cognitive deficit, involving auditory-verbal short-term memory, language, visuo-spatial processing and general intelligence (review in Vallar and Papagno, 1993).

Exceptions, however, are on record. A clear-cut dissociation between language and vocabulary acquisition on the one hand and intelligence on the other is illustrated by the case of Nigel Hunt (1967). This person suffering from Down's syndrome was able to write a book, which gives an account of happenings, travels and visits. The book, which has been referred to as marked by the 'total absence of interpretations and abstractions' (Zellweger, 1977: 404) shows how a someone with Down's syndrome and defective general intelligence may achieve good vocabulary and linguistic skills.

FF, by contrast, has a normal phonological short-term memory. We investigated the operation of this system in more detail by studying the effects of two variables: phonological similarity and word length, upon immediate serial recall (see a discussion of these effects in Vallar and Baddeley, 1984a). FF showed a clear-cut detrimental effect of phonological similarity in four-, five- and six-item sequences, in both the auditory and the visual modalities of presentation of the stimuli. This is the usual pattern of normal controls. To assess the word length effect we used two- and four-syllable words, matched for frequency. As in normal subjects, FF's recall was better for sequences of auditorily presented short words, compared with long. The effect of word length was not tested with visual presentation, since FF proved to be extremely slow in reading the words, preventing a meaningful interpretation of the memory experiment.

In conclusion, FF's phonological short-term memory is preserved. Her auditory-verbal digit span (5.75) is normal. The presence of the phonological similarity effect in immediate serial recall shows that FF, like normal subjects, holds both auditory and visual information in the phonological short-term store component of the system. The presence of the word-length effect indicates that she is able to prevent the decay of memory items by making use of the rehearsal component. However, not all aspects of phonological processes are spared. FF showed defective performance in tasks requiring phonological judgements, such as deciding whether or not two words have the same stress pattern [for example, same: tàvolo–zòccolo' (table–hoof), vs. different: 'fucile–vìgile' (rifle–policeman): see Burani et al., 1991], or phonological parsing (exchanging the initial phonemes from pairs of words; for example, from 'Dino Zoff' to 'Zino Doff').

FF can learn foreign languages: an experimental study

If FF's normal phonological short-term memory has played a role in her good acquisition of vocabulary in both Italian, English and French, she should perform well in paired-associate learning of novel words, which can be regarded as an experimental analogue of vocabulary acquisition (Baddeley et al., 1988; Papagno et al., 1991; Papagno and Vallar, 1992). We explained to FF that we wanted her to learn some Russian words. FF was auditorily presented with eight pairs of words, at the rate of one pair per two seconds: the first item was an Italian word, the second was its Russian translation. Such novel words were Russian words transliterated into Italian (Baddeley et al., 1988). The pair rosa *(rose)–svieti* is an illustrative example. Two- and three-syllable items were used. FF was very motivated, thinking that she was going 'to study Russian'. As shown in figure 22.1, FF was able to learn seven pairs over ten trials, a performance comparable to that of the control group. In contrast, in a task requiring the acquisition of pairs of Italian words, FF's learning rate was much slower than that of controls, although she was able to memorize all eight words in ten trials (Vallar and Papagno, 1993).[1]

The main result of this study is the association of a remarkably good developmental acquisition of vocabulary and language (in the presence of widespread cognitive deficits) with an entirely normal function of the phonological short-term store and articulatory rehearsal components of verbal short-term memory. These findings verify the prediction that vocabulary learning requires the integrity of phonological short-term memory, and may occur even in the presence of defective verbal learning and retention.

PV: Phonological Short-term Memory Selectively Impaired

PV is an Italian woman (born 1951) who in February 1977, when 26 years old, suffered a cerebrovascular attack in the left cerebral hemisphere. The occurrence of a stroke at such a young age was probably due to heart disease (stenosis of the mitralic valve), for which PV underwent in April 1977 a successful surgical operation of mitral commissurotomy.

Immediately after the stroke, PV had a right hemiparesis, which fully recovered in about one month, and some mild dysphasic disorders. We first met PV nine months

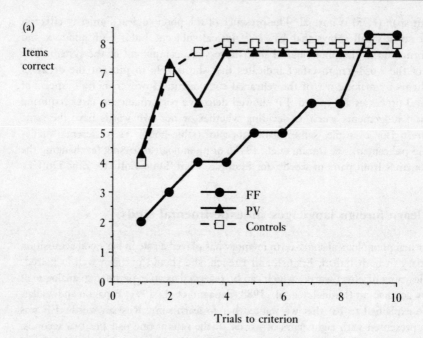

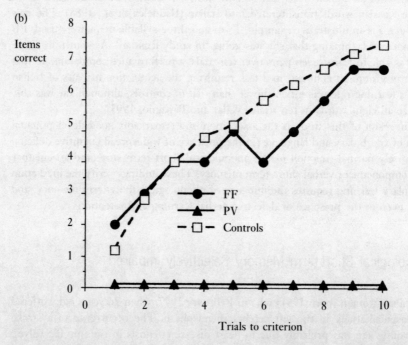

Figure 22.1 Paired-associate learning by normal Italian control subjects and by FF and PV: (a) auditorily presented Italian word-word pairs; (b) auditorily-presented Italian word-Russian new word pairs

Source: Baddeley et al. (1988); Vallar and Papagno (1993)

later, in November 1977. During the acute stage of her disease PV was supported by her parents, but, as soon as her physical recovery was complete, she lived on her own with her two children. PV had been referred to the Neuropsychology Centre of the University of Milan (Italy) for a general evaluation of her dysphasic disturbances (see Basso et al., 1982).

PV lives in a town in the north of Italy. Travelling by car from PV's town to Milan takes about two hours. When PV came to Milan for the first visit, she travelled alone, driving her own car. In November 1977, she spent three full days, in our laboratory, during which she underwent a neurological and neuropsychological assessment. Every day in the late afternoon, when the examination was over, she drove back home, because she wished to spend the evening with her children. The following day she was back in Milan to complete the assessment. The final day of this first study was extremely foggy, and driving in the motorway might have been very dangerous due to the low visibility and the frequent accidents. We warned PV, but she could not be persuaded, and returned home safely. We realized later that PV was a skilled and fast driver: sometimes she drove one of us (GV) to the railway station of her town, coping with the traffic with considerable ability.

A few months after this first assessment, PV set up as a dealer in pottery that she painted herself: she had attended courses on the making and painting of pottery. A few years later she gave up this small business, to be able to spend as much time as possible with her two sons. Since then, one of us (GV) has had the opportunity to meet PV many times, and to assess various aspects of her memory deficit in more detail.

PV had no primary sensory and motor deficits and her neurological examination was within the normal range. A computerised tomography scan showed an extensive ischaemic lesion in the fronto-temporo-parietal regions of the left hemisphere.

The assessment of PV's speech revealed minimal abnormalities: during spontaneous speech she made a few phonological errors (misproductions of words, which typically involve omitted, extraneous or duplicated sounds) and sometimes showed difficulties in finding the appropriate word; she also made a few errors in spontaneous writing; her comprehension of spoken language was defective only in the case of relatively complex commands, such as 'Touch the white small circle and the red large square'.

PV's mild disorders of speech production recovered in a few months. Her mild deficit of speech comprehension was further explored in the following years (see, for example, Vallar and Baddeley, 1984b, 1987): it was confined to long sentences, exceeding the abnormally reduced capacity of her phonological short-term memory, provided the linear arrangement of words conveyed crucial information. Examples of sentences PV failed to understand are: 'One could reasonably claim that *sailors* are often lived on by *ships* of various kinds', or 'The *world* divides the *equator* into two hemispheres, the northern and the southern', where PV's task was to verify whether or not the sentence was true. By contrast PV was able to judge with nearly complete accuracy whether a sentence of comparable length, such as 'It is true that *physicians* comprise a profession that is *manufactured in factories*, from time to time' is true or false. In this type of material the anomaly is produced by a semantic mismatch between relevant items in the sentence.

This comprehension deficit did not interfere substantially with her everyday life. PV's main subjective report was the inability to 'understand' (this was the term she used) even short sequences of digits (prices of goods, telephone numbers) spoken to her. The difficulty was considerably minor, however, when she read similar sequences. PV also complained about her inability to perform mental arithmetic. For instance, when shopping, she had problems in checking that she was paying the right amount of money, due to a difficulty in computing the value of the coins.

The subjective difficulty of dealing with sequences of heard digits had a dramatic experimental counterpart. As assessed by a span task, her ability to repeat digits, letters or words read aloud by the examiner was consistently errorless only in the case of *single* stimuli. This, together with her preserved performance in tasks assessing phonological analysis (Vallar and Baddeley, 1984b), rules out the possibility that her defective span may be interpreted in terms of a perceptual, rather than mnestic, deficit. When sequences of two or more items were presented PV's repetition performance deteriorated. If, however, the same stimuli were presented visually, printed on cards, PV was able to repeat longer sequences. When the summed probabilities of correct performance for all lengths of lists were used as a measure of span, PV's digit span was 3.1 with auditory presentation, and 4.5 with visual input (Shallice and Vallar, 1990). Span of normal subjects is typically greater than four digits, with a superior performance when the material is presented auditorily (the 'modality effect': see ibid.).

This selective inability to recall auditory stimuli immediately after presentation is due to the pathologically reduced capacity of the auditory-verbal (phonological) short-term store component of memory. This was confirmed by her failure in a number of different tests assessing immediate retention of verbal material presented auditorily (see Basso et al., 1982; Vallar and Papagno, 1986). PV's forgetting of even a single letter was abnormally rapid: within a few seconds. When she was required to repeat, immediately after presentation, a list of words exceeding her defective span, retention of the final words in the list was defective. This defective recency effect indicates a reduced capacity of the phonological short-term store. By contrast, recall of the initial words in the list, which represent the output of long-term memory processes, was within the normal range. Level of performance was much better with visual presentation. The forgetting curve for single letters over 15 seconds was much less steep. Free recall of lists of visually presented words was preserved in both the recency and the prerecency portions of the curve.

Her deficit can not be attributed to damage to other systems (Basso et al., 1982; Vallar and Baddeley, 1984b). PV's perceptual processes were unimpaired, and her ability to provide responses to auditory-verbal stimuli was not affected by the modality of output, such as oral repetition vs. manual pointing. Her verbal long-term learning and retention of individual words and connected discourse, such as a short story, were normal. PV's short- and long-term memory for visuo-spatial information, such as sequences of positions, was preserved. General intelligence was also within the normal range. For instance, PV's score in the Raven Progressive Matrices 47 was 32 out of 36 (cut off 18).

PV cannot learn foreign languages

PV, in addition to Italian, spoke a little French. Once she briefly mentioned that, after the onset of her disease, she attempted to study French again, but gave up because it was too difficult. The precise reasons for this failure were however unclear to PV, and we decided to investigate her ability to learn words in a foreign language by an experimental study (Baddeley et al., 1988). We (Vallar and Baddeley, 1984b) had previously shown that PV was able to read aloud pronounceable nonwords with complete accuracy. Her immediate repetition of nonwords was errorless for two-syllable items, and 80 per cent correct for three-syllable items; she was however unable to repeat four- and five-syllable nonwords (Baddeley et al., 1988). During this repetition experiment, PV reported that she treated nonwords as sequences of meaningless syllables. PV has a comparable span for auditorily presented two-syllable nonwords (1.70) and for names of individual letters (1.60: see Shallice and Vallar, 1990) which comprise one or two syllables.

Having assessed that PV was able to repeat individual two- and three-syllable nonwords immediately after presentation, we used the paired-associate paradigm described above. We asked PV to learn eight two- and three-syllable Russian words unknown to her. She was unable to learn a single novel Russian word over ten trials (see figure 22.1). In this task we used a rate of presentation of two seconds per pair. This fast rate could minimize PV's possibility to set up and utilize long-term learning strategies, forcing her to rely upon the defective phonological short-term store. In a second experiment presentation rate was therefore slowed down to five seconds per pair, and a parallel but different set of material was used. PV, however, again showed a total lack of learning, failing to recall a single pair on any of the ten learning trials.

As mentioned previously, PV has a visual memory span that is consistently greater than her auditory span (see Basso et al., 1982). If retention in a short-term storage system contributes to the acquisition of new words, visual presentation of the material might improve PV's ability to learn new words. With visual presentation PV was able to learn six out of eight words over ten trials. This performance level is greater than the total absence of learning found with auditory presentation (see figure 22.1), but is still defective as compared with normal subjects, who were able to acquire all eight new words over ten trials. These findings suggest that phonological short-term memory contributes also to the learning of visually presented new words. PV's impaired learning of new words may be contrasted with her normal acquisition of Italian words, both with auditory (see the figure) and with visual presentation.

A Conclusion

These two cases of broken memories show how selective the patient's deficit may be. FF's phonological short-term memory and most linguistic abilities are preserved. She is however impaired in a wide range of tasks assessing reasoning, visuo-spatial processing and long-term memory. FF, making use of her spared skills, is able to do a number of things, such as learning foreign languages, but not others. For instance, she is highly dependent on her family for many aspects of everyday life.

PV has a dramatic deficit in the immediate retention of auditory-verbal information, in the absence of any other cognitive impairment. PV, unlike FF, can not learn foreign languages and has some problems in speech comprehension and mental arithmetic. PV, however, is able to take care of herself and her two sons, and does not require any specific assistance or help.

These two case stories illustrate, as do many other neuropsychological studies of individual patients, the multicomponential organization of the brain. They also show, however, how individuals with brain damage and selective deficits of cognitive functions do their best to live a decent life.

Note

1   This task might make use of knowledge of the world in a creative way to enhance the new 'links' between known single items: knowledge that is out of reach of FF's intellectual capacities.

Further Reading

Vallar, G. and Papagno, C. (1995) 'Neuropsychological impairments of short-term memory', in A. Baddeley, B. Wilson and F. Watts (eds), *Handbook of Memory Disorders* (Chichester, W. Sussex: John Wiley), pp. 135–65.

References

Baddeley, A.D., Papagno, C. and Vallar, G. (1988) 'When long-term learning depends on short-term storage', *Journal of Memory and Language*, **27**: 586–95.
Basso, A., Spinnler, H., Vallar, G. and Zanobio, M.E. (1982) 'Left hemisphere damage and selective impairment of auditory-verbal short-term memory', *Neuropsychologia*, **20**: 263–74.
Burani, C., Vallar, G. and Bottini, G. (1991) 'Articulatory coding and phonological judgements on written words and pictures: the role of the phonological output buffer', *European Journal of Cognitive Psychology*, **3**: 379–98.
Hunt, N. (1967) *The World of Nigel Hunt* (New York: Garret).
Papagno, C. and Vallar, G. (1992) 'Phonological short-term memory and the learning of novel words: the effects of phonological similarity and word length', *Quarterly Journal of Experimental Psychology*, **44A**: 47–67.
Papagno, C., Valentine, T. and Baddeley, A.D. (1991) 'Phonological short-term memory and foreign language vocabulary learning', *Journal of Memory and Language*, **30**: 331–47.
Shallice, T. and Vallar, G. (1990) 'The impairment of auditory-verbal short-term storage', in G. Vallar and T. Shallice (eds), *Neuropsychological Impairments of Short-term Memory* (Cambridge: Cambridge University Press), pp. 11–53.
Vallar, G. (1994) 'Left spatial hemineglect: an unmanageable explosion of dissociations? No', *Neuropsychological Rehabilitation*, **4**: 209–12.
Vallar, G. and Baddeley, A.D. (1984a) 'Fractionation of working memory: neuropsychological evidence for a phonological short-term store', *Journal of Verbal Learning and Verbal Behavior*, **23**: 151–61.
Vallar, G. and Baddeley, A.D. (1984b) 'Phonological short-term store, phonological processing and sentence comprehension', *Cognitive Neuropsychology*, **1**: 121–41.
Vallar, G. and Baddeley, A.D. (1987) 'Phonological short-term store and sentence processing', *Cognitive Neuropsychology*, **4**: 417–38.
Vallar, G. and Papagno, C. (1986) 'Phonological short-term store and the nature of the recency effect: evidence from neuropsychology', *Brain and Cognition*, **5**: 428–42.

Vallar, G. and Papagno, C. (1993) 'Preserved vocabulary acquisition in Down's syndrome: the role of phonological short-term memory', *Cortex*, **29**: 467–83.

Zellweger, H. (1977) 'Down's syndrome', in P.J. Vinken, G.W. Bruyn and N.C. Myrianthopoulos (eds), *Handbook of Clinical Neurology: Congenital Malformations of the Brain and Skull*, vol. 31, part II (Amsterdam: North-Holland), pp. 367–469.

23 'I Know It, but I Can't Write It': Selective Deficits in Long- and Short-term Memory

Argye E. Hillis and Alfonso Caramazza

Introduction

We have known Jeanette since the day after her stroke in July of 1984. The etiology of her thrombo-embolic stroke involving the left fronto-parietal area was a bit of a mystery; she was a healthy, active, 43-year-old librarian without high blood pressure or cardiac disease. The stroke mostly affected her language skills; a mild arm weakness resolved within 24 hours. At that time her speech was fluent, limited to perseverative phrases like 'now, now, now,' 'let's see', and 'I wouldn't know'. She communicated her ideas mostly through complex drawings or pointing to printed words in a book. Her auditory comprehension was limited to words and simple sentences. However, she improved rapidly, and was discharged from the hospital with resolving 'word-retrieval' difficulties in speech and writing and persisting difficulties in comprehension/retention of spoken sentences. It was expected that she would recover sufficient language skills for independent interactions in the community (banking, shopping, and so on), but no one expected her to return to work.

We lost contact with Jeanette for a few years, until one of us ran into her in February 1987 in the public library where she was again working as a librarian. She conversed without difficulty and recalled her experiences in the hospital in great detail. A few days later we received a letter from her, which included the following excerpt:

It was nice seeing you again at the library. . . . I would love to attend your stroke club meetings. My progress has been good, but I have trouble with writing more than anything. (My husband is writing this note, for example.)

After she began attending stroke club meetings Jeanette expressed an interest in participating in our research on aphasia. She also sought some ideas as to how she might improve in writing and in telephone interactions. She said that her success on her job was limited by the fact that she could not consistently assist callers who wished to place books on hold, check the availability of specific books, or have their call returned by another staff member. She complained that people 'talked too quickly' for her to understand, and that she would often become 'confused' about what they wanted. She also admitted to making errors in writing down simple messages, especially if she had to include a telephone number or an unusual name.

We tried some mock telephone calls to determine the problem underlying her difficulty in telephone communications. She was called from a separate office and asked to check or hold certain titles, find books by a given author or to take messages. Her accuracy was dismal. In light of her essentially normal interaction in the stroke club and other face-to-face conversations, her complete inability to carry out these simple and very familiar tasks was somewhat surprising. But her errors were very enlightening. To illustrate, when asked to hold a book entitled *Human Visual Cognition* by Seymour, she wrote down the title as *Seeing Psychology*. She had asked for the author's name to be spelled, and had written down 'Se__'. She had also attempted to take down the telephone number to call when the book came in, but had correctly transcribed only the first three digits. On another occasion, when asked to have a specified person return the call of Cathy Mort, she wrote down; 'Cindy____came. Please____her call.' She subsequently said that she was trying to write, 'Cindy *Mort called* Please *return* her call.'

These errors provided initial indications of what turned out to be Jeanette's most striking language impairments: (a) reduced auditory-verbal short-term memory, which interfered with her recall of telephone numbers, precise names and titles (even when she recalled the approximate meaning of the title, as in '*Seeing Psychology*'); (b) difficulty in writing verbs (note that she correctly wrote, 'her call' – the noun form of call – 'but wrote 'came' instead of 'called – the verb form of call); and (c) impaired ability to convert a spoken form of an unfamiliar name (like Mort) to a plausible written form. Each of these problems will be discussed in greater detail below, as we describe Jeanette's performance on research batteries and illustrate how her pattern of performance not only pointed to ways in which she could become more successful at work but also helped to reveal aspects of the representation and processing of language in the brain.

Overall Language Skills

When Jeanette began to participate in our research in early 1987, a set of screening tests was given to evaluate aspects of language that were currently being studied by various members of our laboratory. On the reading screener she made morphological errors (for example, *conquer* → 'conquered'[1]) and functor substitutions (with visually/phonologically similar functors, such as *whenever* → 'wherever') and was unable to correctly read aloud any pseudowords (for example, *reat* → 'I don't know how I would do that – Rita or red'). On the spelling screener she had trouble spelling verbs, functors and pseudowords (described in detail below), but wrote single nouns flawlessly. No dictated sentence was written accurately. For example, she wrote the dictated sentence, 'He should teach you how to swim' as: He can keep you to swim and 'The packages were brought by the men' as: The package are sold/bring when the men. On the comprehension screener she was only 60 per cent correct in pointing to one of two pictures corresponding to a spoken sentence when the foil depicted a syntactically related sentence (for example, 'the man is chasing the bull' vs. 'the man is being chased by the bull'), but was 100 per cent accurate when the foil depicted the semantically related sentence (for example, 'the man is driving the car' vs. 'the man is washing the car'). She accurately repeated words and pseudowords, but had trouble repeating sentences. On the morphology screener, Jeanette often substituted, deleted or added suffixes or prefixes in oral reading and repetition of affixed (suffixed or prefixed) and unaffixed words. For example, she read dangle as 'dangling', and repeated 'baker' as 'baking'. Her best performance was on the naming screener, in which she self-corrected her only error in naming verbally 25 pictures and six objects presented for tactile exploration.

Jeanette's spontaneous speech was fluent and usually grammatical, although she made morphological errors and rare phonemic or semantic errors (see appendix A). In general, however, her speech sounded normal, if a bit less eloquent than one might expect for her occupation and education level (a master's degree in library science). In summary, her main persisting problems in language included: (a) difficulty in writing verbs, functors and pseudowords; (b) production of morphological errors in speech, as well as in writing; (c) difficulties in repeating sentences and in processing the syntax of spoken sentences.

These problem areas were reflected quantitatively in her scores on the Boston Diagnostic Aphasia Examination (BDAE; Goodglass and Kaplan, 1972). Her only percentile scores that were below or at the 50th percentile for aphasic subjects were in following spoken commands (6/15 points), repetition of high probability sentences (2/8 sentences correct; see errors in appendix A), and writing sentences to dictation (0/12). Her performance was errorless on subtests of word discrimination, paragraph comprehension, responsive and confrontation naming, reading comprehension, serial writing and primer-level dictation.

On more detailed testing, Jeanette's score of 50 on the Boston Naming Test (Goodglass et al., 1983) and her score of 166 (scaled score of 110) on the Peabody Picture Vocabulary Test (Dunn and Dunn, 1981) were within the normal range. Performance on the Wechsler Memory Scale (Wechsler, 1972) was normal except on digit span (in which she did not achieve the minimum score of 4 on forward recall or 3 on backward recall).

Jeanette's problems in writing, morphological processing and auditory short-term memory (as the proposed underlying basis for her problems in repetition and processing syntax of spoken sentences) are described in detail in separate sections.

Grammatical Category-specific Deficit in Writing

We have already mentioned that Jeanette had difficulty in retrieving the spellings of words, particularly of verbs and functors. This problem was the one which seemed most troublesome to her because it precluded success in most daily tasks that required any writing, such as taking telephone messages for co-workers (as exemplified above) or writing letters to communicate specific needs or complaints. As an illustration of the latter, Jeanette attempted to express in writing a specific complaint in her work setting:

that the air conditioner in the library had been malfunctioning for some time and telephone requests for repair had not been satisfactorily addressed. After accurately addressing the letter, she wrote:

Dear Sir:
   My complaint is about communication. Parkville library cannot____the workers why the air conditioner is on the fritz. The____the air conditioner will be____. I can____
   The building management shall us with respect.
   Call me if you____any____explanation.

She read aloud her attempt, filling in the missing words, in this way: 'My complaint is about communication. Parkville librar*ians* cannot *explain to* the workers why the air conditioner is on the fritz (because we don't know). *When will* the air conditioner be *repaired?* I can *wait* (if the part is in Moscow or something), *but I need to be able to explain*. The building management *should treat* us with respect (when we call). Call me if you *need* any *further* explanation.'

Clearly Jeanette's written version would not have met her needs. In view of her concerns, we studied Jeanette's writing first. As a means of obtaining a good sample of her writing, and as a means of following any changes in her writing skills over time, she was asked to write an entry in a journal each day. At first she wrote about her daily activities, but as this topic became boring she began to include summaries of interesting articles she had read in the newspaper that day. She kept the journal for more than a year. Excerpts are included in appendix B, along with her spoken version of what she had attempted to write.

Experimental studies

Jeanette's spelling was evaluated for effects of task (oral spelling to dictation, written spelling to dictation, written picture naming, and delayed copying) and effects of stimulus dimensions (lexical parameters, such as frequency) with the Johns Hopkins University Dysgraphia Battery (Goodman and Caramazza, 1986). There were no significant differences between oral spelling and written spelling, or between writing to dictation and written naming, when lists were matched for grammatical word class. Delayed copy transcription (from upper to lower case or vice versa) was errorless. In spelling to dictation there were no significant effects of concreteness, sound-to-spelling regularity or frequency, but there was an important effect of grammatical word class: she spelled 100 per cent of the nouns, 90 per cent of the adjectives, 75 per cent of the verbs, and 70 per cent of the functors on a list of 28 words of each class matched for length and frequency. Her errors included omissions, semantically related words (for example, 'faith' → *belief*; 'bring' → *carried*), morphological errors (for example, 'speak' → *speech*), and visually/ phonologically similar words (for example, 'reveal' → *resolve*), along with occasional unrelated word responses (such as 'begin' → *rail*) and phonologically implausible nonword responses (that is, spellings that do not reflect the pronunciation of the word, such as 'while' → *ciqui*). She was always aware of her errors, but never produced a phonologically plausible spelling of the stimulus (for example, supe for soup), suggesting that she was

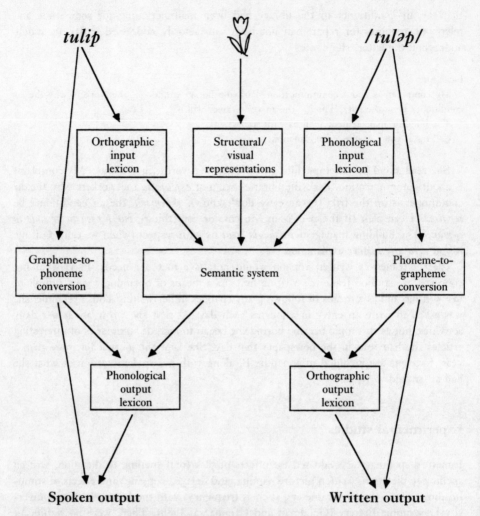

Figure 23.1   A schematic representation of the cognitive processes involved in lexical tasks

unable to use sublexical mechanisms for converting from sound to print in order to produce a plausible spelling when she could not retrieve the stored spelling. In keeping with this conclusion, Jeanette correctly spelled only 7 per cent of the pseudowords (for example, remmun) dictated to her, compared to 88 per cent of words of the same length.

The fact that Jeanette showed unimpaired comprehension of single words (of all grammatical word classes) suggests that the cognitive mechanisms underlying her writing are intact at least through the level of the lexical-semantic component in the model of lexical processing depicted in figure 23.1. Additional evidence that her errors occurred following activation of an intact semantic representation of the stimulus is that Jeanette orally produced the correct names of pictures (of actions) even when she could not write the names. Therefore, her errors in spelling words had to arise in output – either in accessing the lexical orthographic representation (that is, the stored representation of the spelling of the word, in the orthographic output lexicon in the figure) or in peripheral

Table 23.1   Percentage correct performance in written and oral naming

	N	*Jeanette*	HW	EBA
Written picture naming				
Nouns	30	97	97	8
Verbs	30	53	97	10
Oral picture naming				
Nouns	30	100	53	10
Verbs	30	97	20	70

writing processes. The latter is unlikely, because she made the same errors in oral spelling, and because her errors were frequently semantically related or visually/phonologically related real words.[2] Thus, her difficulty in spelling words was attributed to the level of accessing lexical orthographic representations (the orthographic output lexicon in the figure). An additional deficit, at the level of sound-to-print conversion, interfered with her ability to spell pseudowords correctly and to spell words plausibly when she failed to access the stored spelling of the word in the output lexicon.

If Jeanette's errors in spelling words resulted from damage at the level of the ortho-graphic output lexicon, then the substantial effect of grammatical word class must arise at that level of processing. To garner additional evidence for accepting or rejecting this hypothesis, the influence of grammatical word class was further investigated. Jeanette's pattern of performance was contrasted to that of HW, a patient we were studying concurrently, who showed the same advantage for nouns over verbs, but in spoken output only (see Caramazza and Hillis, 1991, for details).

A list of 98 nouns and 98 verbs, matched for frequency and length, was presented for both spelling to dictation and oral reading. Jeanette correctly wrote all of the nouns, but only 76 per cent of the verbs; but she showed no effect of word class in reading – she read 98 per cent of the nouns and 95 per cent of the verbs correctly. The patient HW showed the same effect of word class but the opposite pattern with respect to modality; that is, her performance was better on nouns than verbs only in spoken, not written, output.

Similarly, in naming 30 objects and 30 actions, Jeanette was more accurate on objects than on actions (97 per cent vs. 53 per cent, respectively) in written naming but nearly flawless in spoken naming; by contrast, HW was more accurate on objects than actions (53 per cent vs. 20 per cent, respectively) in spoken naming, but nearly flawless in written naming (table 23.1). The differences between nouns and verbs in these tasks cannot be simply due to 'greater difficulty' of verbs compared to nouns in the impaired output modality, since a third patient, EBA, showed the opposite dissociation between nouns and verbs (in spoken output only) using the same stimuli (Hillis and Caramazza, in press). For example, on the naming task, EBA's oral naming was less accurate for the objects than the actions (10 per cent vs. 70 per cent, respectively).

Furthermore, Jeanette showed a dissociation in performance between nouns and verbs in the impaired modality even when the form of the word was the same for the two word classes; that is, when homonyms were tested. This result was demonstrated by testing written and verbal naming of homonyms, for which one meaning is a noun and the other meaning is a verb, in a sentence context. To illustrate, for written naming, the following sentence frames were presented on separate occasions, and Jeanette was asked to fill in the blank with the dictated word. Each frame was presented along with the corresponding spoken sentences:

> *Please sign the*——. 'Please sign the check. Write the word "check".'
> *Please*——*the time.* 'Please check the time. Write the word "check".'

Jeanette correctly wrote 98 per cent (49/50) of the words when used as nouns, but only 56 per cent (28/50) of the words (with the same spellings) when used as verbs. In contrast, HW correctly wrote more than 95 per cent of the words whether they were used as nouns or verbs. But in a comparable oral reading task (asked to read the underlined word in the same sentences, in which the target word was written in the blank), Jeanette's performance was flawless, whereas HW showed a word-class effect: 88 per cent correct for the noun forms vs. 46 per cent for the verb forms. EBA again showed the opposite word-class effect on a similar task: impaired verbal naming of homonyms in response to definitions of the noun form, but more accurate naming in response to definitions of the verb form (19 per cent vs. 75 per cent correct, respectively).

Implications of Jeanette's pattern of performance in writing for theories of lexical representation

The dissociation between nouns and verbs in a single output modality – writing in Jeanette's case, speaking in HW's case – along with the opposite dissociation in one output modality in EBA, provide compelling evidence that stored knowledge of the spellings of words (lexical orthographic representations) and stored knowledge of the pronunciations of words (lexical phonological representations) is organized in such a way that brain damage can affect one grammatical class of words more than another. The data from testing homonyms in particular suggest that the representation of a specific sequence of letter identities (for example, c–h–e–c–k) must be separately stored or processed for the noun form and the verb form, such that the information can be available for use as one form but not the other. This conclusion is consistent with previous reports of differentially impaired production of nouns and verbs as a result of brain damage (Baxter and Warrington, 1985; Miceli et al., 1984, 1988; Zingeser and Berndt, 1988). Along with a multitude of case studies of patients with naming and comprehension deficits in selective semantic categories (see Warrington and McCarthy, 1987; Damasio, 1990, for review), these cases provide ample evidence of a remarkably fine-grained organization of lexical knowledge in the brain.

Implications of Jeanette's pattern of performance in writing for improving her communication skills

Analysis of the cognitive mechanisms that underlie Jeanette's pattern of writing performance was useful not only in terms of its implications for understanding how lexical knowledge is represented in the brain, but also in terms of providing ideas to help her write more successfully. For example, documenting her ability to produce a word orally when she could not retrieve the spelling of the word provided impetus for teaching her to convert the phonological form of the word to the written form through phonology-to-orthography conversion (POC) mechanisms. Unfortunately, Jeanette was impaired in the use of POC mechanisms, as indicated by: (a) her very poor performance in spelling pseudowords plausibly; and (b) her phonologically implausible spellings of words when she could not access the stored spelling. However, the possibility that POC mechanisms could improve with training was indicated by a number of case reports of writing therapy for patients with similar writing difficulties (Carlomagno and Parlato, 1989; Hillis Trupe, 1986).

Hence, Jeanette was taught specific POC, or speech sound–letter translation, rules by relying on her intact access to both the spelling and the pronunciation of nouns. For example, teaching her that /b/ is associated with the letter b relied on her knowledge that /b/ is the initial phoneme of 'baby' and *b* is the initial letter of *baby*. In this way, when she could not retrieve the spelling of a verb that she wanted to write, she identified the initial sound and converted it to the initial letter of a noun with the same first sound. Her ability to retrieve a letter associated with a particular sound required use of the intervening 'key word' (the noun she could spell) only for a few trials. That is, she demonstrated rapid learning of the direct association between the sound and the letter. Furthermore, she rarely needed to use this individual sound-to-letter conversion approach for each sound in the word, since obtaining the first few letters of the word often 'cued' access to the complete spelling (the lexical orthographic representation of the word). In other words, her learned skill allowed her to convert the first sound of a successfully retrieved oral name to the initial letter(s), which in turn served to cue retrieval of the lexical orthographic representation. Thus, use of learned POC rules or strategies allowed her to use her more intact oral naming of verbs to self-cue written naming of verbs.

Auditory Comprehension and Short-term Memory

In contrast to her normal comprehension of single words, Jeanette's comprehension of spoken sentences was markedly impaired. For example, she scored 21/36 (moderate impairment) on the Modified Token Test (DeRenzi and Faglioni, 1978). Performance on a written version of this test, and on all reading comprehension tasks of the BDAE, was flawless. Hence, her impaired comprehension of spoken sentences cannot be attributed to a modality-independent deficit in processing the syntax or the meaning of the sentences, since she understood the very same sentences when they were written. Alternatively, her poor sentence comprehension might be due to impaired auditory short-term memory (STM), or storage of the string of words while it is being analysed by a syntactic processing mechanism (Caramazza et al., 1981; Saffran and Marin, 1975; McCarthy and Warrington, 1987). If Jeanette's errors were a consequence of reduced auditory STM, we would expect her to show other manifestations of reduced auditory STM, such as impaired sentence repetition, and reduced auditory word and digit span. As we have noted, her repetition was strikingly impaired; for example, on the BDAE she correctly repeated only 2/8 high-probability and 2/8 low-probability sentences. Auditory digit span and auditory word span were 3–4 (normal spans = 5–9). Consistent with impaired STM in the auditory modality only, Jeanette's visual spans for digits and words were normal (5–7).

Caramazza et al. (1981) have argued that a specific pattern of errors in sentence comprehension would be expected as a consequence of reduced auditory STM. If normal syntactic processing is assumed to require storing the sentence input and/or results of syntactic analyses, pathologically limited storage would give rise to a pattern of 'asyntactic' comprehension – understanding of the sentence based primarily on the lexical–semantic information and pragmatic constraints. Thus, the patient should misunderstand only those sentences in which semantic interpretation requires appreciation of the syntactic relationships among major lexical items. For instance, unless one is able to hold the sequence of words in the sentence and their relationship to functors, it should be difficult to differentiate the sentence, 'The boy was hit by the girl', from the sentence, 'The boy hit the girl'. In fact, it has been argued that the former type of sentence (passive reversible sentence) is more difficult to understand than the latter type (active reversible sentence), because in the absence of a stored representation of the precise sentence form (including word order and functors), both sentences would be understood as the active form (Bever, 1970). In contrast, both passive and active semantically irreversible sentences should be easier to understand than reversible sentences, because pragmatic constraints rule out alternative readings of the sentence. To illustrate, the sentence 'The apples were bought by the woman' could be understood simply on the basis of semantic processing of the major lexical items, 'apple', 'bought' and 'woman', irrespective of the order in which they are heard, since the alternative order (The apples bought the woman) is pragmatically impossible.

Other types of sentences that should be difficult to understand in the presence of an auditory STM deficit are those with relative clauses, not only because they are longer and contain more information to be processed, but also because their interpretation is not always possible on the basis of 'local analyses' of parts of the sentence. That is, in the presence of a reduced span, only a few words can be held in short-term storage, so syntactic analysis can operate over only a few (successive) words at a time. Consider the consequences for interpreting the sentence, 'The girl that was watched by the boy was eating an apple'. Local analyses of strings of 4–5 words at a time might result in 'the boy' being incorrectly assigned the grammatical role of subject of 'eating an apple'. Thus, these types of sentences should be particularly difficult to understand when only local analyses of the sentences are possible, due to a reduced STM store.

Experimental studies

To see if these predictions would be borne out in Jeanette's sentence comprehension, several tests were administered. Most of these tests were administered again nearly three years later (after a period of therapy, followed by two years without therapy).

Jeanette's scores on tests of auditory discrimination and auditory-verbal span are shown in table 23.2. Her word and digit span was 100 per cent correct for three items

Table 23.2   Accuracy on auditory discrimination and span

Auditory discrimination test (Wepman, 1973): score = 27/30 (WNL)

Rhyming word discrimination (from JHU Dyslexia Battery, presented auditorily) score = 40/40

Auditory sequential memory test (Wepman and Morency, 1975)
   Form I (digits): total score = 30/70 (43% correct)
   Form II (words): total score = 46/60 (77% correct)

	2 items (%)	3 items (%)	4 items (%)	5 items (%)
Auditory word recall (span)				
Immediate recall: verbal response				
phonologically dissimilar words	100	100	30	0
phonologically dissimilar words	100	0	0	
Immediate recall: pointing to words				
phonologically dissimilar words	100	100	30	0
Immediate recall: pointing to pictures				
phonologically dissimilar words	100	100	40	0
Auditory digit recall: verbal response				
Immediate recall	100	100	40	0
Delayed recall				
5-second filled delay	100	100	40	0
10-second filled delay	100	100	40	0
Visual digit recall; verbal response				
Immediate recall	100	100	100	100
Delayed recall				
5-second filled delay	100	100	100	100
10-second filled delay	100	100	100	100

and 30–40 per cent for four items, irrespective of the modality of output (excluding a speech output deficit as the basis for limitation) and irrespective of the type of stimulus (words or digits). Her digit span was also unchanged when she was asked to say the alphabet repeatedly for five seconds or for ten seconds before recalling the digits. In the digit span tasks she showed a primacy effect: recall was 100 per cent correct for the first digit, 90 per cent correct for the second and third digits, and 50 per cent correct for the fourth digit.

Jeanette's span was affected by the modality of input: substantially better for visual than for auditory input. Together, the results of span tasks demonstrate that Jeanette's visual short-term span is normal, whereas her auditory short-term span is consistently below the normal span of 5–9. This limitation is not due to more general problem in auditory-verbal discrimination or of spoken output.

We have noted that Jeanette's repetition of sentences of the BDAE was quite impaired, although single word repetition was flawless for lists that contained no morphologically

Table 23.3 Error rate in repetition of various sentence types in January 1988
(% of total responses in parentheses)

	N	Total errors	Errors that changed meaning
Embedded relative clause (e.g. The giraffe that has the bow is watching the monkey.)	64	9 (14.1)	6 (9.4)
Right-branching relative clause (e.g. The giraffe is watching the monkey that has the bow.)	64	13 (20.3)	8 (12.5)
Subject relative clause (e.g. The monkey that is watching the giraffe has the bow.)	64	28 (43.8)	17 (26.6)
Object relative clause (e.g. The monkey that the giraffe is watching has the bow.)	32	19 (59.4)	5 (46.9)

complex words. Sentence repetition was further assessed using sentences with relative clauses that were tested in sentence comprehension tasks (as described below). She made errors on all types of sentences, but she had more difficulty with sentences containing relative clauses that referred to a subject and object than with sentences containing embedded or right-branching clauses that referred to an attribute ($\chi^2 = 26.0$; $df = 1$; $p \ll 0.0001$; see table 23.3 for scores and examples of each sentence type). Some of her errors paraphrased the sentence adequately. For example, she repeated the sentence 'The bull that is chasing the man has the flower' as 'The bull has a flower, and he's running after the man'. Other errors changed the meaning of the sentence. Thus, 'The boy that the girl was touching has the hat' was repeated as 'The boy was touching the girl that has a hat'.

Auditory comprehension of sentences was evaluated by presenting a sentence verbally, and then presenting a picture that depicted either the meaning of the sentence or the meaning of a related sentence. The first set of 240 sentences were simple active or passive sentences. Half the foils were 'semantic foils' (which depicted a sentence in which the agent, object or action were replaced), and half the foils were 'syntactic foils' (which depicted a sentence with the same lexical items, but a different syntactic form). As shown in table 23.4, Jeanette had more trouble with semantically reversible sentences, and she rarely accepted a semantic foil. When these sentences were retested nearly three years later her primary difficulty concerned passive reversible sentences. But when the same sentences were presented in print along with the same pictures her performance was flawless.

The stimuli for the second set consisted of sentences with relative clauses and pictures that depicted the corresponding sentence, a subject–object reversal, or a shifted attribute. 'Filler sentences' consisted of simple sentences and sentences with semantic foils, on which Jeanette consistently answered correctly. As shown in table 23.5, she had most difficulty understanding sentences with object relative clauses.[3] To illustrate, she accepted a picture of a bull (with a flower) chasing a man as corresponding to the sentence, 'The bull that the man is chasing has the flower' (an example of subject–object reversal).

Table 23.4 Simple sentence/picture verification

	N	*Jan. 1988*	*Dec. 1990*
		Total errors (%)	
Auditory stimuli			
Nonreversible active	60	1 (2)	0
(e.g. The man is painting the wall.)			
Nonreversible passive	60	4 (7)	0
(e.g. The wall is painted by the man.)			
Reversible active	60	9 (15)	1 (2)
(e.g. The boy is kissing the girl.)			
Reversible passive	60	8 (13)	7 (12)
(e.g. The girl is kissed by the boy.)			
Total	240	22 (9)	8 (3)
Error types			
Rejection of correct picture	120	10 (8)	3 (3)
Verification of semantic foil	90	2 (2)	0
Verification of syntactic foil	30	8 (27)	5 (17)
Printed stimuli			
Total	240	0	DNT

Note: DNT = Did not test.

Table 23.5 Auditory sentence/picture verification

	N	*Jan. 1988*	*Dec. 1990*
		Total errors (%)	
Embedded relative clause	64	6 (9)	2 (3)
Right-branching relative clause	64	4 (6)	14 (22)
Subject relative clause	64	24 (38)	18 (24)
Object relative clause	32	14 (44)	18 (56)
Total	224	48 (21)	52 (23)
Error types			
Rejection of correct picture	120	26 (22)	25 (21)
Verification of foil depicting			
subject/object reversal	52	9 (17)	12 (23)
Verification of foil depicting			
shifted attribute	52	13 (25)	15 (29)

Table 23.6   Reading comprehension: errors in sentence–picture verification
(% of total responses in parentheses)

Set 1

Date	Dec. 1987
Condition	(No delay between sentence and picture presentation, unlimited time for sentence presentation)

Nonreversible active	0
Nonreversible passive	0
Reversible active	0
Reversible passive	0
Total	0

Set 2

Date	Jan. 1988	Dec. 1990	Oct. 1990
Condition	(No delay, unlimited time)	(No delay, limited time)	(With delay, limited time)
Embedded relative clause	0 (0)	0 (0)	2 (3)
Right-branching relative clause	1 (2)	0 (0)	0 (0)
Subject relative clause	0 (0)	3 (5)	2 (3)
Object relative clause	1 (3)	5 (16)	6 (19)
Total	2 (1)	8 (4)	10 (4)

Clearly, these are difficult sentences to understand. Normal subjects make about 5 per cent errors on these sentences with subject and object relative clauses, and 1–2 per cent errors on the other sentences (Romani, unpublished data). Nevertheless, Jeanette's comprehension of these sentences when presented auditorily is significantly poorer than normal. In contrast, her comprehension of the very same sentences presented in print was normal (in 1988). On this administration, the sentences were presented for an unlimited time, along with the same pictures as in the auditory task. Hence, we could not be sure whether the striking difference in her performance on the auditory version and the printed version was due to the difference in modality (auditory vs. visual), or the increased time allowed for processing the written sentence. When she was retested in 1990 (when her performance on other tasks was somewhat better than in 1988), we made the two versions more comparable. The auditory version was presented in the same way as in 1988. However, for the printed version, the sentences were presented only for approximately the same time as they were in the auditory version (as the examiner subvocalized the sentence), and the picture was presented only after completion of the sentence presentation (as in the auditory version). As shown in table 23.6, her reading comprehension was no longer normal, but still remarkably better than her understanding of the same sentence presented auditorilly (4 per cent errors vs. 23 per cent errors; $\chi^2 = 33.0$, $df = 1$, $p \ll 0.0001$). To determine whether the difference between her 1988 and 1990 performance was due to the shorter duration of the sentence presentation or due to the delay between the presentation of the sentence and presentation of the picture, the entire task was repeated, but the picture was now presented along with the sentence. (And the sentence was again presented only while it was subvocalized by the examiner.) In fact, it made no difference whether the picture was presented along with the sentence or only after it; it seems that the duration of the sentence presentation made more of a difference (3 per cent errors with no time constraints vs. 19 per cent errors with time constraints, on the sentences with object relative clauses; $\chi^2 = 4.0$, $df = 1$, $p \ll 0.05$).

In summary, Jeanette has trouble understanding spoken sentences that substantially exceed her verbal span of 3–4 words, at least when a correct response cannot be made on the basis of lexical information and pragmatic constraints. She has particular difficulty if a correct response cannot be made on the basis of combined local analyses of strings of contiguous words. However, she can understand all types of sentences normally if they are presented visually for an unlimited time. Furthermore, visual presentation, even for a limited time, allows her to understand most types of sentences.

Jeanette's problem in understanding sentences cannot be accounted for by an impairment in lexical semantics (or accessing lexical semantics in the auditory modality), because her single word comprehension is excellent; it also cannot be accounted for a deficit in modality-independent syntactic processing, since she understood the printed sentences. However, her problem can be accounted for by her well-documented auditory STM deficit (in span and repetition tasks), on the assumption that at least certain types of syntactic processing, such as assigning attributes to the correct subject or object in the sentence, require short-term storage of the sequence of morphemes. This need for short-term storage in sentence processing seems to have been alleviated by presenting the sentence in print for an unlimited time for her to analyse.

Implications of Jeanette's pattern of performance for models of language processing

We have argued that Jeanette's errors in sentence comprehension tasks are a consequence of her auditory STM deficit. The precise nature of the role of auditory STM in sentence processing has received considerable attention, and is beyond the scope of this chapter (see Vallar and Shallice, 1990, for review). However, a few points can be made. Jeanette's accuracy in understanding at least simple spoken sentences in active voice even when the sentence length exceeds her span, suggests that the phonological sequence she is able to store is adequate for syntactic processing in these cases, but may be insufficient when the sentence cannot be understood on the basis of local analyses of component strings of lexical items (Caramazza et al., 1981), or when the initial attempt to process the sentence sequentially fails so that comprehension requires 'retracking' the sentence (see McCarthy and Warrington, 1987, for discussion).

Although a crucial role for STM in auditory comprehension of sentences has been previously proposed on the basis of similar patterns of performance on auditory tasks (see, for example, Caramazza et al., 1981; Saffran and Marin, 1975; but see Butterworth et al., 1986, for an alternative view), the sparing of reading comprehension in the face of impaired STM has not been previously documented. In fact, it is often assumed that comprehension of printed sentences, just as comprehension of spoken sentences, requires auditory-verbal STM (Caramazza et al., 1981). But if we are correct that Jeanette's pattern of performance is a consequence of her impaired auditory STM, then we must propose that processing some types of sentences (for example, simple passive reversible sentences and sentences with embedded attribute clauses) is highly dependent on normal auditory STM only when the sentence is spoken, and not when it is printed. This proposal is not incompatible with the sorts of hypotheses we have cited about the role of STM in sentence comprehension. If STM is only required when local analyses of component word strings of the sentence fail to yield a correct interpretation, or when initial sequential processing of the sentence fails so that it must be retracked, then presentation of the printed string for unlimited time might compensate for a limited auditory STM, either by allowing the reader to extend the individual analyses of strings to include words that are more separated in the sentence (for example, by ignoring the intervening clause), or by allowing the reader to backtrack in the printed stimulus. The fact that Jeanette's performance was somewhat less accurate when the printed sentences were presented for limited durations suggests that additional time or additional attempts may have been needed to determine words to include in local analyses or to backtrack to previous parts of the sentences with object relative clauses.

Consistent with the hypothesis that the printed sentence (which remains available for analysis) can compensate for impaired storage of the spoken sentence in this way, Jeanette was sometimes observed physically to cover a clause in the middle of a printed sentence when she was given unlimited time. For example, she might have covered *that was watched by the boy* in attempts to understand *The girl that was watched by the boy was eating an apple*. On this view, Jeanette's relatively intact printed sentence comprehension does not rule out a role of auditory-verbal STM in normal reading, but suggests that at least some readers (like Jeanette, who was well-educated, highly motivated and good at problem-solving) can compensate for an impairment in STM while reading, but not while listening, by relying on the persisting availability of the printed sentence.

Implications of Jeanette's pattern of performance for improving her communication skills

We have described how documenting an impairment in STM memory as a plausible basis for her sentence comprehension difficulty constrains models of sentence processing. But how did all this testing help Jeanette? To begin with, the realization that her 'confusion' that developed when people cited unfamiliar titles of books or sequences of numbers such as book accession numbers or telephone numbers was due to a highly circumscribed deficit in auditory STM assuaged her feelings of 'stupidity', and provided the impetus for employing specific strategies to assure more successful interactions. For instance, she began to ask people to write down titles, authors, accession numbers, and so on, for her to look up. When that was not possible, for example, in telephone calls, Jeanette asked the person to give her the title or sequence of numbers one item at a time, and to pause as she wrote down each word or digit. Of course, these strategies required assertiveness on Jeanette's part and patience on the part of the speaker. When she could not convince callers to speak sufficiently slowly, she had to ask them to call back when another librarian was available.

What about therapy to improve her impairment? Although it is frequently assumed that STM is unremediable (O'Connor and Cermak, 1987), some authors have described successful improvement in word or digit span with specific strategies designed to improve immediate recall of sequences (see, for example, Peach, 1987). Whether the documented improvement is a result of increased STM *per se*, or a result of more general benefits of therapy like increased attention or motivation has often been difficult to determine. Nevertheless, single-subject multiple-baseline studies have sometimes shown a functional relationship between a specific intervention and improvement in digit span and other STM memory tasks, while other aspects of language or cognitive function have remained stable (until these other aspects were addressed via different strategies).

In view of these optimistic reports of 'STM therapy' and Jeanette's strong motivation to improve, she was provided with drills of the type that had been described in the literature. These tasks included repeating strings of four words; pointing to series of four words; and pointing to series of four pictures named. After three baseline sessions (in which no feedback was provided), her errors on these tasks were followed by a sequence of prompts or cues until the correct response was elicited.

Jeanette improved significantly in all of the practice drills. (However, it is not apparent that the specific cues or prompts made any difference, since she began to improve in some tasks during 'baseline' sessions; see Hillis, 1989, for details). She also improved significantly in auditory comprehension of all types of sentences, except those with object relative clauses. She showed some gains in scores on standardized tests, such the Modified Token Test (from 21/36 to 24/36), but her scores remained below normal levels, and were not statistically significant. The retesting we have reported that took place more than two years later showed that she maintained some improvement in understanding passive, reversible sentence; but her performance on sentences with relative clauses was at her pretreatment levels.

Nevertheless, Jeanette was not discouraged; her gains on tests that were associated with the practice drills were less important to her than her improved understanding of her comprehension difficulties and her use of strategies to compensate for her limited span. She also reported that the practice drills had helped her learn to 'concentrate' and to use visual imagery to retain a sequence of words. By the time of retesting Jeanette had moved to another library, where she had greater responsibilities, and she felt more confident in her job performance.

Conclusions

To sum up 'story', Jeanette is an intelligent (and good-humoured!) lady who had the misfortune to incur brain damage at a relatively young age. She has had the determination and energy needed to alleviate and/or compensate for her persisting deficits in language processing sufficiently to resume her previous roles not only as a librarian but also as a homemaker and mother of two teenage boys. It has been our good fortune that she has also elected to participate in our extensive studies in several domains of language. Her patterns of performance in these studies have provided evidence for specific claims about the organization of lexical knowledge in the brain, about the representation of morphologically complex words (as constituent morphemes) in spoken output mechanisms, and about the role of auditory STM in sentence comprehension.

Notes

1   Written stimuli or responses are printed in italics; spoken stimuli or responses are given in quotes. The word preceding an arrow is the stimulus; the word following an arrow is the response.
2   Similar errors in oral and written spelling could have arisen in the short-term storage of the activated orthographic lexical representation while output processes for oral or written spelling are implemented (i.e., at the level of a graphemic buffer). But impairment at this level was ruled out because Jeanette made no errors in delayed copy transcription – a task that relies on such short-term storage, and because semantically related word substitutions could not arise at this level.
3   The difference between sentences with subject relative clauses and sentences with object relative clauses was significant only on the later administration ($\chi^2 = 7.2$, $df = 1$, $p < 0.01$). On the earlier date, both sentences with subject relative clauses and those with object relative clauses were understood significantly less often than either of the other types ($\chi^2 = 14.1$, $df = 1$, $p < 0.001$ for the *smallest* difference).

Appendix A: Examples of Jeanette's Spontaneous Speech, Writing and Repetition (June 1986)

Verbal description of the 'cookie theft' picture

Mother is washing dishes, and the sink is overflowed onto the floor. The little boy is on the stool, trying to get cookies from the cookie jar, and give it to his sister. While he's doing this, the stool is going to fall right down onto the floor, with the little boy with him.

Written description of the 'cookie theft' picture

Mother and the children in the kitchen. The boy is standing on the stool. The stool———. The sink is overflows. Mother looks mad. The boy____the cookie to his sister.

She read her description as follows:

Mother and the children *are* in the kitchen. The boy is standing on the stool. The stool *is falling*. The sink is overflowing. Mother looks mad. The boy *is handing* the cookie to his sister.

Repetition of sentences from the BDAE

Stimulus	*Response*
You know how.	Do you know.

Down to earth.	Down . . . I know it's earth.
I got home from work.	I got home last night.
The spy fled to Greece.	Something to Greece.
Pry the tin lid off.	Pry it.
Go ahead and do it if possible.	I know you can.
The Chinese fan had a rare emerald.	The Chinese emerald had a flaw.
Near the table in the dining room.	On the table near the door.
The barn swallow captured a plump worm.	The barn swallow swallowed a fat worm.
The lawyer's closing argument convinced him.	The lawyer closed the argument.
I stopped at the front door and rang the bell.	I can't remember . . . at the front door and ringed.
The phantom soared across the foggy heath.	The phantom soared over the valley in the fog.

Appendix B: Excerpts from Jeanette's Journal (with her verbal corrections in parentheses)

10 February 1987
Milt and I went to the bank. We____the stock. We____at the bank for an hour. The red tape was unbeiefable. (We *sold* the stock. We *waited* at the bank . . .)

12 February 1987
I will/would____the night. Greg worked until 7:30 and Milt went to a meeting with unmpire. *I*____leftovers in the refrigerators. (I *slept through* the night . . . I *ate* leftovers . . .)

26 March 1987
Andy and I went to the mall. For a birthday gift Andy wants a softball bat. We____at Champs. (. . . We *ate* at Champs.)

30 March 1987
Winter will____to Baltimore this week. Andy____to Virginia Tech for eleven weeks. (Winter will *return* to Baltimore this week. Andy *went* to Virginia Tech for eleven weeks.)

21 April 1987
It is too hot at the library. The county government has the library do air conditioners until May 1. The temperature on the third floor was 84 at 5 o'clock. It will____overnight. (The county government has the library *keep the* air conditioners *off* until May 1 . . . It will *cool down* overnight.)

13 June 1987
There is cooler at the library. The repairmen at on Thursday. Ronnie said the repairmen____on and down the stairs and said, 'The air conditioner is on the fritz. They were

here last month. (*It isn't* cooler at the library. The repairmen *came* on Thursday. Ronnie said the repairmen *just went up* and down the stairs and said, 'The air conditioner is *broken. . . .*)

17 June 1987
The track at the high school is closed. County government has the budget of the years have been spent. Many people called Rassmussen did office to should the money. Taxpayers are angry. (. . . *The* County government *said* the budget *for* the years *has* been spent. Many people called Rassmussen's office to *request* the money.) [She did not correct 'years' (for year)].

18 July 1987
Because paper napkins in vogue, families spent cloth napkins with a napkins ring for everybody. Some napkins ring were engraved with a name or initials. The napkins could used several times because washings.
(*Before* paper napkins *were* in vogue, families *bought* cloth napkins with a napkins ring for everybody. Some napkins ring*s* were engraved with a name or initials. The napkins could *be* used several times *between* washings.) [She did not correct 'napkins rings' (for napkins rings).]

20 July 1987
The Model T Ford convened is in Easton, MD last weeks. Many owners used a trailer to bring their cars. The automobiles were built from 1908 to 1927. The cars made a sound like a tin can. (The Model T Ford *convention was* in Easton, MD last *week . . .*)

29 July 1988
The 'War of the Roses' is over in Annapolis. The Historic District Commission in Annapolis agreed that Ms. Lavies had a plastic rose trellis instead of a wood trellis. The legal battle between the commission and Ms. Lavies laid three years.
(. . . Annapolis agreed that Ms. Lavies *can have* a plastic rose trellis instead of a wood trellis. The legal battle between the commission and Ms. Lavies *lasted* three years.)

31 July 1987
The National Weather Service reported that the 31 was the 22nd day of July that the temperature hit 90 degree or higher. The average high temperature of 92.4 degree is also high temperature of July on record.
(The National Weather Service reported that the 31*st* was the 22nd day of July that the temperature hit 90 degrees or higher. The average high temperature of 92.4 degrees is also the higher temperature of July on record.) [She did not correct 'higher' (for highest)].

1 December 1987
Charles Osbourne lived with his hiccups for 65 years. His hiccups are muffled now only by pauses in speech. He hiccups are louder when he's asleep. His diets consists of liquids. Osbourne said he contracted the hiccups while butching the hog. He is 93 Years old.

(. . . *His* hiccups are louder when he's asleep . . .). [She did not correct 'diet*s* consists' or 'butching' (for butchering).]

13 January 1988
In Florida, three resident will not get $5000 in the state lottery. Any person who owes money to pay child support will not receive winnings. One citizen lives in Pompano Beach and two lives in Hollywood. One person owes $3,000, another owes $ 2,000, and another owes $150, according to state records. [She did not correct 'three resident' or 'two lives in'.]

15 March 1988
A girl in Valencia, California was ordered by an employee of McDonald's before a meal was finished. The restaurant has a curfew for youngsters under 16. Tracey Tellez is 13. Tracey left and wait for her mother in the parking lot. Tracey is suing McDonald's.
(A girl in Valencia, California was ordered *to leave* by an employee of McDonald's before *her* meal was finished . . .) [She did not correct 'She left and wait for'.]

15 April 1988
Chewing gum came from Mexico. Santa Anna, the Mexican General, lived on Staten Island, New York. The general was exiled from his native land. His interpreteer and secretary was an american, James Adams. Santa Anna chewed the tropical fruit called, 'chicle'. The general left in May, 1866, and Adams persuaded him to leave the chicle behind. Adams began experimented with the chicle including sweeting agents. The Adams chewing gum company was started.
[She did not correct 'began experimented' or 'sweeting agents'.]

Acknowledgements

The research reported in this chapter was supported by NIH grants RIO 19330, DC00366, and NS22201 to the Johns Hopkins University. The authors are grateful to Jeanette for her cheerful hard work throughout these studies and for allowing us to include excerpts from her journals, as well as research data, in this chapter. We are also grateful to Brenda Rapp for helpful comments on an earlier draft.

Further Reading

Damasio, A. and Damasio, H. (1992) 'Brain and language', *Scientific American*, **267**: 88–109.
Kosslyn, S. and Koenig, O. (1992) *Wet Mind* (New York: The Free Press).
McCarthy, R.A. and Warrington, E.K. (1990) *Cognitive Neuropsychology: A Clinical Introduction* (San Diego, Cal.: Academic Press).

References

Baxter, D.M. and Warrington, E.K. (1985) 'Category-specific phonological dysgraphia', *Neuropsychologia*, **23**: 653–66.

Berndt, R.S. (1988) 'Category-specific deficits in aphasia', *Aphasiology*, 2: 337–40.

Bever, T.G. (1970) 'The cognitive basis for linguistic structures', in J.R. Hayes (ed.), *Cognition and the Development of Language* (New York: John Wiley), pp. 279–352.

Butterworth, B., Campbell, R. and Howard, D. (1986) 'The uses of short-term memory: a case study', *Quarterly Journal of Experimental Psychology*, 38A: 705–38.

Caramazza, A. and Hillis, A.E. (1991) 'Lexical organization of nouns and verbs in the brain', *Nature*, 349: 788–90.

Caramazza, A., Basili, A.G., Koller, J.J. and Berndt, R.S. (1981) 'An investigation of repetition and language processing in a case of conduction aphasia', *Brain and Language*, 14: 235–71.

Carlomagno, S. and Parlato, V. (1989) 'Writing rehabilitation in brain-damaged aphasic patients: a cognitive approach', in X. Seron and G. Deloche (eds), *Cognitive Approaches in Neuropsychological Rehabilitation* (Hillsdale, N.J. Lawrence Erlbaum Associates), pp. 175–209.

Damasio, A.R. (1990) 'Category-related recognition defects as a clue to the neural substrates of knowledge', *Trends in Neuroscience*, 13: 95–8.

De Renzi, E. and Faglioni, P. (1978) 'Normative data and screening power of a shortened version of the Token Test', *Cortex*, 14: 41–9.

Dunn, L.M. and Dunn, L.M. (1981) *Peabody Picture Vocabulary Test-Revised*. Circle Pines, MN: American Guidance Service.

Goodglass, H. and Kaplan, E. (1972) *The Boston Diagnostic Aphasia Examination* (Philadelphia, Penn.: Lea and Febiger).

Goodglass, H., Kaplan, E. and Weintraub, S. (1983) *The Revised Boston Naming Test* (Philadelphia, Penn.: Lea & Febiger).

Goodman, R.A. and Caramazza, A. (1986). *The Johns Hopkins Dysgraphia Battery* (Baltimore, MD: Johns Hopkins University).

Hillis Trupe, A.E. (1986) 'Effectiveness of retraining phoneme to grapheme conversion', in R.H. Brookshire (ed.), *Clinical Aphasiology, 1986* (Minneapolis, Minn.: BRK Publishers), pp. 163–71.

Hillis, A.E. (1989) 'The effects of a 'short-term memory treatment approach' on language deficits associated with impaired short-term memory', paper presented at Clinical Aphasiology Conference, Lake Tahoe N.V., June 1989.

Hillis, A.E. and Caramazza, A. (1994) 'Theories of lexical processing and theories of rehabilitation', in G. Humphreys and M.J. Riddoch (eds), *Cognitive Neuropsychology and Cognitive Rehabilitation* (Hove, Sussex: Lawrence Elbaum Associates).

Hillis, A.E. and Caramazza, A. (in press) 'The representation of grammatical categories of words in the brain', *Journal of Cognitive Neuroscience*.

McCarthy, R.A. and Warrington, E.K. (1987) 'Understanding: a function of short-term memory?', *Brain*, 110: 1565–8.

Miceli, G., Silveri, M.C., Villa, G. and Caramazza, A. (1984) 'On the basis of agrammatics' difficulty in producing main verbs', *Cortex*, 20: 217–20.

Miceli, G., Silveri, M.C., Nocentini, U. and Caramazza, A. (1988) 'Patterns of dissociation in comprehension and production of nouns and verbs', *Aphasiology*, 2: 351–8.

O'Connor, M. and Cermak, L.S. (1987) 'Rehabilitation of organic memory disorders', in M. Meier, A. Benton and L. Diller (eds), *Neuropsychological Rehabilitation* (New York: Guilford Press), pp. 260–79.

Peach, R. (1987) 'A short-term memory treatment approach to the repetition deficit in conduction aphasia', I.R. Brookshire (ed.), *Clinical Aphasiology*, vol. 17 (Minneapolis, Minn.: BRK Publishers), pp. 35–45.

Saffran, E.M. and Marin, O.S.M. (1975) 'Immediate memory for word lists and sentences in a patient with a deficient auditory short-term memory', *Brain and Language*, 2: 420–33.

Shallice, T. (1988) *From Neuropsychology to Mental Structure* (Cambridge: Cambridge University Press).

Vallar, G. and Shallice, T. (1990) *Neuropsychological Impairments of Short-term Memory* (Cambridge: Cambridge University Press).

Warrington, E.K. and McCarthy, R.A. (1987) 'Categories of knowledge: further fractionations and an attempted explanation', *Brain*, **110**: 1273–96.

Wechsler, D. (1972) *The Wechsler Memory Scale* (New York Psychological Corporation).

Wepman, J.M. (1973) *Auditory Discrimination Test* (Palm Springs, Cal.; Language Research Associates).

Wepman, J.M. and Morency, A. (1975) *Auditory Sequential Memory Test* (Palm Springs, Cal.: Language Research Associates).

Zingeser, L.B. and Berndt, R.S. (1988) 'Grammatical class and context effects in a case of pure anomia: implications for models of language production', *Cognitive Neuropsychology*, **5**: 473–516.

24 How Names Are Special: Neuropsychological Evidence for Dissociable Impairment and Sparing of Proper Name Knowledge in Production

Carlo Semenza

The use of proper names is a necessary part of social life despite variations due to different contexts and cultures. However, proper names seem to be more elusive than other names and temporary failures to retrieve them occur more often than we want. Indeed these failures, besides affecting the success of communication (it may be unclear who is being addressed or spoken of), may cause confusion, embarrassment or even offence. Attempts to circumvent these problems require painstaking work or result in ambiguous identification. Elderly people are especially prone to retrieval failures for proper names as a consequence of age-related changes in memory ability, thus adding a nontrivial difficulty to their social adjustment. Quite aside from social concerns, the function of proper names has been fascinating philosophers for over a hundred years, and a related interest in the same issues lies in modern linguistics. There seems to be a case, therefore, for wanting to know more about the processing of proper names within the cognitive system and, ultimately, in the brain.

Only recently, however, have proper names become of interest to psychologists, and some remarkable findings in brain-damaged patients have put neuropsychologists in the front line of this kind of research. Some of the most important cases will be reported in this chapter, with equal concern for clinical and theoretical aspects.

The Patients

The patients that I shall describe in this chapter have been observed and studied by me in collaboration with my colleagues Marina Zettin and Teresa Sgaramella. The first two patients, PC and LS, were selectively anomic for proper names and were the first patients to exibit this disturbance ever described (Semenza and Zettin, 1988, 1989). A third patient had the mirror problem: under certain circumstances he could only retrieve proper names, while he failed with all other words, producing in their place an incomprehensible sequence of phonemes (Semenza and Sgaramella, 1993).

I shall mention finally a recently observed patient who had problems both with proper names and with faces; this will tell us a few important things about how information about personal identity is stored in memory.

Anomias for Proper Names

Clinical histories

When PC was introduced to Dr Marina Zettin, he was referred to as 'a typical case of *nominal aphasia*'. This term is commonly used among neuropsychologists to indicate a well-known type of aphasia whereby, despite good articulation and intact syntactic abilities, a patient has major difficulty in retrieving certain types of words, especially substantives (nouns). It took Marina no time to understand that she was facing a much more peculiar and rare case. Two years previously, PC had suffered a stroke, resulting in permanent damage in the left parieto-occipital area (as documented by a computed tomography (CT) scan). For a few months he had been severely aphasic, showing the pattern of 'jargonaphasia', a condition where the patient produces a continuous flow of meaningless utterances, full of phonemic as well as semantic errors, accompanied in general (including PC) by poor auditory comprehension. But when Marina first met him he no longer seemed aphasic and only the most sensitive tests could detect some mild signs of language disability. Even these had disappeared six months later, when we tested him more thoroughly. He never showed motor or sensory deficits except for a right hemianopia, a deficit compatible with the occipital lesion. Any neurologist or speech therapist (and indeed Marina and myself) would consider this outcome a surprisingly favourable one: most patients of this sort never fully recover and are doomed to communication problems all their lives. PC, a 62-year-old businessman with university education, who had been active in politics and who for a long time had held an executive position in a large state-owned company, was however understandably unaware of his relative luck compared to other cases, and he was naturally upset with the only disturbance still persisting: a complete inability to retrieve the names of persons and places. Unlike the nominal aphasia, with which he had been first diagnosed, this disturbance did not affect common names. As Marina Zettin immediately saw, this condition was not known to neuropsychologists. Marina contacted me in Padua; I went to Trieste, and we started to study the patient.

We met LS a few years later. Again it was Marina Zettin who spotted the case, this time in Turin, where she had just started working at the Clinica Maria Ausiliatrice. LS, then 41 and with eight years of education, went there to be rehabilitated after he had suffered a brain injury after a riding accident. Three months after the trauma he was totally free of neurological and cognitive symptoms but, as with PC, he was absolutely unable to produce proper names. He did not have a social life as active as PC's, but he was quite disturbed by this inability and by some other subtle, previously unobserved difficulties that emerged when he went back to the hardware store where he worked. His lesion was localized in the fronto-temporal area, as documented by both an immediate CT scan and by an nuclear magnetic resonance (NMR) scan performed a year later. It is clear that this lesion is very different from that affecting PC; we shall comment later on this curious fact.

Neuropsychological findings

At the time we conducted our study, both PC and LS appeared to be free of neuro-psychological symptoms apart from their anomia for proper names. They complained of nothing else. No conventional neuropsychological battery nor a careful observation of their behaviour in everyday life showed any disturbance. In particular, they scored perfectly or well within normal limits in tests measuring language abilities (the Milano Aphasia Battery and an Italian version of the Boston Diagnostic Aphasia Examination), visual recognition (including faces), spatial orientation and imagery, short- and long-term memory, and calculation (although a moderate acalculia had persisted in both cases several months after the reacquisition of all other abilities).

We shall see, however, that LS had a very special complaint once he went back to work. We shall also see that he had some subtle deficits of which he was unaware that could not be demonstrated with routine neuropsychological testing and that for this reason we had failed to show in PC. We shall however postpone the description of associated deficits to later in the chapter and give here only a full account of the patient's selective anomia. Before this description we just want to make clear that the deficit affected only the production side (oral and written word retrieval, with equal severity), because the patients' auditory and written comprehension of proper names were both intact.

Naming must be tested in at least three ways: confrontation naming, naming from definition, and naming by category, usually allowing one minute to produce as many items as possible (fluency of naming).

Confrontation naming with real objects (50 items) and pictures (100 items), some of which were uncommon, did not present a problem for either PC, who scored perfectly, or for LS, who made only two errors on pictures of very difficult items. We even specifically tested the patients' ability to name items from categories such as vegetables, fruits, body parts, colours and letters, which can sometimes be compromised selectively (see, for example, Hart et al., 1985). A minimum of ten items for each category was administered: neither patient made a single mistake. Finally, they did not fail to name items from other categories which we thought might be (semantically, if not visually) confusable, such as 'pasta types' (a very Italian test indeed).

However, when we started testing proper names the performance of both patients changed dramatically. With real people, PC could name his wife and son (who both had relatively uncommon names), while LS, who had a larger family, correctly named a few relatives. Apart from this, they could not retrieve any other names, including, much to their embarrassment, those of other relatives and of very old friends. With pictures of famous people, PC scored 0/20 and LS 2/25. In all cases both patients provided a fair amount of information about people whose names they failed to retrieve. These descriptions included details unique to each specific individual. This was not a failure in memory concerning information about the person, only access to the phonological form of the name. No difficulty was observed in matching spoken or written names with the pictures in a multiple-choice test, again indicating that both patients had good recognition of identity through pictures.

The ability to retrieve geographical names on confrontation was tested using a blank atlas and pictures of the sites of well known cities. PC could not produce a single name correctly from 15 map sites for cities, nor he could name rivers (eight items), countries (ten items) or mountains (eight items). He was, however, able to match the pictures of city sites correctly with the corresponding location on the map and produced a vast amount of information on nearly all the rivers, countries and mountains. When given the name of each of these geographical sites as a label, he never failed to locate it correctly on the map. LS was slightly better, but by no means unimpaired. He could name only 6/15 pictures and 4/5 map sites of cities but could match them all correctly in pairs. He correctly named 3/8 countries and 2/8 mountains. For all items he demonstrated perfect recognition by providing full information and by correctly matching spoken or written names.

An important observation is that here and in the following tasks the patients' only failures were omissions ('don't know' responses).

In naming to definition (for example, 'What is a means of transportation with two wheels?') both patients were very good, provided proper names were not the target. Stimuli included various categories of nouns (including animate beings, inanimate objects and abstract nouns), adjectives, verbs and numbers. PC was perfect (103/104) and LS scored 75/80. By contrast, their performance with proper names was extremely poor. PC named again only his wife and his son out of eight relatives and friends and none out of 15 famous persons, although it was demonstrated in various ways that he knew who was being described. The same happened for cities (0/15), mountains (0/15) and countries (0/10). He could point correctly to all geographical locations on the blank atlas. LS scored 5/8 for relatives, 2/15 for famous persons, 3/5 for cities, 1/5 for mountains and 3/5 for countries. He also had no problem in pointing correctly to geographical locations on the blank atlas and showed clear knowledge about the people described in the definitions.

Phonemic cueing (consisting of the first phoneme of the name) alone never improved the patients' performance in generating proper names either on confrontation or definition. Semantic cueing was more effective, but only in the particular case in which the proper name also had a real meaning. For instance, Colombo (Columbus) in Italian means 'pigeon'. Both PC and LS seemed to be helped if the description included a cue to the meaning of the name ('Tell me who discovered America. He had the name of a bird'.) PC answered 4/15 correctly and, when phonemic cueing was also provided, he was successful in 8 out of 15 cases. LS performed similarly, being correct in 4/15 cases and improving to 9/15 with phonemic cueing.

Naming by category in one minute was also tested; table 24.1 reports the performance of both patients in several categories. The performance with proper names, at least when specific categories were required (as opposed to the category 'any name'), was much lower than common names and certainly significantly lower than that of normal subjects matched for age and education. Furthermore, additional time did not improve their

Table 24.1 PC's and LS's performance in naming by category in one minute

	PC	LS
Relatives	5	n.t.
Musicians	n.t.	1
Sportsmen	n.t.	2
Actors	n.t.	2
Politicians	n.t.	2
Any person's names	n.t.	12
Cities	5	n.t.
Rivers	1	n.t.
Vegetables	20	11
Fruits	25	12
Birds	6	9
Clothes	12	13
Footwear	10	6
Body parts	15	16
Means of transportation	7	15
Occupations	20	13
Sports	15	12
Carpenter's tools	n.t.	7
Types of trains	6	n.t.
Types of pasta	n.t.	10
Types of pots	6	n.t.
Common names beginning with F	13	13
Common names beginning with M	13	9
Common names beginning with S	n.t.	10

Note: n.t. = not tested.

performance with proper name categories, whereas for all other categories they continued to give new correct items. They did not commit class inclusion errors.

As far as immediate memory for names is concerned, both patients were able to repeat immediately any proper name and to retrieve it if allowed to rehearse silently without interference. Any interference procedure (such as counting backwards), however, caused their performance to drop to zero in 10–15 seconds. In this task PC forgot my name ten times in a row. He looked so frustrated that I interrupted the test before he could retrieve my name. The same happened to LS with Marina (eventually he learned her Christian name after realizing that 'marina' was also a common name, meaning navy or seaside; however, he never managed to remember Zettin).

Are Proper Names Independently Processed?

The dissociation exhibited by PC and LS, anomia for proper names and sparing of common names, is a simple one. Simple dissociations between two tasks are assumed to reflect either the fact that one task is more difficult than the other (so that, when cognitive sources decrease, one task is disturbed and the other is not) or an at least relative, genuine independence in the processing necessary for the two tasks. Without the demonstration of the opposite dissociation (in our case sparing of proper names and deficit of common ones) it is impossible to decide in favour of the second alternative and it is usually wise to stick to the more conservative conclusion that one task is more difficult than the other. In the case of proper names, their relative difficulty with respect to common ones had been shown in the past by several investigations via questionnaires and experimental tasks (see, for instance, Reason and Lucas, 1984; Young et al., 1985; Cohen and Faulkner, 1986; McWeeny et al., 1987). However, PC and LS suggest that simple difficulty of name, compared with word, recall might not underlie their problem. Their anomia did not seem to follow a gradient of difficulty; rather it occurred, unlike in most neuropsychological cases, in an almost all-or-none fashion. As we have seen, the patients could retrieve virtually 100 per cent of common names, while their performance with proper names was close to zero. Indeed, no account based on a frequency or a difficulty factor could convincingly explain, for example, why PC could retrieve on definition the word 'exegesis', while he could not come up with his best friend's name. The hypothesis according to which proper names might enjoy independent processing in the cognitive (and in the nervous) system was therefore still to be kept very much alive. (As we shall see there were also other more theoretical reasons to keep thinking of it as a serious possibility.) It should also be noted here that independence of processing need not contradict a theory based on differential difficulty: proper names might indeed be more hard to retrieve overall, just because the independent process they require is more demanding (we shall also consider later why this may have its advantages). However, strong disconfirmation of the relative difficulty hypothesis would be provided by a double dissociation.

A patient featuring selective *sparing* of proper names was eventually found. His fascinating case, described in detail in Semenza and Sgaramella (1993), will now be summarized.

Sparing of Proper Names

Clinical history

In 1988 my colleague Teresa Sgaramella and I were collecting cases of jargonaphasia in order to compare their oral production with their usually equally disturbed written production. In order to study as many cases as possible we asked our students (we have many from all parts of Italy) to travel to hospitals in their home regions and report tapes and written samples documenting jargonaphasia.

Maria Rosa Petracca, then a final-year student, reported the case of RI, a right-handed farmer, 66 years old, who lived in a small village in the province of Brindisi, in the south of Italy. RI had been a very active person, with some experience in small business, but limited formal education (five years). In September 1988 he suffered an ischaemic attack which led to an aphasia with mild hemiparesis and oral apraxia. A left-occipital lesion could be demonstrated (CAT scan). His extremely severe aphasia concerned virtually only the production side and he could be characterized as a 'phonemic jargon' patient, a condition where the speech output consists virtually only of meaningless phonemes. Although otherwise co-operative, his awareness of the linguistic impairment probably contributed to his unwillingness to provide long pieces of spontaneous speech. Maria Rosa Petracca was kind enough to follow the patient for us and we were able to study him longitudinally, with the intention of tapping the course of his jargonaphasia and of the similar jargonagraphia that affected his writing output.

We were able to examine his speech production in September 1988, September 1989 and December 1990. For unknown reasons, in the last period his reading comprehension, which had been very good, and the mechanics of his writing underwent a severe deterioration so we had no written sample for December 1990. But his oral production contained a new, very surprising element that made us want to examine the patient more closely. So Teresa added a week to her Christmas holiday and went to meet him. She saw and tested him at length on two different occasions in two consecutive weeks (all data shown in this chapter refer to this latter period).

What had led us to decide to pursue the case had been a finding in the tape that Maria Rosa had sent us. Our standard procedure with tapes recording aphasics' oral production is to transcribe each sample carefully. Segmentation is decided on prosodic cues and with the help of real word boundaries. If necessary we use the International Phonetic Alphabet to be able to account for all possible linguistic sounds. We did not, however, use this precaution with RI since he produced exclusively Italian phonemes. More importantly, the transcription has to be agreed upon by at least three independent judges and then examined by a reliable speaker of the dialect in the patient's area. This was important for RI since, in the villages nearby, dialects with Albanian and Greek influences occur. When we were finally reasonably sure that RI was not speaking any known language, we realized that about one-quarter of his production consisted of proper names. This led Teresa to her long but profitable journey to the south of Italy: just in time, because a few weeks later RI had another stroke which unfortunately caused him to lose his articulation capacities for ever.

Neuropsychological findings

Although produced with evident effort and at a slow rate, RI's spontaneous speech was well articulated and consisted of monosyllabic segments which accounted for about three-quarters of the total speech segments. The remaining speech output consisted of word-like polysyllabic segments, the majority of which were either real names or literal paraphasias of persons' names. For instance, in the longest single sample of uninterrupted speech (consisting of 209 segments), where he was answering questions about his job, the only real words were 49 persons' names (including 40 real names and nine literal paraphasias of proper names), consisting of 11 different types, two numbers ('eight' and 'five'), one adverb (*intanto* – while), one noun (*barba* – beard) that he repeated twice, and two literal paraphasias (*scrita*, instead of *scritta* – written; *tuto* instead of *tutto* – all)[1], consisting of the simplification of geminate phonemes. Most of the proper names he produced turned out to be those of relatives and friends. These names, as well as the few other words, were not appropriate to the context but seemed to emerge randomly in the output.

RI was unable to repeat the sounds of single letters (vowels or consonant sounds followed by schwa) although he was 4/20 correct in the repetition of consonant – vowel (CV) syllables. He was totally unable to repeat any word, including proper names, that he produced spontaneously or in the naming conditions. His comprehension was quite good as measured by the Milano Aphasia Battery: he correctly matched 20/20 spoken words to one of four pictures without specific distractors, and 16/20 when phonemic and semantic distractors were included in the alternatives. He correctly executed 10/10 spoken orders of a complex sort (for example, 'Fold a piece of paper and throw it into the basket'). He did not show any great difficulty (18/22) in matching spoken names to pictures of famous people, where the task was to pick the right one from four people of similar occupation and age. In the four instances in which he failed, he managed to convey the idea that he really did not know the person and refused to guess. His poor education did not allow him to be tested reliably on geographical names in any condition. In everyday life he appeared to have intact comprehension.

Reading aloud was nil and resulted, for any type of material, in a phonemic jargon intermixed with proper names, just as in his spontaneous speech. In particular he could not read proper names. His reading comprehension was also virtually absent.

RI's ability to name objects and animals was then tested in both a confrontation condition (30 items) and to definition (15 items). The remarkable abundance of well-formed proper names in his otherwise disturbed spontaneous output led us to the suspect that he might have been spared in retrieving the phonological form of proper names. He was therefore also separately tested for proper names on picture confrontation (relatives and friends: 10 items; and famous persons: 22 items). None of these naming tests was successful: RI responded to each item with randomly chosen monosyllables.

Naming was then tested in a (phonemic) cued condition where the cue consisted of the first sound of the name (a vowel or a consonant followed by a schwa). RI's performance was still nil in cued naming of very high frequency objects or animals (0/30 on confrontation and 0/15 from definitions) and did not change when retested a week later. However, he now scored 10/10 in cued naming of pictures of relatives and friends and 18/22 in cued naming of pictures of famous persons (the same ones he recognized in the comprehension test). He omitted to name the remaining four items, making again a clear display of the fact that he did not know the people at all. He gave exactly the same performance a week later. In tests of naming proper names from definitions, aided by phonemic cueing, he scored 10/10 in both weeks.

A Double Dissociation: Further Evidence and Complications

We have just described the two sides of a double dissociation in speech production between common and proper names. Observations of anomias for proper names were soon replicated and reliable cases are described in Lucchelli and De Renzi (1992), Carney and Temple (1993)[1] and recently by Hittmair-Delazer et al. (1994).

Selective sparing of proper names seems to be rarer thus far. RI's case is furthermore complicated by the fact that appropriate name production was spared with the aid of phonemic cueing. A thorough discussion of the reasons for RI's pattern of performance may be found in the original report of the case (Semenza and Sgaramella, 1993). The other similar reported case (Cipolotti et al., 1993) has been observed only in the written modality, the oral modality being too impaired because of articulation problems. The main aspect of these cases is that they help to constitute a convincing double dissociation, testifying that, while in some cases proper names may be specifically lost (LS, PC), in others they can be specifically spared (RI).

An unsolved problem is that observed cases of proper name anomia dissociate with regard to geographical names. While, in fact, Semenza and Zettin's first two cases, as reported above, were impaired also with the names of countries, rivers, mountains, and so on, in three other reported cases geographical names were retrieved almost as well as common names. This may well be the result of a gradient of difficulty: Semenza and Zettin's cases were indeed more severe than the others. The possible influence of other factors cannot, however, be easily discarded: for instance, I would suspect a role of a purely linguistic factor: the possibility for geographical names to be adjectivized (for example Japan: Japanese).

Testing the Arbitrary Link Hypothesis: More Data on LS and Other Anomics – The Pathological Anatomy of Proper Name Anomias

The link between a proper name and its bearer is, we suggest, more arbitrary than the link between a common name and the entity or event it represents. LS's case first offered supporting empirical evidence for this notion. While anomia for proper names was, in fact, the patient's only complaint, further testing revealed other subtle deficits, whose association with such anomia may not be a pure coincidence. LS was demonstrated to have a particular difficulty in learning arbitrary links between words. This was proved by his performance on the paired-associate learning task from the Wechsler Memory Scale and similar tests requiring the retrieval of one component of a word pair. He quickly learned the 'easy' pairs (in which the two words have a semantic relation to each other, such as 'pear/apple') but he showed chance performance over several attempts in retrieving the second member of the pair, given the first, when the relation between the two was totally arbitrary, such as 'dog/clock'. By contrast, he had no difficulty in tasks requiring the learning of supraspan lists of words. Converging evidence for the importance of this insight also came when he went back to work. He found great difficulty in learning the labelled numbers needed for hardware stock identification.

One piece of luck in LS's case was that the patient was familiar with classical music. We confronted him with several wordless pieces, some of which he demonstrated he knew very well, by singing along and continuing the melody appropriately when the music stopped. Again, as expected, given the perfectly arbitrary link a title has with a piece of music, LS was unable to retrieve any title nor, of course, any composer's name. He could, however, recognize what he missed in naming in a multiple-choice setting.

This music test could not be performed with cases of proper-name anomia that were observed later. However, when looked for, further evidence in favour of the arbitrary links hypothesis was impressive. Lucchelli and De Renzi's (1992) case showed a clear deficit in learning name–face and number–colour pairs, and also had an inability to recall previously known telephone numbers. Hittmair-Delazers et al.'s (1994) case was also disturbed in paired-associate learning, could not retrieve personal number facts, and had a deficit in matching faces to names and to occupations.

All these cases may then be viewed as constellations of symptoms fitting the idea that anomia for proper names may be associated with difficulty in retrieving meaningless associations which would, in turn, confirm the role of proper names as pure referring expressions. Interpreting groups of symptoms as meaningful may be dangerous (Shallice, 1988) because symptoms may be associated due to mere anatomical contiguity in the neural implementation of different functions that have no relation to each other. There are conditions, however (Semenza, 1993), where associations of symptoms are meaningful, because they can be seen to be functionally connected. The association of anomia for proper names with the inability to deal with arbitrary links would not only be logically expected on a theoretical basis but is also unlikely to have been determined by anatomical contiguity of different functions. In fact, despite the great likeness of symptoms across cases, known cases of proper-name anomia have been determined by very different cerebral lesions. While PC had a left-occipital lesion, LS suffered a lesion of the fronto-temporal region, close to temporal pole. Lucchelli and De Renzi's (1992) case had a lesion in the left thalamus, while Hittmair et al.'s (1994) patient MP had a high fronto-temporal lesion. Carney and Temple's (1993) case had multiple lesions. Anatomical contiguity is not a feature of these cases; functional associations of symptoms *may* be.

Identity-specific Semantics and Proper Names: One More Complex Case

In recent years proper names have also been studied, indirectly, in the context of investigations on recognition and naming of faces. An influential model has been proposed by Bruce and Young (1986), whereby names are stored separately at the terminal node of a person-recognition route and can only be accessed after semantic information about person identity has been retrieved. This model is supported by a considerable number of experimental and clinical observations. In particular, it is consistent with the well-known finding that, although one is often able to remember person identity information when unable to remember the name ('I know who you are but I don't remember your name'), the opposite pattern of remembering the name but not remembering any other information about the person almost never occurs. Up-to-date reports on the development of this model are numerous (see, for instance, Burton and Bruce, 1992; Carney and Temple, 1993; and Cohen, forthcoming), and I shall not discuss it any further here. What I shall do, instead, is to report briefly a yet-unpublished case that nicely supports one of the major implications of the model; that is, that identity-specific semantics is distinct from general semantic knowledge.

CB, a 25-year-old right-handed worker, with eight years of education, suffered a head trauma as a consequence of a road accident. Two small lesions were evidenced by CT scan: the first in the left anterior frontal lobe and the second at the border between the left parietal and occipital lobes. CB was referred to Marina Zettin as an anomic for people's names and, indeed, the discrepancy between his ability to retrieve common names (over 90 per cent correct) and people's names (no more than 15 per cent correct) in confrontation and definition fit the pattern in a convincing way, if not with the purity of previously observed cases.

CB, however, had more problems than simply being unable to retrieve proper names. He also could not retrieve any other type of information about the people he could not name. This happened with pictures and also with real people. For instance, he could never identify at first sight, despite long acquaintance, Marina from two speech therapists, all young, attractive women of about the same age, size and hair colour. He was not, however, affected by the relatively rare disturbance called 'prosopagnosia', the inability to recognize faces, because he could easily distinguish people he knew from those he did not know (he flawlessly passed a 70-item test) and scored within normal limits with Warrington's (1984) face recognition memory test. In this test 50 unfamiliar faces are presented sequentially, and recognition memory for these faces is then tested by a forced-choice procedure in which the target face is paired with a similar new face. Semantic cues about a specific individual did not seem to elicit easily the retrieval of other distinguishing information about that single individual. For instance, if provided with the cue 'president of FIAT', he might say 'very rich' (an easy guess) but not 'white-haired'. When provided with proper names, however, CB could immediately provide full information about the people he knew, including details unique to each individual (he scored 30/32 in this test. He could not, however, match spoken or written names of famous people – even those for whom he had demonstrated full knowledge – to corresponding pictures in a multiple-choice test (eight alternatives). It seems that for CB faces have become *disconnected* from person-specific information that can be accessed if he is given the name.

The case is important because *only* the specific domain of knowledge about individual people is affected in this way.

Conclusions

We have seen how proper names are a very special instance in semantics and how some peculiarities in their processing seem to be uncovered by brain damage.

The first important conclusion we draw from neuropsychological cases is that in producing common and proper names, two separable output routes may be implicated: one for mapping identity-specific semantics to name, and one for mapping general semantic properties to common words. They cannot be separated only at the lexical level, because one would then predict different effects in anomia for proper names depending on whether the answer is spoken or written. A general mechanism for word production indicates that the activation of the lexical level from semantics (Butterworth et al., 1984) proceeds by matching semantic information with the appropriate entry in the lexicon. Now, it seems, two such procedures are required: one for common words and one for proper names. This view is compatible with a recent model of speech production due to Levelt (1989), whereby lexical production is in two stages. The first stage consists of the retrieval of a 'lemma', that is, an abstract lexical item supplied with both syntactic and semantic features. The second stage accesses the morphophonological form, the 'lexeme'. Each lemma points to its corresponding form: that is, it can refer to the address in the form lexicon, the lexeme, where the information for that item is stored. The first stage includes tagging of the syntactic class of a lexical item. The class of nouns is, indeed, divided into two major classes: proper nouns and common nouns, that have different syntactic functions. It is possible, therefore, that the place where processing is different from the two classes of nouns is within the lemma stage.

Why a name is processed in one way or the other is probably determined by the amount of descriptive value or 'sense', as opposed to 'reference' in Frege's (1892) terms. What is the usefulness of having two different types of processes? One can speculate that such a bipartite mechanism may favour the labelling of individuals and would naturally follow an organization of the semantic system whereby identity-specific semantic information is stored and accessed separately from more generic knowledge. An organization of the semantic system in these terms is supported by the observation of patients like CB. In his case, in fact, identity-specific semantic information is clearly cut off from other types of information such as face identification, and is accessed only via the corresponding proper names, which are reliable pointers to the individual token's address in memory.

Note

1   The authors call it a case of 'prosopoanomia', a specific inability to put names to faces: the critical test for this claim, however, naming from definition (that at variance with confrontation naming should not be impaired if a true prosopoanomia was there), was not performed.

Further Reading

Cohen, G. and Burke, D.M. (1993) *Memory for Proper Names*: a special issue of *Memory* (Hove, Sussex: Lawrence Erlbaum Associates).

References

Bruce, V. and Young, A. (1986) 'Understanding faces recognition', *British Journal of Psychology*, 77: 305–27.
Burton, A.M. and Bruce, V. (1992) 'I recognize your face but I can't remember your name: a simple explanation?', *British Journal of Psychology*, 83: 45–71.
Butterworth, B.L., Howard, D. and McLoughlin, P. (1984) 'The semantic deficit in aphasia: the relationship between semantic errors in auditory comprehension and picture naming', *Neuropsychologia*, 22: 409–26.
Carney, R. and Temple, C.M. (1993) 'Prosopoanomia? A possible category specific anomia for faces', *Cognitive Neuropsychology*, 10(2): 185–95.
Cipolotti, L., McNeil, J.E. and Warrington, E.K. (1993) 'Spared written naming of proper names: a case report', *Memory*, 4(1): 289–312.
Cohen, G. (forthcoming) 'Age-related problems in the use of proper names in communication', in

M.L. Hummert, J.M. Wiemann and J.F. Nussbaum (eds), *Interpersonal Communication and Older Adulthood: Interdisciplinary Research* (Beverly Hills, Cal.: Sage).

Cohen, G. and Faulkner, D. (1986) 'Memory for proper names: age differences in retrieval', *British Journal of Developmental Psychology*, 4: 187–97.

Frege, G. (1892) 'Uber Sinn und Bedeutung [On sense and meaning]', in G. Patzig (ed.), *Funktion, Begriff, Bedeutung* (Gottingen: Vandenhoek and Ruprecht), pp. 40–65.

Hart, J., Berndt, R.S. and Caramazza, A. (1985) 'Category-specific naming deficit following cerebral infarction', *Nature*, 316: 439–40.

Hittmair-Delazer, M., Denes, G., Semenza, C. and Mantovani, M.C. (1994) 'Anomia for people's names', *Neuropsychologia*, 32(4): 465–76.

Levelt, W.J.M. (1989) *Speaking: From Intention to Articulation* (Cambridge, Mass.: MIT Press).

Lucchelli, F. and De Renzi, E. (1992) 'Proper name anomia', *Cortex*, 28: 221–30.

McWeeny, K.H., Young, A., Hay, D.C. and Ellis, A.W. (1987) 'Putting names to faces', *British Journal of Psychology*, 78: 143–4.

Reason, J.T. and Lucas, D. (1984) 'Using cognitive diaries to investigate naturally occurring memory blocks', in J.E. Harris and P.E. Morris (eds), *Everyday Memory, Actions and Absentmindedness* (London: Academic Press).

Semenza, C. (1993) 'Methodological issues', in G.J. Beaumont and J. Sergent (eds), *A Dictionary of Neuropsychology* (Oxford: Basil Blackwell).

Semenza, C. and Sgaramella, T.M. (1993) 'Proper names production: a clinical study of the effects of phonemic cueing', *Memory*, 1(4): 265–80.

Semenza, C. and Zettin, M. (1988) 'Generating proper names: a case of selective inability', *Cognitive Neuropsychology*, 5(6): 711–21.

Semenza, C. and Zettin, M. (1989) 'Evidence from aphasia for the role of proper names as pure referring expressions', *Nature*, 342(6250): 678–9.

Shallice, T. (1988) *From Neuropsychology to Mental Structure* (Cambridge: Cambridge University Press).

Warrington, E.K. (1984) *Recognition Memory Test* (Windsor, Berks.: NFER–Nelson).

Young, A.W., Hay, D.C. and Ellis, A.W. (1985) 'The faces that launched a thousand slips: everyday difficulties and errors in recognizing people', *British Journal of Psychology*, 76: 495–523.

Part VII   Developments and Declines

Impairments Across the Lifespan

Introduction

In her chapter Temple describes the case of John, a 13-year-old boy who suffered from a developmental anomia and somewhat selective inability to develop normal conceptual knowledge, particularly in the domain of animals. John was known to have abnormalities on the left side of the brain including the left temporal lobes, and two isolated cases of epileptic seizure when he was between the ages of four and eight years suggested that the brain injury may have occurred during this period. On tests of semantic knowledge, such as naming pictures and providing definitions of concepts, John was clearly abnormal. For instance, he often made semantic errors, naming 'strawberry' as 'orange'. Such errors are comparatively rare in young children although they do sometimes occur. John, however, also made rather more unusual errors, such as naming a 'turtle' as an 'octopus', and gave anomalous definitions to many animal names. More generally, John showed a markedly disjunctive pattern of intellectual impairment across a range of intellectual skills, being close to his range on some tests and up to eight years behind on others. He also had a general memory impairment and found it difficult to retain many everyday facts, such as his birth date. This pattern of findings suggests a sharp dissociation between different aspects of memory both across general memory skills and in the more proscribed area of semantic knowledge.

The decline of cognition in abnormal ageing, for example in dementia, such as Alzheimer's disease, is also associated with progressive deterioration of various aspects of memory. Rusted, Ratner, and Sheppard provide an account of an ongoing project following a small group of initially mildly dementing elderly patients who, over a period of years, developed Alzheimer's disease. In their chapter they focus on just one of their patients, an elderly and cheerful man (AH) whose dementia gradually worsened over the testing period. In their studies they focus on memory for routine actions, such as making a cup of tca, and show how this is comparatively well preserved even though other aspects of memory have become massively impaired. For instance, AH could still actually make a cup of tea even past the point where he had developed a dense anterograde amnesia and could retain new information for a few seconds only. This preservation of basic stereotypical action sequences is important theoretically as it once again suggests a fractionation of memory, and it is also important practically as it demonstrates that even in the severest stages of dementia there may be some behaviours which are preserved and which the patient can still usefully perform.

Progressive brain disease need not, of course, afflict only the elderly, and Della Sala, Lucchelli, Lunghi, and Spinnler report the case of a man in his late forties who began to show signs of memory failures. Initially this started with frequently forgetting everyday appointments and errands and over a period of five years or so declined into something like a dense anterograde amnesia. At this point the patient was still working under the close and frequent instruction of colleagues, but over the next ten years his condition deteriorated into Alzheimer's disease and he lost his ability to drive, find his way round the city in which he lived, his anterograde amnesia became almost total, and intellectual impairments became apparent. Interestingly, his spatial memory did not decline at the same rate as his other memory abilities, and his work skills appeared to be preserved for an even longer period of time. This case, then, illustrates a very slow onset of dementia and shows how memory abilities can be selectively lost over a long period of illness.

25   The Kangaroo's a Fox

Christine M. Temple

A lion is 'fat and eyes and ears and he's brown and black lines and eats apples'. This description of a lion was given by a 13-year-old boy, John, who has a poor memory and has particular difficulty in naming, recognizing and remembering animals. We know that for most children animal names are learnt relatively early. In a study conducted in 1973, Nelson looked at 80 infants and noted the first words which these young children produced. When the first ten words were compared it was found that the most common words were animals, foods and toys. Studying slightly older children, who were aged between one and two years, Nelson looked at the words produced when the children were able to generate about 50 different words. Animals were again one of the basic categories of words in these early vocabulary items. We know, therefore, that if John was a typical child he would have started to learn animal names relatively early in life.

It would be possible for John's difficulty with animals to result from unusual experience in life in which he had very little encounter with animals. Such a possibility can be imagined for certain inner-city children if they had also been deprived of books and the experience of television and film. However, in John's case the family lives on a farm and their home is close to a wildlife park which they visit from time to time. There is nothing unusual about the environment in which John grew up. Moreover, his twin sister, with whom he has shared much family life and day-to-day experience, does not have the problems which John experiences with animals and animal names.

Another interesting aspect to John's description of the lion is that he produces a series of explicit statements about the lion. Usually, if you ask a child to tell you about an animal which they do not know, the child will simply say that they do not know what the animal is like. This was a pattern of behaviour that we observed frequently amongst young four-year-old children attending nursery school whose performance we compared with John and who we shall describe in more detail later. When John is asked about the lion he does not say that he does not know what a lion is, he produces a set of descriptors, some of which are reasonable and some of which are inaccurate or improbable. This suggests that John does have some type of representation of knowledge about a lion. He is able to produce a description of something which appears to be a living creature with facial features and an appetite. However, the features that are described are not simply a subset of correct features about lions. It is not that he simply has partial knowledge of lions. He seems to be activating elements of information that might be appropriate for another creature. For example, he says that the lion has black lines, which would be an accurate feature in association with a zebra. He also says that the lion eats apples, which is an uncommon suggestion in association with a large game animal. The description which he produces does not seem to identify any specific animal. John is not merely describing an incorrect animal.

Despite John's poor description of a lion, he is able to name one correctly when presented with a line drawing of the creature. Unfortunately, this does not indicate that he really knows the identity of the lion since he also calls other things lions. When he incorrectly names pictures of a leopard and a tiger, he sometimes says that they are lions. These might seem reasonable confusions because there are a variety of semantic features in common between lions, leopards and tigers. They look rather similar and have similar body sizes and proportions. They are all large, wild cats, live in similar habitats and may be seen in similar areas in a zoo. However, John also produces the name 'lion' on occasions when he is presented with a picture of a kangaroo, an owl and a seal. In these cases, there is much less semantic similarity or visual similarity between the picture and the response. Kangaroos and owls do not look like lions. Nor do they live in similar habitats to lions. Nor do they move like lions or have lifestyles similar to lions. However, in the case of the response 'lion' to seal, it is possible that the similarity in appearance between a seal and a sealion may contribute to the response.

Does John know that the picture of a lion is more like a lion than the pictures of a leopard, tiger, kangaroo, owl or seal? What happens if John is asked to point to a lion when there are other animals also present in the array that he is studying? When he was asked to point to a lion, and included amongst the distracter pictures were a leopard, a tiger and a kangaroo, John was correctly able to point to the lion. He was also able to correctly point to the leopard and the tiger. This might suggest that he is able to understand these items and his difficulty is simply in naming. However, when he is asked to point to the kangaroo he points to the camel. Moreover, when he is asked to point a rhinoceros he picks the lion, and when he is asked to point a fox he picks the lion.

One reason for our interest in John is that this difficulty in identifying and distinguishing between animals was not a difficulty which extended to identifying and distinguishing objects. We can contrast the description he produced of the lion with the description that he produced of an ashtray. In this case John said, 'It's glass. It's got a big round in it. You can put your ash in it.' Moreover, he can accurately name an ashtray and point to it correctly when he is presented with an array of pictures of objects. Indeed, when presented with an array of 24 items that would be found in a house, John is able to point to all of them correctly and names all but two correctly. He made two minor errors: a chest of drawers named as cupboard; and a toaster named as a grill. In this chapter we shall discuss in more detail the way in which we investigated John's difficulties and the things that we learnt from our studies of him. First, we shall say a little more about John himself and his history.

Who is John?

John's mother was healthy during the pregnancy in which she carried him. John was born at 39 weeks of gestation by a normal delivery and there were no complications at birth. The only atypical aspect to John's initial development was that he was one of twins, both of whom appeared healthy at birth. There were no problems with John in his early infancy and no particular concerns until he went to school. He walked when he was about a year old and there were no difficulties with toilet training or learning to dress. His motor milestones were good and there were no early reports of concern over speech development, though no systematic testing by any psychologist or paediatrician took place in the early years. Hearing and vision were both said to be normal and there were no concerns at any time about either of these modalities. John had no head injury or serious illness in his early childhood. The only suggestion of any possible neurological abnormality was that at the age of three years and five months an episode occurred whilst at school which was believed to be an epileptic seizure. No subsequent seizure disorder developed, but a second comparable episode occurred at five years and seven months when John was in his first year at school. An electroencephalogram (EEG) was taken to record the electrical activity across the cortex and determine whether there were any spikes which would be typical of a seizure disorder. Abnormalities were seen in the right central area, posterially, bilaterally and in the left temporal area. Despite the absence of on-going epilepsy, a decision was then taken to administer a low dose of anticonvulsive therapy. This was withdrawn after two years as no further seizures had occurred. EEGs taken since this time have continued to indicate left temporal abnormality and left-sided abnormality.

The first concern about behaviour at school arose at about six years of age. John's mother was not particularly worried about the school's concerns as she felt patterns of John's development were similar to her own. She also felt that since he had spent so much time with his twin, this might have affected his development and made him slightly different from other children. When John was eight years old he was given an intellectual assessment on the Wechsler Intelligence Scale which suggested that he was a child with generalized learning difficulties, and he was moved into a special unit within an integrated school. However, three years later intellectual assessment suggested an IQ twenty points higher than on the eight-year-old assessment. At this time a very marked scatter in the subtest scores on Wechsler was indicated. On the eleven-year-old assessment some subtests of the IQ scale suggested that John's intellectual level was in the mid-sixties, but on other tests he scored normally. It was this atypical scatter of scores and concern about John's memory in the classroom that led to the referral for further neuropsychological assessment. The neurologist who saw him at this time noted that

He simply cannot carry information over from one minute to the next. . . . during the assessment he was unable to tell me when his birthday was. What he did remember was that his birthday date was printed somewhere in his maths book and he hunted through this and found it.

His support teacher at school also wrote: 'He seems to forget what one has told him from one week to the next.'

John's Memory

John's short-term memory was assessed by his ability to recall a sequence of digits which had been spoken to him at a rate of approximately one per second. It was slightly low for age, but not markedly so. His digit span assessed in this way was five for remembering digits forward and two for remembering digits backward. John's ability to remember a short story, immediately after he has heard it, is again low for age but not markedly so. He was read one of the short Taylor stories, which is as follows:

Three boys built a house in the woods. They put a table and two old chairs in it. There was a basket full of apples under the table. One afternoon they went away and left the door open. When they came back they found two little pigs eating the apples.

When John recalled this story he said the following:

Doing it, they built a house. They put a table and they left the door open and then the pigs ate all the apples and they came back and see two pigs in there.

John's rendition is not grammatical but it does convey the main points of the story. After a delay of half an hour John still remembers some of the main features of the story. He says the following:

They skipped away and they left the door open and the pigs went to get the apples and when they come back they see two pigs in there.

John has forgotten the earlier portion of the story but does recall the element that relates to the pigs and the apples. The slight loss of information may provide some evidence of the beginnings of a process of deterioration. For it seems that, although John is able to recall some information briefly after it is presented, with longer delays some loss of knowledge must occur since John's knowledge of the facts of the world and his own life are very limited. He has had clear difficulty in establishing these semantic stores of knowledge.

On intellectual assessment John's score on the information subtest, which requires recall of factual knowledge about the world, was the lowest of all subtest scores. He attained a scaled score of only 4 which is well below a normal level for his age. Poor knowledge is also apparent on day-to-day questions. Despite John's age of twelve years and his residence for most of his life in the same farm cottage, he is unable to indicate his address. He is also unable to indicate his birthday. Moreover, when offered a series of dates from which to pick his birthday, he is correctly able to pick the month but is incorrect in his selection of the date. So even in a recognition task which we generally consider to be much easier than a recall task, he does not recognize his birthday.

At the time of John's assessment Margaret Thatcher was the Prime Minister of Great Britain, and those who work with neurological patients are well aware she had a sufficiently dominant personality and presence that even severely impaired neurological patients and currently dementing adults tend to know her identity well after they have lost extensive amounts of semantic information. Children also tended to be very familiar with the identity of Margaret Thatcher when she was the Prime Minister, and John's twin knew about her. However, John was unable to name the Prime Minister. He also had poor knowledge of the Royal Family and other famous people. When asked the name of the Queen, John replied 'Lady Di', and when asked to name pictures of famous pop stars he could name none correctly. In contrast, his sister could name 12 out of the 14 pictures of pop stars which had been selected for use with children by Edward De Haan. John's difficulty in naming the faces of the pop stars could reflect a memory impairment, but it could also reflect difficulty with face recognition itself, that is developmental prosopagnosia. These two possibilities are not mutually exclusive. John's memory for other visual patterns was also very poor. On Benton's Visual Retention Test presented in its multiple-choice recognition format, John's performance was severely impaired. He also had great difficulty in copying diagrams from memory.

When studying adult neurological patients who have sustained brain injury, disorders of memory are frequently considered as quite distinct from disorders of language. Individuals with memory disorders, that is, those with acquired amnesias, may retain good language skills and their language does not usually have aphasic characteristics. These acquired amnesic patients have a memory disorder whose onset occurs after childhood. At the time of language acquisition in infancy and childhood, their memory is presumed to have been intact. Only after the language system has become fully developed and established has the amnesia developed. We know that their amnesia does affect the acquisition of subsequent linguistic knowledge since they have difficulty incorporating into their vocabulary new words which have only entered the language system in recent years. Indeed, the ability to recognize words which have entered the vocabulary at different dates and in different decades is sometimes used as a test to assess whether there is any temporary gradient associated with their memory loss.

For a child with a developmental disorder of memory, which in John's case may be associated with abnormal functioning of the temporal lobe systems which subserve memory, the deficient memory system may be present at the time of language acquisition and language development. Thus, a developmental amnesia may have a direct impact upon the acquisition of language as well as factual knowledge about the world. In particular, it may affect the acquisition of semantic information which is important for the development of vocabulary items. Thus, in some cases where there is a developmental amnesic disorder, a presenting characteristic may be developmental anomia in which there are apparent difficulties in retrieving the names for items. These difficulties with naming may arise because of impoverished establishment of the semantic representations for the items or difficulty in accessing such representations. We now go on to discuss the nature of John's difficulties with naming, and the interesting characteristics associated with its pattern, within which difficulties in naming animals are much severe than difficulties in naming everyday objects.

Naming Levels

John was given a series of standardized tests of naming in which line drawings of items are presented in confrontation naming tasks. The child is simply requested to name the picture which he is shown. On these tasks, John's naming abilities on average were appropriate to a child of about four years to five years of age. Occasionally John made errors in naming which indicated that he was able to activate some of the sound characteristics associated with the word, but not all of them. Thus, he made occasional phonemic paraphasias, for example, he named a cigarette as 'a cevarette'. Such errors were comparatively rare, as were his occasional perceptual errors, for example, the naming of a pea pod as a mouth, presumably based upon the misperception that the peas were like individual teeth and the overall shape of the pod was similar to the overall shape of lips. The majority of John's errors, however, were semantic paraphasias, in that they shared some elements of meaning in common with the correct target. Errors of this sort included 'finger' named as 'thumb', 'parachute' named as 'kite', and 'arrow' named as 'nail'. Within these semantic paraphasias it was also rapidly evident that animals were a particular problematic group for John. For example, he named a bear as a sheep, a kangaroo as a goat, a squirrel as a mouse and a goat as a cow. This aspect of behaviour seems particularly interesting.

Preparing Test Material and Selecting Controls

For our initial investigations we decided to use a set of test material which had been published by Snodgrass and Vanderwart (1980). This consisted of a set of pictures, all of which were line drawings and which were depicted in so far as was possible with a similar degree of complexity and with similar size and general characteristics. Since the standard data associated with the responses to these stimuli came from America and the test was to be carried out in Britain, we tested a number of normal British adults on the pictures to determine typical British responses to some items. For example, whereas in America one of the pictures is named as a wrench, in English the normal name is a spanner. Five adults were tested and any variation which they produced in naming these items was considered as a correct response when it came to scoring John's performance and the other children with whom he was compared. From the Snodgrass and Vanderwart stimuli, 48 items were picked which showed living creatures, including animals, birds, insects and sea creatures. A further 48 items were selected which depicted objects generally found inside a house. Sets of 24 items of food and 24 items of clothing were also picked.

From John's standardized assessment we have been able to derive a precise naming age for him, on a test which had norms from the local area in which he lived: John had a naming age of 4 years 5 months. Using this as a standard we decided to compare his performance with normal children who had developed to a comparable naming level. Our aim was to determine whether John had just been very slow in acquiring his naming skills while his development was normal in its pattern but simply delayed in its characteristics. Alternatively, John's naming skills might be unusual in their pattern of strengths and weaknesses. In order to do this we compared John with ten nursery school children who also had an average naming age of 4 years 5 months but whose chronological age was very different from John: they were aged four years. If, when we compared John with these control children, his pattern of performance was very similar to theirs we would have described his performance as reflecting developmental lag. He would have been delayed in his development but the pattern of the delay would have been like that of normal children. If, in contrast, his pattern of development was very different from that of normal children, we would know that he had a deviant developmental path and the interpretation of his performance would differ.

Testing the Naming of Living Creatures and Objects

As predicted, John had difficulty in naming our pictures of animals. He named only 18/48 pictures correctly. This contrasted with his good naming of the indoor objects for which he was able to name 41/48 stimuli. Thus, on this first test it was evident that there was a statistically significant difference between his ability to name animals and indoor objects. One possibility could be that this difference resulted from a difference in the stimuli that was unrelated to their category of membership. For example, it could be that the animals were less common that the indoor objects.

In order to test for this possibility, we eliminated from the set of items the seven most unusual animals, which were leopard, kangaroo, giraffe, beetle, ostrich, grasshopper and penguin. We also excluded the seven most common indoor objects, which were telephone, bed, table, chair, book, saw and knife. We were left with two sets of 34 stimuli in which the frequency bias now strongly favoured the animals; that is, by removing the unusual animals and the common indoor objects we had developed two sets of stimuli for which the average frequency of the animals was much higher than the average frequency of the objects. If frequency was an important determiner of the ability to name, then John should have become better at naming this set of animals than the indoor objects. However, his pattern of performance was as before, with only 41 per cent of animals named correctly and 83 per cent of indoor objects. These levels of performance were almost identical to the previous comparison, in which 38 per cent of animals and 85 per cent of indoor objects were named correctly. We concluded that the difference between John's ability to name the two categories was not the result of some intrinsic difference in the frequency of the names that had to be produced. We were also able to compare the items on their familiarity and again found that differences in familiarity were insufficient to account for John's difficulty with the animal names.

Would this difficulty in naming animals also be found amongst the young four-year-old control children. The answer was no. Whilst John was only able to name 18/48 animals, all of our control children were able to name more animals than this. The average number of animals which they were able to name was 31, and even the child who was poorest at naming animals did better than John. This difference between John and the controls was statistically significant. In contrast, the young children were not as good as John at naming the indoor objects. John was able to name 41 of them, but the best naming performance from the control children was not as good as this: on average they named only 26 of the indoor objects. The control children were statistically significantly poorer than John at naming indoor objects. Overall, the level of performance of the control children on the animals and the indoor objects was much more even than for John. Thus, John was able to name 23 more indoor objects than animals. For the controls the largest difference between the ability to name indoor objects and the ability to name animals was only nine items and in this case a single child named nine more animals than indoor objects; the opposite direction of difference to John. Every control child except one was able to name more animals than indoor objects correctly. It looks as if frequency of word occurrence was a better predictor of naming than was the class of object – for most children. On average, the children named six animals more than the number of indoor objects they were able to name. For no child was there anything approaching the pattern seen in John's case, with an ability to name 23 more indoor objects than animals. When the control children were compared with John on the naming of foods and clothing, their performance was much more similar and there were no significant differences between the groups. Thus, John's pattern of development is not simply like that of a young child developing naming a very slow rate. His performance is atypical. He has been much better than his naming age controls in learning how to name indoor objects such as envelopes, cookers, sofas, ironing boards, screwdrivers and spanners, but he has been much poorer than the control children at learning to name animals and insects such as lion, fox, kangaroo, fly, duck, swan, pig and caterpillar.

Looking at Errors

When John was unable to name a picture his responses also differed from the responses of the younger children when they were unable to name a picture: it was common for them, if they did not know the name of a picture, to simply say that they did not know. In comparison to John they produced more refusals in their patterns of response and far fewer overt errors. John showed a statistically significantly increased tendency to produce a response even though it was an inaccurate response.

A further difference between John's responses and the controls' responses was evident when the errors were examined in a different way. In this comparison we looked at what John and the controls actually said when they made an overt error. We found that the controls tended to make similar types of responses to each other. In order to investigate this systematically we used both published information from the Snodgrass and Vanderwart (1980) study and also the responses of our subjects. Published with the pictures are lists of responses which at least one of Snodgrass and Vanderwart's 42 control adults used to name a picture. These are incorrect responses but they are errors that are generated by normal adults. For example, a normal adult studied by Snodgrass and Vanderwart named a needle as a pin and another named a stool as a chair. There were also normal errors to the pictures of animals. For example, a normal adult named a sheep as a lamb and another named an eagle as a parrot. These responses are classified as nondominant responses. In addition to these nondominant responses, we also classified as a nondominant any response which at least two of the ten control children produced. Thus for example, at least two of our controls named a donkey as a horse and called a picture of bread, toast.

We then looked again at all the overt errors made by John and the controls and counted those that were of this nondominant character. That is, we were interested in the number of errors that seemed to be reasonable or common errors. Roughly three-quarters of the controls' responses were nondominant. However, in contrast, only a

Table 25.1   John's naming errors

Indoor objects

Chest of drawers → cupboard   thimble → basket
rolling-pin → rolling   paintbrush → pencil
broom → brush*   pliers → spanner

Animals

donkey → rabbit   beetle → bee
camel → zebra   eagle → blackbird
leopard → tiger   duck → goat
squirrel → mouse   cockerel → chicken*
sheep → cow   ostrich → goat
kangaroo → cat, lion   grasshopper → wasp
deer → goat   fly → wasp*
rhinoceros → cow   owl → lion
tiger → lion*   ant → wasp
giraffe → zebra*   crocodile → octopus
butterfly → spider   tortoise → octopus
spider → wasp   snail → shell*
frog → octopus   seal → lion

Note:
* Nondominant responses.
Source: Adapted from Temple (1986).

quarter of John's responses were of this sort. This indicates that when John makes an overt error he tends to produce a response which is more atypical than that of normal children. This was true in all categories but was particularly apparent in the animal and food categories for which more errors were generated. For example, amongst the food-stuffs John named a strawberry as an orange and a pear as a pineapple. None of the control children, nor any of the 42 normal adults tested by Snodgrass and Vanderwart, made an error of this sort.

Amongst John's errors in naming animals were many which were not nondominant responses. These and his nondominant responses are listed in table 25.1, where they are contrasted with his errors in identifying indoor objects. We shall give some examples contrasting these types of response and the responses produced by the controls. When asked to name a picture of a tortoise, of the ten controls eight were able to identify it correctly. Two of the controls made mistakes and they both produced a similar error. They said turtle instead of tortoise. In contrast to this pattern, John said octopus. The normal children's errors are consistent with the visual similarity between the tortoise and a turtle. However, an octopus has very different characteristics to a tortoise.

Even when the control children produced responses which were not nondominant, they tended to have semantic features in common with the stimulus. For example, the picture of the ostrich was difficult for the young children: only one child of the ten controls identified it correctly. Six children said that they did not know and could not hazard a guess as to the identity of the creature. There were three children who made attempts to name the ostrich, each of which was incorrect. However, in each case the response that was produced was another bird: dodo, goose, and swan. All are creatures with long necks. In contrast, John misnamed an ostrich as a goat.

John had difficulty even with the relatively easy items on the test. All of the control children were able to identify a butterfly and all were able to identify a spider. In contrast, John called the butterfly a spider and named the spider as a wasp. This production of an incorrect name to an item and yet the inability to produce that same name to the correct item indicates that John does not simply fail to name items because he does not know some of these words. He does have a representation for the word spider but he does not produce it in response to the correct picture.

Understanding Names

We have suggested that for John the problems with memory and naming may be connected. That is, although he may have been able to learn some of the words for animals' names, he may have had difficulty in learning the full set of semantic features associated with these items and this may be linked to his memory difficulties. This means that the anomia is not simply a language-based deficiency. It is not the case that we believe that he has a full representation of these vocabulary items and just has difficulty in activating the items in specific circumstances as is possible in cases of acquired anomias in adults with aphasic disorders. One way to determine the extent to which vocabulary knowledge has become established is to ask John to listen to the names of living creatures and other items and then to select their picture from an array of different choices. An anomic person who simply has difficulty finding a name in their vocabulary ought not to have so much difficulty in selecting an item from an array because here there is no necessity to retrieve the object name itself. If John's ability to point to objects is better than his ability to name, then we know that there is an anomic aspect to his performance. However, if he remains significantly poorer at pointing to animals than at pointing to indoor objects, we know that the distinction in his ability to carry out these two sets of tasks cannot be reduced simply to a generalized anomic aspect.

When we carried out the pointing-to-an-array task with John, we found that he was better at pointing to animals than at naming them. This indicated that when he did not have to retrieve the name for the item, he did have a better performance level and confirmed that there was an anomic aspect to his performance. Specifically, where he had been able to name only 18 animals he was able to point to 29 of the pictures of animals. However, this ability to point to animal pictures was still significantly poorer than the ability to point to indoor objects. Pointing to indoor objects was fractionally better than naming of the same objects but performance was getting close to ceiling. John was able to point to 44 of the indoor objects, having been able to name 41 previously. John's ability to point to the indoor objects remains better than his ability to point to the animals. Thus, the distinction between dealing with indoor object names and dealing with animal names is not simply an impairment which is related to anomic difficulties; it is something more pervasive.

Development over Time

John was retested one year after the initial assessment of his naming and memory skills to determine whether the pattern of the deficit had persisted. Both verbal and nonverbal memory remained poor, although there had been some improvement in general language skills and these and literacy acquisition were closer to a six-year than a five-year level. The developmental anomia remained marked and naming age on standardized testing had increased from four years five months to only five years. The same category-specific deficiency in animal naming was evident and, although performance had improved slightly, John had remained significantly poorer than the $4^1/2$-year-olds who had been tested the previous year. His naming of indoor objects had also improved and remained markedly better than his animal naming.

Identifying Descriptions

On our first assessment of John we had only asked him to name items in response to pictures. One way of distinguishing between a recognition disorder (an agnosia) and a naming disorder is that agnosic disorders are often modality-specific. Somebody with a visual object agnosia may have difficulty in naming a visually presented object but may be able to do so quite easily from a verbal description of that object when the visual modality is not involved. We wanted to determine whether there was a similar dissociation in the case of John. Alternatively, if as hypothesized it was the representations of knowledge and the memory for the semantic features of the items which was problematic, then we would expect that there would also be difficulty in naming from descriptions. We therefore constructed verbal descriptions of 47 of the indoor objects and 44 of the animals, omitting the other items for which it was problematic to produce a readily identifiable and concise description. An example of a verbal description of an animal was: 'It's a four-legged animal that lives on a farm. We get milk from it and it goes moo.' An example of a description of an indoor object was: 'It's long and flat and it's used for drawing straight lines.' The descriptions were read to John and he was asked to name the items. On this task, as with the naming of pictures, John was significantly better at naming indoor objects than at naming animals. He named 77 per cent of the indoor objects but only 36 per cent of the animals. The category-specific aspect to his anomia is therefore not modality specific.

Naming Photographs

We know from studies of adults who have neurological injuries that some patients with parietal lobe injuries have particular difficulty in identifying objects if the visual information associated with the object is degraded. Patients studied by Warrington and Taylor (1973) had difficulty in identifying line drawings of items. We wondered whether the impoverished nature of the visual information which was present in the line drawings with which we had been testing John was contributing to his naming difficulties. Again, we were trying to determine whether there was an aspect of his difficulties which reflected an apperceptive agnosic component rather than any fundamental difficulty with the semantic representations for these items. We therefore selected a subgroup of the animals which had been used in the previous investigations for which it was possible to find both a colour photograph and also a small model of the animal in children's toy shops. We then presented these stimuli to John for naming. In fact, we presented the line drawing twice, the photographs once and the models once. We were then able to compare both overall accuracy and the consistency of response across the different stimuli. Accuracy of performance was identical. Of our 16 items, John was able to name nine black and white drawings, nine photographs and eight models correctly. The kangaroo was named as a fox in both line drawing presentations, as a rabbit when it was presented as a photograph, and as a mouse when presented as a model. Since John has a difficulty in naming photographs comparable to the difficulty he has in naming line drawings, we know that his difficulty with naming is not related to the degraded element of the information present in the line drawing pictures.

Describing Animals and Objects

As a final test we asked John to produce descriptions, one of which started this chapter. We gave him the names of objects and of animals and asked him to describe them. Here we were trying to determine explicitly what semantic features John could activate in association with these items. As discussed at the start of the chapter, his descriptions of indoor objects were richer and had greater complexity and greater accuracy than his descriptions of animals. In the comparisons of the productions associated with these items, it seems that semantic information associated with objects has been more clearly and readily established in an accessible way than the information associated with the living creatures.

Speculations

Why should difficulty with memory which affects the acquisition of language have more impact in the development of vocabulary items which are living creatures than vocabulary items which are indoor objects? In the discussion of the neurological adults who have displayed such category specific dissociations, one suggestion has been that the distinctions between animals are based on visual features. We know that for John the visual information associated with animals seems to be less salient than for young normal children in that his responses often share very few visual characteristics with the stimulus pictures, whereas when normal children make errors they often produces responses of items that are rather similar in appearance to the stimulus. However, it might have been argued that if John has difficulty in making such visual distinctions, he would tend to show an increased rate of error where he would produce items that shared some visual features with the stimulus rather than producing such atypical responses.

In the discussions of acquired category-specific disorders, the functional significance of indoor objects has also been stressed. In John's case we wondered whether this distinction between animal and indoor object naming, which we argued tied in with his memory impairment, might be similar to the distinctions seen in acquired amnesia between memory for procedural knowledge and memory for factual knowledge. In many cases of acquired amnesia it has been shown, for example by Brooks and Baddeley (1976), that procedural learning remains intact. People are able to learn skills and learn aspects of motor acquisition despite the inability to acquire new semantic information. We have therefore hypothesized that John's better ability to name indoor objects than to name animals may be related to the inclusion of such objects in his motor activities. Thus, he uses and acts upon many of these indoor objects and perhaps this ability to incorporate them into his motor systems enables some element of encoding associated with them which he does not have available in relation to animals. This would predict that those animals, if any, with which he might have had physical contact on the farm might also be more easily remembered. We do not have any empirial data to test this prediction. It would also suggest that he should have relatively good ability to name body parts which are things that are incorporated into his movements and routines, and on this we do have data available. John is good at naming body parts and the errors that he makes are logical and reasonable. Presented with 25 pictures of body parts to name he made only four errors: forehead named as head; lips named as mouth; eyebrow named as eye; and elbow named as arm. All errors except the last would be taken as correct under certain scoring criteria. He is also able to point to body parts from an array with high accuracy. We therefore argue that John's distinction between the ability to name indoor objects and the ability to name animals is similar to the distinctions between procedural and declarative knowledge that are discussed in cases of acquired amnesia, and that in John's case his underlying amnesic impairment has contributed to the specific impairments of language leading to greater impact on the acquisition of certain categories of knowledge and information than on others.

Note

This case is described more formally and in more detail, including statistical details, in C.M. Temple (1986) 'Anomia for animals in a child', *Brain*, **109**: 1225–42.

Further Reading

Ostergaard, A.L. (1987) 'Episodic, semantic and procedural memory in a case of amnesia at an early age', *Neuropsychologia*, **25**: 341–57.

Ostergaard, A.L. and Squire, L.R. (1990) 'Childhood amnesia and distinctions between forms of memory', *Brain and Cognition*, **14**: 127–33.

Temple, C.M. (1992) 'Developmental and acquired disorders of childhood', in I. Rapin and S.J. Segalowitz (vol. eds), F. Boller and J. Grafman (series eds), *Handbook of Neuropsychology*, vol. 6: *Child Neuropsychology* (Amsterdam: Elsevier).

References

Brooks, D.N. and Baddeley, A.D. (1976) 'What can amnesic patients learn?', *Neuropsychologia*, **14**: 111–22.

Nelson, K. (1973) 'Structure and strategy in learning to talk', *Monographs of the Society for Research in Child Development*, **38**: serial no. 149: 1–138.

Snodgrass, J.G. and Vanderwart, M. (1980) 'A standardised set of 260 pictures: norms for name agreement, image agreement, familiarity, and visual complexity', *Journal of Experimental Psychology: Human Learning and Memory*, **6**: 174–215.

Temple, C.M. (1986) 'Anomia for animals in a child', *Brain*, **109**: 1225–42.

Warrington, E.K. and Shallice, T. (1984) 'Category specific semantic impairments', *Brain*, **107**: 829–54.

Warrington, E.K. and Taylor, A.M. (1973) 'The contribution of the right parietal lobe to object recognition', *Cortex*, **9**: 152–64.

26   When All Else Fails, We Can Still Make Tea: a Longitudinal Look at Activities of Daily Living in an Alzheimer Patient

Jennifer Rusted, Hilary Ratner and Linda Sheppard

Introduction

Dementia is the most common cause of cognitive impairment in the elderly population. Approximately 15 per cent of individuals over the age of 65 years will suffer some form of dementia, and approximately half of these individuals will have dementia of the Alzheimer type (DAT) (Terry and Katzman, 1983). First described by Alois Alzheimer in 1907, clinical diagnosis of this particular dementia depends on a history of progressive cognitive impairment in the absence of infectious, nutritional, vascular, endocrinological or toxic causes. Clinical diagnosis is confirmed at autopsy by the presence of a specific set of neuropathological markers: the degenerative processes lead to cortical and subcortical brain cell abnormalities, neurofibrillary tangles and neuritic plaques, and chronic reductions in Central Nervous System (CNS) neurotransmitter function. These changes in the structure and functional integrity of the brain are responsible for the global changes observed in memory, information processing capacity and, in the later stages of the disorder, mood and personality.

In recent years, increased interest in this particular form of dementia has generated an enormous body of literature documenting the progressive deterioration of cognitive function on a wide range of experimental tests of information processing. These studies report that AD patients show deficits on tasks of short-term memory (Morris, 1986), visuo-spatial memory (see, for example Morris et al., 1987) and attention (for example, Baddeley et al., 1986). They are unable to acquire new information (for example, Kopelman, 1985), or to actively retrieve information from recent (for example, Martin and Fedio, 1983) or remote memory (for example, Wilson et al., 1981; Corkin, 1982). Semantic memory is impaired (for example, Weingartner et al., 1983), individuals are grossly deficient on tests which require generation of item names on request (for example,

Martin et al., 1985), and performance on tests of priming and implicit memory also reveal significant deficits (for example, Grafman et al., 1990).

In the light of such global deterioration of memory skills, it is perhaps surprising that many AD patients continue accurately to complete routine tasks of daily living long after the emergence of significant deficits on assessment tests such as those listed above, even though the everyday tasks make demands upon many of the same components of memory (for location, temporal sequence, intention) and require not insignificant periods of directed attention.

The issue of whether formal tests of performance accurately reflect functional status of memory is a contentious one. While early experimental studies suggested that memory for activities of daily living was predicted by mental status tests (Lawton and Brody, 1969; Wilson et al., 1973), subsequent studies questioned that link. Baddeley et al. (1982) argued that the predictive value of verbal memory for everyday memory function largely depends on the tasks selected, and Reed et al. (1989) pointed out that the relationship between these measures was also affected by the severity of the population tested. Ratner et al. (1988) reported that verbal memory does not correlate significantly with recall of action sequences; and Skurla et al. (1988) that mental status does not predict AD patients' ability to re-enact routine activities, such as tea-making, shopping or telephoning. In short, it would seem that factors which determine verbal memory performance are not identical to those which determine functioning on activities of daily living, and that assessments based on verbal memory skills may significantly underestimate action memory performance.

There are a number of reasons why this should be the case. Among healthy individuals, memory for actions or events is generally superior to verbal memory (Poon, 1985; Ratner et al., 1988; Backman et al., 1990), and psychological studies of action memory have suggested a number of characteristics which contribute to that superiority.

First, action memory benefits from the hierarchical nature of action sequences, which provides a structure for organizing recall of individual actions required to achieve a predetermined goal or outcome (Mandler, 1984). All actions are linked in so far as they contribute to the achievement of a particular goal, but the actions differ in their importance with respect to the achievement of that goal and the enabling subgoals. This relational hierarchy will in turn influence the centrality, and the recall probability, of individual actions within the sequence (Trabasso and van den Broeck, 1985; van den Broeck, 1988). The value of this hierarchical organization has been frequently demonstrated: adults reliably recall more actions from a structured than an unstructured event (Kausler et al., 1985), while superordinate events are better recalled, and make better cues for recall, than do subordinate actions (Mandler, 1984). Individual actions within an activity are of course related to one another linearly as well as hierarchically. The linear ordering reflects both temporal and causal links, and beneficial effects on recall probability have been demonstrated for both of these: memories for actions with constrained logical sequences are better remembered than activities with variable or arbitrary sequences in infancy and early childhood (Fivush et al., 1992; Bauer, 1992; Bauer & Mandler, 1992), and adults recall more actions when there are causal connections among them than when there are not (Padgett and Ratner, 1987).

A second characteristic which distinguishes action memory from verbal memory is the existence of contextual cues that prime established temporal sequences of actions associated with a particular physical or social context (Reason and Mycielska, 1982). In a large-scale study in 1979, Reason asked individuals to monitor 'slips of action' made over a period of two weeks in well-established routine activities of everyday life. From these diaries, he identified four of the most common categories of errors which occurred for familiar activities: repetitions of actions within a sequence; goal switches, in which individuals began with the intention of completing one activity and found themselves switching to a second one half-way through; omissions and reversal of actions; and confusions and blends of actions from different activities. He suggested that slips of actions occur primarily for highly practised, overlearned routines which are completed automatically and only monitored intermittently at critical points in the action sequence. Where a stronger, established programme exists for an activity, it may override a weaker one involving some of the same actions. That is, shared components may prime the stronger sequence and result in a switch from one activity to another if insufficient monitoring of the weaker routine occurs in the course of its execution. For example, commission errors when completing a new routine in an old setting may frequently involve intrusions from the formerly established sequence which occurred in that same context (G. Cohen, 1989).

A third characteristic which contributes to the superiority of action memory is the elaborated encoding of the memory trace as an automatic consequence of executing that act. In recent years, a large number of research studies have suggested that memory for actions incorporates motoric information in the form of the motor programme required for accurate completion of the action. Because these motor programmes are encoded in addition to the symbolic representation of the information, the memory trace is qualitatively distinct from a memory trace based on either visual or verbal information (see Engelkamp and Zimmer, 1989; and Engelkamp and Cohen, 1991, for overviews of this literature). Action memory recall benefits from the availability of motoric memory traces to supplement verbal memory: healthy adults recall more unrelated actions if they perform them (subject-performed tasks, or SPTs) than if they simply encode a verbal description of each (Cohen, 1981, 1983; Engelkamp and Zimmer, 1984; Backman et al., 1986). Various selective interference studies have provided evidence for the specifically motoric nature of the encoded trace, demonstrating that action memory is selectively disrupted by completing additional motor activity in the intervening retention period (Saltz and Donnenwerth-Nolan, 1981; Zimmer and Engelkamp, 1984; Kausler et al., 1992).

A number of studies have demonstrated that these attributes of action memory influence performance in AD patients. Dick et al. (1988) demonstrated that AD patients, like healthy adults, do encode motoric information in a spatial memory task, and that self-determined actions promote better recall than experimenter-determined ones. Karlsson et al. (1989) examined performance of AD patients on SPT tasks and have found that, while patients make proportionally more errors than the elderly control sample, they did recall performed actions better than actions verbally described.

These SPT studies, however, may still underestimate residual action memory: they rely exclusively on verbal recall, although verbal skills are greatly impaired in AD patients; they assess memory for recently acquired actions presented in sequences never experienced before, although memory for daily activities involves retrieval, not acquisition, of familiar action sequences; SPT actions do not accomplish an overall goal, are context-independent and unrelated to one another, although events experienced in everyday life are goal-directed, with causal connections between actions.

A *post hoc* comparison of AD patients' recall of SPT and daily-activities tasks indicates the significance of these differences for AD patients. Skurla et al. (1988) examined memory for everyday events (dressing, coffee-making, shopping and telephoning) in a group of mild to moderate AD patients. Although they recalled fewer actions than healthy elderly subjects, the AD patients correctly performed 78 per cent of the actions involved in these events. On the SPT task reported by Karlsson et al. (1989), a comparable group of AD patients recalled an average of only 10 per cent of the actions presented.

Most of the remembering AD patients require in everyday life is activity based. A better understanding of the nature of memory for everyday activities in AD patients is a prerequisite for the development of strategies for optimizing functional independence, particularly since AD patients have frequently been shown to be insensitive to other strategies (for example, semantic encoding and retrieval strategies) which have been used successfully to improve memory performance in the healthy elderly (Backman et al., 1990).

In the following pages, we present a study of the declining performance of one of our AD volunteers on an activity of daily living. Interest in the theory of action and activity memory has centred around the issue of which features contribute most to its well-documented superiority over verbal memory. We chose to address the question from the other side: when activity memory does break down, what are the salient features of the memory that remains? We can expect that the strongest features of those traces will be most resistant to disruption, and that those features which contribute to its uniqueness will drive residual memory in individuals with chronic and progressive memory impairment.

Experimental Design and Methods Used

Population

Despite the large numbers of individuals who are eventually diagnosed as having AD, the majority of these are not diagnosed until impairments are severe. We feel that more information can be obtained from longitudinal data on a small, homogeneous group of individuals who are monitored from the early stages of the disease, than from a much larger group of patients who have already deteriorated substantially on performance measures before they are seen. We have therefore chosen to work with a small group of AD patients in the East Sussex region. Volunteers are recruited on the basis of a clinical diagnosis of AD made by consultant psychogeriatricians attached to local medical centres. All are subsequently administered the Cambridge Examination for Mental Disorders of the Elderly (CAMDEX) test battery (Roth et al., 1988) to exclude individuals with multi-infarct or mixed multi-infarct/Alzheimer-type dementias. Premorbid IQ measures for all volunteers were established by administration of the National Adult Reading Test (NART) (Nelson and Willison, 1991).

General procedures

The main focus of the work involves monitoring performance on a tea-making task, and evaluating errors which emerge with the progression of the disease. Individuals are monitored at regular intervals from recruitment. In the first instance, we visit every 6–8 weeks; as the disease progresses and performance deteriorates more quickly, the interval between visits decreases to 4 weeks.

In the project we set out to study activity memory under conditions which optimized performance for the patient. In order to minimize the stress involved (which would be likely to impair performance within the session), we were concerned to recruit individuals who were still living at home under the care of a spouse or near relative, and to monitor performance within the familiar environment of the patient's own kitchen. Individuals were recruited early in the development of their memory disorder. In this way, we were able to establish a clear protocol for each individual which reflected their own idiosyncratic tea-making routine, and against which subsequent changes and errors could be unambiguously classified. Preliminary testing established that at recruitment the volunteer was able to name spontaneously all items and actions associated with the experimental task, and to perform those actions accurately. Although each individual had a different protocol, the individual actions could be grouped into common subgoals: boiling the kettle, preparing the cups, making/pouring the tea.

All sessions were discretely videotaped; in addition to providing a better basis for detailed analysis of performance (Smith et al., 1987), this also frees the researcher to interact naturally with the patient, without being preoccupied with the session events.

At each session, volunteers were required to make tea under a number of different conditions. In this chapter, we shall examine the verbal recall (VR), patient reenactment (PR) and patient-directed re-enactment (PDR) measures. In the PR condition, the volunteer is asked if s/he would 'make a cup of tea, just as you normally do it'. The PDR condition was included to examine the effectiveness of *observed* enactment on accuracy and detail of the patient's verbal recall. The volunteer is told that the experimenter wants to make a cup of tea, but doesn't know how to do it; the volunteer is asked to give very detailed instructions, such that the researcher can produce a cup of tea 'just the way you normally do it'. The researcher makes no move and completes no action which is not expressly indicated by the volunteer. Neutral cues are used in all procedures if the volunteer loses track of the goal before completing the sequence (for example, 'What do we need next?' 'What were you going to do next?').

All sessions included a verbal recall (VR) by the volunteer of his/her method of making tea. Instructions encourage the volunteer to provide 'as much detail as possible' about how s/he makes a cup of tea in her/his own kitchen. Since even the healthy elderly greatly abbreviate verbal descriptions of activities (Ratner et al., 1988), performance of AD patients was compared with recall performance of a healthy elderly control group asked to recall their tea-making routines under the same instructions. This group of 13 individuals was matched to AD volunteers on age, educational and socio-economic background, and IQ.

All sessions also included a traditional short assessment test of cognitive status, the Mini Mental State Examination (MMSE) (Folstein et al., 1975). This was selected because of its brevity, established reliability and ease of administration. Volunteers were often unhappy with formal assessment procedures of any duration, and we were concerned not to jeopardize our relationship with the volunteers by employing more formal testing than was absolutely necessary to provide us with a measure of cognitive decline. The test provides a measure of immediate and delayed memory, orientation and manual dexterity. Clinical impairment is indicated by a score of less than 24 out of 30.

All action memory procedures used in the project have been used in earlier studies with healthy elderly populations (Padgett and Ratner, 1987; Ratner et al., 1988) and were extensively piloted with AD volunteers. Videotapes from the sessions were scored by two independent raters for actions completed. Differences between raters were minimal; where they occurred they were resolved by discussion. For each session, the action and its order of occurrence within the sequence were ranked against the volunteer's established protocol. We also scored (a) total number of actions completed; (b) maximum length of correct sequence; (c) number of sequence breaks (forward jumps + regressions); (d) number of omissions; and (e) number of repetitions.

Patient AH

In 1991, when we first saw AH, he was 71 years old, and had been suffering from memory problems for around nine years, though his first formal assessment and diagnosis of a memory problem was not made until 1986. CAT scans completed in 1986 revealed some atrophy of the brain, but no specific lesion sites. This was consistent with the CAMDEX diagnostic assessment of progressive memory decline which indicated dementia of the Alzheimer's type. Personally, AH was an outgoing, jolly, sociable and active man, who moved with speed and confidence through routine activities of daily living such as dressing, toileting and short kitchen routines. His MMSE score was 19/30. In the two years since we began visiting him, his ability to complete activities of daily living has progressively declined; one of the few activities which he is still performing independently, though with some loss of accuracy, is tea-making.

Results

In this chapter, we shall present and discuss data from a representative subset of the sessions which we have completed with AH over the past two years. Figure 26.1 shows AH's tea-making routine, involving a total of 26 actions in three subgoals. Table 26.1 presents a summary of information on the dates and intervals between sessions, MMSE scores and total number of actions recalled at each of the sessions on VR, PR and PDR tasks.

Although there are no universally accepted criteria for categorizing the stages of AD, we have adopted, on the basis of a review of its usage within the literature, the following MMSE score equivalents: mild (19+), moderate (15–18), and severe (<15). The session data have been grouped accordingly. The regularity of sessions was interrupted in the early stages of monitoring when the volunteer underwent surgical procedures for a medical problem. We visited him immediately prior to the event (session 4) and re-established testing after a recuperation period some 30 weeks later (session 5).

1	Lift lid of kettle
2	Monitor water level
3	Fill
4	Replace lid
5	Switch on at plug
6	Turn kettle on
7	Locate saucer
8	Place on worktop
9	Locate cup
10	Place on worktop
11	Locate spoon
12	Place on worktop
13	Locate sugar
14	Spoon into cup
15	Locate caddy
16	Put tea-bag in cup
17	Replace lid of caddy
18	Locate milk (in fridge)
19	Pour milk in cup
20	Replace milk in fridge
21	Take cup to kettle
22	Wait for kettle to boil
23	Turn kettle off
24	Pour water into cup
25	Stir tea-bag in cup
26	Remove tea-bag

Figure 26.1   AH's tea-making routine

From table 26.1, it is clear that verbal recall protocols are significantly reduced relative to enactment estimates of memory; this was confirmed by a Wilcoxon signed ranks test ($N = 11$, $T = 0$, $p < 0.01$). Although the control sample of healthy elderly ($n = 13$) showed a similar tendency to produce abbreviated protocols in verbal recall, with an average of 12.9 actions recalled, this was still substantially better than AH could achieve. It is interesting to note that for AH verbal recall is impaired from very early on in the course of the disorder, and correlates significantly with performance decline on the MMSE (rank order correlation coefficient: rho $= 0.69$, $p < 0.05$).

Patient-directed tea-making was established for this individual from session 5 onwards. Despite the fact that this requires verbal recall by the volunteer, we see relatively stable and accurate performance through all sessions. AH recalls in the region of three times as many actions when those actions are enacted in front of him than he can in the absence of such feedback; and unlike the VR scores, PDR scores do not correlate with the MMSE measure. In fact, while PDR scores are generally lower than PR scores, the difference is not significant on a Wilcoxon signed ranks test ($N = 6$, $T = 9$).

The highest number of correct actions are recalled by AH when he is performing the actions to make the tea himself (PR). Under these conditions, accurate completion of the

Table 26.1   Total number of actions recalled under verbal (VR), patient re-enactment (PR) and patient-directed re-enactment (PDR) conditions, across a representative subset of sessions run with AH over two years

| Interval (weeks) | | MMSE | Number of actions | | |
			VR	PR	PDR
1	0	19	6	26	—
2	13	19	6	25	—
3	13	20	6	29	—
4	6	19	6	27	—
5	31	17	8	21	18
6	15	16	7	23	16
7	15	16	5	35	—
8	15	16	4	24	26
9	8	15	0	22	16
10	4	11	2	16	18
11	4	13	2	12	22

tea-making activity is maintained through the mild and moderate stages of the disorder (the slight decrease in overall number of correct actions reflects a dropout of noncritical actions, with no critical errors). There is a marked and significant break in his ability in the two most recent sessions, where corresponding MMSE scores indicate movement into the severely impaired phase of the disorder. This produces a significant correlation between PR performance and MMSE scores across the sessions (rho = 0.72, $p < 0.05$). We can look at the source of this change, that is, what exactly is lost in the sessions where total number of correct actions decline by studying the details of the recall protocols for these sessions.

Table 26.2 classifies the changes observed in PR tea-making performance across the sessions. We see that the gradual decline in number of correct actions completed in the course of the activity is not mirrored by any of the more obvious potential sources of declining performance. So neither action repeats (rho = −0.26), number of sequence breaks (rho = −0.31), nor changes in maximum sequence length (rho = 0.50) correlate significantly with the decrease in the number of actions completed. Errors of commission of novel actions, whether appropriate or inappropriate, were too infrequent to warrant report, even in the later sessions with AH. Number of omissions is the only significant indicator of change, increasing across sessions and correlating with the decline in total actions completed (rho = 0.72, $p < 0.05$). In the more severe phase, changes in performance involved almost exclusively increases in omissions.

Interestingly, maximum length of correct sequence was disrupted early in the development of the dementia, falling rapidly from 26 to 6 actions in the first two sessions, after which there is little further change. In fact, the number of sequence breaks in the original 26-action protocol (that is the total number of forward or backward jumps in sequence) across the moderate and severe phases of dementia also remained relatively stable,

Table 26.2 Detailed breakdown of the patient-enacted tea-making performance for each of the sessions represented in table 26.1

Total number of actions	MMSE	Longest sequence of correct actions	Number of breaks in sequence	Number of actions omitted	Number of action repeats
26	19	26	0	0	0
25	19	15	4	1	0
29	20	6	11	2	5
27	19	6	8	1	2
21	17	5	9	9	4
23	16	8	6	4	1
35	16	5	13	5	14
24	16	6	8	2	0
22	15	5	9	7	3
16	11	5	7	13	3
12	13	3	6	14	0

indicating that the stability of the maximum length sequence does not mask an otherwise more fragmented performance. Neither action repeats, number of breaks in sequence nor maximum sequence length correlate with changes in MMSE scores.

While it is hard to find consistent indicators of change in cognitive status within the activity recall data, there are a number of pointers which emerge in the detailed analyses. The mild-to-moderate phase incorporates the sudden and dramatic reduction in the maximum length of sequentially correct actions, along with a significant increase in the number of actions being omitted. In contrast, the moderate-to-severe change is characterized solely by the twofold increase in the number of actions omitted from the activity altogether. The omissions occur across a number of subgoals, but are largely accounted for by the disruption and eventual loss of one specific subgoal: filling and boiling the kettle. For AH, this subgoal involves a sequence of six actions, and his protocols indicate that, prior to dropping this sequence altogether, it was a subset of actions which had become increasingly unstable within the activity: in session 2 it slipped from its initial position and was completed after preparation of the cups. In session 4, some of the actions were repeated, in session 6 and 8 it occurred increasingly late in the activity, and by sessions 9 and 10, it had been dropped completely: AH made the tea with cold water from the tap.

One of the most interesting elements to emerge is the occasional occurrence of chaotic and fragmented performance when the volunteer seems to lose the activity completely. Session 7 provides an example of this. In this session, the total number of actions performed was 35; performance was characterized by frequent sequence breaks and multiple repeats of short sequences. In this instance, AH located and added sugar to the teacups four times and added teabags to the teacups twice. Despite the visual, kinaesthetic and temporal cues which were available to him, he showed no awareness of these repetitions, and no hesitancy in his tea-making routine. These chaotic sessions punctuate his otherwise stable and competent performance at tea-making. We were surprised by the re-establishment of accurate tea-making in subsequent sessions. For AH, at least, these sessions seem to occur in transition phases, around the time of change in the MMSE score, and may prove to be a significant anticipatory marker for change.

Discussion

Despite extensive verbal memory impairments and an almost complete inability to retain information provided only seconds before, AH has maintained certain activity-based memories in an accurate and implementable form well into the course of his dementia. This residual memory for actions is likely to be vastly underestimated by procedures which rely on verbal recall. It is most effectively tapped by conditions which allow AH to perform the actions which he is trying to recall. However even his verbal recall skills far exceed those predicted by his verbal memory performance, and are comparable to his enactment performance, when he simply observes each of his recalled actions being performed by a third party. Most of the literature concerned with the superiority of action memory in healthy individuals has indicated that experimenter-enacted events are far less effectively recalled than subject-performed ones (see, for example, Backman et al., 1986), and that imagined actions produce fewer accessible memory traces than do subject-performed ones (e.g. Saltz and Donnenwerth-Nolan, 1981). The indicators from this study are that individuals with impaired memory skills may benefit more than healthy elderly in conditions which explicitly involve motoric information, *whether subject-generated or observed*.

This differential effect may have been masked by floor effects in previous action memory studies which employ standard SPT paradigm with AD patients (for example, Karlsson et al., 1989). In those studies, enactment occurs at encoding but retrieval is purely verbal. Research studies from our laboratory (Hutton and Rusted, 1993) indicate that considerably higher recall performance is obtained in the standard SPT paradigm if volunteers perform the actions at recall as well as at encoding. The equivalence of the patient and patient-directed re-enactment conditions in the present study may also reflect the significance or familiarity of the particular goal. That is, the supplementary contribution of personally completing the action and accessing motor programmes may be less important when the activity has a salient and well-established goal which unambiguously directs the sequence of the actions recalled. Ratner et al. (1993) reported that children recall action sequences better if the goals and the enabling subgoals produce tangible or observable outcomes, rather than outcomes which change or mask the component processes. We intend to re-examine the individual protocols and videotapes to determine whether differential error patterns occur in subgoals which have different outcome characteristics. The evidence suggests that for AH at least, the *object + outcome* cues and the anticipatory planning are more important determinants of accurate recall than the actual activation of motor programmes; if confirmed, this finding has important implications for the sorts of cues which would promote accurate completion of the activity.

The early breakdown in maximum sequence length is another interesting feature of the preliminary analysis. Although at first glance it might look like evidence for impaired attentional capacity, it could also suggest quite the opposite: AH continues to complete his tea-making activity accurately, and attains his goal, despite the frequent breaks in sequence and inability to hold the temporal sequence of actions. This requires a significant degree of attention to the final goal, and the ability to pick up and sort out fragmented sequences in order to establish what has and has not been done. AH managed this, in the early sessions, with relatively few omissions or action repeats.

As more substantial numbers of omission errors do occur in AH's tea-making, we can look for the *cues* to these changes retrospectively: the sudden dropout of the kettle subgoal, for example, followed an increasingly unstable position of that subgoal within the action sequence. The predictive value of this early change will become clearer as we examine the changes observed with other volunteers. For AH, the first substantial breakdown in his ability to make tea has been this selective loss of the initial subgoal. This reflects the hierarchical organization of activity memory, and suggests a highly systematic breakdown in retrieval.

The changes taking place in the PR protocols as the dementia progresses were not as dramatic nor as predictable as we had anticipated. The errors which reportedly characterize event memory in healthy adults, that is, blending subgoals, switching goals and errors of commission, were markedly absent in AH's performance. It may be that the patterns of errors in volunteers with severe memory defects are qualitatively different from those observed in healthy adults. Certainly, it seems intuitively plausible that errors of blending, switching and commission might characterize a more active mind, when parallel processing of current activities and anticipated ones is more likely. The pathological reduction in capacity for processing which AH is exhibiting may encourage the single-minded maintenance of the anticipated goal.

This preliminary work has generated many questions and many interesting issues. We have, in the short space of time in which the project has been running, learned an enormous amount about the pitfalls of longitudinal studies, the hazards of home-based testing, and the unpredictability of human beings. We have learned to accommodate laboratory-based paradigms and principles within the broader needs of greater face validity. The emerging results will, we hope, provide an insight into the processes behind the catastrophic deterioration in memory and their functional consequences for activities of daily living in individuals with progressive dementia.

Acknowledgements

The authors wish to acknowledge the help and support of the local branches of the Alzheimer Society in Sussex, and Drs Venkateswarlu, Aldrich and Pendlebury; technical assistance from George Mather and Pennie Smith, and the unfailing good cheer and co-operation shown by Olive and Arthur through our endless visits. The work is supported by a grant from the Wellcome Trust.

Further Reading

Backman, L. (1992) 'Memory training and memory improvement in Alzheimer's disease: rules and exceptions', *Acta Neurologica Scandinavica*, Suppl., **139**: 84–9.

Hutton, S., Sheppard, L., Rotner, H.H. and Rusted, J.M. (forthcoming) 'Structuring the acqui-sition and retrieval environment to facilitate learning in individuals with dementia of the Alzheimer type', *Memory*.

Ratner, H.H. and Foley, M.A. (forthcoming) 'A unifying framework for the development of children's activity memory', in H. Reese (ed.), *Advances in Child Development and Behaviour*, vol. 25 (Orlando: Academic Press).

References

Backman, L., Nilsson, L.-G. and Chalom, D. (1986) 'New evidence on the nature of the encoding of action events', *Memory and Cognition*, 14: 339–46.

Backman, L., Mantyla, T. and Herlitz, A. (1990) 'The optimization of episodic remembering in old age', in P.B. Baltes and M.M. Baltes (eds), *Successful Aging: Perspectives from the Behavioral Sciences* (New York: Cambridge University Press), pp. 118–63.

Baddeley, A., Sunderland, A. and Harris, J. (1982) 'How well do laboratory-based psychological tests predict patients' performance outside the laboratory?', in S. Corkin, K.L. Davis, J.H. Growdon, E. Usdin and R.J. Wurtman (eds), *Alzheimer's Disease: A Report of Progress* (New York: Raven Press), pp. 141–9.

Baddeley, A., Logie, R., Bressi, S., Della Sala, S. and Spinnler, H. (1986) 'Dementia and working memory', *Quarterly Journal of Experimental Psychology*, 36A: 603–18.

Bauer, P. (1992) 'Holding it all together: how enabling relations facilitate young children's event recall', *Cognitive Development*, 7: 1–28.

Bauer, P. and Mandler, J. (1992) 'Putting the horse before the cart: the use of temporal order in recall of events by one-year-old children', *Developmental Psychology*, 28: 441–52.

Cohen, G. (1989) *Memory in the Real World* (London: Lawrence Erlbaum Associates).

Cohen, R. (1981) 'On the generality of some memory laws', *Scandanavian Journal of Psychology*, 22: 267–82.

Cohen, R. (1983) 'The effect of encoding variables on the free recall of words and action events', *Memory and Cognition*, 11: 575–82.

Corkin, S. (1982) 'Some relationships between global amnesias and memory impairments in Alzheimer's disease', in S. Corkin, K.L. Davis, J.H. Growdon, E. Usdin and R.J. Wurtman (eds), *Alzheimer's Disease: A Report of Progress* (New York Raven Press), pp. 149–64.

Dick, M.B., Kean, M.-L. and Sands, D. (1988) 'The preselection effect on the recall facilitation of motor movements in Alzheimer type dementia', *Journal of Gerontology*, 43: 125–35.

Engelkamp, J. and Cohen, R. (1991) 'Current issues in memory of action events', *Psychological Research*, 53: 175–81.

Engelkamp, J. and Zimmer, H.D. (1984) 'Motor program information as a separable memory unit', *Psychological Research*, 46: 283–99.

Engelkamp, J. and Zimmer, H.D. (1985) 'Motor programs and their relation to semantic memory', *German Journal of Psychology*, 9: 239–54.

Engelkamp, J. and Zimmer, H.D. (1989) 'Memory for action events: a new field of research', *Psychological Research*, 51: 153–7.

Fivush, R., Kuebli, J. and Clubb, P.A. (1992) 'The structure of events and event representations: a developmental analysis', *Child Development*, 63: 188–201.

Folstein, M.E., Folstein, S.E. and McHugh, P.R. (1975) 'Mini-mental state: a practical method for grading the cognitive state of patient for clinician', *Journal of Psychiatry Research*, 12: 189–98.

Grafman, J., Weingartner, H., Newhouse, P.A., Thompson, K., Lalonde, F., Litvan, L., Molchan, S. and Sunderland, T. (1990) 'Implicit learning in patients with AD', *Pharmacopsychiatry*, 23: 94–101.

Hutton, S. and Rusted, J.M. (1993) 'A role for enactment at encoding and at retrieval in normal and abnormal ageing', paper presented at the annual meeting of the American Gerontological Society, New Orleans, USA.

Karlsson, T., Backman, L., Herlitz, A., Nilsson, L.-G., Winblad, O. and Osterlind, P.-O. (1989) Memory improvement at different stages of Alzheimer's disease', *Neuropsychologia*, **27**: 737–42.

Kausler, D.L., Lichty, W. and Davis, R.T. (1985) 'Temporal memory for performed activities: intentionality and adult age differences', *Developmental Psychology*, **21**: 1132–8.

Kausler, D.L., Wiley, J.G. and Lieberwitz, K.J. (1992) 'Adult age differences in short-term memory and subsequent long-term memory for actions', *Psychology and Aging*, **7**: 309–16.

Kopelman, M.D. (1985) 'Rates of forgetting in Alzheimer-type dementia and Korsakoff's syndrome', *Neuropsychologia*, **23**: 23–30.

Lawton, M.P. and Brody, E. (1969) 'Assessment of older people: self-maintaining and instrumental activities of daily living', *Gerontologist*, **9**: 179–86.

Mandler, J. (1984) *Stories, Scripts and Scenes: Aspects of Schema Theory* (Hillsdale, N.J.: Lawrence Erlbaum Associates).

Martin, A. and Fedio, P. (1983) 'World production and comprehension in Alzheimer's disease: a breakdown of semantic knowledge', *Brain and Language*, **25**: 323–41.

Martin, A., Brouwers, P., Cox, C. and Fedio, P. (1985) 'On the nature of the verbal memory deficit in Alzheimer's disease', *Brain and Language*, **25**: 323–41.

Morris, R. and Kopelman, M.D. (1986) 'The memory deficits in Alzheimer-type dementia: a review', *Quarterly Journal of Experimental Psychology*, **38A**: 49–76.

Morris, R.G. (1986) 'Short-term forgetting in senile dementia of the Alzheimer's type', *Cognitive Neuropsychology*, **3**: 77–97.

Morris, R.G., Evenden, J.L., Sahakian, B.J. and Robbins, T.W. (1987) 'Computer-aided assessment of dementia: comparative studies of neuropsychological deficits in Alzheimer-type dementia and Parkinson's disease', in S.M. Stahl, S.D. Iversen and E.C. Goodman (eds), *Cognitive Neurochemistry* (London: Oxford University Press).

Moscovitch, M. (1982) 'A neuropsychological approach to perception and memory in normal and pathological aging', in F.I.M. Craik and S. Trehub (eds), *Aging and Cognitive Processes* (New York: Plenum Press).

Nelson, H.E. and Willison, J. (1991) *National Adult Reading Test (NART)* (Windsor, Berks: NFER–Nelson).

Norman, D. (1981) 'Categorization of action slips', *Psychological Review*, **88**: 1–15.

Padgett, R. and Ratner, H.H. (1987) 'Older and younger adults' memory for structured and unstructured events', *Experimental Aging Research*, **13**: 133–9.

Poon, L.W. (1985) 'Differences in human memory with ageing: nature, causes and clinical implication', in J.E. Birren and K.W. Schaie (eds), *Handbook of the Psychology of Aging* (New York: Van Nostrand Reinhold), pp. 427–62.

Ratner, H.H., Padgett, R.J. and Bushey, N. (1988) 'Old and young adults' recall of events', *Developmental Psychology*, **24**: 664–71.

Ratner, H.H., Foley, M.A., Mathog, A. and Jorgenson, J. (1993) 'The role of action results in children's event memory', poster presented at the meeting of the American Psychological Association, Toronto, Canada.

Reason, J. and Mycielska, K. (1982) *Absentminded? The Psychology of Mental Lapses and Everyday Errors* (Englewood Cliffs, N.J.: Prentice-Hall).

Reed, B.R., Jagust, W.J. and Seab, J.P. (1989) 'Mental status as a predictor of daily function in progressive dementia' *Gerontologist*, **29**: 804–7.

Roth, M., Huppert, F., Tym, E. and Mountjoy, C.Q. (1988) *Cambridge Examination for Mental Disorders of the Elderly (CAMDEX)* (Cambridge: Cambridge University Press).

Saltz, E. and Donnenwerth-Nolan, S. (1981) 'Does motoric imagery facilitate memory for sentences?: a selective interference test', *Journal of Verbal Learning and Verbal Behaviour*, **20**: 322–32.

Skurla, E., Rogers, J.C. and Sunderland, T. (1988) 'Direct assessment of activities of daily living in Alzheimer's disease', *Journal of the American Geriatric Society*, **36**: 97–103.

Smith, B., Ratner, H.H. and Hobart, C. (1987) 'The role of cuing and organization in children's memory for events', *Journal of Experimental Child Psychology*, **44**: 1–24.

Terry, R.D. and Katzman, R. (1983) 'Senile dementia of the Alzheimer type', *Annals of Neurology*, **14**: 497–506.

Trabasso, T. and van den Broeck, P. (1985) 'Causal thinking and the representation of narrative events', *Journal of Memory and Language*, **24**: 612–30.

van den Broeck, P. (1988) 'Causal networks versus goal hierarchies in summarizing text', *Journal of memory and Language*, **27**: 1–22.

Weingartner, H., Kaye, W., Smallberg, S.A., Ebert, H., Gillin, J.C. and Sitaram, N. (1983) 'Memory failures in progressive idiopathic dementia', *Journal of Abnormal Psychology*, **90**: 187–96.

Wilson, L.A., Grant, K. and Witney, P.M. (1973) Mental status of elderly hospital patients related to occupational therapists' assessment of activities of daily living', *Gerontologia Clinica*, **15**: 197–222.

Wilson, R.S., Kasniak, A.W. and Fox, J.H. (1981) 'Remote memory in senile dementia', *Cortex*, **17**: 41–8.

Zimmer, H.D. and Engelkamp, J. (1985) 'An attempt to distinguish between kinematic and motor memory components', *Acta Psychologica*, **58**: 81–106.

27 Fifteen-year-long Isolated Amnesia: an Unusual Onset of Alzheimer's Disease?

Sergio Della Sala, Federica Lucchelli, Alessandro Lunghi and Hans Spinnler

Introduction

In the last decade, slowly progressive deterioration of a specific, single cognitive function has been reported in the domain of language output (Mesulam, 1982; Poeck and Luzzatti, 1988), semantic knowledge (Basso et al., 1988; Hodges et al., 1992), visual perception (Magnani et al., 1982; De Renzi, 1986), and praxis (De Renzi, 1986; Dick et al., 1989). Whether all these cases represent an unusual onset of dementia or whether they are in fact separate entities remains to be seen.

It is only recently that similar, slowly progressive selective memory impairments have been described (Kritchevsky and Squire, 1993), although a number of earlier studies of mildly deteriorated Alzheimer (AD) patients have documented individual cases of selective deficits of memory (Capitani et al., 1986; Della Sala et al., 1986; Becker, 1988; Baddeley et al., 1991; Haxby et al., 1992). Della Sala et al. (1986) reported the psychometric pattern of deterioration in a group of 39 AD patients: 22 of them (56 per cent) exhibited homogeneous deterioration of their cognitive functions, whereas the remaining 17 showed a less-global progression of deterioration. In nine cases (23 per cent) the deficit was restricted to a single cognitive domain. Four AD patients of this latter subgroup exhibited a pure amnesic deficit when they were first tested, at which time their mean length of illness was 1.5 (sd 0.6) years. More recently, Haxby et al. (1992) reported five AD patients, out of a group of 16, who had a history of progressive isolated memory impairment lasting up to 35 months.

This chapter describes a relatively young patient with slowly progressive amnesia which, after 15 years, evolved to dementia of Alzheimer type. In an attempt to determine whether this case can be traced back to an unusual history of dementia or whether it is a separate nosological entity, we investigated the incidence of selective memory impairment and its duration in a group of patients diagnosed as having either AD or benign forget-fulness (Kral, 1978; Crook et al., 1986).

Clinical History

MZ, a 57-year-old man with five years of education, was first referred for neuro-psychological evaluation in 1984, at the age of 49. At that time, both he and his wife drew attention to the memory difficulties he had been having for many years. His previous clinical history was completely uneventful, with no history of alcohol or drug abuse, or episodes traceable to encephalitic illness (Damasio et al., 1985) or to major seizures (Victor and Agamanolis, 1990). Nor was there a history of developmental learning disabilities (Ostergaard, 1987). The neurological examination was negative.

The first symptoms in this previously normal subject became apparent when he was about 40 years old (that is, 17 years before our last assessment) and consisted in forget-ting errands and appointments with increasing frequency, so that he spontaneously began to make use of written reminders. In the following years, he noticed that he easily forgot about recent events, such as visits from friends and relatives. He used to watch soccer on TV, but shortly after doing so, would be unable to remember which team had won. At that time, he was working in a factory as a welder; such was his expertise that he was often called to other factories for special jobs and, despite his low education, was promoted foreman.

Between 40 and 49 years of age, his memory worsened considerably. He was often unable to remember what he had to do at work and had to ask his fellow-workers. After a few minutes, he would forget what they had said and had to repeat the question several times over. Shortly after the time of our first formal examination (at the age of 49), MZ agreed with his boss that his memory problems were severely obstructing his ability to act as foreman, and consequently he gave up the position. Because of severe amnesia, he progressively lost the ability to work autonomously as a welder and was reduced to merely following his fellow-workers instructions. None the less, his welding skills were unimpaired and, provided somebody reminded him of what he had to do, he was still very much in demand for his dexterity.

On the whole, his deficit seemed to concern primarily the learning and retention of new information, while no impairment of remote memory was evident. He showed no difficulty in remembering details about his past. He was easily able to find his way around in his home town, but reported some feeling of uncertainty when driving in other towns that he had visited on previous occasions. No general cognitive deterioration was evident in everyday life; all difficulties were accounted for by his memory deficit. Lan-guage was fluent and syntactically correct, with no signs of anomia or lexical difficulties. He was well aware of his problems and was able to give articulate accounts of them.

When he was next seen in 1988 (at the age of 53), both he and his wife reported a gradual worsening of his problems. Impairment was still limited to memory and no other cognitive symptoms had emerged. His amnesia had worsened to the stage where he was rarely able to retain information for more than a few minutes and he was constantly disorientated in time. His mnestic impairment had made a profound impact on his everyday life, but he was still able to work under supervision, and had no difficulty in driving. His language was normal. He was interested in hobbies (for example, he still sang with a group without any apparent difficulty) and was involved in family life.

At the time of our third examination (1990, when MZ was 55 years old) a dramatic change was reported to have occurred in the few previous months (after about 15 years of isolated amnesia), when more widespread involvement of cognitive functions had become evident. Several events marked this accelerated evolution of his illness. He had lost his job, because he was no longer able to follow his fellow-workers instructions and his craftsmanship had deteriorated. Spatial disorientation had become manifest in familiar surroundings, so that he could not go out unaccompanied, though orientation in his own home was still intact. Driving was now impossible, not only because of topographical disorientation, but also because of motor awkwardness. Subtle language disturbances were noticed, such as difficulty in planning a complex discourse and mild word-finding difficulties. He was markedly impaired in recalling people's names. He was still aware of his deficits, which he reported accurately, giving clear evidence of being both worried and depressed about his condition.

The neurological examination was still completely normal. A tentative diagnosis of probable AD was advanced.

At the time of the most recent follow-up examination (September 1992, when MZ was 57 years old), we learnt that the course of the disease had been marked by a rapid decline in everyday functioning, evolving to a picture of severe dementia. Language had worsened gradually to the stage where communication was virtually impossible. His speech was reduced to stereotyped utterances, severe anomia and verbal paraphasias. He had been forced to give up his hobby as a singer, because of his inability to follow the songs and the tunes. Dressing apraxia and motor awkwardness were evident (for example, in grooming and eating) as well as constant disorientation in his own home. Activities of daily living are so impaired that he now requires continual supervision. He is now very apathetic and seemingly unaware of his condition. He shows no interest in the environment and, although very quiet, spends most of his time at home in purposeless activities (such as moving objects). His neurological examination is still normal.

In summary, MZ's clinical history consists of 15-year-long slowly progressive amnesia followed by the rapid deterioration of all his cognitive functions, evolving to full-blown severe dementia.

Neuroradiological Evaluation

A first CT scan performed in 1984 was normal; atrophic changes were not even mentioned by the neuroradiologist. A second CT scan performed in 1989 showed mild, symmetric atrophy, without focal abnormalities; this examination showed little change with respect to the previous one performed five years earlier (figure 27.1).

In order to investigate functional derangements not detected by CT scans or MRI, in May 1990 a PET study (figure 27.2) was performed to measure the local metabolic rate for 2-[^{18}F]fluoro-2-deoxy-D-glucose ([^{18}F]FDG). This demonstrated bilateral parietal and temporal hypometabolism and left frontal hypometabolism, a pattern considered indicative of Alzheimer's disease (Friedland et al., 1985; Haxby et al., 1986).

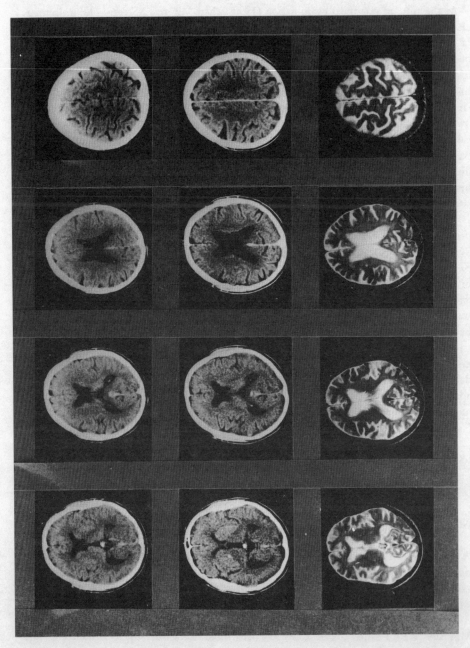

Figure 27.1 Axial section from CT scans (top: 1984; middle: 1989) and MR scans (bottom: 1992)

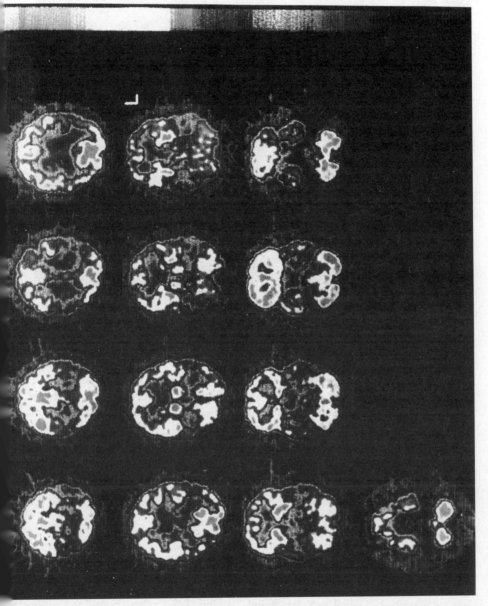

Figure 27.2 PET scans (1990)

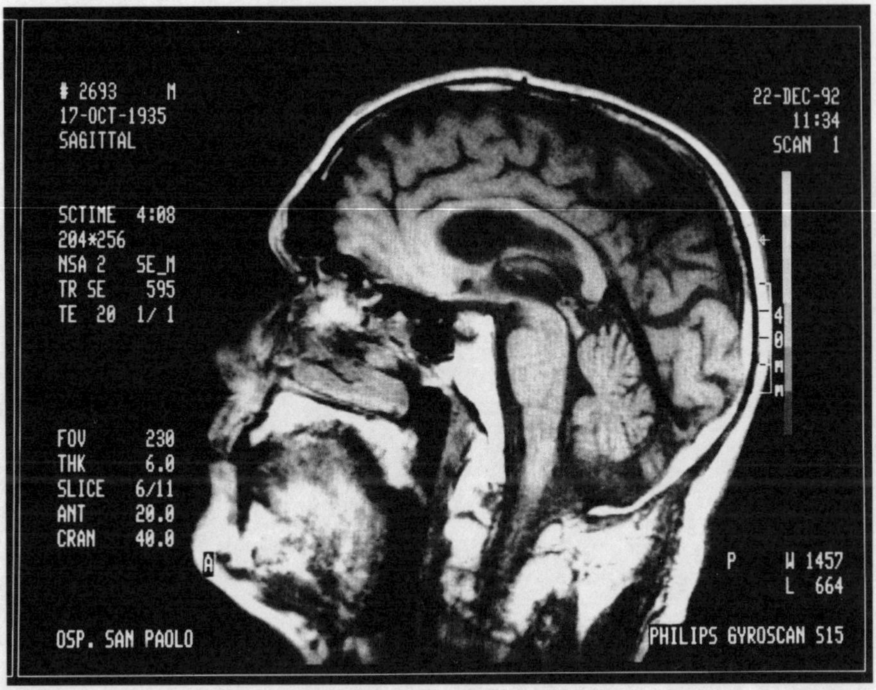

Figure 27.3   Sagittal section from MR scans (1992)

A spin-echo MRI scan (figures 27.1 and 27.3) was performed in December 1992, with sagittal T_1 weighted images plus axial and coronal proton density and T_2 weighted images. MRI showed extensive areas of abnormal signal intensity, hypointense in T_1 weighted images and hyperintense in T_2 weighted images, interpreted as severe diffuse atrophy, with relative sparing of the occipital lobes. No specific involvement of the medial temporal lobe structures was evident at this stage.

On the whole, neuroimaging studies revealed no focal lesions of the brain but in the advanced stages showed a picture compatible with a diagnosis of probable Alzheimer's disease. No evidence of selective damage to memory-related structures was ever reported.

Neuropsychological Assessment

Formal neuropsychological assessments were performed in 1984, 1988, 1989 and 1990 and attempted in 1992, using standardized tests available from previous studies. Most tests are described in detail in Spinnler and Tognoni (1987), where norms and adjustment criteria for age and education (and sex when appropriate) are set out. Story recall, serial position curve, paired associates, naming, autobiographical memory, colour-figure matching, Towers of Hanoi and digit cancellation tests are described elsewhere (Barigazzi et al., 1987; Capitani et al., 1992; Novelli et al., 1986a, 1986b; Borrini et al., 1989; Della

Sala et al., 1992, submitted): their standardization and norms follow the same procedure as the tests described in Spinnler and Tognoni (1987). For all of them an inferential cut-off score corresponding to the worst 5 per cent of the healthy Italian population was chosen. With a 5 per cent risk, adjusted scores below the cut-off were considered to correspond to an impaired performance. In this way, irrespective of intertest and interscale differences of difficulty and scores, the criterion of impairment is conceptually the same (Capitani and Laiacona, 1988). The famous events questionnaire was administered in the version devised by Costa et al. (1989) and pathological performance was indicated by the cut-off score (adjusted for age, sex and education) found in normal controls.

In 1988, MZ's score on a screening test devised to assess global cognitive functioning (MODA: Milan Overall Dementia Assessment; Brazzelli et al., 1994) fell within the moderate pathological range (77.4, adjusted for age and education, cut-off: 85.5, score range: 0–100). This was fully accounted for by his poor performance on the memory and orientation items. In the following sessions his general cognitive performance worsened slowly (74.8 in 1989 and 68.7 in 1990), but eventually nose-dived (14 in 1992).

MZ's performances on memory and other cognitive tests are reported in tables 27.1 and 27.2. It is unfortunate that some tests became available for use only late in the course of MZ's disease. The tables also report the 5th lower centile and the median scores of the normal population.

It is clear that MZ's verbal memory was severely impaired from the first examination, while his spatial memory was preserved until at least 1989. By and large, all the other cognitive test scores were within the normal range until 1989, when a slight attention and language impairment emerged. In the last formal session, carried out in 1990, clear-cut global deterioration was evident, with involvement of all cognitive functions except visual perceptual abilities. A formal language examination (the Italian version of the Aachener Aphasie Test; De Bleser et al., 1986) was also carried out on that occasion and documented moderate aphasia, with more marked involvement of repetition.

MZ was next seen in September 1992, as a 57-year-old, and found to be virtually incapable of undergoing formal testing. Communication was almost impossible due to severe aphasia, impairment in discourse planning and marked difficulty in understanding all but the simplest verbal and nonverbal instructions.

On the whole, MZ's formally assessed cognitive profile is consistent with clinical evidence of pure progressive amnesia eventually evolving to dementia.

Discussion

Amnesic features

MZ presented a picture of amnesia that was characterized from its onset (at the age of 40) by severe progressive impairment of verbal episodic memory. Spatial memory was spared until MZ was 54 years old, at which time more widespread cognitive impairment began to show up in formal testing.

On the other hand, there was indirect evidence (for example, lexical competence,

Table 27.1   Memory tests

(MZ's age)	Sessions				Controls' inferential 5th centile	Controls' median score
	1 Nov. 1984 (49)	2 Mar. 1988 (52)	3 Jul. 1989 (53)	4 Jun. 1990 (54)		
Episodic memory						
Verbal span (0–inf.)	2.75*	2.75*	2*	2*	2.75	4.50
Supraspan verbal learning (Buschke-Fuld) (0–180)	5*	0*	1*	0*	36	111
Story recall (0–150)	12*	0*	0*	0*	24	60
Serial position						
Primacy (0–70)	4.5	0*	—	0*	4.5	15.5
Recency (0–30)	9.5	10.5	—	10	7.5	18.5
Paired associates (0–22.5)	—	0.5*	—	3*	6	12.5
Spatial span (0–9)	4.75	4	4	2.75*	3.5	4.75
Supraspan spatial learning (0–29.16)	7.9	5.7	—	1.08*	5.5	18.5
Semantic memory						
Verbal fluency (semantic cue) (0–inf.)	9.5	8.75	7.5	4*	7	17
Free word association (0–inf.)	6.25	6.25	—	2.5*	3.75	9.5
Colour-figure matching (0–16)	—	—	—	14	10	16
Map of Italy (0–15)	—	11	6*	6.25*	7.25	13.75
Retrograde memory						
Famous events questionnaire (0–80)	—	—	—	31.43*	(41.53)	
Autobiographical memory (0–45)	—	—	—	12*	19	38

Notes: Scores are adjusted for age, education and sex. Range is indicated in brackets. See text for references.

* pathological score, i.e., below the inferential 5th centile of normal population.

— not performed

Table 27.2   General cognitive tests

(MZ's age)	Sessions				Controls' inferential 5th centile	Controls' median score
	1 *Nov. 1984* *(49)*	*2* *Mar. 1988* *(52)*	*3* *July 1989* *(53)*	*4* *Jun. 1990* *(54)*		
Intelligence						
Raven PM 1938 set A,B,C,D (0–48)	21.25	18.25	20	8.75*	14.75	28.75
Weigl's Sorting Test (0–15)	11.25	13.25	9.25	—	4.25	10.75
Elithorn's perceptual maze (0–16)	8.75	—	—	1*	7.25	14.25
Verbal judgement	41.75	—	39.25	—	32	50
Attention						
Digit cancellation test (0–50)	31.5	24.5	13.1*	8.1*	23.9	40.5
Reversal learning (0–24)	23	21.5	—	—	18.25	23.25
Language						
Token test (0–36)	32.75	34.75	24.5*	18*	26.25	33
Naming (0–32)	32	—	—	27.75*	28	31
Praxis						
Ideomoor apraxia (0–72)	71	—	65	42*	52	69
Orofacial apraxia (0–20)	20	—	—	—	17	20
Finger agnosia (0–24)	19.25	21.25	—	16.25	13.75	22
Visual perception						
Constructional apraxia (0–14)	10.75	10.75	—	1*	7.75	12.5
Street's completion test (0–14)	6.25	5.25	—	7.75	2	7.25
Scrawls discrimination (0–32)	31	32	—	—	20.75	31.25
Length of segment discrimination (0–32)	29	26	—	29	17	26
Gottschaldt's hidden figures (0–34)	31.15	—	—	—	16.75	29.5

Notes: See table 27.1.

verbal fluency) that semantic memory was largely preserved until late in the disease. Procedural memory was also spared, as evidenced by MZ's preserved ability to drive and perform his work activities skilfully. Anterograde memory appeared to be more severely affected than retrograde memory. Memory problems were confirmed by formal neuropsychological assessment.

In summary, MZ's amnesia may be described as a rather selective impairment of verbal learning abilities, which remained remarkably pure for years.

Co-existing cognitive defects

The involvement of nonverbal memory coincided with the first signs of other cognitive deficits not involving memory (unfortunately, data pertinent to this stage of his illness are incomplete). This occurred about 15 years after the behavioural onset. Since then, his cognitive functions have deteriorated with alarming rapidity, evolving to very severe dementia in less than a year.

The diagnosis of AD seems indisputable, given that the final picture was virtually indistinguishable from severe AD and that there was no evidence (clinical or neuroradiological) of other diseases known to cause mental deterioration. As a matter of fact, his clinical history was negative and his neurological examination has always been unremarkable, thus ruling out pathological events (such as amnesic stroke) which are usually accompanied by additional signs. Moreover, the neuroradiological examination revealed neither focal abnormalities nor a differential distribution of atrophic changes, as observed in temporal and frontal Pick's disease or frontal lobe degeneration. Apart from his amnesia, which could be interpreted as a manifestation of a specific dysfunction of hippocampal structures, his final behavioural picture was not indicative of prominent or selective involvement of certain areas of the brain (for example, language disturbances or 'frontal' symptoms).

What is remarkable about this case is not the endpoint of the illness but its most unusual course, characterized by an exceedingly early onset (40 years) and exceptionally long duration (about 15 years) of isolated though progressive amnesia, eventually leading to rapidly evolving, full-blown dementia.

An unusual presentation of AD?

Memory disturbance is an early feature and a constant characteristic of Alzheimer's disease (McKhann et al., 1984; Nebes, 1992; Della Sala et al., 1986; Spinnler and Della Sala, 1988). However, by the time the patient comes to the neurologist's attention the impairment is usually more widespread.

The loss of memory of sufficient severity to interfere with social and occupational functioning with relatively preserved other cognitive abilities is the most common dementia profile (Morris and Kopelman, 1986; see Carlesimo and Oscar-Berman, 1992, for a review). Weintraub and Mesulam (forthcoming) labelled this typical picture as 'progressive amnestic dementia'. Among 21 autopsied cases of their series, one patient's amnesia was 'distinctly more salient than any other deficit throughout most of the 13 years of her illness'; unfortunately, the authors make no mention of how long amnesia presented as the only deficit before dementia.

It could be surmised that an isolated memory deficit is in fact the most common early sign of Alzheimer's disease (present in 32 per cent of the 129 AD patients reported by Della Sala et al., 1986), but in most cases this early stage would just escape relatives' notice and neurologists' evaluation. It might well be that patients are referred to the physician only at an advanced stage, when the mnestic deficit is of sufficient severity to impair everyday functioning or when additional cognitive deficits emerge. In fact, in Italy more than 40 per cent of AD patients are referred for neurological consultation some three years after the onset of symptom(s) (Della Sala et al., 1986). Memory disturbance is still isolated in very few patients by the time they seek medical advice, but in the follow-up other cognitive abilities soon deteriorate, thus establishing a diagnosis of dementia.

Data from the literature indicate that it is highly uncommon for progressive amnesia to persist as an isolated deficit for more than three years in Alzheimer's disease (Haxby et al., 1992). Our recent experience confirms this claim. From 1987 to 1993 (June) a series of 500 subjects were referred to our laboratory for cognitive evaluation, 301 of whom were finally diagnosed as AD. Only seven subjects in the whole sample presented with isolated memory deficit at the first examination and a provisional diagnosis of senile benign forgetfulness (SBF; Kral, 1978; Crook et al., 1986) was advanced. In four, the evolution to dementia, as documented in follow-up sessions, occurred after 2–6 years (mean: 4.0 years). Three patients are still purely amnesic (duration range: 2–5 yrs; mean: 3.6 years) and still carry a diagnosis of SBF. In 121 out of the 301 AD cases, memory disturbance was reported as the only symptom at onset, but a generalized cognitive impairment was found from the first examination. In all these 121 patients the duration of the isolated amnesia before global deterioration became apparent could not be assessed reliably. In most cases the evolution to dementia occurred early in the course of the disease, confirming that the observation of patients in the purely amnesic stage is a rare occurrence. MZ can be clearly differentiated form all these patients by the exceptionally long duration of his progressive amnesia before dementia.

We could hypothesize that focal onset (aphasia, apraxia or agnosia or, as in the present case, pure amnesia characterizes a subgroup of AD patients who will undergo a much slower progression of disease, with dementia supervening after a long period marked by a restricted cognitive deficit. In fact, the rate of decline in AD is reported to be quite variable from subject to subject (Katzman et al., 1988).

On the other hand, there is a paucity of relevant data from the literature on the focal onset of AD. In most cases of progressive focal cognitive disturbances follow-up observation was not carried out for more than five years from the onset, so that in many cases later global deterioration cannot be ruled out. In cases in which spreading of cognitive impairment was observed and progression to AD was therefore documented (reinforced, in some cases, by pathological confirmation), this occurred after a highly variable interval from the onset, although a few cases with a long history (up to 15 years) of an isolated neuropsychological deficit are reported (Duffy and Petersen, 1992; Kempler et al., 1990; Leger et al., 1991; Deruaz et al., 1993). On the whole, no consistent pattern of evolution emerges from the available data. Moreover, to the best of our knowledge, there have been no reports of cases of long-standing isolated amnesia evolving to dementia.

MZ could be seen as an extreme variation of AD, that is, an instance of exceptionally slow disease, where the slowly progressive course appears to be due to an unusually long amnesic stage (while, on the other hand, the 'demential' stage of the disease appears to be particularly fast). Alternatively, MZ's disease could be described as a different, as yet unknown, nosological entity of cortical dementia, clinically distinct from AD on the basis of its extremely early onset and unusual course.

The clinical diagnosis of AD is relatively straightforward in typical cases, but much less so when atypical features are present. One of the proposed diagnostic criteria is evidence of an increasingly typical picture of AD by serial observation. An obvious limit to this practice is the relative aspecificity of the final picture of severe dementia, which, in the absence of pathological evidence, renders differentiation between nosological entities a major diagnostic problem. So far, AD would appear to be the most plausible clinical diagnosis of MZ's dementia, since there are no signs of any other known patho-logical processes. Data from the literature are consistent, at least in part, with the possibility of focal degenerative changes extending to other parts of the cortex at a late stage of illness. This has been most convincingly demonstrated in cases of progressive aphasia, with reference to a preferential involvement of language areas. We can hypoth-esize that MZ's progressive amnesia was brought out by slowly evolving pathological changes that were restricted to memory-related structures (possibly the hippocampus) for a very long time and eventually extended to other cortical areas.

It appears that no specific features predict the course of the disease, although it is possible that in future, long-term follow-up studies of similar cases of isolated amnesia without dementia will further improve our understanding of this syndrome.

Acknowledgements

We thank Dr D. Perani, S. Raffaele Hospital, for performing the PET study and Ms Gillian Jarvis for revising the English in our paper.

Further Reading

Kritchevsky, M. and Squire, L.R. (1993) 'Permanent global amnesia with unknown etiology', *Neurology*, **43**: 326–332.
Weintraub, S. and Mesulam, M.M. (1993) 'Four neuropsychological profiles in dementia'. In H. Spinnler and F. Boller (eds) *Handbook of Neuropsychology*, vol. 8, 253–282.

References

Baddeley, A.D., Della Sala, S. and Spinnler, H. (1991) 'The two-component hypothesis of memory deficit in Alzheimer's disease', *Journal of Clinical and Experimental Neuropsychology*, **13**: 341–9.
Barigazzi, R., Della Sala, S., Laiacona, M., Spinnler, H. and Valenti, V. (1987) 'Esplorazione testistica della memoria di prosa', *Ricerche di Psicologia*, **1**: 49–80.
Basso, A., Capitani, E. and Laiacona, M. (1988) 'Progressive language impairment without dementia:

a case with isolated category specific semantic defect', *Journal of Neurology, Neurosurgery and Psychiatry*, **51**: 1201–7.

Becker, J.T. (1988) 'Working memory and secondary memory deficits in Alzheimer's disease', *Journal of Experimental and Clinical Neuropsychology*, **10**: 739–53.

Borrini, G., Dall'Ora, P., Della Sala, S., Marinelli, L. and Spinnler, H. (1989) 'Autobiographical memory: sensitivity to age and education of a standardized enquiry', *Psychological Medicine*, **19**: 215–44.

Brazzelli, M., Capitani, E., Della Sala, S., Spinnler, H. and Zuffi, M. (1994) 'A neuropsychological instrument adding to the description of patients with suspected cortical dementia: the "Milan Overall Dementia Assessment"', *Journal of Neurology, Neurosurgery and Psychiatry*, **57**: 1510–17.

Capitani, E. and Laiacona, M. (1988) 'Aging and psychometric diagnosis of intellective impairment: some considerations on test scores and their use', *Developmental Neuropsychology*, **4**: 325–30.

Capitani, E., Della Sala, S. and Spinnler, H. (1986) 'Neuropsychological approach to dementia', in K. Poeck, H.J. Freund and H. Gaensehirt (eds), *Neurology* (Berlin/Heidelberg/New York: Springer), pp. 61–9.

Capitani, E., Della Sala, S., Lucchelli, F., Soave, P. and Spinnler, H. (1988) 'Gottschaldt's hidden figure test: sensitivity of perceptual attention to aging and dementia', *Journal of Gerontology*, **43**: 157–63.

Capitani, E., Della Sala, S., Logie, R. and Spinnler, H. (1992) 'Recency, primacy and memory: reappraising and standardising the serial position curve', *Cortex*, **28**: 315–42.

Carlesimo, G.A. and Oscar-Berman, M. (1992) 'Memory deficits in Alzheimer's patients: a comprehensive review', *Neuropsychology Review*, **3**: 119–69.

Costa, M., De Renzi, E. and Faglioni, P. (1989) 'Un questionario italiano per lo studio della memoria retrograda', *Archivio di Psicologia, Neurologia e Psichiatria*, **50**: 735–55.

Crook, T., Bartus, R.T., Ferris, S.H., Whitehouse, P., Cohen, G.D. and Gershon, S. (1986): 'Age-associated memory impairment: proposed diagnostic criteria and measures of clinical change: report of a National Institute of Mental Health Work Group', *Developmental Neuropsychology*, **2**: 261–76.

Damasio, A.R., Eslinger, P.J., Damasio, H., van Hoesen, G.W. and Cornell, S. (1985) 'Multimodal amnesic syndrome following bilateral temporal and basal forebrain damage', *Archives of Neurology*, **42**: 252–9.

De Bleser, R., Denes, F., Luzzatti, C., Mazzucchi, A., Poeck, K., Spinnler, H. and Willmes, K. (1986) 'L'Aachener Aphasie Test (AAT). Problemi e soluzioni per una versione italiana del test e per uno studio crosslinguistico dei disturbi afasici', *Archivio di Psicologia, Neurologia e Psichiatria*, **47**: 209–37.

Della Sala, S., Nichelli, P. and Spinnler, H. (1986) 'An Italian series of patients with organic dementia', *Italian Journal of Neurological Sciences*, **7**: 27–41.

Della Sala, S., Laiacona, M., Spinnler, H. and Ubezio, C. (1992) 'A cancellation test: its reliability in assessing attentional deficits in Alzheimer's disease', *Psychological Medicine*, **22**: 885–901.

Della Sala, S., Spinnler, H. and Stangalino, C. (submitted) 'Colour-figure matching and language defects are dissociated in Alzheimer dementia'.

De Renzi, E. (1986) 'Slowly progressive visual agnosia or apraxia without dementia', *Cortex*, **22**: 171–80.

Deruaz, J.P., Assal, G. and Peter-Favre, Cl. (1993) 'Un cas clinico-pathologique d'aphasie progressive', *Revue neurologique*, **149**: 186–91.

Dick, J.P.R., Snowden, J., Northen, B., Goulding, P.J. and Neary, D. (1989) 'Slowly progressive apraxia', *Behavioral Neurology*, **2**: 101–4.

Duffy, J.R. and Petersen, R.C. (1992) 'Primary progressive aphasia', *Aphasiology*, **1**: 1–15.

Friedland, R.P., Budinger, T.F., Koss, E. and Ober, B.A. (1985) 'Alzheimer's disease: anterior-posterior and lateral hemispheric alterations in cortical glucose utilization', *Neuroscience Letters*, 53: 235–40.

Haxby, J.V., Grady, C.L., Duara, R., Schlageter, N.L., Berg, G. and Rapoport, S.I. (1986) 'Neocortical metabolic abnormalities precede non-memory cognitive deficits in early Alzheimer type dementia', *Archives of Neurology*, 43: 882–5.

Haxby, J.V., Raffaele, K., Gillette, J., Schapiro, M.B. and Rapoport, S.I. (1992) 'Individual trajectories of cognitive decline in patients with dementia of Alzheimer type', *Journal of Clinical and Experimental Neuropsychology*, 14: 575–92.

Hodges, J.R., Patterson, K., Oxbury, S. and Funnel, E. (1992) 'Semantic dementia: progressive fluent aphasia with temporal lobe atrophy', *Brain*, 115: 1783–806.

Katzman, R., Brown, T., Thal, L.J., Fuld, P.A., Aronson, M., Butters, N., Klauber, M.R., Wiederholt, W., Pay, M., Renbing, X., Ooi, W.L., Hofstetter, R. and Terry, R. (1988) 'Comparison of rate of annual change of mental status score in four independent studies of patients with Alzheimer's disease', *Annals of Neurology*, 24: 384–9.

Kempler, D., Metter, E.J., Riege, W.H., Jackson, C.A., Benson, D.F. and Hanson, W.R. (1990) 'Slowly progressive aphasia: three cases with language, memory, CT and PET data', *Journal of Neurology Neurosurgery and Psychiatry*, 53: 987–93.

Kral, V.A. (1978) 'Benign senile forgetfulness', in R. Katzman, R.D. Terry and K.L. Bick (eds), *Alzheimer's Disease: Senile Dementia and Related Disorders*, vol. 7: *Aging* (New York: Raven), pp. 47–51.

Kritchevsky, M. and Squire, L.R. (1993) 'Permanent global amnesia with unknown etiology', *Neurology*, 43: 326–32.

Leger, J.M., Levasseur, M., Benoit, N., Baron, J.C., Tran Dinh, S. Bolgert, F., Cohen, L., Brunet, P. and Signoret, J.L. (1991) 'Apraxie d'aggravation lentement progressive: étude par IRM et tomographie à positons dans 4 cas', *Revue neurologique*, 147: 183–91.

Magnani, G., Bettoni, L. and Mazzucchi, A. (1982) 'Lesioni atrofiche biooccipitali di incerta natura all'origine di una agnosia visiva', *Rivista di Neurologia*, 52: 137–48.

McKhann, G., Drachman, D., Folstein, M., Katzman, R., Price, D. and Stadlan, E.M. (1984) 'Clinical diagnosis of Alzheimer's disease: report of the NINCDS–ADRDA Work Group under the auspices of the Department of Health and Human Services Task Force on Alzheimer's disease', *Neurology*, 34: 939–44.

Mesulam, M.M. (1982) 'Slowly progressive aphasia without generalized dementia', *Annals of Neurology*, 11: 592–8.

Morris, R. and Kopelman, M.D. (1986) 'The memory deficits in Alzheimer-type dementia: a review', *Quarterly Journal of Experimental Psychology*, 38A: 575–602.

Nebes, R.D. (1992) 'Cognitive dysfunction in Alzheimer's disease', in F.I.M. Craik and T.A. Salthouse (eds), *The Handbook of Aging and Cognition* (Hillsdale, N.J.: Lawrence Erlbaum Associates), pp. 373–446.

Novelli, G., Papagno, C., Capitani, E., Laiacona, M., Cappa, S.F. and Vallar, G. (1986a) 'Tre test clinici di memoria verbale a lungo termine', *Archivio di Psicologia Neurologia e Psichiatria*, 2: 278–96.

Novelli, G., Papagno, C., Capitani, E., Laiacona, M., Vallar, G. and Cappa, S.F. (1986b) 'Tre test clinici di ricerca e produzione lessicale. Taratura su soggettie normali', *Archivio di Psicologia, Neurologia e Psichiatria*, 4: 477–506.

Ostergaard, A.L. (1987) 'Episodic, semantic and procedural memory in a case of amnesia at an early age', *Neuropsychologia*, 25: 341–57.

Poeck, K. and Luzzatti, C. (1988) 'Slowly progressive aphasia in three patients: the problem of accompanying neuropsychological deficits', *Brain*, 111: 151–68.

Spinnler, H. and Della Sala, S. (1988) 'The role of clinical neuropsychology in the neurological diagnosis of Alzheimer's disease', *Journal of Neurology*, 235: 258–71.

Spinnler, H. and Tognoni, G. (eds) (1987) 'Standardizzazione e taratura italiana di test neuro-psicologici', *Italian Journal of Neurological Sciences*, Suppl. 8.

Victor, M. and Agamanolis, D. (1990) 'Amnesia due to lesions confined to the hippocampus: a clinical-pathologic study', *Journal of Cognitive Neuroscience*, **2**: 246–57.

Weintraub, S. and Mesulam, M.-M. (1993) 'Four neuropsychological profiles in dementia', in F. Boller and H. Spinnler (eds), *Handbook of Neuropsychology*, vol. 8 (Amsterdam: Elsevier Science), pp. 253–82.

Patient Index

Nancy (pp. 255–66)
A 67-year-old former mathematics teacher with a specific impairment in working-memory functioning.

NH (pp. 121–2)
An amnesic who presented a form of visual confabulation.

Mrs P (pp. 225–35)
A 62-year-old retired teacher diagnosed as having semantic dementia.

PC (pp. 366–71)
A 62-year-old businessman who suffered a stroke resulting in nominal aphasia.

PS (pp. 32–44)
A 67-year-old garage proprietor who, following a stroke, exhibited features of a profound memory disorder.

PV (pp. 337–42)
A 26-year-old Italian woman who suffered a stroke in the left cerebral hemisphere which resulted in a severe disorder of short-term verbal memory.

RI (pp. 371–4)
A 66-year-old Italian farmer who, due to an ischaemic attack, is aphasic and has mild hemiparesis and oral apraxia.

RW (pp. 318–23)
A 62-year-old man who suffered a small stroke resulting in him showing symptoms of aphasia.

SD (pp. 104–5)
A 37-year-old man who, due to an open head injury, became severely amnesic and presented a form of confabulation.

Sheila (pp. 1–7)
A young woman who, following a viral infection of the brain, suffered a dense and intractable anterograde amnesia.

Mr Smith (pp. 196–207)
A 65-year-old man who, following some apparent narrowing of the right carotid artery, showed symptoms of topographic amnesia.

SS (pp. 45–53)
The president of an optical physics firm who contracted herpes simplex encephalitis resulting in a dense anterograde and retrograde amnesia.

TC (pp. 125–8)
A 34-year-old man suffering from chronic schizophrenia.

WF (pp. 118–21)
A 42-year-old man who suffered a ruptured aneurysm resulting in a dense amnesia.

WM (pp. 145–9)
A 47-year-old chronic schizophrenic woman.

Subject Index

Author Index